P9-CQK-243

SELLING TODAY

Sixth
Canadian
Edition

PARTNERING TO CREATE VALUE

GERALD L. MANNING
DES MOINES AREA COMMUNITY COLLEGE

MICHAEL AHEARNE
UNIVERSITY OF HOUSTON

BARRY L. REECE
VIRGINIA POLYTECHNIC INSTITUTE AND STATE UNIVERSITY

H. F. (HERB) MACKENZIE
BROCK UNIVERSITY

PEARSON

Toronto

Vice-President, Editorial Director: Gary Bennett
Editor-in-Chief: Nicole Lukach
Acquisitions Editor: Nick Durie
Marketing Manager: Leigh-Anne Graham
Supervising Developmental Editor: Suzanne Schaan
Developmental Editor: Pamela Voves
Project Manager: Ashley Patterson
Manufacturing Manager: Susan Johnson
Production Editor: Niraj Bhatt/Aptara®, Inc.
Copy Editor: Jennifer McIntyre
Proofreader: Sally Glover
Compositor: Aptara®, Inc.
Photo Researcher: Karen Hunter
Art Director: Julia Hall
Interior Designer: Julia Hall
Cover Designer: Black Eye Design/Michel Vrana
Cover Image: iStock

Credits and acknowledgments of material borrowed from other sources and reproduced, with permission, in this textbook appear on the appropriate page within the text [or on page 484].

Original edition published by Pearson Education, Inc., Upper Saddle River, New Jersey, USA. Copyright © 2013 Pearson Education, Inc. This edition is authorized for sale only in Canada.

If you purchased this book outside the United States or Canada, you should be aware that it has been imported without the approval of the publisher or the author.

Copyright © 2013 Pearson Canada Inc. All rights reserved. Manufactured in the United States of America. This publication is protected by copyright and permission should be obtained from the publisher prior to any prohibited reproduction, storage in a retrieval system, or transmission in any form or by any means, electronic, mechanical, photocopying, recording, or likewise. To obtain permission(s) to use material from this work, please submit a written request to Pearson Canada Inc., Permissions Department, 26 Prince Andrew Place, Don Mills, Ontario, M3C 2T8, or fax your request to 416-447-3126, or submit a request to Permissions Requests at **www.pearsoncanada.ca.**

10 9 8 7 6 5 4 3 2 1 [TBD]

Library and Archives Canada Cataloguing in Publication

   Selling today : partnering to create value / Gerald L. Manning . . . [et al.]. — 6th Canadian ed.

Includes index.
ISBN 978-0-13-216108-4

1. Selling—Textbooks.   I. Manning, Gerald L.

HF5438.25.S45 2012   658.85   C2011-906904-0

ISBN 978-0-13-2161

Contents

Part V Developing a Presentation Strategy 226

Preface

As the Western world completes its transition from a production focus to a sales-and-service focus, it is clear that today's business people are required to have a better understanding of the fundamentals of personal selling than those of the past. This push to a more sales-and-service-dominant logic is particularly strong in North America. According to the U.S. Bureau of Labor Statistics, seven of the top ten largest occupations have a significant selling component.

In order to *create and deliver superior value* to their customers, more and more salespeople are adopting a partnering style of selling to build long-term, strategic relationships with their customers. Having these long-term relationships is important, as it is more profitable for companies to retain existing customers than it is to acquire new ones. The pivotal role of a *partnering style of selling* in today's highly competitive business environment is a common theme throughout the 6th Canadian Edition of *Selling Today: Partnering to Create Value*.

The primary goal of each revision of *Selling Today* is to develop the finest research-backed and most practical and applied text available in the marketplace. The revision process begins with a thorough review of several hundred articles, books, and research reports. The authors also study popular sales training programs such as Conceptual Selling, SPIN Selling, Integrity Selling, and Solution Selling. These training programs are used by major corporations such as Microsoft, Marriott, UPS, SAS Institute, Purolator, and Xerox Corporation. Of course, reviews and suggestions by professors and students influence decisions made during the revision process.

STAYING ON THE CUTTING EDGE: NEW TO THIS EDITION

Since our last edition, the business environment and research on professional selling have undergone significant changes. As active researchers, practitioners, and consultants in the field of selling, our primary goal is to provide an up-to-date and cutting-edge treatment of the field. At the same time, we painstakingly incorporate more "learning by doing" materials to equip you with hands-on experience that is not available—at least to the best of our knowledge—in any other books on the market. The 6th Canadian Edition of *Selling Today* describes how sales professionals must cope with new forces shaping the world of sales and marketing with a balanced blend of cutting-edge academic and practical materials. The most significant changes in the new edition include:

- The new subtitle—***Partnering to Create Value***—reflects a reoccurring theme that is present in the 6th Edition and new to the *Selling Today* series. That is, in today's competitive market a "partnering style of selling" creates a competitive advantage for sales organizations that translates into increased customer value.

- Chapter 1 of the 6th Canadian Edition—***Relationship Selling Opportunities in the Information Economy***—has been reorganized and rewritten in order to immediately engage you in the field of personal selling. Exciting information-age selling careers are highlighted to educate you on the career paths available to you when you enter the workforce. In addition, the pressing need for selling skills in most 21st-century knowledge worker careers is outlined to solidify the importance of personal selling in today's information economy.

■ The 6th Canadian Edition of *Selling Today* is the first textbook to include a complete chapter on how salespeople ***"Determine Customer Needs Using a Consultative Questioning Strategy"*** (Chapter 11). The advent of the Marketing Concept some 50 years ago initiated a focus on meeting customer needs; however, until now the execution of this strategy from a personal selling standpoint has not been clearly explained in a single chapter. With a close correlation to the questioning strategy of Neil Rackham's number one-selling book *Spin Selling*, this new 6th Canadian Edition chapter is the first to illustrate the application of these questions to a college classroom setting. Highlighted in this chapter is the importance of discovering customer needs and configuring value-added product solutions to meet those needs. Being the first to cite results of major research studies conducted on the strategic use of questions by high-performing salespeople, *Selling Today* is at the forefront of personal selling books in terms of academic research. A professionally produced training video entitled *Questions, Questions, Questions* complements these research findings and illustrates the imperative use of questions in a consultative selling setting.

■ Further documenting the impact of the marketing concept on the sales force, Chapter 2—***Evolution of Selling Models That Complement the Marketing Concept***—is the first chapter to explain how the marketing concept has produced the new personal selling models and strategies used by high-performing salespeople and sales organizations today.

■ The 6th Canadian Edition features a reorganized and rewritten chapter titled ***"Creating Value with the Consultative Sales Presentation/Demonstration"*** (Chapter 12) with new research illustrating the value that ethically used persuasion can have on helping customers make effective buying decisions.

■ The 6th Canadian Edition features new boxed features in many chapters. We would like to point your attention to those titled **Social Media and Selling Today, From the Field,** and **Global Business Insight**—all new to this edition. Please also note the many chapter references on how social media is used by today's sales organizations and individual salespeople.

■ Academic articles and research from professional journals such as Journal of Professional Selling and Sales Management, Journal of Marketing, and Harvard Business Review is referenced throughout the text.

BUILDING ON TRADITIONAL STRENGTHS

Selling Today: Partnering to Create Value has been successful because the authors continue to build on strengths that have been enthusiastically praised by instructors and students. Speaking to these strengths, *Selling Today* has become the standard for personal selling textbooks internationally. International editions of the book have been sold in over 30 different countries, including China, Croatia, Indonesia, and Spain, to help attain this leadership position. Of particular note, recent success is due in large part to the research focus applied to the content herein. *Selling Today* is the premier research-backed textbook in the marketplace for personal selling.

Previous editions of *Selling Today* have chronicled the evolution of consultative selling, strategic selling, partnering, customer relationship management, and value-added selling. This edition provides new material on each of these important concepts.

1. **The four broad strategic areas of personal selling,** introduced in Chapter 2, serve as a catalyst for skill development and professional growth throughout the textbook. Future success in selling depends heavily on your ability to develop relationship, product, customer, and presentation strategies. Salespeople who have achieved long-term success in personal selling have mastered the skills needed in each of these four strategic areas.

2. **The partnering era is described in detail.** Partnership selling principles, so important to today's successful selling and marketing strategies, are presented and clearly illustrated throughout the text. Strategic alliances—the highest form of partnering—are also discussed in detail.

3. **Value-added selling strategies** are presented throughout the text. Salespeople today are guided by a new principle of personal selling: *Partnerships are established and maintained only when the salesperson creates customer value.* Customers have fundamentally changed their expectations. They want to partner with salespeople who can create value, not just communicate it. Value creation involves a series of improvements in the sales process that enhance the customer's experience.

4. **Real-world examples**, a hallmark of previous editions and a continued focus in this edition, build the reader's interest in personal selling and promote an understanding of the major topics and concepts. With opening vignettes at the beginning of each chapter that put you in the shoes of the salesperson, and role plays that allow you to utilize the skills you have learned, the real-world examples truly enrich the overall learning experience. The Reality Selling Today Video Series features successful young salespeople and provides real-world examples of sales careers and presentations. *Five new Reality Selling Today Videos have been added to this series for the 6th Canadian Edition.* Additional real selling examples have been obtained from a range of progressive organizations, large and small, such as Xerox, Hilti, UPS, Tenrox, WFS Ltd., and more.

5. In addition to the role-play exercises and video case problems, the **Reality Selling Today Video Role Plays**—which feature 11 role-play scenarios—remain an invaluable resource. Found in Appendix 1, these scenarios give you the chance to assume the role of a salesperson in selling situations that are relevant to today's competitive environment. These role-play scenarios build on what you have learned in the **Reality Selling Today Video** sales presentations and interviews. The 11 detailed salesperson/customer role-play scenarios use the actual products and sales positions of the salespeople who appeared in the Reality Selling Today Videos. Websites of the companies you will be using to role-play sales presentations are supplied so that you can learn appropriate amounts of product and company information. The Reality Selling Today Video interviews and sales presentations provide the necessary background and contextual information for you to use in both selecting the scenario and conducting the role play. The role plays are also specifically designed to prepare you for professional selling role-play competitions at annual college and university conventions.

6. The **knowing-doing gap,** common in personal selling classes, is closed by having you, the student, participate in the comprehensive role play/simulation "Partnership Selling: A Role Play/Simulation for Selling Today," available on the companion website to the text. You assume the role of a new sales trainee employed by the Park Inn International Convention Centre. Serving as an excellent capstone experience, you develop the critical skills needed to apply relationship, product, customer, and presentation strategies.

7. **Four professionally produced sales training videos** titled *The Adaptive Selling Today Training Video Series* are featured in the 6th Canadian Edition, including a new *Adaptive Selling Today Training Video* that presents *negotiating challenges and strategies* vital to success in personal selling (Chapter 13). These videos—*Communication Styles: A Key to Adaptive Selling; Questions, Questions, Questions: Adapting Your Questions to Customer's Needs; Negotiations: Solving the Tough Problems and Adapting Negotiations for Win-Win Solutions; and Closing the Sale with Questions: Adapting Your Close to Your Customer's Needs*—demonstrate important skills presented in the text. In addition to the *Communication Styles* video, *Selling Today* is the only text to provide **a comprehensive online adaptive communication/behavioural style assessment, free to users of the text** (Chapter 4). The Selling Today Adaptive/ Communication Style Assessment Exercise not only helps students discover and enhance their own communication style, but can also be used to assess customers' and colleagues' styles. Detailed suggestions for improving relationships are also provided.

8. **New Decision-Making Mini Simulations and BizSkill Simulations** are available with the 6th Canadian edition. These simulations showcase real-world decision-making scenarios that challenge students to make critical choices in a business context. Students receive feedback for each choice that they make, and this feedback helps to illustrate how everyday decisions impact businesses.

9. **The following high-interest boxed inserts** are presented throughout the text:

    ■ **From the Field.** These real-world examples explain how selling skills affect the success of persons who may or may not consider themselves salespeople.

    ■ **Selling in Action.** These concise inserts feature contemporary issues in selling to keep the readers of *Selling Today* abreast of the latest developments.

    ■ **Global Business Etiquette.** These brief inserts provide practical tips on how to build global relationships. Most inserts focus on a specific country.

    ■ **Social Media.** Informing you how social networking applies to personal selling, these succinct inserts identify how social media networks such as Facebook, Twitter, LinkedIn, and YouTube can be used effectively in the selling process.

10. **End-of-chapter summaries are now organized into bullet points** corresponding to the key points that appear in the Chapter Preview of each chapter. These summaries provide you with a review tool that can be used to understand how the concepts and themes covered are related to one another—i.e., the "big picture."

11. A **complete update** of key terms for selling appears in each chapter. These terms are boldfaced and defined throughout the text.

ORGANIZATION OF THIS BOOK

The material in *Selling Today* continues to be organized around the four pillars of personal selling: relationship strategy, product strategy, customer strategy, and presentation strategy. The first two chapters set the stage for an in-depth study of these strategies. The first chapter gives you the opportunity to explore career opportunities in the four major employment areas: services, retail, wholesale, and manufacturing, while the second chapter describes the evolution of personal selling.

Research indicates that high-performance salespeople are better able to build and maintain relationships than are moderate performers. Part 2, **Developing a Relationship Strategy**, focuses on several important person-to-person relationship-building practices that contribute to success in personal selling. Chapter 3 is entitled "Creating Value with a Relationship Strategy" and Chapter 4 is entitled "Communication Styles: A Key to Adaptive Selling. Chapter 5 examines the influence of ethics on relationships between customers and salespeople.

Part 3, **Developing a Product Strategy**, examines the importance of complete and accurate product, company, and competitive knowledge in personal selling. A well-informed salesperson is in a strong position to configure value-added product solutions for customers' unique needs.

Part 4, **Developing a Customer Strategy**, presents information on why and how customers buy and explains how to identify prospects. With increased knowledge of the customer, salespeople are in a better position to understand customers' unique wants and needs and create customer value in the multi-call, lifetime customer setting.

The concept of a salesperson as an advisor, consultant, value creator, and partner to buyers is stressed in Part 5, **Developing a Presentation Strategy**. As was the case in the 5th Canadian Edition, emphasis is placed on the need-satisfaction presentation model. New to the 6th Canadian Edition is a chapter titled "Determining Customer Needs Using a Consultative Questioning Strategy" (Chapter 11), which is unique to this book and cannot be found in any other personal selling textbook. Part 6 includes two chapters: "Opportunity Management: The Key to Greater Sales Productivity" and "Management of the Sales Force."

The new edition features an improved Appendix 1, "Reality Selling Today Role-Play Scenarios," which now includes 11 role-play scenarios that provide you with the opportunity to—of course—sell.

A SPECIAL NOTE TO STUDENTS ON HOW TO USE THE BOOK

This 6th Canadian Edition of *Selling Today* has several new features that distinguish it from other texts. Here we offer you a few tips to make the most out of the materials presented in the new edition.

Selling is fun. That does not mean it is easy to close a deal. Each chapter in this new edition has been reorganized with the sole goal of providing you with a systematic summary of key concepts related to the topic area and ample application exercises. While there are different ways you can approach the text, we believe it is most effective to start each chapter with a concrete understanding of how the chapter fits into the big picture of selling through value creation, the overriding theme of this textbook. In this regard, we have extensively revised and updated the chapter previews, chapter summaries, key terms, review questions, and cross-references among the chapters to assist you in integrating key concepts.

Practice makes perfect. We have created numerous role-play exercises that resemble real-life selling situations. In our experience, some students may dismiss these exercises as easy. Try one of the exercises and you will see how these students could not be more wrong. Don't be mistaken—the exercises are not that difficult, but we do inject a great deal of reality into them to make them complex enough to provide you with the opportunity to hone your selling skills. So practise them with a friend, a family member, or in front of a mirror.

Finally, **observe, analyze, and think about your experiences with salespeople in everyday life**, using the concepts and themes you have learned from the text. Think about how those salespeople sell to you, or how you would do it differently if you were them.

We encourage you to write to us regarding your experience with this new edition.

SELLING TODAY SUPPLEMENTS

Selling Today: Partnering to Create Value, 6th Canadian Edition, is accompanied by a complete supplements package. The instructor resources listed below are password protected and available for download via **www.pearsoncanada.ca**

Instructor's Resource Manual. The comprehensive Instructor's Manual includes detailed presentation outlines, answers to review questions, a trainer's guide for the *Grey Issues* selling ethics game, suggested responses to learning activities, instructions for using the case problems, and a complete trainer's guide for using the role play/simulation.

Test Item File. More than 1000 test questions—including multiple-choice, true/false, and essay questions—are provided in Microsoft Word format. The Test Item File enables instructors to view and edit the existing questions, add new questions, and generate tests. This robust test bank is also available in My Test format (see below).

My Test. The new edition test bank comes with *My Test*, a powerful assessment-generation program that helps instructors easily create and print quizzes, tests, and exams as well as homework or practice handouts. Questions and tests can all be authorized online, allowing instructors ultimate flexibility and the ability to efficiently manage assessments at any time, from anywhere.

PowerPoint Slides. A collection of more than 200 transparencies—culled from the textbook or specifically designed to complement chapter content—is also available electronically in PowerPoint software.

Companion Website. The companion website (**www.pearsoncanada.ca/manning**) offers students valuable resources, including chapter quizzes and exercises, Decision-Making Mini Simulations and BizSkill Simulations, Adaptive Selling videos, role-play videos, a Virtual Marketing Library, and an online assessment tool for better understanding one's own style as well as the adaptive selling communication style of others. Sales literature and support materials for completing role plays as part of "Partnership Selling: A Role Play/Simulation for Selling Today" is also supplied on the companion website.

DVD Videos. There are several new videos available with the 6th Canadian Edition that will be invaluable tools in the classroom.

Reality Selling Today Video Series—In response to high demand from instructors, the Reality Selling Today Video Series, introduced in the 5th Canadian

Edition, was expanded. The 6th Canadian Edition offers five new video sets with accompanying chapter opening vignettes, case problems, and role-plays that demonstrate how recent college graduates are using their selling skills to pursue rewarding sales careers. A comprehensive listing of these videos is presented in Appendix 1.

Adaptive Selling Today Training Video Series—This four-video series now includes a new sales training video based on the content of Chapter 13, "Negotiating Buyer Concerns." For the first time, students can view the types of negotiating situations salespeople encounter—in a classroom setting. Based on extensive research in selling organizations, students learn how to negotiate win-win solutions to overcome the price problem.

Pearson Custom Library. For enrollments of at least 25 students, you can create your own textbook by choosing the chapters that best suit your own course needs. To begin building your custom text, visit www.pearsoncustomlibrary.com. You may also work with a dedicated Pearson Custom editor to create your ideal text—publishing your own original content or mixing and matching Pearson content. Contact your local Pearson Representative to get started.

Technology Specialists. Pearson's Technology Specialists work with faculty and campus course designers to ensure that Pearson technology products, assessment tools, and online course materials are tailored to meet your specific needs. This highly qualified team is dedicated to helping schools take full advantage of a wide range of educational resources, by assisting in the integration of a variety of instructional materials and media formats. Your local Pearson Education sales representative can provide you with more details on this service program.

CourseSmart for Instructors. CourseSmart goes beyond traditional expectations to provide instant online access to the textbooks and course materials you need at a lower cost for students. And even as students save money, you can save time and hassle with a digital eTextbook that allows you to search for the most relevant content at the very moment you need it. Whether it's evaluating textbooks or creating lecture notes to help students with difficult concepts, CourseSmart can make life a little easier. See how when you visit www.coursesmart.com/instructors.

CourseSmart for Students. CourseSmart goes beyond traditional expectations to provide instant online access to the textbooks and course materials you need at an average savings of 60 percent. With instant access from any computer and the ability to search your text, you'll find the content you need quickly, no matter where you are. And with online tools like highlighting and note-taking, you can save time and study efficiently. See all the benefits at **www.coursesmart.com/students**.

THE SEARCH FOR WISDOM IN THE AGE OF INFORMATION

The search for the fundamentals of personal selling has become more difficult in the age of information. The glut of information threatens our ability to identify what is true, right, or lasting. The search for knowledge begins with a review of information, and wisdom is gleaned from knowledge. Books continue to be one of the best sources of wisdom. Many new books, and several classics, were used as references for the 6th Canadian Edition of

Selling Today, Partnering to Create Value. A sample of the more than 40 books used to prepare this edition follows:

The Tipping Point by Malcolm Gladwell
Integrity Selling for the 21st Century by Ron Willingham
A Whole New Mind by Daniel H. Pink
Rethinking the Sales Force by Neil Rackham and John R. DeVincentis
Business Ethics by O. C. Ferrell, John Fraedrich, and Linda Ferrell
Negotiating Genius by Deepak Malhotra and Max H. Bazerman
Blur: The Speed of Change in the Connected Economy by Stan Davis and Christopher Meyer
Close the Deal by Sam Deep and Lyle Sussman
Complete Business Etiquette Handbook by Barbara Pachter and Marjorie Brody
Effective Human Relations: Personal and Organizational Applications by Barry L. Reece and Rhonda Brandt
First Impressions: What You Don't Know About How Others See You by Ann Demarais and Valerie White
Hug Your Customers by Jack Mitchell
Keeping the Funnel Full by Don Thomson
Marketing Imagination by Ted Levitt
Marketing: Real People, Real Choices by Michael R. Solomon, Greg W. Marshall, and Elnora W. Stuart
Megatrends by John Naisbitt
Personal Styles and Effective Performance by David W. Merrill and Roger H. Reid
Psycho-Cybernectics by Maxwell Maltz
Questions—The Answer to Sales by Duane Sparks
Re-Imagine! Business Excellence in a Disruptive Age by Tom Peters
Self Matters by Phillip C. McGraw
SPIN Selling by Neil Rackham
SPIN Selling Fieldbook by Neil Rackham
Strategic Selling by Robert B. Miller and Stephen E. Heiman
The 7 Habits of Highly Effective People by Stephen R. Covey
The Customer Revolution by Patricia Seybold
The Double Win by Denis Waitley
The New Conceptual Selling by Stephen E. Heiman and Diane Sanchez
The New Professional Image by Susan Bixler and Nancy Nix-Rice
The New Solution Selling by Keith M. Eades
The Power of 5 by Harold H. Bloomfield and Robert K. Cooper
The Sedona Method by Hale Dwoskin
The Success Principles by Jack Canfield
Value-Added Selling by Tom Reilly
Working with Emotional Intelligence by Daniel Goleman
Zero-Resistance Selling by Maxwell Maltz, Dan S. Kennedy, William T. Brooks, Matt Oechsli, Jeff Paul, and Pamela Yellen

ACKNOWLEDGMENTS

Many people have made contributions to the 6th Canadian Edition of *Selling Today: Partnering to Create Value.* We thank award-winning video producer Art Bauer for his creativity, dedication, and attention to detail in the production of the Adaptive Selling Today Training Video Series. We also thank Son Lam for his help and contributions with the Reality Selling Video Series, Cases, and Role-Play exercises. Throughout the years the text has been improved as a result of numerous helpful comments and recommendations by both students and faculty. We extend special appreciation to the following reviewers:

Andrea Ely, Capilano University; Don Hill, Langara College; Athean Hurezeanu, Seneca; Frank Maloney, George Brown; David Moulton, Douglas College; Wendy Threader, Algonquin College; Duane Weaver, Vancouver Island University.

About the Authors

Gerald L. Manning
Des Moines Area Community
College

Mr. Manning served as chair of the Marketing/Management Department for more than 30 years. In addition to his administrative duties, he has served as lead instructor in sales and sales management. The classroom has provided him with an opportunity to study the merits of various experimental learning approaches such as role plays, simulations, games, and interactive demonstrations. *Partnership Selling: A Role Play/Simulation for Selling Today*, included in the 11th U.S. edition, was developed and tested in the classroom by Mr. Manning. He has applied numerous personal selling principles and practices in the real world as the owner of a real estate development and management company.

Mr. Manning has served as a sales and marketing consultant to senior management and owners of over 500 businesses, including several national companies. He appears regularly as a speaker at national sales conferences. Mr. Manning received the Outstanding Instructor of the Year award given annually by his college.

Dr. Michael Ahearne
University of Houston

Dr. Ahearne is the C.T. Bauer Chaired Professor in Marketing and the Executive Director of the Sales Excellence Institute. The SEI is widely recognized as the leading university-based sales institute in the world, training more than 2000 sales students, placing PhD students at top research universities, and working with more than 200 major corporations annually. He earned his PhD in Marketing from Indiana University. He has also served on the faculty at the University of Connecticut and Pennsylvania State University. In addition, he has internationally lectured about sales and sales management in such countries as Austria, Belgium, France, Germany, India, Italy, Spain, and Russia.

Dr. Ahearne has published articles in leading academic journals on factors influencing the performance of salespeople, sales teams, and sales organizations. His work has appeared in the *Journal of Marketing, Journal of Marketing Research, Management Science, Journal of Applied Psychology, International Journal of Research in Marketing,* and *Journal of the Academy of Marketing Science*. In addition to reviewing for the top marketing and management journals, he currently serves as the editor of the *Journal of Personal Selling and Sales Management*—the leading international scholarly journal in the sales field. His work has also been featured in numerous trade and popular press publications, including *Business 2.0, Business Investors Daily, U.S. News & World Report,* and *INC Magazine*.

Before entering academia, Dr. Ahearne played professional baseball for the Montreal Expos Organization and worked in the health care industry for Eli Lilly and PCS Healthcare. He actively consults in many industries, including insurance, health care, consumer packaged goods, technology, and transportation.

Dr. Barry L. Reece
Virginia Polytechnic Institute
and State University

Dr. Reece has devoted more than three decades to teaching, researching, consulting, and developing training programs in the areas of sales, leadership, human relations, and management. He has conducted over 600 seminars and workshops for public and private sector organizations. He has written extensively in the areas of sales, supervision, communications, and management. Dr. Reece was named Trainer of the Year by the Valleys of Virginia Chapter of the American Society for Training and Development and was awarded the Excellence in Teaching Award by the College of Human Sciences and Education at Virginia Polytechnic Institute and State University.

Dr. Reece has contributed to numerous journals and is author or co-author of 30 books, including *Business, Human Relations—Principles and Practices, Supervision and Leadership in Action,* and *Effective Human Relations—Personal and Organizational Applications.* He has served as a consultant to Lowe's Companies, Inc.; Wachovia; WLR Foods; Kinney Shoe Corporation; Carilion Health System; and numerous other for-profit and not-for-profit organizations.

Dr. H. F. (Herb) MacKenzie
Brock University

Dr. MacKenzie is currently Chair, Marketing, International Business, and Strategy and an associate professor of marketing at Brock University in St. Catharines, Ontario. He has taught in the undergraduate, graduate, and executive education programs at universities in Canada, Europe, and the Middle East, and has been consulting to both private- and public-sector businesses since 1985. He has over 15 years of industrial sales and sales management experience and has published many cases, conference proceedings, and articles in the areas of sales management, buyer-seller relationships, and distribution channel management. He has authored and co-authored textbooks on introduction to business, personal selling, sales management, and marketing, and has edited four Canadian marketing casebooks. He has been recognized by his students in recent years as Professor of the Year and Marketing Professor of the Year and was twice the winner of the Faculty of Business Faculty Award of Excellence.

KEEPING CURRENT IN A CHANGING WORLD

Throughout the past decade, Professors Manning, Ahearne, Reece, and MacKenzie have relied on three strategies to keep current in the dynamic field of personal selling. First, they are actively involved in sales training and consulting. Frequent interaction with salespeople and sales managers provides valuable insight regarding contemporary issues and developments in the field of personal selling. A second major strategy involves extensive research and development activities. The major focus of these activities has been factors that contribute to high-performance salespeople. The third major strategy involves completion of training and development programs offered by North America's most respected sales training companies. Professors Manning, Ahearne, Reece, and MacKenzie have completed seminars and workshops offered by Wilson Learning Corporation,

Forum Corporation, Franklin-Covey, Sedona Training Associates, the Association for Humanistic Psychology, and several other organizations.

AN INVESTMENT IN THE FUTURE

Charles Schwab, the great industrialist and entrepreneur, said, "We are all salespeople every day of our lives, selling our ideas and enthusiasm to those with whom we come in contact." As authors, we suggest that you retain this book for future reference. Periodic review of the ideas in this text will help you daily in areas such as:

- interacting more effectively with others
- interviewing for new jobs in the future
- understanding and training salespeople who work for you or with you
- selling new ideas to senior management, co-workers, or employees you might be supervising
- selling products or services that you represent as a salesperson

We wish you much success and happiness in applying your knowledge of personal selling.

Gerald L. Manning
Michael Ahearne
Barry L. Reece
H. F. (Herb) MacKenzie

SELLING TODAY

Sixth
Canadian
Edition

Part I
Developing a Personal Selling Philosophy

I knew early in my studies that I wanted to be in sales, and earning the CPSA Sales Excellence Award helped confirm my career choice. I get tremendous personal satisfaction helping customers solve buying problems.

—Mariola Czarniak, Regional Accounts Manager, Xerox Canada Ltd., Advanced Office Solutions

Canadian Professional
Sales Association
L'association canadienne
des professionnels
de la vente

SELL MORE. SELL SMARTER.

**CPSA
ACPV**

VENDEZ PLUS. VENDEZ MIEUX.

cpsa.com

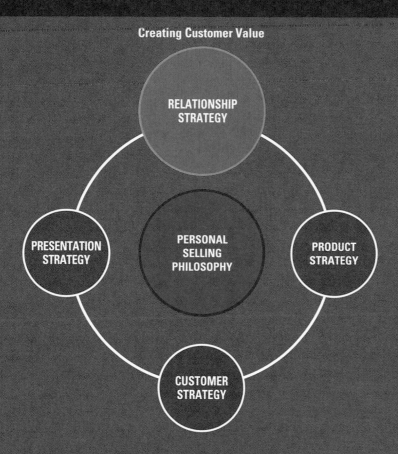

Creating Customer Value

RELATIONSHIP STRATEGY

PRESENTATION STRATEGY

PERSONAL SELLING PHILOSOPHY

PRODUCT STRATEGY

CUSTOMER STRATEGY

The two chapters that make up Part 1 establish a foundation for the entire textbook. Chapter 1 provides a contemporary definition and description of personal selling and describes information-age personal selling career opportunities. Sales training programs offered by academic institutions, sales training companies, and employers are also presented. In response to the developments associated with the information economy, Chapter 2 presents the evolution of contemporary selling models that complement the marketing concept. Chapter 2 also introduces the major themes that connect all of the chapters.

Chapter 1
Relationship Selling Opportunities in the Information Economy

Learning Objectives

After studying this chapter, you should be able to

1 Define *personal selling* and describe the three prescriptions of a personal selling philosophy.

2 Describe the emergence of relationship selling in the age of information.

3 Discuss the rewarding aspects of a career in selling today.

4 Discuss the different employment settings in selling today.

5 Explain how personal selling skills have become one of the master skills needed for success in the information age and how personal selling skills contribute to the work performed by knowledge workers.

6 Identify the four major sources of sales training.

 Reality Selling Today Video Series

Job seekers who visit websites such as Monster.ca are usually surprised to discover that sales careers represent one of the largest job-posting categories. The next big surprise comes when they discover the great variety of companies that hire salespeople. Alex Homer (pictured above) is a professional clothier for the Tom James Company (www.tomjames.com), the world's largest manufacturer and retailer of custom-made, luxury clothing. Tom James has sales offices in Canada, the United Kingdom, France, Germany, the Netherlands, Australia, and across the United States. Each Tom James client purchases directly from one of the company's well-trained professional clothiers, who provide clients with wardrobe consultation on a variety of fashion topics such as wardrobe coordination, current trends, proper fit, pattern and cloth selection, necessary collection pieces, and attire for specific occasions. Tom James clothiers like Alex always come to their clients because appointments are conducted at the client's location of choice.

Alex Homer discovered the Tom James Company in 2007 after he placed second in the national sales competition for students. Tom James took interest in Alex, and Alex decided to learn more about Tom James by participating in ride-alongs with the company's existing sales representatives. He liked it and decided to accept the job offer. Before starting to actually call on customers, Alex received training in selling, product knowledge,

and prospecting. Regarding career development, Tom James offers new hires the necessary training to build a successful selling career regardless of their level of past experience. It also offers opportunities for net worth building, such as profit sharing, retirement plans, and stock plans. In 2009, 30 percent of Tom James sales professionals earned $100 000 or more in commissions, leadership pay, bonuses, and stock dividends.

PERSONAL SELLING TODAY—A DEFINITION AND A PHILOSOPHY

Personal selling OCCURS WHEN A COMPANY REPRESENTATIVE INTERACTS DIRECTLY WITH a customer or prospective customer to present information about a product or service.[1] It is a process of developing relationships; discovering needs; matching the appropriate products with those needs; and communicating benefits through informing, reminding, or persuading. The term **product** should be broadly interpreted to encompass information, services, ideas, and issues. Increasingly, personal selling is viewed as a process that adds value. In an ideal situation, the salesperson builds a mutually rewarding relationship, diagnoses the customer's needs, and custom-fits the product to meet those needs. Having knowledge of these customer needs will lead to higher customer satisfaction and willingness to purchase a product.[2]

personal selling Involves person-to-person communication with a prospect. It is a process of developing relationships; discovering customer needs; matching appropriate products with those needs; and communicating benefits through informing, reminding, or persuading.

product Should be broadly interpreted to encompass physical goods, services, and ideas.

Strategic/Consultative Selling Model	
Strategic step	**Prescription**
Develop a personal selling philosophy	• Adopt marketing concept • Value personal selling • Become a problem solver/partner

Figure 1.1 Today, salespeople use a strategic plan based on a personal philosophy that emphasizes adopting the marketing concept, valuing personal selling, and becoming a problem solver/partner.

Preparation for a career in personal selling begins with the development of a personal philosophy or set of beliefs that provides guidance. To some degree, this philosophy is like the rudder that steers a ship. Without a rudder, the ship's direction is unpredictable. Without a personal philosophy, the salesperson's behaviour also is unpredictable.

The development of a **personal selling philosophy** involves three prescriptions: adopt the marketing concept, value personal selling, and assume the role of a problem solver or partner in helping customers make buying decisions (Fig. 1.1). These three prescriptions for success in personal selling are presented here as part of the Strategic/Consultative Selling Model. This model is expanded in future chapters to include additional strategic steps in the selling process. Chapter 2 will illustrate how the marketing concept has produced an evolving set of improvements to the sales process, moving it from peddling to value-added partnering.

EMERGENCE OF RELATIONSHIP SELLING IN THE INFORMATION ECONOMY

THE RESTRUCTURING FROM AN INDUSTRIAL ECONOMY TO AN **information economy** began approximately 50 years ago (Fig. 1.2). During this period, our economy began shifting from an emphasis on industrial activity to an emphasis on information processing. We were giving way to a new society where most of us would work with information instead of producing goods.[3] Today we live in an age in which the effective exchange of information is the foundation of most economic transactions, and the implications for personal selling are profound. We will describe the four major developments that have shaped the information economy and discuss the implications for personal selling.

Major advances occur in information technology and electronic commerce. The information age has spawned an information technology revolution. Salespeople and other players in today's information age use personal computers, mobile phones, smartphones, websites, Customer Relationship Management (CRM) applications with cloud computing, email, instant messaging, blogging, social media—including Facebook, YouTube, Twitter, etc.—and other forms of technology. Referred to as **selling 2.0**, these information technology tools, along with innovative sales practices, are used to create value for both the buyer and seller by improving the speed, collaboration, customer engagement, and accountability of the sales process.

personal selling philosophy A salesperson's commitment to value personal selling, adopt the marketing concept, and become a problem solver and partner to help customers make better buying decisions.

information economy An economy where there is an emphasis on information processing.

selling 2.0 Information technology tools along with innovative sales practices used to create value for both buyers and sellers by improving the speed, collaboration, customer engagement, and accountability of the sales process.

Industrial Economy 1860–1960	Information Economy 1960–2020
Major advances in manufacturing and transportation	Major advances in information technology
Strategic resources are capital and natural resources	Strategic resource is information
Business is defined by its products and factories	Business is defined by customer relationships
Sales success depends on meeting sales quotas	Sales success depends on adding value

INCREASES IN RELATIONSHIP SELLING AND RELATIONSHIP MARKETING →

Figure 1.2 The age of information has greatly influenced personal selling. Salespeople today use a variety of technological tools to gather and process information to create customer value. They recognize that information is a strategic resource and that relationship skills are needed to build trust for information acceptance.

The explosive growth of electronic commerce and other Internet activities has changed the way we use computers. Stan Davis, futurist and co-author of *Blur: The Speed of Change in the Connected Economy*, notes that in today's information economy, we use computers less for data crunching and more for connecting. These connections involve people to people, company to customer, machine to machine, product to service, organization to organization, and all these in combination.[4] Without these connections, information-age workers cannot do their jobs. People who work extensively with information, such as salespeople, need these electronic connections to conduct their information gathering, information sharing, and information management responsibilities.

Information is a strategic resource. Advances in information technology have increased the speed by which we acquire, process, and disseminate information. David Shenk, author of *Data Smog: Surviving the Information Glut*, notes that we have moved from a state of information scarcity to one of information overload.[5] In an era of limitless data, informed salespeople can help us decide which information has value and which information should be ignored. Salespeople are the eyes and ears of today's marketplace. They collect a wide range of product, customer, and competitive intelligence.[6]

Business is defined by customer relationships. Michael Hammer, consultant and author of *The Agenda*, says the *real* new economy is the customer economy. As scarcity has given way to abundance, as supply has exceeded demand, and as customers have become better informed, we have seen a power shift. Customers have taken more control of their own destinies.[7]

On the surface, the major focus of the age of information seems to be the accumulation of more and more information and the never-ending search for new forms of information technology. It's easy to overlook the importance of the human element. Humans, not computers, have the ability to think, feel, and create ideas. It is no coincidence that relationship selling and relationship marketing, which emphasize long-term, mutually satisfying buyer–seller partnering relationships, began to gain support at the beginning of the information

Social Media and Selling Today

Creating Customer Value with Social Media

Popular business strategies such as "Selling is a Contact Sport" and "Speed is Life" describe the value of social media in the selling process. Being immediately available to a customer is essential to a salesperson's success for many reasons, including providing information at the moment the customer needs it; responding to a customer's relationship-building contact; and obtaining and following up on leads. Instant outreach to one or more customers is also critical for high-performing salespeople. This instant contact capability empowers salespeople to quickly send notices of price changes, product modifications, product operation tips, service alerts, website updates, and invitations to events, both business and socially related.

Advances in communication technology enhance the value of salesperson availability and outreach by dramatically reducing the time required for salesperson and customer interactions. Among these advances is the category generally referred to as *social media*. Facebook, Twitter, YouTube and smartphones are frequently identified as key components of this category.

Facebook can be used by a salesperson to expand his or her personal information that may be found on the company's website. Products or services are also found on Facebook, allowing customers and others to learn about and discuss a salesperson's offerings. Twitter can instantly move business and relationship messages between the salesperson and the customer. Smartphones and similar mobile devices allow communications to include still and moving images designed to improve recipients' understanding and acceptance of the accompanying messages.

High-performing salespeople and their organizations are well advised to carefully study the continuous advances in communication technologies and rapidly adopt the advantages they offer.[a] Playing the serious sport of "Contact with Customers" at the fastest possible speed is now a critical necessity in a salesperson's life.

age. Companies such as DuPont, Kraft Foods, and General Electric have adopted a philosophy that focuses on customer satisfaction, team selling, and relationship selling.[8]

value-added selling Improving the sales process to create value for the customer. Salespeople add value when they offer better advice and product solutions, carefully manage customer relationships, and provide better service after the sale.

Sales success depends on adding value. Value-added selling can be defined as a series of creative improvements within the sales process that enhance the customer experience. Salespeople can create value by developing a quality relationship, carefully identifying the customer's needs, and then configuring and presenting the best possible product solution. Value is also created when the salesperson provides excellent service after the sale. Neil Rackham, author of *Rethinking the Sales Force*, and other experts in sales and marketing say that success no longer depends merely on communicating the value of products and services. Success in personal selling rests on the critical ability to create value for customers.

The value added by salespeople today is increasingly derived from intangibles such as the quality of the advice offered and the level of trust that underlies the relationship between the customer and the salesperson. The value of these intangibles can erode with shocking speed when the customer feels deceived or discovers that the competition is able to add more value to the sales process.[9]

CONSIDERATIONS FOR A FUTURE IN PERSONAL SELLING

JOB SEEKERS WHO VISIT **Monster.ca** OR **CareerBuilder.ca** ARE USUALLY SURPRISED TO discover that sales careers represent one of the largest job posting categories. Many thousands of entry-level sales positions are listed every day. The next big surprise comes when they discover the great variety of companies that hire salespeople. Some companies, such as Procter & Gamble, Purolator, and Dell, are well known across Canada. But there are many smaller, more regional companies that advertise for salespeople, as well as many foreign-owned companies that have sales forces in Canada and that may be unfamiliar to people seeking sales jobs. Toronto-based BlueSky Personnel Solutions helps companies solve their human resources needs and uses field salespeople to sell its services to prospective businesses. Würth Canada is a division of Würth Group, the world's largest fastener company. It has 447 employees, and 368 of them are salespeople. They sell to small and large customers in the automotive/trucking and maintenance/metals markets across Canada.[10]

From a personal and economic standpoint, selling can be a rewarding career. Careers in selling offer financial rewards, recognition, security, and opportunities for advancement to a degree that is unique when compared to other occupations.

Wide Range of Employment Opportunities

There are more than a million people employed in sales positions across Canada—approximately 10 percent of the Canadian workforce. In addition, the number of sales positions is increasing in most industrialized countries. Sales positions commonly rank among the jobs considered most in demand.[11] A close examination of these positions reveals that there is no single "selling" occupation. Our labour force includes hundreds of different selling careers, and chances are there are positions that match your interests, talents, and ambitions. The diversity within selling will become apparent as you study the career options discussed in this chapter.

While many college and university students ultimately become salespeople, often it's not their first career choice. Students tend to view sales as dynamic and active but feel that a selling career will require them to engage in deceitful or dishonest practices. The good news is that old stereotypes about sales are gradually going by the wayside. Students who study the careers of highly successful salespeople discover that ethical sales practices represent the key to long-term success.

Everyone Sells

Selling Is a Life Skill

Many business students who have no intention of pursuing a career in sales will eventually have successful sales careers. Some students will begin their careers in sales and then move on—sometimes to management positions in their company. Some students will begin their careers in other areas and will find that the opportunities and benefits of being in sales will motivate them to switch to sales careers. Many students will spend their whole lives in non-sales careers, but most will find that the skills they learn from selling will benefit them throughout their working lives. As we point out in this chapter, selling skills are needed by management personnel, entrepreneurs, and professionals.

Eddie Greenspan, Canada's best-known criminal lawyer, has been practising law for more than 30 years. He has many of the personal characteristics of superior salespeople: He loves what he does and he hates to lose. While salesmanship is not a word he would ascribe to as solemn a situation as a jury trial, he says, "In a court of law, you're in the business of selling the truth. . . . You have to make the listeners believe that you believe what you are selling."[b]

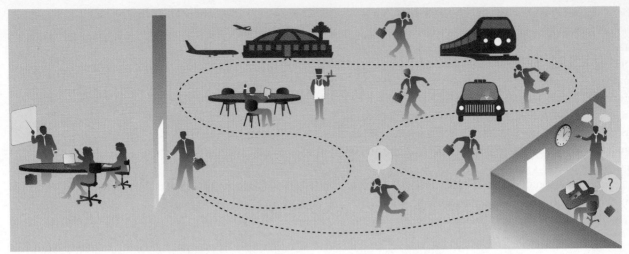

Sales is the lifeblood of any business. According to 2008 Yankee Group research study titled. "Mobile CRM Tipping Point Finally Arrives", sales representatives spend their time on the following activities:

- Face-to-face selling 26%.

- Sales prep 16%
- Administrative tasks 26%
- Travel and waiting 32%

Figure 1.3 How Salespeople Spend Their Time
A professional selling position encompasses a wide range of tasks and, as such, salespeople must possess a variety of skills.
Source: Sybase Inc., www.sybase.com/files/Thankyou_Pages/Sybase_Mobile_Solutions_for_SAP_Sales_Reps_print.pdf (accessed June 21, 2010).

Activities Performed by Salespeople

A professional selling position encompasses a wide range of tasks and, as such, salespeople must possess a variety of skills. Figure 1.3 provides important insight about how many outside salespeople spend their time on the job. Note the time spent in administrative tasks, servicing, and telephoning. This, along with face-to-face selling and travelling time, provides a large amount of variety for salespeople. In some selling positions, such as retail selling, more time may be spent in face-to-face selling.

A salesperson representing Federal Express (FedEx) makes numerous sales calls each day in an attempt to establish new accounts and provide service to established accounts. There is a wide range of potential customers who can use FedEx delivery services. A salesperson working for a Caterpillar construction equipment dealer may make only two or three sales calls per day. The products offered by the dealer are expensive and are not purchased frequently.

Freedom to Manage One's Own Time and Activities Because of the wide range of activities, most selling positions allow salespeople to be in control of how they use their time, decide what activities they will prioritize in their work schedules, and interact with a wide range of people. This contrasts with many careers where people are assigned to a particular location, assigned specific tasks, and directly supervised by others. This freedom to plan activities and prioritize the use of time, not unlike that of an entrepreneur, is high on the list of why many successful salespeople have chosen sales as a career. However, the ability to manage one's time, set priorities, and execute successfully on these priorities is critical to success in selling. We will present more on the subject of opportunity management in Chapter 16.

Titles Used in Selling Today Just as selling occupations differ, so do the titles by which salespeople are known. Their titles reflect, in part, the variety of duties they perform. A survey of current job announcements indicates that companies are using titles such as these:

Account Executive	Sales Consultant
Account Representative	Business Development Manager
Account Manager	Sales Associate
Relationship Manager	Marketing Representative
District Representative	Territory Manager
Marketing Partner	Channel Partner

Two factors have contributed to the creation of new titles. First, we have seen a shift from "selling" to "partnering." When salespeople assume a consulting or partnering role, the value of the relationship often exceeds the value of the transaction. Second, the new titles reflect a difference in education and skill sets needed for the sales position.[12] It is important to recognize, however, that there are still a large number of individuals employed in selling who prefer, and are proud, to be called "salespeople."

Salespeople, regardless of title, play an important role in sustaining the growth and profitability of organizations of all sizes. They also support the employment of many nonselling employees.

Above-Average Income

Studies dealing with incomes in the business community indicate that salespeople earn significantly higher incomes than most other workers. Some salespeople actually earn more than their sales managers and other executives within the organization. In fact, a successful career in sales and sales management can result in earnings similar to doctors, lawyers, and chief executives.[13,14] This high level of compensation—whether from base salary, bonus, or incentives—is justified for good performance. Table 1.1 provides information on sales compensation in Canada. Executive and sales force compensation continue to climb despite uncertain economic conditions.[15]

In recent years, we have seen new ways to report sales compensation for salespeople. The Hay's Group, working with C&C Market Research, developed a reporting method that tracks earnings for different types of sales approaches. Research indicates that salespeople involved in transactional sales, which generally focuses on selling products at the lowest price, also earned the lowest compensation. Sales personnel involved in value-added sales earned the highest level of compensation. These highly paid salespeople created improvements and therefore value in the sales process that enhanced the customer experience.[16]

Above-Average Psychic Income

Two major psychological needs common to all people are recognition and security. **Psychic income**, which consists of factors that provide psychological rewards, helps satisfy these important needs and motivates us to achieve higher levels of performance. The

psychic income Consists of factors that provide psychological rewards; it helps to satisfy the need for recognition and security, and motivates us to achieve higher levels of performance.

Table 1.1 Sales Compensation, Canada, $000's

Sales Compensation, Canada $000's	Base Salary			Total Cash		
	25%ile	50%ile	75%ile	25%ile	50%ile	75%ile
Sales trainee	$43.3	$47.9	$56.9	$47.7	$55.1	$63.3
Sales representative—intermediate	$50.0	$57.8	$66.8	$57.2	$66.8	$80.0
Sales representative—senior	$64.7	$77.0	$87.3	$77.1	$92.4	$112.3
Inside sales—associate	$31.7	$40.7	$42.6	$33.7	$42.1	$51.9
Inside sales—intermediate	$38.2	$44.1	$50.9	$41.0	$49.7	$59.5
Inside sales—senior	$48.9	$53.3	$58.9	$52.9	$61.5	$77.7

In addition to base salary, sales positions are generally eligible to earn annual incentive or bonus. The median target incentive opportunity for these roles, as a percentage of base salary, is 13.5%, $15.0%, 23.0%, 10.0%, 10.0%, and 10.0% for each of the above roles, respectively. The median organization size (in terms of revenues) is about $500 million.

©2010 Mercer Benchmark Database, Mercer (Canada) Limited. Printed with permission.

need for recognition has been established in numerous studies that have examined human motivation. Workers from all employment areas indicate that recognition for work well done is an important morale-building factor.

In selling, recognition will come more frequently and with greater intensity than in most other occupations. Because selling contributes so visibly to the success of most business firms, the accomplishments of sales personnel will seldom go unrecognized. Most people want to achieve some measure of security in their work. Selling is one of those occupations that usually provide job security during both good and bad times.

Opportunity for Advancement

Each year, thousands of openings appear in the ranks of supervision and management. Because salespeople work in positions of high visibility, they are in an excellent position to be chosen for advancement to positions of greater responsibility. The top executives of many of today's companies began their careers in the ranks of the sales force. Theodore Kinni, in *Selling Power*, notes, "Today's C-suites are literally bursting with sales professionals."[17] Of course, not every salesperson can become president of a large corporation, but, in the middle-management ranks, there are numerous interesting and high-paying positions in which experience in selling is a prime requisite for advancement. We present information on careers in sales management in Chapter 17.

Opportunities for Women

Prodded by a growing awareness that gender is not a barrier to success in selling, business firms are recruiting qualified women in growing numbers. The percentage of women in the sales force has increased considerably. In fact, in sales and related occupations, women comprise approximately 50 percent of the workforce.[18] Although women are still relative newcomers to industrial sales, they have enjoyed expanded career opportunities in such areas as real estate, insurance, advertising services, investments, and travel services. A growing number of women are turning to sales employment because it offers excellent economic rewards and in many cases a flexible work schedule. Flexible schedules are very appealing to women who want to balance career and family.

At Pitney Bowes, a major provider of corporate mail services, about 24 percent of the top employees are women. Many of the top salespeople are women who were formerly teachers.[19] About 20 percent of all financial advisers are women.[20]

In recent years, the labour market has become a place of churning dislocation caused by the heavy volume of mergers, acquisitions, business closings, bankruptcies, and downsizings. Personal selling careers, as well as those career areas that value selling skills, have become attractive employment options to the thousands of professionals who walk away from—or are pushed out of—corporate jobs.

EMPLOYMENT SETTINGS IN SELLING TODAY

CAREERS IN SALES INCLUDE BOTH INSIDE AND OUTSIDE SALES POSITIONS. An **inside salesperson** is one who performs selling activities at the employer's location, typically using the telephone and email. Many manufacturers and wholesalers have developed inside sales forces to take orders, make calls on customers, and provide support for outside salespeople. In some cases, the inside salespeople are called *customer service representatives* and provide a number of support services on behalf of outside salespeople.

Inside sales can be either *inbound* or *outbound*. Inbound inside salespeople respond to calls initiated by the customer. **Telemarketing** is a common form of outbound inside sales that serves several purposes, including sales and service. In some cases, this includes technical support personnel who provide technical information and answer questions. Some companies utilize sales assistants to confirm appointments, conduct credit checks, and follow up on deliveries.[21] The use of telemarketing, websites, and the Internet has grown rapidly as businesses use these methods to contact potential new customers and to follow up on current small customers or customers in distant areas.

Unlike inside sales, an **outside salesperson** travels to meet prospects and customers in their place of business or residence. Information technology companies such as Hewlett-Packard and Dell employ thousands of salespeople to sell computer systems, peripherals, and integrated technology solutions to other companies, large and small. Wholesalers across Canada, such as Sysco Canada and Acklands-Grainger, employ outside salespeople who, in addition to selling products, offer a variety of services to their customers, such as maintaining inventories, merchandising, providing promotional support, gathering and interpreting market information, extending credit, and distributing goods. In addition, many direct-to-consumer salespeople engage at least partially in outside sales—for example, interior designers, financial planners, and insurance agents.

Inside and outside salespeople for the same company often work together and rely heavily upon each other. For example, inside salespeople often prospect, generating and qualifying leads for outside salespeople to call on personally. Also, once an initial sale is made by an outside salesperson, inside salespeople are asked to provide ongoing customer contact and service, taking responsibility for meeting customer needs while being alert for opportunities to sell additional products or services.

inside salesperson A salesperson who performs selling activities at the employer's location, typically using the telephone and email.

telemarketing A common form of outbound inside sales that serves several purposes, including sales and service.

outside salesperson A salesperson who travels to meet prospects and customers in their place of business or residence.

Selling Through Channels

Many times people mistakenly think of selling jobs as being limited to the interaction between the company and the end user of a good or service. However, goods and services flow from manufacturer to end user through a *channel of distribution*.

As can be seen in Figure 1.4, sales jobs exist throughout this distribution chain.[22] In fact, many of the most promising sales careers in terms of career advancement and compensation exist at the beginning of the channel flow in the form of *business to business*, or "B2B," sales. **Trade selling** refers to the sale of a product or service to another member of the channel of distribution. For example, a manufacturer of household goods may employ sales representatives to sell its products to retailers. It may instead (or also) sell its products to wholesalers that warehouse the product and in turn the wholesaler employs sales representatives to sell these and other products to retailers that the manufacturer does not want to service directly. In the latter part of the channel flow, we find retail salespeople and, in some cases, service salespeople selling to consumers. This is often referred to as *business-to-consumer*, or "B2C" sales. As you can see, selling careers may be classified in several ways.

Similar scenarios exist with industrial products where the end user is a business rather than an individual consumer and with services where the end user is either a consumer or business user. Another example of B2B sales is **missionary**, or **detail, sales.** Rather than selling directly to the end user, the missionary salesperson attempts to generate goodwill and stimulate demand for the manufacturer's product among channel members.

Career Opportunities in the Service Channel

Sales careers in service sales include both business-to-business and business-to-consumer sales. Today nearly 80 percent of the Canadian labour force is employed in some capacity in the service sector of the economy. The growth rate for the service industry is much higher than the growth rate for goods companies. Service companies provide career opportunities in a variety of settings.

- *Hotel, motel, and convention centre services.* Each year, thousands of seminars, conferences, and business meetings are held throughout Canada. Most of these events are hosted by hotels, motels, or convention centres. The salespeople employed by these firms play an important role in attracting clients to utilize these facilities. Salespeople diversify markets and upgrade services to sell room space, food, beverages, entertainment, and other services to create an attractive atmosphere for potential clients.

  Typical of the salespeople employed in this sector are Samantha Cheuk and Erin Munro, part of the sales team at the Westin Grand in Vancouver. Samantha is a sales and catering coordinator. She works with customers to establish their meeting and food service needs when they also plan to book sleeping accommodations as part of their meeting or conference package. Erin is a catering manager. She works with customers who do not have accommodations needs but who require the hotel's meeting or dining facilities. Both Samantha and Erin must communicate effectively with customers, completely understand their specific needs, and then ensure that the hotel delivers on any promises made.[23] In the selling of hotel and convention centre sales, as well as a number of the other types of service selling, salespeople may be involved in both B2B and B2C selling, depending upon whether they are selling to a business

trade selling Refers to the sale of a product or service to another member of the channel of distribution.

missionary, or **detail, sales** Refers to sales made when the manufacturer's salesperson generates goodwill and stimulates demand among channel members, rather than through selling direct to end users.

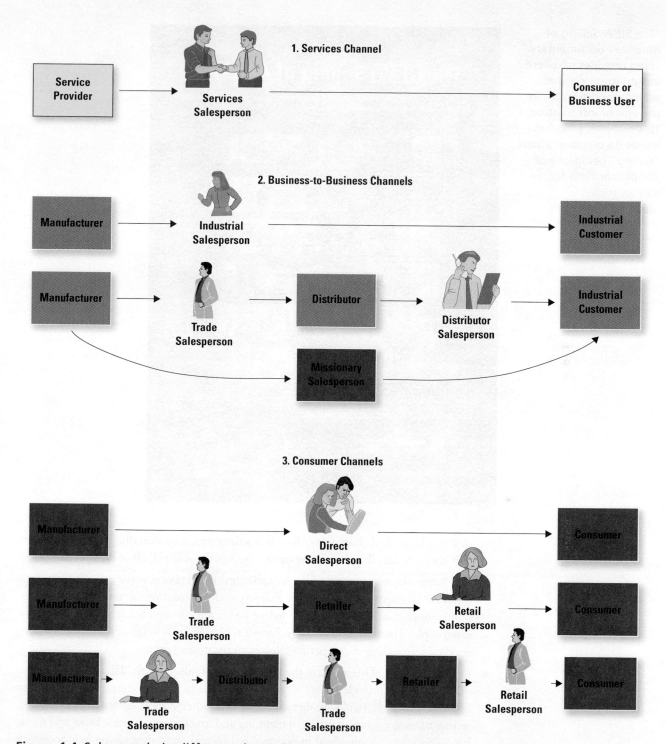

Figure 1.4 Salespeople in different channels

"The NEW Selling of America" documentary video provides excellent insight into personal selling opportunities in the age of information. This five-part program leaves no question about "selling" being one of the master skills for success today.

Source: Courtesy of The University Sales Education Foundation.

or to an individual. Buying motives and selling strategies described in later chapters will vary considerably depending upon whether the sale is B2B or B2C.

■ *Telecommunications services.* The deregulation of telephone service resulted in considerable fragmentation within the industry and the creation of numerous new communications companies. This has led to an increased need for telecommunications salespeople. These individuals must have a thorough knowledge of their system and a good understanding of competing telecommunications systems.

■ *Financial services.* This is one of the hottest areas of sales growth. There are more than 3000 firms that provide financial services in Canada, directly employing more than 550 000 people.[24] Banks, brokerage firms, and other businesses are branching out, selling a broader range of financial planning and investment services. More and more, bank employees are involved in personal selling activities, developing new accounts, and servicing existing ones. Bank personnel are completing sales training courses in record numbers these days.

■ *Media sales.* Revenue from advertising supports the radio, television, newspaper, and magazine industries and is also a major source of profit for the Internet. Amy Vandaveer, a salesperson featured in Chapter 6, sells advertising space for *Texas*

Monthly. Both local and national advertising supports each of these and each must sell advertising to remain in business. In fact, newspapers and magazines generate far more revenue from the sale of advertising than from subscriptions. The wide variety of client needs and the task of meeting these needs make the work of media sales representatives interesting. Additionally, the requirement for members of the media sales staff to develop or to help the client develop commercials makes this work very interesting.

■ *Real estate*. The purchase of a home is usually the single largest expenditure in the average person's lifetime. The purchase of commercial property by individual investors or business firms is also a major economic decision. Therefore, the thousands of Canadian real estate salespeople assume an important responsibility. Busy real estate salespeople often hire sales associates to conduct open houses or perform other tasks. Real estate salespeople must obtain listings, advertise the properties, conduct visits with potential clients, and sell properties. Pearl Paul moved to Canada from Trinidad in 1972. She decided to get into real estate sales when her husband wanted to return to his hometown—Winnipeg—in search of work. In 2008, after only three years in sales, Pearl Paul became the top-selling salesperson among approximately 150 salespeople in her Royal LePage office. Honesty helped Pearl establish trust and build good relationships. The backside of Pearl's business card states, "The referral of your friends and family is the greatest compliment you can give me."[25]

■ *Insurance*. Selling insurance has always been one of the most rewarding careers in sales. Common forms of insurance sold include life, liability, fire, health, automobile, casualty, homeowner, and business. There are two broad groups of insurance salespeople. Employees of major companies such as Manulife Financial, Liberty Mutual, Sun Life Financial, or State Farm make up one group. Marcus Smith, whom we introduce in Chapter 2, is an excellent example of this type of salesperson who sells various insurance products but only for his company, Liberty Mutual. In one recent

Pearl Paul's success comes from establishing and maintaining good client relationships.

year, Canadians purchased 757 200 individual life insurance policies with an average value of $271 600.[26] The second type consists of independent agents who represent a number of insurance companies. The typical independent agency sells a broad line of personal and commercial insurance services offered by many companies.

■ *Business services.* The great number of new businesses and the expansion of existing businesses have resulted in an increase in the demand for business services provided by outside contractors. Some of these services include computer programming, training, printing, credit reporting, payroll and accounting, payment processing, recruiting, transportation, and security. Many other sales careers involving the sale of services exist. The field is increasing at a rapid pace and sales positions become available in services sales every day.

Career Opportunities in the Business Goods Channel

Manufacturers employ sales and sales support personnel in a variety of different positions in outside and inside sales. Outside salespeople interact with potential customers on a face-to-face basis. Some of the categories of outside salespeople include field salespeople, sales or application engineers, and missionary or detail salespeople. Inside salespeople include customer service representatives (CSRs) who rely primarily on the telephone and the Internet to communicate with customers, to identify new prospects, and to carry out other sales activities.

■ *Industrial salespeople.* Industrial salespeople include both technical salespeople (sales engineers or application engineers) and nontechnical salespeople. Sales engineers or technical salespeople sell heavy equipment, machinery, chemical products, aircraft, complex electronic equipment, and military equipment. Such salespeople must have a good technical understanding of their products and customer needs. Nontechnical salespeople generally sell office equipment; disposable goods such as adhesives, cleaners, and packaging; and office supplies.

■ *Sales engineers or applications engineers.* Sales or applications engineers must possess a detailed and thorough technical knowledge of their products as well as competing products. These salespeople must be able to identify and analyze customer problems and develop solutions to these problems that meet the customer's needs. Sales engineers must be technically proficient in all aspects of their products and in communicating the merits and advantages of their products to the customer.

Steve Tice, president of Sim Graphics Engineering Corporation, and Steve Glenn, vice president for new business development, are the primary sales engineers for the corporation.[27] Sim Graphics develops automated graphic simulation systems for use in industry, hospitals, and educational institutions. Their company utilizes customized demonstration presentations for potential customers. Many potential customers fail to understand the complexity of the systems so demonstrations are needed to show what is actually available. On some occasions it is necessary to build and demonstrate a prototype or to make a full-blown presentation. Customers who do not understand the product will be reluctant to purchase something they don't comprehend.

■ *Field salespeople.* **Field salespeople** interact with new customers and current customers. They must be able to identify customer needs and requirements and to recommend the proper product or service to meet the customer's needs. Field salespeople who provide

field salespeople Salespeople who regularly visit face-to-face with new customers and current customers.

excellent service often receive information from their satisfied customers on new leads. These customers often provide recommendations to other potential customers for the field salesperson.

Betty Robertson, president of Lyncole Industries, is also the field sales representative for her company. Lyncole sells piping and associated supplies to contractors. Betty states that following up on the installation of the equipment is very important. The contractors she sells to are potential repeat customers; it is essential to follow-up and make certain that the customer is satisfied.[28]

■ *Missionary salespeople.* **Missionary salespeople**, also known as *detail salespeople*, serve to develop goodwill, provide information, and stimulate demand for the manufacturer's products. A missionary salesperson does not sell the product but receives recognition for increasing the sale of products indirectly. Missionary salespeople must be able to provide technical product information and offer sound advice in areas such as credit policies, pricing, display, layout, and storage.

Deborah Karish, a sales representative for Amgen, stresses relationship selling in her work with medical facilities while selling to both medical staff and physicians. She had to learn the technology of her products, how they were manufactured, and how the medicines could be utilized most effectively in treating patients. She went through a pairing program with physicians to learn how the products are used. Deborah knows it is necessary to establish good relationships with the medical staff. Failing to establish good relationships generally means that the people will not work with the salesperson.

missionary, or detail, salespeople Salespeople who attempt to generate goodwill and stimulate demand for the manufacturer's product among channel members, rather than selling direct to the end user.

Career Opportunities in the Consumer Goods Channel

Sales careers in the consumer goods channel, referred to earlier as "B2C" selling, include both retail selling and direct selling careers. Conventional retailers face increased competition from online retailers. Consumers spend billions of dollars on Internet purchases. Traditional retailers are forced to offer customers more than products in order to compete effectively against online sellers. Well-trained salespeople can add value to the traditional shopping experience.

■ *Retail salespeople.* A large number of salespeople work in retail. Retail selling is an excellent area for gaining initial sales experience. Retail selling careers abound in a number of product areas.

Global Business Insight
What Motivates Salespeople

A study of nearly 41 000 salespeople across nine countries found that U.K. and U.S. salespeople were most likely to be motivated by income: 36 percent and 33 percent, respectively. However, they differed greatly when they were asked whether selling was a stepping stone to management. Eleven percent of U.K. salespeople thought so, but only 6.1 percent of U.S. salespeople

agreed. Canadian salespeople, at 8.8 percent, were in the middle.

George F. Dudley, one of the research co-authors, suggested why the percentage might be so low in the United States: "In the U.S.," Dudley said, "good salespeople are likely to see management as a step backward, not forward, because they can make more money in sales."[c]

Jacqueline Irish is a sales associate who has helped Stoney Creek Furniture gain recognition as an outstanding retailer.

When he was still in secondary school, Chris Mckee worked on weekends and evenings washing motor homes. By age 18, Chris had received his Ontario motor vehicle certification, which allowed him to sell motor homes and other recreational vehicles while still a student in business administration at Georgian College. Chris sells motor homes ranging in price from $70 000 to more than $650 000 for Ontario's largest motor home dealership—The Hitch House. He regularly participates in factory training programs, where he has become an expert in motor homes and their systems.[29]

Stoney Creek Furniture in Stoney Creek, Ontario, is Canada's largest furniture showroom. The company's sales associates—dedicated to superior customer service—helped the retailer win the National Home Furnishings Association North American Retailer of the Year 2010. This was the first time the award was given to a Canadian retailer. The company's non-commissioned sales associates have been described as "well-trained, experienced, and among the best in the world."[30]

direct salespeople Independent contractors who represent manufacturers selling products or services directly to consumers, usually face-to-face but also via the telephone or Internet.

■ *Direct salespeople.* **Direct salespeople** are independent contractors who represent manufacturers selling products or services directly to consumers, usually face-to-face but also via the telephone or Internet. There are an estimated 900 000 such salespeople in Canada, with total estimated annual sales of more than $2 billion. Approximately 60 percent of these salespeople—accounting for an estimated 70 percent of sales—are employed by Direct Sellers Association of Canada member companies.[31] Personal care, home/family care, wellness, and leisure/educational products, along with services such as utilities, phone, legal, etc., are the major industries represented by this form of selling.

A rapidly growing form of direct sales is network (or multilevel) marketing. In this form of distribution, manufacturers eschew advertising and other trade/promotional spending, relying instead on a large network of independent consultants or distributors to sell the product or service directly to consumers or businesses. The independent consultant builds his or her business not only through the direct sales of the product or service to consumers, but also by sponsoring new consultants to sell the company's products or services. The sponsoring consultant then earns commissions on the product/service sales generated by the new consultant, in addition to what he or she personally sells. The number of levels on which a consultant is paid varies by company, but the benefit to the consultant is the ability to leverage both his or her own efforts plus that of other consultants in his or her "downline." These types of organizations are highly reliant on socialization communication and cooperation between consultants for successful sales results.[32]

Knowledge Workers in the Information Economy

The late Stanley Marcus, Chairman Emeritus of the prestigious Neiman Marcus company, said, "Sooner or later in business, everybody has to sell something to somebody." He noted that even if you are not in sales, you must know how to sell a product, a service, an idea, or yourself.[33] Marcus's views have garnered a great deal of support among observers of the information age. Today's workforce is made up of millions of knowledge workers who succeed only when they add value to information. **Knowledge workers** are individuals whose work effort is centred around creating, using, sharing, and applying knowledge. The information economy is about the growing value of knowledge, making it the most important ingredient of what people buy and sell.[34] One way to add value to information is to collect it, organize it, clarify it, and present it in a convincing manner. This skill, used every day by professional salespeople, is invaluable in a world that is overloaded with information.

knowledge workers Individuals whose work effort is centred around creating, using, sharing, and applying knowledge.

As noted earlier, relationships have become more important in the information age. In many cases, information does not have value unless people interact effectively. Creating networks with social ties allows knowledge workers to acquire and provide information more successfully.[35] For example, a salesperson may possess information concerning an important new technology, but that information has no value until it is communicated effectively to an investor, a customer, or someone else who can benefit from knowing more about his product. A bank loan officer may have the resources needed to assist a prospective homeowner in reaching her dream, but in the absence of a good relationship, communications may break down. Thus, in the information age, it becomes important for firms to create structures to encourage knowledge sharing.[36]

SELLING SKILLS—ONE OF THE "MASTER SKILLS FOR SUCCESS" FOR THE KNOWLEDGE WORKER

In his best-selling book Megatrends, John Naisbitt noted that "the game of life in the information age is people interacting with other people."[37] With its emphasis on effective and adaptive interpersonal interaction, selling has become one of the "master skills for success in the information economy." Furthermore, individuals who have developed skills associated with careers in sales are more likely to be successful when they decide to go out on their own because more often than not, those skills translate very well to other businesses.[38] Today, personal selling skills contribute in a major way to four groups of knowledge workers who may not consider themselves salespeople:

- Managerial personnel
- Professionals (accountants, consultants, lawyers, architects, engineers, etc.)
- Entrepreneurs
- Marketing personnel and customer service representatives

Managerial Personnel

People working in managerial occupations represent a large group of knowledge workers. They are given such titles as "executive," "manager," or "administrator." Leaders are constantly involved in capturing, processing, and communicating information. Some of the most valuable information is acquired from customers. This helps explain the rapid growth in what is being described as "executive selling." Chief executive officers and other executives often accompany salespeople on sales calls to learn more about customer needs and in some cases to assist with presentations. Manny Fernandez of the Gartner Group, a technology consulting firm based in Stamford, Connecticut, spends more than half his time travelling on sales calls.[39] Leaders also must articulate their ideas in a persuasive manner and win support for their vision. Brian Tracy, author of *The 100 Absolutely Unbreakable Laws of Business Success*, says, "People who cannot present their ideas or sell themselves effectively have very little influence and are not highly respected."[40]

Professionals

Today's professional workers include lawyers, designers, programmers, engineers, consultants, dentists, counsellors, doctors, accountants, and many other specialized knowledge workers. Our labour force includes nearly 20 million professional service providers, persons who need many of the skills used by professional salespeople. Clients who purchase professional services are usually more interested in the person who delivers the service than in the firm that employs the professional. They seek expert diagnosticians who are truly interested in their needs. The professional must display good communication skills and be able to build a relationship based on trust.

business or client development
Bringing in new business, from new or existing clients or customers.

Technical skills are not enough in the information age. Many employers expect the professional to bring in new business, often referred to as **business** or **client development**, in addition to keeping current customers satisfied. Employers often screen professional applicants to determine their customer focus, ability to interact well with people, and client development skills.

Many firms are providing their professional staff with sales training. The accounting firm Ernst & Young sets aside several days each year to train its professional staff in personal selling. The National Law Firm Marketing Association recently featured Neil Rackham, author of *Spin Selling*, as keynote speaker at its national conference. The Wicker Corporation, a manufacturer of equipment for the plastics industry, has initiated a program designed to motivate its researchers, engineers, and manufacturing staff members to get involved in sales. Faced with increased competition and more cost-conscious customers, a growing number of law, accounting, engineering, and architectural firms are discovering the merits of personal selling as an auxiliary activity.[41]

Jimmy Is a Salesperson

Who is Jimmy Pattison? Depending on where in Canada you are located, he may or may not be well known. You might recall seeing the Pattison name underneath many billboards across this country.

However, Jimmy Pattison is much bigger than a billboard. From a humble Saskatchewan beginning, Jimmy Pattison demonstrated his entrepreneurial calling at a very early age. He started by selling packets of seeds door-to-door; eventually graduated to selling pots and pans, also door-to-door; and then, while in university, graduated to selling used cars. While a student at UBC, Jimmy Pattison would buy a used car in the evening, drive it to school the following day, sell it at a modest profit, and return home by bus. Eventually, he bought a share in his fist GM dealership. Today, the Pattison Group is involved in the automotive, media, packaging, food sales and distribution, entertainment, export, and financial industries.

The Pattison Group's sales reached $7.1 billion in 2009; the number of employees 33 000; and the number of worldwide locations 449. As one of Canada's richest people and the owner of Canada's third largest private company, Jimmy Pattison describes himself as someone "having no other skills except as a salesman."[d]

Entrepreneurs

Thousands of new businesses are started each year in Canada. As noted previously, people who want to start a new business frequently need to sell their plan to investors and others who can help get the firm established. Once the firm is open, owners rely on personal selling to build their businesses.

James Koch, chief executive officer of the Boston Beer Company (brewer of Samuel Adams beer), makes a strong case for personal selling. Like most new companies, his started with no customers. To get the new company established, he assumed the role of salesperson and set a goal of establishing one new account each week.

Today Koch continues to spend time on the street visiting convenience stores, supermarkets, and taverns. Competition from popular craft beers such as Fat Tire and Magic Hat, and imports such as Stella Artois and Beck, present a major challenge. He's also trying to get the attention of young men who think of Samuel Adams as their father's beer. He readily admits that selling his beer is the most rewarding part of his job. Koch could have sold his company to a megabrewer long ago, but that option is not appealing to this wealthy entrepreneur who loves to sell.[42]

Marketing Personnel and Customer Service Representatives

Because of the close working relationships of marketing directors, product managers, marketing research specialists, warehouse and shipping specialists, and others working with customers in the marketing efforts of companies, it is imperative for these personnel to understand, and in most cases to acquire, the skills of personal selling. This generally results in a much more productive sales and marketing effort and a satisfied customer base.

The assignment of selling duties to employees with customer service responsibilities has become quite common today. The term **customer service representative (CSR)** is

customer service representative (CSR) Knowledge workers who process reservations, accept orders by phone or other means, deliver products, handle customer complaints, provide technical assistance, and assist full-time sales representatives.

used to describe knowledge workers who process reservations, accept orders by phone or other means, deliver products, handle customer complaints, provide technical assistance, and assist full-time sales representatives. Some companies are teaming CSRs and salespeople. After the sale is closed, the CSR helps process paperwork, check on delivery of the product, and engage in other customer follow-up duties. In addition to increased service quality, the improved customer expertise from this process improves customer loyalty.[43]

Assigning sales duties to customer service representatives makes sense when you consider the number of contacts customers have with CSRs. When a customer seeks assistance with a problem or makes a reservation, the CSR learns more about the customer and often provides the customer with needed information. Customer needs often surface as both parties exchange information. It is important to keep in mind the advice offered by the authors of *Selling the Invisible*: "Every act is a marketing act. Make every employee a marketing person."[44]

Increasingly, work in the information economy is understood as an expression of thought. At a time when people change their careers eight or more times during their lives, selling skills represent important transferable employment skills.

LEARNING TO SELL

"ARE SALESPEOPLE MADE OR ARE THEY BORN?" THIS CLASSIC QUESTION SEEMS TO IMPLY THAT some people are born with certain qualities that give them a special advantage in the selling field. This is not true. The principles of adaptive selling, listening, and customer orientation can be learned and applied by people whose personal characteristics are quite different.[45]

In the past few decades, sales training has been expanded on four fronts. These four sources of training are corporate-sponsored training, training provided by commercial vendors, certification studies, and courses provided by colleges and universities.

Corporate-Sponsored Training

Hundreds of business organizations, such as Apple Computer, IBM, Maytag, Western Electric, and Zenith, have established training programs. These large corporations spend millions of dollars each year to develop their salespeople. *Training* magazine, which conducts annual analyses of employer-provided training, indicates that salespeople are among the most intensively trained employee groups. A new salesperson preparing for a consultative selling position may spend a few months to a year or more in training. For many salespeople, the training is as close as their laptop computer. Lucent Technologies, for example, uses web-based training for about one-third of its training courses.[46]

Training Provided by Commercial Vendors

The programs designed by firms specializing in the development of sales personnel are a second source of sales training. Some of the most popular courses are offered by the Canadian Professional Sales Association, the Richardson Company Training Media, Acclivus Corporation, Wilson Learning Corporation, Miller Heiman Inc., Dale Carnegie Training, and AchieveGlobal (see Table 1.2.) The legendary Professional Selling

Table 1.2 Sales Training Offered by Commercial Vendors

Training programs provided by commercial vendors are very popular. This table introduces a few of the well-established sales training programs offered to salespeople who are interested in improving their selling skills.

Company	Training Programs	Description
Canadian Professional Sales Association www.cpsa.com	• Professional Selling • Strategic Account Management	Provides in-class and online sales training with emphasis on consultative selling and building value-based partnerships
Sales Performance International	• Solution Selling • Opportunity Selling	Provides sales training based on concepts explained in *The New Solution Selling,* by Keith Eades
Integrity Systems, Inc. www.integritysystems.com	• Integrity Selling • The Customer	Provides sales training based on concepts explained in *Integrity Selling for the 21st Century,* by Ron Willingham
Huthwaite, Inc. www.huthwaite.com	• Spin Selling Certificate • Creating Client Value	Provides sales training based on concepts in *The Spin Selling Fieldbook,* by Neil Rackham
Miller Heiman, Inc. www.millerheiman.com	• Strategic Selling • Conceptual Selling	Provides sales training based on concepts presented in *Strategic Selling* and *The New Conceptual Selling*
AchieveGlobal www.achieveglobal.com	• Professional Selling • Professional Sales	Provides the original Xerox Skills (PSS) *Professional Selling Skills (PSS)* sales training; *Course Content Coaching* has been updated
Wilson Learning Worldwide www.wilsonlearning.com	• The Versatile Salesperson	Provides updated sales training based on the original Larry Wilson *Counselor Selling Training Program*
Dale Carnegie Training, Inc. www.dalecarnegie.com	• Sales Advantage • How to Sell Like a Pro	One of the largest international training companies providing sales training using many of the concepts presented in the Dale Carnegie books, such as *How to Win Friends and Influence People*
Richardson E Learning www.richardson.com	Richardson Quick Learning	*Richardson QuickSkills™* 5.0 incorporates a set of online tools that allows for improved efficiency in developing and delivering customized and tailored online sales training courses

Skills (PSS) course, developed in the late 1960s by Gene Keluche, is still offered by AchieveGlobal. This carefully designed course, once owned by Xerox, has been completed by millions of salespeople in Canada, the United States, and around the world.[47]

Certification Programs

The trend toward increased professionalism in personal selling has been the stimulus for a third type of training and education initiative. Many salespeople are returning to the classroom to earn certification in a sales or sales-related area. In the United States, many salespeople earn the Certified Medical Representative (CMR) designation. The CMR curriculum includes nearly 40 courses that are delivered to more than 9000 students. The National Automobile Dealers Association in the United States sponsors the Code of Conduct Certification program for automotive sales representatives. Both of these

CSP
Certified Sales Professional

The recognized standard of sales excellence

CSP - When these three letters follow your name, they pack a powerful message

- 86% gained a competitive advantage in the marketplace
- 72% rank in the top 25% of sales within their respective organizations
- More than half earn personal annual incomes over $75,000 per year
- 9 out of 10 CSPs recommend becoming a Certified Sales Professional (CSP) to others

FIND OUT MORE about the CSP designation. Call 1-888-267-2772 or visit us at www.cpsa.com/CSP

"
Achieving my CSP designation through the CPSA program has been invaluable as it relates to both my sales career and my personal life. I have applied the various principles and processes which substantially increased my sales productivity! I am more focused and goal-oriented."
L. Lang, CSP

The Canadian Professional Sales Association provides professional accreditation for salespeople who complete its Certified Sales Professional program.

certification programs require extensive study of modules and the completion of rigorous examinations. The Canadian Professional Sales Association offers the Certified Sales Professional (CSP) designation to sales professionals in Canada who meet the highest standards of education, experience, and ethical conduct.

Some companies have developed their own sales training certification programs. The Pitney Bowes Certified Postal Consultant (CPC) program is designed to improve the level of assistance given to customers who want to upgrade their mail process. It is available to members of the 4000-person Pitney Bowes sales force who sell both products (postage meters) and services. Freightliner developed a certification program for its 1800-member sales force. The various courses include topics ranging from product knowledge to truck-selling skills.[48]

College and University Courses

The fourth source of sales training is personal selling courses offered by colleges and universities throughout Canada. These courses are attracting an increasing number of students interested in careers in accounting, entrepreneurship, and finance, as well as sales and marketing. Although there is no formulaic answer that can be applicable to all selling situations, these courses provide students with a repertoire of skills that help them become more effective.[49] Sales training has also become an important part of the MBA curriculum at several elite universities.[50] The business community, in general, is increasingly asking for more selling skills from graduates of business programs.

REVIEWING KEY CONCEPTS

- Define personal selling and describe the three prescriptions of a personal selling philosophy.

  Personal selling occurs when a company representative interacts directly with a customer or prospective customer to present information about a product or service. Salespeople are encouraged to develop a personal selling philosophy based on three prescriptions: adopt the marketing concept, value personal selling, and assume the role of a problem solver or partner.

- Describe the emergence of relationship selling in the age of information.

  Restructuring from an industrial economy to an information economy began in the 1950s. We now live in an age in which the effective exchange of information is the foundation of most economic transactions. Salespeople use a variety of information technology tools to gather and process information of value to customers.

- Discuss the rewarding aspects of a career in selling today.

  Selling careers offer many rewards not found in other occupations. Income, both monetary and psychic, is above average, and there are many opportunities for advancement. Salespeople enjoy job security, mobility, and independence. Opportunities in selling for members of minority groups and for women are growing. In addition, selling is very interesting work, because a salesperson is constantly in contact with people. The adage "no two people are alike" reminds us that sales work is never dull or routine.

- Discuss the different employment settings in selling today.

  The text describes each of the three major career options and employment opportunities in the field of personal selling—namely, services, business goods, and consumer goods. Keep in mind that each category features a wide range of selling positions, varying in terms of educational requirements, earning potential, and type of customer served. The discussion and examples should help you discover which kind of sales career best suits your talents and interests.

- Explain how personal selling skills have become one of the master skills needed for success in the information age and how personal selling skills contribute to the work performed by knowledge workers.

  Today's workforce is made up of millions of *knowledge workers* who succeed only when they add value to information. The new economy rewards salespeople and other knowledge workers who collect, organize, clarify, and present information in a convincing manner. Selling skills contribute in a major way to four groups of knowledge workers who usually do not consider themselves salespeople: customer service representatives, professionals (accountants, consultants, lawyers, etc.), entrepreneurs, and managerial personnel.

- Identify the four major sources of sales training.

  Sales training can be acquired from four key sources: corporate-sponsored training, training provided by commercial vendors, certification programs, and courses offered by colleges and universities. Many MBA programs now include professional selling and sales management in the curriculum.

Key Terms

business or client development **22**

customer service representative (CSR) **23**

direct salespeople **20**

field salespeople **18**

information economy **6**

inside salesperson **13**

knowledge workers **21**

missionary, or detail, sales **14**

missionary, or detail, salespeople **19**

outside salesperson **13**

personal selling **5**

personal selling philosophy **6**

product **5**

psychic income **11**

selling 2.0 **6**

telemarketing **13**

trade selling **14**

value-added selling **8**

Review Questions

1. Explain how personal selling can help solve the problem of information overload.

2. According to the Strategic/Consultative Selling Model (Fig. 1.1), what are the three prescriptions for developing a successful personal selling philosophy?

3. List and describe the four employment settings for people who are considering a selling career.

4. What future is there in selling for women?

5. Some salespeople have an opportunity to earn certification in a sales or sales-related area. How can a salesperson benefit from certification?

6. Explain why high-performance value-added salespeople earn much more than high-performance transactional salespeople.

7. List three titles commonly used to describe manufacturing salespeople. Describe the duties of each.

8. Develop a list of eight selling career opportunities in the service field.

9. Explain why personal selling is an important auxiliary skill needed by lawyers, engineers, accountants, and other professionals.

10. List and briefly describe the four major sources of sales training.

Application Exercises

1. Examine a magazine or newspaper ad for a new product or service that you have never seen. Evaluate its chances for receiving wide customer acceptance. Does this product require a large amount of personal selling effort? What types of salespeople (service, manufacturing, wholesale, or retail) are involved in selling this product?

2. For each of the following job classifications, list the name of at least one person you know in that field:

   a. Full-time person who sells a service

   b. Full-time inside wholesale salesperson

   c. Full-time manufacturer's salesperson

   d. Full-time retail salesperson

   Interview one of the people you have listed and ask the following questions concerning their duties and responsibilities:

   a. What is your immediate supervisor's title?

   b. What would be a general description of your position?

   c. What specific duties and responsibilities do you have?

   d. What is the compensation plan and salary range for a position like yours?

   Write a job description from this information.

3. When Shelly Jones, a vice president and partner in the consulting firm Korn/Ferry International, looks into the future, he sees some new challenges for salespeople. He recently shared the following predictions with *Selling Power* magazine:

   a. Salespeople will spend more time extending the range of applications or finding new markets for the products they sell.

   b. The selling function will be less pitching your product and more integrating your product into the business equation of your client. Understanding the business environment in which your client operates will be critical.

   c. In the future you will have to be a financial engineer for your client. You need to understand how your client makes money and be able to explain how your product or service contributes to profitable operation of the client's firm.

   Interview a salesperson who is involved in business-to-business selling—a manufacturer's representative, for example—and determine whether this person agrees with the views of Shelly Jones.

4. There are many information sources on selling careers and career opportunities on the Internet. Two examples include Monster.ca and CareerBuilder.ca. Search the Internet for information on selling careers.

   Use your search engine to find career information on a pharmaceutical representative, a field sales engineer, and a retail salesperson.

5. Sales managers are frequently asked what personal characteristics are most important to success in selling. Among the criteria often cited are sociability, aggressiveness, enthusiasm, empathy, verbal ability, and time management. Which of these do you believe are the most important? Least important? Are there important personal characteristics that are missing from this list?

⟳ ROLE-PLAY EXERCISE

This role play will let you practise selling your knowledge, skills, and experience to a prospective employer. You will be meeting with a class member who will assume the role of an employer who is developing a new sales team. Prior to this interview, reflect on the courses you have completed, work experience, and other life experiences that may have value in the eyes of the employer.

You may also want to reflect on any volunteer work you have completed and any leadership roles you have held. Be prepared to discuss the personal selling skills you are developing in this course, skills you have learned in previous employment settings, and related skills you have learned in other courses you have taken, such as psychology, communications, sociology, etc.

🎥 Reality Selling Today Video Case Problem

Alex Homer, featured at the beginning of this chapter, works as a professional clothier for the Tom James Company (www.tomjames.com). Alex sells a comprehensive collection of high-quality attire: formal (black tie/tuxedo), business (suits), business casual (sport coats, slacks, etc.), and weekend (jeans, sport shirts, shorts, khakis, etc.). His clients are typically gentlemen and ladies who do not have time to go to the store, dislike the idea of store shopping, or have fit characteristics that present challenges for purchasing clothing "off-the-peg."

For Alex, it is important to call on existing customers as well as prospects and to be aware of the different approaches used in each type of sales call. Typically, prior to visiting with an existing customer, he puts together clothing ideas for the season that make sense for the client based on how she/he dresses and how much her/his closet is lacking in a particular area (such as shirts or slacks). For new prospects, Alex contacts them by telephone. Realizing that cold-calling is an antiquated way of building a long-standing and fruitful sales career, the Tom James Company emphasizes the importance of referrals to build a business. Referrals tend to be easier to contact by phone and they typically purchase more in-person, due to the strength of the referrer's name. All in all, referrals remove many obstacles to turning a person who is completely unaware of one's business into a client.

According to Alex, the biggest challenge in his business is getting in front of people. This challenge stems from many possible sources: lack of time for the prospect, perceived price/value imbalance, lack of experience in in-office clothing shopping, and being perceived as a "suit" company rather than an all-inclusive clothing provider.

Especially for repeat clients, who represent 80 percent of the company's annual business, Alex Homer describes solid call preparation as key for successful selling. If the salesperson is unprepared and shows up in the client's office with a bag in hand and a "what are you buying today?" attitude, clients can sense this and become frustrated. They understand that professional clothiers provide a service and expect them to be prepared as a partner/problem solver regarding their wardrobes. As Alex puts it, "Stores provide clothing. Tom James provides a service."

When it comes to understanding the needs of a prospect, Alex follows a certain sales process: He first asks his clients what is most important to them when they go clothing shopping. For most of his clients, it is one of four things: price, quality, fit, or trend-sensitivity. Based on that, he determines what clothing the client wears during the vital parts of their business (client meetings, board meetings, trials, close-the-sale presentations, speaking engagements, and so forth). Then he asks how they would evaluate their closet (excellent, good, fair, or poor). Finally, if applicable, he finds out what it would take to make a slight improvement in their closet. (See the chapter opener on page 4 and Reality Selling Today Role Play 1 in Appendix 1 on page 434 for more information.)

Questions

1. Does it appear that Tom James and Alex Homer have a personal selling philosophy like that described in this chapter? Provide examples that support each of the three prescriptions.

2. Put yourself in the position of Alex Homer. What might be the most rewarding and the most adverse aspects of his sales job?

3. Describe how Alex uses personal selling skills in utilizing existing knowledge and gathering new information from the customer in order to advance the sales process.

4. Discuss different ways in which Alex can actively generate good customer referrals.

5. What skills are particularly important for Alex's sales job? Which of the four major sources of sales training outlined in this chapter would you recommend for acquiring those skills?

Chapter 2
Evolution of Selling Models That Complement the Marketing Concept

Learning Objectives

After studying this chapter, you should be able to

1   Discuss the evolution of personal selling models as an extension of the marketing concept.

2   Describe the evolution of consultative selling from the marketing era to the present.

3   Define *strategic selling* and name the four broad strategic areas in the Strategic/ Consultative Selling Model.

4   Describe the evolution of partnering and the nature of a strategic selling alliance.

5   Explain how value-added selling strategies enhance personal selling.

 Reality Selling Today Video Series

Successful salespeople who sell financial services products—such as those employed by Manulife Financial, London Life, Sun Life Financial, or State Farm—are masters of consultative selling. Marcus Smith one of the most productive sales representatives of Liberty Mutual (**www.libertymutual.com**), uses the consultative relationship selling approach exclusively. He believes that excellence in selling starts with an in-depth understanding of what customers value most. After gaining a careful understanding of their needs, he works closely as a partner with his customers in selecting the right products that will solve their buying problems and satisfy their long-term needs.

Founded in 1912, Liberty Mutual is an important player in the highly competitive insurance market. The three pillars of the company's culture consist of behaving with integrity, treating people with dignity and respect, and providing superior products and services. Smith is a strong believer in those corporate values. Yet implementing this relationship-oriented selling approach represents a challenge, given the constraints of resources and the competitive intensity of the insurance market. Smith's strategy is simple yet effective: placing emphasis on tracking and forecasting market information, focusing on identifying profitable customers, and directing resources to those customers.

Smith does not start conversations with his new customers with a sales pitch. Instead, he spends time building rapport with each customer and finding some beliefs and opinions that he and his customers have in common. These icebreakers go a long way toward

making customers feel comfortable sharing with Smith what their actual needs are. Then he asks permission to ask questions to fully understand his customer's unique needs. After confirming what the customer needs, he presents a balanced comparison between his offers and those of competitors. Being empathetic and honest with customers lies at the heart of his consultative relationship selling.

MARKETING CONCEPT REQUIRES NEW SELLING MODELS

A CAREFUL EXAMINATION OF PERSONAL SELLING PRACTICES DURING THE PAST 50 YEARS reveals some positive developments. We have seen the evolution of personal selling through several stages. The early *persuader stage* that was popular prior to the emergence of the marketing concept emphasized pushing or peddling products. At this stage, with little regard for long-term, mutually rewarding customer relationships, salespeople attempted to convince any and all market members to buy products offered. Over the years, personal selling evolved to the *problem-solver stage*, obtaining the participation of buyers in identifying their problems, which could then be translated into needs. At this stage the salesperson attempts to present products that correspond with customer needs.[1] Today, salespeople are no longer the flamboyant product "peddlers" of the past. Instead, they are increasingly becoming diagnosticians of customers' needs and problems. A growing number of salespeople recognize that the quality of the partnerships they create is as important as the quality of the products they sell. This sweeping change in personal selling models, from peddling to long-term consultative problem solving and value-added partnering, was prompted by the emergence of the marketing concept.

Evolution of the Marketing Concept

marketing concept A philosophy that says the firm should co-ordinate all its activities to satisfy its customers while achieving its own goals.

What is the **marketing concept**? It is a principle that holds that achieving organizational goals depends on knowing the needs and wants of target markets and delivering the

Table 2.1 Evolution of Personal Selling (1950 to Present)

Sales and Marketing Emphasis	Selling Emphasis
Marketing Era Begins (1950s) Organizations determine needs and wants of target markets and adapt themselves to delivering desired satisfaction; product orientation is replaced by a customer orientation	• More organizations recognize that the salesperson is in a position to collect product, market, and service information concerning the buyer's needs
Consultative Selling Era Emerges (Late 1960s to early 1970s) Salespeople are becoming diagnosticians of customers' needs as well as consultants offering well-considered recommendations; mass markets are breaking into target markets	• Buyer needs are identified through two-way communication • Information giving and negotiation tactics replace manipulation
Strategic Selling Era Emerges (Early 1980s) The evolution of a more complex selling environment and greater emphasis on market niches create the need for greater structure and more emphasis on planning	• Strategy is given as much attention as selling tactics • Product positioning is given more attention • Greater emphasis on account management and team selling
Partnering Era Emerges (1990 to the present) Salespeople are encouraged to think of everything they say or do in the context of their long-term, high-quality partnership with individual customers; sales force automation provides specific customer information	• Customer supplants the product as the driving force in sales • Greater emphasis on strategies that create customer value • Adaptive selling is given greater emphasis

desired products. Under the marketing concept, customer focus and value are the paths to sales and profits.[2]

The era of marketing and the age of information began in the early 1950s (Table 2.1). A General Electric executive is credited with making one of the earliest formal statements indicating corporate interest in the marketing concept. In a paper heralding a new management philosophy, he observed that the principal marketing function of a company is to determine what the customer wants and then develop the appropriate product or service. This view contrasted with the prevailing practice of that period, which was to develop products and then build customer interest in those products.[3]

The foundation for the marketing concept is a business philosophy that leaves no doubt in the mind of every employee that customer satisfaction is of primary importance. All energies are directed toward satisfying the customer. As Peter Drucker once observed, "The customers define the business."

Although the marketing concept is a business fundamental, some companies ignore it and suffer the consequences. Ford Motor Company was a leader in quality control during the 1980s and early 1990s but then seemed to shift its focus to other areas. The result was a drop in J. D. Power and Associates' quality rankings, and a drop in sales. Ford also failed to stay in touch with consumer tastes.[4] With renewed insight into the marketing concept, Ford now appears to be reconnecting with its customers.[5]

Business firms vary in terms of how strongly they support the marketing concept. Some firms have gone the extra mile to satisfy the needs and wants of their customers:

■ UPS founder Jim Casey adopted the marketing concept when the company was first established. He described the firm's customer focus this way: "Our real, primary objective is to serve—to render perfect service to our stores and their customers. If we keep that objective constantly in mind, our reward in money can be beyond our fondest dreams."[6]

■ Marriott Hotels uses a blend of "high tech" and "high touch" to build customer goodwill and repeat business. Each of the 8500 sales representatives can sell the services of 10 motel brands in Marriott's portfolio. The customer with a small meeting budget might be encouraged to consider a Fairfield Inn property. The customer seeking luxury accommodations might be introduced to a Ritz-Carlton hotel (acquired a few years ago). All reservations go through the same system, so that if one Marriott hotel is full, the sales representative can cross-sell rooms in another Marriott hotel in the same city.[7]

Marketing Concept Yields Marketing Mix

Once the marketing concept becomes an integral part of a firm's philosophy, its management seeks to develop a network of marketing activities that maximize customer satisfaction and ensure profitability. The combination of elements making up a program based on the marketing concept is known as the **marketing mix** (Fig. 2.1). The marketing mix is a set of controllable, tactical marketing tools that consists of everything the firm can do to influence the demand for its product. The many possibilities can be organized into four groups of variables: *product*, *price*, *place*, and *promotion*.[8]

One of the four Ps shown in Figure 2.1—promotion—can be further subdivided into advertising, sales promotion, personal selling, and public relations. When a company adopts the marketing concept, it must determine how some combination of these elements can result in maximum customer satisfaction.

Important Role of Personal Selling

Every marketer must decide how much time and money to invest in each of the four areas of the marketing mix. The decision must be objective; no one can afford to invest money in a marketing strategy that does not provide a good return on money invested. *Personal selling is often the major promotional method used—whether measured by people employed, by*

marketing mix A set of controllable, tactical marketing tools that consists of everything the firm can do to influence the demand for its product. These can be organized into four sets of variables: product, price, place, and promotion.

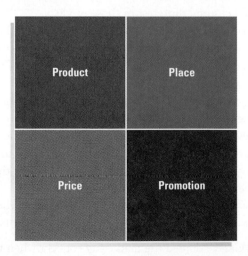

Figure 2.1 Each of the elements that make up the marketing mix must be executed effectively for a marketing program to achieve the desired results.

total expenditures, or by expenses as a percentage of sales. More than 10 percent of the total workforce in Canada and the United States are employed in sales positions, and about 40 percent of them have field sales responsibility. They cost their companies well over a trillion dollars every year and represent by far the largest marketing expenditure. This is more than four times what is spent on advertising.[9]

Firms make large investments in personal selling in response to several major trends: Products and services have become increasingly sophisticated and complex; competition has greatly increased in most product areas; and demand for quality, value, and service by customers has risen sharply. In response to these trends, personal selling has evolved to a new level of professionalism. Since the beginning of the information age, personal selling has gone through three distinct developmental periods: the consultative selling era, the strategic selling era, and the partnering era.

EVOLUTION OF CONSULTATIVE SELLING

Consultative selling, WHICH EMERGED IN THE LATE 1960S AND EARLY 1970S, IS AN EXTENSION of the marketing concept (see Table 2.1). This approach emphasizes need identification, which is achieved through effective communication between the salesperson and the customer. The salesperson establishes two-way communication by asking appropriate questions and listening carefully to the customer's responses. The salesperson assumes the role of consultant and offers well-considered recommendations. Negotiation replaces manipulation as the salesperson sets the stage for a long-term partnership. Salespeople who have adopted consultative selling possess a keen ability to listen, define the customer's problems, and offer one or more solutions.

Although consultative selling is emphasized throughout this text, it is helpful to understand the role of transactional selling in our economy. **Transactional selling** is a sales process that most effectively matches the needs of the value-conscious buyer, who is primarily interested in price and convenience. Many transactional buyers are well aware of their needs and may already know a great deal about the products or services they intend to purchase. Because the transaction-based buyer tends to focus primarily on low price, some marketers are adopting lower-cost selling channels. Low-cost transaction selling strategies include telesales, direct mail, and the Internet. This approach to selling is usually employed by marketers who do not see the need to spend very much time on customer need assessment, problem solving, relationship building, or sales follow-up.[10,11]

The decline in popularity of transactional sales approaches is due to two industry trends: the rise of e-commerce, which displaces transactional sales managed by people, and the increasing complexity of businesses. As more business supplier-related transactions are managed through portals and online bidding, businesses have a diminished demand for salespeople to manage the transactional sale.[12]

Service, retail, wholesale, and manufacturing firms that embrace the marketing concept have already adopted or are currently adopting consultative selling practices. The major features of consultative selling are as follows:

1. The customer is seen as *a person to be served*, not a prospect to be sold. Consultative salespeople believe their function is to help the buyer make an intelligent decision. They use a four-step process that includes need discovery, selection of the solution, a need-satisfaction presentation, and servicing the sale (see Fig. 2.2). These customer-centred strategies will be explained in Chapters 10 to 15.

consultative selling An approach to personal selling that is an extension of the marketing concept. Emphasis is placed on need identification, need satisfaction, and the building of a relationship that results in repeat business.

transactional selling A sales process that most effectively matches the needs of the value-conscious buyer, who is primarily interested in price and convenience.

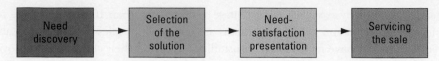

Figure 2.2 The Consultative Sales Presentation Guide. This contemporary presentation guide emphasizes the customer as a person to be served.

2. The consultative salesperson, unlike the peddler of an earlier era, does not try to overpower the customer with a high-pressure sales presentation. Instead, the buyer's needs are identified through *two-way* communication. The salesperson conducts precall research and asks questions during the sales call in an attempt to develop a relationship and learn as much as possible about the person's needs and perceptions.

3. Consultative selling emphasizes *need identification*, *problem solving*, and *negotiation instead of manipulation*. This approach is very compatible with the *problem-solver stage* of personal selling discussed in Chapter 1.[13] Helping the buyer make an informed and intelligent buying decision adds value to the sales process.

4. Consultative selling emphasizes *service* at every phase of the personal selling process. Several important research studies indicate the strong, positive impact of customer satisfaction on company profits.[14] The relationship between a seller and a buyer seldom ends when the sale is made. In most cases, customer expectations increase after the sale.

At first glance, it may appear that consultative selling practices can be easily mastered. The truth is, consultative selling is a complex process that puts great demands on sales personnel. This approach to personal selling requires an understanding of concepts and principles borrowed from the fields of psychology, communications, and sociology. It takes a great deal of personal commitment and self-discipline to become a sales consultant/adviser.

THE EVOLUTION OF STRATEGIC SELLING

STRATEGIC SELLING BEGAN TO RECEIVE CONSIDERABLE ATTENTION DURING THE 1980S (SEE Table 2.1). During this period we witnessed the beginning of several trends that resulted in a more complex selling environment, owing to increased global competition, broader and more diverse product lines, more decision makers involved in major purchases, and greater demand for specific, custom-made solutions. These trends will continue to influence personal selling and sales training in the age of information.

As companies face increased levels of complexity in the marketplace, they must give more attention to strategic planning. The strategic planning done by salespeople is often influenced by the information included in their company's strategic market plan. **Strategic planning** is the process that matches the firm's resources to its market opportunities. It takes into consideration all of the major functional areas of the business that must be coordinated, such as financial assets, workforce, production capabilities, and marketing.[15] Almost every aspect of strategic planning directly or indirectly influences sales and marketing.

The strategic plan should be a guide for a strategic selling plan. This plan includes strategies that you use to position yourself with the customer before the sales call even begins. The authors of *Strategic Selling* point out that there is a difference between a *tactic* and a *strategy*.[16] **Tactics** are techniques, practices, or methods you use when you are face-to-face with a customer. Examples are the use of questions to identify needs, presentation skills, and various types of closes. These and other tactics will be discussed in Chapters 10 to 15.

strategic planning The process that matches the firm's resources to its market opportunities.

tactics Techniques, practices, or methods that a salesperson uses during face-to-face interactions with customers.

Sales success in the new economy requires us to think of ourselves as problem solvers/partners throughout the sales process.

Strategies, on the other hand, are prerequisite to tactical success. If you develop effective strategies, you are more likely to make your sales presentation to the right person, at the right time, in a manner most likely to achieve positive results.

A selling strategy is a carefully conceived plan that is needed to accomplish a sales objective. Let's assume you are a sales representative employed by a pharmaceutical company. In an ideal situation, you want to establish a dialogue with the physician and learn about the types of patients she sees, diseases she treats, and challenges she faces in her practice. However, you do not want to call on busy doctors who may have no use for the drugs offered by your company. A strategy might include a careful study of the entire physician population in your territory. This analysis will help you identify those who need information about the drugs your company offers.[17] With this information, you can select the most appropriate selling tactic (method), which might be to present samples to doctors who are not currently prescribing your drug.

strategies The things that salespeople do as the result of precall planning to ensure that they call on the right people, at the right time, and with the right tactics to achieve positive results.

Selling Today

The War between Sales and Marketing

Within many companies there is little alignment between sales and marketing. In fact, a real turf war often exists between these two functions. One source of friction is *economic*. Senior management must make decisions regarding budget allocation for each function. The folks in marketing may want to spend large amounts of money on advertising to generate customer awareness of a new product. The folks in sales may feel this money would be better spent by increasing the size of the sales force.

The second source of conflict is *cultural*. Sales and marketing attract different types of people who spend their time in different ways. The marketing staff may be focused on program elements (product warranty, price, placement of the product, etc.). Salespeople, in contrast, want to focus their attention on existing and potential customers. One way to end the war between sales and marketing is to encourage more joint planning and information sharing. The leaders of both functions must try to achieve common ground in terms of philosophies and values.[a]

adaptive selling Altering sales behaviours during a customer interaction in order to improve communication.

Strategic planning, an important element of the *problem-solver stage*, sets the groundwork for a value-added form of consultative selling that is more structured, more focused, and more efficient. The result is better time allocation, more precise problem solving, and a greater chance that there will be a good match between your product and the customer's needs.

Adaptive selling is another key element of the *problem-solver stage*. **Adaptive selling** can be defined as altering sales behaviours during a customer interaction in order to improve communication. It relates to a salesperson's ability to collect information regarding the customer's needs and respond appropriately. Adaptive selling frequently requires complex behavioural adjustments.[18]

Many companies have discovered that specialized sales training is an effective strategy. When Microsoft wanted to build a stronger partnership with its customers, all of its 5000 sales professionals completed the Solution Selling sales training course. This training, based on concepts presented in *The New Solution Selling* by Keith Eades, helped Microsoft salespeople create greater value for its customers.[19]

The Strategic/Consultative Selling Model

When you study a value-added approach to personal selling that combines strategic planning, consultative selling practices, and partnering principles, you experience a mental exercise that is similar to solving a jigsaw puzzle. You are given many pieces of information that must form a complete picture. Putting the parts together isn't difficult, however, if you can see the total picture at the beginning. Therefore, a single model has been developed to serve as a source of reference throughout the entire text. Figure 2.3 shows this model.

The Strategic/Consultative Selling Model features five steps, each based on three prescriptions. The first step involves the development of a personal selling philosophy, which was introduced in Chapter 1. Each of the other four steps relates to a broad

Salespeople who build partnering relationships are rewarded with repeat business and referrals. These relationships require a strategic approach to selling.

strategic area of personal selling. Each step makes an important and unique contribution to the selling/buying process.

Developing a Relationship Strategy Success in selling depends heavily on the salesperson's ability to develop, manage, and enhance interpersonal relations with the customer. People seldom buy products or services from someone they dislike or distrust. Harvey B. Mackay, founder of Mackay Envelope Corporation, says, "People don't care how much you know until they know how much you care." Most customers

Strategic/Consultative Selling Model*	
Strategic step	**Prescription**
Develop a personal selling philosophy	• Adopt marketing concept • Value personal selling • Become a problem solver/partner
Develop a relationship strategy	• Adopt win-win philosophy • Project professional image • Maintain high ethical standards
Develop a product strategy	• Become a product expert • Sell benefits • Configure value-added solutions
Develop a customer strategy	• Understand the buying process • Understand buyer behaviour • Develop prospect base
Develop a presentation strategy	• Prepare objectives • Develop presentation plan • Provide outstanding service

* Strategic/consultative selling evolved in response to increased competition, more complex products, increased emphasis on customer needs, and the growing importance of long-term relationships.

Marketing Concept

• coordinate all activities

• to create satisfied customers

• and achieve company goals

Figure 2.3 The Strategic/Consultative Selling Model is an extension of the marketing concept.

Adaptive selling requires a strategic selling plan. Adaptive selling can be defined as altering sales behaviours during a customer interaction in order to improve communication. It relates to a salesperson's ability to collect information regarding the customer's needs and respond appropriately. Adaptive selling frequently requires complex behavioural adjustments.

relationship strategy A well-thought-out plan for establishing, building, and maintaining quality relationships.

relationship selling A form of personal selling that involves securing, developing, and maintaining long-term relationships.

are more apt to discuss their needs and wants openly with a salesperson with whom they feel comfortable.

A **relationship strategy** is a well-thought-out plan for establishing, building, and maintaining quality relationships. This type of plan is essential for success in today's marketplace, which is characterized by vigorous competition, look-alike products, and customer loyalty dependent on quality relationships as well as quality products. The relationship strategy must encompass every aspect of selling, from the first contact with a prospect to servicing the sale once this prospect becomes an established customer. The relationship strategy is an integral dimension of **relationship selling**. Relationship selling is a form of personal selling that involves securing, developing, and maintaining long-term relationships with customers.[20] Increased support for relationship selling recognizes the growing importance of partnerships in selling. The primary goal of the relationship strategy is to create rapport, trust, and mutual respect, which ensures a long-term partnership. To establish this type of relationship, salespeople must adopt *a win-win philosophy—that is, if the customer wins, I win; project a professional image; and maintain high ethical standards* (see Fig. 2.3). Chapters 3, 4, and 5 provide important information on development of the relationship strategy.

Some people think that the concept of *relationships* is too soft and too emotional for a business application; these people think it's too difficult to think about relationships in strategic terms. In fact this is not the case at all. Every salesperson can and should formulate a strategic plan that builds and enhances relationships.

product strategy A well-conceived plan that emphasizes acquiring extensive product knowledge, learning to select and communicate appropriate product benefits that will appeal to the customer, and configuring value-added solutions.

Developing a Product Strategy Products and services represent problem-solving tools. The **product strategy** is a plan that helps salespeople make correct decisions concerning the selection and positioning of products to meet identified customer needs. The three prescriptions for the product strategy are *become a product expert, sell benefits, and configure value-added solutions.* The development of a product strategy begins with a thorough study of one's product (see Fig. 2.3) using a feature–benefit analysis approach. Such product features as technical superiority, reliability, fashionableness, design integrity, or guaranteed availability should be converted to benefits that appeal to the customer. Today's high-performance salespeople strive to become product experts. Chapter 6 focuses on company, product, and competition knowledge needed by salespeople.

Product knowledge is not the only important element of a product strategy. In fact, salespeople who are too focused on selling products often fail to identify complete solutions to the customer's problem. Stephen Covey, author of the best-selling book *The 7 Habits of Highly Effective People*, says, "Diagnose before you prescribe." If the salesperson does not deeply engage the customer and fails to diagnose the problem correctly, chances are the solution recommended may not be the best one.[21]

The development of a product strategy often requires thoughtful decision making. Today's more knowledgeable customers seek a cluster of satisfactions that arise from the product itself, from the manufacturer or distributor of the product, and from the salesperson. The "new" product that customers are buying today is the sum total of the satisfactions that emerge from all three sources. The cluster of satisfactions concept is discussed in more detail in Chapter 7.

Developing a Customer Strategy Patricia Seybold, author of *The Customer Revolution*, says we are in the midst of a profound revolution—the customer revolution. And it's bigger than the Internet revolution:

> Customers have taken control of our companies' destinies. Customers are transforming our industries. And customers' loyalty—or lack thereof—has become increasingly important. . . .[22]

Customers have become increasingly sophisticated in their buying strategies. More and more, they have come to expect value-added products and services, and long-term commitments. Selling to today's customer starts with getting on the customer's agenda and carefully identifying his or her needs, wants, and buying conditions. Salespeople who have a better understanding of customer needs are better able to produce satisfied customers who are willing to pay more![23]

A **customer strategy** is a carefully conceived plan that will result in maximum responsiveness to the customer's needs. This strategy is based on the fact that success in personal selling depends, in no small measure, on the salesperson's ability to learn as much as possible about the prospect. It involves the collection and analysis of specific information on each customer. When developing a customer strategy, the salesperson should *develop an understanding of the customer's buying process, understand buyer behaviour*, and *develop a prospect base*. The first two parts of the customer strategy are introduced in Chapter 8. Suggestions concerning ways to develop a solid prospect base are discussed in Chapter 9.

The customer strategy is dictated by the needs of the customer. For example, it's best to consider relationship formation from the customer's perspective. When a *consultative* selling approach is required, the customer strategy will usually encompass a long-term relationship and ongoing collaboration. If a *transactional* approach is required, the customer strategy would not, in most cases, emphasize need assessment, problem solving, relationship building, and sales follow-up.[24]

Developing a Presentation Strategy Typical salespeople spend about 30 percent of their time in actual face-to-face selling. However, the sales presentation is a critical part of the selling process. The **presentation strategy** is a well-developed plan that includes

customer strategy A carefully conceived plan that will result in maximum responsiveness to the customer's needs.

presentation strategy A well-developed plan that includes preparing the sales presentation objectives, preparing a presentation plan that is needed to meet these objectives, and renewing one's commitment to provide outstanding customer service.

From the Field

Sales Success Paves the Way for Young Entrepreneur

At age 19, Rosado Shaw wanted to be a salesperson, but the company she worked for wouldn't let her sell. She had recently dropped out of college and taken a job with a company that makes umbrellas and tote bags. One day she took a sick day and called on the marketing staff at a museum of natural history. The result of this impromptu sales call was a $140 000 order. She then went to the president of the company and asked, "Are you going to let me sell now, or what?" After two years in sales, Shaw moved to a rival firm, Umbrellas Plus, and acquired more experience. She eventually purchased a controlling interest in the company and turned it into a $10 million enterprise.[b]

preparing the sales presentation objectives, preparing a presentation plan that is needed to meet these objectives, and *renewing one's commitment to provide outstanding customer service* (see Fig. 2.3).

The presentation strategy usually involves developing one or more objectives for each sales call. For example, a salesperson might update personal information about the customer, provide information on a new product, and close a sale during one sales call. Multiple-objective sales presentations, which are becoming more common, are discussed in Chapter 10. Presale presentation plans give salespeople the opportunity to consider those activities that take place during the sales presentation. For example, a salesperson might preplan a demonstration of product features to use when meeting with the customer. Presale planning ensures that salespeople are well organized during the sales presentation and prepared to offer outstanding service.

Interrelationship of Basic Strategies The major strategies that form the Strategic/Consultative Selling Model are by no means independent. The relationship, product, and customer strategies all influence development of the presentation strategy (see Fig. 2.4). For example, a salesperson might develop one relationship-building tactic for use during

Figure 2.4 The major strategies that form the Strategic/Consultative Selling Model are by no means independent of one another. The focus of each strategy is to satisfy customer needs and build quality partnerships.

the initial face-to-face meeting with the customer, and another for use during the negotiation of buyer resistance. Another relationship-building method might be developed for use after the sale is closed. The discovery of customer needs (part of the customer strategy) will greatly influence planning for the sales presentation.

EVOLUTION OF PARTNERING

PARTNERING BECAME A BUZZWORD IN THE 1990S, AND IN THE 2000S IT BECAME A BUSINESS reality.[25] Partnering has been driven by several economic forces. One is the demise of the product solution in several industries. When products of one company are nearly identical to those of the competition, the product strategy becomes less important than the relationship, customer, and presentation strategies. In contrast, some partnerships grow out of the need for customized products or services. Many manufacturers have formed partnerships with companies that offer flexibility in terms of product configuration, scheduling of deliveries, or some other factor.

Today's customer wants a quality product *and* a quality relationship. Salespeople willing to abandon short-term thinking and invest the time and energy needed to develop high-quality, long-term relationships with customers are greatly rewarded. A strong partnership serves as a barrier to competing salespeople who want to sell to your accounts. Salespeople who are able to build partnerships enjoy more repeat business and referrals. Keeping existing customers happy also makes a great deal of sense from an economic point of view: Experts in the field of sales and marketing know that it costs four to five times more to get a new customer than to keep an existing one. Therefore, even small increases in customer retention can result in major increases in profits.[26]

Partnering is a strategically developed, long-term relationship that solves the customer's problems. A successful long-term partnership is achieved when the salesperson is able to skilfully apply the four major strategies and, thus, add value in various ways (Fig. 2.5). Successful sales professionals stay close to the customer and constantly search for new ways to add value.

partnering A strategically developed, long-term relationship that solves the customer's problems.

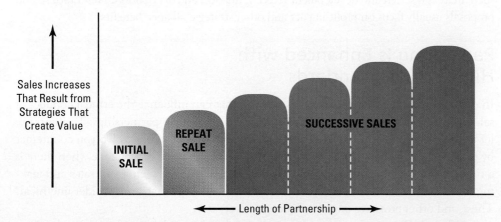

Figure 2.5 Partnering is a strategically developed, long-term relationship that solves the customer's problems. A successful partnering effort results in repeat sales and referrals that expand the prospect base. The strength of the partnership increases each time the salesperson uses value-added selling strategies.

The salespeople at Mackay Envelope Corporation achieve this goal by making sure they know more about their customers than the competitors know. Salespeople who work for Xerox Corporation are responding to a sales orientation that emphasizes postsale service. Bonuses are based on a formula that includes not only sales but also customer satisfaction.

Strategic Selling Alliances—The Highest Form of Partnering

strategic selling alliance
Alliances that are achieved by teaming up with another company whose products or services fit well with your own.

Throughout the past decade we have seen the growth of a new form of partnership that often is described as a **strategic selling alliance**. The goal of strategic selling alliances is to achieve a marketplace advantage by teaming up with another company whose products or services fit well with your own.[27] Alliances often are formed by companies that have similar business interests and, thus, gain a mutual competitive advantage. It is not uncommon for a company to form several alliances. Corning, a maker of glass products, has formed partnerships with several companies that need innovative glass technology. For example, Corning formed an alliance with Samsung, a Korean manufacturer of television screens. Burlington, Ontario–based Jenex Corporation formed a strategic selling alliance with U.S.-based Competitive Technologies, giving that company the right to sell Jenex's Thermapik® in specified geographic territories around the world. Competitive Technologies must guarantee a specified sales volume of the product—designed to relieve pain and itch caused by insect stings and bites—in order to maintain its exclusive rights to sell the product.[28]

Strategic alliances have created a new selling environment. The first step in building an alliance is to learn as much as possible about the proposed partner. This study takes place long before face-to-face contact. Alliances that are formed between companies that vary greatly in such areas as customer focus, financial stability, or ethical values will likely fail.[29] The second step is to meet with the proposed partner and explore mutual benefits of the alliance. At this point the salesperson (or account manager) is selling advice, assistance, and counsel, not specific products. Building win-win alliances requires the highest form of consultative selling. Very often, the salesperson is working with a company team made up of persons from such areas as research and development (R&D), finance, and distribution. Presentations and proposals usually focus on profit impact and other strategic alliance benefits.[30]

Partnering Is Enhanced with High Ethical Standards

In the field of selling there are certain pressures that can influence the ethical conduct of salespeople, and poor ethical decisions can weaken or destroy partnerships. To illustrate, let us assume a competitor makes exaggerated claims about a product. Do you counteract by promising more than your product can deliver? What action do you take when there is a time management problem and you must choose between servicing past sales and making new sales? What if a superior urges you to use a strategy that you consider unethical? These and other pressures must be dealt with every day.

Although Chapter 5 is devoted entirely to ethical considerations in personal selling, it should be noted that ethics is a major theme of this text as a whole, with the topic interwoven throughout several chapters. The authors believe that ethical decisions must be made every day in the life of a salesperson, so this important topic cannot be covered in a single chapter.

Partnering Is Enhanced with Customer Relationship Management

Many companies have adopted some form of customer relationship management. **Customer relationship management (CRM)**, sometimes referred to as *sales automation*, is the process of building and maintaining strong customer relationships by providing customer value.[31] A modern CRM program relies on a variety of technologies to improve communications in a sales organization and enhance customer responsiveness. A variety of CRM applications will be discussed throughout the text.

customer relationship management (CRM) The process of building and maintaining strong customer relationships by providing customer value.

VALUE CREATION—THE NEW SELLING IMPERATIVE

WE HAVE DEFINED VALUE-ADDED SELLING AS A SERIES OF CREATIVE IMPROVEMENTS WITHIN the sales process that enhance the customer experience. The *information economy* will reward those salespeople who have the skills, the knowledge, and the motivation to determine how to create value at every step of the sales process.

As Figure 2.6 shows, value creation begins with an understanding of the customer's value needs. Salespeople can create value in many ways: by establishing a relationship based on trust; by carefully identifying the customer's needs; and by identifying the best possible product solution. In the case of a complex sale, understanding the customer's

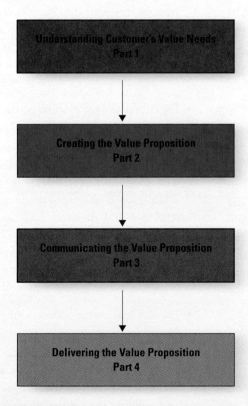

Figure 2.6 Creating and Delivering Customer Value Model
The salesperson's role in value creation is illustrated in this figure.
Adapted from Figure 1.2, Making and Delivering Value, Solomon, Marshall, and Stuart, *Marketing: Real People, Real Choices,* Prentice Hall, Upper Saddle River NJ, 2008, page 23.

value needs may take a great deal of time and may involve bringing in team members who have specific technical expertise.

Creating an appealing value proposition (Part 2) requires a detailed study of the customer's value needs. If you discover that timely delivery of your product is of critical importance, you must give the customer what they want. And if you promise on-time delivery, you must back up your claims.

Communicating the value proposition (Part 3) presents another major challenge. Traditional selling has too often emphasized communicating only the value that lies in the product. The focus of the sales call has too often been the product, not creating value for the customer.[32]

Delivering value (Part 4) can be very challenging. It may require coordination of credit approval, training, installation, service, and other aspects of the sale. Of course, each element of the selling process provides an opportunity to add value.

REVIEWING KEY CONCEPTS

- Discuss personal selling as an extension of the marketing concept.

  The *marketing concept* is the belief that a firm should dedicate all its policies, planning, and operations to the satisfaction of the customer. Salespeople today are problem solvers who obtain the participation of buyers in identifying their problems, which can then be translated into needs.

- Describe the evolution of consultative selling from the marketing era to the present.

  The *marketing era* that began in Canada in the 1950s looked first at customer needs and wants and then created goods and services to meet those needs and wants. *Consultative selling* emerged in the late 1960s and early 1970s as an approach that emphasizes the identification of customer needs through effective communication between the salesperson and customer. The evolution of selling continued with the development of *strategic selling* and *partnering*.

- Define strategic selling and name the four broad strategic areas in the Strategic/Consultative Selling Model.

  Strategic selling evolved in the 1980s and involves the preparation of a carefully conceived plan to accomplish sales objectives. Strategic selling is based on a company's *strategic market plan*, which takes into consideration the coordination of all the major functional areas of the business—production, marketing, finance, and personnel. The four broad strategic areas in the Strategic/Consultative Selling Model (after the development of a personal selling philosophy) are developing a relationship strategy, developing a product strategy, developing a customer strategy, and developing a presentation strategy.

- Describe the evolution of partnering and the nature of a strategic selling alliance.

  Partnering is a strategically developed, long-term relationship that solves the customer's problems. The long-term partnership is achieved when the salesperson is able to skilfully apply the four major strategies and therefore add value in various ways. The *strategic selling alliance* is the highest form of partnering. The goal of this type of alliance is to achieve a marketplace advantage by teaming up with another company whose products fit well with your own.

- Explain how value-added selling strategies enhance personal selling.

  Value-added selling has emerged as a major response to the customer economy. This approach to personal selling is defined as a series of creative improvements that enhance the customer's experience. The information economy rewards those salespeople who have the skills, the knowledge, and the motivation to determine how to create value at every step of the sales process.

Key Terms

adaptive selling **38**

consultative selling **35**

customer relationship management (CRM) **45**

customer strategy **41**

marketing concept **32**

marketing mix **34**

partnering **43**

presentation strategy **41**

product strategy **40**

relationship selling **40**

relationship strategy **40**

strategic planning **36**

strategic selling alliance **44**

strategies **37**

tactics **36**

transactional selling **35**

Review Questions

1. Why is peddling or "pushing products" inconsistent with the marketing concept?

2. Describe how new models of selling emerged in response to the marketing concept.

3. Describe the importance of personal selling as a part of the marketing concept.

4. What is consultative selling? Give examples.

5. Diagram and label the four-step Consultative Sales Presentation Guide.

6. List and briefly explain the four broad strategic areas that make up the selling process.

7. Briefly describe the evolution of partnering. Discuss the forces that contributed to this approach to selling.

8. Provide a brief description of value-added selling. What economic forces have motivated companies to adopt value-added selling?

9. Briefly explain why some organizations are developing strategic selling alliances.

10. Explain why the ethical conduct of salespeople has become so important.

Application Exercises

1. Assume that you are an experienced professional salesperson. A professor who teaches at a nearby university has asked you to speak to a consumer economics class about the benefits of personal selling. Make an outline of what you will say.

2. A friend of yours has invented a unique and useful new product. This friend, an engineer by profession, understands little about marketing and selling this new product. She does understand, however, that "nothing happens until somebody sells the product." She has asked you to describe the general factors that need to be considered when you market a product. Prepare an answer to her question.

3. When Brenda Fisher received her B.Ed., she thought she would like to teach. However, a pharmaceutical firm offered her a sales position that would require her to call on doctors and pharmacists to explain her firm's product line. Describe the similarities and differences between personal selling and teaching.

4. To learn more about industry-based global sales training programs, access www.wilsonlearning.com. Click on the "Sales Effectiveness" link and examine the content of the various sales courses offered throughout the world by this company. From this review, describe the similarities between what this company offers and the material in this chapter.

5. One of the topics frequently debated among salespeople and sales managers is whether men or women are better suited to sales positions. Where do you stand on this issue? Find support for your position and then be prepared to defend your views in class.

ROLE-PLAY EXERCISE

The purpose of this role play is to provide you with an opportunity to engage in a basic need identification exercise. You will be meeting with someone (a class member) who is preparing for an important job interview and needs to buy a pen and/or pencil. Prior to the meeting, make a list of the questions you will ask. Then pair off with the class member and ask your questions. Be sure to take notes. At the end of the interview, be prepared to recommend the most appropriate pen and/or pencil.

Reality Selling Today Video Case Problem

At the beginning of this chapter, you were given an introduction to Marcus Smith, who is employed by Liberty Mutual, a successful insurance company. Smith is responsible for introducing a very large number of products and services and he must always keep one eye on the competition. He must be prepared to answer questions about his own products and services and those of the competition. He must also be prepared to discuss the intricacies of the insurance terms and possible bundles of insurance policies in order to offer his customers the best value.

Like every other professional salesperson, Smith is constantly involved in learning. We now know that the principles of selling can be learned and applied by people whose personal characteristics are quite different. Most successful salespeople spend considerable time acquiring product knowledge, keeping up to date in their industry and related industries, and learning more about their customers. Smith acquired his formal training in professional selling from the Program in Excellence in Selling while he attended university. In the insurance industry, salespeople often go through industry-related training and a formal exam to acquire a license to sell personal and property insurance. Smith also undergoes Liberty Mutual's rigorous training program, which provides courses in four concentrations: products and services, company, competition, and quoting.

Smith realizes the importance of a relationship strategy that is built on a win-win philosophy. In addition to building a strong relationship with the customer, he must be able to work effectively with others who directly or indirectly influence the sale. He shares market information with his peers periodically because a broad view of the market as a whole is crucial in the highly competitive insurance industry. The salesperson who is honest, accountable, and sincerely concerned about the customer's welfare brings added value to the sales. (See chapter opener on page 31 and Reality Selling Today Role Play 2 in Appendix 1 on page 435 for more information.)

Questions

1. Does it appear that Smith has adopted the three prescriptions of a personal selling philosophy? (See Strategic/Consultative Selling Model.) Explain.

2. What prescriptions of the relationship strategy (see Strategic/Consultative Selling Model) have been adopted by Marcus Smith? Describe why a relationship strategy is especially important in personal selling.

3. Value-added selling is defined as a series of creative improvements in the sales process that enhance the customer's experience. Describe the various ways in which Marcus Smith can create value for his customers.

4. Why would it be important for the marketing support personnel (marketing research, product managers, advertising and sales promotion, etc.) employed by Liberty Mutual to understand personal selling? Can you describe any marketing support people who would benefit from the acquisition of personal selling skills?

PART I

ROLE-PLAY EXERCISE
Developing a Personal Selling Philosophy

SCENARIO

You are currently working part-time at the Best Buy store located in Three Rivers Mall. You are a full-time student majoring in marketing at Red River College. The manager of your store wants you to identify potential customers on your campus and sell Dell laptop computers to those individuals who have a need for this product.

CUSTOMER PROFILE

Theresa Feng is a full-time commuter student who lives with her parents and shares the family's one computer with her mom. Each morning she drives about 32 kilometres to the campus and spends most of the day attending classes, working in the library, and visiting with friends. She currently spends about two hours each evening on the computer at home.

SALESPERSON PROFILE

You started working at the Best Buy store shortly after graduating from high school. The store manager was impressed with your computer expertise and your friendly manner. Although you are able to sell any type of computer, you tend to specialize in laptop computers, which are ideal for college students who have mobile computing needs. Your personal computer is a new Dell laptop, which replaced your desktop computer.

PRODUCT

You sell several different laptop computers that vary in price from $799 to $1499. Each laptop is equipped with specific, easily accessible ports to interact with a variety of external components. All of your laptops offer both productivity and entertainment applications. Services offered by Dell include helpful assistance via telephone or online tutorials at **www.support.dell.com**. Dell's warranty provides service and support to be handled by the Geek Squad (**www.geeksquad.ca**), which is located in the store.

INSTRUCTIONS

For this role play, you will meet with Theresa Feng, played by another student, and determine her interest in and need for a laptop computer. Prior to meeting with Theresa, preplan your relationship strategy, product strategy, customer strategy, and presentation strategy. Chapter 1 provides a description of each strategic area. Be prepared to close the sale if you feel that the customer will benefit from this purchase.

Part II
Developing a Relationship Strategy

All selling is ultimately relationship selling.
This is especially true in complex sales where
the relationship continues after the sale.

—Brian Tracy, The 100 Absolutely Unbreakable Laws of Business Success

Creating Customer Value

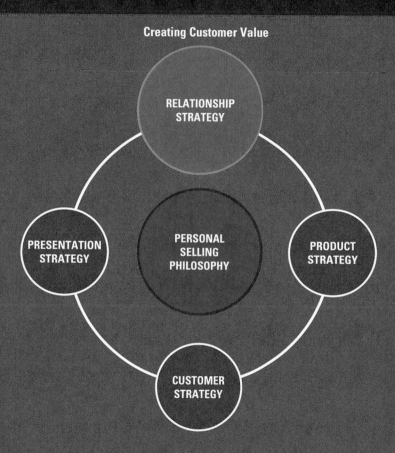

High-performance salespeople are generally better able to build and maintain relationships than moderate performers. Part II includes three chapters that focus on person-to-person relationship-building strategies. Chapter 3 explains how to create value with a relationship strategy. Chapter 4 introduces communication-style bias and explains how to build strong interpersonal relationships with style flexing. The influence of ethical decisions on relationships in selling is discussed in Chapter 5.

Chapter 3
Creating Value with a Relationship Strategy

Learning Objectives

After studying this chapter, you should be able to

1   Explain the importance of developing a relationship strategy.

2   Discuss how thought processes can enhance your relationship strategy.

3   Identify and describe the major nonverbal factors that shape our sales image.

4   Describe conversational strategies that help us establish relationships.

5   Explain how to establish a self-improvement plan based on personal development strategies.

 Reality Selling Today Video Series

The salespeople who work for CB Richard Ellis (**www.cbre.com**) understand the importance of developing relationship strategies. This successful commercial real estate services company, with 14 Canadian sales offices from Halifax to Vancouver and more than 300 offices in some 50 countries, strives to build a long-term partnership with each customer.

Susana Rosas (see page 53), a real estate broker at CB Richard Ellis (**www.cbre.com/usa/us/tx/houston+galleria**), places a great deal of emphasis on building rapport during the first contact. She, like most other real estate professionals, knows that rapport with commercial real estate clients is of critical importance. She knows that to build relationships with clients, a good knowledge of the market is necessary but not sufficient. She has to master a multitude of skills, among which keeping an open and empathetic conversation style with her clients is the key. Above all, listening closely to everything that prospects say helps a salesperson to accurately identify their wants and needs. Furthermore, she works closely with her team members in the same collaborative manner to make sure all of those identified needs are met.

DEVELOPING A RELATIONSHIP STRATEGY

DEVELOPING AND APPLYING THE WIDE RANGE OF INTERPERSONAL SKILLS NEEDED in today's complex sales environment can be challenging. Daniel Goleman, author of the bestselling books *Emotional Intelligence* and *Working with Emotional Intelligence*, notes

that there are many forms of intelligence that influence our actions throughout life. One of these, **emotional intelligence**, refers to the capacity for monitoring our own feelings and those of others, for motivating ourselves, and for managing emotions well in ourselves and in our relationships. People with a high level of emotional intelligence display many of the qualities needed in sales work: self-confidence, trustworthiness, adaptability, initiative, optimism, empathy, and well developed social skills.[1]

Goleman and other researchers state that there are widespread exceptions to the rule that IQ predicts success. In the field of personal selling and most other business occupations, emotional intelligence is a much greater predictor of success.[2] The good news is that emotional intelligence can be enhanced with a variety of self-development activities, many of which are discussed in this chapter.

Information-age selling involves three major relationship challenges. The first major challenge is building new relationships. Salespeople who can quickly build rapport with new prospects have a much greater chance of achieving success in personal selling. The second major challenge is transforming relationships from the personal level to the business level. Once rapport is established, the salesperson is in a stronger position to begin the need identification process. The third major challenge is the management of relationships. Successful salespeople must manage many different relationships.[3] Salespeople must develop relationship management strategies that focus on four key groups. These groups are discussed later in this chapter.

In this chapter we introduce the win-win philosophy and discuss the importance of projecting a professional image. Chapter 4, on adaptive selling, explains how an understanding of our own communication style and that of the customer can help us better manage the relationship process. Chapter 5 focuses on the importance of maintaining high ethical standards in order to build long-term relationships with the customer (see Fig. 3.1).

emotional intelligence The capacity for recognizing our own feelings and those of others, for motivating ourselves, and for managing emotions effectively in ourselves and our relationships.

Daniel Goleman, author of the bestselling book *Working with Emotional Intelligence,* defines emotional intelligence as the capacity for monitoring our own feelings and those of others, for motivating ourselves, and for managing emotions well in ourselves and in our relationships. People with a high level of emotional intelligence, which he says can be learned and improved on, display many of the qualities needed in sales work: self-confidence, trustworthiness, adaptability, initiative, optimism, empathy, and well developed social skills.

Relationships Add Value

Ron Willingham, author of *Integrity Selling for the 21st Century*, says there is a relationship between the salesperson's achievement drive and their view of personal selling. Salespeople who feel a professional responsibility to create as much value for customers as possible exhibit more energy, a stronger work ethic, and a greater eagerness to ask customers for decisions.[4]

The manner in which salespeople establish, build, and manage relationships is not an incidental aspect of personal selling; in the information age it is the key to success.

Strategic/Consultative Selling Model	
Strategic step	**Prescription**
Develop a personal selling philosophy	✔ Adopt marketing concept ✔ Value personal selling ✔ Become a problem solver/partner
Develop a relationship strategy	• Adopt win-win philosophy • Project professional image • Maintain high ethical standards

Figure 3.1 Every salesperson should have an ongoing goal of developing a relationship strategy that adds value to the sale.

In the information economy, business is defined by customer relationships and sales success depends on adding value (see Fig. 1.2 on page 7). Daniel Pink, author of *A Whole New Mind*, says we are moving from the information age to the conceptual age. He predicts that one of the major players in the conceptual age will be the **empathizer**. Empathizers have the ability to imagine themselves in someone else's position and understand what that person is feeling. They are able to understand the subtleties of human interaction.[5]

We have defined value-added selling as *a series of creative improvements in the sales process that enhance the customer experience*. Customers perceive that value is added when they feel comfortable with the relationship they have with a salesperson. A good relationship encourages customers to feel that if a problem arises, they will receive a just and fair solution. A good relationship creates a clear channel of communication about issues that might surface during each step of the sales process. Len Rodman, CEO of a large engineering and construction company, recalls a problem in one particular region: Earnings were minimal and the person in charge could not sell to high-tier clients. Len put a different salesperson in charge whose strength was building relationships and, within an 18-month period, that region became one of the most profitable.[6]

The salesperson who is honest, accountable, and sincerely concerned about the customer's welfare adds value to the sale. These characteristics give the salesperson a competitive advantage—an advantage that is becoming increasingly important in a world of "look-alike" products and similar prices.

empathizer Someone who has the ability to imagine themselves in someone else's position and understand what that person is feeling.

Partnering—The Highest-Quality Selling Relationship

Salespeople today are encouraged to think of everything they say or do in the context of their relationship with the customer. They should constantly strive to build a long-term partnership. In a marketplace characterized by increased levels of competition and greater product complexity, we see the need to adopt a relationship strategy that emphasizes the "lifetime" customer. High-quality relationships result in repeat business and important referrals. A growing number of salespeople recognize that the quality of the partnerships

Today's customer wants a quality product and a quality relationship. This means that salespeople can create value with a well developed relationship strategy.

they create is as important as the quality of the products they sell. Today's customer wants a quality product *and* a quality relationship. One example of this trend is the J. D. Power and Associates customer satisfaction studies. J. D. Power conducts customer satisfaction research in several different industries; for example, the Domestic Hotel Guest Satisfaction Study measures guest satisfaction among frequent business travellers.[7]

In Chapter 1 we defined partnering as a strategically developed, high-quality, long-term relationship that focuses on solving the customer's buying problems.[8] This definition is used in the sales training video entitled *Partnering—The Heart of Selling Today*. Traditional industrial-age sales training programs emphasized the importance of creating a good first impression and then "pushing" your product. Partnering emphasizes building a strong relationship during every aspect of the sale and working hard to maintain a quality relationship with the customer after the sale. Today, personal selling must be viewed as a process, not an event.[9]

Larry Wilson, noted author and founder of Wilson Learning Worldwide, identifies partnering as one of the most important aspects of strategic thought processes needed by salespeople. He points out that the salesperson who is selling a "one-shot" solution cannot compete against the one who has developed and nurtured a long-term, mutually beneficial partnership. Wilson believes there are three keys to a partnering relationship:

- *The relationship is built on shared values.* If your client believes that you both share the same ideas and values, it goes a long way toward creating a powerful relationship.

- *Everyone needs to clearly understand the purpose of the partnership and be committed to the vision.* Both the salesperson and the client must agree on what they are trying to do together.

- *The role of the salesperson must move from selling to supporting.* The salesperson in a partnership is actively concerned with the growth, health, and satisfaction of the company to which she or he is selling.[10]

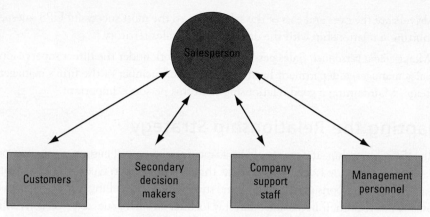

Figure 3.2 An effective relationship strategy helps high-performing salespeople build and maintain win-win relationships with four key groups.

Salespeople willing to abandon short-term thinking and invest the time and energy needed to develop a high-quality, long-term relationship with customers are rewarded with greater earnings and the satisfaction of working with repeat customers. Sales resulting from referrals also increase.

Relationship Strategies Focus on Four Key Groups

Establishing and maintaining a partnering-type relationship internally as well as with customers is a vital aspect of selling. High-performance sales personnel build strong relationships with four groups (see Fig. 3.2):

1. *Customers.* As noted previously, a major key to success in selling is the ability to establish working relationships with customers in which mutual support, trust, and goals are nurtured over time. Research suggests that salespeople who maintain regular contact with their customers and develop sound business relationships based on mutual trust are able to drive up sales productivity.[11] Cisco Systems is one of many companies that now measure themselves by the quality of their relationships with their customers. Salespeople earn their bonuses in large part based on customer satisfaction rather than on gross sales or profit.[12]

2. *Secondary decision makers.* High-performance salespeople understand the importance of building relationships with the people who work with customers. In many selling situations, the first person the salesperson meets is a receptionist, a secretary, or an assistant to the primary decision maker. These persons can often facilitate a meeting with the prospect. Also, the prospect may involve other people in making the buying decision. For example, the decision to buy new office furniture may be made by a team of persons, including the buyer and the people who will actually use the furniture.

3. *Company support staff.* The maintenance of relationships internally is a vital aspect of selling. Support staff may include persons working in the areas of market research, product service, credit, training, or shipping. Influencing these people to change their priorities, interrupt their schedules, accept new responsibilities, or fulfill any other request for special attention is a major part of the salesperson's job. At UPS, the

drivers are the eyes and ears of the sales force, so the most successful UPS salespeople nurture a relationship with the drivers in their sales territory.[13]

4. *Management personnel.* Sales personnel usually work under the direct supervision of a sales manager, a department head, or some other member of the firm's management team. Maintaining a good relationship with this person is important.

Adapting the Relationship Strategy

Ideally, the relationship strategy should be adapted to the type of customer you are working with. Chapter 1 provided a description of the three most common types of selling situations: transactional selling, consultative selling, and strategic alliance selling. Transactional buyers are usually aware of their needs and often stay focused on such issues as price, convenience, and delivery schedules. They usually know a great deal about the products or services they wish to purchase. In the transactional sale, the relationship strategy is often secondary.

In the consultative sale, however, the impact of relationships on the sale is quite important. A consultative sale emphasizes need identification, which is achieved through effective communication and a relationship built on mutual trust and respect. The consultative salesperson must display a keen ability to listen, define the customer's problem, and offer one or more solutions. The opportunity to uncover hidden needs and create custom solutions is greatly enhanced by a well conceived relationship strategy.[14]

In terms of relationship building, strategic alliance selling is often the most challenging. Very often the salesperson is working with a company team made up of people from such areas as research and development (R&D), finance, and distribution. The salesperson must build a good working relationship with each team member. Forming an alliance with another company involves building relationships with several representatives of that buying organization.

We will revisit these three types of selling situations later in Chapter 5 when we discuss the trust factor. In the meantime, keep in mind that customers almost never buy products from someone they dislike. A salesperson who is not viewed as helpful and trustworthy will not succeed in any type of selling situation.

THOUGHT PROCESSES THAT ENHANCE YOUR RELATIONSHIP STRATEGY

INDUSTRIAL-AGE FOLKLORE CREATED THE MYTH OF THE "BORN" SALESPERSON—A DYNAMIC, outgoing, highly assertive individual. Experience acquired during the age of information has taught us that many other factors determine sales success. Key among these factors are a positive self-image and the ability to relate to others in effective and productive ways. With the aid of knowledge drawn from the behavioural sciences, we can develop the relationship strategies needed in a wide range of selling situations.

Self-Concept—An Important Dimension of the Relationship Strategy

self-concept Bundle of facts, opinions, beliefs, and perceptions about yourself that are present in your life every moment of every day.

Your **self-concept** is the bundle of facts, opinions, beliefs, and perceptions about yourself that are present in your life every moment of every day.[15] The self-concept you have today reflects information you have received from others and life events that occurred throughout childhood, adolescence, and adulthood. You are *consciously* aware of some of the things you have been conditioned to believe about yourself. But many comments and events that have shaped your self-concept are processed at the *unconscious* level and continue to influence your judgments, feelings, and behaviours whether you are aware of them or not.[16]

Phillip McGraw, author of *Self Matters*, says we often sabotage our own success by adopting limiting beliefs. These are the specific things we think about that cause us to conclude that we are not capable of achieving success. These beliefs restrict our thinking and our actions.[17] McGraw, better known as "Dr. Phil," has developed a one-sentence guide to understanding the importance of your self-concept: *The past reaches into the present, and programs the future, by your recollections and your internal rhetoric about what you perceive to have happened in your life*.[18] Past experiences and events, which McGraw describes as "defining moments," can influence your thinking for a lifetime.

How can you develop a more positive self-concept? How can you get rid of self-destructive ways of thinking? Bringing your present self-concept out into the open is the first step in understanding who you are, what you can do, and where you are going. Improving your self-concept will not happen overnight, but it can happen. A few practical approaches are summarized as follows:

1. *Focus on the future and stop being overly concerned with past mistakes or failures.* You should learn from past errors, but they should not immobilize you.

2. *Develop expertise in selected areas.* By developing "expert power," you not only improve your self-image but also increase the value of your contributions to your employer and your customers.

3. *Learn to develop a positive personal attitude.* To develop a more positive outlook, read books or listen to audio presentations that describe ways to develop a positive personal attitude.

Consider materials developed by Jack Canfield, Stephen Covey, Brian Tracy, Dale Carnegie, and Phillip McGraw.

Later in this chapter you will learn how to develop and initiate a plan for self-improvement. If you want to improve your self-concept, consider adopting this plan.

The Win-Win Philosophy

As noted in Chapter 1, the marketing concept is a philosophy that leaves no doubt in the mind of every employee that customer satisfaction is of primary importance. Salespeople who work closely with customers are in a position to monitor customer satisfaction.

Adopting the win-win philosophy is the first step in developing a relationship strategy. Stephen Heiman and Diane Sanchez, authors of *The New Conceptual Selling*, describe the "win-win" approach as follows:

> In Win-Win selling, both the buyer and seller come out of the sale understanding that their respective best interests have been served—in other words, that they've both won. It is our firm conviction, based on thousands of selling situations, that over the long run the only sellers who can count on remaining successful are the ones who are committed to this Win-Win philosophy.[19]

From the Field

Adding Value Builds Strong Relationships

Janssen Inc., an innovative, research-based pharmaceutical company located in Toronto, has been servicing the Canadian market for more than 50 years. Its salespeople are among the best in the industry and adhere to the values and leadership standards promoted by its parent company, Johnson & Johnson.

Dean Keating, a primary care sales representative, focuses his efforts on working to develop value-added solutions for his physician customers. Many busy physicians do not have the resources to provide additional support

and education for patients with Alzheimer's disease or their caregivers, for example. Dean helps arrange the availability of nurses specially trained in Alzheimer's disease to provide this support.

Is this focus on understanding customer needs valued by doctors? As a result of this solution-oriented approach, Dean is seen as a true partner by his customers.

Today, salespeople who can demonstrate that they deliver understanding and value to their customers are able to build superior relationships. Everyone wins.[a]

The win-win strategy is based on such irrefutable logic that it is difficult to understand why any other approach would be used. The starting point to the development of a win-win philosophy is to compare the behaviours of persons who have adopted the win-lose approach with the behaviours of persons who have adopted the win-win approach (see Fig. 3.3).

Empathy and Ego Drive

We have described the growing importance of the *empathizer*—someone with the ability to imagine themselves in someone else's position and to understand what that person is feeling. A salesperson simply cannot sell well without the invaluable ability to get critical feedback from the client through empathy. When you sense what the customer is feeling, you can change pace and make whatever modifications are needed in your sales presentation.[20] Fortunately, the ability to relate to and connect with customers can be learned.

ego drive An inner force that makes the salesperson want and need to make the sale.

Ego drive is another basic quality that is of critical importance in personal selling. **Ego drive** is an inner force that makes the salesperson want and need to make the sale. Closing the

Win-lose people	Win-win people
• See a problem in every solution	• Help others solve their problem
• Fix the blame	• Fix what caused the problem
• Let life happen to them	• Make life a joyous happening for others and themselves
• Live in the past	• Learn from the past, live in the present, and set goals for the future
• Make promises they never keep	• Make commitments to themselves and to others and keep them both

Figure 3.3 The starting point to developing a win-win philosophy is to compare behaviours of win-lose salespeople with those of win-win salespeople.
(Adapted from a list of losers, winners, and double winners in *The Double Win* by Denis Waitley.)

sale provides a powerful means of enhancing the salesperson's ego. Research indicates that top salespeople have both the motivation to make the sale and the empathy that gives them the connecting tool with which to do it. Therefore, empathy and ego drive reinforce each other.[21]

Character and Integrity

Shoshana Zuboff, contributing columnist for *Fast Company* magazine, sees widespread acceptance of wrong as normal. She points to acceptance in some industries of the belief that "It's not wrong because everyone is doing it."[22] Employees working for prominent companies such as Merck, WorldCom, Putman Investments, Tyco, and Edward D. Jones & Company have been involved in ethical lapses.[23] Most white-collar crime is committed by persons who lack character and integrity.

Character is composed of personal standards, including honesty, integrity, and moral strength. It is a quality that is highly respected in the field of personal selling. **Integrity**, the basic ingredient of character, is exhibited when you achieve congruence between what you know, what you say, and what you do.[24] Toronto-based clinical psychologist Barbara Killinger says, "Integrity is built one small step at a time, yet it can slip away seemingly overnight."[25] In a world of uncertainty and rapid change, integrity has become a valuable character trait. Salespeople with integrity can be trusted to do what they say they will do. One way to achieve trustworthiness in personal selling is to avoid deceiving or misleading the customer. More will be said about this topic in Chapter 5, which examines the ethical conduct of salespeople.

character Your personal standards of behaviour, including honesty and integrity. Your character is based on your internal values and the resulting judgments you make about what is right and what is wrong.

integrity Part of your character; what you have when your behaviour is in accordance with your professed standards and personal code of moral values.

VERBAL AND NONVERBAL STRATEGIES THAT ADD VALUE TO YOUR RELATIONSHIPS

THE FIRST CONTACT BETWEEN A SALESPERSON AND A PROSPECT IS VERY IMPORTANT. DURING the first few minutes—or seconds, in some cases—the prospect and the salesperson form impressions of each other that will either facilitate or detract from the sales call. Malcolm Gladwell, author of the bestselling book *Blink*, says that when two people meet for the first time, both will make very superficial, rapid judgments about the other person. This decision-making process, he argues, usually happens subconsciously in a split second (in the blink of an eye).[26]

Every salesperson projects an image to prospective customers, and this image influences how a customer feels about the sales representative. The image you project is the sum total of many verbal and nonverbal factors. The quality of your voice, the clothing you wear, your posture, your manners, and your communication style represent some of the factors that contribute to the formation of your image. We discuss several forms of verbal and nonverbal communication in this chapter. Communication style is examined in Chapter 4.

Nonverbal Messages

When we attempt to communicate with another person, we use both verbal and nonverbal communications. **Nonverbal messages** are "messages without words" or "silent messages." These are the messages—other than spoken or written words—that we communicate through facial expressions, voice tone, gestures, appearance, posture, and other nonverbal means.[27]

nonverbal message A form of communication that has been defined as "messages without words" or "silent messages."

Nonverbal communication, such as facial expressions, voice tone, handshakes, gestures, appearance, and posture, are all important aspects of the relationship strategy. Research indicates that these nonverbal messages convey much more than verbal messages.

Research indicates that when two people communicate, *nonverbal messages convey much more impact than verbal messages*. Words play a surprisingly small part in the communication process. Every spoken message has a vocal element, coming not from *what* we say, but from *how* we say it. The voice communicates in many ways: through tone, volume, and speed of delivery. A salesperson wishing to communicate enthusiasm needs to use a voice that is charged with energy.

As we attempt to read nonverbal communication, it is important to remember that no *one* signal carries much meaning on its own. If a person you meet for the first time displays a weak grip during the handshake, for example, don't let this one signal shape your first impression. Such factors as posture, eye contact, gestures, clothing, and facial expressions must all be regarded together.[28]

Nonverbal messages can reinforce or contradict the spoken word. When your verbal message and body language are consistent, they give others the impression that you can be trusted and that what you say reflects what you truly believe. When there is a discrepancy between your verbal and nonverbal messages, you are less apt to be trusted.[29]

Entrance and Carriage As noted earlier, the first impression you make is very important. The moment a salesperson walks into a client's office, the client begins making judgments. Susan Bixler, author of *The Professional Image* and *Professional Presence*, makes this comment:

> All of us make entrances throughout our business day as we enter offices, conference rooms, or meeting halls. And every time we do, someone is watching us, appraising us, sizing us up, and gauging our appearance, even our intelligence, often within the space of a few seconds.[30]

Bixler says that the key to making a successful entrance is simply believing—and projecting—that you have a reason to be there and have something important to offer the client. You can communicate confidence with a strong stride, good posture, and a friendly smile. A confident manner communicates to the client the message, "This meeting will be beneficial to you."

Shaking Hands An inadequate handshake is like dandruff: No one will mention it, but everyone will notice it. The handshake is an important symbol of respect and, in most business settings, it is the proper greeting.[31] In the field of selling, the handshake is usually the *first* and frequently the *only* physical contact you make during a sales call. The handshake can communicate warmth, genuine concern for the prospect, and an image of strength. It can also communicate aloofness, indifference, and weakness to the customer. The message we communicate with a handshake is determined by a combination of five factors:

1. *Eye contact during handshake.* Eyes transmit more information than any other part of the body, so maintain eye contact throughout the handshaking process and display a pleasant smile.

2. *Degree of firmness.* Generally speaking, a firm handshake communicates a caring attitude, while a weak grip (the dead-fish handshake) communicates indifference.

3. *Depth of interlock.* A full, deep grip communicates friendship to the other person.

4. *Duration of grip.* There are no specific guidelines to tell us what the ideal duration of a grip should be. However, by extending the duration of the handshake we can often communicate a greater degree of interest in and concern for the other person. Do not pump up and down more than once or twice.

5. *Degree of dryness of hands.* A moist palm not only is uncomfortable to handle but also can communicate the impression that you are quite nervous. Some people have a physiological problem that causes clammy hands, and they should keep a handkerchief within reach to remove excess moisture.[32]

The best time to present your name is when you extend your hand. When you introduce yourself, state your name clearly and then listen carefully to be certain you hear the customer's name. To ensure that you will remember the customer's name, repeat it. In some cases, you will need to check to be sure you are pronouncing it properly.

Selling Today

Remembering Names

In the field of personal selling, remembering a person's name is very important. To improve your ability to recall names, use one or more of these memory aids.

- *Verify the spelling.* After hearing the name, ask, "Is that Reece with a 'c' or an 's'?" Repetition helps you remember the name.

- *Ask how the person wants to be addressed.* Ask, "Should I call you Miss Thomas, Ms. Thomas, or Mrs. Thomas?" This is another opportunity for repetition.

- *Relate the name to something easy to remember.* If the person's last name is Park, connect this name with

"Algonquin Park(Ontario)" in your mind. Some aspect of appearance (hair style, eyeglasses, etc.) might serve as a connecting reference.

- *Use the name quickly.* Work the person's name into the conversation right away: "Ms. Thomas, may I ask you a few questions?"

- *Use the name frequently.* During and at the end of the meeting, work the name into the conversation: "Ms. Thomas, thank you for meeting with me."[b]

Facial Expressions If you want to identify how another person is feeling, watch facial expressions closely. The face is a remarkable communicator, capable of accurately signalling emotion in a split second and capable of concealing emotion equally well. You can tell in a blink of an eye if your customer's face is registering surprise, pleasure, or skepticism (see Fig. 3.4). Facial expressions are largely universal, so people around the world tend to "read" faces in a similar way. It is worth noting that the smile is the most recognized facial signal in the world and it can have a great deal of influence on others. George Rotter, professor of psychology at Montclair University, says, "Smiles are an enormous controller of how people perceive you." People tend to trust a smiling face.[33] Get in the habit of offering a sincere smile each time you meet with a prospect.

Eye Contact When the customer is talking, eye contact is one of the best ways to say, "I'm listening." If you are looking across the room or at papers in your briefcase, the customer will assume you are not listening. However, prolonged eye contact can send the wrong message. A prolonged direct stare can be threatening. To avoid the prolonged stare, take fleeting glances at your notes. As the customer speaks, nod occasionally to indicate agreement or interest.[34]

Effect of Appearance on Relationships

We form opinions about people based on a pattern of immediate impressions conveyed by appearance. The clothing we wear, the length and style of our hair, the fragrances we use, and the jewellery we display all combine to make a statement about us to others—a statement of primary importance to anyone involved in selling.

unconscious expectations
Certain views concerning appropriate dress.

We all have certain views, or **unconscious expectations**, concerning appropriate dress. In sales work we should try to anticipate the expectations of our clientele. The clothing worn by salespeople does make a difference in terms of customer acceptance because it communicates powerful messages. The clothing we wear can influence our credibility and likeability.

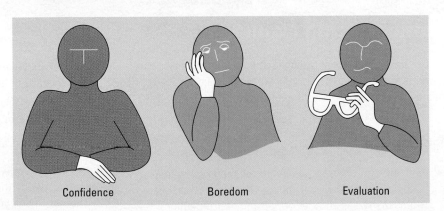

Confidence   Boredom   Evaluation

Figure 3.4 Our subtle facial gestures are continuously sending messages to others.

Spending an afternoon with a customer on the golf course is part of the relationship strategy of this salesperson. Many companies support this approach to building and maintaining relationships.

Most image consultants agree that there is no single "dress for success" look. The appropriate wardrobe will vary from one city or region to another and from company to company. However, there are some general guidelines that you should follow in selecting clothing for sales work. Four key factors should govern your decisions: simplicity, appropriateness, quality, and visual integrity.[35]

Simplicity The colour of your clothing, as well as the design, will communicate a message to the customer. Some colours are showy and convey an air of casualness. In a business setting we want to be taken seriously, so flashy colours should usually be avoided.

Appropriateness Selecting appropriate clothing for sales work can be a challenge. We must carefully consider the clients we serve and decide what will be acceptable to them. Many salespeople are guided by the type of products they sell and the desired image projected by their employers. Deciding what constitutes appropriate attire in today's business-casual world begins with an understanding of what it means to "dress down." **Business casual** is clothing that allows you to feel comfortable but look neat and professional. Pay close attention to the clothing your clients wear.[36] If a client is wearing a nice sport coat, a collared long-sleeved shirt, and dress slacks, don't wear khaki trousers and a short-sleeve polo shirt. In recent years, the casual dress trend has reversed at many companies and workplace dress codes have become more formal.[37]

business casual Clothing that allows you to feel comfortable but looks neat and professional.

Quality The quality of your wardrobe will also influence the image you project to customers. A salesperson's wardrobe should be regarded as an investment, with each item carefully selected to look good and fit well. Susan Bixler says, "If you want respect, you have to dress as well as or better than your industry standards."[38]

Visual Integrity Visual presence must have a certain amount of integrity and consistency. The images you project are made up of many factors, and lack of attention to important details can negate your effort to create a good impression. Too much jewellery, a shirt that does not fit well, or shoes that are not shined can detract from the professional look you want to project. People are often extra alert when meeting someone new, and this heightened consciousness makes every detail count.[39] Many young people today have tattoos or body piercings. While these may be considered fashionable among friends, they may be problematic for salespeople as some customers will hold other views. Like dandruff on your collar or stale tobacco on your breath, they may not be mentioned, but they will most certainly be noticed, and they are likely to have a negative impact on your sales. Keep in mind that customer contact often takes place in several settings. The first meeting with a customer may take place in his or her office, but the second meeting may be on the golf course. And the third meeting may take place at a nice restaurant. The clothing you wear in each of these settings is important.

Effect of Voice Quality on Relationships

As noted previously, every spoken message has a vocal element. What we hear is greatly influenced by the speaker's tone of voice, vocal clarity, and verbal expressiveness. On the telephone, voice quality is even more important because the other person cannot see your facial expressions, hand gestures, and other body movements. You cannot trade in your current voice for a new one; however, you can make your voice more pleasing to others. How? Consider these suggestions.

1. *Do not speak too quickly or too slowly.* Rapid speech often causes customers to become defensive. They raise psychological barriers because a "rapid-fire monologue" is associated with high-pressure sales methods. Many salespeople could improve their verbal presentation by speaking more slowly. The slower presentation allows others to follow, and it allows you, the speaker, time to think ahead—to consider the situation and make judgments. Another good tip is to vary the speed of your speech, leaving spaces between thoughts. Crowding too many thoughts together may confuse the listener.[40]

2. *Avoid a speech pattern that is dull and colourless.* The worst kind of voice has no colour and no feeling. Enthusiasm is a critical element of an effective sales presentation. It is also contagious. Your enthusiasm for the product will be transmitted to the customer.

3. *Avoid bad speech habits.* Kristy Pinand, a youthful-looking 23-year old, routinely used "teen speak." For example, she described a recent promotion as "so cool." Her supervisor felt she not only looked young but sounded very young, and this image could potentially hurt her ability to win the respect of clients. She urged Ms. Pinand to select her words more carefully. Ms. Pinand heeded the constructive advice and now rehearses her remarks aloud before she calls a client.[41]

Some speech habits can make us sound poorly educated and inarticulate. At age 22, Mike White learned that his unique regional accent and colourful speech patterns created problems at work. He recognized this was a "turnoff" to some of the image-conscious people he worked with. One day, his sales manager asked him if he had his racquetball equipment with him and White replied, "Yeah, I brung it." Fortunately, White's supervisor was willing to tactfully correct his grammatical problems and help him communicate with greater clarity. Today, Mike White is CEO of a successful company and a frequent speaker at trade shows.[42]

Effect of Etiquette on Your Relationships

The study of etiquette (sometimes called manner or protocol) reveals a number of ways to enhance your relationship strategy. Salespeople who possess knowledge of the rules of etiquette can perform their daily work with greater poise and confidence. Think of etiquette as a universal passport to positive relationships and respect.

With practice, anyone can develop good etiquette without appearing to be "stiff" and at the same time win the respect and admiration of others. Space does not permit a complete review of this topic, but we cover some of the rules of etiquette that are especially important to salespeople.

1. *Avoid the temptation to address a new prospect by first name.* In a business setting, too much familiarity too quickly can cause irritation.

2. *Avoid offensive comments or stories.* Never assume that the customer's value system is the same as your own. Rough language, off-colour stories, or personal views on political issues can do irreparable damage to your image.

3. *Recognize the importance of punctuality.* Ann Marie Sabath, owner of a firm that provides etiquette training for business employees, says, "We teach people that if you're early, you're on time, and if you're on time, in reality, you're late." Showing up late for an appointment will be viewed as rudeness by most clients.[43]

4. *When you invite a customer to lunch, do not discuss business before the meal is ordered unless the client initiates the subject.* Also, order food that is easily controlled and avoid such items as ribs, chicken, or lobster.

5. *When you use voice mail, leave a clear, concise message.* Do not speak too fast or mumble your name and number.

6. *Avoid cell phone contempt.* Turn off the cell phone ringer any time you are with a client. Never put your phone on the table during a meal.

It has been said that good manners make other people feel better. This is true because good etiquette requires that we place the other person's comfort ahead of our own. One of the best ways to develop rapport with a customer is to avoid behaviour that might be offensive to that person.

Social Media and Selling Today

Enhancing Your Relationship Strategy with Social Media

It is likely that your sales contacts and others associated with your accounts are using social media. This means that their postings will appear occasionally on Facebook, LinkedIn, and other similar sites. Most of these online services permit you to be notified by email when such postings occur. Many entries in most social sites are frivolous, so a review of every post may be unnecessary. However, it is wise to monitor these posts carefully enough to detect important relationship information.

You may wish to make note of many of these postings in your sales database. A sales contact may mention recent activities such as events attended, hobbies, or notable experiences. Someone might make reference to

an alma mater or to a friend who is well known. You can use this kind of information to add value to subsequent conversations with the person who posted. The information may give you a chance to point out interests or friends you have in common. You may also take note of issues to avoid, such as commenting on a recent varsity game your contact's school may have lost.

Your own entries on social websites can also add value to your relationship with sales contacts. Usually, you can directly comment on a sales contact's post instead of waiting until a subsequent conversation. You might comment that you agree with the entry or add helpful—and positive—information that supports the contact's comment.

CONVERSATIONAL STRATEGIES THAT ENHANCE RELATIONSHIPS

THE FOUNDATION FOR A LONG-TERM RELATIONSHIP WITH THE CUSTOMER IS FREQUENTLY A "get acquainted" type of conversation that takes place before any discussion of business matters. Within a few minutes it is possible to reduce the relationship tension that is so common when two people meet for the first time. This informal visit with the customer provides the salesperson with an opportunity to apply three guidelines for building strong relationships featured in *How to Win Friends and Influence People*, the classic book written by Dale Carnegie.

- *Become genuinely interested in other people*. Tim Sanders, Chief Solutions Officer at Yahoo!, says, "How we are perceived as human beings is becoming increasingly important in the new economy."[44] When you become genuinely interested in the customer, you create an experience that is long remembered.

- *Be a good listener; encourage others to talk about themselves*. Stephen Covey, the noted author and consultant, recommends empathetic listening. This requires listening with your ears, your eyes, and your heart.[45] We live in a culture in which empathic listening is quite rare. Interrupting has become all too common as people rush to fill every gap in the conversation.

- *Talk in terms of the other person's interests*.[46] When you are initiating a conversation with a customer, don't hesitate to use small talk to get the conversation started. This may involve current events, business, or sports. Be sure to focus on topics in which the customer is interested.

The length of this conversation depends on your sense of the prospect's reaction to your greeting, how busy the prospect appears to be, and your awareness of topics of mutual interest. The following three areas should be considered in developing conversation.

Comments on Here and Now Observations

Observant salespeople are aware of the things going on around them. These observations can be as general as unusual developments in the weather or as specific as noticing unique artefacts in the prospect's office. These observations often provide the basis for *small talk*, which can break the ice and speed up the building of a relationship.

Compliments

When you offer a *sincere* compliment to your prospect, you are saying, "Something about you is special." Most people react positively to compliments because they appeal to the need for self-esteem. Your admiration should not be expressed, however, in phony superlatives that will seem transparent. Jack Canfield, author of *The Success Principles*, reminds us that everything we say to a customer produces an effect: "Know that you are constantly creating something—either positive or negative—with your words."[47]

Search for Mutual Acquaintances or Interests

A frequent mode for establishing rapport with a new prospect is to find friends or interests you have in common. If you know someone with the same last name as your prospect, it may be appropriate to ask whether your friend is any relation. Anything you observe in the prospect's office or home might suggest an interest that you and your prospect share. A strong bond often develops between two persons who share the same interest or hobby. Estate planner Frances Carlisle says her love of animals lands her many clients. Some of these clients wish to include provisions for the care of pets in their estate plans. Sometimes an unusual hobby (skydiving, mountain climbing, auto racing, etc.) is the perfect way to stand out and cultivate relationships with clients.[48]

STRATEGIES FOR SELF-IMPROVEMENT

ORSON WELLES, A WELL KNOWN AND HIGHLY RESPECTED ACTOR, ONCE SAID, "EVERY ACTOR is very busy getting better or getting worse." To a large extent, salespeople are also "very busy getting better or getting worse." To improve, salespeople must develop an ongoing program for self-improvement (see Chapter 16). It is important to keep in mind that all improvement is self-initiated. Each of us controls the switch that allows personal growth and development to take place.

At the beginning of this chapter, when we introduced the concept of emotional intelligence, we noted that it can be increased with the aid of self-development activities. Would you like to develop a more positive self-concept? Improve your ability to develop win-win relationships? Develop effective nonverbal communication skills? Improve your speaking voice? These relationship-building strategies can be achieved if you are willing to follow these four steps:

Step one: Set goals. The goal-setting process begins with a clear, written statement that describes what you want to accomplish. If your goal is too general or vague, progress toward achieving that goal will be difficult to observe. Next, you must identify the ways in which you plan to achieve your goal. Perseverance is the key to goal achievement.

Step two: Use visualization. To **visualize** means to form a mental image of something. The power to visualize (sometimes called guided imagery) is in a very real sense the power to create. If you really want to succeed at something, picture yourself doing it successfully. For example, spend time developing mental pictures of successful sales presentations or visualizing yourself as one of the top salespeople in your organization. Once you have formed a clear mental picture of what you want to accomplish, identify the steps needed to get there and then mentally rehearse them. The visualization process needs to be repeated over and over again.[49]

visualize Form a mental image of something.

Step three: Use positive self-talk. People with a strong inner critic will receive frequent negative messages that can erode their self-esteem. It helps to refute and reject those negative messages with positive self-talk. **Self-talk** takes place silently in the privacy of your mind—a series of personal conversations you have with yourself continually throughout the day. Just like statements from other people, your self-talk can dramatically affect your behaviour and self-esteem.[50]

self-talk An effort to override past negative mental programming by erasing or replacing it with conscious, positive, new directions.

Step four: Reward your progress. When you see yourself making progress toward a goal, or achieving a goal, reward yourself. This type of reinforcement is vital when you are trying to change a behaviour. There is nothing wrong with taking pride in your accomplishments.

This salesperson has set a fitness goal. Physical fitness can be an important part of a self-improvement program.

Self-improvement efforts can result in new abilities or powers, and they give us the motivation to draw more fully on the talents we already have. As a result, our potential for success is greater.

REVIEWING KEY CONCEPTS

- Explain the importance of developing a relationship strategy.

  The manner in which salespeople establish, build, and maintain relationships is a major key to success in personal selling. The key relationships in selling include management personnel, company support staff, secondary decision makers, and customers.

  The concept of *partnering* is revisited and discussed in detail. Partnering emphasizes building a strong relationship during every aspect of the sale and working hard to maintain a quality relationship with the customer after the sale. Partnerships can be strengthened when salespeople use value-added relationship strategies.

- Discuss how thought processes can enhance your relationship strategy.

  An understanding of the psychology of human behaviour provides a foundation for developing relationship strategies. In this chapter, we discuss the link between self-concept and success in selling. Self-imposed fears can prevent salespeople from achieving success. The relationship strategy is built on the win-win philosophy, empathy and ego drive, and character and integrity.

- Identify and describe the major nonverbal factors that shape our sales image.

  We describe several factors that influence the image we project to customers. The image others have of us is shaped to a great extent by nonverbal communication. We may choose the right words to persuade a customer to place an order, but aversive factors communicated by our clothing, handshake, facial expression, voice quality, and etiquette miscues may prejudice the customer against us and our product or service.

- Describe conversational strategies that help us establish relationships.

  The various conversational strategies that enhance relationships are reviewed. These include comments on "here and now" observations, compliments, and the search for mutual acquaintances. Dale Carnegie's guidelines for building strong relationships are discussed.

- Explain how to establish a self-improvement plan based on personal development strategies.

  We discussed the importance of adopting strategies for self-improvement. A four-step self-improvement plan is the key to relationship building.

Key Terms

business casual **65**

character **61**

ego drive **60**

emotional intelligence **53**

empathizer **55**

integrity **61**

nonverbal message **61**

self-concept **58**

self-talk **69**

unconscious expectations **64**

visualize **69**

Review Questions

1. List the three prescriptions that serve as the foundation for development of a relationship strategy.
2. How important are establishing, building, and maintaining relationships in the selling process? List the four groups of people with whom sales personnel must be able to work effectively.
3. Why is *partnering* described as the highest-quality selling relationship? Why has the building of partnerships become more important today?
4. Defend the statement, "Successful sales relationships depend on a positive self-concept."
5. Describe the win-win approach to selling.
6. How is our self-concept formed? Why is a positive self-concept so important in personal selling?
7. Describe the meaning of the term *emotional intelligence*.
8. Identify three conversational methods that can be used to establish relationships.
9. Describe the meaning of *nonverbal messages*. Why should salespeople be concerned about these messages?
10. List and describe each step in the four-step self-improvement plan.

Application Exercises

1. Select four salespeople you know and ask them if they have a relationship strategy for working with customers, management personnel, secondary decision makers, and company support staff. Ask each salesperson to give you two or three specific examples of steps they have taken to build and maintain a positive relationship with their customers.
2. The partnering style of selling is emphasized throughout the book. To gain more insight into the popularity of this concept, use an Internet search engine of your choice and key in the words "partnering + selling." Notice the large number of documents related to this query. Click on and examine several of these documents to learn more about this approach to selling.

3. Complete the following etiquette quiz. Your instructor will provide you with answers so you can check your responses.
   a. On what side should you wear your name tag?
   b. Is it appropriate to drink beer from a bottle at a reception?
   c. When introducing a female salesperson to a male prospect, whose name should be spoken first?
   d. At the table, when should you place your napkin in your lap?
   e. Is it ever proper to comb, smooth, or touch your hair while seated at a restaurant table?
4. In October, people of the Hindu religion celebrate Diwali, the festival of lights. The festival of lights is one

of the most important and most beautiful Indian festivals. Rick Saulle, a pharmaceutical sales representative employed by Pifzer, knew that one of the most important physicians he called on was Indian and would celebrate Diwali. He also knew that it is commonplace to provide sweets to Indians who celebrate Diwali. Saulle visited an Indian grocery store and purchased a plate of Indian sweets. When he presented these to the physician, the response was very positive. The doctor grabbed Saulle's hand, shook it forcefully, and sincerely thanked him for honouring this important holiday.[51]

Canada is host to a kaleidoscope of the world's cultures, and the trend toward greater diversity will accelerate in the years ahead. Reflect on the gift given by Mr. Saulle and then answer these questions.

a. Is it appropriate for a salesperson to give a gift to someone who is celebrating a religious holiday?

b. In addition to giving a gift, what are some other ways to recognize a religious festival or holiday?

c. List and describe three holidays or festivals celebrated by religions other than Christian.

5. Move quickly through the following list of traits. Use a check mark beside those that fit your self-image. Use an X to mark those that do not fit. If you are unsure, indicate with a question mark.

—— I like myself.

—— I trust myself.

—— People trust me.

—— I often do the wrong thing.

—— I usually say the right thing.

—— People avoid me.

—— I dislike myself.

—— I enjoy work.

—— I waste time.

—— I control myself.

—— I put up a good front.

—— I enjoy nature.

—— I use my talents.

—— I am dependent on others for ideas.

—— I feel hemmed in.

—— I am involved in solving community problems.

—— I use time well.

—— I do not use my talents fully.

—— I enjoy people.

—— I do not like myself.

—— I usually say the wrong thing.

—— I do not like to be around people.

—— I am discouraged about life.

—— I have not developed my talents.

—— People like to be around me.

Now look at the pattern of your self-assessment.

a. Is there a pattern?

b. Is there a winner or loser pattern?

c. What traits would you like to change? List them.

d. Pick the trait you would like to change the most and prepare a plan to achieve this change. Your plan should include specific goal statements.

6. It is pointed out in this chapter that clothing communicates strong messages. In this exercise you will become more aware of whether your clothes communicate the messages you want them to communicate.

a. Make a chart like the one that follows:

Item of clothing being analyzed	What I want my clothes to say about me to others	What others think my clothing says about me

b. In the first column, list the clothing you are now wearing (e.g., dress slacks, dress shoes, and sweater; athletic shoes, jeans, and T-shirt; or suit, dress shirt, and dress shoes).

c. In the middle column, describe the message you would like the clothes you have chosen to say (e.g., "I want to be comfortable," "I want people to trust me," or "I want people to take me seriously.").

d. Have somebody else fill in the third column by describing what they think your clothes say about you.

e. Compare the last two columns. Do your clothes communicate what you want them to? Do the same exercise for social dress, casual dress, business attire, and hair style.

Note: If you are currently employed, analyze the clothing you wear at work.

↻ ROLE-PLAY EXERCISE

This is a two-part role-play exercise. Part one involves preparation for a sales call on a new prospect you have not met previously. The primary objective of this meeting is to get acquainted with the prospect and begin the process of building a long-term relationship. You anticipate that this prospect will become a very good customer. Review the text material on thought processes that will enhance your relationship strategy, nonverbal strategies that add value to your relationships, and conversational strategies that enhance relationships. Prepare a written outline of what you plan to say and do during the first five to ten minutes of the meeting. Think of this outline as your "strategic plan." Part two involves a role play with a class member who will play the role of the prospect. Throughout the role play, try to say and do everything that was part of your plan. At the end of the role play, give your strategic plan outline to the prospect and request feedback on your performance.

Reality Selling Today Video Case Problem

The commercial real estate services industry is highly competitive. CBRE, the firm featured at the beginning of this chapter, offers a wide variety of services such as industrial and logistical services, real estate consulting, investment properties services, and global corporate services.

When clients want to find an office space, they hold their realtor to high standards. After all, the term of a lease contract is a long one, and the stakes are high. CBRE salespeople understand the magnitude and trend of the commercial real estate market. They know that the customers are anxious to partner with someone who can be trusted to look after their best interests.

When new salespeople join the CBRE sales force, they usually work under a senior broker. The mentor helps these recruits form a professional image that appeals to the type of clientele served by the company. In the end, there is a direct link between the image projected by the salespeople and the success of the company. CBRE also adopts a team-based selling approach to ensure that the client is in the good hands as the relationship between CBRE and the client develops. Susana Rosas, an experienced CBRE broker, believes that working under a mentor to learn how to process a deal with a relationship orientation is invaluable. That mentality is part of CBRE's culture and success. Susana works closely with her team members through several stages of the relationship with CBRE clients, from prospecting to post-sales follow-up. When working with new recruits and her team members, she emphasizes the following points:

- Customers notice even the little details such as the firmness of a handshake or simply the properness of an introduction.

- Salespeople at CBRE must be able to build rapport with a variety of personality types. Some customers are quiet, reserved, and somewhat guarded when expressing their views. Others are more impulsive and express their views openly. Salespeople are encouraged to alter their communication style to increase the comfort level of the customer. Susana believes that it is always important for a salesperson to gauge how his or her communication style impacts the prospect. A positive attitude is another important aspect of the relationship-building process at CBRE.

- Susana is a strong believer that salespeople should find out what customers value. Most of the time, a salesperson must come up with innovative solutions to seemingly irreconcilable needs, such as the need to have a large space to accommodate cyclical ups and downs of the customer's industry and the need for efficiency. What is the most important aspect of commercial real estate sales? Most customers do not open up and share important information until they trust the salesperson. (See the chapter opener on p. 52 and Reality Selling Today Role Play 2 in Appendix 1 on page 435 for more information.)

Questions

1. Does it appear that the CBRE salesperson supports the three prescriptions that serve as a foundation of the relationship strategy? (See Strategic/ Consultative Selling Model in Figure 3.1.) Explain your answer.

2. Why should real estate salespeople spend time developing a relationship strategy? What might be some long-term benefits of this strategy?

3. Is it ever appropriate to touch your client other than with a handshake? Explain your answer.

4. How would you behave differently when dealing with a return client versus a new client?

5. What are some precautions to take when preparing for a meeting with a foreign-born prospect?

Chapter 4
Communication Styles: A Key to Adaptive Selling

Learning Objectives

After studying this chapter, you should be able to

1   Discuss how communication style influences the relationship process in sales.

2   Identify the two major dimensions of the communication-style model.

3   Explain the four communication styles in the communication-style model.

4   Learn how to identify your preferred communication style and that of your customer.

5   Learn to achieve interpersonal versatility and build strong selling relationships with style flexing.

 Adaptive Selling Today Training Video Series

COMMUNICATIONS STYLES—A KEY TO ADAPTIVE SELLING

COMMUNICATION STYLES—OR BEHAVIOUR STYLES, AS THEY ARE SOMETIMES CALLED—HAVE been described as one of the most popular training topics in sales and management.

In this two-part Adaptive Selling Today training video, you'll meet Lana, a senior salesperson. While working with Ron, Sandra, and Raymond (one of her top customers, her sales team member, and her marketing manager, respectively), Lana shares what she has learned about building selling relationships with communication styles. We will learn how Lana and her team take a "No, this won't work" response from Ron and, with the adaptive selling "Platinum Rule," attempt to build a mutually rewarding relationship.

Every year publications such as *Canadian Business, Fortune,* and *Fast Company* feature profiles of well-known business leaders. These articles often focus on the communication styles of the executives who provide leadership in companies across North America. Who can forget Al "Chainsaw" Dunlap, who was described as aggressive, frank, opinionated, and impatient? He earned his nickname by ordering huge layoffs when he was the CEO responsible for restructuring companies such as Scott Paper and Sunbeam Corporation. Deborah Hopkins earned the nickname "Hurricane Debby" for the way she conducted business while holding leadership positions at Unisys, GM Europe, Boeing, and Lucent Technologies. Her demanding, ambitious, and sometimes emotional style occasionally

created personality clashes. In contrast, Bill Gates is described as a quiet, reflective person who often seems preoccupied with other matters. And then there is Jeff Bezos, the founder and CEO of Amazon.com, who is often described as the happy extrovert. He seems to enjoy being with other people and often displays spontaneous, uninhibited behaviour.[1]

We form impressions of people by observing their behaviour. The thoughts, feelings, and actions that characterize someone are generally viewed as their **personality**.[2] Communication style is an important aspect of our personality.

personality The thoughts, feelings, and actions that characterize someone.

COMMUNICATION STYLES—AN INTRODUCTION TO MANAGING SELLING RELATIONSHIPS

ALMOST EVERYONE HAS HAD THE PLEASANT EXPERIENCE OF MEETING SOMEONE FOR THE FIRST time and developing instant mutual rapport. There seems to be something about some people that makes you like them instantaneously—a basis for mutual understanding that is difficult to explain. On the other hand, we can all recall meeting people who "turn us off" almost immediately. Why do these things happen during the initial contact?

The impressions that others form about us are based on what they observe us saying and doing. They have no way of knowing our innermost thoughts and feelings, so they make decisions about us based on what they see and hear.[3] The patterns of behaviour that others observe can be called **communication style**. *Behaviour style* and *social style* are additional terms frequently used to describe these patterns of behaviour.

communication style Patterns of behaviour that others observe. Voice patterns, eye movement, facial expression, and posture are some of the components of our communication style.

Adaptive selling, introduced in Chapter 1, is defined as altering sales behaviours in order to improve communication with the customer. It relates to a salesperson's ability to collect information regarding the customer's needs and respond appropriately. Adaptive selling frequently requires complex behavioural adjustments.[4] Adjusting one's communication style in order to fit individual customer needs and preferences is an important element of adaptive selling.

adaptive selling Altering sales behaviours in order to improve communication with the customer.

We form impressions of others by observing their behaviour. Jeff Bezos, founder of Amazon.com, is often described as the happy extrovert who frequently displays spontaneous, uninhibited behaviour. In contrast, Microsoft's Bill Gates is described as a quiet, reflective person who often seems preoccupied with other matters.

Communication-Style Bias

Bias in various forms is quite common in our society. In fact, governments at all levels have passed many laws to curb blatant forms of age, ethnic, religious, and gender discrimination. We also observe some degree of regional bias when people from various parts of Canada meet.

The most frequently occurring form of bias is not commonly understood in our society. What has been labelled **communication-style bias** is a state of mind that almost every one of us experiences from time to time, but we usually find it difficult to explain the symptoms. Communication-style bias can develop when we have contact with another person whose communication style is different from our own. For example, a purchasing agent was overheard saying, "I do not know what it is, but I just do not like that sales representative." The agent was no doubt experiencing communication-style bias but could not easily describe the feeling.

Your communication style is the "you" that is on display every day—the outer pattern of behaviour that others see. If your style is very different from another person's, it may be difficult for the two of you to develop rapport. All of us have had the experience of saying or doing something that was perfectly acceptable to a friend or co-worker and being surprised when the same behaviour irritated someone else. However, aside from admitting that this happens, most of us are unable to draw meaningful conclusions from these experiences to help us perform more effectively with people in the future.[5]

In recent years, thousands of sales professionals have learned to manage their selling relationships more effectively through the study of communication styles. Books such as *I'm Stuck, You're Stuck* by Tom Ritchey, *People Styles at Work* by Robert Bolton and Dorothy Grover Bolton, and *The Versatile Salesperson* by Roger Wenschlag serve as good references. Many training companies offer seminars that provide enrolees with a practical understanding of communication-style theory and practice. Wilson Learning (**www.wilsonlearning.com**) offers a program entitled *The Versatile Salesperson*. This program

communication-style bias
A state of mind we often experience when we have contact with another person whose communication style is different from our own.

helps salespeople develop the interpersonal skills necessary to work effectively with customers whose communication style is different than their own. Over 7 million people worldwide have completed Wilson Learning programs that focus on communication styles.[6]

Communication-Style Principles

The theory of behavioural- or communication-style bias is based on a number of underlying principles. A review of these principles will be beneficial before we examine specific styles.

1. *Individual differences exist and are important.* It is quite obvious that we all differ in terms of such physical characteristics as height, shoe size, facial features, and body build, but the most interesting differences are those patterns of behaviour that are unique to each of us. Voice patterns, eye movement, facial expressions, and posture are some of the components of our communication style. Additional characteristics are discussed later in this chapter. Research by Swiss psychoanalyst Carl Jung and others has helped us understand the importance of individual differences.

2. *A communication style is a way of thinking and behaving.* It is not an ability, but instead a preferred way of using the abilities one has. This distinction is very important. An ability refers to how well someone can do something. A *style* refers to how someone likes to do something.[7]

3. *Individual style differences tend to be stable.* Our communication style is based on a combination of hereditary and environmental factors. Our style is somewhat original at the time of birth; it takes on additional individuality during the first three to five years of life. By the time we enter elementary school, the teacher should be able to identify our preferred communication style. While an individual's communication style tends to remain fairly constant throughout life, adapting to different communication counterparts or the ability to "flex" can be enhanced.

From the Field

Some Accountants Communicate

In a famous Monty Python skit, John Cleese describes an accountant he is interviewing as dull, unimaginative, humourless, tedious, and drab, and says that while in most professions these would be considered drawbacks, not so in accounting. But the reality today is that highly successful professional accountants do not match the stereotype that Cleese describes.

Today's best chartered accountants know they must manage relationships with clients, and that means regularly communicating with them. Ruth Todd is a partner at KPMG LLP (Canada) and has been a chartered accountant for nearly 20 years. Ruth says that KPMG promotes a culture of "client service excellence," and that means staying in touch with clients so they always know you are interested in their business and that you wish to help them find solutions that meet their needs. Some clients call Ruth on a regular basis; some almost never call. Ruth says, "I regularly go through my portfolio of clients and ensure that none get ignored. I contact some by phone, some by email, and some in person, depending on their preference. I find that when I regularly call them, many reciprocate and call me when they have a question because they know I want to help." Ruth also points out that she does not invoice a client for every phone call. She says, "If you are too focused on billing, the client will become hesitant to call for advice. You need to think about adding value and building long-term relationships."[a]

Group sales presentations can be very challenging because, in most cases, you are attempting to adapt to several different communication styles.

4. *There are a finite number of styles.* Most people display one of several clusters of similar behaviours, and this allows us to identify a small number of behavioural categories. By combining a series of descriptors, we can develop a single "label" that describes a person's most preferred communication style.

5. *To create the most productive relationships, it is necessary to get in sync with the communication style of the people you work with.*[8] Differences between people can be a source of friction unless you develop the ability to recognize and respond to the other person's style.

The ability to identify another person's communication style, and to know how and when to adapt your own preferred style to it, can afford you a crucial advantage in dealing with people. Differences between people can be a source of friction. The ability to "speak the other person's language" is an important relationship-management skill.[9]

Improving Your Relationship Selling Skills

Anyone who is considering a career in selling will benefit greatly from the study of communication styles. These concepts provide a practical method of classifying people according to communication style and give the salesperson a distinct advantage in the marketplace. A salesperson who understands communication-style classification methods and learns how to adapt them can avoid common mistakes that threaten interpersonal relations with customers. Awareness of these methods greatly reduces the possibility of tension arising during the sales call.

The first major goal of this chapter is to help you better understand your own most preferred communication style. The second goal is to help you develop greater understanding and appreciation for styles that are different from your own. The third goal is to help you manage your selling relationships more effectively by learning to adapt your style to fit the communication style of the customer. This practice is called **style flexing**.

style flexing The deliberate adjustment of one's communication style to accommodate the needs of the other person.

COMMUNICATION-STYLE MODEL

THIS SECTION INTRODUCES YOU TO THE FOUR BASIC COMMUNICATION STYLES. ONE OF THESE will surface as your most preferred style. The communication-style model that defines these styles is based on two important dimensions of human behaviour: dominance and sociability. We look at the dominance continuum first.

Dominance Continuum

dominance Reflects the tendency to influence or exert one's will over others in a relationship. Each of us falls somewhere on this continuum.

Dominance can be defined as the tendency to control or prevail over others.[10] Dominant people tend to be quite competitive. They also tend to offer opinions readily and to be decisive, opinionated, self-assertive, and vocal. Each of us falls somewhere on the dominance continuum illustrated by Figure 4.1.

A person classified as high in dominance is generally a "take charge" type of person who makes a position clear to others. A person classified as low in dominance is usually more reserved, unassertive, and easygoing. Dominance has been recognized as a universal behavioural characteristic. David W. Johnson developed the Interpersonal Pattern Exercise to help people achieve greater interpersonal effectiveness. He believes that people fall into two dominance categories:

1. *Lower dominance:* These people have a tendency to be quite cooperative and let others control things. They tend to be lower in assertiveness.

2. *Higher dominance:* These people tend to like to control things and frequently initiate demands. They are more aggressive in dealing with others.[11]

The first step in determining your most preferred communication style is to identify where you fall on the dominance continuum. Do you tend to rank low or high on this scale? To answer this question, complete the Dominance Indicator form in Table 4.1. Rate yourself on each scale by placing a check mark on the continuum at the point that represents how you perceive yourself. If most of your check marks fall to the right of centre, you are someone who is higher in dominance. If most of your check marks fall to the left of centre, you are someone who is lower in dominance. Is there any best place to be on the dominance continuum? The answer is no. Successful salespeople can be found at all points along the continuum.

Sociability Continuum

sociability Reflects the amount of control one exerts over emotional expressiveness. People who are high in sociability tend to express their feelings freely, while people who are low on this continuum tend to control their feelings.

Sociability reflects the amount of control we exert over our emotional expressiveness.[12] People who are high in sociability tend to express their feelings freely, while people who are low in this dimension tend to control their feelings. Each of us falls somewhere on the sociability continuum illustrated in Figure 4.2.

Sociability is also a universal behavioural characteristic. It can be defined as the tendency to seek and enjoy interaction with others. Therefore, high sociability is an

Low ████████████████████████████ High

Figure 4.1 The first step in determining your most preferred communication style is to identify where you are on the dominance continuum.

Table 4.1 Dominance Indicator

Rate yourself on each scale by placing a check mark on the continuum at the point that represents how you perceive yourself.

I Perceive Myself as Somewhat

Cooperative	/	/	/	/	/	Competitive
Submissive	/	/	/	/	/	Authoritarian
Accommodating	/	/	/	/	/	Domineering
Hesitant	/	/	/	/	/	Decisive
Reserved	/	/	/	/	/	Outgoing
Compromising	/	/	/	/	/	Insistent
Cautious	/	/	/	/	/	Risk-taking
Patient	/	/	/	/	/	Hurried
Complacent	/	/	/	/	/	Influential
Quiet	/	/	/	/	/	Talkative
Shy	/	/	/	/	/	Bold
Supportive	/	/	/	/	/	Demanding
Relaxed	/	/	/	/	/	Tense
Restrained	/	/	/	/	/	Assertive

High

Low

Figure 4.2 The second step in determining your most preferred communication style is to identify where you are on the sociability continuum.

indication of a person's preference to interact with other people. Lower sociability is an indicator of a person's desire to work in an environment where he or she has more time alone instead of having to make conversation with others. The person who is classified as being lower in the area of sociability is more reserved and formal in social relationships.

The second step in determining your most preferred communication style is to identify where you fall on the sociability continuum. To answer this question, complete the Sociability Indicator form shown in Table 4.2. Rate yourself on each scale by placing a check mark on the continuum at the point that represents how you perceive yourself. If most of your check marks fall to the right of centre, you are someone who is higher in sociability. If most of your check marks fall to the left of centre, you are someone who is lower in sociability. Keep in mind that there is no best place to be. Successful salespeople can be found at all points along this continuum.

As you reflect on your dominance and sociability ratings, keep in mind that self-ratings can be misleading. Many people do not see themselves in the same way that others see them. Friends and co-workers who frequently observe your behaviours may be in a better position to identify your communication style.

With the aid of the dominance and sociability continuums we can now discuss a relatively simple communication-style classification plan that has practical application in the field of selling. We will describe the four basic styles: Emotive, Directive, Reflective, and Supportive.

Table 4.2 Sociability Indicator

Rate yourself on each scale by placing a check mark on the continuum at the point that represents how you perceive yourself.

I Perceive Myself as Somewhat

Disciplined	/	/	/	/	/	Easygoing
Controlled	/	/	/	/	/	Expressive
Serious	/	/	/	/	/	Lighthearted
Methodical	/	/	/	/	/	Unstructured
Calculating	/	/	/	/	/	Spontaneous
Guarded	/	/	/	/	/	Open
Stalwart	/	/	/	/	/	Humorous
Aloof	/	/	/	/	/	Friendly
Formal	/	/	/	/	/	Casual
Reserved	/	/	/	/	/	Attention-seeking
Cautious	/	/	/	/	/	Carefree
Conforming	/	/	/	/	/	Unconventional
Reticent	/	/	/	/	/	Dramatic
Restrained	/	/	/	/	/	Impulsive

Four Styles of Communication

By combining the two dimensions of human behaviour—dominance and sociability—we can form a partial outline of the communication-style model (Fig. 4.3). Dominance is represented by the horizontal axis and sociability is represented by the vertical axis. Once the two dimensions of human behaviour are combined, the framework for communication-style classification is established.

The Emotive Style The upper right-hand quadrant of Figure 4.4 defines a style that combines higher sociability and higher dominance. We call this the **Emotive style** (see Fig. 4.5). Emotive people are expressive and willing to spend time maintaining and enjoying a large number of relationships. Television personalities Rick Mercer and Oprah Winfrey provide excellent models of the Emotive communication style. Sports personality Don Cherry and actors Jim Carrey, Mike Myers, and Robin Williams also project the Emotive communication style. They are outspoken, enthusiastic, and stimulating. The Emotive person wants to create a social relationship quickly and usually feels more comfortable in an informal atmosphere. Some of the verbal and nonverbal clues that identify the Emotive person follow:

1. *Appears quite active.* This person gives the appearance of being busy. A person who combines higher dominance and higher sociability often displays spontaneous, uninhibited behaviour. The Emotive person is likely to express feelings with vigorous movements of the hands and a rapid speech pattern.

Emotive style A communication style that displays the following characteristics: appears to be quite active, takes the social initiative in most cases, likes to encourage informality, and expresses emotional opinions.

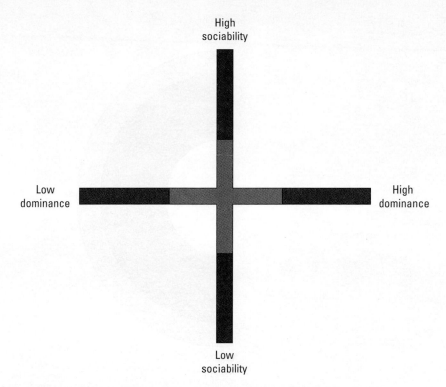

Figure 4.3 When the dominance and sociability dimensions of human behaviour are combined, the framework for communication-style classification is established.

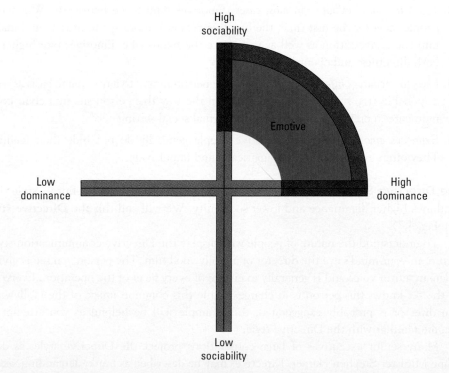

Figure 4.4 The Emotive style combines high sociability and high dominance.

Sociable	Unstructured
Spontaneous	Excitable
Zestful	Personable
Stimulating	Persuasive
Emotional	Dynamic

Figure 4.5 Key words for the Emotive style.

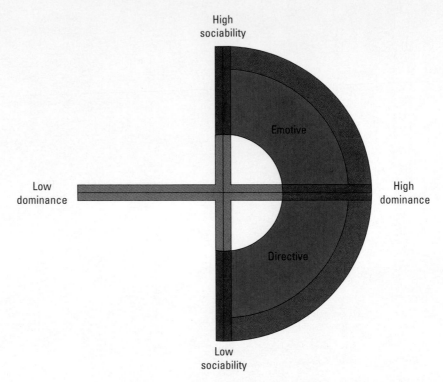

High
sociability

Low
dominance

High
dominance

Emotive

Directive

Low
sociability

Figure 4.6 The Directive style combines high dominance and low sociability.

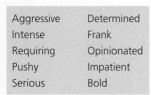

Aggressive	Determined
Intense	Frank
Requiring	Opinionated
Pushy	Impatient
Serious	Bold

Figure 4.7 Key words
for the Directive style.

Directive style A communication style that displays the following characteristics: appears to be businesslike, displays a serious attitude, and voices strong opinions.

2. *Takes the social initiative in most cases.* Emotives tend to be extroverts. When two people meet for the first time, the Emotive person is more apt to initiate and maintain the conversation as well as to initiate the handshake. Emotives rate higher in both directness and openness.

3. *Likes to encourage informality.* The Emotive person moves to a first-name basis as soon as possible (too soon in some cases). Even the way this person sits in a chair communicates a preference for a relaxed, informal social setting.

4. *Expresses emotional opinions.* Emotive people generally do not hide their feelings. They often express opinions dramatically and impulsively.

The Directive Style The lower right-hand quadrant of Figure 4.6 defines a style that combines higher dominance and lower sociability. We will call this the **Directive style** (see Fig. 4.7).

To understand the nature of people who display the Directive communication style, picture in your mind's eye the director of a Hollywood film. The person you see is giving orders in a firm voice and is generally in charge of every facet of the operation. Everyone on the set knows this person is in charge. While this common image of the Hollywood film director is probably exaggerated, this example will be helpful as you attempt to become familiar with the Directive style.

Many senior executives of large corporations project the Directive style, as does Prime Minister Stephen Harper. Directives may be described as frank, demanding, assertive, and determined.

Emotive people like Oprah Winfrey and Robin Williams are stimulating, excitable, and spontaneous. Emotives generally do not hide their feelings and often express opinions dramatically and impulsively.

Judith Sheindlin, better known as Judge Judy, uses a brash "take no prisoners" approach to handling disputes on the *Judge Judy* television show. She is frank, assertive, and very focused.

In the field of selling you will encounter a number of customers who are Directives. How can you identify these people? What verbal and nonverbal clues can you observe? A few of the behaviours displayed by Directives follow:

1. *Appears to be quite busy.* The Directive generally does not like to waste time and wants to get right to the point. Judy Sheindlin of the *Judge Judy* television show displays this behaviour.

2. *May give the impression of not listening.* In most cases the Directive feels more comfortable talking than listening.

3. *Displays a serious attitude.* A person who is lower in sociability usually communicates a lack of warmth and is apt to be quite businesslike and impersonal.

4. *Likes to maintain control.* The person who is higher on the dominance continuum likes to maintain control. During meetings the Directive often seeks to control the agenda.[13]

The Reflective Style The lower left-hand quadrant of the communication-style model features a combination of lower dominance and lower sociability (Fig. 4.8). People who regularly display this behaviour are classified as having the **Reflective style** (see Fig. 4.9).

The Reflective person tends to examine all the facts carefully before arriving at a decision. Like a cautious scientist, this individual wants to gather all available information and weigh it carefully before taking a position. The Reflective type is usually a stickler for detail.[14] The late physicist Albert Einstein fits the description. Rex Murphy, the journalist who hosts CBC's *Cross Country Checkup*; David Suzuki, the scientist who hosts CBC's *The Nature of Things*; and CBC news anchor Peter Mansbridge, who hosts *Mansbridge One on One*, all display the characteristics of the Reflective type.

Reflective style A communication style that displays the following characteristics: controls emotional expression, displays a preference for orderliness, tends to express measured opinions, and seems difficult to get to know.

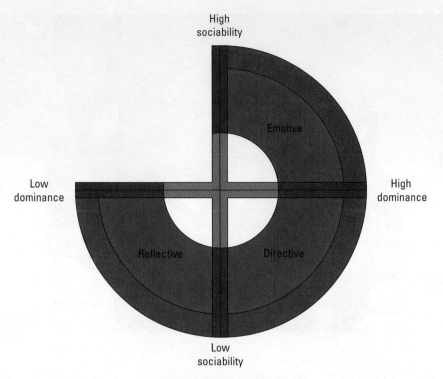

High
sociability

Emotive

Low
dominance

High
dominance

Reflective

Directive

Low
sociability

Figure 4.8 The Reflective style combines low dominance and low sociability.

Precise	Scientific
Deliberate	Preoccupied
Questioning	Serious
Disciplined	Industrious
Aloof	Stuffy

Figure 4.9 Key words for the Reflective style.

The Reflective communication style combines lower dominance and lower sociability; therefore, people with this classification tend to be reserved and cautious. Some additional behaviours that characterize this style follow:

1. *Controls emotional expression.* Reflective people tend to curb emotional expression and are less likely to display warmth openly. Bill Gates displays this personality trait.

2. *Displays a preference for orderliness.* The Reflective person enjoys a highly structured environment and generally feels frustration when confronted with unexpected events.

3. *Tends to express measured opinions.* The Reflective individual usually does not express dramatic opinions. This communication style is characterized by disciplined, businesslike actions.

4. *Seems difficult to get to know.* The Reflective person tends to be somewhat formal in social relationships and therefore can be viewed as aloof by many people.

In a selling situation the Reflective customer does not want to move too fast. This person wants the facts presented in an orderly and unemotional manner and does not want to waste a lot of time socializing.

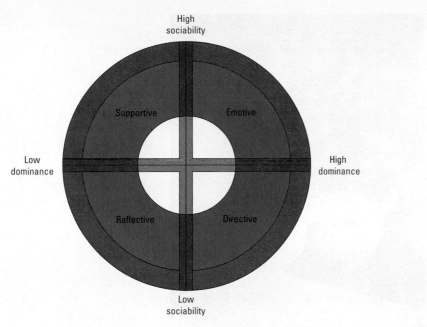

High
sociability

Low
dominance

Supportive   Emotive

Reflective   Directive

High
dominance

Low
sociability

Figure 4.10 The Supportive style combines low dominance and high sociability.

The Supportive Styles The upper left-hand quadrant shows a combination of lower dominance and higher sociability (Fig. 4.10). This communication style is called the **Supportive style** (see Fig. 4.11) because these people find it easy to listen and usually do not express their views in a forceful manner. Canadian singers Anne Murray and Rita MacNeil both display the characteristics of the Supportive style, as did the late Diana, Princess of Wales.

Supportive style A communication style that displays the following characteristics: appears quiet and reserved, listens attentively to other people, tends to avoid the use of power, and makes decisions in a thoughtful and deliberate manner.

Persons with the Reflective style, such as David Suzuki, tend to control their emotions and examine all the facts when making a decision.

Lighthearted	Patient
Reserved	Sensitive
Passive	Relaxed
Warm	Compliant
Docile	Softhearted

Figure 4.11 Key words for the Supportive style.

People with the Supportive communication style are usually quiet and unassuming.

Low visibility generally characterizes the lifestyle of Supportive people. They complete their tasks in a quiet, unassuming manner and seldom draw attention to what they have accomplished. In terms of assertiveness, persons with the Supportive style rank quite low. Someone who ranks higher on the dominance continuum is likely to view the Supportive individual as being too easygoing. Other behaviours that commonly characterize the Supportive person follow:

1. *Gives the appearance of being quiet and reserved.* People with the Supportive communication style can easily display their feelings, but not in the assertive manner common to the Emotive individual.

2. *Listens attentively to other people.* In selling, good listening skills can be a real asset. This talent comes naturally to the Supportive person.

3. *Tends to avoid the use of power.* Whereas the Directive may rely on power to accomplish tasks, the Supportive person is more likely to rely on friendly persuasion.

4. *Makes decisions in a thoughtful and deliberate manner.* The Supportive person usually takes longer to make a decision.

Popularity of the Four-Style Model

We are endlessly fascinated by ourselves, and this helps explain the growing popularity of the four-style model presented in this chapter. To satisfy this insatiable appetite for information, many training and development companies offer training programs that present the four social or communication styles. Figure 4.12 features the approximate

Supportive (Manning/Reece/Ahearne/MacKenzie)	Emotive (Manning/Reece/Ahearne/MacKenzie)
Amiable (Wilson Learning)	Expressive (Wilson Learning)
Supportive-Giving (Stuart Atkins Inc.)	Adapting-Dealing (Stuart Atkins Inc.)
Relater (People Smarts)	Socializer (People Smarts)
Steadiness (Personal Profile System)	Influencing (Personal Profile System)
Supportive (DiSC)	Influencing (DiSC)
Reflective (Manning/Reece/Ahearne/MacKenzie)	Directive (Manning/Reece/Ahearne/MacKenzie)
Analytical (Wilson Learning)	Driver (Wilson Learning)
Conserving-Holding (Stuart Atkins Inc.)	Controlling-Taking (Stuart Atkins Inc.)
Thinker (People Smarts)	Directive (People Smarts)
Cautiousness/Compliance (Personal Profile System)	Dominance (Personal Profile System)
Conscientious (DiSC)	Dominance (DiSC)

Figure 4.12 The four basic communication styles have been used in a wide range of training programs. For comparison purposes, the approximate equivalents to the four communication styles discussed in this chapter are listed.

equivalents of the four styles presented in this chapter. Although four-style programs were initially created and marketed in the United States, they have become a global phenomenon, according to staff at the Wilson Learning.[15] Inscape Publishing, the company that developed the DiSC learning instrument over three decades ago, reports that more that 40 million people worldwide have completed DiSC workshops.[16]

Determining Your Communication Style

You now have enough information to identify your own communication style. If your location on the dominance continuum is right of centre and your position on the sociability continuum is below the centre mark, you fall into the Directive quadrant. If your location on the dominance continuum is left of centre and your position on the sociability continuum is above the centre mark, then your most preferred style is Supportive. Likewise, lower dominance matched with lower sociability forms the Reflective communication style, and higher dominance matched with higher sociability forms the Emotive communication style.

An Online Assessment of Your Communication Style You can gain further insight into your communication style by accessing the **www.pearsoncanada.ca/manning** website and clicking on the Online Assessment of Your Communication Style link. After completing the assessment, you will be supplied with a profile indicating your most preferred communication style. You will also be presented with a profile of your secondary style. See application exercises 1, 2, 3, and 4 on page 98 for more ways to use this online assessment tool.

Of course, all of us display some characteristics of the Emotive, Directive, Reflective, and Supportive communication styles. However, one of the four styles is usually predominant and readily detectable.[17] This is your preferred style.

Some people who study the communication-style model for the first time may initially experience feelings of frustration. They find it hard to believe that one's behavioural

Tom Ritchey's book *I'm Stuck, You're Stuck* presents the theory behind the popular DiSC Behavioral Style Model. The DiSC model was first introduced under the name Performax by Carlson Learning.

Reprinted with permission of the publisher. From I'm Stuck, You're Stuck: Breakthrough to Better Work Relationships and Results by Discovering your DiSC® Behavioral Style, copyright © 2002 by Tom Richey, Berrett-Koehler Publishers, Inc., San Francisco, CA. All rights reserved. www.bkconnection.com.

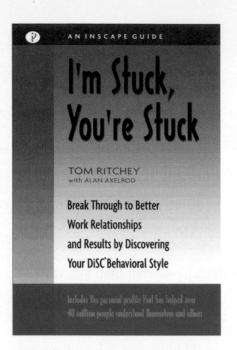

style tends to remain quite uniform throughout life. People often say, "I am a different person each day!" It is certainly true that we sometimes feel different from day to day, but our most preferred style remains stable.

The Supportive person might say, "I sometimes get very upset and tell people what I am thinking. I can be a Directive when I want to be!" There is no argument here. Just because you have a preferred communication style does not mean you will never display the behavioural characteristics of another style. Some people use different styles in different contexts and in different relationships.[18] Reflective people sometimes display Emotive behaviour, and Emotive people sometimes display Reflective behaviour. We are saying that each person has one most-preferred and habitually used communication style.

MINIMIZING COMMUNICATION-STYLE BIAS

SALESPEOPLE OFTEN MAKE THE MISTAKE OF FOCUSING TOO MUCH ON THE CONTENT of their sales presentation and not enough on how they deliver their message.[19] Communication-style bias is a barrier to success in selling. This form of bias is a common problem in sales work simply because salespeople deal with people from all four quadrants. You cannot select potential customers on the basis of their communication style. You must be able to develop rapport with people from each of the four quadrants. When people of different styles work together but don't adapt to one another, serious problems can develop.[20]

How Communication-Style Bias Develops

To illustrate how communication-style bias develops in a sales situation, let us observe a sales call involving two people with different communication styles. Lana Wheeler entered the office of Ron Harrington, one of her large accounts, with a feeling of optimism.

She was sure that her product would save Ron's company several thousand dollars a month. She was 99 percent certain that, this being her third call on Ron, the sale would be closed. Ten minutes after meeting Ron, she was walking out of his office without an order. What went wrong?

Lana Wheeler is an engaging type who is an Emotive in terms of communication style. Her sales calls are typically fast-paced. She entered Ron's office and immediately began to close the sale. Ron interrupted and told Lana he couldn't commit to her proposal. Lana appeared to ignore Ron's response and told him she could put some more figures together on pricing and then used another trial close. Ron finally told Lana, "Look, you don't understand the way I do business. We have bigger issues than additional figures. As I said, this is a 'no go' project."

Ron's communication style is Directive. He feels uncomfortable when someone is making a decision for him. He wants to maintain control and be in charge of making his own decisions. He felt tension when Lana tried to get him to make a decision on her terms. If Lana had spent more time asking questions, listening more closely, and allowing Ron to feel like the decision was his, she may have found out what "the bigger issues" were. The approach she used would have been more appropriate for the Supportive or Emotive communication style.

A salesperson who is highly adaptable can usually build rapport with customers regardless of their communication style. Style flexing is a sales strategy that can be learned.

Adaptive Selling Requires Versatility

Personal selling has become more customer focused than ever before, so every effort should be made to reduce the tension between the salesperson and customer. Dr. David Merrill, one of the early pioneers in the development of communication-style instruments and training programs, uses the term **versatility** to describe our ability to minimize

versatility Our ability to minimize communication-style bias.

In the training video *Communication Styles: A Key to Adaptive Selling Today,* Lana, Ron, Raymond, and Sandra all moved into their excess zones before learning about the platinum rule and developed communication-style bias. After learning flexibility and versatility, salespeople can adapt to the style of others and then build the kind of rapport that adds value to the sale.

Selling Today

Closing the Sale with Adaptive Selling

Rich Goldberg, CEO of Warm Thoughts Communications, a marketing communications company, sensed he was about to lose an important client. He met with his staff and together they created a profile based on their knowledge of the client's communication style. It soon became apparent that there was a mismatch between the client and the salesperson who called on that person. The customer was low in sociability but high in dominance. The customer was also described as someone who needed facts and figures. The salesperson was working on relationship building, and this approach was agitating the client. Goldberg counselled his staff to keep conversations with this customer brief, use facts and figures frequently, and clearly spell out the company's commitment to the client.[b]

communication-style bias.[21] Roger Wenschlag, author of *The Versatile Salesperson*, describes versatility as "the degree to which a salesperson is perceived as developing and maintaining buyer comfort throughout the sales process." *Adapting* to the customer's preferred communication style can enhance sales performance.[22]

Mature and Immature Behaviour There is a mature and an immature side to each behavioural style. Let us examine the Emotive style to illustrate this point. People with this style are open, personable individuals who seem genuinely friendly. The natural enthusiasm displayed by the mature Emotive is refreshing. On the other hand, an Emotive person who is too talkative and too emotional may have difficulty building rapport with some customers; this is the immature side of the Emotive communication style.

You will recall that we used the words "industrious" and "precise" to describe the Reflective style. These are words that apply to the mature side of the Reflective person. We also used the words "aloof" and "stuffy." These words describe the immature side of the Reflective.

The good news is that we all have the potential for developing the mature side of our communication style.

Strength/Weakness Paradox It is a fact of life that your greatest strength can become your greatest weakness. If your most preferred style is Reflective, people are likely to respect your well-disciplined approach to life as one of your strengths. However, this strength can become a weakness if it is exaggerated. The Reflective person can be too serious, too questioning, and too inflexible. Robert Haas, former CEO of Levi Strauss & Company, is known for extraordinary—some say obsessive—attention to detail. Those who work with him say an offhand conversation can sound like a lecture. This Reflective, however, has the ability to flex his style. Levi's employees are fiercely loyal to Haas and describe him as compassionate to a fault.[23]

People with the Directive style are open and frank. They express their true feelings in a direct manner. In most cases we appreciate candour, but we do not like to be around people who are too straightforward or too blunt in expressing their views. Steven Ballmer, CEO of Microsoft, was known as a very demanding executive during his early years with the company. His explosive temper was legendary and he often put the fear of God into his staff members. He once needed throat surgery because he yelled so much. Later he

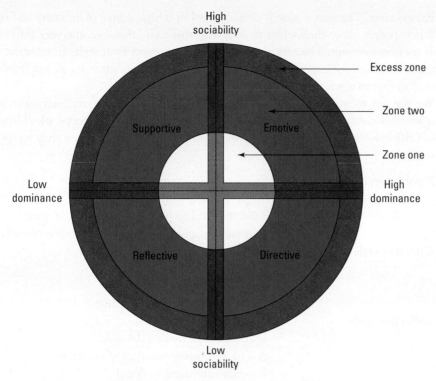

Figure 4.13 The completed communication-style model provides important insights needed to manage the relationship process in selling.

became more diplomatic and less domineering.[24] When people come across as opinionated, they tend to antagonize others. We should avoid pushing our strengths to the point of unproductive excess.[25]

To illustrate how strengths become weaknesses in excess, let us add more detail to our communication-style model. Note that it now features three zones that radiate out from the centre (see Fig. 4.13). These dimensions might be thought of as intensity zones.

Zone one. People who fall within this zone display their unique behavioural characteristics with less intensity than those in zone two. The Emotive person, for example, is moderately high on the dominance continuum and moderately high on the sociability continuum. As you might expect, zone one communication styles are more difficult to identify because there is less intensity in both dimensions (dominance and sociability).

Zone two. Persons who fall within this zone display their unique behavioural characteristics with greater intensity than persons in zone one. The zone two Reflective, for example, falls within the lowest quartile of the dominance continuum and the lowest quartile of the sociability continuum. The boundary line that separates zone one and zone two should not be seen as a permanent barrier restricting change in intensity. Under certain circumstances we should abandon our most preferred style temporarily. A deliberate move from zone one to zone two, or vice versa, is called style flexing.

Excess zone. The excess zone is characterized by a high degree of intensity and rigidity. When people allow themselves to drift into this zone, they become very inflexible, which is often interpreted by others as a form of bias toward their style. In addition, the strengths of the inflexible person become weaknesses. Extreme intensity in any quadrant is bound to threaten interpersonal relations.

We are apt to move into the excess zone and exaggerate our style characteristics under stressful conditions. Stress tends to bring out the worst in many people. Here are some of the behaviours that salespeople and customers may display when they are in the excess zone:

Emotive style	Expresses highly emotional opinions
	Stops listening to the other person
	Tries too hard to promote own point of view
	Becomes outspoken to the point of being offensive
Directive style	Gets impatient with the other person
	Becomes dictatorial and bossy
	Does not admit being wrong
	Becomes extremely competitive
Reflective style	Becomes stiff and formal
	Is unwilling to make a decision
	Avoids displaying any type of emotion
	Is overly interested in detail
Supportive style	Agrees with everyone
	Is unable to take a strong stand
	Becomes overly anxious to win approval of others
	Tries to comfort everyone

The excess zone is characterized by a high degree of intensity and rigidity. We are more apt to move into the excess zone under very stressful conditions.

ACHIEVING VERSATILITY THROUGH STYLE FLEXING

Style flexing IS THE DELIBERATE ATTEMPT TO ADAPT ONE'S COMMUNICATION STYLE TO accommodate the needs of the other person. You are attempting to communicate with the other person on his or her own "channel." Ron Willingham, in his book *Integrity Selling*, reminds us that "people are more apt to buy from you when they perceive you view the world as they view the world."[26] In a selling situation, you should try to determine the customer's most preferred style and flex your own accordingly. If your preferred communication style is Directive and your customer is a Supportive, try to be more personal and warm in your presentation. Once you know the customer's style, flexing your style can make the difference between a presentation that falters and one that exceeds your expectations.[27] Style sensitivity and flexing add value to the sales process.

Throughout the preapproach, you should learn as much as possible about the customer and try to determine his style. Once you are in the customer's presence, do not become preoccupied analyzing the person's style. If you are trying hard to analyze the person's style, you may not listen closely enough to what she is trying to tell you. If you are truly tuned in to the customer, you can absorb many clues that will help you determine her style. After the sales call, analyze the communication and record your findings. Use this information to plan your next contact with the customer.[28] Listen closely to the customer's tone of voice. A Supportive person sounds warm and friendly. The Reflective customer's voice is more likely to be controlled and deliberate. Pay particular attention to gestures. The Emotive individual uses his hands to communicate thoughts and ideas. The Directive also uses gestures to communicate but is more controlled and less spontaneous. The Reflective person appears more relaxed, less intense. The Emotive individual is an open, impulsive communicator, while the Reflective person is quite cautious. The Supportive type is personal and friendly, while the Reflective person may seem difficult to get to know. To avoid relationship tension, consider the following suggestions for each of the four styles.

Selling to Emotives

If you are attempting to sell products to an Emotive person, keep in mind the need to move at a pace that will hold the attention of the prospect. Be enthusiastic and avoid an approach that is too stiff and formal. Take time to establish goodwill and build relationships. Do not place too much emphasis on the facts and details. To deal effectively with Emotive people, plan actions that will provide support for their opinions, ideas, and

The Platinum Rule Do Unto Others As They Want Done Unto Them.

Selling Today

The Platinum Rule®

The Platinum Rule®, created many years ago by Dr. Tony Alessandra, provides each of us with the motivation we need to treat others the way they want to be treated. This rule is a simple, proven method for building strong relationships with our customers.

"Do Unto Others As They Want Done Unto Them."

The Platinum Rule® (www.platinumrule.com) is at the heart of the style-flexing sales strategy. When we take time to determine if the customer is behaving as an Emotive, Directive, Reflective, or Supportive, we can then treat them the way they want to be treated.[c]

dreams.[29] Plan to ask questions concerning their opinions and ideas, but be prepared to help them get "back on track" if they move too far away from the topic. Maintain good eye contact and, above all, be a good listener.

Selling to Directives

The key to relating to Directives is to keep the relationship as businesslike as possible. Developing a strong personal relationship is not a high priority for Directives. In other words, friendship is not usually a condition for a good working relationship. Your goal is to be as efficient, time disciplined, and well organized as possible, and to provide appropriate facts, figures, and success probabilities. Most Directives are goal-oriented people, so try to identify their primary objectives and then determine ways to support and help with these objectives. Early in the sales presentation, ask specific questions and carefully note responses. Look for specific points you can respond to when it is time to present your proposal.

Selling to Reflectives

The Reflective person will respond in a positive way to a thoughtful, well-organized approach. Arrive at meetings on time and be well prepared. In most cases it is not necessary to spend a great deal of time building a social relationship. Reflective people appreciate a no-nonsense, businesslike approach to personal selling. Use specific questions that show clear direction. Once you have information concerning the prospect's needs, present your proposal in a slow, deliberate way. Provide as much documentation as possible. Do not be in too big a hurry to close the sale. Never pressure the Reflective person to make quick decisions.

Selling to Supportives

Take time to build a social relationship with the Supportive person. Spend time learning about the things that are important in this individual's life—family, hobbies, and major interests. Listen carefully to personal opinions and feelings. Supportive individuals like to conduct business with sales personnel who are professional but friendly. Therefore, study their feelings and emotional needs as well as their technical and business needs. Throughout the presentation, provide personal assurances and support for their views. If you disagree with a Supportive person, curb the desire to disagree too assertively; Supportive people tend to dislike interpersonal conflict. Give them the time to comprehend your proposal. Patience is important.

As you develop your communication-style identification skills and become more adept at style flexing, you are better able to manage the relationship process. With these skills, you should be able to open more accounts, sell more to established customers, and more effectively meet the pressures of competition. Most important, your customers will view you as a person better able to understand and meet their needs.

Word of Caution

It is tempting to put a label on someone and then assume the label tells you everything you need to know about that person. If you want to build an effective sales partnership with a prospect, you must acquire additional information about that person. Stuart Atkins, a respected authority on communication styles and author of *The Name of Your Game*, says we should be careful not to use labels that make people feel boxed in, typecast, or judged. He believes we should not classify *people*; we should classify their *strengths* and *preferences* to act one way or another under certain circumstances.[30] You must also be careful not to let the label you place on yourself become the justification for your own inflexible behaviour. Try not to let the label justify or reinforce why you are unable or unwilling to communicate effectively with others.

REVIEWING KEY CONCEPTS

- Discuss how communication style influences the relationship process in selling.

  Many sales are lost because salespeople fail to communicate effectively with the prospect. Communication-style bias contributes to this problem. Every salesperson who is willing to develop style sensitivity and engage in appropriate style flexing can minimize one of the most common barriers to success in selling.

- Identify the two major dimensions of the communication-style model.

  The communication-style model is based on two continuums that assess two major aspects of human behaviour: dominance and sociability. By combining them as horizontal and vertical continuums we create quadrants that define four styles of communication. We have called these the Emotive, Directive, Reflective, and Supportive styles.

- Explain the four communications styles in the communication-style model.

  The Emotive style combines high sociability and high dominance, whereas the Directive style combines high dominance and low sociability. The Reflective style combines low dominance and low sociability, whereas the Supportive style combines low dominance and high sociability.

- Learn how to identify your preferred communication style and that of your customer.

  With practice you can learn to identify your preferred communication style. The starting point is to rate yourself on each scale (dominance and sociability) by placing a check mark at a point along the continuum that represents how you perceive yourself. Completion of the dominance and sociability indicator forms will help you achieve greater awareness of your communication style. This same approach can be used to identify the customer's preferred style.

- Learn to achieve interpersonal versatility and build strong selling relationships with style flexing.

  A third dimension of human behaviour—versatility—is important in dealing with communication styles that are different from your own. You can adjust your own style to meet the needs of others—a process called *style flexing*. Style flexing is an attempt to change or alter your style to meet the needs of the customer.

Key Terms

Review Questions

1. What is the meaning of the term *communication style*?

2. Describe the five major principles that support communication-style theory.

3. What are the benefits to the salesperson who understands communication style?

4. What two dimensions of human behaviour are used to identify communication style?

5. Describe the person who tends to be high in sociability.

6. What are the four communication styles? Develop a brief description of each.

7. What is the reaction of most people who study communication styles for the first time? Why does this reaction surface?

8. Define *style flexing*. How can style flexing improve sales productivity?

9. Explain the statement, "Your greatest strength can become your greatest weakness."

10. What suggestions would you give to a salesperson who is planning to meet a new prospect who displays the Reflective communication style?

Application Exercises

1. Communication, or behaviour, styles are the basis for one of the most popular training programs. Worldwide, 47 million people have participated in Wilson and DiSC programs. An understanding of communication styles assists us in building better personal and business relationships. As indicated in this chapter, the first step in applying what you have learned about communication styles is to identify and understand your own style. Using the Online Communication Style Assessment tool at www.pearsoncanada.ca/manning, assess your communication style.

   a. Do you agree with your assessment of your most preferred style? How about your results on your secondary style?

   b. Referring back to the material presented in this chapter, identify the strengths and weaknesses of your style.

   c. Identify the styles you enjoy working with best. Identify the styles you enjoy working with least.

   d. Referring to the behaviours listed on page 94, can you identify those behaviours you tend to exhibit when you feel stressed?

   e. Explain why you think so many individuals and companies have participated in these programs. From Figure 4.12 on page 89, list the names of other training programs you could use to identify your most preferred style.

2. Self-awareness is important in personal selling. As we get to know ourselves, we can identify barriers to acceptance by others. Once you have identified your most preferred communication style, you have taken a big step in the direction of self-awareness. We have noted that self-ratings can sometimes be misleading because some people lack a high degree of self-awareness. They do not see themselves as others see them. Consider asking four or five people, co-workers for example, to assess and print the profile of your communication style using the online assessment. Then compare these ratings with your self-rating.

3. Many salespeople, after being introduced to communication-style concepts, attempt to categorize each of their customers. They report that their relationships become mutually more enjoyable and productive. Select four people whom you know quite well (e.g., supervisor, subordinate, customer, teacher, friend, or member of your sports team). Using the two behavioural continuums in this chapter, determine these people's communication styles. Using your own descriptive terminology in conjunction with terminology in this chapter, develop a descriptive behavioural profile of each of these people. Explain how this information could improve your relationship with each of these people.

4. To assess your ability to style flex, assume you are going to make four sales calls on customers displaying each of the four communication styles. For purposes of illustration, consider your first call is on an Emotive customer with a communication style like Rick Mercer's. The second call is on a Supportive customer with a communication style like Rita MacNeil's, the third is on a Reflective customer with a communication style like Bill Gates's, and the last is on a Directive customer like Prime Minister Stephen Harper. For each of these customers, refer to the online communication style assessment and assess the behaviours you would demonstrate as you established your relationship with them. Print each of

the profiles and compare them to one another. Did you flex your style of communication to better interact with the customer representing Rick Mercer's style versus the customer representing Rita MacNeil's style? Did you flex differently for the customers representing Bill Gates and Prime Minister Stephen Harper?

5. Myers-Briggs Personality Types and Jungian Personality Types are two very popular descriptions of the material in this chapter. Using your search engine, access the Internet sites that refer to these concepts. Type in "Jungian + personality profiles" to access the Jungian personality types. To access the Myers-Briggs types, type in "Myers-Briggs + personality profiles." Does the number of hits indicate anything about the validity and popularity of these theories? Examine specific queries about both. Do you see the relationship between the theories and the material in this chapter? Each year, about 2.5 million North Americans complete the Myers-Briggs Type Indicator (MBTI). Why is this psychological assessment instrument so popular?

ROLE-PLAY EXERCISE

For the purpose of this role play, assume the role of Ray Ito, who is described in the case problem below. Ray is described as a quiet, amiable person who displays the Supportive communication style. You will meet with Vera Maynard, who is also described in the case problem.

For the purpose of this role play, assume that Vera displays the characteristics of the Directive communication style. Prior to the role play, study the chapter material on style flexing and information on how to sell to persons who have the Directive communication style.

CASE PROBLEM

Ray Ito has been employed at CanTrust Real Estate for almost two years. Prior to receiving his real estate licence, he was a property manager with a large real estate agency in another community. During his first year with CanTrust, he was assigned to the residential property division and sold properties totalling $3 875 000. He then requested and received a transfer to the commercial division.

Three months ago, Ray obtained a commercial listing that consisted of 10.5 hectares (26 acres) of land near a growing residential neighbourhood. The land is zoned commercial and appears to be ideally suited for a medium-sized shopping centre. Ray prepared a detailed prospectus and sent it to Vera Maynard, president of Consumer Growth Corporation, a firm specializing in development of shopping centres. One week later he received a letter from Ms. Maynard requesting more information. Shortly after receiving Ray's response, Ms. Maynard called to set up an appointment to inspect the property. A time and date were finalized, and Ray agreed to meet her plane and conduct a tour of the property.

Ray is a quiet, amiable person who displays the Supportive communication style. Friends say that they like to spend time with him because he is a good listener.

Questions

1. If Ms. Maynard displays the characteristics of the Directive communication style, how should Ray Ito conduct himself during the meeting? Be specific as you describe those behaviours that would be admired by Ms. Maynard.

2. If Ms. Maynard wants to build rapport with Ray Ito, what behaviour should she display?

3. It is not a good idea to put a label on someone and then assume the label tells us everything about the person. As Ray attempts to build rapport with Ms. Maynard, what other personal characteristics should he try to identify?

Chapter 5
Ethics: The Foundation for Relationships in Business

Learning Objectives

After studying this chapter, you should be able to

1 Describe how ethical decisions influence relationships in selling.

2 Discuss factors that influence character development.

3 Describe the factors that influence the ethical conduct of sales personnel.

4 Discuss guidelines for developing a personal code of ethics.

5 Describe ethical and legal issues in international business.

 Reality Selling Today Video Series

Edith Botello started her career as a salesperson with Mattress Firm (**www.mattressfirm. com**), one of the world's largest and most successful retailers in the specialty bedding market. Edith is currently the assistant manager of one of the company's 560 stores. She is responsible for the sales productivity, maintenance, and merchandising of the store. Within her district, she is also an in-market trainer, recruiter, and intern coordinator.

Edith believes that qualifying (the term used by Mattress Firm to describe need identification) and listening are the most important skills to be a successful salesperson in her industry. Therefore, she really tries to understand why customers come to visit her and what will make them get a great night's sleep. People come into her store with a wide variety of different needs: Their bed is 20 years old; they are upgrading to a different size; they are buying a college bed; they need a bed for a guest bedroom; their current bed has dips and sags; they are going in for surgery next week and would like to recover on a supportive mattress; and so forth. Accordingly, Edith's goal is to ask the right questions so that she can sell them a solution based on their individual needs. Mattress Firm has taught Edith techniques on how to sell to different types of people. Edith believes that the main reason why many salespeople are successful is that they get their customer to believe in them by educating them and making them feel great about their purchase. Edith feels very fortunate to work for a company that values training and customer service.

Building relationships with customers is very important for Edith because people typically buy from salespeople they like and trust. One way she builds relationships is by getting to know her customers and talking to them about things that interest them.

As Edith puts it, you cannot expect your customers to open up to you unless you kick things off by asking questions. Edith also makes use of testimonials to demonstrate how previous customers have resolved their needs with particular sleep products. Customers like to hear that their salesperson has experience dealing with, and finding solutions to, problems they are encountering.

MAKING ETHICAL DECISIONS

Business ethics COMPRISE PRINCIPLES AND STANDARDS THAT GUIDE BEHAVIOUR IN THE world of business. They help translate your values into appropriate and effective behaviours in your day-to-day life. Whether a specific behaviour is right or wrong, ethical or unethical, is often determined by company leaders, customers, investors, the legal system, and the community.[1] Of course, the views of various stakeholders may be in conflict. Kickbacks and secret payoffs may be acceptable practices to the vice president of sales and marketing, yet may be viewed as unethical by members of the sales force, the board of directors, investors, and the general public.

There is no one uniform code of ethics for all salespeople as societal and relational norms can vary from person to person.[2] However, numerous business organizations, professional associations, and certification agencies have established written codes. The Canadian Professional Sales Association (CPSA), introduced in Chapter 2, requires all

business ethics Comprise principles and standards that guide behaviour in the world of business. They help translate your values into appropriate and effective behaviours in your day-to-day life.

persons seeking to become a Certified Sales Professional to agree to abide to the CPSA Sales Institute Code of Ethics (see Fig. 5.1).

Today, we recognize that character and integrity strongly influence relationships in personal selling. As noted in Chapter 3, character is composed of your personal standards of behaviour, including your honesty and integrity. Your character is based on your internal values and the resulting judgments you make about what is right and what is wrong. The ethical decisions you make reflect your character strength.

We are indebted to Stephen Covey, author of *The 7 Habits of Highly Effective People*, for helping us to better understand the relationship between character strength and success in personal selling. In his bestselling book, Stephen Covey says there are basic principles that must be integrated into our character. One example is to always do what you say you are going to do. "As we make and keep commitments, even small commitments, we begin to establish an inner integrity that gives us the awareness of self-control and

The CPSA Sales Institute Code of Ethics is the set of principles and standards that a certified sales professional will strive to adhere to with customers, organizations, competitors, communities and colleagues.

The Certified Sales Professional pledges and commits to uphold these standards in all activities.

I will:

1. Maintain honesty and integrity in all relationships with customers, prospective customers, and colleagues and continually work to earn their trust and respect.
2. Accurately represent my products or services to the best of my ability in a manner that places my customer or prospective customer and my company in a position that benefits both.
3. Respect and protect the proprietary and confidential information entrusted to me by my company and my customers and not engage in activities that may conflict with the best interests of my customers or my company.
4. Continually upgrade my knowledge of my products/services, skills and my industry.
5. Use the time and resources available to me only for legitimate business purposes. I will only participate in activities that are ethical and legal, and when in doubt, I will seek counsel.
6. Respect my competitors and their products and services by representing them in a manner which is honest, truthful and based on accurate information that has been substantiated.
7. Endeavor to engage in business and selling practices which contribute to a positive relationship with the community.
8. Assist and counsel my fellow sales professionals where possible in the performance of their duties.
9. Abide by and encourage others to adhere to this Code of Ethics.

As a certified sales professional, I understand that the reputation and professionalism of all salespeople depends on me as well as others engaged in the sales profession, and I will adhere to these standards to strengthen the reputation and integrity for which we all strive. I understand that failure to consistently act according to this Code of Ethics may result in the loss of the privilege of using my professional sales designation.

Figure 5.1 The CPSA Sales Institute Code of Ethics
Source: www.cpsa.com/institute.html. Reprinted with permission.

courage and strength to accept more of the responsibility for our own lives."[3] Fulfilling your commitments builds trust, and trust is the most important precondition of sales partnering.

CHARACTER DEVELOPMENT

COLLEGES AND UNIVERSITIES ARE BEGINNING TO PLAY A MORE ACTIVE ROLE IN CHARACTER development, and many now offer courses that focus on ethics. When a new ethics course was developed at the University of Virginia, the faculty indicated that the purpose of the course is not to point out what is right and what is wrong. Rather, the course is designed to help students understand the consequences of their actions when they face an ethical dilemma.[4]

Despite growing interest in business ethics, unethical behaviour has become all too common. A survey conducted by *Newsweek* suggests that the current generation of workers may be more tolerant of deception. Many of those involved in the survey did not view lying and cheating as unacceptable.[5] Employees who are involved in unethical behaviour often report that they were under pressure to act unethically or illegally on the job.

The Erosion of Character

As the past decade unfolded, many large inflexible corporations were transformed into smaller, more nimble competitors. "New economy" thinking prevailed as business firms, large and small, worked hard to become lean, innovative, and profitable. We witnessed an almost unrelenting emphasis on earnings that was driven, in many cases, by executive greed. During this period, some of the most respected companies began to cross the ethical divide.[6]

A company cannot enjoy long-term success unless its employees are honest, ethical, and uncompromising about values and principles. Yet many employees engage in dishonest

Social Media and Selling Today

The Ethical Use of Social Media

When new, the Internet was often looked upon as an unregulated "Wild West," harbouring users of unknown identities with questionable motives. As people grew more familiar with the Internet, it became easier to identify some of the disreputable sites, yet user skepticism continued. Dishonest personas and practices can frequently be found on the Internet. Emails from strangers still improperly solicit money, and the true motives of bloggers may not be known. Originators of Twitter messages (tweets) are often not who they appear to be.

This means that users of social media should be skeptical. Their biases must be managed by salespeople using social media for promotion. The burden is on the sales-person to establish and maintain high ethical standards in all presentations and messages. It is not difficult for a user to discover discrepancies among the websites, Facebook pages, emails, and tweets generated by a salesperson and his or her sales organization. Just like a reputation, one's social media credibility is difficult to repair once damaged.

Social media is a two-edged sword regarding one's business reputation and credibility. Postings and messages can reach hundreds of people within a very short period of time. This can be advantageous for a sales organization when the communication is positive. It can also be extremely damaging if the information is negative.

practices that erode character. The collapse of Lehman Bros., one of the largest U.S. corporations, can be traced to a culture that emphasized risk-taking, personal ambition over teamwork, and earnings growth at any cost. The new economy depends on innovation and aggressive development of markets, but actions that weaken the moral contract with employees, customers, and shareholders can have serious consequences. Let's examine some half-truths that have influenced the erosion of moral character in business settings.

- *We are only in it for ourselves.* Some critics of today's moral climate feel that the current moral decline began when society's focus shifted from "what is right" to "what is right for me." In personal selling, this point of view can quickly subtract from rather than add value to a customer relationship. Fortunately, there are many salespeople for whom integrity and self-respect are basic values. Darryl Ashley, a pharmaceutical representative for Eli Lilly Company, suspected that a pharmacist (a customer) was diluting chemotherapy drugs in order to increase profit margins. Darryl shared his suspicions with one of the cancer doctors who was purchasing the drug from the pharmacist. Tests indicated that the drug had indeed been diluted.[7]

- *Corporations exist to maximize shareholder value.* In the past, corporations were often viewed as economic and social institutions—organizations that served a balanced group of stakeholders. In recent years, analysts, stock traders, CEOs, and the media have too often focused on a single standard of performance—share price.[8] Marjorie Kelly, editor of *Business Ethics*, says, "Managing a company solely for maximum share price can destroy both share price and the entire company."[9]

  Pressure to increase "numbers" led to sales abuses at WorldCom Incorporated. Some salespeople double-booked accounts in order to make their quota and collect increased commissions. The false reporting was identified by an internal company probe and the guilty sales representatives were fired.[10] The same pressure led financial executives at Canada's Nortel Networks to report forecast revenues and earnings that were "out of touch with reality"; as a result, the company's CEO and a number of senior financial executives were fired.[11]

- *Companies need to be lean and mean.*[12] Downsizing has become a common practice even when the economy is strong. After layoffs, companies must deal with serious problems of low morale and mistrust of management. Those employees who remain after a company reduces its ranks often feel demoralized, overworked, and fearful. The stress of long hours and a faster pace can result in losses in quality and bad service that alienate customers. Richard Sennett, author of *The Corrosion of Character*, says that the decline of character strength can be traced to conditions that have grown out of our fast-paced, high-stress, information-driven economy. He states that character strength builds as we display loyalty, mutual commitment, and the pursuit of long-term goals.[13] These are the qualities needed to build strong buyer–seller relationships.

Today many business firms are struggling to align their values, ethics, and principles with the expectations of their salespeople and their customers. The process of negotiating ethical standards and practices must be ongoing. Citigroup Incorporated, the world's largest financial services firm, is working hard to move beyond regulatory scandals. Charles Prince, Citigroup CEO, wants the company to better balance its "delivering-the-numbers" culture with a long-term attention to reputation. He readily admits that "at

Character strength builds as we display loyalty, mutual commitment, and the pursuit of long-term goals. These are the qualities needed to build strong buyer–seller relationships.

times, our actions have put at risk our most precious commodity—the trust of our clients, the patience of our employees, and the faith of our shareholders."[14]

Can moral behaviour be taught? The National Business Ethics Survey, conducted annually by the Ethics Resource Center (**www.ethics.org**), found that 90 percent of employees said that ethics training is useful or somewhat useful to them. A growing number of students are completing business ethics courses as part of their business programs.[15]

FACTORS INFLUENCING THE ETHICS OF SALESPEOPLE

IN THE FIELD OF PERSONAL SELLING, THE TEMPTATION TO MAXIMIZE SHORT-TERM GAINS BY some type of unethical conduct is always present. Salespeople are especially vulnerable to moral corruption because they are subject to such temptations. Here are a few examples:

The competition is using exaggerated claims to increase the sale of its product. Should you counteract by using exaggerated claims of your own to build a stronger case for your product?

You have visited the buyer twice and, each time, the person displayed interest in your product. During the last visit the buyer hinted that the order might be signed if you provide a small gift. Your company has a policy that gifts are not to be given under any circumstances. What do you do?

Your sales manager is under great pressure to increase sales. At a recent meeting of the entire sales staff, this manager said, "We have to beat the competition no matter what it takes!" Will this emotional appeal change your way of dealing with customers?

During a recent business trip, you treated a good friend who is not a customer to lunch. You paid for the entire meal and left a generous tip. Do you put these non–business-related expenses on your expense account?

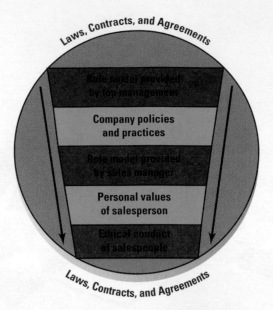

Figure 5.2 Factors determining ethical behaviour of salespeople.

These ethical dilemmas arise frequently in the field of selling. How do salespeople respond? Some ignore company policy, cast aside personal standards of conduct, and yield to the pressure. However, most salespeople are able to resist. They are aided by numerous factors that help them distinguish right from wrong. Figure 5.2 outlines the forces that help them deal honestly and openly with prospects at all times. We will discuss each of these factors.

Top Management as Role Model

Ethical standards tend to filter down from the top of an organization. Employees look to company leaders for guidance. The organization's moral tone, as established by management personnel, is the most important single determinant of employee ethics. Richard Schulze, Best Buy founder and chairman, is the person who must put ethics concerns on the front burner and make sure that employees stay focused on that priority. The most influential ethics spokesman at Timberland is CEO Jeffrey Swartz, a third generation CEO whose grandfather founded the company. With pride, he points out Timberland's slogan: "Boots, Brand, Belief."[16]

In recent years, top management has often been guided by advice from professional service firms such as McKinsey & Company and Arthur Anderson. Too often these firms are recommending strategies that result in quick, short-term gains. Alan M. Webber, who has been studying professional service firms for 20 years, notes, "They want the money right now." He says, "[T]o make the most money, you actually have to believe in the product or service you offer and care for the customers or clients whom you serve."[17]

Company Policies and Practices

Company policies and practices can have a major impact on the ethical conduct of salespeople. Al Rosen, who taught accounting at York University for 30 years, says that once you are hired, you become a product of your company and its ethics drift through you. He

Doing Business in China

China has entered the World Trade Organization and its leaders have promised to tear down the barriers that have frustrated foreign business representatives for so long. This country provides a huge market for foreign brands. However, doing business in China begins with a careful study of Chinese business customs.

- Patience is critical when doing business in China. Avoid taking the initiative until you fully understand the rules.

- Business entertaining is frequently done banquet style. If you host a banquet, plan your menu carefully because foods have different meanings. You will be in complete control and no one will eat or drink until you give the signal. Toasting is a ritual in China.

- Chinese businesspeople do not make deals quickly. They prefer to spend time building relationships that will last for years. Harmony is important.

- When making introductions, the oldest and highest-ranking person is introduced first. Chinese bow slightly when greeting another person and the handshake follows.

- Gift giving is a complex process in China. Gifts should be given after all business transactions have been completed.

- Avoid gifts that suggest death in the Chinese culture: clocks, knife openers, and handkerchiefs, for example.[a]

says, "People are telling you to forget this and that—it becomes a birds-of-a-feather atmosphere."[18] Many employees do not have well developed moral sensitivity and, therefore, need the guidance of ethics policies. These policies should cover distributor relations, customer service, pricing, product development, and related areas.[19]

Developing policy statements forces a firm to "take a stand" on various business practices. Distinguishing right from wrong can be a healthy activity for any organization. The outcome is a clearer philosophy of how to conduct business transactions. Furthermore, the efforts of salespeople can be compromised by the unethical actions of their companies. Selling products for a company that condones unethical practices is very difficult for the salesperson who maintains high ethical standards.[20]

Sun Life Financial—headquartered in Toronto, with offices in 22 countries serving millions of customers—provides its employees with a carefully worded document entitled "Code of Business Conduct." Employees must affirm annually their commitment to these values. Several of these values form the foundation for a corporate culture that encourages ethical behaviour:[21]

- **Integrity** We are committed to the highest standards of business ethics and good governance.

- **Customer Focus** We provide sound financial solutions for our customers and always work with their interests in mind.

- **Value** We deliver value to the customers and shareholders we serve and to the communities in which we operate.

Most marketing companies provide salespeople with guidelines in such areas as sharing confidential information, reciprocity, bribery, gift giving, entertainment, and business defamation.

Sharing Confidential Information Personal selling, by its very nature, promotes close working relationships. Customers often turn to salespeople for advice. They disclose confidential information freely to someone they trust. It is important that salespeople preserve the confidentiality of information they receive.

It is not unusual for a customer to disclose information that may be of great value to a competitor. This might include development of new products, plans to expand into new markets, or anticipated changes in personnel. A salesperson may be tempted to share confidential information with a representative of a competing firm. This breach of confidence might be seen as a means of gaining favour. In most cases this action will backfire. The person who receives the confidential information will quickly lose respect for the salesperson. A gossipy salesperson will seldom develop a trusting relationship with a customer.

reciprocity A mutual exchange of benefits, as when a firm buys products from its own customers.

Reciprocity **Reciprocity** is a mutual exchange of benefits, as when a firm buys products from its own customers. Some business firms actually maintain a policy of reciprocity. For example, a manufacturer of commercial sheets and blankets may purchase hotel services from firms that use its products. Is there anything wrong with the "you scratch my back and I'll scratch yours" approach to doing business? The answer is sometimes yes. In some cases, the use of reciprocity borders on commercial blackmail. Salespeople have been known to approach firms that supply their company and encourage them to buy out of obligation. The firm may be forced to buy products of questionable quality at excessive prices. A business relationship based on reciprocity often has drawbacks, such as the ever-present temptation to take reciprocal customers for granted. A customer who buys out of obligation may take a back seat to customers who were won in the open market.

Personal selling, by its nature, promotes close working relationships. It is important that salespeople preserve the confidentiality of information they receive. Violation of this ethical responsibility will quickly erode a relationship with the customer.

Selling Today

Ethics: Increasingly Becoming Front and Centre

Customers today are more likely to demand proof of integrity, particularly when choosing important vendors that must be capable of providing long-term support. Many salespeople simply try to refer customers to their company websites, where they can find statements of company values and ethics practices. However, many customers are now demanding more. Requests for proposals are increasingly requiring vendors to sign documents that explicitly outline their good ethical practices.

Experts in business ethics suggest four things common to vendors that follow "best practices":

1. A top-level business executive responsible for ethics, business conduct, and compliance. These executives are increasingly responsible for reporting directly and regularly to company boards of directors.

2. The ability for all employees to be able to report, anonymously and confidentially, any suspected wrongdoing. At Nortel Networks, employees are now able to call a confidential advice line, email the business ethics department, or communicate directly with anyone in the organization, including individual members of the board or the board as a whole.

3. The ability to monitor and assess their ethics program effectiveness. Vendors need more than simple statements of ethical conduct and values.

4. Ethics training for all employees, including senior executives. Sun Microsystems provides a basic online ethics training program for all of its 35 000 employees worldwide and requires that they take ongoing training. In addition, about 1200 top executives and some staff members are required to participate each year in a two-day workshop. Before Brian Conlon, Chief Information Officer at Howrey, Simon, Arnold & White, a large international law firm, awarded a contract to Sun Microsystems to overhaul his company's IT infrastructure, he carefully scrutinized Sun's business conduct and compliance programs. As justification, he says, "The things we are doing with Sun are not one-offs. It will be our partner for a long time, and we need to make sure it will stay in business."[b]

Bribery The book *Arrogance and Accords: The Inside Story of the Honda Scandal* describes one of the largest commercial corruption cases in North American history. Over a 15-year period, Honda officials received more than US$50 million in cash and gifts from dealers anxious to obtain fast-selling Honda cars and profitable franchises. When the bribery became public, 18 former Honda executives were convicted of obtaining kickbacks; most went to prison.[22] In some cases, a bribe is wrong from a legal standpoint. In almost all cases, the bribe is wrong from an ethical point of view. However, bribery does exist, and a salesperson must be prepared to cope with it. It helps to have a well established company policy to use as a reference point for what is not acceptable.[23]

Salespeople who sell products in foreign markets need to know that giving bribes is viewed as an acceptable business practice in some cultures. However, bribes or payoffs may violate federal government legislation. Canada has the *Corruption of Foreign Public Officials Act*, and for Canadian salespeople who work for U.S. companies, the *U.S. Foreign Corrupt Practices Act* (FCPA) may also be relevant. Lucent Technologies dismissed two high-ranking executives in China after it found potential violations of the FCPA.[24]

Gift Giving Gift giving is a common practice in Canada. However, some companies do maintain a "no gift" policy. Many companies report that their policy is either no gifts or nothing of real value. Some gifts, such as advertising novelties, planning calendars, or a meal, are of limited value and cannot be construed as a bribe or payoff.

There are some grey areas that separate a gift from a bribe. Most people agree that a token of insignificant value, such as a pen imprinted with a company logo, is an appropriate way to foster goodwill. A bribe, on the other hand, is an attempt to influence the person who is receiving the gift.

Are there right and wrong ways to handle gift giving? The answer is yes. The following guidelines will be helpful to any salesperson who is considering giving gifts to customers:

1. Do not give gifts before doing business with a customer. Do not use the gift as a substitute for effective selling methods.

2. Never convey the impression you are "buying" the customer's business with gifts. When this happens, the gift becomes nothing more than a bribe.

3. When gift giving is done correctly, the customer will clearly view it as symbolic of your appreciation—a "no strings attached" goodwill gesture.

4. Be sure the gift is not a violation of the policies of your firm or of your customer's firm. Some companies will not allow employees to accept gifts at all; others place a dollar limit on a gift's value.

In summary, if you have second thoughts about giving a gift, do not do it. When you are sure some token is appropriate, keep it simple and thoughtful.

Entertainment Entertainment is a widespread practice in the field of selling but may be viewed by some people as a bribe. The line dividing gifts and entertainment from bribes is often quite arbitrary. Salespeople must frequently decide how to handle entertaining. A few industries see entertainment as part of the approach used to obtain new accounts. This is especially true when competing products are nearly identical. A good example is the cardboard box industry. These products vary little in price and quality. Winning an account may involve knowing who to entertain and how to entertain.

Entertainment is a highly individualized process. One customer might enjoy a professional football game while another might be impressed most by a quiet meal at a good restaurant. The key is to get to know your customer's preferences. How does the person spend leisure time? How much time can the person spare for entertainment? You will need to answer these and other questions before you invest time and money in entertainment.

Business Defamation Salespeople frequently compare their product's qualities and characteristics with those of a competitor during the sales presentation. If such comparisons are inaccurate, are misleading, or slander a company's business reputation, such conduct is illegal. Competitors have sued hundreds of companies and manufacturer's representatives for making slanderous statements while selling.

What constitutes business defamation? Steven M. Sack, co-author of *The Salesperson's Legal Guide*, provides the following examples:

1. *Business slander*. This arises when an unfair and untrue oral statement is made about a competitor. The statement becomes actionable when it is communicated to a third party and can be interpreted as damaging the competitor's business reputation or the personal reputation of an individual in that business.

2. *Business libel.* This may be incurred when an unfair and untrue statement is made about a competitor in writing. The statement becomes actionable when it is communicated to a third party and can be interpreted as damaging the company.

3. *Product disparagement.* This occurs when false or deceptive comparisons or distorted claims are made concerning a competitor's product, services, or property.[25]

Use of the Internet Use of the Internet offers salespeople many advantages, but it can also create a number of ethical dilemmas. For example, email abuse has become a modern-day problem because some employees forget that their employer owns the email system. Email messages that contain inflammatory or abusive content, embarrassing gossip, or breaches of confidentiality can lead to legal liabilities. A growing number of companies are developing policies that define permissible uses of their email system.[26]

Some resourceful salespeople have created their own websites to alert, attract, or support clients. The rise of these "extranets" has created some problems because they often function outside of the company's jurisdiction. What should top management do if a salesperson encourages her customers to participate in a special web auction for a backlogged product? What if the salesperson makes exaggerated claims about a new product? Every marketing firm needs to carefully monitor the development and use of extranets.[27]

The effectiveness of company policies as a deterrent to unethical behaviour depends on two factors. The first is the firm's attitude toward employees who violate these policies. If violations are routinely ignored, the policy's effect soon erodes. Second, policies that influence personal selling need the support of the entire sales staff. Salespeople should have some voice in policy decisions; they are more apt to support policies they have helped develop.

Sales Manager as Role Model

The salesperson's actions often mirror the sales manager's behaviour and expectations. This is not surprising when you consider the relationship between salespeople and their supervisors. They look to their supervisors for guidance and direction. The sales manager is generally the company's closest point of contact with the sales staff. This person is usually viewed as the chief spokesperson for top management.

Sales managers generally provide new salespeople with their first orientation to company operations. They are responsible for interpreting company policy. On a continuing basis the sales manager monitors the salesperson's work and provides important feedback regarding conduct. If a salesperson violates company policy, it is usually the sales manager who is responsible for administering reprimands. If the moral fibre of a sales force begins to break down, the sales manager must shoulder a great deal of responsibility, even if it goes against "standard practice."[28]

Sales managers influence the ethical behaviour of salespeople by virtue of what they say and what they do. From time to time, managers must review their expectations of ethical behaviour. Salespeople are under continual pressure to abandon their personal ethical standards to achieve sales goals. Values such as integrity and honesty must receive ongoing support from the sales manager. The role of the sales manager will be discussed in more detail in Chapter 17.

Sales managers influence the ethical behaviour of salespeople by virtue of what they say and what they do.

The Salesperson's Personal Values

Ann Kilpatrick, a sales representative in the transportation industry, encountered something unexpected when entertaining a potential client. The client said, "Let's go to Johnny's." She was not familiar with Johnny's but, on arrival, discovered it was a raunchy bar. Kilpatrick related that she sat there for five minutes and then said, "This is not what I was expecting. This is a sleazy place. Let's go somewhere else where we can talk." She was not willing to compromise her personal values to win a new account.[29]

values Your deep personal beliefs and preferences that influence your behaviour.

Values represent the ultimate reasons people have for acting as they do. **Values** are your deep personal beliefs and preferences that influence your behaviour. To discover what really motivates you, carefully examine what it is you value.[30] Values serve as a foundation for our attitudes, and our attitudes serve as a foundation for our behaviour (see Fig. 5.3). We do not adopt or discard values quickly. In fact, the development of values is a lifelong process.

Customers have a very negative view of salespeople who lack integrity. Yet the temptation to lie about a product's features or benefits grows when you are trying to meet sales quotas. Pharmacist John Craig describes a meeting with a pushy sales representative employed by a pharmaceutical company. The salesperson emphasized the wonders of a powerful, expensive painkiller but failed to describe its side effects. Craig said, "He was very pushy at the beginning," and this behaviour revealed a character flaw.[31]

Values Conflict Values help us establish our own personal standards concerning what is right and what is wrong. Ron Willingham, author of *Integrity Selling for the 21st Century*,

Figure 5.3 The relationship of values, attitudes, and behaviour.

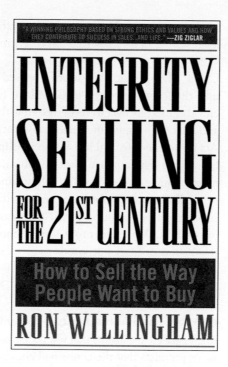

Ron Willingham says a salesperson's ethics and values contribute more to sales success than do techniques and strategies.

says, "Selling success is more an issue of who you are than what you know."[32] A salesperson's ethics and values contribute more to sales success than do techniques or strategies. Some salespeople discover a values conflict between themselves and their employer. If you view your employer's instructions or influence as improper, you have three choices:

1. Ignore the influence of your values and engage in unethical behaviour. The end result will likely be a loss of self-respect and a feeling of guilt. When salespeople experience conflicts between their actions and values, they also feel a loss of confidence and energy.[33] Positive energy is the result of creating value for the customer. Negative energy emerges when salespeople fail to honour and embrace their ethical values.

2. Voice strong opposition to the practice that is in conflict with your value system. Take a stand and state your beliefs. When ethical infractions occur, it's best to bring them up internally and try to influence decisions made by your peers or superiors. In some cases, doing the right thing may not be popular with others. Price Pritchett, author of *The Ethics of Excellence*, says, "Not everybody will be on your side in your struggle to do the right thing."[34]

3. Refuse to compromise your values and be prepared to deal with the consequences. This may mean leaving the job. It may also mean that you will be fired.

Salespeople face ethical problems and decisions every day. In this respect they are no different from doctors, lawyers, teachers, or any other professional. Ideally, they will make decisions on the basis of the values they hold.[35]

Laws, Contracts, and Agreements

Take another look at Figure 5.2 and notice that all of the key elements, personnel, and policies are influenced by laws, contracts, and agreements. Everyone involved in sales and marketing is guided by legal as well as ethical standards. We live in a society in which the legal system plays a key role in preventing people from engaging in unethical behaviour.

Laws The specific obligations imposed by government on the way a business operates take the form of statutes. In Canada, it is necessary for salespeople not only to know federal statutes but also to recognize that there are many provincial and territorial statutes, and that important differences exist between provinces and territories. The *Competition Act* is the major federal legislation in Canada that defines illegal practices, including price fixing, bid rigging, price discrimination, predatory pricing, double ticketing, resale price maintenance, bait and switch selling, and pyramid selling.

All Canadian provinces and territories have passed legislation that establishes a cooling-off period during which the consumer may void a contract to purchase goods or services. While the provisions of **cooling-off laws** vary from jurisdiction to jurisdiction, their primary purpose is to give customers an opportunity to reconsider a buying decision made under a salesperson's persuasive influence. In most jurisdictions, this legislation is referred to as either *The Direct Sellers Act* or *The Consumer Protection Act*.

cooling-off laws Provincial and territorial laws that give customers an opportunity to reconsider a buying decision made under a salesperson's persuasive influence.

contract An oral or written promise enforceable by law.

Contracts and Agreements The word *contract* may bring to mind the familiar multipage, single-spaced documents that few people seem able to understand. A **contract** is simply a promise or promises that the courts will enforce. Oral contracts are enforceable, but written contracts are preferable, as they reduce the possibility of disagreement; courts give written contracts great weight in a lawsuit. A written contract can consist of a sales slip, a notation on a cheque, or any other writing that offers evidence of the promises that the parties made.[36]

Salespeople are sometimes the legal representatives of their company and, therefore, must be careful when signing written contracts. They often oversee contracts with customers, suppliers, and resellers. A salesperson may be asked to sign an employment contract at the time he or she is hired. Most of these agreements include a noncompete clause. One of the most common clauses, a noncompete clause prohibits salespeople from joining a competing firm for a year after they leave. Most clauses are legally binding even when an employee's position is cut. Employers see employment contracts as an effective way to protect intellectual property, customer lists, and other resources an employee might take to a competing firm.[37]

Many companies are learning that resolving legal disputes can be very costly and time-consuming. Resolving a dispute in the courts can sometimes take several years. A serious effort to prevent unethical activities can prevent costly litigation.

Ethics beyond the Letter of the Law Too often, people confuse ethical standards with legal standards. They believe that if they are not breaking the law, then they are acting in an ethical manner.[38] A salesperson's ethical sense must extend beyond the legal definition of what is right and wrong. To view ethics only in terms of what is legally proper encourages the question, "What can I get by with?" A salesperson must develop a personal code of ethics that extends beyond the letter of the law.

Bruce Weinstein, a professional ethicist who is often introduced as "The Ethics Guy," offers sound advice on living an ethical life. He says we should do the right thing simply because it's the right thing to do. The only way you can build a loyal and growing client base is to demonstrate that you have the customer's own best interests at heart. You are trying to make things better for them: "Here is where ethics differs from the law. It demands more of us," says Weinstein.[39]

From the Field

She Quits Her Job over Her Personal Code of Ethics

Birgitta Jonsdottir, during a whirlwind tour in Toronto in 2011, disclosed that she has had a varied career bouncing between her home country of Iceland and North America. The 43-year-old mother of three has been a nanny, a retail sales clerk, and a door-to-door salesperson, and is now a prominent member of parliament in Iceland.

Describing her short career in door-to-door selling, she says she "pushed a vacuum cleaner on an elderly couple that had never bought anything on a payment plan." As she was returning home after the sale, she had misgivings about what she had done. She realized that she used her persuasive ability for her personal benefit, selling something to someone who didn't need it. At that point, she quit and returned to Iceland.[c]

A PERSONAL CODE OF ETHICS THAT ADDS VALUE

MANY PEOPLE CONSIDERING A CAREER IN SELLING ARE TROUBLED BY THE THOUGHT THAT THEY may be pressured into compromising their personal standards of right and wrong. These fears may be justified. The authors of *The Ethical Edge*, a book that examines organizations that have faced moral crises, contend that business firms have given too little thought to the issue of helping employees to function ethically within organizations.[40] Many salespeople wonder whether their own ethical philosophy can survive in the business world. These are some of their questions:

> "Can a profitable business and good ethics coexist?"
> "Are there still business firms that value adherence to high ethical standards?"
> "Is honesty still a valued personal trait in the business community?"

In the field of athletic competition, the participants rely heavily on a written set of rules. The referee or umpire is ever-present to detect rule violations and assess a penalty. In the field of personal selling, there is no universal code of ethics. However, some general guidelines can serve as a foundation for a personal code of business ethics.

1. *Personal selling must be viewed as an exchange of value.* Salespeople who maintain a value focus are searching for ways to create value for their prospects or customers. This value may take the form of increased productivity, greater profit, enjoyment, or security. The value focus motivates the salesperson to carefully identify the prospect's wants and needs.[41] Salespeople who accept this ethical guideline view personal selling as something you do *for* customers, not something you do *to* customers. The role of the salesperson is to diagnose buyer needs and determine whether value can be created. Always be prepared to add value.

2. *Relationship comes first, task second.* Sharon Drew Morgan, author of *Selling with Integrity*, says you can't sell a product unless there is a level of comfort between you and the prospect. She encourages salespeople to take the time to create a level of comfort, rapport, and collaboration that encourages open communication.[42] Placing task before relationship is based on the belief that the salesperson knows more than the customer. Morgan reminds us that "the buyer has the answers; the seller has the questions."[43] These answers will surface only when the buyer–seller relationship is characterized by rapport and trust.

3. *Be honest with yourself and with others.* To achieve excellence in terms of ethical practices, you have to believe that everything you do counts. Tom Peters, in *Thriving on Chaos*, says, "Integrity may be about little things as much as or more than big ones."[44] It's about accuracy in completing your expense account—and resisting the temptation to inflate the expense report for personal gain. It's about avoiding the temptation to stretch the truth, to exaggerate, or to withhold information. Paul Ekman, author of *Telling Lies*, says that withholding important information is one of the primary ways of lying.[45] A complete and informative sales presentation may include information regarding the product's limitations. If you let your character and integrity be revealed in the little things, others will see you as someone who acts ethically in all things. Any violation of honesty, however small, dilutes your ethical strength, leaving you weaker for the big challenges you will face sooner or later.[46]

The Trust Factor

Everyone involved in personal selling must work hard to build relationships based on trust. Customers are more apt to trust salespeople they believe to be ethical, leading to a much more productive partnership.[47] Although trust is an essential element of every sale, the meaning of trust changes with the type of sale.[48]

- *Trust in transactional sales.* The primary customer focus in this type of sale is trust in the product. Is the product reliable? Is the product priced as low as possible? Can the product be delivered in a timely fashion? The transactional buyer may purchase a product from a salesperson with whom they do not feel totally comfortable if it meets their purchase criteria.

- *Trust in consultative sales.* In a consultative sale, the customer focus shifts from the product to the person who sells the product. The consultative buyer is thinking, "Can I trust this salesperson to identify my problem and offer me one or more solutions?" Customers involved in a consultative sale usually do not separate the product from

Personal selling must be viewed as an exchange of value. Salespeople who accept this ethical guideline view personal selling as something you do for customers, not something you do to customers.

the person selling it. They want to do business with a salesperson who displays such positive qualities as warmth, empathy, genuineness, competence, and integrity.

- *Trust in strategic alliance sales*. The strategic alliance buyer wants to do business with an institution that can be trusted. This buyer looks beyond the well qualified salesperson and assesses the entire organization. A strategic alliance customer will not feel comfortable partnering with a company whose values differ greatly from their own. Ethical accountability will greatly influence the way a partner is judged and valued.

Trust exists when we strongly believe in the integrity, ability, and character of a person or an organization. Although trust is intangible, it is at the very core of all meaningful relationships. Trust is quickly lost and slowly won.[49]

ETHICAL AND LEGAL ISSUES IN INTERNATIONAL BUSINESS

ETHICAL AND LEGAL ISSUES THAT ARE QUITE COMPLEX ON THE DOMESTIC SCENE BECOME even more complicated at the international level. International business is growing and Canada is deeply involved in the global marketplace. Thomas Friedman, author of the bestselling book *The World Is Flat: A Brief History of the Twenty-First Century*, says today's highly competitive and global marketplace is flattening the world of international business. Our companies must adopt a more aggressive global focus in order to compete with China, India, and other dynamic economies.[50]

Cultural Issues

Today's global marketplace reflects a kaleidoscope of cultures, each with its own unique qualities. **Culture** is the sum total of beliefs, values, knowledge, ethnic customs, and objects that people use to adapt to their environment. Cultural barriers can impede acceptance of products in foreign countries and weaken interpersonal relationships. When the salesperson understands the cultural background of the foreign customer, communication problems are less likely. Many people from Asia, Arab countries, and much of Africa prefer a more indirect style of communication and therefore value harmony, subtlety, sensitivity, and tact more than brevity.[51] The customer who seems to be agreeing with everything you say may have no intention of buying your product. This person may simply be displaying polite and tactful behaviours.

> **culture** The sum total of beliefs, values, knowledge, ethnic customs, and objects that people use to adapt to their environment.

Perceptions of time differ from country to country. Canadians value promptness, but businesspeople from other countries often approach meetings in a more relaxed manner. Arriving late for a meeting may not be viewed as a problem. Many companies are spending thousands of dollars to make sure that employees sent abroad are culturally prepared. Eastman Chemical Company, for example, has developed a highly successful orientation program for employees who have accepted overseas assignments.[52]

Legal Issues

Doing business in the global marketplace continues to be an ethical minefield. Illegal demands for bribes, kickbacks, or special fees may stand in the way of successful transactions. The Canadian and U.S. governments have enacted legislation that prohibits companies from using bribes or kickbacks to influence foreign officials. But monitoring illegal activities throughout the world is a very difficult task.[53] Motorola, for example, uses software to analyze invoices and payments in order to uncover possible payoffs. Gifts from suppliers to Canadian and U.S. companies can also be a problem. United Technologies sends a letter to foreign suppliers each year saying, "We don't want gifts."[54]

Canadian and U.S. businesses acknowledge that it is difficult to compete with organizations from other countries that are not bound by our laws. However, the International Business Ethics Institute (**www.business-ethics.org**) believes our companies have been a very positive role model for the rest of the business world. As noted previously in this chapter, high ethical standards depend on strong leadership provided by management personnel at all levels of the organization. Integrity starts at the top.

REVIEWING KEY CONCEPTS

- Describe how ethical decisions influence relationships in selling.

  Character and integrity strongly influence relationships in personal selling. Unethical sales practices will ultimately destroy relationships with customers. These practices undermine trust, which is at the very core of all meaningful relationships.

- Discuss factors that influence character development.

  Many colleges and universities are playing a more active role in character development. Character education is often integrated into courses that focus on ethics. Character is composed of personal standards of behaviour, so all of us can do things that build character. Keeping our commitments to others provides just one example of how character is built.

- Describe the factors that influence the ethical conduct of sales personnel.

  Salespeople can benefit from the stabilizing influence of good role models. Although top management personnel are usually far removed from day-to-day selling activities, they can have a major impact on salespeople's conduct. Dishonesty at the top of an organization can cause an erosion of ethical standards at the lower echelons. Sales managers provide another important role model. They interpret company policies and help establish guidelines for acceptable and unacceptable selling practices.

- Discuss guidelines for developing a personal code of ethics.

  Salespeople must establish their own standards of personal conduct. They must decide how best to serve their company and build strong partnerships with their customers. The pressure to compromise one's ethical standards surfaces almost daily. The primary deterrent is a strong sense of right and wrong. Three general guidelines that can serve as a foundation for a personal code of ethics are:

  a. Personal selling must be viewed as an exchange of value.

  b. Relationship comes first, task second.

  c. Be honest with yourself and with others.

- Describe ethical and legal issues in international business.

  At the international level, ethical and legal issues can be very complex. The global marketplace reflects a great number of cultures, each with unique qualities. Coping with illegal activities throughout the world is also very challenging. Illegal demands for bribes, kickbacks, or special fees can serve as a barrier to business transactions.

Key Terms

business ethics **101**

contract **114**

cooling-off laws **114**

culture **117**

reciprocity **108**

values **112**

Review Questions

1. What is the definition of *business ethics*? Why is this topic receiving so much attention today?

2. Carefully review Figure 5.1, the CPSA Sales Institute Code of Ethics. Select the three standards you feel would present the greatest challenge to salespeople. Explain your choices.

3. How does business slander differ from business libel?

4. What major factors help influence salespeople's ethical conduct?

5. What are cooling-off laws? How do they protect consumers?

6. Why must a salesperson's ethical sense extend beyond the legal definition of what is right and wrong?

7. Explain why the sales manager plays such an important role in influencing the ethical behaviour of salespeople.

8. A company policy on ethics will usually cover several major areas. What are they?

9. Is it ever appropriate to give gifts to customers? Explain.

10. List and describe three guidelines used as a foundation of a self-imposed code of business ethics.

Application Exercises

1. You find that you have significantly overcharged one of your clients. The error was discovered when you received payment. It is unlikely that the customer or your company will become aware of the overcharge. Because of this error, the company realized a high net profit on the sale. Your commissions are based on this profit. What, if anything, will you do about the overcharge?

2. Access the Canadian Professional Sales Association website at **www.cpsa.com**. Click on "Training" and then on "Sales Designation." Examine the steps to becoming a Certified Sales Professional (CSP) by clicking on "CSP Process" in the drop-down menu under "Sales Designation." Review the CPSA Sales Institute Code of Ethics printed in this chapter (or through the link on step 4 of the CSP Process). Discuss your views on the impact professional certification has on the ethical behaviour of salespeople. Do you think the designation CSP would affect the impression a customer might have of a salesperson?

3. You work for a supplier of medical equipment. Your sales manager informs you that he wants you to capture a certain hospital account. He also tells you to put on your expense account anything it costs to secure the

hospital as a client. When you ask him to be more specific, he tells you to use your own judgment. Up to this time you have never questioned your sales manager's personal code of ethics. Make a list of the items you feel can be legitimately charged to the company on your expense account.

4. For some time, your strongest competitor has been making untrue derogatory statements about your product and about you as a salesperson. You know for a fact that her product is not as good as yours, yet hers has a higher price. Several of your best customers have confronted you with these charges. Describe how you plan to answer them.

5. Sales managers must approve expense reports turned in by members of the sales force. Assume the role of sales manager for a sales force that includes 12 salespeople who travel frequently and average about two overnight trips each week. Recently you noticed that the expense reports turned in by two of your salespeople seem quite high. You suspect that these salespeople are padding their expense reports. What steps should you take to determine if cheating is occurring? How can a sales manager prevent the padding of expense reports?

This morning you met with a customer who has purchased office supplies from you for almost three years. You are quite surprised when she says, "I am prepared to place an order worth $10 500, but you must match an offer I received from a competitor." She then explains that the competitor is offering new customers a seven-day, all-expenses-paid trip to Quebec City if they place an order for more than $10 000. What would you do?

Prepare to role-play your response with another student. Review the material in this chapter, paying special attention to ways you can add value and build long-term relationships with ethical decision making.

Reality Selling Today Video Case Problem: Mattress Firm

Mattress Firm (www.mattressfirm.com) is one of the largest and most successful specialty bedding companies in the world. It offers sleep solutions, including conventional and specialty mattresses, as well as bedding-related products. The company has grown to become one of the largest and fastest growing retailers in the nation. The company operates more than 560 stores in 38 markets nationwide and carries the top mattress brands. From the very beginning, the company set out to be a different kind of mattress retailer, focused on creating a unique shopping experience.

According to Edith Botello, featured at the beginning of this chapter, the biggest differentiator between Mattress Firm and its competitors is the sales process. As Edith puts it, buying a mattress can be overwhelming: How do you know which one is the best if all you see when you walk into a store are dozens of white rectangles? At Mattress Firm, sales reps make it simple for their customers to pick out their mattress without trying out every single bed. The process invites customers to get fitted for a mattress, just as with suits, shoes, and gowns. This is done through the company's Sleep Diagnostic System, which asks the customer a series of questions about their sleep quality and then measures their weight distribution and postural alignment. The system then recommends a type of support and eliminates 80 percent of the beds in the showroom. Taking the risk out of buying a mattress by letting the customer know what mattresses are best for them is something that only Mattress Firm offers.

How can ethical aspects of selling come into play in Edith's job as a retail salesperson? One example would be that sometimes salespeople have the opportunity to write up a sale where they would get credit but have not earned the right to do so. At times, customers shop around but eventually end up at the same store and want the same product that was offered to them previously. In such a case, the customer may request the particular salesperson who helped him or her previously. If that salesperson is not there, the new salesperson could choose to not give her/him credit. Another example might be a customer who tries to get greater price discounts by making untrue statements about a competitor's price offering or shopping around at different Mattress Firm locations in order to get the lowest possible price. In many cases, however, the salesperson will recognize this behaviour and act accordingly.

Being ethical is a core value at Mattress Firm. New hires are made aware of Mattress Firm's expectations from the beginning of their employment to ensure that they are ethical with their customers and other salespeople. Mattress Firm's Code of Conduct is a guide to the general principles that permeate the employees' relationships with customers, business partners, and, last but not least, each other. The Code goes far beyond compliance with laws and regulations. It is also a set of practical instructions to help employees in their day-to-day work. It explains, for example, how to manage potential conflicts of interest and how to report suspected violations of the rules.

At Mattress Firm, several policies and elements in the incentive compensation system exist that also help to safeguard ethical behaviour. The Standard Operating Procedure (SOP) dedicates an entire section to commission sales and how to handle different situations such as team selling, ticket trading, SPIFFS, bonuses, etc. For example, the commission system encourages sales reps to hold the line on price concessions. National sales contests are also audited to ensure ethical behaviour. The SOP and Employee Code of Conduct are housed on the company's intranet and are available to view at any time. (See the chapter opener on page 100 and Reality Selling Today Role Play 4 in Appendix 1 on page 438 for more information.)

Questions

1. Put yourself in Edith Botello's place as a sales rep selling mattresses. Can you imagine situations in your job that might challenge your ethical conduct?

2. For retailers such as Mattress Firm, what are the major areas that should be covered in a company policy on ethics?

3. Revenue-based incentive compensation plans, by their very nature, pressure sales reps to generate high sales, which might cause unethical sales practices. How could an incentive compensation system be designed that stimulates sales generation but safeguards ethical sales behaviour at the same time?

4. Image you were a salesperson for Mattress Firm, just like Edith Botello. A customer walks into your store and, after a while, shows great interest in a specific Tempur-Pedic. When it comes to the price, the customer mentions that your competitor across the street offered him exactly that mattress at a 10 percent lower price than Mattress Firm. You have some doubts that this statement is actually true, but you do not want to disgruntle the customer and compromise the sale. How would you react?

PART II

ROLE-PLAY EXERCISE
Developing a Relationship Strategy

SCENARIO

You are an experienced sales representative employed by Canadian Steel Processing, a company that has been in business for nearly 70 years. Your company is an ISO 9002-certified manufacturing company that has earned many accolades, including three consecutive J. D. Power & Associates awards for customer satisfaction. Over the years the company has invested heavily in automation technology as a means of ensuring consistent manufacturing quality. The Canadian Steel Processing sales force understands that the company will not be the lowest bidder in most sales situations because the highest quality can never be obtained at the lowest price.

CUSTOMER PROFILE

Tyler Hensman has held the position of senior purchasing agent at Regina Steel Fabricators for several years. Throughout this period, Tyler has negotiated over a dozen purchase agreements with Dana Davis, senior account representative with Canadian Steel Processing. Tyler takes pride in purchasing quality steel products at the best price.

SALESPERSON PROFILE

Dana Davis began working for Canadian Steel Processing about four years ago. After completion of an extensive sales training program, Dana was assigned to a territory in Saskatchewan. After three successful years, Dana was promoted to senior account representative.

PRODUCT

Canadian Steel Processing sells a wide range of steel products. Many of the orders filled are for high stress steel beams, stainless steel bolts and nuts, and structural tubing used in commercial building construction. Most orders specify a certain quality of steel.

INSTRUCTIONS

For this role play you will assume the role of Dana Davis, senior account representative employed by Canadian Steel Processing. To prepare for the role play, you should carefully read the case problem at the end of Chapter 5. This information will help you understand the issues that need to be addressed during the role play.

During the early stages of the role play, you will want to obtain more information from the customer and resolve any misunderstandings. You want to obtain an order for type 316 stainless steel bolts and nuts, and maintain a good relationship with this important customer. Keep in mind that ethical decisions can greatly influence the relationship between a salesperson and the customer. Reflect on the important information covered in Chapter 5 prior to your meeting with Tyler Hensman.

Part III
Developing a Product Strategy

Service is not a competitive edge, it is the competitive edge. People do not buy just things; they also buy expectations. One expectation is that the item they buy will produce the benefits the seller promised. Another is that, if it doesn't, the seller will make good on the promise.

—Karl Albright and Ron Zemke, Service America: Doing Business in the New Economy

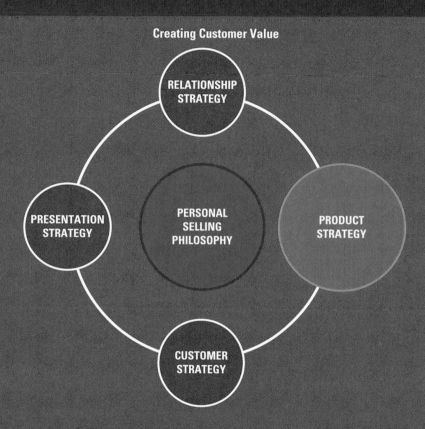

Creating Customer Value

RELATIONSHIP STRATEGY

PRESENTATION STRATEGY

PERSONAL SELLING PHILOSOPHY

PRODUCT STRATEGY

CUSTOMER STRATEGY

Part III examines the important role of complete and accurate product, company, and competitive knowledge in personal selling. Lack of knowledge in these areas impairs the salesperson's ability to configure value-added solutions. Part III also describes several value-added selling strategies.

Chapter 6
Creating Product Solutions

Learning Objectives

After studying this chapter, you should be able to

1   Explain the importance of developing a product strategy.

2   Describe product configuration.

3   Identify reasons why salespeople and customers benefit from thorough product knowledge.

4   Discuss the most important kinds of product and company information needed to create product solutions.

5   Describe how knowledge of competition improves personal selling.

6   List major sources of product information.

7   Explain how to add value with a feature–benefit strategy.

 Reality Selling Today Video Series

For more than 10 years, Amy Vandaveer has had a highly successful sales career. She has a bachelor's degree in marketing and has sold sales technology software, sales training programs, and media services. Currently, Amy is a sales representative for *Texas Monthly* (**www.texasmonthly.com**), a magazine that focuses largely on leisure activities and events in Texas. *Texas Monthly*'s sales staff is responsible for selling the large amount of advertising space available in the magazine. It may sound like a relatively easy job; after all, *Texas Monthly* has a large, loyal reader base and would be an attractive advertising outlet for many businesses. Remember, though, that *Texas Monthly* has many direct and indirect competitors, all of whom are trying to sell their services to the same group of businesses Amy works with.

Because of the many options available to a prospective advertiser, Amy must become an expert on what her customers want, what *Texas Monthly* can offer them, and what *Texas Monthly*'s competitors can offer. By doing so, she can improve her ability to answer customers' questions and emphasize the benefits—in the context of her customers' needs—of choosing *Texas Monthly* over other advertising outlets. She is no longer just selling advertising space; instead, she can offer her customers her own knowledge and experience in creating solutions that address their needs.[1]

DEVELOPING A PRODUCT SOLUTION
THAT ADDS VALUE

As NOTED IN CHAPTER 1, A PRODUCT STRATEGY HELPS SALESPEOPLE MAKE CORRECT decisions concerning the selection and positioning of products to meet identified customer needs. The **product strategy** is a well-conceived plan whereby a sales representative becomes a product expert, selling product benefits and creating value-added solutions (see Fig. 6.1). Configuring value-added solutions is discussed in detail in Chapter 7.

Selling Solutions

A **solution** is a mutually shared answer to a recognized customer problem. In many selling situations, a solution is more encompassing than a specific product. It often provides measurable results such as greater productivity, increased profits, or less employee turnover. Selling a solution, versus selling a specific product, usually requires a greater effort to define and diagnose the customer's problem.[2] Think of **solution selling** as a process by which the salesperson uncovers and clarifies a customer's problem, works with the customer to create a vision of how things could be better, and then develops a plan for implementing the vision.[3]

product strategy A well-conceived plan for sales that emphasizes acquiring extensive product knowledge, learning to select and communicate appropriate product benefits that will appeal to the customer, and creating value-added solutions.

solution A mutually shared answer to a recognized customer problem.

solution selling A process by which the salesperson uncovers and clarifies a customer's problem, works with the customer to create a vision of how things could be better, and then develops a plan for implementing the vision.

Strategic/Consultative Selling Model	
Strategic step	Prescription
Develop a personal selling philosophy	✓ Adopt marketing concept ✓ Value personal selling ✓ Become a problem solver/partner
Develop a relationship strategy	✓ Adopt win-win philosophy ✓ Project professional image ✓ Maintain high ethical standards
Develop a product strategy	• Become a product expert • Sell benefits • Configure value-added solutions

Figure 6.1 Developing a product strategy enables the salesperson to custom-fit products or services to the customer's needs.

Most salespeople have adopted a broad definition of the term *product* to encompass information, services, ideas, tangible products, or some combination of these that satisfies the customer's needs, with the right solution.[4] Let's look at the sales process at two firms.

Strategic Vista International, a Markham, Ontario-based technology leader in video security and surveillance, has begun manufacturing and distributing a new line of digital video monitoring solutions that allows customers to view multiple camera locations from anywhere in the world at any time. Salespeople can configure a range of product solutions to satisfy the needs of most consumers and small- and medium-sized businesses.[5]

Loki Management Systems, a Delta, B.C.-based software developer, provides workforce management solutions to customers in the healthcare, hospitality, and tele-

According to Keith Eades, author of *The New Solution Selling*, a solution is a mutually shared answer to a recognized customer problem. It is more encompassing than a specific product and it provides measurable results. Eades states that more than 500 000 individuals worldwide have been trained in solution selling. Solution selling forms the core of Microsoft's selling processes.

Source: Book Cover from *The New Solution Selling,* 2e by Keith Eades. Copyright © 2004. Reprinted by permission of The McGraw-Hill Companies, Inc.

THE NEW SOLUTION SELLING

The Revolutionary Process That is Changing the Way People Sell

KEITH M. EADES

Foreword by **KEVIN JOHNSON** Group VP Worldwide Sales, Marketing, & Services, Microsoft

communications industries. Its product solutions help companies create employee work schedules, increase employee satisfaction and retention, reduce staffing and overtime costs, save management time, and reduce payroll errors.[6]

From the customer's point of view, salespeople employed by Strategic Vista International and Loki Management Systems are primarily selling information and expertise. Customers view the problem-solving ability these salespeople provide as the product. When you sell a complex product, it is knowledge and expertise that create value.

Tailoring the Product Strategy A product strategy should be tailored to the customer's buying needs. Transactional buyers are usually well aware of their needs. Most of these customers have conducted their own research and have a good understanding of the product that will meet their needs. The office manager who frequently buys a large amount of copy paper knows that this standard item can be purchased from several vendors, and that the quality of the paper usually does not vary from one vendor to another. The consultative buyer may lack needs awareness and will want help to evaluate possible solutions. This customer usually needs a customized product solution, as it appeals to the customer's desire for choices that are tailored to his or her needs. Developing a product strategy for the strategic alliance customer usually offers the greatest challenge. Study of the proposed alliance partner can be very time-consuming, but the rewards of a successful partnership may be substantial. In some cases, the company that wishes to form an alliance with a new customer must be prepared to make a large investment in capital-intensive technology and additional personnel.[7]

Explosion of Product Options

Domestic and global markets are overflowing with a vast array of goods and services. In some industries the number of new products introduced each year is mind-boggling. Makers of consumer products, for example, churn out as many as 30 000 new products each year. Want to buy a product in the securities and financial services field? In the fastest-growing segment—mutual funds—there are now approximately 80 fund management companies and 144 dealer firms in Canada that sell 1800 different mutual funds.[8] For the customer, this much variety creates a "good news–bad news" situation. The good news is that almost all buyers have a choice when it comes to purchasing a product or service; people like to compare various options. The bad news is that having so many choices often complicates the buying process.

One of the most important roles of the salesperson is to simplify the customer's study of the product choices. Later in this chapter we discuss how product features (information) can add value when converted into specific benefits (knowledge) that can help the buyer make an intelligent buying decision.

Creating Solutions with Product Configuration

The challenge facing both customers and salespeople in this era of information overload is deciding which product applications, or combination of applications, can solve the customer's buying problem. If the customer has complex buying needs, then the salesperson may have to bring together many parts of the company's product mix to develop a custom-fitted solution. The product selection process is often referred to as **product configuration**.

product configuration The solution of complex buying needs; for instance, when the salesperson brings together many different parts of the company's product mix or uses specialized software to develop a custom-fitted solution.

Salespeople representing Cisco Systems are often involved in the sale of new products to new and established customers. They use Cybrant Solutions Architect software to quickly identify solutions. The software helps salespeople ask prospects the right questions to discover their needs and then configures a solution that best meets those needs.[9]

Amy Vandaveer takes pride in her ability to create solutions based on product configuration. In fact, every proposal she prepares is customized to fit the needs of a *Texas Monthly* customer.

Many companies use product configuration software to develop customized product solutions quickly and accurately. It incorporates product selection criteria and associates them directly with customer requirements. Members of the sales force can use the sales configurator to identify product options, prices, delivery schedules, and other parts of the product mix, while working interactively with the customer. Most of today's product configuration software can be integrated with contact management software programs such as Salesforce, ACT!, and NetSuite. In addition to improving the quality of the sales proposal, this software reduces the time-consuming process of manually preparing written proposals.

A major element of product configuration is *quotation management*. Quick and accurate pricing is critical in today's fast-paced sales environment. Leading companies are aggressively automating their quotation management process.[10]

Preparing Written Proposals

written proposal A specific plan of action based on the facts, assumptions, and supporting documentation about a buying solution that are included in the sales presentation. Written proposals vary in terms of format and content.

Written proposals are frequently part of the salesperson's product strategy. It is only natural that some buyers will want the proposed solution put in writing. A **written proposal** can be defined as a specific plan of action based on the facts, assumptions, and supporting documentation about a buying solution that are included in the sales presentation.[11] A well-written proposal adds value to the product solution and can set you apart from the competition. It offers the buyer reassurance that you will deliver what you have promised. Written proposals, which are often accompanied by a sales letter, vary in terms of format and content. Many government agencies, and some large companies, issue a request for proposal (RFP) that specifies the format of the proposal. Most effective proposals include the following parts:

Budget and overview. These tell the prospect the cost of the solution you have prescribed. Be specific as you describe the product or service features to be provided, and itemize the price. When you confirm pricing with a proposal, misunderstandings and mistakes can be avoided.

Objective. The objective should be expressed in terms of benefits. A tangible objective might be "to reduce payroll expense by 10 percent." An intangible objective might be stated as "to increase business security offered by a company with a reputation for dependability." Focus on specific benefits that relate directly to the customer's needs.

Strategy. Briefly describe how you will meet your objective. How will you fulfill the obligations you have described in your proposal? In some cases this section of your proposal includes specific language: "Your account will be assigned to Sue Zhou, our senior lease representative."

Schedule. Establish a time frame for meeting your objective. This might involve the confirmation of dates with regard to acquisition, shipping, or installation.

Rationale. With a mixture of logic and emotion, present your rationale for taking action now. Once again, the emphasis should be on benefits, not features.[12]

This salesperson is making a follow-up call to determine if the customer needs any additional information regarding the written proposal, which was sent earlier.

Some written proposals follow a specific format developed by the company. The length of a proposal can vary from a single page to dozens of pages for a complex product.

The proposal should be printed on quality paper and be free of any errors in spelling, grammar, or punctuation. Before completing the proposal, review the content one more time to be sure you have addressed all of the customer's concerns. Bob Kantin, author of *Sales Proposals Kit for Dummies*, says the proposal is really the first "product" that the customer receives from you, so be sure it is perfect.[13] Neil Rackham, noted author and sales consultant, recommends addressing your proposal to the "invisible" customer. Very often the proposal will be reviewed by individuals the salesperson has never met. And these are often the people who will make or break the deal.[14]

The remainder of this chapter is divided into five major sections. The first two examine the kinds of product information and company information required by the salesperson. The third section describes the type of information about the competition that is helpful to salespeople. Sources of information are covered in the fourth section, and the fifth section describes how product features can be translated into buyer benefits.

BECOMING A PRODUCT EXPERT

ONE OF THE MAJOR CHALLENGES FACING SALESPEOPLE IS WINNING THE CUSTOMER'S TRUST. A survey reported in *Sales & Marketing Management* ranked product knowledge as the number one characteristic of salespeople who are able to build trust.[15] Ideally, a salesperson will possess product knowledge that meets and exceeds customer expectations, increasing sales effectiveness and willingness to pay.[16]

Tom Peters says that when it comes to product knowledge, remember: "More, more, more. And, more important: Deeper, deeper, deeper." In summary: "He or she who has the largest appetite for Deep Knowledge wins."[17] This section reviews some of the most

Writing Effective Sales Letters

Salespeople are increasingly using sales letters to describe features and benefits, to position products, to build relationships, and to provide assurances to customers. There are several standard rules that apply to all written sales letters. These include:

1. Sales letters should follow the standard visual format of a business letter. They should contain, in the following order, either a letterhead or sender's address, the date, the inside address (the same as on the outside of the envelope), a salutation, the body, a complimentary closing, a typed name and handwritten signature of sender, and a notation of enclosures (if there are any).

2. Placement of the letter on the paper should provide balanced white space bordering the entire letter. Three to five blank lines should separate the date and inside address; a single blank line should separate the inside address and the salutation, the salutation and the opening paragraph of the letter, and each paragraph. A single blank line should separate the last paragraph and the complimentary closing. Single spacing should generally be used within the paragraphs.

3. Proper business punctuation includes a colon after the salutation and a comma after the complimentary close.

4. Most sales letters include at least three paragraphs. The first paragraph should indicate why you are writing the letter, the second paragraph should be a summary of the benefits proposed, and the third paragraph should state what the next action step will be for the salesperson, the customer, or both.

5. Proper grammar and spelling must be used throughout the entire letter. Business letters provide opportunities to build a stronger relationship with the customer and to close the sale. Improper placement, punctuation, spelling errors, or weak content conveys a negative impression to the reader and may result in a lost sale.

6. The use of the personal pronoun "I" should be minimized in the sales letter. To keep the letter focused on the customer's needs, the pronouns "you" and "your" should appear throughout the body of the letter.

common product information categories: (1) product development and quality improvement processes, (2) performance data and specifications, (3) maintenance and service contracts, and (4) price and delivery. Each is important as a potential source of knowledge concerning the product or service.

Product Development and Quality Improvement Processes

product development The testing, modifying, and retesting of an idea for a product several times before offering it to the customer.

Companies spend large amounts of money in the development of their products. In **product development**, the original idea for a product or service is tested, modified, and retested several times before it is offered to the customer. Each modification is made to improve the product. Salespeople should be familiar with a product's development history. Often this information will set the stage for stronger sales appeals.

quality control The evaluation or testing of products against established standards. This has important sales appeal when used by the salesperson to convince a prospect of a product's quality.

Quality improvement continues to be an important long-term business strategy for most successful companies. Salespeople need to identify processes for quality improvement that provide a competitive advantage and be prepared to discuss this information during the sales presentation. Toyota, Ritz-Carleton Hotels, and Xerox are examples of companies that have won awards for implementing important quality controls. **Quality control**, which involves measuring products and services against established standards, is one dimension of the typical quality improvement process.

Product knowledge training is an ongoing activity in the life of a salesperson.

Winnipeg-based Reimer Express and its parent company, Roadway Express, have together received ISO 9002 certification for the system-wide management and operation of their transportation services across Canada and the United States. This certification, from the International Organization for Standardization (ISO), assures customers of a high level of quality service from these companies. Vice President of Operations John Bronneck says, "To achieve this class of service is a massive endeavour. Especially when you look at the need to coordinate the operations of a network that includes

From the Field

Writing Spreads the Word

Rudolf Melik, CEO of Laval, Quebec–based Tenrox Inc., recognized he had a problem common to many smaller businesses: How do you compete with large competitors who can spend millions of dollars on marketing when you can afford only a much smaller amount? His solution: Write a book. His company makes software that tracks time and expenses for project-driven businesses. With his brother Ludwig, Vice President of Sales and Marketing, Rudolf wrote a book on streamlining consulting processes.

Within only a few months, about a hundred companies requested a copy. Rudolf says, "Some of those are new customers who are being courted by our sales reps. The book helps them understand our products and explains the benefits." Rudolph has also been invited to speak at Boston's Project Management Institute, where he will get to talk to 60 decision makers from major U.S. companies. "The same exposure would cost millions in advertising," says Melik.[a]

over 380 terminals, 9500 tractors, 34 000 trailers, 900 000 customer sites and 59 000 shipments that enter our system every day. And, it's all done with one focus: customer service." Reimer Express has previously won the Canada Award for Business Excellence in Quality.[18]

Performance Data and Specifications

Most potential buyers are interested in performance data and specifications. Here are some typical questions that might be raised by prospects:

> "What is the frequency response for this stereo loudspeaker?"
> "What is the anticipated rate of return on this mutual fund?"
> "What is the energy consumption rating for this appliance?"
> "Are all of your hotel and conference centre rooms accessible to persons with physical disabilities?"

A salesperson must be prepared to address these types of questions in the written sales proposal and the sales presentation. Performance data are especially critical when the customer is attempting to compare the merits of one product with another.

To become familiar with the performance of Whirlpool appliances, salespeople literally "live" the brand. The company rented and redesigned an eight-bedroom farmhouse near corporate headquarters and outfitted it with Whirlpool dishwashers, refrigerators, washers, dryers, and microwaves. Salespeople, in groups of eight, live at the house for two months and use all of the appliances. Whirlpool engineers visit the home and present information on design, performance data, and specifications. A recent graduate of the training program says, "I have a confidence level that's making a difference in my client contacts."[19]

Maintenance and Service Contracts

Prospects often want information concerning maintenance and care requirements for the products they purchase. The salesperson who can quickly and accurately provide this information will have the edge. Proper maintenance will usually extend the life of the product, so this information should be provided at the time of the sale.

Today, many salespeople are developing customized service agreements that incorporate the customer's special priorities, feelings, and needs. They work hard to acquire a real understanding of the customer's specific service criteria. If call-return expectations are very important to the customer, the frequency and quantity of product-related visits per week or month can be included in the service contract. Customized service agreements add value to the sale and help protect your business from the competition.[20]

Price and Delivery

Potential buyers expect salespeople to be well versed in price and delivery policies and be in a position to set prices and plan deliveries. If a salesperson has pricing authority, buyers perceive the person as someone with whom they can really talk business. The ability to set prices puts the salesperson in a stronger position.[21] Decision-making authority in the area of pricing gives the salesperson *more power and responsibility*. If the salesperson negotiates

Sea Ray Boats, a quality leader in the pleasure boat industry, worked hard to become an ISO 9002 certified builder. Sea Ray has also earned two consecutive J.D. Power and Associates awards for customer satisfaction. Highperforming salespeople are familiar with these important product knowledge achievements and able to communicate the benefits to prospective boat buyers.

a price that is too low, the company may lose money on the sale. Price objections represent one of the most common barriers to closing a sale, so salespeople need to be well prepared in this area.

In most situations, the price quotation should be accompanied by information that creates value in the mind of the customer. The process of determining whether or not the proposal adds value is often called **quantifying the solution**. When the purchase represents a major buying decision, such as the purchase of a new computer system, quantifying the solution is important. One way to quantify the solution is to conduct a cost–benefit analysis to determine the actual cost of the purchase and savings the buyer can anticipate from the investment (see Table 6.1).

Another way to quantify the solution is to calculate return on investment (ROI). As products and services become more complex and more expensive, customers are more

quantifying the solution The process of determining if a sales proposal adds value. Quantifying the solution is especially important in situations where the purchase represents a major buying decision.

Table 6.1 Quantifying the Solution with Cost–Benefit Analysis

Quantifying the solution often involves a carefully prepared cost-benefit analysis. This example compares the higher-priced Phoenix semitruck trailer with the lower-priced FB model, which is a competing product.

Cost Savings of the Phoenix Versus FB Model for a 10-Year Period (All Prices Are Approximate)	Cost Savings
Stainless steel bulkhead (savings on sandblasting and painting)	$ 425.00
Stainless steel rear door frame (savings on painting)	425.00
Air ride suspension (better fuel mileage, longer tire life, longer brake life)	3 750.00
Hardwood or aluminum scuff (savings from freight damages and replacement of scuff)	1 000.00
LED lights (last longer; approximate savings: $50 per year 10 years)	500.00
Light protectors (save $50 per year on replacement 10 years)	500.00
Threshold plate (saves damage to entry of trailer)	200.00
Internal rail reinforcement (saves damage to lower rail and back panels)	500.00
Stainless steel screws for light attachment (savings on replacement cost)	200.00
Domestic oak premium floor—1 (should last 10 years under normal conditions)	1 000.00
Doors—aluminum inner and outer skin, outside white finish, inside mill finish, fastened by five aluminum hinges (savings over life of trailer)	750.00
Five-year warranty in addition to standard warranty covers bulkhead rust, LED lights, floor, scuff liner, glad hands, rear frame, mud flap assembly, and threshold plate (Phoenix provides a higher trade-in value)	1 500.00
Total approximate savings of Phoenix over 10-year period (All the preceding is standard equipment on a Phoenix; this trailer will sell for $23 500; an FB standard trailer would sell for $19 500)	$10 750.00
Less additional initial cost of Phoenix over FB standard	4 000.00
Overall cost savings of Phoenix over FB trailer	$ 6 750.00

likely to look at the financial reasons for buying. This is especially true in business-to-business selling. Salespeople who can develop a sales proposal that contains specific information on ROI are more likely to get a favourable response from key decision makers. Chief financial officers, for example, are more inclined to approve an expensive purchase if it results in a good return on investment.[22]

Performing accurate ROI calculations typically requires the collection of detailed financial information. You may need to help the prospect collect information within the company to build a case for the purchase. BAX Global, with offices throughout Canada and the United States, offers customers multi-modal shipping solutions. It has the capability to employ more than one mode of transportation for a customer. In order to develop a customized solution for the customer, the sales representative must collect a great deal of data from the prospect. Transportation modes (e.g., trucks, trains, ships, airplanes) vary in terms of cost, speed, dependability, frequency, and other criteria, so preparation of the sales proposal can be a complicated process.[23]

The use of ROI selling requires more work up front, but it may lead to shorter sales cycles. The salesperson who is not well schooled in financial issues or who cannot compute and supply price information accurately may be at a serious disadvantage. In Chapter 7, we discuss how to position products according to price.

KNOW YOUR COMPANY

WE SHOULD NEVER UNDERESTIMATE INFORMATION ABOUT THE COMPANY ITSELF AS A STRONG appeal that can be used during the sales presentation. This is especially true when the customer is considering a strategic alliance. Before teaming up with another company, the strategic alliance buyer will want to learn a great deal about the firm the salesperson represents. In many cases, you are selling your company as much as or more than you are selling a product.[24]

Some companies, such as Microsoft, Four Seasons Hotels, and TD Waterhouse, have what might be called "brand power," because these companies and the products they sell are well known. However, if you are selling teak outdoor furniture made by Rock Wood Casual Furniture of Oakville, Ontario, or outsourced email services offered by The Electric Mail Company Inc. of Burnaby, B.C., you may find it necessary to spend time providing information about your company. In this section we examine the types of information needed in most selling situations.

Company Culture and Organization

Many salespeople take special pride in the company they work for. Salespeople employed by Research In Motion feel good that the company was recognized by *The Financial Post* as one of the top 10 Canadian companies to work for in 2011. It survived the dot-com bubble to become "an incredible Canadian success story that continues to expand and develop new markets worldwide."[25]

As noted in Chapter 5, character and integrity are the hallmarks of a successful sales organization. UPS Incorporated chairman and CEO Michael L. Eskew says, "[S]trategies change and the purpose changes, but the values never change."[26]

Every organization has its own unique culture. **Organizational culture** is a collection of beliefs, behaviours, and work patterns held in common by people employed by a specific firm. Most organizations over a period of time tend to take on distinct norms and practices. At Lowe's Canada, a statement of core values communicates what the company holds important and guides everyone in the organization as they serve the company's customers (see Fig. 6.2). Research indicates that the customer orientation of a firm's salespeople will be influenced by the organization's culture. A supportive culture that encourages salespeople to offer tailor-made solutions to buyer problems will set the stage for long-term partnerships.[27]

organizational culture A collection of beliefs, behaviours, and work patterns held in common by people employed by a specific firm.

Many prospects will use the past performance of a company to evaluate the quality of the current product offering. If the company has enjoyed success in the past, there is good reason to believe that the future will be bright.

Company Support for Product

Progressive marketers support the products they sell. In some cases, product support takes the form of sales tools that can be used in preparation for a sales call or during a sales call. Salespeople for Hunter Douglas Canada, a manufacturer of window fashions,

Figure 6.2 Companies such as Lowe's Canada communicate their core values to customers, suppliers, employees, and other stakeholders.

have a Dealer Merchandising Portfolio. With this aid, salespeople can help dealers select and order sample books, brochures, videos, in-store display material, and many other items.[28]

Company support after the sale is also important. Tool-and-die firm Jagemann Stamping Company often uses a sales team made up of a salesperson, an engineer, and line workers. Line workers can often answer the technical questions raised by a customer. Whenever there is a problem or defect, a small group of line workers is sent out with either a salesperson or an engineer to investigate. This involvement raises the workers' commitment to the customer.[29]

A quick response to a customer's questions about product configurations or pricing can serve as a product strategy improvement within the sales process. This salesperson is adding value by using his notebook computer and cell phone to access and quickly communicate information.

KNOW YOUR COMPETITION

ACQUIRING KNOWLEDGE OF YOUR COMPETITION IS ANOTHER IMPORTANT STEP TOWARD developing complete product knowledge. Salespeople who have knowledge of their competitors' strengths and weaknesses are better able to emphasize the benefits they offer and add value. Prospects often raise specific questions concerning competing firms. If you cannot provide answers or if your answers are vague, the sale may be lost.

Global Business Insight

Doing Business in Australia

Canadian and Australian businesspeople have a lot in common. Everyone in Australia speaks English and business dress is similar in both countries. However, subtle differences do exist.

■ When you greet an Australian businessperson, give your full name and then firmly shake hands.

■ Australians tend to be modest people who often root for the underdog. Keep information about your power and wealth to yourself.

■ Although Australian businesspeople tend to be informal and friendly, they still expect you to be a good listener and be completely familiar with your product.

■ Keep your presentations simple. Australians want you to get to the point.[b]

Your Attitude toward Your Competition

Regardless of how impressive your product is, the customer will naturally seek information about similar products sold by other companies. Therefore, you must acquire facts about competing products before the sales presentation. It has never been easier to obtain information about competing products. Check the competitor's website, annual reports, press releases, and marketing material. Once armed with this information, you will be more confident in your ability to handle questions about the competition.

The attitude you display toward your competition is of the utmost importance. Every salesperson should develop a set of basic beliefs about the best way of dealing with competing products. Here are a few helpful guidelines:

1. *In most cases, do not refer to the competition during the sales presentation.* This shifts the focus of attention to competing products, which is usually not desirable.

2. *Never discuss the competition unless you have all your facts straight.* Your credibility will suffer if you make inaccurate statements. If you do not know the answer to a specific question, simply say, "I do not know."

3. *Never criticize the competition.* You may be called on to make direct comparisons between your product and competing products. In these situations, stick to the facts and avoid emotional comments about apparent or real weaknesses.

4. *Be prepared to add value.* The competition may come to your prospect with a comparative advantage in price, delivery, or some other area. Be prepared to neutralize the competitor's proposal with a value-added approach. If your competitor has slow delivery, encourage the customer to talk about why prompt delivery is important.[30]

Customers appreciate an accurate, fair, and honest presentation of the facts. They generally resent highly critical remarks about the competition. Avoid mudslinging at all costs. Fairness is a virtue that people greatly admire.

Become an Industry Expert

Salespeople need to become experts in the industry they represent. In many cases this means moving beyond the role of product specialist and becoming a business analyst. Staying current and developing an understanding of business processes takes time and may require additional education.[31] If your clients work in the banking industry, read the appropriate trade journals and become active in professional associations that serve bankers' needs.

SOURCES OF PRODUCT INFORMATION

THERE ARE SEVERAL SOURCES OF PRODUCT INFORMATION AVAILABLE TO SALESPEOPLE. SOME of the most common include: (1) product literature developed by the company, (2) sales training programs, (3) plant tours, (4) internal sales and sales support team members, (5) customers, (6) the product, and (7) publications.

Product Literature, Catalogues, and Web-Based Sources

Most companies prepare materials that provide a detailed description of their product. This information is usually quite informative, and salespeople should review it carefully. If the company markets a number of products, a sales catalogue is usually developed. To save salespeople time, many companies give them computer software that provides a constantly updated, online product catalogue. Advertisements, promotional brochures, and compact discs can also be a valuable source of product information.

Mitsubishi Caterpillar Forklift America presents its basic product information online, so it's available to dealer representatives in the privacy of their homes, hotel rooms, or wherever else they bring their laptops. Each of the seven product information courses takes about an hour. To reinforce basic product knowledge, the company offers advanced instructor-led courses.[32] Some companies are using interactive distance learning (delivered via satellite) to present different types of sales training.

Plant Tours

Many companies believe that salespeople should visit the manufacturing plant and see the production process firsthand. Such tours not only provide valuable product information but also increase the salesperson's enthusiasm for the product. A new salesperson may spend several days at the plant getting acquainted with the production process. Experienced personnel within the organization can also benefit from plant tours.

Knowing, understanding, and being able to clarify information in product literature adds value within the sales process. Customers seek out the "product experts" who can assist them in making intelligent buying decisions.

Internal Sales and Sales Support Team Members

Team selling has become popular in part because many complex sales require the expertise of several sales and sales support personnel. Expertise in the areas of product design, finance, or transportation may be needed to develop an effective sales proposal. Pooled commissions are sometimes used to encourage team members to share information and work as a team.

Customers

Persons who actually use the product can be an important source of information. They have observed its performance under actual working conditions and can provide an objective assessment of the product's strengths and weaknesses. Some companies collect testimonials from satisfied customers and make this persuasive information available to sales staff. Wabi Iron and Steel Corp. in New Liskeard, Ontario, manufactures components for machinery that must operate under adverse conditions. The company keeps ahead of its competitors by systematically developing and testing improved alloys in close cooperation with one of its major customers. It has been able to develop components exclusively for this customer, and its success has given Wabi the profile it needs to compete in new markets. In recognition of its sales success, Wabi won an Ontario Global Traders Award.[33]

Salespeople employed by semiconductor manufacturer Intel Corporation are expected to take the company's business customers from the conceptual stage of their purchase all the way to delivery of the finished product. Dialogue with customers begins very early in the sales cycle when customers need help designing their end product.[34] This approach requires the empowerment of the sales force with greater depth and breadth of product information.

Product

The product itself should not be overlooked as a source of valuable information. Salespeople should closely examine and, if possible, use each item they sell to become familiar with its features. Investigation, use, and careful evaluation of the product will provide a salesperson with additional confidence.

Publications

Trade and technical publications such as *Canadian Grocer* and *Advertising Age* provide valuable product and industry information. Popular magazines and the business section of the newspaper also offer salespeople considerable information about their products and their competition. Publications such as *Consumer Reports* test products extensively and report the findings in nontechnical language for the benefit of consumers. These reports are a valuable source of information.

Word of Caution

Is it possible to be overly prepared? Can salespeople know too much about the products and services they sell? The answer to both questions is generally no. Communication

E-learning has become popular because it is inexpensive and fast, and it can be geared to the flexible schedules of salespeople. This regional sales team is receiving sales training from the company's home office.

problems can arise, however, if the salesperson does not accurately gauge the prospect's level of understanding.[35] There is always the danger that a knowledgeable salesperson will overwhelm the potential buyer with facts and figures. This problem can be avoided when salespeople adopt the feature–benefit strategy.

ADDING VALUE WITH A FEATURE–BENEFIT STRATEGY

FREDERICK W. SMITH, FOUNDER OF FEDERAL EXPRESS, FIRST PROPOSED THE CONCEPT OF overnight delivery in a paper that he wrote as an undergraduate at Yale University. The now-famous paper was given a "C" by his professor. Many years later, Smith said, "I don't think that we understood our real goal when we first started Federal Express. We thought that we were selling the transportation of goods; in fact, we were selling peace of mind."[36]

Throughout this chapter we emphasize the importance of acquiring information on the features of your product, company, and competition. Now it is important to point out that successful sales presentations translate product features into benefits that meet a specific need expressed by the customer. The "peace of mind" that Frederick W. Smith mentioned is a good example of a buyer benefit. Only when a product feature is converted to a buyer benefit does it make an impact on the customer.

Distinguish between Features and Benefits

To be sure we understand the difference between a product feature and a buyer benefit, let us define these two terms.

A **feature** is data, facts, or characteristics of your product or service. Features often relate to craftsmanship, design, durability, and economy of operation. They may reveal how the product was developed and manufactured. Product features are often described in the technical section of the written sales proposal and in the literature provided by the manufacturer.

A **benefit** is whatever provides the consumer with personal advantage or gain. It answers the question, "How will I benefit from owning or using the product?" If you mention to a prospect that a certain tire has a four-ply rating, you are talking about a product feature. If you go on to point out that this tire will provide greater safety, last longer, and improve gas mileage, you are pointing out benefits.

General versus Specific Benefits Neil Rackham, author of *The SPIN Selling Fieldbook*, says that a statement can only be a benefit if it meets a specific need expressed by the buyer. When you link a benefit to a buyer's expressed need, you demonstrate that you can help solve a problem that has been described by the customer. A general benefit shows how a feature can be helpful to a buyer, but it does not relate to a specific need expressed by the buyer. Here are two examples of specific benefits:

> "Our water purification system meets the exact specifications you have given us for environmental compliance."
>
> "Our XP400 model meets the safety criteria you've spelled out."

Rackham says that benefit statements linked to the customer's expressed need are especially effective in large and complex sales.[37]

Some sales training programs suggest that salespeople need to include advantages in the sales presentation. Advantages are characteristics (i.e., features) of the product that can be used or will help the buyer. Consider the following statement:

> "Prior to shipping, all of our containers are double wrapped. This means that our product is completely free from contamination when it arrives at your hospital."

Some salespeople develop an advantage statement for each important product feature. Unfortunately, these advantages are often included in the sales presentation even when the buyer has not expressed a need for this information. When this happens, the advantage can be described as a general benefit.

Successful salespeople focus on specific benefits that relate to a need explicitly expressed by the customer. Less successful salespeople take the position that the best way to create value is to present as many benefits as possible. Today's customer measures value by how well your product benefits fit their needs. They use a "shotgun" approach to benefits, assuming that more benefits create higher volume. High-performance salespeople work hard to discover which benefits the customer really cares about.[38]

Use Bridge Statements

We know that people buy benefits, not features. One of the best ways to present benefits is to use a bridge statement. A **bridge statement** is a transitional phrase that connects a statement of features with a statement of benefits. This method permits customers to connect

feature Anything that a customer can feel, see, hear, taste, smell, or measure to answer the question, "What is it?" Features often relate to craftsmanship, durability, design, and economy of operation.

benefit Something that provides the customer with personal advantage or gain to answer, for the customer, the question, "How will I benefit from owning or using the product?"

bridge statement A transitional phrase that connects one or more product features with potential customer benefits.

the features of your product to the benefits they will receive. A sales representative for a food wholesaler, for example, might use a bridge statement to introduce a new snack food:

> "This product is nationally advertised, *which means* you will benefit from more presold customers."

Some companies prefer to state the benefit first and the feature second. When this occurs, the bridge statement may be a word such as "because."

> "You will experience faster turnaround and increased profits *because* the first order includes point-of-purchase advertising materials that focus on the Valentine's Day promotion you have planned."

Identify Features and Benefits

A careful analysis of the product will help identify both product features and customer benefits. Once all the important features have been identified, arrange them in logical order. Then write beside each feature the most important benefit the customer will derive from that feature. Finally, prepare a series of bridge statements to connect the appropriate features and benefits. Using this three-step approach, a hotel selling conference and convention services and a manufacturer selling electric motors used to power mining equipment developed feature–benefit worksheets (see Tables 6.2 and 6.3). Notice how each feature is translated into a benefit that would be important to someone purchasing these products and services. Table 6.3 reminds us that company features can be converted to benefits.

Avoiding Information Overload

Knowing your product has always been essential to good selling, but concentrating on product alone can be a serious mistake. Salespeople who love their products and possess vast product knowledge about them may overload their customers with product data

Table 6.2 Convert Product Features to Benefits

Salespeople employed by a hotel can enhance the sales presentation by converting product features to benefits.

Feature	Benefit
Facilities	
Our hotel conference rooms were recently redecorated.	Which means all your meetings will be held in rooms that are attractive and comfortable.
Our rooms were completely redecorated this year and many are now designated non-smoking.	Which means your people will find the rooms clean and attractive. In addition, those who wish can select a non-smoking room.
Food Services	
We offer four different banquet entrées prepared by our executive chef, who was recently selected Chef of the Year by the Canadian Federation of Chefs and Cooks.	Which means your conference will be enhanced by delicious meals served by a well-trained staff.
Our hotel offers 24-hour room service.	Which means your people can order food or beverages at their convenience.

Table 6.3 Convert Company Features to Benefits	
Here we see company features translated into customer benefits.	
Feature	**Benefit**
Our company has the largest selection of motors in the area.	Which means you will have an excellent choice of models to interface with your equipment.
We hire only certified service technicians.	Which means your equipment will be kept running in peak condition by well-qualified service personnel.
Our company has an inventory of all major spare parts.	Which means you will have less equipment downtime and will make higher profits.

they neither need nor want. This practice is sometimes described as a "data dump." With the aid of specific types of questions (see Chapter 11), the customer's needs can be identified. Once the customer's needs are known, the salesperson can develop a customized sales presentation that includes selected features that can be converted to specific benefits.

REVIEWING KEY CONCEPTS

- Explain the importance of developing a product strategy.

  A product strategy helps salespeople make the right decisions concerning the selection and positioning of products to meet specific customer needs. It is a carefully conceived plan that emphasizes becoming a product expert, selling specific benefits, and configuring value-added solutions.

- Describe product configuration.

  Product configuration involves decisions regarding which product applications, or combination of applications, can solve the buying problem. In the era of information overload, product selection has become more challenging. In some cases product configuration software is used to develop customized product solutions.

- Identify reasons why salespeople and customers benefit from thorough product knowledge.

  A salesperson whose product knowledge is complete and accurate is better able to identify and satisfy customer needs. Additional advantages to be gained from thorough product knowledge include greater self-confidence, increased enthusiasm, improved

ability to develop stronger selling appeals, and improved ability to overcome objections.

- Discuss the most important kinds of product and company information needed to create product solutions.

  Salespeople should possess product knowledge that meets or exceeds customer expectations. Some important product information categories include product development and quality improvement processes, performance data and specifications, maintenance and service contracts, and price and delivery.

  Information about the company can be used to develop strong appeals that can enhance the sales presentation. This is especially true when the customer is considering a strategic alliance. Important company information includes an understanding of the firm's culture and organization and company support for products offered.

- Describe how knowledge of competition improves personal selling.

  Prospects often raise specific questions concerning competing firms. Salespeople who have knowledge of their competitors' strengths and weaknesses are better able to emphasize the benefits they offer and add value. The attitude you display toward your competition is of the utmost importance.

- List major sources of product information.

  Salespeople gather information from many sources. Company literature and sales training programs are among the most important. Other sources include factory tours, customers, trade and technical publications, and actual experience with the product itself.

- Explain how to add value with a feature–benefit strategy.

  In the sales presentation and in preparing the written sales proposal, your knowledge of the product's features and your company's strengths must be presented in terms of the resulting benefits to the buyer. We distinguished between general and specific benefits. Specific benefits, linked to a customer's expressed need, are very effective.

Key Terms

benefit **142**

bridge statement **142**

feature **142**

organizational culture **135**

product configuration **127**

product development **130**

product strategy **125**

quality control **130**

quantifying the solution **133**

solution **125**

solution selling **125**

written proposal **128**

Review Questions

1. What is a *product strategy*? Why is it important for salespeople to have a clearly defined product strategy?

2. Distinguish between *product features* and *buyer benefits*.

3. What is *product configuration*? Provide an example of how this practice is used in the sale of commercial stereo equipment.

4. Review the Lowe's Canada statement of corporate values on page 136 and then identify the two items that you believe contribute the most to a salesperson's career success.

5. Define *organizational culture*. How might knowledge of a company's organizational culture benefit a salesperson?

6. Basic beliefs underlie the salesperson's method of handling competition. What are four guidelines a salesperson should follow in developing basic beliefs in this area?

7. Explain what the customer's expectations are concerning the salesperson's attitude toward competition.

8. List and briefly describe the five parts included in most written sales proposals.

9. What are the most common sources of product information?

10. Distinguish between a general benefit and a specific benefit. Why do customers respond positively to specific benefits?

Application Exercises

1. Obtain, if possible, a copy of a customer-oriented product sales brochure or news release that has been prepared by a marketer. (Many salespeople receive such selling tools.) Study this information carefully; then develop a feature–benefit analysis sheet.

2. Today many companies are automating their product configuration and proposal-writing activities. Go to the Internet and find these software providers: **www.bigmachines.com/salesforce.php** and **www.results-online.com**. Click on each company's demonstration software and study the design of each product.

3. Select a product you are familiar with and know a great deal about. (This may be an item you have shopped for and purchased, such as a compact disc player or an automobile.) Under each of the categories listed, fill in the required information about the product.

   a. Where did you buy the product? Why?

   b. Did product design influence your decision?

   c. How and where was the product manufactured?

   d. What different applications or uses are there for the product?

e. How does the product perform? Are there any data on the product's performance? What are they?

f. What kinds of maintenance and care does the product require? How often?

g. Could you, as a sales representative, sell the product you have written about in categories (a) through (f)? Why or why not?

4. Visit Dell Canada (**www.dell.ca**) and click on a product solution. You have decided that you want a desktop computer, and your primary needs are preparing paper assignments, spreadsheets, and class presentations and doing Internet searches. You do not have a lot of extra money to spend, so you are searching for an inexpensive product solution. Notice that Dell quantifies the solution for you as you click on it. Print out your solution and bring it to class, and be prepared to compare your quantified solution with that of other students.

5. With the product solution you created for the previous application exercise, prepare a list of product features and the benefit or benefits associated with each feature. If you were a salesperson selling this product solution to a customer, which benefits would you emphasize? Explain.

↻ ROLE-PLAY EXERCISE

Study the convention centre information included in "Partnership Selling: A Role Play/Simulation" on your companion website **www.pearsoncanada.ca/manning**. Pay particular attention to pricing on the meals and meeting rooms. Click on the sales proposal link and configure a sales proposal for your instructor (using your school name and address), who is responsible for setting up a student awards meeting. The meeting includes a banquet-style meal of chicken Wellington for 26 attendees from 5:30 to 8:00 p.m. on the last Wednesday of next month. The meal will be served at 5:45 p.m., and the awards session is scheduled from 6:45 to 8:00 p.m. in the same room. The seating should be banquet style. Present the completed proposal to another student (acting as your customer) and communicate the features and benefits of your proposal.

 Reality Selling Today Video Case Problem

Texas Monthly is a regional magazine covering politics, business, and culture, but focusing largely on leisure activities and events in Texas. The magazine has a large real estate advertising section, as well as classified sections in which nearly all advertisers are Texas-based businesses appealing to a prospective buyer who is interested in connecting with Texas history and culture. It also has a large, loyal reader base all over Texas, mostly urban, well-educated, and affluent, and the magazine's salespeople pride themselves on their ability to find creative solutions for their customers.

Today, Amy Vandaveer, a sales representative for *Texas Monthly*, is meeting with the marketing director for the Woodlands Town Center, a major community development organization. The Woodlands is a planned community outside of Houston and the recently added Woodlands Town Center includes restaurants, shops, and a hotel and convention centre.

The marketing director's goal is to make the Woodlands Town Center a destination for Houston residents, rather than another area serving people who already live in the Woodlands. Up to this point, the Woodlands Town Center has mostly relied on word of mouth and the positive publicity that it received after winning awards to attract visitors; now, the marketing director is interested in using more print advertising and has scheduled this meeting with Amy to learn more about the possibilities of advertising with *Texas Monthly*.

As a rule, Amy uses relatively informal presentations on her sales calls. The most significant part of her presentation is a copy of *Texas Monthly*; showing potential customers a recent issue gives them the opportunity to see the magazine's overall look and feel and gives them a good look at the context in which their ads would appear. Over the course of the informal presentation, Amy also shows the customer statistics on the reader base of *Texas*

Monthly and the ways in which they respond to ads in the magazine, as well as a price sheet for various types of ads.

After listening to what the Woodlands Town Center needs, Amy proposes a four-page colour ad, which can also be printed separately from the magazine for use as a brochure. Although the price depends on the number of stand-alone brochures that are ordered, she estimates that the cost of the ad would be about $50 000. She and the marketing director agree on a timeline for a more formal proposal that can be shared with the rest of the Woodlands Town Center board, and Amy moves on to the rest of her day. (See chapter opener on page 124 and Reality Selling Today Role Play 3 in Appendix 1 on page 440 on for more information.)

Questions

1. Explain how Amy Vandaveer can use the three prescriptions for a product-selling strategy in preparing and presenting product solutions.

2. What are the major benefits that Amy incorporates into her presentation?

3. What are the most likely objections that the marketing director might raise?

4. In addition to the actual product strategy, how important will information about *Texas Monthly* (its history, mission, past performance, etc.) be in closing the sale?

PARTNERSHIP SELLING: A ROLE PLAY/SIMULATION

Visit the role play simulation materials provided in the Student Resources section of your companion website at **www.pearsoncanada.ca/manning**. *A Contents page lists appropriate page references for the activities.*

Read *Employment Memorandum 1* (p. 5), which introduces you to your new training position with the Hotel Convention Centre. You should also study the product strategy materials that follow the memo to become familiar with the company, product, and competitive knowledge you will need in your new position.

Read *Customer Service/Sales Memorandum 1* (p. 26) and complete the two-part customer/service assignment provided by your sales manager. In item 1, you are to configure a price–product sales proposal; in item 2, you are to write a sales cover letter for the sales proposal. Note that the information presented in the price–product sales proposal will consist of product facts or features, and the information presented in your sales cover letter should present specific buyer benefit statements. These forms should be custom-fitted to meet your customer's— B. H. Riveras—specific needs. All the product information you will need is in the product strategy materials provided as enclosures and attachments to *Employment Memorandum 1*.

Chapter 7
Product-Selling Strategies That Add Value

Learning Objectives

After studying this chapter, you should be able to

1   Describe positioning as a product-selling strategy.

2   Explain the cluster of satisfactions concept.

3   Discuss product-positioning options.

4   Explain how to sell your product with a price strategy.

5   Explain how to sell your product with a value-added strategy.

 Reality Selling Today Video Series

You have just finished paying off your college loans and it's time to replace that old rust bucket with a new car. You have looked at the sport-compact cars available, but they all seem so small. Now you are eagerly looking at cars in the sports sedan category. The cars in this niche offer a good blend of comfort, design, and performance. However, there are almost too many choices. *Road & Track* says there are 11 different automobiles in this group. The list price starts at $71 425 for the Cadillac CTS-V. The Audi A4 and Jaguar X-Type offer all-wheel drive; all the rest offer front- or rear-wheel drive. As you learn more about the choices available, it becomes clear that each manufacturer has taken steps to differentiate its product.[1]

Several years ago automobile manufacturers from around the world began to develop and position cars for the sports sedan segment. Research indicated that demand for these cars would increase. The result was the introduction of 11 different marques, each with its own unique characteristics. At the dealer level, the process of product differentiation continues. If you want something more than standard equipment, the salesperson can describe a variety of options that can add $10 000 or more to the price. Each car can be accessorized to meet your personal needs. The dealer can also help position this product with modern facilities, customer-friendly service policies, and a reputation for honesty and integrity.

Some automobile manufacturers see the sports sedan category as critical to their success. At BMW, the 3 Series sports sedan accounts for nearly half of the company's sales worldwide. Sports sedans can be very profitable because many buyers purchase expensive options such as special wheel and tire packages, anti-skid electronics, ground-effects trim, and top-of-the line audio systems.

Salespeople at the dealer level in the crowded sports-sedan market play an important role in positioning their brand for competitive advantage. Adding value depends on the salesperson's ability to provide a competitive analysis using knowledge of the manufacturer, the automobile, and the dealership.

Design can play a major role in the sports sedan market segment. BMW and Audi recently unveiled completely redesigned cars. These new cars will face off against the Infiniti G37 and the Cadillac CTS, two cars noted for advanced design.[2]

Salespeople at the dealer level can play an important role in positioning the automobile for competitive advantage. They can describe the quality control process that ensures the build quality of the BMW 330i or demonstrate the sports car driving characteristics of the Lexus IS 350. Adding value depends on the salesperson's ability to provide a competitive analysis using knowledge of the manufacturer, the automobile, and the dealership.

PRODUCT POSITIONING—A PRODUCT-SELLING STRATEGY

LONG-TERM SUCCESS IN TODAY'S DYNAMIC GLOBAL ECONOMY REQUIRES THE CONTINUOUS positioning and repositioning of products.[3] **Positioning** involves those decisions and activities intended to create and maintain a certain conception of the firm's product in the customer's mind. It requires developing a marketing strategy aimed at influencing how a particular market segment perceives a product in comparison to the competition.[4] In a market that has been flooded with a variety of sport-utility vehicles (SUVs), Land Rover has been positioned as a dependable vehicle that can climb a steep, rock-covered hillside with ease. Every effort has been made to create the perception of safety, durability, and

positioning Decisions and activities intended to create and maintain a certain conception of the firm's product in the customer's mind.

security. To give sales representatives increased confidence in the Land Rover, the company has arranged plant tours and the opportunity to observe actual testing of the Land Rover under extremely demanding conditions. Good positioning means that the product's name, reputation, and niche are well recognized. However, a good positioning strategy does not last forever. The positioning process must be continually modified to match the customer's changing wants and needs.[5]

The Essentials of Product Positioning

Most companies use a combination of marketing and sales strategies to give their products a unique position in the marketplace. Every salesperson needs a good understanding of the fundamental practices that contribute to product positioning. This chapter begins with a brief introduction to the concept of product differentiation. This is followed by an explanation of how products have been redefined in the age of information. The remainder of the chapter is devoted to three selling strategies that can be used to position a product. Emphasis is placed on positioning your product with a value-added strategy. In the age of information, salespeople who cannot add value to the products they sell will diminish in number and influence.

Achieving Product Differentiation in Personal Selling

differentiation Your ability to separate yourself and your product from that of your competitors.

One of the basic tenets of sales and marketing is the principle of product differentiation. **Differentiation** refers to your ability to separate yourself and your product from that of your competitors. It is the key to building and maintaining a competitive advantage.[6] The competitors in virtually all industries are moving toward differentiating themselves on the basis of quality, price, convenience, economy, or some other factor. Salespeople, who are on the front line of many marketing efforts, assume an important role in the product differentiation process. Differentiating your product helps you stand out from the crowd. It often allows you to distance yourself from the competition. In many cases, the process of differentiation creates barriers that make it difficult for the buyer to choose a competing product simply on the basis of price.[7]

Global Business Insight

Doing Business in India

India is a very large country that is growing in importance in terms of international trade. Indians' customs are often dictated by their religious beliefs. In addition to Hindus and Muslims, there are dozens of other religious groups. Study the Indian culture carefully before your first business trip to this country.

■ Customs of food and drink are an important consideration when you do business in India. Avoid eating meat in the presence of Hindus because they are vegetarians and consider the cow a sacred animal. Muslims will not eat pork or drink alcoholic beverages.

■ There is a very strict caste system in India so be aware of the caste of the clients with whom you are dealing and any restrictions that may apply to that caste.

■ Most members of the Indian business community speak English.

■ Indians tend to be careful buyers who seek quality and durability. They respect a caring and well informed salesperson. Personal relationships in business transactions are very important.

Creating a Value Proposition

A well-informed customer will usually choose the product that offers the most value. Therefore, salespeople need to position their product with a value proposition. A **value proposition** is the set of benefits and values the company promises to deliver to customers to satisfy their needs. The value proposition presented by Porsche promises driving performance and excitement.[8] Kinko's, which is now part of FedEx, is attempting to differentiate itself from Sir Speedy, AlphaGraphics, and print shops found at Office Depot, OfficeMax, and Staples. The new value proposition promises that 1200 FedEx Kinko's locations offer a breadth of services unparalleled in the industry. These new centres leverage the traditional strengths and brand awareness of FedEx and Kinko's.[9]

In many situations, salespeople must quantify the value proposition. This is especially true when the customer is a business buyer. (Business buyer behaviour will be discussed in Chapter 8.) The value quantification process raises customer comprehension levels as they discover the merits of buying your product or service.[10] Let's assume you are selling Kenworth trucks and one of your customers is Day & Ross Transport, based in Hartland, New Brunswick. This large company is planning to purchase 200 new trucks. Your Kenworth diesel trucks cost 10 percent more than rivals' trucks. Within your proposal you should try to quantify the benefits of buying Kenworth trucks, which may include greater reliability, higher trade-in value, and plush interiors that will help the buyer attract better drivers.[11]

> **value proposition** Set of benefits and values the company promises to deliver to customers to satisfy their needs.

THE CLUSTER OF SATISFACTIONS CONCEPT

TED LEVITT, FORMER EDITOR OF *Harvard Business Review*, SAYS THAT PRODUCTS ARE problem-solving tools. People buy products if they fulfill a problem-solving need. Today's better-educated and more demanding customers are seeking a *cluster of satisfactions*. **Satisfactions** arise from the product itself, from the company that makes or distributes the product, and from the salesperson who sells and services the product.[12] Figure 7.1 provides a description of a three-dimensional *Product-Selling Model*. As noted in Chapter 6, many companies are attempting to transform themselves from *product selling* to *solution selling*. To develop and sell solutions, salespeople must be familiar with the satisfactions that meet the needs of each customer.

To illustrate how the concept of a cluster of satisfactions works in a business setting, let us examine an important buying decision. Elaine Parker, a sales representative for Elmore Industries Incorporated, sells metals for manufacturing operations. Over a period of six months, she frequently called on a prospect that had the potential to become a valued customer. During every call, the buyer's receptionist told her the company was happy with its present supplier. Elaine refused to give up and finally the buyer agreed to see her. At first, she was greeted with cool silence, so she decided to ask him some questions about his business, such as: "How's the slow economy affecting your sales?" The buyer's answers focused on materials costs. He said his company could not raise prices nor cut quality. He wanted to lower costs but was unsure how it could be done. Elaine suggested he consider trying some new alloys that were less expensive than the standard metals he had been purchasing. As she described the new alloys, the buyer's interest began to build. She offered to make a full presentation to the buyer and his engineers at a follow-up meeting. The second meeting was a success. Soon after that meeting, Elaine received her first order from the customer. Within a year, she had become the customer's most trusted adviser on technological developments in the industry and his exclusive supplier.[13]

> **satisfactions** The positive benefits that customers seek when making a purchase. Satisfactions arise from the product itself, from the company that makes or distributes the product, and from the salesperson who sells and services the product.

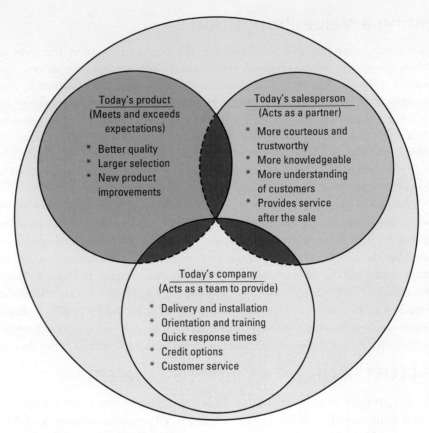

Figure 7.1 Product-Selling Model

The product strategy should include a cluster of satisfactions that meet the needs of today's better-educated and more demanding customers. Drawing from this cluster, the salesperson can custom-fit presentations to meet a wide range of customer needs.

Elaine Parker used questions to engage the customer and identify his problem. She also provided answers to questions raised by the customer:

Questions related to the product

What product is best for our type of operation?

Does the product meet our quality standards?

Given the cost of this product, will we maintain our competitive position in the marketplace?

Questions related to the company

Does this company provide the most advanced technology?

What is the company's reputation for quality products?

What is the company's reputation for standing behind the products it sells?

Questions related to the salesperson

Does the salesperson possess the knowledge and experience needed to recommend the right product?

Can the salesperson clearly communicate specific buyer benefits?

Can the salesperson serve as a trusted adviser?

Will this salesperson provide support services after the sale?

Salespeople who are knowledgeable in all areas of the Product-Selling Model are better able to position a product. Knowledge helps you achieve product differentiation, understand the competition, and prepare an effective value proposition. The competitive analysis worksheet (Table 7.1) can help you discover ways to position your product as the superior choice over your competition.

Table 7.1 Competitive Analysis Worksheet

A value-added product-selling strategy is enhanced when salespeople analyze product, company, and salesperson attributes of the competition in relation to benefits they offer. This information helps the salesperson create value within the sales process.

	My Company	Competitor A	Competitor B
Product Attributes			
Quality			
Durability			
Reliability			
Performance			
Packaging flexibility			
Warranty			
Brand			
Company Attributes			
Reputation			
Industry leadership			
Facilities			
Ease of doing business			
Distribution channels			
Ordering convenience			
Returns, credits, etc.			
Salesperson Attributes			
Knowledge/Expertise			
Responsiveness			
Pricing authority			
Customer orientation			
Honesty/integrity			
Follow-through			
Presentation skills			

A Word of Caution Because many of today's information-age products are very complex, product differentiation must be handled with care. Salespeople are sometimes tempted to use technical lingo—real and invented—to impress the buyer. This problem often surfaces in a situation in which the salesperson is not sure how to describe the value-added features of the product. Robert Notte, technology chief for travel outfitter Backroads, says that during the telecom boom, salespeople representing WorldCom (now MCI) and other firms babbled endlessly, using industry jargon that was often unintelligible. "They wanted you to be impressed," Robert Notte says. Some customers were so intimidated that they were afraid to ask questions—or make a buying decision.[14]

PRODUCT-POSITIONING OPTIONS

PRODUCT POSITIONING IS A CONCEPT THAT APPLIES TO BOTH NEW AND EXISTING PRODUCTS. Given the dynamics of most markets, it may be necessary to reposition products several times during their lifespan, because even a solid popular product can lose market position quickly. Salespeople have assumed an important and expanding role in positioning products. To succeed in our information-drenched society, marketers must use a more direct and personalized form of communication with customers. Advertising directed toward a mass market will often fail to position a complex product.

Throughout the remainder of this chapter, we discuss specific ways to use various product-positioning strategies. We explain how salespeople can (1) position new and emerging products versus mature and well-established products, (2) position products with price strategies, and (3) position products with value-added strategies.

Selling New and Emerging Products versus Mature and Well-Established Products

product life cycle Stages of a product from the time it is first introduced to the market until it is taken off the market, including the stages of introduction, growth, maturity, and decline.

Products, like human beings, are born, grow up, mature, and grow old. In marketing, this process is known as the **product life cycle**; it includes the stages a product goes through from the time it is first introduced to the market until it is discontinued. As the product moves through its cycle, the strategies relating to competition, promotion, pricing, and other factors must be evaluated and possibly changed. The nature and extent of each stage in the product life cycle are determined by several factors:

1. the product's perceived advantage over available substitutes;
2. the product's benefits and the importance of the needs it fulfills;
3. competitive activity, including pricing, substitute product development and improvement, and effectiveness of competing advertising and promotion; and
4. changes in technology, fashion, or demographics.[15]

As we attempt to develop a product-selling strategy, we must consider where the product is positioned within its life cycle. The sales strategy used to sell a new and emerging product will be much different from the strategy used to sell a mature, well-established product (see Fig. 7.2).

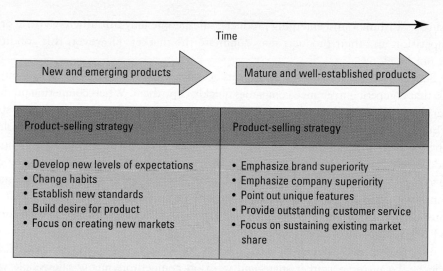

Figure 7.2 Product-selling strategies for positioning new and emerging products versus mature and well-established products.

Selling New and Emerging Products Selling strategies used during the new and emerging stage (see Fig. 7.2) are designed to develop a new level of expectation, change habits, and in some cases establish a new standard of quality.[16] The goal is to build desire for the product. Highly talented and resourceful salespeople are needed during the product initiation phase.[17] Salespeople must be resourceful, possess information regarding every aspect of the product, and be able to present a convincing value proposition.[18]

When Brother International Corporation introduced its line of Multi-Function Centre (MFC) machines, the goal was to convince buyers that one machine could replace five separate machines. However, before buyers would give up their copy machine, fax machine, laser printer, and other machines, they asked some hard questions. Is a multi-function machine reliable? Does the quality match that of the current machines? Finding the best machine for each customer is challenging because Brother offers more than 10 different MFC models to choose from.

In some cases the new product is not a tangible item. Several years ago, IntraLinks closed its first big sale, a $50 000 contract, with J.P. Morgan. The company got its start providing the financial services industry with the secure transmission of highly confidential information across the Internet. Patrick Wack and his business partners convinced J. P. Morgan and other financial firms that they did not need to rely on an army of foot messengers and FedEx trucks to deliver sensitive documents. They were not only selling a new product, they were selling a vision that included new levels of expectations. The value proposition focused on faster, more secure document transfer, which, in the customer's mind, translated into improved customer service and cost savings. Today Patrick Wack is selling this document transfer concept to customers in a variety of business communities.[19]

Selling Mature and Well-Established Products Mature and well-established products are usually characterized by intense competition as new brands enter the market. Customers who currently buy your product will become aware of competing products. With new and emerging products, salespeople may initially have little or no competition and their products may dominate the market. However, this condition may not last long.

Sun Life Financial regularly provides its agents with new products. Yet the company finds that competing insurance companies quickly copy them. When competing products enter the market, Sun Life sales agents must adopt new strategies. One positioning strategy Sun Life uses is to emphasize the company's history of superior service to policyholders for nearly 150 years and its undeniable financial strength. It is a growth-focused company headquartered in Canada but with offices in 22 countries. Agents often describe Sun Life as a supportive company that gives high priority to service after the sale and a stable organization that will be around to service future needs.[20] The objective is to create an awareness in the customer's mind that Sun Life is a solid company with a long history of good service to policyholders.

The relationship strategy is often critical in selling mature and well-established products. To preserve market share and ward off competitors, many salespeople work hard to maintain a strong relationship with the customer. At Sun Life, salespeople have found that good service after the sale is one of the best selling strategies because it builds customer loyalty.

Selling Products with a Price Strategy

Product, promotion, distribution, and price are the four elements that make up the marketing mix. Pricing decisions must be made at each stage of the product life cycle. Therefore, setting the price can be a complex process. The first step in establishing price is to determine the firm's pricing objectives. Some firms set their prices to maximize their profits; they aim for a price as high as possible without causing a disproportionate reduction in unit sales. Other firms set a market share objective; management may decide that the strategic advantage of an increased market share outweighs a temporary reduction in profits. Many of the new companies doing business on the Internet have adopted this approach.

Pricing strategies often reflect the product's position in the product life cycle. When large high-definition flat-screen televisions were in the new and emerging stage, customers who wanted this innovative product were willing to pay $5000 or more for a unit.

Transactional Selling Tactics That Emphasize Low Price Some marketers have established a positioning plan that emphasizes low price and the use of transactional selling tactics. These companies maintain a basic strategy that focuses on meeting competition. If the firm has meeting competition as its pricing goal, it makes every effort to charge prices that are identical or close to those of the competition. Once this positioning strategy has been adopted, the sales force is given several price tactics to use. Salespeople can alter (lower) the base price through the use of discounts and allowances. Discounts and allowances can take a variety of forms. A few of the more common ones follow:

quantity discount A price reduction made to encourage a larger volume purchase than would otherwise be expected.

> **Quantity discount.** The quantity discount allows the buyer a lower price for purchasing in multiple units or above a specified dollar amount.

Seasonal discount. With seasonal pricing, the salesperson adjusts the price up or down during specific times to spur or acknowledge changes in demand. Off-season travel and lodging prices provide examples.

Promotional allowance. A promotional allowance is a price reduction given to a customer who participates in an advertising or a sales support program. Many salespeople give supermarkets promotional allowances for advertising or displaying a manufacturer's products.

Trade or functional discount. Channel intermediaries, such as wholesalers, often perform credit, storage, or transportation services. Trade or functional discounts cover the cost of these services.[21]

seasonal discount Adjusting prices up or down during specific times to spur or acknowledge changes in demand.

promotional allowance A price reduction given to a customer who participates in an advertising or sales support program.

trade or **functional discount** A discount given to channel intermediaries to cover the cost of the services they provide.

Another option available to salespeople facing a buyer with a low-price buying strategy is to "unbundle" product features. Let's assume that a price-conscious customer wants to schedule a conference that will be accompanied by a buffet-style meal. To achieve a lower price, the salesperson might suggest a cafeteria-style meal, thereby eliminating the need for servers. This product configuration involves less cost to the seller and the cost savings can be passed on to the buyer. Timken Company, a century-old bearing maker, has adopted bundling as a way to compete with other manufacturers around the world. The company now surrounds its basic products with additional components in order to provide customers with exactly what they need. These components can take the form of electronic sensors, lubrication systems, castings, or installation and maintenance. Giving customers bundling options has given Timken a big advantage over foreign competitors who often focus on the basic product. Salespeople who represent Timken have flexible pricing options.[22]

These examples represent only a small sample of the many discounts and allowances salespeople use to compete on the basis of price. Price discounting is a competitive tool available to large numbers of salespeople. Excessive focus on low prices and generous discounts, however, can have a negative impact on profits and sales commissions.

Consequences of Using Low-Price Tactics

Pricing is a critical factor in the sale of many products and services. In markets where competition is extremely strong, setting a product's price may be a firm's most complicated and important decision. The authors of *The Discipline of Market Leaders* encourage business firms to pick one of three disciplines—best price, best product, or best service—and then do whatever is necessary to outdistance the competition. However, the authors caution us not to ignore the other two disciplines: "You design your business to excel in one direction, but you also have to strive to hit the minimum in the others."[23] Prior to using low-price tactics, everyone involved in sales and marketing should answer these questions:

- *Are you selling to high- or low-involvement buyers?* Some people are emotionally involved with respected brands, such as BMW, Sony, and BlackBerry. A part of their identity depends on buying the product they consider the best. Low-involvement buyers care mostly about price.[24]

- *How important is quality in the minds of buyers?* If buyers do not fully understand the price–quality relationship, they may judge the product by its price. For a growing

How Do Customers Judge Service Quality?

In the growing service industry, there is intense price competition. From a distance, one gets the impression that every buyer decision hinges on price alone. However, a closer examination of service purchases indicates that service quality is an important factor when it comes to developing a long-term relationship with customers.

How do customers judge service quality? Researchers have discovered valuable insights about customer perceptions of service quality. They surveyed hundreds of customers in a variety of service industries and discovered that five service-quality dimensions emerged:

1. *Tangibles:* Details the customers can see, such as the appearance of personnel and equipment.

2. *Reliability:* The ability to perform the desired service dependably, accurately, and consistently.

3. *Responsiveness:* The willingness of sales and customer service personnel to provide prompt service and help customers.

4. *Assurance:* The employees' knowledge, courtesy, and ability to convey trust and confidence.

5. *Empathy:* The provision of caring, individualized attention to customers.

Customers apparently judge the quality of each service transaction in terms of these five quality dimensions. Companies need to review these service-quality dimensions and make sure that each area measures up to customers' expectations. Salespeople should recognize that these dimensions have the potential to add value to the services they sell.[a]

number of customers, long-term value is more important than short-term savings that result from low prices.

■ *How important is service?* For many buyers, service after the sale is a critical factor. Even online customers, thought to be very interested in price, rate quality of service very highly. This is especially true in business-to-business sales. A survey conducted

Edgar Argo *Agency*
Sales Magazine from the
Manufacturing Agent
National Association (MANA).

"WE HAVE QUALITY AND WE HAVE LOW PRICES...
WHICH DO YOU WANT?"

by Accenture reported that 80 percent of nearly 1000 corporate buyers rate a strong brand and reliable customer service ahead of low prices when deciding which companies to do business with online.[25]

Influence of Electronic Business on Pricing Companies large and small are racing to discover new sales and marketing opportunities on the Internet. Products ranging from personal computers to term insurance can now be purchased from various websites. Salespeople who are involved primarily in transactional selling and add little or no value to the sales transaction will often not be able to compete with online vendors. To illustrate, consider the purchase of stocks online from one of Canada's many discount brokers. At the present time, it's possible to make an online purchase for a fraction of the cost of using a full-service broker. A well-informed buyer, willing to visit several websites, can make decisions based on online information and investing tools that were considered to be beyond the understanding of the average investor only a few years ago. Persons who need little or no assistance buying stocks can visit Canada's largest discount broker, TD Waterhouse Discount Brokerage, or one of the many others, including Scotia iTrade, RBC Direct Investing, and CIBC Investor's Edge, to name only a few of the many choices available to informed consumers. The person who wants help selecting a stock can turn to a full-service broker such as BMO Nesbitt Burns or Scotia McLeod. Full-service brokers can survive and may prosper as long as they can add value to the sales transaction. The new economy is reshaping the world of commerce, and every buyer continues to have more choice.

Selling Your Product with a Value-Added Strategy

Many progressive marketers have adopted a market plan that emphasizes **value-added strategies**. Companies can add value to their product with one or more intangibles, such as better-trained salespeople, increased levels of courtesy, more dependable product deliveries, better service after the sale, and innovations that truly improve the product's value in the eyes of the customer. In today's highly competitive marketplace, these value-added benefits give the company a unique niche and a competitive edge. Companies that don't make selling and delivering high-value solutions a high priority will consistently lose sales to competitors.[26]

> **value-added strategies** Relationship, product, or service strategies that a company uses to add value for the customer.

To understand fully the importance of the value-added concept in selling and how to apply it in a variety of selling situations, it helps to visualize every product as being dimensional. The *total product* is made up of four "possible" products: the generic product, the expected product, the value-added product, and the potential product (see Fig. 7.3).[27]

Generic Product The **generic product** is the basic, substantive product you are selling. Generic product describes only the product category—for example, life insurance, rental cars, clothing, hotels, or personal computers. Every Ritz-Carlton hotel offers guest rooms, food and beverage service (i.e., restaurants, bars, and banquet space), meeting rooms, guest parking, and other basic services. For customers who visit Tilley Endurables, the generic product is the men's and women's travel and adventure clothing and accessories they find there. The generic products at a bank are money that can be loaned to customers and basic chequing account services. The capability of delivering a generic product gives

> **generic product** The basic, substantive product being sold.

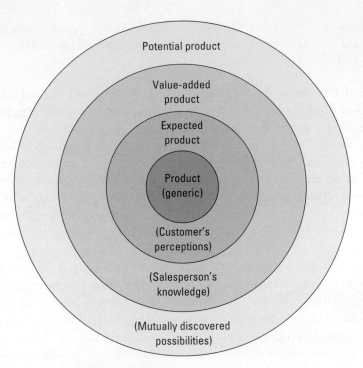

Figure 7.3 The Total Product Concept
An understanding of the four possible products is helpful when the salesperson develops a presentation for different customers.

the marketer the right to play in the game, to compete in the marketplace.[28] Generic products, even the lowest-priced ones, often cannot compete with products that are "expected" by the customer.

Expected Product Every customer has minimal purchase expectations that exceed the generic product itself.[29] Ritz-Carlton must offer not only a comfortable guest room, but also a clean one. Some customers expect a "super" clean room. The **expected product** is everything that represents the customer's minimal expectations. The customer at Tilley Endurables will expect quality products, a good selection, fashionable accessories, and well-informed salespeople.

The minimal purchase conditions vary among customers, so the salesperson must acquire information concerning the expected product that exists in the customer's mind. When the customer expects more than the generic product, the product can be sold *only* if those expectations are met. Every customer perceives the product in individualized terms, which a salesperson cannot anticipate.

Determining each customer's expectations requires the salesperson to make observations, conduct background checks, ask questions, and listen to what the customer is saying. You are attempting to discover both feelings and facts. Top salespeople encourage the customer to think more deeply about the problems they face and discover for themselves the value of a solution. They *avoid* offering solutions until the needs are clearly spelled out. If the buyer says, "The average gas mileage for our fleet of delivery trucks is only 3.4 km per litre," the salesperson might respond with this question: "How does this low mile-

expected product Everything that represents the customer's minimal expectations.

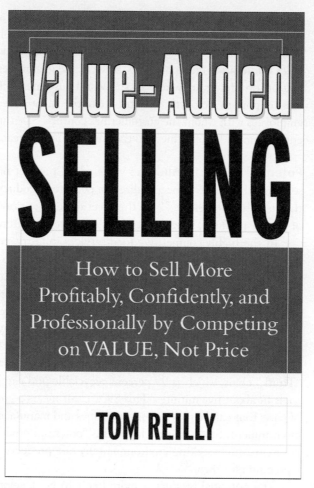

In his book *Value-Added Selling,* Tom Reilly states that "Value-added selling is a business philosophy. It's proactively looking for ways to enhance, augment, or enlarge your bundled package for the customer. Value-added salespeople sell a three-dimensional bundle of values: the product, the company, and themselves."

Source: Book cover of *Value-Added Selling* by Tom Reilly. Copyright © 2003. Reprinted by permission of The McGraw-Hill Companies, Inc.

age rate affect your profitability?" To move the customer's attention from the expected product to a value-added product, you need to keep the customer focused on solutions.[30]

Research reported in the *Harvard Business Review* indicates that it is very difficult to build customer loyalty if you are selling only the expected product. Customer satisfaction and loyalty do not always move in tandem.[31] The customer who purchases the services of Ernst & Young Consulting may feel satisfied after the project is completed but may never do business with the company again. Customer loyalty is more likely to increase when the purchase involves a value-added product.[32]

Value-Added Product The **value-added product** exists when salespeople offer customers more than they expect. Coupling CRM with a differentiation strategy provides one way for a salesperson to add value.[33] When you make a reservation at one of the Ritz-Carlton hotels and request a special amenity such as a tennis lesson, a record of this request is maintained in the computer system. If you make a reservation at another Ritz-Carlton at some future date, the agent will inform you of the availability of a tennis court. The guest who buys chocolate-chip cookies in the gift shop at one location may find some waiting in the room for his or her next stay weeks later. The hotel company uses modern technology to surprise and delight guests.[34] Tilley Endurables provides many things to

value-added product Product that exists when salespeople offer the customer more than they expect.

enhance customers' shopping experiences. At their retail store locations, customers get free cookies, shop in an engaging environment, and can have alterations to clothing done in minutes. Even at its online location, the company adds value for its customers. It provides information on its products, service, and guarantees, and even provides travel information on almost anywhere in the world customers might be travelling.[35] Among the most important factors that contribute to the value-added product is the overall quality of employees with whom the customer has contact. Sales and sales support staff who display enthusiasm and commitment to the customer add a great deal of value to the product.[36]

potential product What may remain to be done to a product—that is, what is possible.

Potential Product   After the value-added product has been developed, the salesperson should begin to conceptualize the **potential product**—what may remain to be done; that is, what is possible.[37] As the level of competition increases, especially in the case of mature products, salespeople must look into the future and explore new possibilities.

In the highly competitive food services industry, restaurant owners like to do business with a distribution sales representative (DSR) who wants to help make the business profitable. The DSR who assumes this role becomes a true partner and looks beyond the customer's immediate and basic needs. The potential product might be identified after a careful study of the restaurant's current menu and customer base. To deliver the potential product, a salesperson must discover and satisfy new customer needs, which requires imagination and creativity.

Steelcase Incorporated, a leading manufacturer of office furniture, has developed the "Think" chair, which is 99 percent recyclable and can be disassembled with basic hand tools in about five minutes. This $900 chair meets a growing demand for products made of parts that can be recycled several times and manufactured in ways least harmful to the environment. Steelcase developed this "potential product" after learning that customers are increasingly seeking environmentally safe products and are sometimes willing to pay a premium for them.[38]

The potential product is more likely to be developed by salespeople who are close to their customers. Many high-performing salespeople explore product possibilities with their customers on a regular basis. Potential products are often mutually discovered during these exchanges.

Every indication points toward product-selling strategies that add value becoming more important in the future. New product life cycles are shrinking, so more companies are searching for ways to add value during the new and emerging stage. Some companies that have experienced low profits selling low-priced products are reinventing those products. They search for product features that provide benefits customers think are worth paying for. Maytag Corporation developed the expensive, environment-friendly Neptune washing machine for customers who will pay more for a washer that uses less water. Tilley Endurables continues to create value for customers by regularly adding new and better products to its product lines.

Value Creation Investments for Transactional, Consultative, and Strategic Alliance Buyers

In most cases, investments in value creation during the transactional sale are minimal. With such sales, salespeople usually place emphasis on finding ways to eliminate any unnecessary costs and on avoiding delays in processing the order. Technology investments

Pricing Your Professional Fees

The age of information has created many career opportunities for people who want to sell professional services. Strong demand for professional services has surfaced in such diverse fields as business consulting, telecommunications, banking, computer technology, training, and health care. When Laura Ricciuto began her career as a consultant, she did not have to decide how to price her services. As part of an MBA small business consulting group, Laura's clients were charged $250 per day for her time. Upon graduation, Laura decided to start her own consultancy: Kaizen Marketing & Creative Design House. Laura initially focused on market research, business planning, and strategy development. She has since expanded into a number of more tactical marketing-related issues: brand development, graphic design, advertising campaigns, Web development, and more. Laura had to decide how much to charge for her various services. Should she price them on an hourly basis or on a project basis? Here are some things she had to consider when determining her fees:

- *Experience:* In the case of Laura Ricciuto, new clients benefit from what she has learned from her many previous consulting contracts.

- *Exclusivity:* Having her office in a smaller Canadian city, Laura is one of few people with expertise in certain aspects of business consulting, and she can charge more for these. Specialists often charge higher fees than generalists.

- *Target Market:* Some markets are less price sensitive. Laura could probably charge higher prices to larger corporations as they are often accustomed to paying higher fees. Smaller business clients are more price-sensitive and resist higher fees.

- *Value:* Ultimately, Laura had to judge how important her service is to particular clients. She understood that the greater the value she could provide to her clients, the higher the fees she could charge.[b]

WHAT IS LEXUS?

Lexus is... Engineering sophistication and manufacturing quality.

Lexus is... Luxury and performance.

Lexus is... An image and an expectation of excellence.

Lexus is... Valuing the customer as an important individual.

Lexus is... Treating customers the way THEY want to be treated.

Lexus is... A total experience that reflects professionalism and a sincere commitment to satisfaction.

Lexus is... "Doing it right the first time".

Lexus is... Caring on a personal level.

Lexus is... Exceeding customer expectations.

And... In the eyes of the customer I AM LEXUS !!!

00-LTT-034

Lexus, a major success story in the automobile industry, offers the customer a value-added strategy that encompasses the product, the company, and the salesperson.

Source: Courtesy of Lexus.

can sometimes play a big role in improving efficiencies.[39] For example, customers may be encouraged to order products online.

A considerable amount of value creation takes place in consultative sales. Higher investments in value creation are permitted because companies need to invest in developing a good understanding of the customer's needs and problems. This is especially true in large, complex sales where creating custom-tailored solutions and delivering more real benefits to the customer provides the opportunity for higher margins. If your company is selling mobile autonomous robots, the sales cycle will be quite long and investments will be quite high. Sales representatives may take several weeks to study the applications of this product in a hospital, a manufacturing plant, or a large warehouse facility. The use of these robots may eventually result in significant cost savings for the customer.[40]

Value creation investments in strategic alliance sales are the highest. As noted in Chapter 1, strategic alliances represent the highest form of partnering. Creating value often requires leveraging the full assets of the company so that investments go well beyond the sales force. Alliances are often developed by a team of specialists from such areas as finance, engineering, and marketing. A proposed alliance may require investments in new technology, manufacturing facilities, and warehouses.[41]

REVIEWING KEY CONCEPTS

- Describe positioning as a product-selling strategy.

  Success in today's dynamic global economy requires the continuous positioning and repositioning of products. Product positioning involves those decisions and activities intended to create and maintain a certain concept of the firm's product in the customer's mind. Salespeople can make an important contribution to the process of product positioning.

- Explain the cluster of satisfactions concept.

  Today's better educated customers are often seeking a cluster of satisfactions. They seek satisfactions that arise from the product itself, from the company that makes or distributes the product, and from the salesperson who sells and services the product.

- Discuss product-positioning options.

  We described the major product-positioning strategies available to salespeople: positioning new and emerging products versus mature and well-established products, positioning with a price strategy, and positioning with a value-added strategy.

- Explain how to sell your product with a price strategy.

  Pricing decisions must be made at each stage of the product life cycle. Some companies use transactional selling tactics that emphasize low price. Salespeople are often given permission to alter (lower) the base price through the use of discounts and allowances. Consequences of using low-price tactics are discussed in this chapter.

- Explain how to sell your product with a value-added strategy.

  To understand fully the importance of the value-added concept in selling, it helps to visualize every product as being four-dimensional. This range of possibilities includes the generic product, the expected product, the value-added product, and the potential product.

Key Terms

differentiation **150**

expected product **160**

generic product **159**

positioning **149**

Review Questions

1. Why has product differentiation become so important in sales and marketing?

2. According to Ted Levitt, what is the definition of a product? What satisfactions do customers want?

3. Explain what is meant by *positioning* as a product- selling strategy. What is a *value proposition?*

4. Why have salespeople assumed an important role in positioning products?

5. Briefly describe the influence of electronic business on pricing. What types of products are sold on the Internet?

6. What are the possible consequences a salesperson might experience when using low-price tactics?

7. What are some of the common ways salespeople add value to the products they sell?

8. What are the four possible products that make up the *total product* concept?

9. Describe the differences between a generic product and a value-added product.

10. Refer to the From the Field boxed feature on page 163. Explain four things that any professional must consider when setting fees for the services they offer.

Application Exercises

1. Obtain catalogues from two competing industrial-supply firms or two competing direct-mail catalogue companies. Assume one of the represented businesses is your employer. After studying the catalogues, make a comparative analysis of your company's competitive advantages.

2. Several weeks ago, Joy Hong fell in love with the Mitsubishi Lancer. After reading about the car in a magazine, she decided to visit a local Mitsubishi dealer. A test drive convinced her to place an order. What happened next was very frustrating. The salesperson immediately started recommending options she should add to the basic car: ABS and air-conditioning package ($2000), automatic transmission ($1200), fog light kit ($434), alloy fuel door ($197), cargo tray ($208), exhaust finisher ($54), cargo organizer ($73), hood protector ($104), and rear and front mud guards ($108). Suddenly the price of $16,598 had approached $21 000 without taxes—not including a destination charge of $1245 and a pre-delivery inspection charge of $250—considerably more than she had planned to spend. Joy returned home without placing an order. Assume the role of sales trainer and suggest ways that the salesperson can improve his ability to position this product so it meets the customer's needs.

3. The Ritz-Carlton hotel chain illustrates the total product concept discussed in this chapter. Research value-added information on the Ritz-Carlton chain by accessing the **www.ritzcarlton.com** website. Choose a location and click "Meetings." Click "Quick Facts" and print the information presented. Circle at least five features you consider to be value-added features. Examine the room rates by clicking on "Accommodations." On the fact sheet you printed, record the room rate for a single- and double-occupancy room.

4. Call a local financial services representative who specializes in stock, bond, or equity fund transactions. Ask what percentage of clients rely on the information given to make complex decisions on their investments. Also ask this person whether customers feel that advice in custom-fit investment programs adds value to their decision making. Find out whether financial products are getting more or less complex, and what effect this will have on providing value-added service in the future.

ROLE-PLAY EXERCISE

Study the convention centre information included in "Partnership Selling: A Role Play/Simulation" online in the Student Resources section at **www.pearsoncanada.ca/manning**. Analyze this information and determine the value-added product that would appeal to the customer, a meeting planner. Prepare a value proposition that summarizes the mix of key benefits on which your product is positioned. The proposition might include the free limousine service to and from the airport. Present your value proposition to another class member who will assume the role of the customer. Consider using information sheets, pictures, and other materials that will enhance your presentation.

CASE PROBLEM

Many of the most profitable companies have discovered that there are "riches in market niches." They have developed products and services that meet the needs of a well-defined or a newly created market. Steelcase Incorporated, a leading source of information and expertise on work effectiveness, has been working hard to develop products that meet the needs of people who do most of their work in an office environment. The company motto is "The Office Environment Company." One of its newest products is the "Think" chair. Steelcase also developed the Personal Harbor Workspace, a self-contained, fully equipped, and totally private pod-like workstation. Steelcase sales literature describes the product as ideal for companies that are tired of waiting for the future: "They were developed to support the individual within a highly collaborative team environment, and they work best when clustered around common work areas equipped with mobile tables, carts, benches, screens, and other Steelcase Activity Products. These 'commons' are meant to be flexible spaces that enhance communication and facilitate interaction."

Steelcase realized that selling this advanced product would not be easy, so a decision was made to develop an advanced sales team to presell the Personal Harbor before its major introduction. Once the team started making sales calls, it became evident that a traditional product-oriented sales presentation would not work. The Personal Harbor was such a departure from conventional office design that many customers were perplexed. Sue Sacks, a sales team member, said, "People acted as if we had fallen from Mars." Team members soon realized that to explain the features and benefits of the product, they had to begin studying new organizational developments such as team-oriented workforces and corporate re-engineering. The advanced sales team was renamed the "advanced solutions" team. Sales calls put more emphasis on learning about the customers' problems and identification of possible solutions. Members of the team viewed themselves as consultants who were in a position to discuss solutions to complex business problems.

The consultative approach soon began to pay off in sales. One customer, a hospital, was preparing to build a new office building and needed workstations for 400 employees. The hospital had formed a committee to make decisions concerning the purchase of office equipment. After an initial meeting between the Steelcase sales team and the hospital committee, a visit to the Steelcase headquarters was arranged. The hospital committee members were able to tour the plant and meet with selected Steelcase experts. With knowledge of the hospital's goals and directions, Sue Sacks was able to arrange meetings with Steelcase technical personnel who could answer specific questions. As a result, the hospital placed an order worth more than a million dollars.[42]

Questions

1. To fulfill a customer's needs, salespeople must be prepared to communicate effectively with customers who are seeking a cluster of satisfactions (see Fig. 7.1). Is it likely that a customer who is considering the Personal Harbor Workspace will seek information concerning all three dimensions of the product-selling model? Explain your answer.

2. What product-selling strategies are most effective when selling a new and emerging product such as Personal Harbor Workspaces?

3. Sue Sacks and other members of her sales team discovered that a traditional product-oriented presentation would not work when selling the workspaces. Success came only after the team adopted the consultative style of selling. Why was the product-oriented presentation ineffective?

4. How would you behave differently when dealing with a return client versus a new client?

PART III

ROLE-PLAY EXERCISE
Developing a Product Strategy

SCENARIO

TD Canada Trust is a full-service bank with a reputation for excellent customer service. Personal selling efforts by customer service representatives, financial advisers, and financial planners are considered an integral part of the bank's customer service program.

CUSTOMER PROFILE

At age 45, Angela Cormier is looking forward to early retirement. To supplement her company-sponsored retirement program, she purchased a guaranteed insurance certificate (i.e., a term deposit) in the amount of $4000 each year. The annual percentage yield earned on these term deposits is currently in the range of 1.2 to 2.4 percent. Angela is not interested in stocks and bonds because she sees these products as high-risk investments.

SALESPERSON PROFILE

Susan Ray is a financial planner with TD Canada Trust. She can provide a wide range of financial products, such as stock and bond mutual funds, blue chip stocks, diversified mutual funds, fixed annuities, money market funds, and guaranteed insurance certificates. Susan feels that Angela Cormier may be a good candidate for investment in fixed annuities. She plans to call Ms. Cormier to request an appointment.

PRODUCT

Susan plans to suggest that instead of purchasing term deposits each year, Angela Cormier purchase a five-year term fixed annuity at an annual yield of 3 percent. The minimum single premium purchase is $5000. This product, offered by General Electric Capital Assurance Company, gives the customer a guaranteed principal and a fixed rate of return. At the contract maturity date, the customer can select several payout options. This is a tax-deferred annuity, which means that the customer won't pay income taxes on earnings until she chooses to withdraw the funds. Angela could add funds to her fixed annuity account throughout the contract period. Also, she need not close the account at the end of the contract period but could allow her money to continue to grow at the same interest rate. If Angela withdraws funds prior to the end of the contract, she would be assessed a withdrawal charge.

INSTRUCTIONS

For this role-play activity, you will assume the role of Susan Ray. You will meet with Angela Cormier, a role played by another student, and determine her current and future financial plans. You will determine if she might benefit by investing in this fixed annuity. Prior to meeting with Angela, review the following material in Chapter 6:

- Adding value with a feature–benefit strategy
- Use of bridge statements
- General versus specific benefits

Also think about the implications of the product-selling model (Fig. 7.1). At the beginning of the role play, use appropriate questions to acquire information regarding Angela's needs. Be prepared to recommend this product and close the sale if you feel that Angela will benefit from this purchase.

Part IV
Developing a
Customer Strategy

One of the two sustainable strategic advantages in the new global marketplace is an obsession with customers. Customers, not markets.

—Tom Peters, Thriving on Chaos

Creating Customer Value

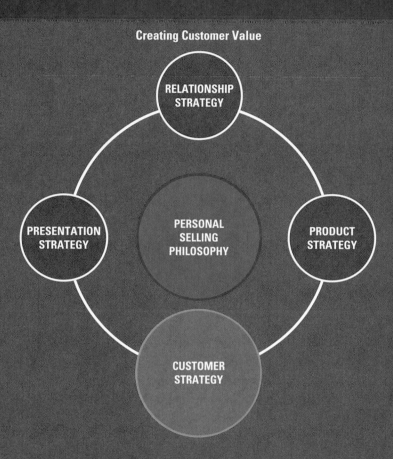

With increased knowledge of the customer, the salesperson is in a better position to achieve sales goals. This part presents information on understanding the buying process, understanding buyer behaviour, and developing a prospect base.

Chapter 8
The Buying Process and Buyer Behaviour

Learning Objectives

After studying this chapter, you should be able to

1   Discuss the meaning of a customer strategy.

2   Explain the difference between consumer and business buyers.

3   Understand the importance of alignment between the selling process and the customer's buying process.

4   Understand the buying process of the transactional, consultative, and strategic alliance buyer.

5   Discuss the various influences that shape customer buying decisions.

 Reality Selling Today Video Series

Ashley Pineda is a new home sales representative for PulteGroup (**www.pultegroupinc. com**). The company offers different product lines: homes for first-time home buyers, move-up homes, and active adult communities. With three different customer groups, Ashley must have a general understanding of the buying motives of each group. In her work with individual customers in each of these groups, she must develop an in-depth understanding of that customer's buying interests.

Most of Ashley's customers are in the first-time home-buyers group who have lived in an apartment but have developed an interest in purchasing a home. Because she has developed an in-depth understanding of this buying group, a central purpose of Ashley's sales presentations is to educate her prospects on renting versus owning and the benefits of owning a home. She also understands that this customer group often knows little about the logistics of owning a home; therefore, she provides her prospects with information and on-site impressions about the neighbourhood, the area, the amenities of the community, as well as shopping areas and schools around the neighbourhood. All these details help Ashley's customers envision raising their children in one of Pulte's neighbourhoods.

Another very important thing Ashley understands about the buying needs of this first-time buying group is the question of the financing of their new home. Ashley typically needs to address the following questions from her customers: What about our credit scores? What qualifies us to buy a new home? Do we need a down payment? What will our

monthly payment be? Will it be comfortable with our budget? PulteGroup supplies Ashley with the knowledge to be able to professionally provide and implement that knowledge and make customers feel comfortable with the financial scenario involved in owning their first home.

Buyers tend to buy from people they like and trust. Considering that many customers buy the largest asset they may ever own from sales professionals like Ashley, trust in the seller becomes especially critical. Therefore, building rapport and trust throughout the whole buying process is essential for Ashley to be successful. Furthermore, Ashley describes having a positive mindset, good time management, and multitasking abilities as the most important skills to be a successful salesperson in her particular business. In essence, sales reps like Ashley have to be able to run their own business in the communities for which they are responsible.

DEVELOPING A CUSTOMER STRATEGY

The greatest challenge to salespeople in the age of information is to improve responsiveness to customers. In fact, a growing number of sales professionals believe that the customer has supplanted the product as the driving force in sales today. This is especially true in those situations in which the products of one company in an industry are becoming more and more similar to those of the competition. Jerry Acuff, author of *Stop*

Acting Like a Seller And Start Thinking Like a Buyer, encourages salespeople to think like buyers. In order to think like a buyer, salespeople must understand the buying process and focus on what the customer is looking for.[1]

Adding Value with a Customer Strategy

customer strategy A carefully conceived plan that will result in maximum customer responsiveness.

A **customer strategy** is a carefully conceived plan that will result in maximum customer responsiveness. One major dimension of this strategy is to achieve a better understanding of the customer's buying needs and motives. As noted in Chapter 1, information has become a strategic resource (see Fig. 1.2). When salespeople take time to discover needs and motives, they are in a better position to offer customers a value-added solution to their buying problem.

Every salesperson who wants to develop repeat business should figure out a way to collect and systematize customer information. The authors of *Reengineering the Corporation* discuss the importance of collecting information about the unique and particular needs of each customer:

> Customers—consumers and corporations alike—demand products and services designed for their unique and particular needs. There is no longer any such notion as the customer; there is only this customer, the one with whom a seller is dealing at the moment and who now has the capacity to indulge his or her own personal tastes.[2]

The first prescription for developing a customer strategy focuses on the customer's buying process (see Fig. 8.1). Buying procedures and policies can vary greatly from one buyer to another. This is especially true in business-to-business selling. If a salesperson

Strategic/Consultative Selling Model	
Strategic step	Prescription
Develop a personal selling philosophy	✓ Adopt marketing concept ✓ Value personal selling ✓ Become a problem solver/partner
Develop a relationship strategy	✓ Adopt win-win philosophy ✓ Project professional image ✓ Maintain high ethical standards
Develop a product strategy	✓ Become a product expert ✓ Sell benefits ✓ Configure value-added solutions
Develop a customer strategy	• Understand the buying process • Understand buyer behaviour • Develop prospect base

Figure 8.1 Strategic/Consultative Selling Model
Today, one of the greatest challenges to salespeople is to improve responsiveness to customers. A well-developed customer strategy is designed to meet this challenge.

fails to learn how the buyer plans to make the purchase, then he or she may find the selling process out of alignment with the customer's buying process. Keith Eades, author of *The New Solution Selling*, says:

> If we haven't defined how our buyers buy, then we make assumptions that throw us out of alignment with our buyers. Misalignment with buyers is one of selling's most critical mistakes.[3]

The second prescription focuses on why customers buy. This topic will be discussed in detail later in this chapter. The third prescription for developing a customer strategy emphasizes building a strong prospect base, which is discussed in Chapter 9.

Complex Nature of Customer Behaviour

The forces that motivate customers can be complex. Arch McGill, a former vice president of IBM, reminds us that individual customers perceive the product in their own terms, and that these may be "unique, idiosyncratic, human, emotional, end-of-the-day, irrational, erratic terms."[4] Different people doing the same thing—such as purchasing a notebook computer—may have different needs that motivate them, and each person may have several motives for a single action. The proliferation of market research studies, public opinion polls, surveys, and reports of "averages" makes it easy to fall into the trap of thinking of the customer as a number. The customer is a person, not a statistic. Companies that fully accept this basic truth are likely to adopt a one-to-one marketing strategy based on a bedrock concept: *Treat different customers differently.*[5]

CONSUMER VERSUS BUSINESS BUYERS

Consumer buyer behaviour REFERS TO THE BUYING BEHAVIOUR OF INDIVIDUALS AND households who buy goods and services for personal consumption. The Canadian consumer market consists of more than 33 million people who purchase many billions of dollars' worth of goods and services each year. **Business buyer behaviour** refers to the buying behaviour of organizations that buy goods and services for use in the production of other products and services that are sold, rented, or supplied to others.[6] In many business buying situations, several people work together to reach a decision. The **buying centre** is a cross-functional team of decision makers who often represent several departments. Each team member is likely to have some expertise needed in a particular purchase decision. Salespeople must continually identify which individuals within a firm will be members of the buying centre.[7]

It is not uncommon for salespeople to sell products and services to both consumer and business buyers. A well-established interior decorating firm will likely work with homeowners as well as commercial clients who own hotels, restaurants, and art galleries. A salesperson employed by an automobile dealership will often sell to corporate customers who maintain a fleet of cars or trucks as well as to consumers who buy vehicles for personal use.

There are some similarities between consumer markets and business markets. Both involve people who assume the role of buyer and make purchase decisions to satisfy needs. These two markets differ, however, in some important areas. Figure 8.2 provides a brief review of some of these differences. A business purchase is likely to involve more participants, who may be well trained, in the decision making process. Most purchasing agents spend time learning how to buy better.[8]

consumer buyer behaviour
Buying behaviour of individuals and households who buy goods and services for personal consumption.

business buyer behaviour
Buying behaviour of organizations that buy goods and services for use in the production of other products and services or for the purpose of reselling or renting them to others at a profit.

buying centre A cross-functional team of decision makers who often represent several departments.

Consumer Buyers	Business Buyers
Purchases made for individual or household consumption	Purchases made for some purpose other than personal consumption
Decisions usually made by individuals	Decisions frequently made by several people
Purchases often made based on brand reputation or personal recommendations with little or no product expertise	Purchases often made according to precise technical specification based on product expertise
Purchases based primarily on emotional responses to product or promotions	Purchases based primarily on rational criteria
Individual purchasers may make quick decisions	Purchasers may engage in lengthy decision process
Products are consumer goods and services for individual use	Products are often complex; classified by how organizational customers use them

Figure 8.2 Differences Between Consumer and Business Buyers

Source: Adapted from Michael R. Solomon and Elnora W. Stuart, *Marketing: Real People, Real Choices,* Third Edition (Upper Saddle River, NJ: Prentice Hall 2003), p. 193. Reprinted and electronically reproduced by permission of Pearson Education, Inc. Upper Saddle River, New Jersey.

Types of Business Buying Situations

There are three major types of business-to-business buying situations. The amount of time and effort organizational buyers spend on a purchase usually depends on the complexity of the product and how often the decision must be made.[9] At one extreme is the *new-task buy,* which may require extensive research. At the other extreme is the *straight rebuy,* which is a fairly routine decision. In the middle is the *modified rebuy,* which will require some research.[10]

new-task buy A first-time purchase of a product or service.

New-Task Buy A first-time purchase of a product or service is a **new-task buy**. Depending on the cost and complexity of this purchase, the buying decision may require several weeks for information gathering and the involvement of numerous participants. In some cases, a buying committee is formed to consider the new product's quality, price, and service provided by suppliers. Salespeople who are involved in new-task buying situations must rely heavily on consultative selling skills.

straight rebuy A routine purchase of previously purchased goods or services.

Straight Rebuy A **straight rebuy** is a routine purchase of items needed by a business-to-business customer. Let's assume you have decided to open a new restaurant and need a steady supply of high-quality cooking oil. After talking to several restaurant suppliers and testing several oils, you select one that meets your needs. Your goal now is to simplify the buying process with the use of a straight rebuy plan. As long as the supplier continues to meet your criteria for price, quality, service, and delivery, future purchases will be routine. Organizations often use the straight rebuy approach for such items as cleaning supplies, copy paper, and cartridges for computer printers. Salespeople must constantly monitor every straight rebuy situation to be sure the customer is completely satisfied. A competing supplier will be quick to exploit any sign of dissatisfaction by the customer.

Modified Rebuy The tide of change is a powerful force in the world of business. From time to time, your customers may wish to modify product specifications, change delivery schedules, or renegotiate prices. Several years ago, the North American automobile manufacturers—faced with greater competitive pressures from China, Germany, Japan, Korea, and other nations—turned to their suppliers and demanded price reductions. Suppliers were required to become involved in a **modified rebuy** or risk loss of the account. A modified rebuy often requires the involvement of several participants. Well-trained professional salespeople work hard to provide outstanding service after the sale and anticipate changes in customer needs. Some salespeople regularly ask their customers what they value most about the existing buying situation and how improvements can be made in this area.

modified rebuy Purchasing when the buyer wants to reconsider product specifications, prices, or suppliers.

Building Strategic Alliances In Chapter 1, we described strategic alliances as the highest form of partnering. Alliances are often formed by companies that have similar business interests and believe the partnership will help them gain a mutual competitive advantage. Large companies often form several alliances. Some strategic alliances take the form of systems selling. **Systems selling** appeals to buyers who prefer a packaged solution to a problem from a single seller, thereby avoiding all the separate decisions involved in a complex buying situation.[11]

Several years ago, Kinko's reinvented itself as a document solutions provider for business firms of all sizes. Full-service Kinko's stores began offering the buyer networks of computers equipped with popular software, ultra-fast colour printers, high-speed Internet

systems selling A type of selling that appeals to buyers who prefer a packaged solution to a problem from a single seller, thereby avoiding all the separate decisions involved in a complex buying situation.

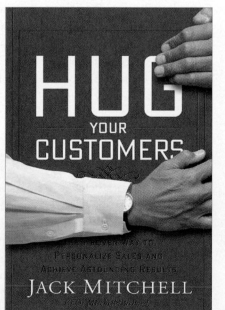

The sales personnel at Mitchells/Richards sell high quality apparel to discriminating customers. Many of these customers are business executives who invest heavily in their business wardrobes. Salespeople at Mitchells/Richards work hard to discover the customer's needs and provide outstanding service after the sale.
Source: Reprinted by permission of Christina B. Bliss.

connections, and, of course, a variety of document preparation services. After Kinko's was purchased by FedEx, a network of 1200 digitally connected FedEx Kinko's locations began offering a wider selection of customized, needs-based document solutions. One large financial institution consolidated the services of 13 vendors by forming an alliance with FedEx Kinko's.[12] Systems selling efforts at FedEx Kinko's have become an important strategy for winning and holding accounts.

Types of Consumer Buying Situations

As noted previously, consumer buying behaviour refers to purchases of products for personal or household use. The amount of time consumers devote to a purchasing decision can vary greatly depending on the cost of the product, familiarity with the product, and the importance of the item to the consumer. Few buyers invest much effort in selecting a tube of toothpaste, but most will devote extensive time to decision making over the purchase of a new automobile or a home. Consumer buying can fall into one of three categories depending on the degree of consumer involvement: habitual, variety-seeking, or complex buying.

habitual buying decision A consumer buying decision that requires very little involvement and in which brand differences are usually insignificant.

Habitual Buying Decisions A **habitual buying decision** usually requires very little consumer involvement and brand differences are usually insignificant.[13] For frequently purchased, low-cost items such as shampoo or paper towels, consumer involvement in the decision-making process is very low. Supermarket shoppers often display habitual buying behaviour as they select items.

variety-seeking buying decision A consumer buying decision motivated by the desire for variety rather than by product dissatisfaction.

Variety-Seeking Buying Decisions A **variety-seeking buying decision** is also characterized by low customer involvement, but also by important perceived brand differences.[14] Brand switching is not uncommon for such decisions because buyers can be influenced by advertising appeals, coupons, or lower prices to try a new brand. Brand switching is usually motivated by the desire for variety rather than dissatisfaction.[15]

complex buying decision An often lengthy consumer buying decision characterized by a high degree of involvement.

Complex Buying Decisions A **complex buying decision** is characterized by a high degree of involvement by the customer. Consumers are likely to be highly involved when the product is expensive, purchased infrequently, and highly self-expressive.[16] The purchase of a vacation home, a long-term care insurance policy, an expensive boat, or a costly piece of art would require a complex buying decision. The learning process for some purchases can be very lengthy.

ACHIEVING ALIGNMENT WITH THE CUSTOMER'S BUYING PROCESS

THE FOUNDATION OF A SUCCESSFUL SALES EFFORT IS KNOWING HOW BUYERS BUY. IF SALES PEOPLE don't know what the customer's decision-making process is and they proceed according to their own agenda, they risk losing the sale. If salespeople have not defined how buyers buy, then they make assumptions that throw their sales process out of alignment with the buyer's buying process.[17] Too often salespeople rely on generalizations about the buyer's decision-making process rather than acquiring specific information.

buying process The stages a buyer goes through when making a buying decision.

The **buying process** is a systematic series of actions, or a series of defined, repeatable steps, intended to achieve a result.[18] Organizational purchasing structures and buying procedures can vary greatly from company to company, so we need to be clear on how decisions are being made within each account. In some cases, the steps in the buying process have been clearly defined by the organization and this information is available to any potential supplier. However, this information may not tell us the whole story. Salespeople need to obtain answers to these types of questions:

How urgent is my proposal to the buyer? When will the buying decision be made?

Will "political" factors within the organization influence how the decision is made?

Has the money needed to purchase my product been allocated?

Which person or persons in the buying organization will actually use or supervise the use of the product I am selling?[19]

Customers make buying decisions in many ways, so understanding each individual buyer's decision-making process is central to success in personal selling. Some buyers will have multiple buying processes. Buying decisions involving a straight rebuy, for example, will likely differ from buying decisions involving a new-task buy.[20]

Steps in the Typical Buying Process

The term "process" brings to mind a set formula that applies to every situation. But buying decisions are made in different ways, so it would be inappropriate to view the buying process as a uniform pattern of decision making. However, there is a model—a form of decision making that buyers usually apply to their unique circumstances. Figure 8.3 shows

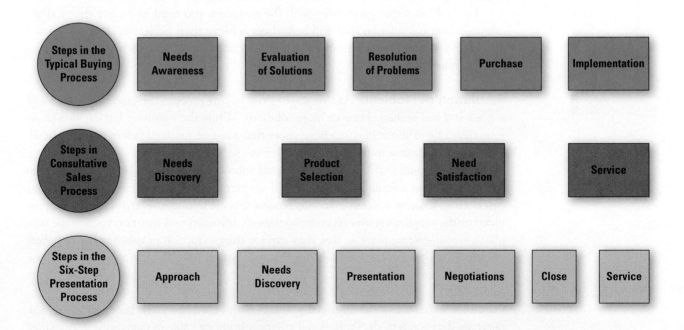

Figure 8.3 Typical Buying Process Model
In this figure, for purposes of illustration, the Typical Buying Process Model is aligned with the two most popular Selling Process Models. It is important for salespeople to understand the customer's unique buying process, and where the customer is in that buying process, and then align the sales process to satisfy their customer's needs.

the typical stages in the buying-decision process: need awareness, evaluation of solutions, resolution of problems, purchase, and implementation. This model is especially helpful in understanding organizational buying decisions and large consumer acquisitions. Consumers who make habitual buying decisions often skip or reverse some of these stages.[21]

Need Awareness Need awareness is the first stage in the buying process. The buyer recognizes that something is imperfect or incomplete. The need for energy conservation technology may surface when oil prices rise to higher levels. The need for a customer service training program may become evident when surveys show a decline in customer satisfaction. Salespeople can create value at this stage of the buying process if they can help determine the magnitude of the customer's problem and identify a solution. For example, a sales representative may be able to help the buyer estimate the cost of poor customer service and recommend a way to improve service. Customers often need help in determining whether they have a problem large enough to justify the cost of a proposed solution.[22]

Evaluation of Solutions Buyers who experience need awareness usually begin searching for information that will help them evaluate possible problem solutions. They realize, at this point, that the problem they face is amenable to some type of solution. In some cases, there are several solutions that the customer needs to study. Salespeople can add value at this stage by providing useful information that helps the customer make an informed choice. In some cases, the value justification can be presented in terms of cost reduction or increased revenue. In other cases, the value justification may be intangible, such as customer satisfaction, improved security, or reduced stress. In business-to-business selling situations, value justification that can be measured is usually the most powerful.

To establish a true partnership with the customer, you need to be sure that you are offering them information that will help them achieve their objectives. If you possess a good understanding of the customer's buying process, you will know what they are trying to accomplish.[23]

Resolution of Problems At this stage of the buying process, the customer is aware of a need and has evaluated one or more solutions. While the customer has decided to do something, he or she is likely to have issues that must be resolved before moving ahead. This is especially true in the case of complex sales.[24]

Some customers will want the proposed solution in writing. Competitors may be invited to submit written proposals. A well-written proposal is one way to add value, as described in Chapter 6. Customers may request specific information that can only be provided by the supplier's engineers or accountants. Customers may insist on visiting the supplier's manufacturing plant so that they can see the production process firsthand. Buyers often need help to overcome obstacles that prevent them from moving to the purchase stage of the buying process.[25]

Purchase After all of the customer's obstacles and concerns have been overcome, the purchase decision is made. Professional salespeople create value in many ways at this stage of the buying process.[26] First, they can make sure the purchase is "hassle free." This may mean working with the customer to arrange the best financing or to supervise delivery and installation of the product. Salespeople can add value by becoming a "customer advocate" within their own organization. This may mean negotiating with various departments to

There is no longer any such notion as *the* customer—there is only *this* customer, the one whom a seller is dealing with at the moment. Discovering the individual needs of this customer can be challenging.

expedite the order. Buyers want to work with salespeople who are able to quickly solve any order fulfillment problems.[27]

Implementation The first sale is only the beginning of the salesperson's relationship with the buyer. Repeat sales occur when your company as supplier has demonstrated the ability to add value in various ways after the sale. Value creation can take the form of timely delivery, superior installation, accurate invoicing, follow-up contacts by the salesperson, or anything else that is important to the customer.

UNDERSTANDING THE BUYING-DECISION PROCESS FOR TRANSACTIONAL, CONSULTATIVE, AND RELATIONSHIP SELLING

THE NEXT STEP IN UNDERSTANDING THE CUSTOMER'S BUYING PROCESS IS TO DISCUSS THREE value creation selling approaches that appeal to certain types of customers. In Chapter 1, we briefly introduced transactional, consultative, and strategic alliance selling. We will now discuss when to work effectively with each type of buyer.[28]

Transactional Process Buyer

Transactional buyers are well aware of their needs and usually know a great deal about the products or services they intend to purchase. In a truly transactional sale, buyers will become frustrated if the salesperson attempts to use needs assessment, problem solving, or relationship building. They are not looking for new information or advice from the salesperson. Most transactional buyers have conducted their own research and, in most cases, have decided which product best meets their needs. They don't want hand-holding and they don't want the salesperson to waste their time.[29]

How can a salesperson add value to a transactional sale? If the buyer is already aware of his or her needs, has evaluated solutions, and has no issues or concerns that need to be resolved, then the salesperson needs to focus on the purchase stage of the five-part buying process model (see Fig. 8.3). Do whatever is necessary to facilitate a convenient and hassle-free purchase. Eliminate any unnecessary costs or delays in processing the order. The transactional buyer may quickly turn to a competitor if he or she experiences unnecessary costs or delays.

Consultative Process Buyer

Consultative selling, a major theme of this text, was described in Chapter 1. This sales approach appeals to buyers who lack needs awareness or need help evaluating possible solutions. Some buying decisions require assistance from a consultative salesperson because the product is very complex or the cost of the product is very high. The purchase of a new home provides a good example in the consumer arena. Home buyers usually seek the assistance of an experienced realtor. The purchase of Internet phone-calling equipment provides a good example in the business-to-business arena. Organizations that are considering the purchase of complex Internet telephone equipment seek answers to several questions: Can we keep a portion of our traditional phone network or must we adopt an all-Internet phone system? Will the new system provide the same voice quality as our traditional system? Internet phone-calling equipment is available from several suppliers, including Avaya Incorporated and Cisco Systems Incorporated. Some customers will need help comparing the technology available from these and other suppliers.[30]

Successful consultative salespeople focus a great deal of attention on needs awareness, which is step one in the buying process model (see Fig. 8.3). This is where salespeople can create the most value by helping customers gain an understanding of their problems and creating solutions that correct these problems.[31] Many customers seek help defining needs and solutions, but avoid dealing with sales representatives who simply want to sell a product.

Consultative selling encompasses the concept that salespeople should conduct a systematic assessment of the prospect's situation. This usually involves collecting as much information as possible prior to the sales call, and using a series of carefully worded questions to obtain the customer's point of view during the sales call. Two-way communication will provide for a mutual exchange of ideas, feelings, and perceptions.

The consultative salesperson will help the customer evaluate solutions and help resolve any problems that surface prior to the purchase stage. Consultative salespeople also work hard to add value at the implementation stage of the sales process. This may involve supervising product delivery and installation, servicing warranties, and providing other services after the sale.

Strategic Alliance Process Buyer

As noted previously, the goal of strategic alliances is to achieve a marketplace advantage by teaming up with another company. Alliances are often formed by companies that have similar business interests and seek to gain a mutual competitive advantage. Dell, for example, formed a partnership with Microsoft and Intel to provide customized e-business solutions. In the highly competitive global market, going it alone is sometimes more difficult.[32]

Step one in building an alliance is a careful study of the proposed partner. This research is often coordinated by senior management and may involve persons working in the areas of sales, marketing, finance, and distribution. At some point, representatives from both companies will meet and explore the mutual benefits of the alliance. Both parties must be prepared to explain how they will add value once the alliance is formed.

The Buyer Resolution Theory

Several theories explain how customers arrive at a buying decision. One traditional point of view is based on the assumption that a final buying decision is possible only after the prospect has answered five logical questions (see Fig. 8.4). This is called the **buyer resolution theory**. One strength of this buying theory is that it focuses the salesperson's attention on five important factors that the customer is likely to consider before making a purchase: need, product, source, price, and time. Answers to these five questions provide valuable insights about the customer's buying strategy. One important limitation of this

buyer resolution theory A selling theory that a purchase will be made only after the prospect has made five buying decisions about need, product, source, price, and time.

Buyer resolution theory recognizes that a purchase is made only after the prospect has made five buying decisions that result from specific, affirmative responses to the five key questions.	
Why should I buy?	Realistically, it is difficult to provide prospects with an answer to this question. In many cases, salespeople fail to help customers become aware of a need. Therefore, large numbers of potential customers are not sufficiently persuaded to purchase products that will provide them with genuine buyer benefits.
What should I buy?	If a prospect agrees that a need does exist, then a sales representative is ready to address this buying decision. He or she must convince the prospect that the product being offered will satisfy the need. In most cases, the buyer can choose from among several competing products.
Where should I buy?	As products become more complex, customers are giving more attention to "source" decisions. In a major metropolitan area someone who wants to buy a LaserJet 3160 or a competing product will be able to choose from several sources.
What is a fair price?	Today's better-educated and -informed consumers are searching for the right balance between price and value (i.e., buyer benefits). They are better able to detect prices that are not competitive or that do not correspond in their minds with the product's value.
When should I buy?	A sale cannot be closed until a customer has decided when to buy. In some selling situations, the customer will want to postpone the purchase because of reluctance to part with the money.

Figure 8.4 Buyer Resolution Theory
This theory, sometimes referred to as "The 5 Ws Theory," focuses attention on questions the customer may need answers to before making a purchase decision. The absence of an answer to any of these questions will likely result in a customer objection.

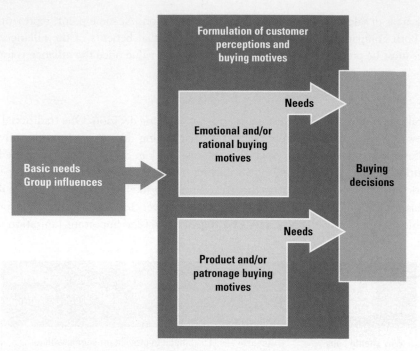

Figure 8.5 The Buyer Behaviour Model
This model illustrates the many complex psychological and sociological forces that influence buyer behaviour.

theory is that a salesperson cannot always anticipate which of the five buying decisions might be most difficult for the prospect to make. If the selling process does not mesh with the buying process, a sale is less likely. There is no established sequence in which prospects make these five decisions, so a highly inflexible sales presentation would not be effective.

UNDERSTANDING BUYER BEHAVIOUR

ALTHOUGH EVERY CUSTOMER IS UNIQUE, SALESPEOPLE NEED TO UNDER-STAND THE IMPORTANT social and psychological influences that tend to shape customer buying decisions. We will review concepts that come from the fields of psychology, sociology, and anthropology. Figure 8.5 illustrates the many forces that influence buying decisions.

Basic Needs That Influence Buyer Behaviour

Basic human needs have changed little throughout our economic history. However, the ways in which needs are fulfilled have changed greatly in the age of information.[33] The starting point for developing an understanding of the forces influencing buying decisions is a review of the individual needs that shape the customer's behaviour. To gain insights into customer behaviour motivated by both physiological and psychological needs, it is helpful to study the popular hierarchy of needs developed by Abraham Maslow.

Selling to Couples

There are many situations in which salespeople sell to a couple rather than to an individual: real estate, mutual funds, cars, wedding rings, insurance. These situations can pose additional challenges for salespeople. Each person in a couple may, for example, bring a hidden agenda to the purchase. An unseasoned salesperson risks alienating or offending one partner and perhaps, as a result, losing the sale.

According to Marilyn Powers, a practising therapist, couples exhibit one of three communications stages: a fusion stage, a power struggle stage, or an independent stage. Couples in the fusion stage think and feel alike and try to avoid conflict. As a result, they make hasty decisions, often without providing adequate information to the salesperson. This may result in the sale being cancelled or in after-sale customer dissatisfaction. To prevent this, the salesperson needs to ask sufficient questions during the need discovery stage of the sales process to be sure he or she fully understands the couple's needs.

Couples in the power struggle stage actively seek a win-lose solution, where one partner's "win" over the other partner is more important than the actual purchase decision. Here, the salesperson needs to slow the sales process and craft a "win-win" solution for the couple. The best way to do this is to focus on each person, being sure to establish and understand each individual's needs. Through active listening—paraphrasing and restating each participant's comments—the salesperson may be able to defuse the emotional situation, keeping the communication lines open and establishing some common ground. Unfortunately, there will be instances where it is apparent that one key decision maker will win the power struggle. Here, some salespeople argue that it is best to align with that person as it will be impossible to keep both participants happy; other salespeople argue that it is best to remain impartial and to avoid getting involved in the power struggle.

Couples in the independent stage often have different opinions about what they should buy, but they are willing to continue their search for a third solution that may be better than either of their independent solutions. A salesperson who encounters this situation may need to give the couple additional time to communicate with each other and should not try to close the sale too quickly.

Judith C. Tingley and Lee E. Robert, authors of *GenderSell: How to Sell to the Opposite Sex*, suggest some tips to use, depending on whether the salesperson is a man or a woman. They suggest that male salespeople must be careful to avoid being patronizing or condescending toward women when trying to sell to a mixed-gender couple. A male salesperson should greet the woman first, keep her involved throughout the sales process, and be careful to use gender-neutral language. Female salespeople need to build credibility quickly, be more rational and less emotional in their selling style, and treat both partners with equal respect.[a]

Maslow's Hierarchy of Needs According to Abraham Maslow, basic human needs are arranged in a hierarchy according to their strength (Fig. 8.6). His theory rests on the assumption that as each lower-level need is satisfied, the need at the next level demands attention.

Physiological Needs. Sometimes called primary needs, **physiological needs** include the needs of food, water, and sleep. Maslow placed our physiological needs at the bottom of the pyramid. He believed that these basic needs tend to be strong in the minds of most people.

physiological needs Primary or physical needs, including food, water, air, warmth, and sleep.

Security Needs. After physiological needs have been satisfied, the next need level that tends to dominate is safety and security. **Security needs** represent our desire to be free from danger and uncertainty. The desire to satisfy the need for safety and security often motivates people to purchase such items as medical and life insurance or a security alarm for their home or business.

security needs These represent our desire for protection from the elements and to be free from danger and uncertainty; buying decisions to support these needs could include clothing, shelter, and insurance.

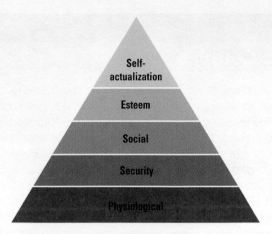

Figure 8.6 Maslow's Hierarchy of Needs Model
The forces that motivate customers to make specific buying decisions are complex. This model illustrates Maslow's hierarchy of needs.

Source: Abraham H. Maslow, Robert D. Frager (editor), and James Fadiman (editor), *Motivation and Personality,* 3rd ed. (Upper Saddle River, NJ: Pearson Education, 1987), p. 193. Reprinted and electronically reproduced by permission of Pearson Education, Inc. Upper Saddler River, New Jersey.

social needs Needs that reflect a person's desire for affection, identification with a group, and approval from others.

Social Needs.   The need to belong, or **social needs**, reflects our desire for identification with a group and approval from others. These needs help explain our continuing search for friendship, social acceptance among one's peers, and long-term business relationships.

esteem needs The desire to feel worthy in the eyes of others, to develop a sense of personal worth and adequacy or a feeling of competence and importance.

Esteem Needs.   At the fourth level of Maslow's needs hierarchy are **esteem needs**, which reflect our desire to feel worthy in the eyes of others. We seek a sense of personal worth and adequacy—a feeling of competence.[34]

self-actualization The need for self-fulfillment; a tapping of one's full potential to meet a goal; the need to be everything one is capable of being.

Self-Actualization.   Maslow defined the term **self-actualization** as a need for self-fulfillment; a tapping of one's full potential. It is the need to "be all that you can be," to have mastery over things you are doing. One goal of consultative selling is to help the customer experience self-actualization in terms of the relationship with the salesperson.

The five-level needs hierarchy model developed by Maslow is somewhat artificial in certain circumstances. At times, several of our needs interact simultaneously. Consider the business lunch where you are not only conducting business with a client but are also satisfying your need to consume food and beverages, to engage in social activities, and perhaps to seem important in your own eyes and, you hope, the eyes of your customer. However, the model does provide salespeople with a practical way of understanding which need is most likely to dominate customer behaviour in certain situations.

Group Influences That Affect Buying Decisions

group influences Forces that other people exert on customers' buying behaviour.

As noted earlier, the people around us influence our buying decisions. These **group influences** can be classified into four major areas: (1) role, (2) reference groups, (3) social class, and (4) culture and microcultures.[35] (See Fig. 8.7.) Salespeople who understand these roles and influences can develop the type of insight customers view as being valuable.

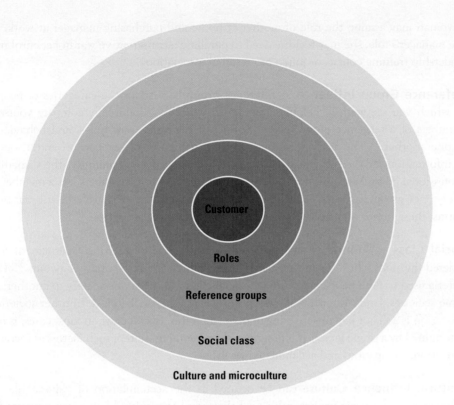

Figure 8.7 Group Influences That Affect Buying Decisions Model
To gain additional insights into customers' motivations, salespeople can study group influences that affect buying decisions.

Role Influence Throughout our lives, we occupy positions within groups, organizations, and institutions. Closely associated with each position is a **role**—a set of characteristics and expected social behaviours based on the expectations of others. All the roles we assume (e.g., student, member of the school board, our position at work) influence not only our general behaviour but also our buying behaviour. In today's society, for example,

role A set of characteristics and expected social behaviours based on the expectations of others. All the roles we assume may influence our buying behaviour.

Selling Today
Selling Across Generation Gaps

It is important to understand the context in which people from different generational groups live and work. After all, success in personal selling requires the ability to create rapport and develop trust with buyers who may differ from us. Picture yourself as a Millennial (Generation Y) who was born between 1977 and 1994. Chances are you welcome the latest high-tech communications technology and do not resent the never-ending sea of information that demands your immediate attention and response. Some of the customers you call on are members of the Baby Boomer Generation, who were born between 1946 and 1964. These individuals may welcome traditional memos, letters, phone calls, and face-to-face communications, and feel uncomfortable working in today's wireless world. Generational differences shaped by sociological, political, and economic conditions can influence our values. Dave Stein, author of *How Winners Sell*, says "Before you ever meet that prospect, understand that 'different' in terms of cross-generational selling is neither right nor wrong; it's just different."[b]

a woman may assume the role of mother at home and purchasing manager at work. In the manager's role, she may feel the need to purchase a conservative wardrobe, enrol in a leadership training course, or join a professional association.

reference group Two or more people who have well-established interpersonal communications and tend to influence the values, attitudes, and buying behaviours of one another. They act as a point of comparison and a source of information for a prospective buyer.

Reference Group Influence A **reference group** consists of the categories of people to which you see yourself belonging and with which you habitually compare yourself. Members of a reference group tend to influence the values, attitudes, and behaviours of one another.[36] The reference group may act as a point of comparison and a source of information for the individual member.[37] In the business community, the Canadian Professional Sales Association may be a reference group for its members. As a member of a reference group, each of us may observe other people in the group to establish our own norms; these norms may become a guide for our purchasing activities.

social class A group of people who share similar values, interests, and behaviours.

Social Class Influence A **social class** is one of society's relatively permanent and ordered divisions whose members share similar values, interests, and behaviours.[38] The criteria used to rank people according to social class vary from one society to another. In some societies, land ownership allows entry into a higher social class. In other societies, education is a major key to achieving upper-class status. Social class, in most cases, is not determined by a single factor. It is determined by a combination of such factors as income, education, occupation, and accumulated wealth.

culture The values, beliefs, institutions, transmitted behaviour patterns, and thoughts of a people or society.

Cultural Influence Culture can be defined as the accumulation of values, rules of behaviour, forms of expression, religious beliefs, and transmitted behaviour patterns for a people or society that shares a common language and environment. Culture tends to encourage or discourage particular behaviours and mental processes.[39] We maintain and transmit our culture chiefly through language. Culture has considerable influence on buying behaviour. Today, culture in Canada is getting more attention because of rapid increases in immigration. As cultural diversity increases, companies must re-examine their sales and marketing strategies. Within most cultures are groups whose members share value systems based on common life experiences and situations. We call such a group a **microculture**. Some microcultures, such as mature consumers, Blacks, Southeast Asians, and Aboriginal Canadians, are important market segments.[40]

microculture Value systems shared by communities based on common life experiences and situations that differ from those of the dominant society's culture.

Perception—How Customer Needs Are Formed

perception A process through which sensations are interpreted using our knowledge and experience.

Perception is the process through which sensations received through sight, hearing, touch, taste, and smell are interpreted using our knowledge and experience. Buyer behaviour is often influenced by perception.[41] When Volkswagen announced that it would build an ultra-luxury car that would sell for more than $100 000, many people questioned the merits of this decision. Could the maker of the Beetle and the Golf compete in the market segment dominated by Lexus, Mercedes Benz, Jaguar, and BMW? After only a few years on the North American market, it was discontinued, although it sold well in other markets. In one year just before it was discontinued, it sold about 140 units in Canada, even though most automobile journalists viewed it as a truly luxury car.[42] Did perception kill the Phaeton in North America?

We tend to screen out or modify stimuli, a process known as *selective attention*, for two reasons. First, we cannot possibly be conscious of all inputs at one time; just the commercial messages we see and hear each day are enough to cause sensory overload. Second, we are conditioned by our social and cultural background, and by our physical and psychological needs, to use selectivity.

Buyers may screen out or modify information presented by a salesperson if it conflicts with their previously learned attitudes or beliefs. For example, the business buyer who feels the new office furniture designs that combine individual work space will only encourage impromptu employee chitchat is apt to use selective attention when the salesperson begins discussing product features. Salespeople who can anticipate this problem of selective attention should acquire as much background information as possible before meeting with the prospect. During the first meeting with the customer, the salesperson should make every effort to build a strong relationship so that the person opens up and freely discusses personal perceptions. Salespeople who do this have accepted one of the great truisms in sales and marketing: "Facts are negotiable. Perception is rock solid."

Buying Motives

Every buying decision has a motive behind it. A **buying motive** can be thought of as an aroused need, drive, or desire that stimulates purchasing behaviour intended to satisfy the aroused need. Our perceptions influence or shape this behaviour. An understanding of buying motives provides the salesperson with the reasons why customers buy. Unfortunately, some buyers will not or cannot tell you their buying motives. A company may be planning a new product launch and wants to keep this initiative a secret. In some cases, revealing important information may make the customer feel vulnerable. And some customers may not be aware of one or more buying motives that will influence the purchase decision.[43]

> **buying motive** An aroused need, drive, or desire that initiates the buying-decision process.

As you might expect, some buying decisions are influenced by more than one buying motive. The buyer of catering services may want food of exceptional quality served quickly so that all the guests can eat together. This customer may also be quite price conscious. In this situation, the caterer should attempt to discover the **dominant buying motive (DBM)**. The DBM will have the greatest influence on the buying decision.[44] If the customer is anxious to make a good impression on guests who have discriminating food tastes, then food quality may be the dominant buying motive. Successful salespeople have adopted a product strategy that involves discovery of the buying motives that influence the purchase decision. In Chapter 10, we describe a need identification process that can be used to discover customers' buying motives.

> **dominant buying motive** The motive that has the greatest influence on a customer's buying decision.

Emotional versus Rational Buying Motives A careful study of buyer perceptions and behaviour reveals that people make buying decisions based on both emotional and rational buying motives. An **emotional buying motive** is one that prompts the prospect to act because of an appeal to some sentiment or passion. When customers buy expensive Harley-Davidson motorcycles, they are paying for much more than a high-flying "hog"; they are purchasing entry into a community of like-minded enthusiasts who share a passion for all things Harley.[45] Emotions can be powerful and often serve as the foundation of the dominant buying motive.[46] A **rational buying motive** usually appeals to the prospect's reason or judgment based on objective thought processes. Some common rational buying motives include quality, price, and availability of technical assistance.

> **emotional buying motive** A motive that prompts the prospect to act as a result of an appeal to some sentiment or passion.

> **rational buying motive** A motive that prompts the prospect to act because of an appeal to the prospect's reason or better judgment such as price, quality, and availability of technical assistance. Generally these result from an objective review of available information.

REFINED ELEGANCE.
RAW POWER.

Some of the most powerful phenomena are the most beautiful. When it comes to the all-new BMW 6 Series Gran Coupé 650i, you will discover that beauty is more than skin deep. The sleek, elegant curves of the 4-door Coupé are powerfully enhanced by the class-leading new BMW TwinPower Turbo 8 cylinder petrol engine with more power and more torque yet far lower emissions. An outstanding car that combines striking design with exceptional power, taking you from 0–100km/h in an impressive 4.6 seconds with only 199–206g CO2/km. For more information on the most exceptional phenomena visit your local BMW dealer or www.bmw.com

THE ALL-NEW BMW 6 SERIES GRAN COUPÉ.

BMW EfficientDynamics

This BMW car ad appeals to a customer's emotional buying motives.

Emotional Buying Motives.   A surprising number of purchases are guided by emotional buying motives. Recent research indicates that buying is a lot more emotional than most marketers thought. Many buyers are guided more by feelings than by logic.[47] Even technology firms sometimes rely on emotional appeals as part of their marketing strategy. Doing business in Canada, or anyplace else in the world, is never purely a rational or logical process. Recognize that there is an emotional component to every sale and tune in to the emotional cues such as body language, tone of voice, and emotive words. With the power of empathy, you can get on the same page, emotionally, as your customer.[48]

Rational Buying Motives.   A purchase based on rational buying motives is generally the result of an objective review of available information. The buyer closely examines product or service information with an attitude that is relatively free of emotion. Business buyers are most likely to be motivated by such rational buying motives as on-time delivery, financial gain, competent installation, saving of time, increased profits, reduced costs, or durability. Business buyers representing large firms, such as Research In Motion, Air Canada, and Canadian National Railways, rely on a buying process that is more formalized than the consumer buying process. Purchases made by these companies usually call for detailed product specifications, written purchase orders, and formal approval. The business buyer and the salesperson work closely during all stages of the buying process, which begins with a precise definition of the customer's problem. Salespeople who sell to business buyers spend a great deal of time gathering, interpreting, and disseminating customer-specific information.[49]

CEO Glenn Sandberg understands that in the business-to-business market, exact specifications and 24-hour support appeal to those customers who are motivated by rational buying motives.

Glenn Sandberg
President/CEO, Formax®, Inc.

Genuine Formax® tooling will save you thousands, and I can prove it.

I know the role of quality in our quest to compete at the highest level. It's why we make every effort to avoid suppliers that can save us a dime but cost us a dollar – a common problem with processors that use knock-off tooling. Did you know that a mold just 1/2 percent oversize can cost your company $20 per hour in product waste? Or that a bargain plate with inferior specifications could actually cost $1,000 per shift? That kind of money adds up fast. Genuine Formax® tooling is manufactured from the finest materials to exacting specifications and is backed by 24/7 support. These differences can save you thousands and are an important part of the value that is Formax®.

Adding Value to Your Business

Formax®

Formax, Inc., 9150 191st Street, P.O. Box 330, Mokena, Illinois 60448 USA (near Chicago)
Phone: (708) 479-3500 Fax: (708) 479-3598
EUROPE: Formax, Inc., Pelikaanweg 6, 1118 DX Schiphol-Z, The Netherlands
Phone: (+31) 20-3161616 Fax: (+31) 20-6480380
Web site: www.formaxinc.com

MEANS YOU GET MORE VALUE FOR YOUR MONEY

Patronage versus Product Buying Motives Another way to help explain buyer perceptions and behaviour is to distinguish between patronage and product buying motives. Patronage buying motives and product buying motives are learned reasons for buying. These buying motives are important because they can stimulate repeat business and referrals.

Patronage Buying Motives. A **patronage buying motive** is one that causes the prospect to buy products from one particular business. The prospect has usually had prior direct or indirect contact with the business and has judged this contact to be beneficial. In those situations where there is little or no appreciable difference between two products, patronage motives can be highly important. At a time when look-alike products are very common, these motives take on extra importance. Some typical patronage buying motives are superior service, complete selection of products, competence of sales representatives, and ability to buy online.

patronage buying motive A motive that causes the prospect to buy a product from one particular company rather than another. Typical patronage buying motives include superior service, attractive decor, product selection, and competence of the salesperson.

Strategic Initiatives Identified	Need Awareness	Evaluation of Solutions	Resolution of Problems	Purchase	Implementation
Present and/or design unique strengths that fit the strategic initiative.	Partner with customers to understand unique needs in new and improved ways.	Configure or adapt superior solutions to unique needs.	Provide assistance and advice to overcome problems and provide solutions.	Adapt and suggest effective methods to purchase and enjoy solutions.	Assist and/or train customers in maximum satisfaction from purchase.

Figure 8.8 Creating Value Throughout the Buying Process Model
A sample list of methods for creating value throughout each of the steps in the buying process. Specific methods should be created after arriving at a careful understanding of the unique needs of the individual customer.

product buying motive A motive that causes the prospect to buy one particular product brand or label over another. Typical product buying motives include brand, quality, price, and design or engineering preference.

Product Buying Motives. A **product buying motive** is one that leads a prospect to purchase one product in preference to another. Interestingly enough, this decision is sometimes made without direct comparison between competing products; the buyer simply feels that one product is superior to another. Numerous buying motives trigger prospects to select one product over another, including brand, quality, price, and design or engineering preference.

It is hard to imagine how salespeople can create value for customers unless they understand the customer's buying motives. Figure 8.8 provides various examples of how salespeople can put this understanding into creating value at different stages of the buying process.

To fully understand the customer's buying strategy, the salesperson must conduct a careful needs discovery or assessment. This is done by asking appropriate questions, listening to the customer's responses, and making careful observations. Chapter 11 provides in-depth coverage of these important adaptive selling skills.

Global Business Insight

Doing Business in France

The French people are very proud of their history, language, social systems, and customs. They expect visitors to respect the many things that make their country unique. Preparation for a business trip to France may take a little extra time.

■ Learn basic French and use it often. Although most French businesspeople speak English, some will not admit it.

■ Introductions should be made by someone (an attorney, banker, or friend) known to the person with whom you want to do business. French people tend to be cautious when meeting someone new.

■ Be prepared to conduct business over meals at nice restaurants. A business lunch might last for two hours. The French rarely invite business guests to their homes.

■ French businesspeople are reluctant to take risks, so negotiations may take a long time. Be well prepared to discuss the merits of your product but avoid the hard sell.

REVIEWING KEY CONCEPTS

- Discuss the meaning of a customer strategy.

  The importance of developing a *customer strategy* was introduced in this chapter. This type of planning is necessary to ensure maximum customer responsiveness. Buying procedures and policies can vary greatly from one buyer to another. If a salesperson does not learn how the buyer plans to make the purchase, then there is the strong possibility that the selling process will be out of alignment with the customer's buying process.

- Explain the difference between consumer and business buyers.

  We looked at business buyer behaviour compared to consumer buyer behaviour. There are three types of business buying situations: straight rebuy, new-task buy, and the modified rebuy. Systems selling is a common business buying strategy. Three types of consumer buying situations were defined: habitual buying decisions, variety-seeking buying decisions, and complex buying decisions.

- Understand the importance of alignment between the selling process and the customer's buying process.

  Customers make buying decisions in many ways, so it would be inappropriate to view the buying process as a uniform pattern of decision making. However, there is a common decision-making model that most buyers apply to their unique circumstances. The typical stages in the buying decision process are needs awareness, evaluation of solutions, resolution of problems, purchase, and implementation.

- Understand the buying process of the transactional, consultative, and strategic alliance buyer.

  Three value-creation selling approaches that appeal to certain types of customers were discussed: the transactional process buyer, the consultative process buyer, and the strategic alliance process buyer. The consultative process buyer offers the greatest challenge to most salespeople.

- Discuss the various influences that shape customer buying decisions.

  Buyer behaviour is influenced in part by individual (physical and psychological) needs. Maslow's popular model ranks these needs. There are also a number of group influences that shape our psychological needs to various degrees. Buyer behaviour is influenced by the roles we assume, reference groups, social class, and culture. *Perception* is defined as the process of selecting, organizing, and interpreting information inputs to produce meaning. We discussed *emotional* and *rational buying motives* and compared patronage and product motives.

Key Terms

Review Questions

1. According to the Strategic/Consultative Selling Model, what are the three prescriptions for the development of a successful customer strategy?

2. List and describe the three most common types of business-to-business buying situations.

3. Describe the five major steps in the typical buying process.

4. List and describe three value-creation selling approaches that appeal to various types of customers.

5. According to the buyer resolution theory, a purchase is made only after the prospect has made five buying decisions. What are they?

6. Explain how Maslow's hierarchy of needs affects buyer behaviour.

7. Describe four group influences that affect buyer behaviour.

8. What is meant by the term *perception*?

9. Distinguish between emotional and rational buying motives.

10. J. D. Power, founder of J. D. Power and Associates, says, "We define quality as what the customer wants." Do you agree or disagree with his observations? Explain your answer.

Application Exercises

1. Select several advertisements from a trade magazine. Analyze each one and determine which rational buying motives the advertiser is appealing to. Explain whether these advertisements also appeal to emotional buying motives. Then select a magazine that is aimed at a particular consumer group—for example, *Chatelaine*, *Canadian Business*, or *Better Homes and Gardens*. Study the advertisements and determine what buying motives they appeal to.

2. The $50 000 Hyundai Genesis 4.6 V8, which entered the North American market as a 2010 model (in 2009), is a far cry from the popular Elantra. Hyundai's new flagship model was designed to compete with Lexus, Mercedes Benz, Cadillac, and BMW. The Genesis is positioned as another choice in the luxury-car market. Will potential customers accept the Genesis as a true luxury car? Will customer perceptions play a role in acceptance of this new model?

3. J. D. Power and Associates is a global marketing information services firm that helps businesses and consumers make better decisions through credible customer-based information. The company provides an unbiased source

of marketing information based on opinions of consumers. Visit **www.jdpower.com/ca** and become familiar with the type of information services offered. View some of the studies done on Canadian consumer satisfaction and be prepared to discuss interesting findings in class.

4. Assume your college or university is considering buying 100 new PCs for student labs throughout the campus. Describe who you think will be involved in the buying centre (by role), and what you think the motives might be for each of them.

5. Assume your college or university is considering replacing its mainframe computer. Its current mainframe computer is now 15 years old and has been creating problems for some time. The cost of a modern replacement is estimated at between $1.5 and $2 million. Will this be a new-task buy, a modified rebuy, or a straight rebuy? If you were a salesperson selling mainframe computers, how would you treat this opportunity? Explain.

ROLE-PLAY EXERCISE

In this role play, you will assume the role of a salesperson working at a clothing store. The inventory includes a wide range of business professional clothing such as suits, sport coats, dress shirts, and accessories; the store also offers a full range of business casual clothing. A member of your class will assume the role of a customer who visits your store for the purpose of buying clothing for work. He or she is about to graduate and will start work at a new job in approximately two weeks. In addition to clothing, your store offers complete alteration services and credit plans. During the role play, you should develop a relationship with the customer using strategies discussed in previous chapters and determine the customer's needs with questions, attentive listening, and observation.

Reality Selling Today Video Case Problem

Ashley Pineda, featured at the beginning of this chapter, is a new home sales representative for the PulteGroup (see website at **www.pultegroupinc.com**). The company engages in the homebuilding and financial services businesses. Its homebuilding business includes the acquisition and development of land primarily for residential purposes and the construction of housing on such land targeted for first-time, first and second move-up, and active adult home buyers. As of March 31, 2010, its homebuilding operations offered homes for sale in 842 communities. The company's financial services business consists of mortgage banking and title operations. It arranges financing through the origination of mortgage loans for its homebuyers, sells such loans and the related servicing rights, provides title insurance policies as an agent, and provides examination and closing services to its home buyers. PulteGroup offers a one-stop shopping experience for prospective customers. Sales reps help clients to finance their homes (with Pulte Mortgage) and to close their homes with PGP Title. One of PulteGroup's key strengths is the ability to provide customers with an exceptional home-buying experience and, ultimately, satisfaction with their homes. Being able to offer everything under one roof and walk the customers through each step of the entire home buying process makes their home-buying experience very comfortable.

Ashley Pineda sells the company's Centex product line, which is primarily geared toward first-time home buyers by delivering quality homes at an affordable price. Ashley describes a typical selling process as follows: When a customer walks in the door, she engages with them by welcoming them and building rapport. The company provides its sales reps with a consultative questioning strategy that allows the reps to smoothly walk the customer through the buying process. The questions, for example, may ask customers about their location preferences or what they consider most important when they buy a home. Ashley asks these types of questions to help her guide first-time home buyers through the variety of different homes available, ranging from one- to two-storey homes, from three to five bedrooms, from 1183 to 2600 square feet, and a price range from $95 000 to $150 000. Across various options, the customers are asked how well the different options align with their needs and wants.

The customers are also given the opportunity to touch and feel their future homes. This process typically involves a car tour through the neighbourhood, where they are shown the different homes' features and colours, and walk-throughs of both completed homes and homes under construction. The latter type helps to demonstrate the quality of Pulte's workmanship, the insulation, and the energy efficiency of a home. Altogether this allows potential customers to feel comfortable with the construction of the homes and the home-buying process.

In the next step, Ashley typically talks about financing issues with first-time homebuyers, such as the amounts of their monthly payments and potential down payments. PulteGroup equips Ashley with the knowledge to be able to professionally provide that information and make customers feel comfortable with the financial scenario involved in owning their first home. Once the customer is comfortable with the financial scenario, Ashley and her customer can move forward toward opening the agreement to buy a home. Generally, when you sign a contract, you are opening the agreement to take the next steps These steps include financing, completing construction, and ultimately closing on the home and moving in. That entire process typically lasts from 45 days to approximately four months. (See the chapter opener on page 170 and Reality Selling Today Role Play 6 in Appendix 1 on page 441 for more information.)

Questions

1. Which of the prescriptions of the Strategic/Consultative Selling Model (see Figure 8.1 on page 172) does Ashley Pineda follow? Please explain.

2. How does Ashley elicit the needs and preferences of the prospective customers? What questions does she ask?

3. Outline a typical buying process that a middle-class couple with two young kids goes through in a first-time home buy. What questions and problems might arise at different stages of the buying process?

4. What might be key influencing factors for the couple's home-buying decisions? To what extent are rational and emotional buying motives important?

5. Put yourself in the position of Ashley Pineda. How can she create value at different stages of the young couple's buying process? Give examples.

6. Ashley sells new homes in the company's Centex product line, which is primarily geared toward first-time home buyers. One of her job responsibilities is to monitor competition. Who might be direct and indirect competitors that Ashley should watch?

Chapter 9
Developing and Qualifying a Prospect Base

Learning Objectives

After studying this chapter, you should be able to

1   Discuss the importance of developing a prospect base.

2   Identify and assess important sources of prospects.

3   Describe criteria for qualifying prospects.

4   Explain common methods of collecting and organizing prospect information.

5   Describe the steps in managing a prospect base.

 Reality Selling Today Video Series

Salesforce.com offers hosted applications that manage customer information for sales, marketing, and customer support, providing clients with a rapidly deployable alternative to buying and maintaining enterprise software. The company's applications are used by more than 90 000 clients for generating sales leads, maintaining customer information, and tracking customer interactions. Dave Levitt (pictured above) joined Salesforce.com as a regional sales manager in 2008 and leads a team of six sales representatives.

With prior experience as a direct salesperson in the enterprise software industry, Levitt has profound knowledge about how to approach and qualify prospects in his business. For his sales representatives, there are various ways to get in touch with potential customers: Some prospects will inquire at the company's website, and that will be forwarded directly to the sales representative so that she can follow up. Direct-response advertising, trade shows, or customer referrals can also be important sources of prospects. Besides having the customers reach out to them, salespeople at Salesforce.com also try to utilize knowledge on the company's many customers. For example, if the sales representative has a chemical company as one of his prospects, he will take a look at the CRM system and ask: What other chemical companies are current customers and how did they benefit from using our services? Then the representative could use reference selling and thus demonstrate credibility to the prospect.

According to Dave Levitt, the key to successful selling is empathy—i.e., the ability to understand the customer's business so that the sales representative can identify areas where he can add value. Levitt points out, "We cannot count on the customer to know

what we offer, because our services can be applied in many different ways. The burden is on the sales representative to use his industry and product knowledge to probe and uncover opportunities, and then to qualify and pursue them accordingly." Hence, the salesperson has to be able to look at accounts holistically, understand what the real business drivers are at a company, and then apply Salesforce.com's service solutions in different areas.

Account-based software vendors such as Salesforce, NetSuite, and Oracle Siebel are helping companies develop effective customer relationship management (CRM) systems. These systems are at the heart of every successful one-to-one marketing initiative.

PROSPECTING—AN INTRODUCTION

prospecting A systematic process of identifying potential customers.

prospect A potential customer who meets the qualification criteria established by you or your company.

GERHARD GSCHWANDTNER, EDITOR OF *Selling Power*, SAYS, "THE MAIN PURPOSE OF A SALESPERSON is not to make sales, but to create customers."[1] Identifying potential customers is an important aspect of the customer strategy. In the terminology of personal selling, this process is called **prospecting**. A potential customer, or **prospect**, is someone who meets the qualification criteria established by you or your company.

Finding prospects who can make the decision to purchase is not as easy as it sounds. This is especially true in business-to-business sales. In many situations, the salesperson must make the sales presentation to multiple decision makers. One of these decision makers might be the technical expert who wants an answer to the question: Does the product meet the company's specifications? Another decision maker may be the person who will actually use the product. The employee who will use the forklift truck you are selling may be involved in the purchase decision. Of course, there is often a "purse-string" decision maker who has the ultimate authority to release funds for the purchase. During periods of economic uncertainty, the decision-making process often moves upward. It is sometimes difficult to make connections with upper-level executives. One solution is to plan a joint sales call involving a higher-level executive from your own company.[2]

The goal of prospecting is to build a qualified **prospect base** made up of current customers and potential customers. Building a prospect base involves the use of CRM software to monitor movement of the customer through the sales process. Many successful companies find that current customers account for a large percentage of their sales. Every effort is made to devise and implement a customer strategy that builds, fosters, nurtures, and extends relationships with established customers. CRM software is critical to building this kind of partnership with a large customer base.[3]

prospect base A list of current and potential customers.

Importance of Prospecting

Every salesperson must cope with customer attrition—that is, the inevitable loss of customers over a period of time, which can be attributed to a variety of causes. Unless new prospects are found to replace lost customers, a salesperson will eventually face a reduction in income and possible loss of employment. Paul Tindall of Toronto-based Coaching Works says, "Top performers prospect consistently. Low performers don't."[4] To better understand the significance of prospecting, let us examine a few common causes of customer attrition.

1. *The customer may have a one-time need or there is an extended period of time between purchases.* Because of this, CB Richard Ellis's Susanna Rosas realizes new prospects for commercial real estate must be continually added to her prospect base.

2. *The customer may move to a new location outside the salesperson's territory.* The Canadian population is very mobile. This cause of attrition is especially common in the retail and service areas and is a major issue experienced by Tom James Clothiers's Alex Homer with many of his successful upwardly mobile clients.

3. *A firm may go out of business or merge with another company.* In some areas of business, the failure rate is quite high. In recent years we have witnessed a record number of mergers, which has caused massive changes in purchasing plans.

4. *A loyal buyer or purchasing agent may leave the position because of promotion, retirement, resignation, or serious illness.* The replacement may prefer to buy from someone else.

5. *Sales are lost to the competition.* In some cases, the competition offers more value. The added value may take the form of better quality, a better price, a stronger relationship, better service, or some combination of these factors.

Some studies reveal that the average company loses 15 to 20 percent of its customers every year. Depending on the type of selling, this figure might be higher or lower. Clearly, many customers are lost for reasons beyond the salesperson's control. If salespeople want to keep their earnings at a stable level, they will need to develop new customers.

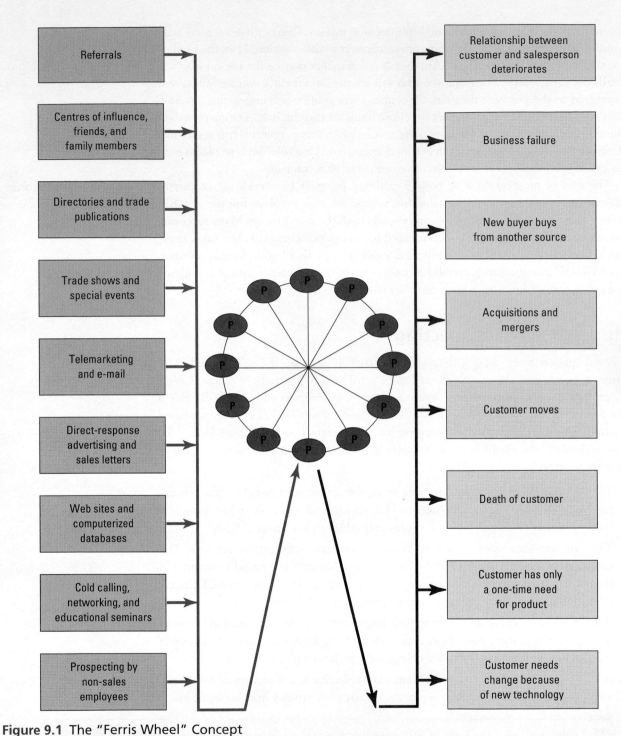

Figure 9.1 The "Ferris Wheel" Concept

The "Ferris wheel" concept, which is aimed at supplying an ongoing list of prospects, is part of world sales record holder Joe Girard's customer strategy.

The boxes on the left side of the figure, from top to bottom, read: Referrals; Centres of influence, friends, and family members; Directories and trade publications; Trade shows and special events; Telemarketing and e-mail; Direct-response advertising and sales letters; Web sites and computerized databases; Cold calling, networking, and educational seminars; Prospecting by non-sales employees.

The boxes on the right side of the figure, from top to bottom, read: Relationship between customer and salesperson deteriorates; Business failure; New buyer buys from another source; Acquisitions and mergers; Customer moves; Death of customer; Customer has only a one-time need for product; Customer needs change because of new technology.

Joe Girard, once recognized by the *Guinness Book of Records* as the world's greatest salesperson, used the "Ferris wheel" concept to illustrate the relationship between prospecting and the loss of customers due to attrition.[5] As people get off the Ferris wheel, the operator fills their seats one at a time, moves the wheel a little, and continues this process until all the original riders have left the wheel and new ones have come aboard (Fig. 9.1). In reality, of course, established customers do not come and go this fast. With the passing of time, however, many customers will be replaced.

PROSPECTING REQUIRES PLANNING

PROSPECTING SHOULD BE VIEWED AS A SYSTEMATIC PROCESS OF LOCATING POTENTIAL customers. Some prospecting efforts can be integrated easily into a regular sales call. Progressive marketers do three things to improve the quality of their prospecting efforts:

1. *Increase the number of people who board the Ferris wheel.* You want to see a continuous number of prospects board the Ferris wheel because they are the source of sales opportunities. If the number of potential prospects declines sharply, the number of sales closed will also decline.

2. *Improve the quality of the prospects who board the Ferris wheel.* Companies often establish quality standards that ensure a steady supply of prospects with high profit potential. For example, some companies focus their prospecting efforts on consultative process buyers. These are prospects who often lack need awareness and need help evaluating possible solutions.

3. *Shorten the sales cycle by quickly determining which of the new prospects are qualified prospects—qualified as to need, authority to buy, ability to pay, and willingness to purchase the product.* Gerhard Gschwandtner says, "Time is the ultimate scorekeeper in the game of selling." He points out that many salespeople do not meet their sales goals because they do not quickly qualify new prospects.[6] Later in this chapter we will examine qualifying practices and discuss how to shorten the sales cycle with sales force automation methods.

Prospecting Plans Must Be Assessed Often

In today's dynamic, ever-changing marketplace, prospecting plans must be monitored continuously. Some prospecting techniques that worked well in the past may become ineffective because of changing market conditions. Midwest Training Institute, a firm that helps companies improve their production and sales efficiency, experienced a dramatic sales decline during the first quarter of the year. This decline came after years of steady sales increases. Joel Pecoraro, president of the company, initiated a thorough investigation and discovered that his sales staff were relying primarily on one prospecting approach that was no longer successful: The salespeople were calling established customers. Pecoraro designed an incentive program that rewarded salespeople who adopted new prospecting techniques, such as attending an association meeting where the salesperson could meet potential prospects or speaking at a meeting attended by persons who might need the services offered by Midwest Training Institute.[7]

SOURCES OF PROSPECTS

EVERY SALESPERSON MUST DEVELOP A PROSPECTING SYSTEM SUITED TO A PARTICULAR selling situation. There are several sources of prospects, and each should be carefully examined.

- Referrals
- Centres of influence, friends, and family
- Directories
- Trade publications
- Trade shows and special events
- Telemarketing and email
- Direct response advertising and sales letters
- Websites
- Computerized databases
- Cold calling
- Networking
- Educational seminars
- Prospecting by non-sales employees

Referrals

referral A prospect who has been recommended by a current customer or by someone who is familiar with the product or service.

The use of referrals as a prospecting approach has been successful in a wide range of selling situations. In most cases, referral leads result in higher close rates, larger sales, and shorter sales cycles. A **referral** is a prospect who has been recommended by a current customer or by someone who is familiar with the product. Satisfied customers, business acquaintances, and even prospects who do not buy can often recommend the names of persons who might benefit from purchasing the product. Liberty Mutual's Marcus Smith realizes that customers are more likely to give a referral if they perceive value in the solution he offers. When you build value into your sales process, you increase the odds that the customer will give you a referral. Jim Domanski, CEO of Teleconcepts Consulting of Kanata, Ontario, says that when you have a referral, there is an explicit or implicit endorsement of you, your company, and your product by the source.[8]

Endless Chain Referrals One approach to obtaining referrals, called the endless chain referral, is easy to use because it fits naturally into most sales presentations. A salesperson selling long-term health care insurance might ask, "Miss Chen, who do you know who might be interested in our insurance plan?" This open-ended question gives the person the freedom to recommend several prospects and is less likely to be answered with no response. Be sure to use your reference's name when you contact the new prospect—"Mary Chen suggested that I call you. . . ."

Referral Letters and Cards The referral letter method is a variation of the endless chain technique. In addition to requesting the names of prospects, the salesperson asks the customer to prepare a note or letter of introduction that can be delivered to the

Your request for a referral is more likely to receive a positive response if made after you have built a strong, trusting relationship. In most cases referral leads result in higher close rates, larger sales, and shorter sales cycles.

potential customer. The correspondence is an actual testimonial prepared by a satisfied customer. Some companies use a referral card to introduce the salesperson. The preprinted card has a place for your customer to sign the new prospect's name and his or her own name, and can be used as part of the sales presentation.

Within the field of personal selling, there is not complete agreement regarding the timing of the referral request. Some sales training programs encourage salespeople to request the referral immediately after closing the sale. Others point out that if you are working with a new customer, it takes time to earn the customer's trust. The customer may feel there is a risk involved in giving you referrals. Once you have built a strong, trusting relationship with the customer, referral requests are more likely to receive a positive response.[9]

Referral Organizations Some salespeople have found that membership in a referral organization is an effective way to obtain good leads. Business Network International (BNI) is one of the largest business networking organizations, with over 3600 chapters worldwide (**www.bni.com**). BNI offers its members the opportunity to share ideas, contacts, and referrals.[10] In addition, some local clubs offer referrals as a member benefit.

Centres of Influence, Friends, and Family Members

The centre-of-influence method involves establishing a relationship with a well-connected, influential person who is willing to provide information about potential prospects. This person may not make buying decisions but has influence on other people who do. To illustrate, consider the challenge facing Gary Schneider, creator of a powerful software product that would help small farmers optimize their crop selection. After spending several years developing the product, Gary and his wife began selling it one copy at a time. During one cold call on a major crop insurer, Gary met a senior researcher who immediately saw the benefits of his product. This respected researcher was in a position to influence buying decisions at his company and to provide prospect information for other crop insurers.[11]

A person who is new to the field of selling often uses friends and family members as sources of information about potential customers. It is only natural to contact people we know. In many cases, these people have contacts with a wide range of potential buyers.

Directories

Directories can help salespeople search out new prospects and determine their buying potential. A list of some of the more popular national directories is provided here.

Canadian Business Resource, published by Canadian Newspaper Services International, maintains a database of 2500 of Canada's largest firms and all 3500 firms listed on the TSX and TSX Venture exchanges. It also maintains more than 40 000 contact names that are downloadable to your contact management software.

Canadian Key Business Directory, available from Dun & Bradstreet Canada, lists and profiles more than 20 000 of Canada's largest companies and maintains more than 60 000 key contact names.

Canadian Trade Index, owned by Owen Media Partners, lists more than 100 000 industrial companies in Canada and more than 50 000 searchable product headings.

ProFile Canada, another Owen Media Partners company, maintains an online database of more than 1 million Canadian businesses. It advertises its database—see **www.profilecanada.com**—as having "the greatest depth of free information on individual companies found on any website in Canada."

Frasers.com provides a comprehensive online directory and search tool for Canadian manufacturers, industrial distributors, and their products and services. It also lists international companies that sell in the Canadian marketplace.

Scott's Directories publishes separate directories for corporate (140 000 manufacturers, distributors, banks, law firms, construction companies, etc.), medical (100 000 doctors, dentists, hospitals, etc.), government (federal, provincial, and municipal), associations (10 000 listings), schools (16 000 colleges, universities, private, Native, special needs, etc.), and residential (12 million listings, available by segment). There are also international directories.

Polk City Directories provide detailed information on 14 million Canadian and U.S. businesses, including 210 million consumers, 13 million executives and professionals, and 75 million homeowners. Polk directories can often be obtained from local government or chamber of commerce offices or seen at your local public library. Polk directories are available in print, on CD-ROM, and online.

There are hundreds of additional directories covering national, regional, and local business and industrial firms. Some directories are free, while others must be purchased for a nominal fee. One of the most useful sources of free information are telephone directories, most of which have a classified section that groups businesses and professions by category (e.g., Yellow Pages).

If you are involved in the sale of products in international markets, International Trade Canada offers several services to assist you, such as the Canadian Trade Commissioner Service. Canada has trade commissions in more than 125 cities throughout the world, which can provide such essential services as market intelligence and identification of potential customers, suppliers, or distributors and agents. Another valuable resource is the Export Development Corporation, a Crown corporation that helps Canadian exporters compete throughout the world. The corporation provides a wide range of financial and risk management services, and country and market information on most countries where Canadians sell. On its website (**www.edc.ca**), you can also view Canadian export performance data by country and view country economic and credit summaries.

Trade Publications

Trade publications provide a status report on every major industry. If you are a sales representative employed by one of the huge food wholesalers that supply supermarkets, then you will benefit from a monthly review of *Canadian Grocer* magazine. Each month, this trade publication reports on trends in the retail food industry, as well as new products, problems, innovations, and related information. Trade journals such as *Women's Wear Daily*, *Home Furnishings*, *Pulp & Paper Canada*, *Purchasing b2b*, *Industrial Distribution*, and *Canadian Underwriter* are additional examples of publications that might help salespeople identify prospects.

Global Business Insight

Doing Business in Germany

Germany represents the world's third largest economy and is an important Canadian trading partner. If you are a salesperson planning a business trip to Germany, keep in mind that there is greater formality in the German business community.

■ Germany has been described as a "low-context" culture in which words carry most of the information. Messages tend to be explicit and direct. In this culture, negotiations (verbal or written) tend to be explicit in defining terms of the agreement. In comparison, China is a high-context culture in which exact phrasing and the verbal part of the messages tend to be less significant than your relationship with the other person.

■ There is a strong emphasis on punctuality, so avoid being late for appointments. Germans tend to make appointments far in advance.

■ Lunch is the most common meal for business meetings. Dining etiquette in Germany involves eating continental style—holding the fork in the left hand continually and the knife in the right hand.

■ The sales presentation should include data and empirical evidence that support your proposal. Brochures and other printed information should be serious and detailed, not flashy.[a]

Research studies indicate that it is much easier to identify good prospects and actually close sales at a trade show.

Trade Shows and Special Events

A trade show is a large exhibit of products that are, in most cases, common to one industry, such as electronics or office equipment. The prospects walk into the booth or exhibit and talk with those who represent the exhibitor. In some cases, sales personnel invite existing customers and prospects to attend trade shows where they will have an opportunity to demonstrate their newest products.

Research studies indicate that it is much easier to identify good prospects and actually close sales at a trade show. In most cases, fewer sales calls are needed to close a sale if the prospect was qualified at a trade show. Once a trade show contact has been identified and judged to be a qualified lead, information regarding the lead should be carefully recorded. When a prospect enters a Xerox Corporation booth, a salesperson uses a few questions to qualify the lead and types the answers into an on-screen form. Xerox uses software developed by NewLeads to record and process data obtained from prospects who have been qualified by a salesperson working in the booth.[12] Special events—such as a hockey game, a golf tournament, a reception for a dignitary, or a charity event—are also great sources for prospects. Bentley Motor Cars invited a number of potential clients to the famous Le Mans 24-hour endurance race, where prospects watched the Bentley race car compete while sipping champagne. In Canada, charity events serve as a venue for cultivating wealthy clientele who can afford a Bentley automobile.[13]

Telemarketing and Email

Telemarketing is the practice of marketing goods and services through telephone contact. It is an integral part of many modern sales and marketing campaigns. One use of telemarketing is to identify prospects. A financial services company used telemarketing to identify prospects for its customized equipment leasing packages. Leads were given to salespeople for consideration. Telemarketing also can be used to quickly and inexpensively qualify prospects for follow-up. Some marketers use the telephone to verify sales leads generated by direct mail, advertisements, or some other method.

telemarketing The practice of marketing goods and services through telephone contact.

Although the response rate for sales emails is quite low, they have proven to be a source of leads for many salespeople. Ideally, sales emails should be sent only to existing customers or others who have "opted in" to receive them. When you use *broadcast* emails, there is a risk that you will be blocked and end up on a spammer blacklist. Online sales specialist Mac MacIntosh says those who use broadcast emails should stay within anti-spam laws by giving recipients the right to opt out of future emails.[14]

Putting your company name in the subject line can help get emails opened by prospects who are familiar with it. Some salespeople send newsletters to current and prospective customers. Lee Levitt, director of sales for software consultant IDC, sends a monthly newsletter to current IDC clients and professionals at large technology companies. He wants to expose them to services his company can provide. Levitt says, "The key is to offer something of value they can quickly digest and use in day-to-day work."[15]

Direct-Response Advertising and Sales Letters

Many advertisements invite the reader to send for a free booklet or brochure that provides detailed information about the product or service. In the category of business-to-business marketing, advertising has the greatest power to generate inquiries. Some firms distribute postage-free response cards (also known as *bingo cards*) to potential buyers. Recipients are encouraged to complete and mail the cards if they desire additional information. In some cases, the name of the person making the inquiry is given to a local sales representative for further action.

Sales letters, sent by email or by Canada Post, can easily be incorporated into a prospecting plan. The prospecting sales letter is sent to persons who are in a position to make a buying decision. Shortly after the letter has been mailed (i.e., three or four days), the prospect is called and asked for an appointment. The call begins with a reference to the sales letter. To make the letter stand out, some salespeople include a promotional item. As noted in Chapter 6, all sales letters must be written with care. To get results, sales letters must quickly get the reader's attention.

Websites

Thousands of companies and businesspeople have established websites on the World Wide Web. A **website** is a collection of web pages maintained by a single person or organization. It is accessible to anyone with a computer and a modem. Large firms, such as Century 21, maintain websites that feature 20 to 30 web pages. Websites frequently offer prospects

website A collection of web pages maintained by a single person or organization.

Locating Prospects with Social Media

Whether seeking business or consumer prospects, a number of social media channels are available to salespeople. The choice of a channel, such as a website, blog, Twitter, or Facebook, depends upon the time the salesperson can commit to the social media prospecting effort.

Websites and Blogs. With websites and blogs, it is important to create a clear identity. Similar to a positioning statement, the appearance and writing style of your Web presence must be designed to be appealing and interesting to your prospective customer visitors. It is well established that visitors expect to find information or entertainment on your site, not the hard sell. It is important to keep your content fresh and reply rapidly to all comments received, which can make this channel time-consuming.

Social Media Sites. Participating in social media sites such as LinkedIn, Facebook, and Twitter can take less time because you can join in a conversation when you wish. LinkedIn is especially attractive to sales professionals. It offers information and tools that can help you conduct research, find new customers, and expand your business contacts and prospects. Much of it is free; however, you may have to pay a subscription fee for some of the advanced features. Search or use an online service to find communities of users with characteristics similar to your best prospect profile. When you join in conversations, you will be influencing people most likely to become customers. When time permits, salespeople also participate in groups that discuss their kinds of products.

Start Your Own Group. If you cannot find a social media community that meets your criteria, start your own. For example, **jmagroup.com** describes the sales representative who started **tweetandgreet.com**. The representative emailed well-known online marketing professionals and Twitter followers, asking them questions about their cars and their memories of them. The excellent responses and stories received provided the representative's site with interesting and attractive content that appealed to potential car buyers and increased the likelihood the website will be cited by others.

Rules of Participation. The rules of participation are to create value with short tips and techniques you've learned as a product/industry expert. Use word-of-mouth promotion by asking readers to share your message with others. When performed effectively, those looking for information about your topic are more likely to follow you and turn to you when it's time to buy.

the opportunity to acquire product information that can help them make a buying decision. Financial services companies describe home financing and refinancing options. Salesforce.com's website provides detailed descriptions of Salesforce.com products and solutions. When someone clicks on a web page and requests information, they will likely become a prospect. Some websites offer an incentive to leave contact information.

Computerized Databases

With the aid of electronic data processing, salespeople can match product features with the needs of potential customers quickly and accurately. In many situations, a firm will develop its own computerized database. In other cases, it is more economical to purchase the database from a company that specializes in collection of such information. One example is Salesgenie, offered by infogroup. With the aid of this software, you can easily obtain lead generation and prospect selection information for different market segments. Gary Hand, president of Alliance Security Systems, needs to keep his sales team supplied with plenty of leads. Salesgenie provides him with a list of prospects by geographical location and by the value of each house. Salesgenie handles these two classifications easily and has therefore become a major time saver.[16] Salesgenie can provide salespeople

*info*CANADA is just one of several companies that maintain databases of consumers and businesses and provide salespeople with an excellent way to prospect for customers.

with leads in such diverse market segments as medical services, engineering, architecture, agriculture, and education.

OneSource, another product available through infogroup, provides in-depth prospect information needed by sales personnel involved in complex, long-cycle sales. Let's assume you are part of a sales team that wants to do business with a group of companies that appear to be highly qualified. OneSource will provide data needed to make sales projections for a specific geographic area and industry type. The real strength of OneSource comes in high-value sales, where a thorough understanding of prospects is needed for the first sales call.[17]

With the aid of a personal computer (PC), salespeople can develop their own detailed customer files. As newer PCs provide expanded storage capacity at lower prices than in the past, salespeople can accumulate a great deal of information about individual customers and use this information to personalize the selling process. For example, a PC can help an independent insurance agent maintain a comprehensive record for each policyholder. As each client's status changes (marriage, birth of children, etc.), the record can easily be updated. With the aid of an up-to-date database, the agent can quickly identify prospects for various existing and new policy options.

Cold Calling

With some products, cold call prospecting is an effective approach to prospect identification. In **cold calling**, the salesperson selects a group of people who may or may not be actual prospects and then calls—by phone or personal visit—on each one. For example, the sales representative for a wholesale medical supply firm might call on every hospital in a given community, assuming that each one is a potential customer. Many new salespeople must rely on cold calling because they are less likely to get appointments through referrals.

Edward Jones Corporation, a financial services company, is a strong supporter of cold calling. Sales representatives knock on doors and introduce themselves with a friendly, professional message: "Hi, my name is Brad Ledwith. I represent the Edward Jones Corporation, and we sell financial services. We're a unique firm because we try to do all of our business face-to-face. I just wanted to stop by and let you know that I've opened up a Jones office in the area and to find out if it's okay to contact you when I have an investment idea."[18] Sales representatives such as Brad Ledwith connect personally with members of their communities.

Successful cold calls do not happen spontaneously. Some strategic thinking and planning must precede telephone calls and personal visits. Who do you contact? What do you say during the first few seconds? In order to appear confident and competent, carefully develop your opening remarks. If you appear to be nervous or unprepared, the prospect will assume you lack experience. Many salespeople who make cold-call phone calls prepare a well-polished script. The script helps keep you on message and guarantees you will not leave out important information.[19]

Canadian sales trainer and coach Steven J. Schwartz suggests that cold calls can be turned into hot calls through a telephone contact system that uses good call planning, strategic scripting, and effective script delivery. His book *How to Make Hot Cold Calls* explains his system, and his website offers a number of personal diagnostic tools for salespeople. (Visit **www.hotcoldcalls.com** and click on "Toolbox.")

Networking

One of the most complete books on networking is *Dig Your Well Before You're Thirsty* by Harvey Mackay. He says, "If I had to name the single characteristic shared by all the truly successful people I've met over a lifetime, I'd say it's the ability to create and nurture a network of contacts."[20] Networking skills are of special importance to new salespeople, who cannot turn to a large group of satisfied customers for referrals and leads. Professionals (accountants, lawyers, consultants, etc.), entrepreneurs, managerial personnel, and customer service representatives must develop networking skills. Networking skills are also

cold calling Method of prospecting in which the salesperson selects a group of people who may or may not be actual prospects, and then calls—by phone or personal visit—on each one.

With computers, salespeople can accumulate a great deal of information about individual customers and use this information to add value during the selling process.

of critical importance to job seekers because at any given time about 80 percent of all available jobs are not posted in the classifieds or on Internet job boards.[21]

In simple terms, **networking** is the art of making and using contacts: people meeting people and profiting from the connections. Barry Siskind, an Ontario-based consultant and author of *Making Contact*, sees networking as a three-act process. In act one, you must be able to approach someone and engage them in conversation. Act two is when you "net-chat," a term Siskind uses to describe the technique of collecting and giving information and finding out as much as you can about the other person in the shortest time possible. Act three is where you disengage. Although networking is one of the premier prospecting methods, some salespeople are reluctant to seek referrals in this manner. In addition, many salespeople do not use effective networking practices. Skilled networkers suggest the following guidelines for identifying good referrals:

networking The practice of making and using contacts. It involves people meeting people and profiting from the connections.

1. *Meet as many people as you can.* Networking can take place on an airplane, at a Rotary Club meeting, at a trade show, or at a professional association meeting. Don't make the mistake of limiting your networking activities to business contacts. The term **social network** refers to your set of *direct and indirect contacts*. An indirect contact might be the brother of a close friend. The brother works for a large company and can help you see more clearly into the operation of this firm.[22]

social network Your set of direct and indirect contacts.

2. *When you meet someone, tell the person what you do.* Give your name and describe your position in a way that explains what you do and invites conversation. Instead of saying, "I am in stocks and bonds," say "I am a financial planner who helps people make investment decisions." Listen more than you talk.

3. *Do not do business while networking.* It usually is not practical to conduct business while networking. Make a date to call or meet with the new contact later.

4. *Offer your business card.* The business card is especially useful when the contact attempts to tell others about your products or services.

5. *Edit your contacts and follow-up.* You cannot be involved with all your contacts, so separate the productive from the nonproductive. Send a short email message to contacts you deem productive and include business information or brochures—anything that increases visibility.[23] Make sure your materials are professional. Use inexpensive contact management software, such as Salesforce.com, to organize your contact information.

There are three types of networks salespeople should nurture (Fig. 9.2). Every salesperson will be well served by networking within his or her own organization. You never know when someone in finance or shipping will be needed to help solve a problem or provide you with important information. A second form of networking involves establishing contacts inside your industry. Make contact with experts in your field, top performers, leaders, successful company representatives, and even competitors. The third form of networking involves business contacts with people outside your industry, such as bankers, government officials, developers, and other people in your community. The local golf course may be a good place to make these contacts.[24]

Educational Seminars

Many salespeople are using educational seminars as a method of identifying prospects. Seminars provide an opportunity to showcase your product without pressuring prospects to buy. Many banks, accounting firms, wine merchants, and consulting companies use

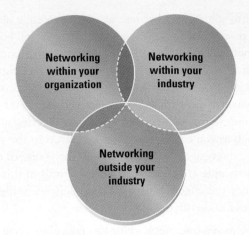

Figure 9.2 Three Types of Networks
Top-performing salespeople recognize that networking can take place in three areas.

seminars to generate new prospects. Previously we mentioned that Edward Jones's sales representatives often make cold calls on prospects. They also schedule seminars that provide prospects with an opportunity to acquire information regarding the potential benefits of investing in a mutual fund, estate planning, or tax-free investing. A complimentary lunch is usually served before the informative presentation. When inviting prospects, be clear about the seminar's content and always deliver what you promise.

Prospecting by Non-Sales Employees

Should service technicians, receptionists, bank tellers, and other non-sales personnel be involved in prospecting? For a growing number of firms, the answer is yes. Prospecting

Selling Today

Develop Your Prospect Base with Seminars

The use of educational seminars has become an important prospecting method. You can educate prospective customers with brochures, news releases, catalogues, or your website, but educational seminars offer the advantage of face-to-face contact. Barbara Siskind, in her book *Seminars to Build Your Business*, identifies 15 objectives for hosting seminars. Here are a few of the most important.

■ *Obtain sales leads.* This is one of the most common objectives for seminars. You can obtain the names of attendees and arrange appointments for future sales calls. Seminars may also help identify actual product users, technical support people, or engineers, who, while they may not be the decision makers, may influence the purchase decision.

■ *Promote your place of business.* Your place of business can become a destination for people who might otherwise not consider visiting it. You have an opportunity to create awareness of your company and develop a positive image for your entire operation and its capabilities.

■ *Showcase and demonstrate your expertise.* Seminars allow you to show a carefully targeted group of people that you really know your stuff. Technical experts and others in the organization who can address clients' specific concerns can support salespeople.

Polaroid Canada used educational seminars where imaging specialists assisted prospective clients in exploring imaging solutions. Toronto-based Charon Systems, Inc., a systems integrator that deploys networks for organizations, regularly organizes seminars for 80 to 100 technology people from mid-sized firms. President David Fung estimates that 25 percent of prospects become clients.[b]

need not be the exclusive responsibility of the sales force. Janet Dixon, a UPS sales representative, needed help making contact with an important prospect. This person wouldn't take her calls. She talked to the UPS service provider (a driver), who called on this account and requested his help. He had serviced this company for years and was like part of the family. He knew the prospect personally and persuaded her to accept a call from the salesperson.[25]

Combination Approaches

In recent years, we have seen an increase in the number of prospecting approaches used by salespeople. In many cases, success in selling depends on your ability to use a combination of the methods described in this chapter. For example, the large number of prospects identified at a trade show might be used to develop an effective telemarketing program. Prospects are called and an effort is made to set up a personal call. Prospects identified at a trade show or educational seminar might also be sent a sales-oriented newsletter, a sales letter, or an email message inviting them to visit your web page.

QUALIFYING THE PROSPECT

ONE OF THE MOST IMPORTANT KEYS TO SUCCESS IN PERSONAL SELLING IS THE ABILITY TO qualify prospects. **Qualifying** is the process of identifying prospects who appear to have a need for your product and should be contacted. Top salespeople use good research and analysis skills to qualify leads effectively.[26]

qualifying The process of identifying prospects who appear to have a need for your product and should be contacted.

    The qualifying process is also the first opportunity to consider what the needs of the buyer might be and how those needs are matched by the characteristics of the product being sold.[27] Some sales organizations link the qualifying process with the need discovery step in the consultative sales process. In most cases, this linkage will depend on the nature and complexity of the prospect's buying process. The more complex the buying process, the more likely these two sales functions will be separate steps in the sales process. We will fully explore the need discovery step in Chapter 11.

    Every salesperson needs to establish qualifying criteria. This process involves finding answers to several basic questions.

1. *Does the prospect have a need for my product?* If you sell copy machines, it might appear that every business firm is a prospect. However, a firm that is outsourcing its copy work to FedEx Kinko's may not be a legitimate prospect. Qualifying involves probing for real needs. Let's assume you sell real estate for a large agency. You receive a call from someone who believes that owning a home is a good investment. At this point, it's important to find out what else makes owning a home important for that person. Get permission to ask questions and then determine the person's real needs. In the final analysis, you may decide it would be a waste of your time and the prospect's time to visit several homes that are on the market.[28]

2. *Does the prospect have the authority to buy my product?* Ideally, you should talk to a person who has authority to buy or who can influence the buying decision. Talking to the right person within a large organization may involve collecting information from

Prospecting for and Qualifying Donors

When Mariya Yurukova graduated from university, she knew what her career would be. An undergraduate degree in psychology gave her many options; however, it was the job she had as a student that turned into her passion and subsequent career choice. Today, with nearly seven years' fundraising experience, she is the Brock University Annual Fund Campaign coordinator.

Fundraising at universities and colleges has become an important source of funds, and most have established advancement offices to encourage donations and manage donor relationships. Fundraising shares a lot of commonalities with marketing and sales, yet few fundraisers consider themselves salespeople. Most advancement offices manage mail and telephone contact with graduates and their families to encourage donations, often through annual campaigns. Many of these campaigns are organized with part-time and student employees. A newer trend, requiring greater coordination, is to encourage "class gifts" from students from a particular year or from a specific program of study.

Mariya, in her role at Brock University, oversees a telemarketing group that solicits funds from Brock University alumni and their parents. Mariya relies on research to identify prospects and continually updates prospect contact information because it is important to the campaign's success. Prospecting for donors has some similarity to prospecting for customers. Donor prospects are researched for *capability*—or *capacity*—which is the same as *ability* (resources and authority). Where do they work and how long have they been working? Potential donors are assessed for *affinity*—or strength of emotional attachment to or relationship with the university. Have they been actively involved in university governance, sports, or student programs? Affinity correlates strongly with *willingness*. Another important indicator of willingness, assuming there is capability, is donation history. Donors who have a history of giving, and particularly if they have been increasing the size of their donations, are more likely to make future and larger donations. Information on prospects is increasingly gathered through online media, combined with news-tracking search engine tools that can deliver information immediately to email inboxes.

When Mariya determines a prospect might be a potential major donor, she passes the information along so that a leadership gifts officer contacts the prospect. Prospects who have very high potential may even receive a face-to-face meeting that could include the vice president of advancement or even the university president. A key to successful university fundraising is how the advancement office approaches, engages, and stewards donors.[c]

several sources. Some buying decisions are made by individuals and others are made by a committee. Expensive products often require the approval of a decision maker higher up in the organization.

3. *Does the prospect have the financial resources to buy my product?* It is usually not difficult to obtain credit information for consumers and business buyers. If you are selling products to a business, the *Dun & Bradstreet Reference Book* is an excellent source of credit information. A local credit bureau can provide credit information for a consumer buyer. While the collection of credit information is not difficult, detecting financial instability can be much more complicated. In recent years, we have seen a steady stream of corporate scandals involving accounting irregularities, inflated balance sheets, and outright fraud.[29] Salespeople must be aware of the possibility that a customer may provide incorrect or misleading information.

4. *Does the prospect have the willingness to buy my product?* Rick Page, author of *Hope Is Not a Strategy*, reminds us that many prospects evaluate products but do not buy. When an evaluation stalls, the prospect may have determined that the need is not of

great enough magnitude or urgency to make the purchase. Also, in some cases there is not enough support within the company to reach closure. Rather than walk away from this situation, some salespeople move higher in the organization to determine the level of support for the purchase.[30]

A large number of senior executives say they get involved in the sale early in the decision process, yet salespeople have difficulty meeting with high-level decision makers. Most senior executives will not meet with salespeople who are making cold calls. When appointments are granted, the time allocated may be very short; five to ten minutes is not uncommon. How do you establish credibility for yourself and your company in a short time period? Be sure you know a great deal about the company before the appointment and be prepared to demonstrate your knowledge of the company and the industry it serves. Do not propose solutions until you fully understand the buyer's problems. Be sure to communicate value.[31]

This list of questions can be revised to meet the needs of many different types of salespeople. A sales representative for an industrial equipment dealer will see the qualifying process differently from the person who sells commercial real estate. The main consideration is providing accurate answers to each question.

COLLECTING AND ORGANIZING PROSPECT INFORMATION

THE INTERNET AND THE INFORMATION REVOLUTION CONTINUE TO MAKE ACQUIRING and managing sales leads much easier.[32] When it comes to collecting and organizing prospect information, salespeople have a large assortment of computer-based systems available. Companies such as Salesforce.com, Oracle, NetSuite, Sage, and Microsoft all offer software applications designed to collect and organize prospect information. Most of these Sales Force Automation (SFA) Systems or Customer Relationship Management (CRM) Systems, as they are now known, have preset categories or fields that contain sales data on the prospect. This **sales data** is the information seen in most CRM systems, including the contact name, title, address, phone number, email address, etc. It may also include information about what products have been purchased, what sales opportunities exist in the future, who the various members or influencers are in the buying centre, their preferred communication styles (refer to Chapter 4), past sales and forecasted sales volume, and percentage change and date of closing the sale. All of the sales data information about the prospect in a CRM system is presented in the account screen report. Figure 9.3 shows an account screen report for Able Profit Machines. The information in this report, including any notes about previous sales calls, is accessed and studied before the salesperson makes a sales call.

sales data Information available from a company's CRM system.

When bringing new prospects into the database, it is expected that the salesperson will acquire this sales data and enter it into the records kept on the prospect. In most CRM systems, this information goes into the shared database that allows other members of the sales team to access information and make additions as they work with prospects. In the event a new salesperson takes over an existing prospect database, all of this information can be accessed quickly and used to plan sales strategies to work effectively with prospects.

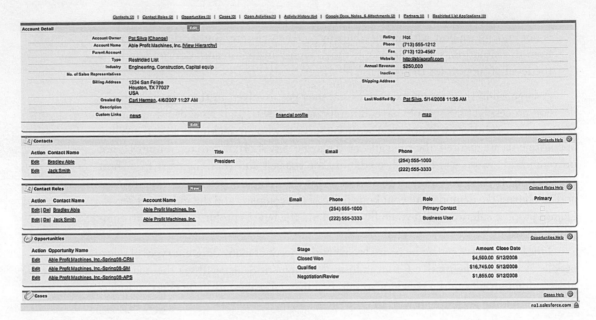

Figure 9.3 The CRM Account Screen Report
This account screen report shows sales data for Able Profit Machines. The sales data, including any notes from previous sales calls, was entered by sales representative Pat Silva of SimNet Systems. Pat Silva has been calling on Able Profit Machines president Bradley Able.

Source: Courtesy of Salesforce.com

Sales Intelligence

sales intelligence Goes beyond data, giving salespeople access to insights into the prospect's marketplace, their firm, their competitors, and even the prospects themselves.

In addition to collecting sales data, the collection of **sales intelligence** is necessary when the sale is complex and requires a long closing cycle. Sales intelligence goes beyond data, giving salespeople access to insights into the prospect's marketplace, their firm, their competitors, and even about the prospects themselves. Sales intelligence is needed today over and above sales data because prospects are looking for insights and knowledge from salespeople above and beyond the product features and benefits. In many buying situations today, prospects using advanced search engines have already learned about features and benefits. In terms of sales intelligence, prospects instead expect salespeople to know answers to many of the following questions. Answers to these questions create much of the value that results in successfully turning prospects into long-term customers.

Do you know me? You need to know more than my name and title. Do you know my role, my goals, how I am evaluated, and how long I have been with the organization? Do you know about the projects I am working on, my style of doing business, and what the requirements are for me to meet my objectives? Do you know about previous dealings I have had with your company? Do I have a favourable opinion of your company and do you know my role and the role of other influencers in the decision-making process?

Do you know my company and my marketplace? Do you know my company mission statement, culture, and vision for the future? Do you know clearly what we are doing, how we are performing in the marketplace, what issues keep us up all night, who our competitors are, and what they are doing? Do you know where we fit into

Your OneSource for Global Business Information

OneSource delivers the most in-depth business information available, providing companies with the data needed to effectively approach targeted markets including; solutions for Sales, Marketing, M&A/Finance, Insurance, Procurement, Recruitment, Legal Compliance, Consulting, Research and more.

Global Business Information

♦Companies ♦Executives ♦Industries ♦Financials ♦Analysis Data ♦News

OneSource enables companies to:

- Access data via your web browser
- Integrate with CRM systems
- View rich company profiles
- Develop quality sales leads
- Improve pre-meeting planning
- Gain competitive intelligence
- Identify key executives
- Target new customers
- Analyze financial performance
- Research industry trends

Global Business Information

866-354-6936

www.onesource.com

OneSource goes beyond sales data and supplies value-adding sales intelligence to salespeople involved in complex sales that have a long closing cycle. This prospect information is loaded into a customer's CRM account detail. Salespeople review this information to plan strategies for successfully moving the sale through the stages in the sales process.

Used with permission.

the existing competitive landscape? Are we the leader or are we in the position of having to play catch-up to survive? Can you relate what you sell directly to what we need to accomplish our goals? Do you know who our partners are or what effect the current economy has on our business?

Do you have any special value-add? You have a product or service you think we need, but what else can you bring to the table? Are there additional resources you can bring to bear to solve my problems or improve my internal business processes? Can you educate me on how you are truly different from the other players in your area of expertise so I can support my recommendation to work with you? Can you help me build a case for return on investment (ROI)?[33]

Answers to these questions come from many sources. CRM suppliers like Salesforce. com, infogroup.ca, Sales-i.com, and Vecta.net have programs that supply this kind of sales intelligence to companies and salespeople. OneSource, mentioned earlier in the chapter, is one example of a supplier of sales intelligence. OneSource supplies sales intelligence to Cardinal Logistics Management, a major provider of logistics, transportation, and supply-chain solutions to large retailers, manufacturers, and distribution companies.

Cardinal's salespeople must know each prospect inside and out in order to sell logistics solutions effectively to their 5000 customers. OneSource supplies 24/7, anywhere access to detailed customer profiles, executive contact data and biographies, financial statements, news trade articles, and analyst reports. A special new-alert feature keeps salespeople up-to-date on any and all developments within their customer's company and their industry, including both their customer's customers and their competitors.[34]

Most importantly, this information must be entered into the company's CRM system to get a 360-degree view of the prospect. The information will also be used to move the prospect through the steps in the sales process.

MANAGING THE PROSPECT BASE

HIGH-PERFORMING SALESPEOPLE TODAY ARE FOCUSED ON EFFECTIVELY MANAGING SALES activities for all prospects in their database. This means that the size and number of prospects are more carefully considered. Too few prospects in various stages of the sales cycle can quickly signal problems. Alternatively, too many customers can drain a salesperson's resources so that too little effort is focused on prospects with the best opportunities. This is a particular problem when salespeople spend too much effort on prospects that have limited potential. CRM software can help organize customer data into meaningful and easy-to-interpret information, as seen in Figure 9.4.

View: Pat Silva Prospects ▾ Edit | Create New View   ‹Previous Page | Next Page›

A | B | C | D | E | F | G | H | I | J | K | L | M | N | O | P | Q | R | S | T | U | V | W | X | Y | Z | Other **All**

Action	Account Name	Amount	Close Date	Stage ▲	Opportunity Name
Edit	Computer Products	$4,500.00	6/24/2008	Qualified	Computer Products-Spring08-APS
Edit	Computer Products	$17,500.00	6/11/2008	Qualified	Computer Products-Spring08-SM
Edit	Quality Builders	$4,500.00	5/13/2008	Qualified	Quality Builders-Spring08-SM
Edit	Ellis Enterprises	$4,500.00	5/13/2008	Qualified	Ellis Enterprises-Spring08-APS
Edit	Lakeside Clinic	$1,855.00	5/13/2008	Qualified	Lakeside Clinic-Spring08-APS
Edit	Johnson and Associates	$750.00	5/13/2008	Qualified	Johnson and Associates-Spring08-APS
Edit	Johnson and Associates	$16,930.00	7/3/2008	Qualified	Johnson and Associates-Spring08-CRM
Edit	International Studios	$4,500.00	5/13/2008	Qualified	International Studios-Spring08-APS
Edit	Landers Engineering	$4,500.00	5/13/2008	Qualified	Landers Engineering-Spring08-APS
Edit	Mercy Hospital	$4,500.00	5/13/2008	Qualified	Mercy Hospital-Spring08-APS
Edit	Murray D'Zines	$4,500.00	5/13/2008	Qualified	Murray D'Zines-Spring08-APS
Edit	Big Tex Auto Sales	$750.00	5/13/2008	Qualified	Big Tex Auto Sales-Spring08-APS
Edit	Excellent Software, Inc.	$4,500.00	5/13/2008	Qualified	Excellent Software,Inc.-Spring08-APS
Edit	Designers Associates	$4,500.00	5/13/2008	Qualified	Designers Associates-Spring08-APS
Edit	Piccadilly Studio	$4,500.00	6/11/2008	Needs Analysis	Piccadilly Studio-Spring08-APS
Edit	General Contractors	$16,745.00	6/12/2008	Needs Analysis	General Contractors-Spring08-CRM
Edit	General Contractors	$1,855.00	6/11/2008	Needs Analysis	General Contractors-Spring08-SM
Edit	Bryan Enterprises	$17,155.00	5/13/2008	Needs Analysis	Bryan Enterprises-Spring08-APS
Edit	Modern Designs	$4,500.00	5/13/2008	Needs Analysis	Modern Designs-Spring08-APS
Edit	Computerized Labs	$4,500.00	7/17/2008	Needs Analysis	Computerized Labs-Spring08-APS
Edit	Media Conglomerate	$4,500.00	7/9/2008	Needs Analysis	Media Conglomerate-Spring08-APS
Edit	Able Profit Machines, Inc.	$16,745.00	5/20/2008	Proposal/Price Quote	Able Profit Machines, Inc.-Spring08-SM
Edit	Murray D'Zines	$16,630.00	6/11/2008	Proposal/Price Quote	Murray D'Zines-Spring08-CRM
Edit	Aeroflot Airlines	$16,520.00	5/13/2008	Proposal/Price Quote	Aeroflot Airlines-Spring08-APS
Edit	Piccadilly Studio	$16,745.00	6/19/2008	Negotiation/Review	Piccadilly Studio-Spring08-CRM
Edit	Able Profit Machines, Inc.	$1,855.00	5/12/2008	Negotiation/Review	Able Profit Machines, Inc.-Spring08-APS
Edit	Bryan Enterprises	$21,020.00	5/13/2008	Negotiation/Review	Bryan Enterprises-Spring08-CRM
Edit	Computer Products	$520.00	5/13/2008	Negotiation/Review	Computer Products-Spring08-CRM

Figure 9.4 The Prospect Base
This CRM record presents a complete list of salesperson Pat Silva's prospects. Note this list includes information on the forecasted dollar amount of each sale, projected date of close, and what stage of the sales process the prospect is in. In CRM systems like Salesforce.com, clicking on any of the prospects on this list will allow the user to drill down into detailed contact information and notes supporting these projections.
Source: Courtesy of Salesforce.com.

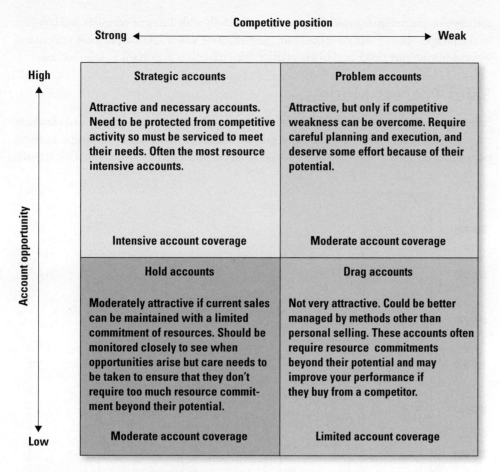

Competitive position

Strong ◄─────────────────────► Weak

High

Account opportunity

Strategic accounts	**Problem accounts**
Attractive and necessary accounts. Need to be protected from competitive activity so must be serviced to meet their needs. Often the most resource intensive accounts.	Attractive, but only if competitive weakness can be overcome. Require careful planning and execution, and deserve some effort because of their potential.
Intensive account coverage	**Moderate account coverage**
Hold accounts	**Drag accounts**
Moderately attractive if current sales can be maintained with a limited commitment of resources. Should be monitored closely to see when opportunities arise but care needs to be taken to ensure that they don't require too much resource commitment beyond their potential.	Not very attractive. Could be better managed by methods other than personal selling. These accounts often require resource commitments beyond their potential and may improve your performance if they buy from a competitor.
Moderate account coverage	**Limited account coverage**

Low

Figure 9.5 The Portfolio Model

This portfolio model uses account opportunity (forecasted sales) and competitive position (the ability to capitalize on opportunity) to classify how much sales effort should be made on individual accounts in the prospect database. Those prospects listed in the strategic accounts cell (high sales forecast and strong position for closing the sale) will receive the largest amount of sales effort, while those in the drag accounts cell will receive little, if any, attention.

To effectively and efficiently manage the prospect base, sales managers and salespeople often conduct an **account analysis** to estimate the sales potential for each prospect. It is a necessary step before deciding how to allocate sales calls across accounts. Portfolio models and the sales funnel are two popular conceptual tools for performing account analyses and deciding how much time and effort, and what sales strategies, to use with the prospects in their database.

account analysis An estimate of the sales potential for each account.

Portfolio Models

Portfolio models involve the use of multiple factors when classifying prospects. Figure 9.5 illustrates a typical four-cell model based on two factors: overall account opportunity for the seller and the seller's competitive position—that is, the ability to capitalize on these opportunities.[35]

The portfolio provides an excellent framework to facilitate communication between salespeople and the various sales support personnel. Teamwork at this stage in the sales cycle can develop improved strategies for working successfully with different accounts and contacts in the prospect base. Portfolio models are most effective where salespeople must understand individual customer needs and where relationship strength is important to sales success.

Sales Process Models

sales process model The total set of prospects being pursued at any given time.

Sales process models, also referred to as sales funnel models, classify prospects based on where they are in the sales process. The **sales process model** is the total set of prospects being pursued at any given time. The sales process model is illustrated in Figure 9.6. This six-step

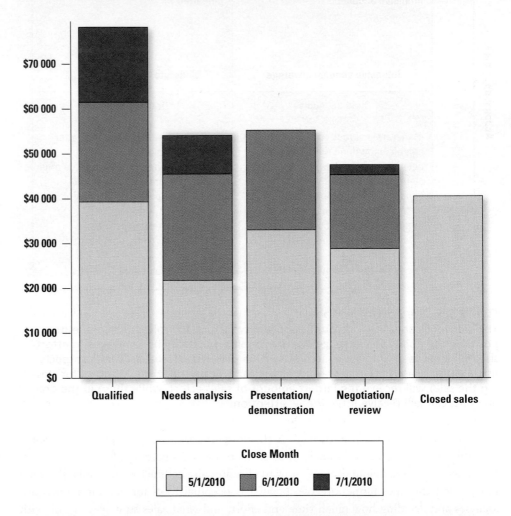

Figure 9.6 The CRM Sales Funnel (or sales process) Dashboard

The sales funnel, or sales process dashboard as it is frequently called, classifies prospects according to where they are in the sales process. In this figure both the total sales potential funnel and the forecasted funnel are presented. The forecasted funnel amounts are arrived at by multiplying the total sale by the forecast amount or likelihood the salesperson projected for successfully closing the sale. The sales forecast needs to be accurate because it is the amount most firms use to project future operating results for the company. You can click any stage on these two charts and drill down to find the underlying data.

Source: Courtesy of Salesforce.com

process model includes Prospect, Qualified, Needs Analysis, Presentation, Negotiations, and Closed/Service. An account might be simply a prospect who has potential but has not been contacted, a qualified prospect ready for a needs analysis, or a prospect in serious negotiations with the salesperson. In sales process model reports such as the one in Figure 9.6, clicking on any part of the bar graph will drill down into and report all the supporting data on prospects in each stage of the sales process. Where an account is in the sales process has implications for if and when the salesperson will be able to close the sale.

The sales cycle for complex technical sales, such as computer networking installations, might be several months in duration. The number of prospects in the funnel for selling such installations may be small compared to the number for an insurance or real estate salesperson. Insurance salespeople know they need to contact a larger number of people to gain permission to make a smaller number of presentations to make an even smaller number of sales. In any selling situation, it is important that salespeople balance their portfolio of prospects that are at various stages of the selling process.[36] A **balanced funnel** enables salespeople to have a sufficiently large number of prospects at each stage in the sales process to meet sales projections and quotas for both the short and the long term.[37] As indicated earlier with Joe Girard's "Ferris wheel" concept, this means that salespeople must ensure that sufficient prospects are regularly added to the funnel to ensure that it does not become empty. In addition to the number of prospects, the quality of the prospects added to the funnel and the ability of the salesperson to manage the sales process will affect the number of sales opportunities that are successfully closed.

Salespeople need to ensure that they "work" the whole funnel so that it is always in balance. They should work on sales opportunities near the bottom of the funnel first; that is, close those that are near the end of the sales process. Then they should work on the top of the funnel; that is, add new prospects. Prospecting is an activity that some salespeople dislike, but if it is not given sufficient attention there is a real danger that the funnel will empty. Finally, salespeople should work on those opportunities that are in the sales process, moving them along through the funnel and ensuring there are regular, predictable sales over time.[38]

CRM Technology for Pipeline Management

This process of managing all the prospects in the salesperson's sales funnel is to ensure that sales objectives are met is called **pipeline management**. CRM software provides an efficient and effective tool for forecasting and managing pipelines. Using sales data entered into the account detail, contact screens, notes applications, etc., sales forecasts can be updated continually as prospects move through the stages in the sales process. Prospects in the database who are no longer qualified, for whatever reason, can be quickly dropped from the sales funnel. Figure 9.7 shows part of a pipeline dashboard produced by a CRM software suite.

Pipeline analytics, defined as the ability to conduct sophisticated data analysis and modelling, are found in most CRM systems. Using pipeline analytics, new reports can be generated regarding the movement of prospects through the sales funnel. These reports can be more clearly presented with the use of dashboards. **Pipeline dashboards** are at-a-glance visualizations that define, monitor, and analyze the relationships existing in the pipeline or sales funnel. Sales team members, including the

balanced funnel A portfolio of prospects where there is a sufficiently large number of prospects at each stage in the sales process.

pipeline management Process of managing all the prospects in the salesperson's sales funnel to ensure that sales objectives are met.

pipeline analytics Ability to conduct sophisticated data analysis and modelling, allowing salespeople to generate new reports regarding the movement of prospects through the sales funnel.

pipeline dashboards At-a-glance visualizations that define, monitor, and analyze the relationships existing in the pipeline or sales funnel.

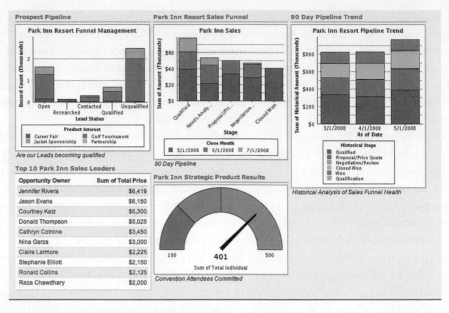

Figure 9.7 Pipeline Dashboards
These additional pipeline dashboards are at-a-glance visualizations that define, monitor, and analyze the relationships existing in the pipeline or funnel. Pipeline analytics exist in most modern CRM systems and are used to produce these important prospect movement reports. The salesperson can quickly and easily access detailed information on specific prospects, and then use this information to plan strategies for moving the prospect to the next stage of the sales process.
Source: Courtesy of Salesforce.com

Most salespeople use CRM software in the development of their prospecting and sales forecasting plan. This software allows the convenient preparation and management of prospect lists.

sales manager, working together from a shared CRM database, can collaborate to create value and enhance the sales strategies to help the salesperson move prospects through the pipeline to a successful sale. CRM pipeline dashboards allow the user to quickly and easily drill down into the reports and records supporting them. This provides for quick updates as prospects move through the sales funnel. Dashboards can also provide insight into the need to add new prospects as existing ones are moved through the sales process.

REVIEWING KEY CONCEPTS

- Discuss the importance of developing a prospect base.

  Prospect identification has been called the lifeblood of selling. A continuous supply of new customers must be found to replace those lost for various reasons. *Prospecting* is the systematic process of locating potential customers. Prospecting requires careful planning.

- Identify and assess important sources of prospects.

  Analysis of both your product and your existing customers can help to identify, locate, and profile your prospects. Important sources of new customers include *referrals* (endless chain referrals and referral letters and cards), centres of influence, friends and family members, directories, trade publications, trade shows and special events, telemarketing and email, direct-response advertising and sales letters, websites, computer databases, cold calling, educational seminars, networking, and prospecting by non-sales employees. Social media can also be used to secure new prospects.

- Describe criteria for qualifying prospects.

  Prospecting techniques produce a list of names that must be evaluated using criteria developed by each salesperson. The process of prospect evaluation is called *qualifying*. The qualifying process involves finding answers to several basic questions: Does the prospect have a need for my product? Can the prospect make the buying decision? Can the prospect pay for the purchase? Does the prospect have the willingness to buy my product? An estimate of the volume of sales that could be generated from this prospect and the prospect's credit rating also should be determined.

- Explain common methods of collecting and organizing prospect information.

  Most companies rely on customer relationship management (CRM) systems to keep track of sales data. The collection of sales intelligence beyond sales data enables salespeople to impress their knowledgeable customers with insights that are above and beyond the product and/or service features and benefits.

- Describe the steps in managing a prospect base.

  Salespeople need to allocate their resources wisely to make the most of the prospect base. They do so by conducting account analyses, using either the portfolio model or the sales funnel model.

Key Terms

account analysis **216**

balanced funnel **219**

cold calling **207**

networking **208**

pipeline analytics **219**

pipeline dashboard **219**

pipeline management **219**

prospect **196**

prospect base **197**

prospecting **196**

qualifying **211**

referral **200**

Review Questions

1. List and briefly explain the common causes of customer attrition.

2. During periods of economic uncertainty, the decision-making process often moves upward. What basic tips would you give a salesperson who is calling on senior executives?

3. Describe three steps progressive marketers take to improve the quality of their prospecting effort.

4. List the major sources of prospects.

5. Explain how the endless chain referral prospecting method works.

6. Discuss how direct-response advertising and sales letters can be used to identify prospects.

7. What is *networking*? How might a real estate salesperson use networking to identify prospects?

8. What does the term *qualifying* mean? What are the four basic questions that should be answered during the qualifying process?

9. When is sales intelligence important? What are the three most important pieces of sales intelligence a salesperson needs to know?

10. Describe two popular models for performing an account analysis.

Application Exercises

1. Prior to getting involved in networking, it's a good idea to prepare an "elevator" presentation. This is a 30-second pitch that summarizes what you want people to know about you. You might think of yourself as a "product" to be sold to an employer who has a job opening. Make your presentation upbeat and brief. Who are you? What are you currently doing? What type of work are you looking for? Practise the presentation alone in front of a mirror and then present it to one or two class members.

2. You are a sales representative for Xerox Canada, which has just designed a new, less expensive, and better quality copying machine. Make a list of 15 prospects you would plan to call about this machine. From the material in this chapter, identify the sources you would use in developing your prospect list.

3. You are in the process of interviewing for a sales position with Sun Life Financial in Toronto. In addition to filling out an application form and taking an aptitude test, one of the tasks the agency manager requests of you is to develop a list of prospects with whom you are acquainted. He informs you that this list will represent the prospects you will be working with during the first few weeks of employment. The agency manager recommends that you list at least 50 names. Prepare a list of 10 acquaintances you have who would qualify as prospects.

4. Sales automation software is most commonly used in the prospecting phase of selling. New-product releases are continually being developed that provide additional features and benefits to salespeople. The software used in this book is marketed by a leader in the field. Access **www.salesforce.com** and research the latest version of Salesforce. Click on and examine the latest demonstration copy of this popular sales automation software.

5. Locating companies to work for is a form of prospecting. Assuming you are interested in changing careers, develop a list of 10 companies for which you would like to work. Assign each company a priority according to your interest, from the most desirable (1) to the least (10). Organize your list into six columns showing the company name, telephone number, address, person in charge of hiring, prospect information, and priority. What sources did you use to get this information?

ROLE-PLAY EXERCISE

For this role play, you will assume a sales position at a Lexus dealership. You have just completed a successful sale by signing the papers for the second new Lexus this customer has purchased in the past four years. Because you know your customer has had a very successful experience with his first Lexus, you have decided to use the referral methods described in this chapter. Review the material on referrals and plan what you will say to your customer to build your prospect base. Pair off with another student who will assume the role of your customer. Explain that satisfied customers often know other people who would consider purchasing a Lexus.

You might say, "Considering the positive experience you have had as a Lexus owner, you probably know others who appreciate fine automobiles. Is there anyone who comes to mind?" If, after probing, your customer doesn't recall someone immediately, ask permission to call him later to see if anyone has come to mind. Ask this person for actual names, addresses, and other qualifying information about prospective customers he knows. Also ask the customer if he would write a referral note or letter that you could use.

CASE PROBLEM

Dave Levitt, featured at the beginning of this chapter, is a regional sales manager for Salesforce.com. The CRM solution provider is exclusively a cloud-computing vendor offering hosted applications. This model sets the company apart from competitors such as SAP, Oracle, or Microsoft, who are predominantly on-premise providers. Cloud-computing systems have a high degree of flexibility as they can be customized for each individual account and implemented within a very short time frame. Salesforce.com's unique selling proposition is therefore closely linked to the speed with which a client can gain the benefit: Cloud-computing implementation times are typically weeks or months, whereas competitive on-premise solutions can take years to be implemented. Therefore, the total cost of ownership is much lower, and the ROI is much higher and comes in faster.

Before getting in touch with a prospect, Levitt's sales representatives typically spend a substantial amount of time preparing for a sales call and keeping up with news releases. Such upfront investigative work is necessary to uncover such things as changes in top management or factors that are driving a company to change a business model. Working for a CRM company, Salesforce.com's salespeople have comprehensive access to additional news and information about each of their customers and prospects. Hence, by the time representatives have decided to pick up the phone to prospect, they already have a sense for why they are

calling and what the value proposition is going to be specifically for that account.

For providers of enterprise software solutions, it is important to have contacts and relationships with three different types of individuals within the prospective customer company: (1) executive financial influencers who have ultimate responsibility for the budget and the project itself, (2) a coach who can give guidance on a day-to-day basis, and (3) IT specialists who can facilitate the process and who would be the custodians after the implementation of the solution. Therefore, the sales representative has to be an orchestrator of resources within Salesforce.com for different buying influencers in the prospect's organization at different points in the sales cycle. For example, the salesperson would include a technical employee from Salesforce.com as part of the sales team who could apply the customer's needs to the product itself and perform demonstrations of software. One would also need to incorporate an internal sales executive that aligns with the customer's executive. Furthermore, the internal services organization or a third-party implementation partner is needed to explain and execute the implementation of the product. There could also be a wide variety of other specialists, depending on which specific tasks have to be accomplished.

Typically, the sales representative would start to qualify the opportunity through conversations with the coach. Using various questioning techniques during the initial discovery process, the sales representative has to understand the following: What is the prospect's business model? Why might the prospect be interested in our offerings? What is their problem and how big is it? What is the complexity of the problem the prospect is trying to address? Will there be a good fit? Is it worth investing the time and money it takes to win the account? What is their time frame? How are they going to measure success?

If the initial discovery shows that the problem can be addressed, the sales representative would then ask for access to the ultimate decision maker and all the other key stakeholders. Then she would perform a similar discovery as was done with the first person (i.e., the coach), constantly trying to qualify the value of the service solution offering and making sure that it is worth pursuing the opportunity (as for large opportunities, it could be a one-year investment to win it). So the sales representative has to make sure and qualify that (1) it is a legitimate opportunity, (2) it can be won, and (3) it is worth winning. As Levitt emphasizes, it has to be a win-win perspective: "We do not sell a commodity, but a specialty. We do not compete on price alone, but on quality and value." (See the chapter opener on page 195 and Reality Selling Today Role Play 7 in Appendix 1 on page 443 for more information.)

Questions

1. Imagine you are in the position of Dave Levitt, selling CRM services to different business clients. What would be the most promising sources of prospects for you?

2. What criteria does Dave Levitt use for qualifying the prospect?

3. What questions does Dave Levitt ask to understand the needs of the customer?

4. What product features does Dave Levitt highlight that will help a user of Salesforce.com improve his business?

5. Does it appear that Dave Levitt is utilizing previously collected sales intelligence to impress the potential buyer with insights that are above and beyond the product features and benefits? Please specify.

PART IV

ROLE-PLAY EXERCISE
Developing a Customer Strategy

SCENARIO

You are a sales representative employed by Park Inn International Hotel and Convention Centre. One of your primary responsibilities is to identify prospects and make sales calls that result in the development of new accounts. During each of these calls, you plan to build a relationship with the customer and describe selected value-added guest services and amenities offered by the Park Inn. You also try to learn as much as possible about the customer's buying process.

CUSTOMER PROFILE

Mohammed Ansari is the founder and Chief Executive Officer of Dynamic Security Inc., a growing high-tech firm with more than 100 employees. The company manufactures and sells security systems for use in residential homes, retail stores, and commercial buildings. According to a recent article in the *Globe and Mail*, Dynamic Security is poised to grow very rapidly in the next year. The article described Mohammed Ansari as a workaholic who usually works 80 hours each week. Delegation does not come easily to this personable, hard-charging entrepreneur.

SALESPERSON PROFILE

You have just completed the Park Inn sales training program and now want to develop some new accounts. In addition to taking care of established customers, you plan to call on at least four new prospects every week.

PRODUCT

Park Inn International is a full-service hotel and convention centre located in Toronto, Ontario. The hotel recently completed a $2.8 million renovation of its meeting and banquet rooms.

INSTRUCTIONS

For this role-play activity, you will meet with Mohammed Ansari, role-played by another student, who appears to be a good prospect. During the first sales call, plan to learn more about Mohammed as an individual and acquire more information about Dynamic Security. This meeting will provide you with the opportunity to begin building a long-term partnership. During the first meeting with a prospect, you like to present a limited amount of important product information. In this case, the length of the appointment is 15 minutes, so you should not try to cover too much information. To prepare for the first sales call,

read *Employment Memorandum Number 1* in "Partnership Selling: A Role Play/Simulation" online in the Student Resources section at **www.pearsoncanada.ca/manning**. This memo describes the value-added guest services and amenities offered by Park Inn. For the purpose of this role play, Mohammed Ansari should be considered a consultative process buyer. You can assume that he will need help identifying and evaluating possible solutions. As you prepare for the first call, think about what may take place during future calls. Review the steps in the typical buying process (see Fig. 8.3). Keep in mind that today's more demanding customers are seeking a cluster of satisfactions. Study the Product-Selling Model (Fig. 7.1) prior to meeting with Mohammed Ansari.

Part V
Developing a
Presentation Strategy

To play any game well, you first have to learn the rules or principles of the game. And second, you have to forget them. That is, you have to learn to play without thinking about the rules. This is true whether the game is chess or golf or selling. Shortcuts won't work.

—From Al Ries and Jack Trout's Marketing Warfare

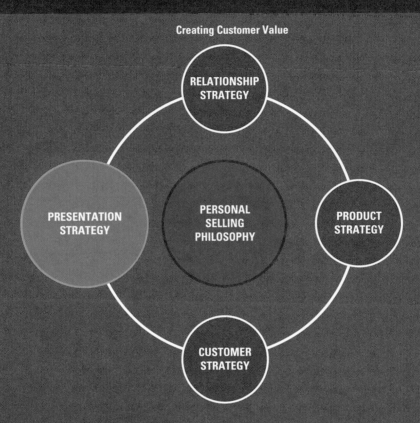

Creating Customer Value

RELATIONSHIP STRATEGY

PRESENTATION STRATEGY

PERSONAL SELLING PHILOSOPHY

PRODUCT STRATEGY

CUSTOMER STRATEGY

The chapters included in Part V review the basic principles used in the Strategic/Consultative Sales Presentation. This information is used as you prepare presentation objectives, develop a presentation plan that adds value, and identify ways to provide outstanding service after the sale.

Chapter 10
Approaching the Customer with Adaptive Selling

Learning Objectives

After studying this chapter, you should be able to

1   Describe the three prescriptions that are included in the presentation strategy.

2   Discuss the two-part preapproach process.

3   Describe team presentation strategies.

4   Explain how adaptive selling builds on four broad strategic areas of personal selling.

5   Describe the six main parts of the presentation plan.

6   Explain how to effectively approach the customer.

7   Describe seven ways to convert the prospect's attention and arouse interest.

 Reality Selling Today Video Series

The worldwide Hilti Group (**www.hilti.com**) specializes in providing leading-edge technology to the global construction industry. With some 20 000 employees in more than 120 countries around the world, Hilti actively pursues a value-added orientation in all of its activities.

As part of this orientation, Hilti puts its new salespeople through a rigorous training curriculum that includes one month of pre-training on Hilti products and services, three weeks of intensive training in product and services sales, and two weeks on software applications. In addition, these salespeople also ride along with experienced sales managers to get hands-on experience. Furthermore, the company offers refresher courses to keep its salespeople updated on Hilti's products and services, the construction market, and corporate strategy. Equipped with this in-depth knowledge and the value orientation that is deeply rooted in the corporate culture, salespeople like Alim Hirani (on the right in the photo at the top of the next page) are always well prepared to approach customers to make sales presentations, demonstrate and explain Hilti's products and services, and show the customers both the tangible and intangible benefits that Hilti can offer.

With a direct sales model, Hilti relies heavily on its salespeople to make the connection and deliver its values to its global customers. Alim is a strong believer that he and his sales team are the face of the company. His credibility is embedded in Hilti's credibility and vice versa. He always makes sure that his sales presentations are well prepared in

advance. More importantly, he builds and maintains rapport with his customers from the very beginning of the business relationship because such partnership mentality motivates the customers to disclose their actual concerns. In the end, customers only value solutions that address their actual needs, and Alim—as a Hilti salesperson—knows that very well.

DEVELOPING THE PRESENTATION STRATEGY

THE PRESENTATION STRATEGY COMBINES ELEMENTS OF THE RELATIONSHIP, PRODUCT, AND customer strategies. Each of the other three strategies must be developed before a salesperson can develop an effective presentation strategy.

The **presentation strategy** is a well conceived plan that consists of three prescriptions: (1) establishing objectives for the sales presentation, (2) developing the presale presentation plan needed to meet these objectives, and (3) renewing one's commitment to provide outstanding customer service (Fig. 10.1).

The first prescription reminds us that we need to establish one or more objectives for each sales call. High-performance salespeople like Alim Hirani understand that it is often possible to accomplish several things during a single call. A common objective of sales calls is to collect information about the prospect's needs. Another common objective is to develop, build, or sustain a relationship with those who will make the buying decision.

A carefully prepared presentation plan ensures that salespeople will be well organized during the sales presentation and prepared to achieve their objectives. A six-step

presentation strategy A well-conceived plan that consists of three prescriptions: establishing objectives for the sales presentation, preparing the presale presentation plan needed to meet these objectives, and renewing one's commitment to provide outstanding customer service.

Selling Power, a magazine with a circulation of over 200 000, understands the importance of value-added selling. This audio sales training program shows how a strategically planned presentation adds value when it is based on carefully developed call objectives and a presentation plan to meet these objectives.

Turn Added Value Into Added Sales

This audio sales-training program is ideally suited for salespeople who want to learn more and earn more.

Salespeople who add real value can justify a higher price and create a strong competitive advantage. Order this new audio sales-training cassette today, and in just 60 minutes you can apply the strategies from the masters to help you add value and multiply sales.

What you'll learn:

■ How to create value-added selling strategies

■ How to see value through your customers' eyes

■ How to create and implement value-added services

■ How to develop a value-focused offer

■ How to negotiate a better price

■ How to create an emotionally valuable buying experience

■ How you can add value to your personal and professional life

Only $12.95
plus $3.50 for shipping and handling.

To order, call 1-800-752-7355, order online at www.sellingpower.com or fax the order form at right to 540/752-7001.

☐ **Yes!** I want "Value-Added Selling: How to Add Value to Multiply Sales"
 ☐ One Cassette – $12.95 plus $1.50 shipping and handling
 ☐ Ten Cassettes – $99 plus $5 shipping and handling

NAME _____
TITLE _____
COMPANY _____
ADDRESS _____
CITY _____ STATE ___ ZIP ___
PHONE _____ FAX _____ EMAIL _____
☐ MASTERCARD ☐ VISA ☐ AMEX ☐ DISCOVER ☐ CHECK ENCLOSED
CARD NUMBER _____ EXP. _____
SIGNATURE _____

Complete and mail to Selling Power, PO Box 5467, Fredericksburg, VA 22403, or call 1-800-752-7355.   0104SLVA

presentation plan is introduced later in this chapter. Establishment of objectives for the sales presentation and preparation of the presale presentation plan must be guided by a strong desire to offer outstanding customer service. Achieving excellence is the result of careful needs analysis, correct product selection, clear presentations, informative demonstrations, win-win negotiations, and flawless service after the sale. Salespeople who are committed to doing their best in each of these areas will be richly rewarded.

Presentation Strategy Adds Value

How does precall planning add value? Value is added when you position yourself as a resource—not just a vendor. You must prove that you have important ideas and advice to offer.[1] A well-planned presentation adds value when it is based on carefully developed

Strategic/Consultative Selling Model	
Strategic step	**Prescription**
Develop a personal selling philosophy	✓ Adopt marketing concept ✓ Value personal selling ✓ Become a problem solver/partner
Develop a relationship strategy	✓ Adopt win-win philosophy ✓ Project professional image ✓ Maintain high ethical standards
Develop a product strategy	✓ Become a product expert ✓ Sell benefits ✓ Configure value-added solutions
Develop a customer strategy	• Understand the buying process • Understand buyer behaviour • Develop prospect base
Develop a presentation strategy	• Prepare objectives • Develop presentation plan • Provide outstanding service
* Strategic/consultative selling evolved in response to increased competition, more complex products, increased emphasis on customer needs, and the growing importance of long-term relationships.	

Figure 10.1 The Strategic/Consultative Selling Model
This model provides the foundation for a value-added consultative presentation strategy.

sales call objectives and on a presentation plan created to meet those objectives. Good planning ensures that the presentation is customized and adapted to meet the needs and time constraints of the prospect. Increasingly, customers' time is very limited and they want a concise and thoughtful presentation. Careful planning is the key to delivering more value and increasing your sales productivity.[2]

Salespeople need to be aware of the changing needs of their customers or risk losing out to their competition. Some salespeople do not pay enough attention to how they conduct business with their established customers. Without a precall plan, it's easy to miss opportunities to increase your knowledge of the customer's business, sell new products, or discover ways to improve service.[3]

PLANNING THE PREAPPROACH

PREPARATION FOR THE ACTUAL SALES PRESENTATION IS A TWO-PART PROCESS. PART one is referred to as the **preapproach**. The preapproach involves preparing pre-sale objectives and developing a presale presentation plan. Part two is called the

preapproach Activities that precede the actual sales call and set the stage for a personalized sales approach, tailored to the specific needs of the prospect. This involves the planning necessary for the actual meeting with a prospect.

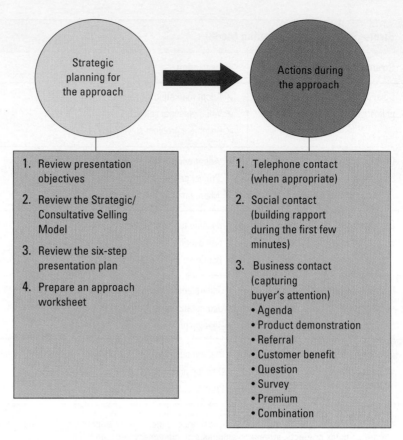

Figure 10.2 Preparing for the Presentation
Preparing for the presentation involves planning for the activities that occur before meeting the prospect and for the first few minutes of actual contact with the prospect.

approach The first contact with the prospect, either face-to-face or by telephone. The approach has three objectives: to build rapport with the prospect, to capture the person's full attention, and to generate interest in the product you are selling.

approach and involves making a favourable first impression, securing the prospect's attention, and transitioning to need identification (Fig. 10.2). The preapproach and approach, when handled correctly, establish a foundation for an effective sales presentation.

The preapproach should be viewed as a key step in preparing for each sales presentation. Professional salespeople complete the preapproach for every presentation whether it involves a new account or an established customer. Top salespeople often spend two or three hours planning for a 25-minute sales call. The preapproach includes the first two prescriptions for developing a presentation strategy: establishing objectives and creating a presale presentation plan.

Establishing Presentation Objectives

Preparation for a sales call is part research, part planning, and part critical thinking. Sales representatives employed by Nalco Chemical Company prepare for each sales call by filling out a 13-point precall planner. One section of this form requires the salesperson to identify the objectives of the call. Nalco is a company that emphasizes professionalism, long-term partnerships, and staying focused on customer needs.[4]

In Chapter 8, we introduced the five stages of the typical buying process (see Fig. 8.3). When you are calling on a *consultative* or *strategic alliance* buyer, you will usually not cover all of these stages during a single sales call. Multi-call sales presentations are especially common in complex sales. Therefore, it's best to develop presentation objectives suitable for each stage of the buying process. During the first stage—need awareness—prospects may or may not be aware of their needs or problems. The need awareness stage is the "investigation" stage. Uncovering and clarifying needs will require the use of appropriate questions (covered in detail in Chapter 11). The following presentation objectives would be appropriate during the first call on a new prospect:

- Establish rapport and begin building a relationship with the prospect.
- Obtain permission to ask need identification questions.
- Obtain personal and business information to establish the customer's profile.

During stage two of the buying process—evaluation of solutions—the customer is ready to consider possible solutions. In some cases, there may be several solutions that must be evaluated. Presentation objectives for stage two might include the following:

- Involve the customer in a product demonstration.
- Provide value justification in terms of cost reduction and increased revenues.
- Compare and contrast the features of, for example, a truck fleet lease plan with a fleet purchase plan.

Every sales call should have an **action objective**. An action objective is something that you want the customer to do during the sales presentation: provide specific financial information; schedule a visit to your manufacturing plant; agree to a trial use of your product; agree to a follow-up meeting; or place an order. An action objective brings a sharp focus to the sales presentation.[5]

Once you have an appointment with the prospect and the presentation objectives have been established, consider sending a fax or email message that outlines the agenda for the meeting. This will confirm the appointment and clarify the topics to be discussed.[6]

action objective Something that you want the customer to do during the sales presentation.

Global Business Insight

Approaching Prospects in Relationship-Focused Countries

In most countries of the world, business is conducted through established relationships and social networks. People in relationship-focused countries—including most of Africa, Central and South America, Arab countries, and the Asia/Pacific region—prefer to do business after personal relationships and trust have been established. It is often difficult to approach prospects directly in these countries, so, if you are trying to make new contacts, you may need a third-party introduction to help bridge the relationship gap. You may use trade associations, chambers of commerce, banks, or even consultants who specialize in arranging introductions in some countries. Attending international trade shows is one of the best ways to make foreign contacts—people attend these shows expressly to make business connections. Another increasingly popular method is to participate in a trade mission. The Department of Foreign Affairs and International Trade (DFAIT) plans, coordinates, and executes trade missions—sometimes led by the prime minister of Canada—to promote Canadian businesses abroad. In recent years, trade missions have been supported by governments at all levels: federal, provincial or territorial, and municipal.[a]

Multi-call sales presentations are common in many areas, including the retail field. The sale of recreational vehicles, leased automobiles, boats, and quality sound systems for home or business typically require more than one sales call. Some clothing stores and independent tailors make office calls to sell tailored clothing. One example is Mitchells/Richards, a progressive retailer with a reputation for superior customer service. Its salespeople will make office calls on request. Working with a customer at his office usually requires more than one sales call.[7]

Team Presentation Strategies

In today's ever-changing business environment, team selling has surfaced as a major development. Team selling is ideally suited to organizations that sell complex or customized products and services that require direct communication between customers and technical experts. Sales teams can often uncover problems, solutions, and sales opportunities that an individual salesperson working alone might not discover.[8] In some situations, the involvement of technical experts can shorten the selling cycle. The team approach often results in more precise need identification, improved selection of the product, and more informative sales presentations.

Team sales presentations require a more detailed precall plan than individual sales calls. Each team member must have a clear understanding of the role he or she will play during the sales call. Sales presentation objectives should be clearly stated. Team

Social Media and Selling Today

Team Selling, Buying Committees, and "Chatter"

Sales of complex or customized products and services invariably involve two teams of people—the selling team and the buying committee or team. Important communications occur between and among members of the two teams. Information about technical and financial matters, information technology, facilities management, and other sales-related issues is exchanged throughout the sales process. Salesforce.com has introduced a system called "Chatter" to facilitate collaborative communication throughout the sales process.

Chatter is linked to the Salesforce.com CRM system and incorporates the benefits of social media. Chatter is a secure, cloud-based online service similar to most social media systems. Members of both teams may create personal profiles. Those creating profiles may introduce themselves in a manner similar to, for example, on Facebook. This personalizes the people working together and makes it easy for anyone with access in both companies to get acquainted with everyone involved in the sales transaction. Users can follow selected personnel in either company, sort the profiles by expertise, and form networks of specialists. Messages are easily transmitted among all participants and recorded for reviewing later. Although it appears to be social media, wise users should retain a "casual business" writing style and avoid too much informality.

Chatter conversations can pertain to specific subjects so users receive real-time news feeds and participate in the development of each part of the solution. This creates value for the total transaction in that anyone in the buying company not involved in the solution development, such as a board of directors, can review the exchanges to understand the results achieved. Sections of the Chatter system are for people within the selling company to confidentially comment and exchange ideas on how to best solve problems and move the sale ahead. When it is time for the sales presentation, everyone following Chatter's continuous collaboration will be well prepared to confirm that the proposed solution is a good fit. The presentation contributions by sales team members can be better organized and coordinated. For more information, go to **salesforce.com/chatter**.

A survey of 19 000 salespeople and sales managers found that about one-fourth of the people contacted use sales teams. A carefully conceived presentation strategy, with each participant having a clear understanding of the role and value he or she will add during the sales call, is essential.

members should share detailed information about the customer, understand the basics of a consultative sales presentation, and be prepared to add value.[9]

Companies that have moved to team sales have discovered that this approach is not easily executed. At Hickok Cole Architects, team selling is the primary approach used to obtain new accounts. However, the team selling process was not easily mastered by staff members. Determining who would communicate when, and determining how presentations would fall into place seamlessly, took months of practice among the company's teams, which often consisted of six or more people. Without sufficient practice, the staff at Hickok Cole discovered that team presentations were sometimes disorganized.[10]

A variation of the team approach to selling is used by some marketers. Salespeople are trained to seek the assistance of another salesperson or to actually turn the customer over to another salesperson when problems surface. The other salesperson may bring to the selling situation a greater ability to identify the customer's needs or to select the appropriate product. Salespeople who have well-prepared presale objectives know when to seek assistance from another professional.

Strategies for Selling to a Buying Committee

In some cases, salespeople must address and satisfy both the individual and collective concerns of each participant in a multi-buyer situation. The decision makers may be members of a well-trained buying team, a buying committee assembled for a one-time purchase, or a board of directors.

As in any type of selling situation, the salesperson should attempt to determine the various buying influences. When possible, the role of each decision maker, the amount of influence he or she exerts, and each decision maker's needs should be determined before the presentation. Careful observation during the presentation can reveal who may use the product (user influencer), who controls the finances (financial influencer), and who can provide the expertise necessary to make the correct buying decision (technical influencer).

When you make a group selling presentation, make sure all parties feel involved. Any member of the group who feels ignored could prevent you from closing the sale. Be sure to direct questions and comments to all potential decision makers in the group. As early as possible, identify the most powerful influences.

Find out if there are any silent team or committee members. A *silent member* is one who will influence the buying decision but does not attend the presentation. Silent members are usually senior managers who have a major influence on the buying decision. If a silent member does exist, you must find a way to communicate, directly or indirectly, with this person.[11]

Adaptive Selling: Builds on Four Strategic Areas of Personal Selling

At the very heart of *adaptive selling* is the belief that every sales call must be tailored to the unique needs, wants, and concerns of the customer. As noted in Chapter 4, adaptive selling involves altering sales behaviours in order to improve communication with the customer. To better identify and respond to the customer's needs frequently requires complex behavioural adjustments before and during the sales call. These adjustments are based on the relationship needs and product needs of the customer. Salespeople today must develop a broader repertoire of selling strategies and apply more effective information-acquisition skills.[12]

The strategic planning that takes place during the preapproach can greatly enhance the adaptive selling process. This plan includes *strategies* that you use to position yourself with the customers and *tactics* you will use when you are face-to-face with a customer. Planning the approach involves consideration of how the *relationship*, *product*, and *customer* strategies can enhance the sales presentation (see Fig. 10.2).

Review the Relationship Strategy As noted in Chapter 3, salespeople need to think of everything they say or do in the context of their relationship with the customer. Customers want a quality product and a quality relationship. Building and nourishing a long-term partnership with the customer often begins with attention to many small details. Confirming an appointment with a brief email message and arriving for the appointment a few minutes early sends a positive message to the customer before the first face-to-face meeting.

The first contact between a salesperson and a prospect is very important. A positive or negative first impression can be formed in a matter of seconds. The customer is receiving

The strategic planning and preparation that takes place during the preapproach can greatly enhance the adaptive selling process. This planning includes a clear understanding of the relationship, product, and customer strategies. This planning and preparation enabled Lana and her sales team to create a presentation strategy that met the relationship and product needs of Ron, one of her largest customers.

a variety of verbal and nonverbal messages that can either facilitate or distract from the sales call. Your behaviours and appearance create an image that others observe and remember. Identification of the customer's preferred communication style should be given a high priority during the initial contact. Once you are in the presence of the customer, absorb the many clues that will help you with style identification. Then use *style flexing* to accommodate the needs of that person.

Review the Product Strategy During the preapproach, you will learn some new things about the potential customer. You will no doubt acquire information that did not surface during the prospecting stage. If this is the case, it pays to take another look at your product. Now it will be easier to identify features with special appeal to the person you are calling on. In addition, you can more accurately identify questions that the prospect might raise.

Product knowledge, combined with knowledge of the customer, builds confidence. Salespeople who are confident in their ability to alter the sales approach as needed are much better prepared to engage in adaptive selling.[13] Customers today are anxious to do business with salespeople who have developed "expert power."

Review the Customer Strategy Personal selling provides us with the opportunity to apply the marketing concept during every contact with the customer. All energies can be directed toward an individual who is likely to think and act differently from anyone else. Customers today have become increasingly sophisticated in their buying strategies. They have higher expectations for value-added products and long-term commitments. A customer strategy focuses on understanding the customer's needs, wants, and buying conditions. A careful review of the information contained in the prospect database is an essential part of reviewing the customer strategy. With this understanding, adaptive selling strategies are formulated to meet both the relationship and product needs of the customer.

DEVELOPING THE SIX-STEP PRESENTATION PLAN

ONCE YOU HAVE ESTABLISHED OBJECTIVES FOR THE SALES PRESENTATION, THE NEXT STEP (prescription) involves developing the presentation plan. This plan helps you achieve your objectives. Today, with increased time constraints, fierce competition, and rising travel costs, the opportunity for a face-to-face meeting with customers may occur less frequently. The few minutes you have with your customers may be your only opportunity to win their business, so careful planning is more critical than ever.

Planning the Presentation

Once you have sufficient background information, you are ready to develop a "customized" presale presentation plan. Preparing a customized sales presentation can take a great deal of time and energy. Nevertheless, this attention to detail gives you added confidence and helps you avoid delivering unconvincing hit-or-miss sales talks. The plan is developed after a careful review of the **six-step presentation plan** (Fig. 10.3). In most cases, the sales process includes the following activities:

six-step presentation plan
Preparation involving consideration of those activities that will take place during the sales presentation.

1. *Approach.* Preparation for the approach involves making decisions concerning effective ways to make a favourable first impression during the initial contact, to secure

The Six-Step Presentation Plan	
Step One: APPROACH	○ Review Strategic/Consultative Selling Model ○ Initiate customer contact
Step Two: PRESENTATION	● Determine prospect needs ● Select solution ● Initiate sales presentation
Step Three: DEMONSTRATION	● Decide what to demonstrate ● Select selling tools ● Initiate demonstration
Step Four: NEGOTIATION	● Anticipate buyer concerns ● Plan negotiating methods ● Initiate win-win negotiations
Step Five: CLOSE	● Plan appropriate closing methods ● Recognize closing clues ● Initiate closing methods
Step Six: SERVICING THE SALE	● Follow-through ● Follow-up calls ● Expansion selling
Service, retail, wholesale, and manufacturer selling.	

Figure 10.3 The Six-Step Presentation Plan
A presale plan is a logical and orderly outline that features a salesperson's thoughts from one step to the next in the presentation. Each step in this plan is explained in Chapters 10 to 15.

the prospect's attention, and to develop the prospect's interest in the product. The approach should set the stage for an effective sales presentation.

2. *Need discovery.* The need discovery process is one of the most critical parts of the selling process. If the salesperson is unable to discover the prospect's buying needs and select a product solution that meets those needs, the sale may be lost. Chapter 11 covers all aspects of the need discovery process and selecting products that meet individual needs.

3. *Presentation.* Three types of need-satisfaction presentation strategies are available to adapt the sales presentation to the needs of the prospect. After deciding which strategy to use, the salesperson carefully prepares the presentations following the guidelines presented. Selling tools or proof devices are used to demonstrate and document the benefits presented. Chapter 12 is devoted exclusively to adapting presentations to meet customer needs.

4. *Negotiation.* Buyer resistance is a natural part of the selling–buying process. An objection, however, does present a barrier to closing the sale. For this reason, all salespeople should become skilful at negotiating resistance. Chapter 13 covers this topic.

5. *Close.* As the sales presentation progresses, there may be several opportunities to close the sale. Salespeople must learn to spot closing clues. Chapter 14 provides suggestions on how to close sales.

6. *Servicing the sale.* The importance of developing a long-term relationship with the prospect was noted in previous chapters. This rapport is often the outgrowth of post-sale service. Learning to service the sale is an important aspect of selling. Chapter 15 deals with activities that build value-adding partnerships.

Adapting the Presentation Plan to the Customer's Buying Process

A truly valuable idea or concept is timeless. The six parts of the presale presentation plan checklist have been discussed in sales training literature for many years; therefore, they might be described as fundamentals of personal selling. These steps are basic elements of most sales and frequently occur in the same sequence. However, the activities included in the six-step presentation plan must be selected with care. Prior to developing the sales call plan, the salesperson must answer one very important question: Do these activities relate to the customer's buying process? As noted in Chapter 8, purchasing structures and buying procedures can vary greatly from company to company. In some cases, the steps in the buying process have been clearly defined by the organization and this information is available to vendors. Selling steps are of little value *unless* they are firmly rooted in your customer's buying process.[14]

THE APPROACH

AFTER A GREAT DEAL OF PREPARATION, IT IS TIME TO COMMUNICATE WITH THE PROSPECT, either by face-to-face contact, by telephone, or by some other appropriate method of communication. We refer to the initial contact with the customer as the *approach*. A high-quality and professional approach is a powerful way to add value and differentiate yourself from your competitors.[15] All the effort you have put into developing relationship, product, and customer strategies can now be applied to the presentation strategy. If the approach is effective, you will be given the opportunity to make the sales presentation. If, however, the approach is not effective, the chance to present your sales story may be lost. You can be the best-prepared salesperson in the business but without a good approach, there may be little chance for a sale.

The approach has three important objectives. First, you want to build rapport with the prospect. This will be accomplished with your *telephone and/or social contact*. Second, you want to capture the person's full attention with your *business contact*. These first two steps are extremely important in establishing how much *influence* you will have throughout the rest of the sales process. Never begin your sales story if the prospect seems preoccupied and is not paying attention. Third, you want to *transition to the next stage of the sales process*. In the early part of the sales process, this will likely be the need discovery; in multi-call presentations it may be one of the other stages in the sales process such as the presentation, negotiations, or closing the sale. In some selling situations, the first contact with the customer is a telephone call. The call is made to schedule a meeting or, in some cases, to conduct the sales presentation. The face-to-face sales call starts with the social contact and continues with the business contact. The telephone contact, social contact, and business contact are discussed in this section.

Establish Your Credibility Early During your approach, everything you do affects the amount of credibility and influence you will have throughout the sales process. Your actions will either increase your perceived value or detract from it.[16] Thomas A. Freese (**www.qbsresearch.com**), author of *Secrets of Question Based Selling*, says credibility is critical to your success in sales. Credibility is an impression that people form of you very early in the sales process.[17] Sometimes little things can erode your credibility before you have a chance to prove yourself. Strategic communications consultant and executive coach Mark Jeffries (**www.markjeffries.com**), in a new training video called *The Art of Networking*, provides examples regarding how misspelled words or grammatical errors in an email, arriving late for an appointment, answering a cell phone or reading an email while with a customer, failing to maintain good eye contact, acknowledging only certain members of a buying group, or failing to send the prospect information that was promised can quickly weaken the amount of influence you have in a relationship. Failure to be well prepared for the sales call will also undermine your credibility. Credibility grows when the customer realizes you are a competent sales representative who can add value throughout the sales process.

The Telephone Contact

A telephone call provides a quick and inexpensive method of scheduling an appointment. Appointments are important because many busy prospects will not meet with a salesperson who drops in unannounced. When you schedule an appointment, the prospect knows about the sales call in advance and can therefore make the necessary preparations.

Some salespeople use the telephone exclusively to establish and maintain contact with the customer. As noted in Chapter 2, inside salespeople rely almost totally on the telephone for sales. **Telesales**—not to be confused with *telemarketing*—includes many of the same elements as traditional sales: gathering customer information, determining needs, prescribing solutions, negotiating buyer concerns, and closing sales. Telesales calls are usually unscripted, as opposed to the scripted calls widely used in telemarketing. In some situations, telesales calls are as dynamic and unpredictable as face-to-face sales calls.

In Chapter 3 we examined some of the factors that influence the meaning we attach to an oral message from another person. With the aid of this information, we can see that communication via telephone is challenging. Since the person who receives the call cannot see our facial expressions, gestures, or posture, he or she must rely wholly on the sound of our voice and the words used. The telephone caller has a definite handicap.

The telephone has some additional limitations. A salesperson accustomed to meeting prospects in person may find telephone contact impersonal. Some salespeople try to avoid using the telephone because they believe it is too easy for the prospect to say no.

telesales Using the telephone to acquire information about the customer, determine needs, suggest solutions, negotiate buyer concerns, and close the sale.

The Definitive Authority on **Solution Selling**

KEEPING THE FUNNEL FULL

Don Thomson

"Excellent coverage of the selling process. A must read for your sales library." — Mike Leavell, Vice President (retired) Hewlett Packard Company

In *Keeping the Funnel Full,* author and award-winning Hewlett-Packard salesperson Don Thomson notes that "every prospect has a preferred method of communication." He states it is important to discover whether that contact method is by telephone, in person, or by email. As one of HP's top-ranked sales pros, Don trail-blazed new markets in the Pacific Northwest (awarded MVP for US Western Sales Region), Western Canada (twice awarded HP Canada's Salesperson of the Year), and the Far East (doubled sales in nine countries in one year).

Book Cover from *"Keeping the Funnel Full"* by Don Thomson, Mardon Publishing Inc. French Creek, British Columbia.

It should be noted that these drawbacks are more imagined than real. With proper training, a salesperson can use the telephone effectively to schedule appointments. When you make an appointment by telephone, use the following practices:

1. *Plan in advance what you will say.* It helps to use a written presentation plan as a guide during the first few seconds of the conversation. What you will say is determined by the objectives of the sales call. Have a calendar available to suggest and confirm a date, time, and place for the appointment. Be sure to write it down.

2. *Politely identify yourself and the company you represent.* Set yourself apart from other callers by using a friendly tone and impeccable phone manners. This approach helps you avoid being shut out by a wary gatekeeper (secretary or receptionist).

3. *State the purpose of your call and explain how the prospect can benefit from a meeting.* In some cases, it is helpful to use a powerful benefits statement that gets the prospect's attention and whets the person's appetite for more information. Present only enough information to stimulate interest.

4. *Show respect for the prospect's time by telling the person how long the appointment will take.* Once the prospect agrees to meet with you, say, "Do you have your appointment calendar handy?" Be prepared to suggest a specific time: "Is Monday at 9:00 a.m. okay?"

5. *Confirm the appointment with a brief note, email message, or letter with the date, time, and place of your appointment.* Enclose your business card and any printed information that may be of interest to the prospect.[18]

Capturing the customer's full attention is a major objective of the approach. Attention has become a very scarce resource in today's fast-paced world.

You should anticipate resistance from some prospects. After all, most decision makers are very busy. Be persistent and persuasive if you genuinely believe a meeting with the prospect can be mutually beneficial.

Effective Use of Voice Mail The growing popularity of voice mail presents a challenge to salespeople. What type of message sets the stage for a second call or stimulates a return call? It's important to anticipate voice mail and know exactly what to say if you reach a recording. The prospect's perception of you is based on what you say and on voice quality. The following message almost guarantees that it will be ignored:

> Ms. Simpson, I am Paul Watson and I am with Elliott Property Management Services. I would like to visit with you about our services. Please call me at 862-1500.[19]

Note that this message provides no compelling reason for the prospect to call back. It offers no valid information that would stimulate interest. The voice-mail message should be similar to the opening statement you would make if you had face-to-face contact with the prospect. For example:

> Ms. Simpson, my name is Paul Watson and I represent Elliott Property Management Services. We specialize in working with property managers. We can help you reduce the paperwork associated with maintenance jobs and provide an easy way to track the progress of each job. I would like the opportunity to visit with you and will call back in the morning.[20]

Note that this message is brief and describes benefits that customers can receive. If Paul Watson wants a call back, then he needs to give the best time to reach him. He should give his phone number slowly and completely. It's usually best to repeat the number. If you are acting on a referral, be sure to say who referred you and why.

Effective Use of Email Many prospects and established customers like the convenience of email correspondence and prefer it to telephone contact. Your challenge is to

During the telephone contact, CRM contact screens and note windows can be important sources of information for making effective value-added calls. The calendar function is being used by this salesperson to schedule and confirm the date, time, and place for the sales call.

make it easy for your correspondents to read and handle your email. Always use a meaningful, specific subject line. People who receive large amounts of email may selectively choose which ones to read by scanning the subject lines and deleting those of no interest. An email with a subject line titled "Action Steps from Our 9/28 Meeting" is more likely to be read than a subject line like "Meeting Notes."[21]

The email message should tell the reader what you want and then encourage a response. Identify the main point of your email within the first or second paragraph. Format the email so it's easy to read. This may require the use of headings (with capitals or boldface print) to identify the main elements of the memo. Proofread all emails for proper grammar, punctuation, and spelling.[22] Always use the grammar and spell check tools. Messages that contain errors may misrepresent your competence. Finally, use a signature file—a small block of text that automatically follows each email you send. A typical signature file includes your full name, title, affiliation, and phone number, and in some cases a slogan.

The Social Contact—Building Rapport

According to many image consultants, "First impressions are lasting impressions." This statement is essentially true, and some profitable business relationships never crystallize because some trait or characteristic of the salesperson repels the prospective customer. Sales personnel have only a few minutes to create a positive first impression. Susan Bixler, author of *The New Professional Image*, describes the importance of the first impression this way:

> Books are judged by their covers, houses are appraised by their curb appeal, and people are initially evaluated on how they choose to dress and behave. In a perfect world this is not fair, moral, or just. What's inside should count a great deal more. And eventually it usually does, but not right away. In the meantime, a lot of opportunities can be lost.[23]

The goal of good social contact is to build rapport. Building rapport leads to credibility, which leads to trust. Once trust is established, the customer is likely to open up and share information.

Building rapport should lead to credibility, which leads to trust. Once trust is established, the prospect is likely to open up and share information. This information will provide clues regarding ways to create value. To be certain that your first impression is appropriate, review the material in Chapters 3, 4, and 5. The information in this chapter is timeless and will serve you well today and in the future.

The brief, general conversation during the social contact should hold the prospect's attention and establish a relaxed and friendly atmosphere for the business contact that is to follow. As mentioned in Chapter 3, there are three areas of conversation that should be considered in developing a social contact:

1. *Comments on here-and-now observations.* These comments may include general observations about the victory of a local athletic team, an article in the *Globe and Mail*, or specific comments about awards on display in the prospect's office. Janis Taylor, sales representative with Trugreen Chemlawn, likes to start each new appointment by seeking "common ground" with her prospects. She looks for such items as a picture of the prospect's children or a trophy.[24]

2. *Compliments.* Most customers will react positively to sincere compliments. Personal items in the prospect's office, achievements, or efficient operation of the prospect's business provide examples of things that can be praised. A salesperson might say, "I learned recently that your company is ranked number one in customer satisfaction by J. D. Power and Associates."

3. *Search for mutual acquaintances or interests.* Discovering that you have mutual friends or interests can serve as the foundation for a strong social contact. Most people enjoy talking about themselves, their hobbies, and their achievements. Debra Fine, author of *The Fine Art of Small Talk*, says, "Small talk isn't stupid. It's the appetizer for all relationships."[25]

Guidelines for Good Social Contact The social contact should be viewed as rapport-building communication on a personal basis. This brief conversation establishes the foundation for the business contact, so it should never be viewed as an insignificant part of the presentation strategy. The following guidelines can help you develop the skills needed to make a good social contact.

1. *Prepare for the social contact.* Conduct a background check on topics of interest to the person you are contacting. This includes reviewing information in the prospect database, reading industry reports, and searching the Internet. Once you arrive at the customer's office, you will discover additional information about the person's interests. Most people communicate what is important to them in the way they personalize their work environment.

2. *Initiate social contact.* The most effective opening comments should be expressed in the form of an open-ended question, such as, "I understand you have just been elected president of the United Way?" You can improve the possibility of a good response to your verbal question by applying nonverbal communication skills. Appropriate eye contact, voice inflections that communicate enthusiasm, and a warm smile will increase the customer's receptivity to your opening comments.

3. *Respond to the customer's conversations.* When the customer responds, it is imperative that you acknowledge the message both verbally and nonverbally. The verbal response might be "That is really interesting" or any other appropriate comment. Nonverbally, let the customer know you are listening by taking notes, maintaining good eye contact, and occasionally nodding your head. These gestures communicate that you want her to continue talking.

4. *Keep the social contact focused on the customer.* Because you cannot control where a conversation might go, you may be tempted to focus the conversation on topics with which you are familiar. A response such as, "Several years ago I was in charge of our company's United Way campaign and we had a difficult time meeting our goal" shifts the focus of the conversation back to you. While an occasional short personal reference may be appropriate, it is best to keep the conversation focused on topics that are of interest to the customer. Dale Carnegie said that one of the best ways to build a relationship is to encourage others to talk about themselves.

Communication on a personal basis is often the first step in establishing a common language that can improve communication between the salesperson and the prospect. How much time should be devoted to the social contact? There is no easy answer to this question. The length of the conversation will depend on the type of product or service sold, how busy the prospect appears to be, and your awareness of topics of mutual interest.

In many cases, the rapport-building conversation will take place over lunch or dinner. Some sales professionals contend that social conversation should occur before the meal is served, reserving business conversation until later. In some cases, it may be during a sporting event, such as a golf outing. It may also occur during a social event, such as a live theatre play that is offered in appreciation of prior or future business. Many successful sales have been closed during or after a social event. This explains why some companies enrol their sales staff and other customer contact personnel in dining etiquette classes.

The Business Contact

Converting the prospect's attention from the social contact to the business proposal is an important part of the approach. When you convert and hold your prospect's attention, you have fulfilled an important step in the selling process. Furthermore, without this step, the door has been closed on completing the remaining steps of the sale.

Some salespeople use a carefully planned opening statement or a question to attract the customer's attention to the sales presentation. A statement or question that focuses on the prospect's dominant buying motive is, of course, more likely to achieve the desired results. Buyers must like what they see and hear, and must be made to feel that it will be worthwhile to hear more.

CONVERTING THE BUYER'S ATTENTION AND AROUSING INTEREST

THROUGHOUT THE YEARS, SALESPEOPLE HAVE IDENTIFIED AND USED A NUMBER OF EFFECTIVE ways to capture the prospect's attention and arouse interest in the presentation. Seven of the most common will be explained in the following material:

- Agenda approach
- Product demonstration approach
- Referral approach
- Customer benefit approach
- Question approach
- Survey approach
- Premium approach

We also discuss combining two or more of these approaches.

Agenda Approach One of the most effective ways to move from the social contact to the business contact is to thank the customer for taking time to meet with you and then review your goals for the meeting. You might say, "Thank you for meeting with me this morning. I would like to accomplish three things during the time you have given me." This statement shows that you value the person's time and have preplanned a specific agenda. Always be open to changing the agenda based on suggestions from the customer.[26] This approach is welcomed by buyers in multi-call situations.

Product Demonstration Approach This straightforward method of getting the prospect's attention can be achieved by showing the actual product, a sample, a mock-up, a video, or a well prepared brochure either in print form or on a computer screen. It is a popular approach used by sales representatives who sell convention services, technical products, pharmaceuticals, photographic equipment, automobiles, construction equipment, office furniture, and many other products. In many multi-call situations, salespeople leave samples for the customer to examine and try at a later date. Trish Ormsby, a sales representative who sells security systems, uses her portable computer to create a visual image of systems that meet the customer's security needs.[27]

Turn up the volume.

Cook's hard-working national consumer campaign will definitely drive up the volume moving through your meat case. Our significant TV presence is a big part of that effort.

Add to that, Cook's print advertising, which will reach your customers through a nonstop media schedule and couponing effort that includes leading national women's magazines, such as *Good Housekeeping, Woman's Day, Family Circle, Rosie* and many more. Plus, our public relations efforts targeting national and local media, and an aggressive Web presence, will maximize the power of our campaign.

And Cook's offers a proven point-of-sale merchandising program tailored to the needs of your store. Of course, as always, our personalized service assures that your orders arrive when you want, the way you want.

We're turning up the volume to your customers. Stay tuned for more year-round exciting action.

Cook's
Cook's ham. Always good to the bone.®

©2001 ConAgra Foods, Inc.

A ConAgra Foods product

A straightforward product demonstration method for getting the grocery store meat manager's attention would be the use of this ad from Cook's (www.cookshams.com), a division of ConAgra. The salesperson can explain the value of featuring meat products that are supported by a strong media promotion and point-of-sale merchandising program.

Referral Approach Research indicates that another person will be far more impressed with your good points if these points are presented by a third party rather than by you. The referral approach is quite effective because a third party—a satisfied customer— believes the prospect will benefit from your product. This type of opening statement has universal appeal among salespeople from nearly every field. When you use the referral approach, your opening statement should include a direct reference to the third party. Here is an example: "Mrs. Follett, my name is Kurt Wheeler, and I represent the Cross Printing Company. We specialize in printing all types of business forms. Mr. Ameno— buyer for Raybale Products, Incorporated—is a regular customer of ours, and he suggested I mention his name to you."

Customer Benefit Approach One of the most effective ways to gain a prospect's attention is to immediately point out one benefit of purchasing your product. Try to begin with the most important issue (or problem) facing the client. When using this approach,

Effective Design and Use of the Business Card

The business card continues to be a powerful tool for salespeople. It provides a personal touch in our high-tech world. The business card is a convenient way to communicate important information to customers and others involved in the sales process. When you develop your business card, keep these tips in mind.

- Use eye-catching items such as your company logo, raised letters, and textured paper. The card should be tasteful and pleasing to the eye. Do use a white background.

- The card should feature all current contact information such as your email address, telephone numbers, and mailing address. List a home phone number only if there's a second line for business calls.

- Consider using both sides of the card. You might print your customer service philosophy on the back of the card or list the products you sell.

Give your cards generously to anyone who might need to contact you later. Always offer your business card when networking. The card is useful when the contact tells others about your products or services. How you respond to someone else's business card is important also. According to communications trainer Mark Jeffries, mentioned earlier, when someone hands you their business card, find something about it you can comment on before putting it away. You can comment on things such as the design, the company, or the individual's title. He contends that people will have a favourable memory of you, if done successfully.[b]

---

the most important buyer benefit is included in the initial statement. For example, the salesperson selling a portable Sony projector might open with this statement:

> The Sony VPL-CS4 lightweight projector strikes a balance among cost, size, brightness, and convenience. It's a good choice for a quick business trip or for a work-at-home presentation.

A company benefit example taken from the financial services field:

> When you meet with a Scotia McLeod investment specialist, you can obtain advice on a family of 48 professionally managed no-load mutual funds.

elevator speech A short, pre-planned and extensively rehearsed speech used to establish credibility and open the door for the salesperson by focusing on the benefit of working with him or her.

The customer benefit approach is also used with what is sometimes referred to as the *elevator speech*. The **elevator speech** focuses on the benefit of working with the salesperson and is used to open the door and establish credibility to meet a need. It is about offering to take excellent care of the prospect. The elevator speech should be short, prepared well in advance, and extensively rehearsed before it is used. It is used most appropriately in the initial call on a prospect where the prequalifying research indicates that the buyer is more interested in the benefits of working with a highly qualified salesperson than finding a new product solution or supplier. Here is an employment services example of a salesperson benefit statement using the elevator speech approach:

> Hello, I'm Kevin Zhang. I partner with companies like yours that need to find talented people to help their business grow and become more profitable.

As noted, the key to achieving success with the customer benefit approach is preparation. Prospects are annoyed when a salesperson cannot quickly communicate the benefits of meeting with them. Bruce Klassen, sales manager for Do All Industrial Supply, says, "Our salespeople begin the sales process by researching the prospect and the company. We need to be sure that our product line is going to benefit that prospect before we make even an initial sales approach."[28]

Question Approach The question approach has two positive features. First, a question almost always triggers prospect involvement. Very few people will avoid answering a direct question. Second, a question gets the prospect thinking about a problem that the salesperson is prepared to solve.

Molly Hoover, a sales training consultant, conducts training classes for sales managers and car dealers who want to better understand the subtleties of selling to the female car buyer. She suggests an approach that includes a few basic questions such as:

> Is the vehicle for business or pleasure?
> Will you be buying within the next week or so?[29]

These opening questions are not difficult to answer, yet they get the customer mentally involved. Some of the best opening questions are carefully phrased to capture attention. The authors of *The Sales Question Book* offer some good examples:

> Are you aware that we just added three new services to our payroll and accounting package? Could I tell you about them?
> We are now offering all our customers a special service that used to be reserved for our largest accounts. Would you be interested in hearing about it?[30]

Once you ask the question, listen carefully to the response. If the answer is yes, proceed with an enthusiastic presentation of your product. If the answer is no, then you may have to gracefully try another approach or thank the prospect for their time and depart. The use of questions will be discussed in detail in the next chapter and will provide information on the specific types of questions to use to approach your customer.

Survey Approach Larry Short, a financial advisor with RBC Dominion Securities and a winner of the Atlantic Canada Award of Distinction by the Investment Dealers Association of Canada, frequently uses the survey approach as part of his customer strategy. He has new clients fill out a detailed questionnaire before he sees them for a first appointment.[31] He studies the completed questionnaire and other documents before making any effort to find a solution to any of the customer's financial planning needs. Data collection through the survey is an important part of the problem-solving philosophy of selling. It is often used in selling office machines, business security systems, insurance, and other products where need cannot be established without careful study.

The survey approach offers many advantages. It is generally a nonthreatening way to open a sales call. You are simply asking permission to acquire information that can be used to determine the buyer's need for your product. Because the survey is tailor-made for a specific business, the buyer is given individual treatment. Finally, the survey approach helps avoid a premature discussion of price. Price cannot be discussed until the survey is completed. We will discuss the survey and needs discovery in detail in Chapter 11.

Premium Approach The premium approach involves giving the customer a free sample or an inexpensive item. A financial services representative might give the customer a booklet that can be used to record expenses. Product samples are frequently used by persons who sell cosmetics. Creative use of premiums is an effective way to get the customer's attention.

The agenda, product demonstration, referral, customer benefit, question, survey, and premium approaches offer the salesperson a variety of ways to set the stage for the presentation strategy. With experience, salespeople learn to select the most effective

The survey approach offers many advantages. It is generally a nonthreatening way to open a sales call. You simply ask permission to acquire information that can be used to determine the buyer's need for the product.

approach for each selling situation. Table 10.1 provides examples of how these approaches can be applied in real-world situations.

Combination Approaches A hallmark of consultative selling is flexibility. Therefore, a combination of approaches sometimes provides the best avenue to need identification.

Table 10.1 Business Contact Worksheet	
This worksheet illustrates how to prepare effective real-world approaches that capture the customer's attention.	
Method of Approach	**What will you say?**
1. Agenda	1. (Office supply) "Thank you for meeting with me, Ms. Zhou. During the next 45 minutes, I plan to accomplish three things."
2. Product demonstration	2a. (Retail clothing) "We have just received a shipment of new fall sweaters from Braemar International."
	2b. (Business forms manufacturer) "Our plant has just purchased a $300 000 Harris Graphics composer, Mr. Reichart. I would like to show you a copy of your sales invoice with your logo printed on it."
3. Referral	3. (Food wholesaler) "Paula Doeman, procurement manager for St. Joseph's Hospital, suggested that I provide you with information about our computerized 'Order It' system."
4. Customer benefit	4. (Real estate) "Mr. and Mrs. Stuart, my company lists and sells more homes than any other company in the area where your home is located. Our past performance would lead me to believe we can sell your home within two weeks."
5. Question	5. (Hotel convention services) "Mrs. McClaughin, will your 2011 Annual Franchisee Meeting be held in April?"
6. Survey	6a. (Custom-designed computer software) "Mr. Pham, I would like the opportunity to learn about your accounts receivable and accounts payable procedures. We may be able to develop a customized program that will significantly improve your cash flow."
	6b. (Retail menswear) "May I ask you a few questions about your wardrobe? The information will help me better understand your clothing needs."
7. Premium	7. (Financial services) "I would like to give you a publication entitled *Guaranteed Growth Annuity*."

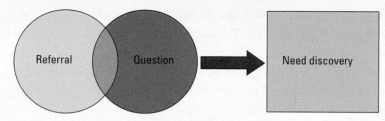

Figure 10.4 Combination Approach
Combination approaches provide a smooth transition to the need discovery part of the consultative-style presentation.

Sales personnel who have adopted the consultative style will, of course, use the question and survey approaches most frequently. Some selling situations, however, require that one of the other approaches be used, either alone or in combination with the question and survey approaches (see Fig. 10.4). An example of how a salesperson might combine referral and question approaches follows:

SALESPERSON: Carl Hamilton at Simmons Modern Furniture suggested that I visit with you about our new line of compact furniture designed for today's smaller homes. He believes this line might complement the furniture you currently feature.

CUSTOMER: Yes, Carl called me yesterday and mentioned your name and company.

SALESPERSON: Before showing you our product lines, I would like to ask you some questions about your current product mix. First, what do you currently carry in the area of bedroom furniture?

Coping with Sales Call Reluctance

The transition from the preapproach to the approach is sometimes blocked by sales call reluctance. Fear of making the initial contact with the prospect is one of the biggest obstacles to sales success. For new salespeople, the problem can be career-threatening. **Sales call reluctance** includes thoughts, feelings, and behavioural patterns that conspire to limit what a salesperson is able to accomplish. It is an internal, often emotional, barrier to sales success. Sales call reluctance can be caused by several different thought patterns:[32]

sales call reluctance Fear of making the initial contact with the prospect.

- Fear of taking risks
- Fear of group presentations
- Lack of self-confidence
- Fear of rejection

Regardless of the reasons for sales call reluctance, you can learn to deal with it. Here are some suggestions:

- *Be optimistic about the outcome of the initial contact.* It is better to anticipate success than to anticipate failure. Martin Seligman, professor of psychology at the University of Pennsylvania and author of the bestselling book *Learned Optimism,* says that success in selling requires a healthy dose of optimism.[33] It is important to frequently recommit yourself to the double win, value-adding approach to working with customers discussed earlier. The anticipation of failure is a major barrier to making the initial contact.

- *Practise your approach before making the initial contact.* A well-rehearsed effort to make the initial contact increases your self-confidence and reduces the possibility that you may handle the situation badly.

- *Recognize that it is normal to feel anxious about the initial contact.* Even the most experienced salespeople experience some degree of sales call reluctance and this reluctance can surface anywhere in the sales process.

- *Develop a deeper commitment to your goals.* Abraham Zaleznik, professor emeritus at Harvard Business School, says, "If your commitment is only in your mind, then you'll lose it when you encounter a big obstacle. If your commitment is in your heart *and* your mind, you'll create the power to break through the toughest obstacles."[34]

Selling to the Gatekeeper

Many decision makers have an assistant or secretary who manages their daily schedule. This person is commonly referred to as the "gatekeeper." If you want to reach the decision maker, work hard to align yourself with the person who schedules this person's appointments. Rule number one is to treat the gatekeeper with respect. Learn his or her name and what he or she does. Keep in mind that this person can be an important source of information. For example, the gatekeeper can tell you how the buying process works and provide information regarding new developments in the company. This person may be able to help you make a preliminary qualification before you reach the decision maker. When you treat this person as an expert by soliciting his or her views, you establish a relationship that can pay big dividends today and in the future.[35] When possible, use personal referrals from someone the prospect knows. If you have met the prospect previously, describe the meeting and tell the gatekeeper why you feel a second meeting would be beneficial.

In some cases a secretary, assistant, or receptionist will screen incoming telephone calls. Be prepared to convince this person that your call is important. Always treat the gatekeeper with respect and courtesy.

Wall Street Journal, March 10, 1999, p. A–23. From the *Wall Street Journal* by permission of Cartoon Features Syndicate.

"I don't think of myself as the Jenkins Doolittle & Bloom gatekeeper. I rather prefer lead blocker."

REVIEWING KEY CONCEPTS

- Describe the three prescriptions that are included in the presentation strategy.

  Developing a presentation strategy involves preparing presale objectives, developing a presale presentation plan, and providing outstanding customer service. The presentation strategy combines elements of the relationship, product, and customer strategies.

- Discuss the two-part preapproach process.

  Preparation for the sales presentation is a two-part process. Part one is referred to as the *preapproach* and involves preparing presale objectives and developing a presale presentation plan. It's best to develop presentation objectives for each stage of the buying process. Part two is called the *approach* and involves making a good first impression, securing the prospect's attention, and transitioning to need identification.

- Describe team presentation strategies.

  In recent years, team selling has surfaced as a major development. Sales teams can often uncover problems, solutions, and sales opportunities that no individual salesperson could discover working alone. Team sales presentations require a more detailed precall plan than individual sales calls. Without careful planning and extensive practice (rehearsal), team presentations are likely to be delivered in a disorganized manner.

- Explain how adaptive selling builds on four broad strategic areas of personal selling.

  Adaptive selling involves altering sales behaviours in order to improve communication with the customer. Salespeople today are challenged to develop a broader repertoire of selling strategies. Salespeople skilled in adaptive selling consider how the relationship, product, and customer strategies can enhance the sales presentation.

- Describe the six main parts of the presentation plan.

  After collecting background information, salespeople need to create a customized presale presentation plan. The plan is developed after careful study of the six-step presentation plan that includes approach, presentation, demonstration, negotiation, close, and servicing the sale.

- Explain how to effectively approach the customer.

  The approach may involve face-to-face contact, telephone contact, or some other appropriate method of communication. If the approach is effective, the salesperson will be given an opportunity to make the sales presentation. A major goal of the *social contact* is to make a good first impression, build rapport, and establish credibility. The *business contact* involves converting the prospect's attention from the social contact to the sales presentation.

- Describe seven ways to convert the prospect's attention and arouse interest.

  Over the years, salespeople have identified several ways to convert the prospect's attention and arouse interest in the presentation. Some of the most common ways include the agenda approach, product demonstration approach, referral approach, customer benefit approach, question approach, survey approach, and premium approach.

Key Terms

action objective **233**

approach **232**

elevator speech **248**

preapproach **231**

presentation strategy **229**

sales call reluctance **251**

six-step presentation plan **237**

telesales **240**

Review Questions

1. What is the purpose of the preapproach? What are the two prescriptions included in the preapproach?

2. Explain the role of objectives in developing the presale presentation plan.

3. Why should salespeople establish multiple-objective sales presentations? List four possible objectives that would be appropriate for stage one and stage two of the buying process.

4. Compare and contrast team sales presentations and individual sales calls.

5. Describe the major steps in the presentation plan. Briefly discuss the role of adaptive selling in implementing the presentation plan.

6. What are the major objectives of the approach?

7. Briefly describe the four guidelines that can help you make a good social contact.

8. What are some rules to follow when leaving a message on voice mail? On email?

9. What methods can the salesperson use to convert the prospect's attention to the sales presentation?

10. Discuss why combination approaches are considered an important consultative-selling practice. Provide one example of a combination approach.

Application Exercises

1. Assume that you are a salesperson who calls on retailers. For some time, you have been attempting to get an appointment with the head buyer for one of the best retailers in the city to persuade her to carry your line. You have an appointment to see her in 90 minutes. You are sitting in your office now and it will take you about 30 minutes to drive to your appointment. Outline what you should be doing between now and the time you leave to meet your prospect.

2. Tom Nelson has just graduated from Algonquin College with a major in marketing. He has three years of experience in the retail grocery business and has decided he would like to work as a salesperson for the district office of Procter & Gamble. Tom has decided to telephone and set up an appointment for an interview. Write out exactly what Tom should *plan* to say during his telephone call.

3. Concepts from Dale Carnegie's *How to Win Friends and Influence People* can help you prepare for the social contact. Access the Dale Carnegie Training website (**www.dalecarnegie.com**) and examine the courses offered. Search for the Sales Advantage Course. Read the course description and review the two main things you will learn in this program.

4. Canadian author and sales trainer Steven J. Schwartz is internationally known for his expertise in helping salespeople get appointments. Visit his website at **www.hotcoldcalls.com** and hit "Toolbox." One of the items here is a 24-question self-assessment tool that can help you identify mistakes you might make when initially contacting prospects by telephone. Complete the survey and assess how well you did. Continue until you get all answers correct.

5. You are being interviewed for a sales position with a national electronics retailer. The job is very important to you as it will help pay your living expenses while you complete your studies. During the interview, the manager says, "We are known for honesty and outstanding service, and we expect any salesperson we hire to sell only products that meet customer needs. Please take 10 minutes and write five questions that you would ask a customer who approaches you in our store and wants to buy a digital camera. I will also want to know why you have chosen the questions you have chosen." What questions will you ask? Defend your choices.

ROLE-PLAY EXERCISE

Research the new computer that you would like to purchase in the future or that you have just purchased. Strategically, prepare to meet a prospect who has been referred to you by a friend and who would like to purchase a similar computer. Using Table 10.1, prepare four different business contact statements or questions you could use to approach your prospect. Review the material in this chapter and then pair off with another student, who will assume the role of your prospect. First, role-play the telephone contact and set up an appointment to get your prospect into your store to meet with you and look at the computer. Second, role-play the approach you will use when the prospect actually comes into the store. Review how well you made the approach.

Reality Selling Today Video Case Problem

The global construction industry is a lucrative market, with customer needs ranging from measuring products to sophisticated construction solutions. Hilti, the company featured in the vignette at the start of this chapter, provides its customers around the world with leading-edge construction products and services with outstanding added value. Hilti prides itself on its direct sales model, which allows its salespeople and service teams to work directly *with* and *for* the customer.

Alim Hirani, an account manager for Hilti, adopts the relationship marketing approach in his selling strategy. He often starts his sales calls, which have been carefully planned, with ice breakers such as asking about the customer's family rather than making the sale immediately. His sales presentations may take place in clients' offices or even at construction sites. Consequently, he must always plan well in advance the best way to make his sales presentations for specific sales calls. At all times, he must attempt to establish his own and his company's credibility by demonstrating the premium value that Hilti's products and services can offer his clients. Whenever possible, Alim tries to get the customer involved in product demonstration "because, after all, 'seeing is believing.'" Once the customers see for themselves the benefits of Hilti's product features, moving the customers from the investigation and evaluation stages to the action stage is just a formality.

Alim sells not only individually but also as part of a team. For major clients who require a complete package

of building/construction, mechanical/electrical, telecom, and interior finishing products and services, Alim works closely with his team members to make sure the information he acquires from the customer during initial contacts is made available to other salespeople and technical personnel on the team. In the construction industry, closing the sale is—most of the time—just the beginning. Well-trained product application specialists join Alim to offer customers after-sale services, technical support, and training. (See the chapter opener on page 228 and Reality Selling Today Role Play 6 in Appendix 1 on page 444 for more information.)

Questions

1. Why should Alim Hirani adopt the three prescriptions for the presentation strategy?

2. Salespeople are encouraged to establish multiple-objective sales presentations. What are some objectives Alim Hirani should consider when he calls on construction managers at the construction site?

3. What are some special challenges Alim Hirani faces when he makes his sales presentations in a non-office setting?

4. Put yourself in the position of a construction salesperson. Can you envision a situation in which you might combine different ways to convert the prospect's attention and interests into action? Explain.

PARTNERSHIP SELLING: A ROLE PLAY/SIMULATION

Developing a Relationship Strategy

Visit the role play/simulation materials provided in the Student Resources section of your companion website at **www.pearsoncanada.ca/manning**. *A Contents page lists appropriate page references for the activities.*

Read *Employment Memorandum 2*, which announces your promotion to account executive. In your new position,

you will be assigned by your instructor to one of the two major account categories in the convention centre market, either the *association accounts market* or the *corporate accounts market*. The association accounts market includes customers who are responsible for planning meetings for their association or group. The corporate accounts market includes customers who are responsible for planning meetings for the company they represent. You will remain in the account category for the rest of the role plays.

Note the challenges you will have in your new position. Each of these challenges will be represented in the future *sales memoranda* you will be receiving from your sales manager. Read *Sales Memorandum 1* for the account category you are assigned. (Note that "A" means association and your customer is Erin Adkins, and "B" means corporate and your customer is Leigh Combs.) Follow the instructions in the sales memorandum and strategically prepare to approach your new customer. Your call objectives will be to establish a relationship (social contact), share an appealing benefit, and find out if your customer is planning any future conventions (business contact).

You may be asked to assume the role of a customer in the account category that you are not assigned as a salesperson. Your instructor will provide you with detailed instructions for correctly assuming this role.

Chapter 11
Determining Customer Needs with a Consultative Questioning Strategy

Learning Objectives

After studying this chapter, you should be able to

1 Outline the benefits of the consultative sales process.

2 Describe the four parts of the need-satisfaction model.

3 Discuss the use of questions to discover customer needs.

4 Describe the importance of active listening and the use of confirmation questions.

5 Select solutions that match customer needs.

 Adaptive Selling Today Training Video Series

QUESTIONS, QUESTIONS, QUESTIONS

THE EFFECTIVE USE OF QUESTIONS IS THE STARTING POINT OF THE CONSULTATIVE SALES process. Questions are used to build adaptive-style selling relationships, discover customer needs, and adapt and present product solutions that meet those needs. Questions span the entire sales process and are also used to successfully negotiate, close, and service a sale.

Questions, Questions, Questions, the second video in our Adaptive Selling Today Training Video Series, introduces and shows how to use the four adaptive selling questions described in this chapter. An Internet telephone systems sales representative featured in the video learns that one of his largest accounts may be going with another supplier. The salesperson's company brought in a new sales training program on how to use questions effectively, and the salesperson is the first to learn the system. With his newly acquired knowledge and skills, the salesperson schedules another call to see if he can, with the use of questions, re-establish his relationship and salvage the sale.

In this follow-up call, we find out how well he has learned to adapt and use questions to discover and better understand the customer's needs, create value, solve the customer's buying problem, and retain the account. Throughout the three-part video, the salesperson learns about the following four-part multiple questioning strategy and what these questions will reveal during the consultative sales presentation.

Extensive research regarding the use of questions in the sales process reveals the importance of developing and perfecting a multiple questioning strategy to understand and solve customer needs. The adaptive questions video dramatically presents how these questions are used in the process.

SURVEY questions	Reveal	Problems and situation
PROBING questions	Reveal	Pain and implications
NEED-SATISFACTION questions	Reveal	Pleasure and need satisfaction
CONFIRMATION questions	Reveal	Mutual understanding

The use of an effective questioning strategy, so important to the consultative sales process, is one of the greatest challenges facing salespeople. Need discovery and questioning will be explored in this chapter (Fig. 11.1), and the sales presentation will be presented in the next chapter.

THE CONSULTATIVE SALES PROCESS ADDS VALUE

A GROWING NUMBER OF SALESPEOPLE, LIKE THE INTERNET TELEPHONE SYSTEM SALESPERSON pictured above, have adopted the consultative sales process. New competitive structures and customer demands have forced companies to continuously adapt and redefine their value-adding processes.[1] Consultative selling, as introduced in Chapter 2, is a value-adding process. Consultative selling involves meeting customer needs by asking strategic questions, listening to customers, understanding—and caring about—their problems, selecting the appropriate solution, creating the sales presentation, and following through after the sale. Consultative selling is a very customer-centric form of selling that creates value for the customer and, in the process, creates value for the firm.[2] This approach is very different from product-oriented selling. As one author noted, "Product-oriented selling can easily lapse into product evangelism." Product-oriented selling is usually inefficient and ineffective.[3,4]

The Six-Step Presentation Plan	
Step One: Approach	☑ Review Strategic/Consultative Selling Model ☑ Initiate customer contact
Step Two: Need Discovery	☐ Ask strategic questions ☐ Determine customer needs ☐ Select Product Solution
Step Three: Presentation	☐ Select presentation strategy ☐ Create presentation plan ☐ Initiate presentation
Step Four: Negotiation	☐ Anticipate buyer concerns ☐ Plan negotiating methods ☐ Initiate win-win negotiations
Step Five: Close	☐ Plan appropriate closing methods ☐ Recognize closing clues ☐ Initiate closing methods
Step Six: Servicing the Sale	☐ Follow through ☐ Follow-up calls ☐ Expansion selling

Service, retail, wholesale, and manufacturer selling

Figure 11.1 Creating the Sales Presentation
A consultative sales process involves adding value by accurately determining the prospect's needs and selecting an appropriate product or service.

New entrants in the field of personal selling sometimes wonder why some people excel in selling products or services, while others, who seem to work just as hard, fall short of meeting company or personal selling goals. The answer can be found by reviewing the behaviours displayed by top sales performers from *Fortune* 500 and smaller entrepreneurial-based companies. High-performance sales personnel have learned how to skilfully diagnose and solve problems better than their competitors.[5] This consultative problem-solving capability translates into the following:

Increased Customer Satisfaction Customers prefer to purchase solutions that truly meet their needs. The solution that is "just right" for the customer adds value, maximizes satisfaction, and sets the stage for a partnership relationship and repeat business. In some cases, the right solution will cost more than the customer planned to pay, but the added value will usually compensate for the higher price.

Jeff Thull, author of *Mastering the Complex Sale* and *The Prime Solution*, states, "In too many buyer–seller relationships, there is a value gap where the customer is not getting the satisfaction they believe was promised."[6] Consultative salespeople with the ability to diagnose and solve customer problems are able to close this value gap.

More Sales Closed The extra time taken to carefully solve the customer's buying problem will set the stage for closing more sales. A certain amount of buyer resistance surfaces in nearly every selling situation. Understanding your customer's needs and configuring the most suitable solution from available options adds value to both your customer and your company. It will help you avoid unnecessary objections from the customer.

Fewer Order Cancellations and Fewer Returns It is always disappointing to have a customer cancel an order a few days after the sale was closed. The frequency of order cancellations can be reduced with consultative-style selling. Returned merchandise is another serious problem. Whether the product is returned or needs to be reconfigured, the expense will often wipe out the profit earned on several sales.

Increased Business and Referrals Many business firms do not make a profit on the first sale. In fact, some firms do not earn a profit until the customer has placed the third or fourth order. The same is true for the salesperson. Without repeat business and a steady list of referrals, the salesperson will generally not experience the financial and psychic rewards described in Chapter 1. If at any point the customer does not feel the treatment was fair, the time and cost invested in partnership building and obtaining the initial order, as well as future sales, may be lost. Repeat business also builds a sense of pride within everyone associated with the business.

Satisfied customers represent a potent form of sales promotion. A group of satisfied customers forms what might be called an "auxiliary" sales force. Through word-of-mouth advertising, especially with the availability of social media and blogging, these people are referring potential customers and building new business for both the salesperson and the firm. Most of us can't resist sharing positive experiences with friends and business acquaintances.

The sales environment is changing. In competitive markets, success increasingly hinges on developing and maintaining mutually rewarding customer relationships.[7] Salespeople using the consultative sales presentation model are able to create more value and gain competitive advantage in their markets.

THE FOUR-PART NEED-SATISFACTION MODEL

To be most effective, the salesperson should think of the sales process as a four-part model. The Consultative Sales Process Guide features these four parts (Fig. 11.2).

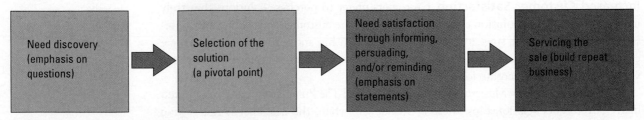

Figure 11.2 The Consultative Sales Process Guide
To be most successful, the salesperson should think of the sales presentation as a four-part process.

Part One—Need Discovery

Since the emergence of the marketing concept discussed in Chapter 2, where the activities of a firm revolve around the needs of the customer, need discovery forms the essence of salespeople being able to create value, meet the needs of their customers, and execute the firm's commitment to the marketing concept. A review of the behaviours displayed by high-performance salespeople helps in understanding the importance of precise need discovery. They have learned how to skilfully diagnose and solve the prospect's problems better than their competitors can. This problem-solving capability translates into more repeat business and referrals, and fewer order cancellations and returns.[8]

Unless the selling situation requires mere order taking (customers know exactly what they want), need discovery in the information economy is a critically important part of the sales process. It may begin during the qualifying stage of building the prospect database or during the approach if the salesperson uses questions or a survey during the initial contact with the customer. Need discovery generally begins after you transition from the approach. In multi-call situations, need discovery may be the primary call objective during the first or second call. In most multi-call settings, it is wise to reconfirm the needs discovered in earlier calls.

The pace, scope, depth, and time allocated to inquiry depend on a variety of factors, including the sophistication of the product, the selling price, the customer's knowledge of the product, the product applications, and, of course, the time available for dialogue between the salesperson and the prospect. Each selling situation is different, so a standard set of guidelines for need discovery is not practical. Additional information on need discovery is presented later in the chapter.

Part Two—Selection of the Solution

The emphasis in sales and marketing today is on determining buyer needs and then selecting or configuring custom-fitted solutions to satisfy these needs. Therefore, an important function of the salesperson is product selection and recommendation. The salesperson must choose the product or service that will provide maximum satisfaction. When making this decision, the salesperson must be aware of all product options, including those offered by the competition.

Salespeople who have the ability to conduct an effective, value-added needs analysis can achieve the status of trusted adviser. Mary Langston is a personal shopper who works in a large department store and helps customers update their wardrobes. When asked what her days are like, she says, "It starts and ends with being a good listener." She promises her customers that she will never let them walk out of the store with clothing that does not look right.[9]

Part Three—Need Satisfaction through Informing, Persuading, or Reminding

The third part of the consultative sales process consists of creating a need-satisfaction sales presentation and communicating to the customer, both verbally and nonverbally, the satisfaction that the product or service can provide. The salesperson places less emphasis on the use of questions and begins making value-adding statements. These

Pharmaceutical salespeople generally have only a short time to present their product. In some situations, the doctor may immediately indicate a willingness to prescribe. However, in other situations the salesperson may be asked to make an informative need-satisfaction presentation to several members of the practice.

value-adding statements are organized into a presentation that informs, persuades, or reminds the customer of the most suitable product or service. In several of the remaining chapters, we discuss specific strategies used in conjunction with the sales presentation/demonstration, negotiating buyer resistance, and closing and servicing the sale.

Part Four—Servicing the Sale

Servicing the sale is a major way to create value. These activities, which occur after closing the sale, ensure maximum customer satisfaction and set the stage for a long-term relationship. Service activities include expansion selling, making credit arrangements, following through on assurances and promises, and dealing effectively with complaints. This topic is covered in detail in Chapter 15.

In those cases where a sale is normally closed during a single sales call, the salesperson should be prepared to go through all four parts of the Consultative Sales Process Guide. However, when a salesperson uses a multi-call approach, preparation for all the parts is usually not practical. The person selling networking systems or investments, for example, almost always use a multi-call sales process. Need discovery (part one) is the focus of the first call.

CREATING VALUE WITH NEED DISCOVERY

A LAWYER DOES NOT GIVE THE CLIENT ADVICE UNTIL THE LEGAL PROBLEM HAS BEEN carefully studied and confirmed. A doctor does not prescribe medication until the patient's symptoms have been identified. In like manner, the salesperson should not recommend purchase of a product without thorough need identification. You start

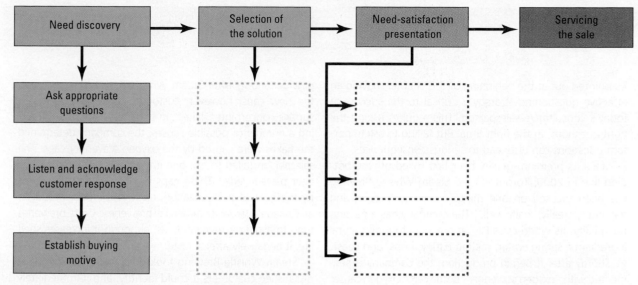

Figure 11.3 Three Dimensions of Need Discovery

with the assumption that the prospect's need or problem is not known. The only way to determine and confirm the need or problem is to get the other person talking. Effective relationship builders are willing to listen to better understand customer challenges. They ask questions that lead to consultative conversations, which open doors to greater opportunities.[10] You must obtain information to properly clarify the need, propose a single solution, or offer a range of solutions.

Customers may not realize that they actually have a problem. Even when they are aware of their need, as noted earlier by Salesforce.com's Dave Levitt, given the wide range of solutions and new products available today they may not realize that an actual solution to their problem exists. Bringing new insights regarding both their buying problem and enhanced solutions creates value for your customer.

Need discovery (sometimes called *need analysis* or *needs assessment*) begins with precall preparation, when the salesperson is acquiring background information on the prospect. As noted in Chapter 9, this part of need discovery is also referred to as *qualifying the prospect*. Need discovery, and in some cases the qualification process, continues once the salesperson and the customer are engaged in a real dialogue. Through the process of need discovery, the salesperson establishes two-way communication by asking appropriate questions and listening carefully to the prospect's responses. These responses will usually provide clues concerning the customer's dominant buying motive (see Fig. 11.3).

need discovery The salesperson establishes two-way communication by asking appropriate questions and listening carefully to the customer's responses.

Need Discovery—Asking Questions

The effective use of questions to achieve need identification and need satisfaction is one of the greatest challenges facing most professional salespeople. The types of questions you ask, the timing of those questions, and how you pose them will greatly affect your ability to create customer value. In many situations, asking high-value-added questions that enlighten your prospect both about their needs and possible solutions results in an immediate sale.

From the Field

The Question Not Asked

As pointed out at the beginning of this chapter, having an effective questioning strategy is critical to the success of today's consultative salesperson. This requires asking the right questions, at the right time. But failing to ask important questions can also lead to serious consequences.

Since its premium-quality beer first rolled off the bottling line in 2000, Toronto-based Steam Whistle Brewing has been focused on one thing: making one beer, and making it "really, really well." The company has a passion for quality. Its world-class Pilsner has only four all-natural ingredients: spring water, malted barley, hops, and yeast.

Shortly after it began production, the company experimented with "oxygen scavenger" bottle caps. Oxygen causes premature quality deterioration of many food products, including beer. The salesperson who sold the caps was excited about the quality improvement his caps would provide. Shortly after Steam Whistle Brewing began using the new caps, however, customer complaints began to surface concerning "flakes" in their beer. After investigating a number of possible causes, the company determined the flakes were caused by the oxygen scavenger caps. The salesperson failed to ask one important question: "Is your beer pasteurized?" These caps work only when activated by the heat of pasteurization, as with the beer produced at Canada's larger commercial breweries. Craft breweries tend to avoid pasteurization as, although it increases shelf life, it negatively affects taste.

Steam Whistle Brewing took quick action to win back dissatisfied customers it could identify, and it immediately improved its filling/capping procedures to ensure its quality was restored. Since then, the "Good Beer Folks" at Steam Whistle have won many awards for their beer.[a]

The strategic approach to asking questions has been the focus of two major studies. These studies were conducted in response to the emergence of the marketing concept and the evolution of the consultative and strategic selling eras discussed in Chapter 2. The research was conducted by Neil Rackham for his book *SPIN Selling* and SPIN Selling Sales Training programs, and Xerox Learning Systems for their successful Personal Selling Skills (PSS) course.

The Spin Selling Model According to research conducted by Neil Rackham during the strategic selling era (see Chapter 2, Table 2.1: Evolution of Personal Selling) on more than 35 000 salespeople, mastering the use of questions can increase one's success in sales by 17 percent.[11] Questions help clarify the exact dimensions of the problem, help the customer evaluate a range of solutions, and assist the customer in evaluating the potential outcome of the solution that is implemented.[12] Rackham's research focused on strategies for making large-ticket sales and is based on a close examination of successful salespeople. Rackham found that the investigative or need discovery stage of the sales process has the most impact on the buyer's decision to purchase a product. He recommends a multiple-question approach that involves using four types of questions in a specific sequence (see Selling Today on p. 272). SPIN sales training programs are presented by Huthwaite, Inc. (**www.huthwaite.com**).

Personal Selling Skills Model The importance of questioning to establishing two-way communication was revealed in another study conducted during the consultative selling era. Research conducted by Xerox Learning Systems was used to develop the original Xerox Personal Selling Skills training program. Sales personnel were interviewed to identify the characteristics of a successful sales call. The results were quite surprising.

A successful sales call lasts an average of 30 minutes. During this period, the salesperson asks an average of 13.6 questions, discusses an average of 7.7 product features, and describes approximately six product benefits. During the successful sales call, the customer asks approximately eight questions.[13] This 18-month study of behavioural differences among high-, average-, and low-performance salespeople illustrates that a successful sales call is a model of good two-way communication. Regarding the specific use of questions, the results revealed high performers:

- Use effective questions to gather information and build a clear, complete, mutual understanding of customer needs.

- Guide the direction of a sales call by striking an appropriate balance between open and closed questions.

- Use their questioning strategy to facilitate an open exchange of information.[14]

This study has been used to create and update the very successful Personal Selling Skills training program, now presented by AchieveGlobal (**www.achieveglobal.com/solutions/sales**).

The art and science of using questions was also discussed by Socrates more than 2500 years ago. He noted, among other things, that questions tend to make people think. It's nearly impossible to remain passive when confronted with a direct question. Today there are sales training programs, such as Michael Hargrove's "Using the Socratic Selling Methods" and books such as Kevin Daley's *Socratic Selling: How to Ask the Questions That Get the Sale*, that include many of the observations of Socrates.[15]

In every selling situation, you want the prospect to be actively thinking, sharing thoughts, and asking questions. Appropriate questions reduce tension and build trust in a selling situation because they communicate interest in the other person's welfare. Until the person begins to talk freely, the salesperson will have difficulty diagnosing and solving the customer's problems.

The Four-Part Consultative Questioning Strategy

Table 11.1 illustrates the use of a multiple questioning strategy to discover customer needs. This strategy is based upon the research studies discussed earlier, as well as that conducted for the *Questions, Questions, Questions* sales training video described in the opening material for this chapter. The four types of questions are situation questions, probing questions, confirmation questions, and need-satisfaction questions. Developing skill in the use of these questions will work best if the consultative salesperson develops the mindset that it is more important to understand the customer than it is to persuade the customer. You will note similarity to the SPIN Selling and Personal Selling Skills questioning strategies, as well as to those found in other popular selling books.

Survey Questions Reveal Customer's Problems At the beginning of most sales presentations, there is a need to collect basic facts about the buyer's existing situation and problem. **Survey questions**—or *information-gathering questions*, as they are sometimes called—are designed to obtain this knowledge. To accomplish this, there are two types of survey questions.

General survey questions help the salesperson discover facts about the buyer's problem and existing situation and are often the first step in the partnership-building process.

survey questions Questions used to help the salesperson collect information about the buyer's existing situation and problem.

general survey questions Questions used early in the sales presentation to help the salesperson discover facts about the buyer's existing situation.

Table 11.1 Types of Questions Used in Conjunction with Consultative Selling

Type of Question	Definition	When Used	Example
Survey	*Discovers basic facts* about the buyer's *problem* and existing situation	Usually at the beginning of a sale	"Can you describe the problems you experience travelling to each of the pro golf tournaments?"
Probing	*Designed to uncover pain and clarify the circumstances and implications* surrounding the customer's problem	When you feel the need to obtain more specific information to fully understand the problem	"Are the travel problems affecting your concentration when you are preparing for the event?"
Confirmation	*Used throughout the sales process to verify* the accuracy and assure a mutual understanding of information exchanged by the salesperson and the buyer	After important information has been exchanged	"So, you think the uncertainty associated with commercial air travel is having some effect on your game?"
Need-Satisfaction	*Designed to move the sales process toward commitment and action;* focuses on the pleasure or payoff achieved from the proposed solution	When you change the focus from the problem to a discussion of the solution	"With fractional ownership of your own jet, what personal benefits would this bring to your performance in the 30 tournaments you play each year?"

(*Note:* Salesperson selling fractional ownership of a jet aircraft to a well-known golf professional on the Professional Golf Association (PGA) Tour who is currently using commercial air travel)

Rackham refers to these as Situation Questions. Here is a sampling of general survey questions that can be used in selected selling fields:

I understand that your regional facilities don't necessarily use the same delivery carriers. Is that correct? (*Shipping service*)

Tell me about the challenges you are facing in the area of data storage. (*File server*)

What is your current rate of employee turnover? (*Customer service training*)

Can you provide me with information on the kinds of meetings and conventions you plan for your clients and employees? (*Hotel convention services*)

Can you describe the style of home furnishings you prefer? (*Retail home furnishings*)

In most selling situations, general survey questions are followed by specific survey questions.

specific survey questions
Questions designed to give prospects a chance to describe in more detail a problem, issue, or dissatisfaction from their point of view.

Specific survey questions are designed to give prospects a chance to describe in more detail a problem, issue, or dissatisfaction they are experiencing from their point of view. These specific survey questions (see Selling Today on page 272), or *problem questions* as they are referred to in the SPIN selling sequence, are designed to delve more deeply into the customer's buying situation. Here are five examples of specific survey questions:

Has it occurred to you that by not consolidating your shipping with one carrier, you're likely spending more than is really necessary? (*Shipping service*)

How do you feel about installing another server to your system? (*File server*)

To what extent is employee turnover affecting your customer service? (*Customer service training*)

What meal function features are most important to your guests? (*Hotel convention services*)

Are you looking for an entertainment centre that blends in with your existing furniture? (*Retail home furnishings*)

Survey questions, general or specific, should not be used to collect factual information that can be acquired from other sources, such as your CRM prospect database, prior to the sales call. The preapproach prospect qualification effort is especially important when the salesperson is involved in a large or complex sale. These buyers expect the salesperson to do his or her homework and to not waste the buyer's time asking general survey questions and discussing basic factual information that is available from other sources. Rackham's research revealed that more experienced salespeople tended to ask more specific survey or problem questions, and ask them sooner.

Although survey questions are most often used at the beginning of the sales presentation, they can also be used at other times. Gaining a better understanding of the customer's situation or buying problem may be necessary at any time during the sales presentation. We present the four types of questions in a sequence that has proven to be effective in most selling situations. However, it would be a mistake to view this sequence as a *rigid* plan for every sales presentation. High-performing salespeople spend time strategically preparing tentative questions before they make the sales call. Table 11.2 provides some examples. Note that both open and closed questions are listed. **Open questions** require the prospect to go beyond a simple yes/no response. **Closed questions** can be answered with a yes or no, or a brief response.

open questions Questions that require the prospect to respond with more than just a yes or no response.

closed questions Questions that can be answered yes or no or with a brief response.

Table 11.2 Need Discovery Worksheet

Preplanned questions—sometimes used in conjunction with company-supplied forms—are often used in service, retail, wholesale, and manufacturer selling. Salespeople who use the consultative approach, such as Johnny in the *Questions, Questions, Questions* video, frequently record answers to their questions and use this information to correctly select and recommend solutions in subsequent calls in their multi-call sales situations. Open and closed questions used in the area of financial services appear in the following list.

Preplanned Questions to Discover Buying Motives	Customer Response
1. "Now, as I understand it, you're currently pursuing an Internet phone system to offset your high cellular costs?"	(Closed/General Survey/Situational)
2. "Are you aware that with the system you are currently using, your brokers may have to keep their laptops on in order to make and receive Internet calls?"	(Closed/Specific Survey/Problem)
3. "So what happens if, say, your broker is waiting for an important return call and then inadvertently logs off his or her laptop without a way to roll over the client's return call into a centralized system?"	(Open/Probing/Pain/Implication)
4. "Let's see if *we* understand this—the brokers won't support the system you're considering because it doesn't include instant messaging. And since the brokers would be the primary users of the new system, you're concerned that the system will fail without their support. Is that correct?"	(Closed/Summary-Confirmation)
5. "What if we could develop a communications system for you that included IM and met the SEC requirements? What positive impact could that have on your situation?"	(Open/Need-Satisfaction/Pleasure)

Open questions are very effective in certain selling situations because they provoke thoughtful and insightful answers. The specific survey question "What are the biggest challenges you face in the area of plant security?" focuses the prospect's attention on problems that need solutions. Closed questions, however, can be equally effective when the sales conversation needs to be narrowed or focused on a specific issue.

Probing Questions Reveal Customer's Pain Early in the sales process, the salesperson should make every effort to fully understand the buying problem and the pain, implications, or consequences surrounding the problem. This is especially important when the problem is difficult to describe, the solution is complex, and the potential impact of a wrong decision is enormous.[16]

probing questions *Questions that help you uncover and clarify the pain, implications, and circumstances surrounding the customer's buying problem. They are used more frequently in large, complex sales. These questions often uncover the current level of customer concern, fear, or frustration related to the problem. The following probing questions, also referred to as* implication *questions in Rackham's* SPIN Selling, *are more focused than the survey questions presented earlier:*

> But doesn't every incorrect label cost you to ship to an incorrect address, then cost you again to have it shipped back to you? (*Shipping service*)
>
> What would the consequences be if you choose to do nothing about your current server situation? (*File server*)
>
> How does senior management feel about employee turnover and the related customer service problem? (*Customer service training*)
>
> Is poor service at the meal function negatively affecting the number of people who will return to your seminar? (*Hotel convention services*)
>
> Is it important that you have easy access for connecting your DVD, TIVO, and wireless LAN network? (*Retail home furnishings*)

Probing or implication questions help the salesperson and customer gain a mutual understanding of *why* a problem is important. Asking effective probing questions requires extensive knowledge of your company's capabilities, much insight into your customer's buying problem, and a great deal of practice.

The best sales presentations are characterized by active dialogue. As the sales process progresses, the customer becomes more open and shares perceptions, ideas, and feelings freely. A series of appropriate probing questions stimulates the prospect to discover things not considered before.

Confirmation Questions Reveal Mutual Understanding Confirmation questions can be used throughout the sales process to verify the accuracy and assure a mutual understanding of information exchanged by the salesperson and the buyer (see Table 11.1). They are used to gain commitment, a critically important part of achieving success in larger complex sales. Without commitment throughout the sales process, the chances of a successful sale evaporate rapidly.

These questions, which are an important update to the research on the use of questioning strategies, help determine whether there is mutual understanding of the problems and circumstances the customer is experiencing, as well as the possibilities for a solution. Throughout the sales process, there is always the potential for a breakdown in communication. Perhaps the language used by the salesperson is too technical. Information

The margin glossary terms:

probing questions Questions that help the salesperson to uncover and clarify the prospect's buying problem and the circumstances surrounding the problem.

confirmation questions Questions used throughout the sales process to verify the accuracy and assure a mutual understanding of information exchanged by the salesperson and the buyer.

Neil Rackham conducted studies of 35 000 sales calls and from this research developed the material for his books *SPIN Selling* and *The New SPIN Selling Fieldbook*. SPIN is an acronym for situational, problem, implication, and need-payoff questions. According to Rackham, "more than half the *Fortune* 100 companies are using the SPIN Selling Model to train their sales forces."

Book cover from *The SPIN Selling Fieldbook* by Neil Rackham. Copyright © 1996. Reprinted by permission of the McGraw-Hill Companies, Inc.

and initial needs discovered during the qualifying stage of the need discovery may have changed. Maybe the prospect is preoccupied and has not listened closely to what has been said. Many confirmation questions are simple and to the point.

> If I understand you correctly, the monitoring system must be set up at both your corporate headquarters and at the manufacturing operation. Is that correct? (*File server*)
>
> I want to be sure I am clear that you feel there is a direct relationship between employee turnover and the problem that exists in customer service. (*Customer service training*)
>
> Did you say your seminar attendance dropped 12 percent last year? (*Hotel convention services*)
>
> So you want a new entertainment centre that blends with your current light-coloured oak furniture? (*Retail home furnishings*)

The length of the sales process can vary from a few minutes during a single-call presentation to weeks or even months in a complex multi-call sales presentation. As the sales process progresses, the amount of information available to the salesperson and the customer increases. As the need discovery progresses, the customer's buying criteria or buying conditions surface. **Buying conditions** are those qualifications that must be available or fulfilled before the sale can be closed. The customer may buy only if the product is available in a certain configuration or can be delivered by a certain date. In some selling situations, product installation or service after the sale is considered an important buying condition by the customer. In a large, complex sale, several buying conditions may surface. The salesperson has the responsibility of clarifying, confirming, and gaining commitment on each condition. The same is true for gaining commitment on each of the specific benefits presented to the customer.

One of the best ways to clarify, confirm, and gain commitment on several buying conditions is with **summary confirmation questions**. To illustrate, let us consider a situation in which Laura Feng, sales manager at a major hotel, has interviewed a prospect who wants to schedule a large awards banquet. After a series of survey, probing, and confirmation

buying conditions Qualifications that must be available or fulfilled before the sale can be closed.

summary confirmation questions Questions used to clarify and confirm buying conditions.

questions, Laura feels confident that the information she collected is sufficient for her to prepare a proposal. However, to be sure all the facts have been collected, Laura asks the following summary confirmation question to gain commitment on the important buying conditions:

> Let me summarize the major items you have mentioned. You want all banquet attendees served within an eight-minute time frame after the opening speaker has finished his speech? And you need a room that will comfortably seat 60 persons banquet-style, and 10 of these persons will be seated at the head table. Is this correct?

Once all the buying conditions are confirmed, Laura can prepare a proposal that reflects the specific needs of her customer. The result is a win-win situation for the customer and the salesperson. The chances of closing the sale greatly improve. In multi-call sales processes, it is wise to begin subsequent calls with summary confirmation questions that re-establish what was discussed during the previous call(s):

> (*Re-qualifying the new prospect*) I would like to revisit the information we have in our database about your company's purchasing procedures. You prefer limiting your suppliers and developing long-term partnerships where they are as committed to your profitability and your customers' total customer satisfaction. You also require e-commerce linkages that allow your people to review the status of their order, delivery dates, and the projected costs, including transportation and financing. Is that correct?
>
> (*The second call in a multi-call sale situation*) Let me begin by going over what we discussed in our last visit. Your current shipper gives you a 50 percent discount and provides a custom-label printer? *If the customer responds in the affirmative, the salesperson continues with another summary-confirmation question.* You also have to buy fairly expensive custom labels and, at around $90 a pack, you're spending over $20 000 just on labels. Is that still correct?

This enables the salesperson to verify that the previously discovered buying conditions have remained the same and not changed since the last meeting. Summary-confirmation questions are also used to effectively clarify, confirm, and gain commitment to several product benefits after they have been presented, generally one at a time. Commitment to the value of the benefits usually results in transitioning the presentation to the closing and servicing of the sale.

Need-Satisfaction Questions Reveal Pleasure The fourth type of question used in the sales process is fundamentally different from the other three. **Need-satisfaction questions** are designed to focus on the solution and the benefits of the solution. These are helpful questions that move the sales process toward commitment and action. The chances of closing the sale greatly improve because need-satisfaction questions—or, as they are sometimes called, *solution* or *pleasure* questions—focus on specific benefits and build desire for a solution.

Survey, probing, and confirmation questions focus on understanding and clarifying the customer's problem. Need-satisfaction questions help the prospect see how your product or service provides a solution to the problem you have uncovered. The opportunity to close the sale greatly improves because you have cast the solution in a pleasurable light.

In most cases, need-satisfaction questions are used after the salesperson has created awareness of the seriousness of the buyer's problem. The questions you ask will replace his or her current levels of concern, pain, or frustration with pleasurable thoughts about

need-satisfaction questions
Questions designed to move the sales process toward commitment and action by helping to clarify the problem in the prospect's mind and by building a desire for your solution.

a solution. The following examples provide insight into the use of need-satisfaction—or, as SPIN Selling refers to them, need-payoff—questions:

> And if I told you that I can offer you cost savings of at least 5 percent over your current shipping expenses, would that be meaningful? (*Shipping service*)
>
> Tests on similar applications show that a new file server can increase data storage by 30 to 40 percent. How much do you feel you would achieve? (*File server*)

In many selling situations, a product demonstration is an essential stage in the sales process. In this case, the salesperson might use the following need-satisfaction question:

> What benefits would you see if we provided a demonstration of one of our training modules to senior management so they can understand what you and I have discovered about reducing employee turnover? (*Customer service training*)

Once the prospect's needs are clearly identified, need-satisfaction questions can be valuable closing tools. Consider this example:

> Considering the benefits we have summarized and agreed on, and noting the fact that our staff will deliver an outstanding meal function, would you like to sign this confirmation so we can reserve the rooms and schedule the meals that you need? (*Hotel convention services*)

Need-satisfaction questions such as these are very powerful because they build desire for the solution and give ownership of the solution to the customer. When the prospect understands which parts of the problem(s) your solution can solve, you are less likely to invite objections. In some cases, you may identify problems that still need to be clarified. When this happens, you can use survey, probing, or confirmation questions to obtain more information.

Lisa Ciampi, account executive for Design Display Inc., believes consultative selling is about being a marketing advisor and problem solver. This approach creates value within the sales process.

Questions, Questions, Everywhere

The use of questions to discover needs and present solutions is discussed in several popular personal selling books. For comparison purposes, the approximate equivalents to the four types of questions described in this chapter are listed.

Selling Today by Manning, Reece, Ahearne, and MacKenzie	The Spin Selling Fieldbook by Rackham	The New Solution Selling by Eades	The New Conceptual Selling by Heiman, Sanchez, with Tuleja	Secrets of Question Based Selling by Freese
Survey	Situation	Open	Confirmation	Status
Probing	Problem	Control	New Information	Issue
Confirmation	Implication	Confirming	Attitude	Implication
Need-Satisfaction	Need-Payoff		Commitment	Solution
			Basic Issue	

The questions above are listed in the sequence presented by the authors. To determine the exact definition of each type of question, check the source.

At this point, you have received only a basic introduction to the four most common types of questions used during the selling process. (For more insight into the application of questions to the sales process, view the three videos in the *Questions, Questions, Questions* series referred to in this chapter's opening vignette. Also refer to the Role-Play Application Exercises on pages 282–283.) We will revisit these important sales tools later in this chapter and in Chapters 12, 13, 14, and 15.

Qualifying to Eliminate Unnecessary Questions

It is important to avoid the use of unnecessary questions during a sales call. Pre-qualifying the prospect, as described in Chapter 9, is especially important when the prospect is a business buyer. Successful salespeople acquire as much information as possible about the prospect before the first meeting. They use sources such as the prospect's website, LinkedIn, previous phone calls or emails, and information recorded in the salesperson's CRM system. This prior understanding of the prospect allows the salesperson to direct the qualifying conversation using effective confirmation questions such as "Your website mentions your company has recently expanded into a new product market. Can you tell me more about that?" Buyers expect the salesperson to be well informed about their operation and not waste time asking a large number of basic survey questions. Confirmation questions communicate this prior knowledge and allow the salesperson and customer to move ahead in the consultative sales process with more important probing and need-satisfaction questions.

Robert Jolles, author of *Customer-Centered Selling*,[17] suggests that salespeople be careful when determining whether the person they are meeting with has the authority to make the purchase decision. According to Jolles, asking a survey question such as

"Are you the one who will be making the decision on this purchase?" encourages prospects without decision-making authority to lie in order to maintain their pride in the situation. Instead, Jolles recommends the question, "Who, besides yourself, will be responsible for this purchase decision?" This subtle yet strategic rephrasing to a confirmation/survey question allows the prospect to tell the truth and maintain his or her dignity.

NEED DISCOVERY—LISTENING TO AND ACKNOWLEDGING THE CUSTOMER'S RESPONSE

TO FULLY UNDERSTAND THE CUSTOMER, WE MUST LISTEN CLOSELY AND ACKNOWLEDGE EVERY response. The authors of *First Impressions* offer these words of advice to salespeople who use questions as part of the need discovery process: "What you do after you ask a question can reveal even more about you than the questions you ask. You reveal your true level of interest in the way you listen."[18] Most of us are born with the ability to hear, but we have to learn how to listen. The starting point is developing a listening attitude. Always regard the customer as worthy of your respect and full attention.[19] Salespeople with high levels of customer orientation truly care about customers, and thus engage in actions that customers value such as listening to customer feedback and solving customer problems. Once you have made a commitment to becoming a good listener, develop active listening skills.

Developing Active Listening Skills **Active listening** is the process of sending back to the prospect what you as a listener think the person meant, in terms of both content and feelings. Active listening requires intense involvement as you concentrate on what you are hearing, exhibit your listening attitude through your nonverbal messages (see Chapter 3), and feed back to the prospect what you think he or she meant.[20] Developing active listening skills involves three practices that can be learned by any salesperson willing to make the commitment:

> **active listening** The process of feeding back to the prospect what you as a listener think the person meant, in terms of both content and feelings. It involves taking into consideration and exhibiting both verbal and nonverbal messages.

- *Focus your full attention.* This is not easy because the delivery of the messages we hear is often much slower than our capacity to listen. Thus, we have plenty of time to let our minds roam, to think ahead, and to plan what we are going to say next. Our senses are constantly feeding us new information while someone is trying to tell us something. Staying focused is often difficult and involves use of both verbal and nonverbal messages.[21] To show that you are paying attention, lean toward the prospect while murmuring "uh-huh," "okay," or "I understand," and nod in agreement when appropriate. Avoid nodding rapidly or saying "uh-huh" loudly or frequently because this will communicate impatience or a desire to turn the conversation back to yourself.[22]

  It is important to listen to the emotion involved in your customer's comments. A poor listener listens to facts; a good listener listens to emotions. Theoretically, 20 percent of communications is strictly facts and 80 percent is emotion—the emotion we all have and put into every thought. Listening for the emotions in your client's conversation enables you to receive the entire message.[23] Emotional buying motives were discussed in detail in Chapter 8.

  Within every sales presentation there will be times when silence should be welcomed. Use silence to control the flow of information and draw out the customer. Customers are often inclined to fill silence by talking. Throughout an effective sales presentation, the customer should be talking more than the salesperson.[24]

In many selling situations, note-taking will demonstrate a high level of professionalism.

■ *Paraphrase the customer's meaning.* After the customer stops talking, pause for two or three seconds and then state in your own words, with a confirmation question, what you think the person meant. This technique not only helps ensure understanding but also is an effective customer relations strategy. The customer feels good knowing that not only are you listening to what has been said, you are also making an effort to ensure accuracy. In addition to paraphrasing the content, use questions to dig for full understanding of the customer's perceptions.[25] The use of survey or probing questions is appropriate any time you need to clarify what is being said by the prospect.

■ *Take notes.* Although note-taking is not necessary in every sales presentation, it is important in complex sales where the information obtained from the customer is critical to the development of a buying solution. Taking accurate notes is a good way to demonstrate to the customer that you are actively listening. When you take notes, you increase your memory of what you heard. Your notes should be brief and to the point.[26] If the information you receive from the customer is too technical or unfamiliar, do not hesitate to ask for clarification of information you don't understand.

Need Discovery—Establishing Buying Motives

The primary goal of questioning, listening, and acknowledging is to uncover prospect needs and establish buying motives. Our efforts to discover prospect needs can be more effective if we focus our questioning on determining the prospect's primary reasons for buying. When a customer has a definite need, it is usually supported by specific buying motives.

The greatest time investment in personal selling is on the front end of the sales process. First you must plan the sales call and then, once you are face-to-face with the customer, you can begin the need discovery stage. It is during the early stage of the sales process that you can create the greatest value for the customer.[27]

SELECTING SOLUTIONS THAT CREATE VALUE

SALESPEOPLE ARE NO LONGER SELLING JUST A "PRODUCT"; INSTEAD THEY ARE PROVIDING a valuable "solution" to customer problems.[28] Consultative salespeople act as product experts and generally provide a customized solution. The second part of the consultative sales process consists of selecting or configuring a solution that satisfies the prospect's buying motives.

As we have noted, most salespeople bring to the selling situation a variety of products and/or services. In today's information economy, salespeople are increasingly selling related services as a part of their product solution. This is especially true in the Western industrialized countries where profit margins on B2B goods-related solutions are declining. In Germany, for example, six of the 30 largest firms have established specific organization units to offer services.[29] The challenge to select the correct solution is growing. Digesting relevant information, perceiving patterns, and determining the unique solution that will work in each unique selling situation requires a considerable amount of time and effort.[30] This process done correctly can create significant value for the customer and build a long-term partnership of repeats and/or referrals.

After identifying the buying motives, the salesperson carefully reviews the available product options. At this point, the salesperson is searching for a specific solution to satisfy the prospect's buying motives. Once the solution has been selected, the salesperson makes a recommendation to the prospect (see Fig. 11.4). The following customer response to this process illustrates the value created when this process is done correctly: "She listened to and worked with the ideas that I had concerning my desires and preferences, as well as made recommendations that complemented and enhanced the vision that I had for my home."[31]

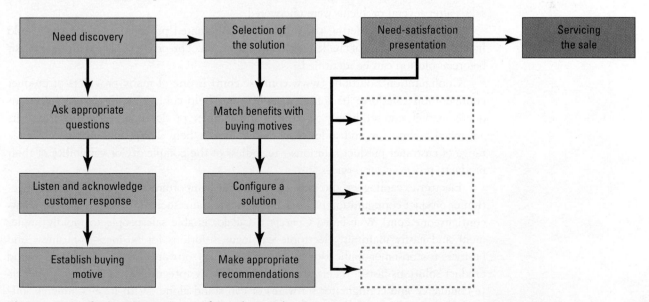

Figure 11.4 Three Dimensions of Product Selection

Selecting Solutions—Match Specific Benefits with Buying Motives

As we noted in Chapter 7, products and services represent problem-solving tools. People buy products when they perceive that they fulfill a need. We also noted that today's more demanding customers seek a cluster of satisfactions that arise from the product itself, from the company that makes or distributes the product, and from the salesperson who sells and services the product (see Fig. 7.1 on p. 152). Tom Reilly, author of *Value-Added Selling*, says, "Value-added salespeople sell three things: the product, the company, and themselves. This is the three-dimensional bundle of value."[32] When possible, the salesperson should focus on benefits related to each dimension of value. Of course, it is a mistake to make benefit statements that do not relate to the specific needs of the customer. High-performance salespeople present benefits that are precisely tailored to the customer's needs. Benefits that are not relevant to the customer's needs waste time and may invite objections.[33]

Selecting Solutions—Product Configuration

Most salespeople bring to the sale a variety of products or services. Salespeople who represent food distributors can offer customers a mix of several hundred items. Most pharmaceutical sales representatives can offer the medical community a wide range of products. Best Buy, a large retailer of electronics, offers customers a wide range of audio and visual entertainment options. The customer who wants to purchase a sound system, for example, can choose from many combinations of receivers, speakers, and so on. Selecting the right solution is referred to by many sales organizations as *product configuration*.

If the sale involves several needs and the satisfaction of multiple buying motives, selection of the solution may take several days or even weeks and may involve the preparation of a detailed sales proposal. In addition, research conducted by Neil Rackham revealed that top-performing salespeople tend to introduce their solutions later in the sale—after several problems were uncovered.

A company considering the purchase of automated production equipment would likely present this type of challenge to the salesperson. The problem needs careful analysis before a solution can be identified.

Configuration Solutions (**www.configsc.com**) is one of many providers of product configuration solutions. Its software applications help configure-to-order organizations quote, market, and sell highly customized and complex products and service offerings. Its advanced technology and industry-focused solutions help salespeople automate a wide range of customer product solutions—regardless of the complexity or variability of their products, processes, or services.[34]

Electronic catalogues also play an increasingly important role in the product selection or product configuration process. Software programs such as Configure One's (**www.configureone.com**) Web-based *Concept E-Catalog* enable salespeople to rapidly implement and easily maintain electronic catalogue solutions for business-to-business and business-to-consumer applications. *Concept E-Catalog* software enables salespeople to find product solutions faster. Its electronic catalogue fully integrates with its other products (e-commerce and configurator software) or can stand alone. With its e-commerce software, salespeople and customers can have access to product solutions 24/7.

Salesforce.com, with its AppExchange integration program, also provides product selection and electronic catalogue capability. BigMachines, voted Best Quote App in 2009, provides on-demand product configuration, pricing, and proposal capabilities that can be easily added to Salesforce.com's on-demand CRM solution. BigMachines enables salespeople to streamline the entire opportunity-to-quote-to-order process, all within the familiar Salesforce.com CRM interface. Capabilities include guided selling, product configuration, complex pricing and discounting, approval workflow, and proposal generation.[35] Electronic product configurators, product catalogues, and e-commerce enable salespeople to create value for the customer by providing time sensitive, professionally prepared, information-rich alternatives in selecting solutions that meet the unique needs established during the need discovery. For many salespeople, the use of sales force technology has changed their methods of selling.[36]

In some selling situations, the salesperson will solely create the solution based on the needs analysis. In more complex selling situations, however,[37] both the salesperson and the customer often play an active role and together co-create the solution. This co-creation process takes place through conversations between the customer and the salesperson. Research reveals this process often helps customers better understand their own needs and conceive of possible solutions that fit those needs. This process creates value and, as a consequence, customers make smarter buying choices that conform to the salesperson's solutions and sales propositions.

Selecting Solutions—Make Appropriate Recommendations

The recommendation strategies available to salespeople are similar to those used by a doctor who must recommend a solution to a patient's medical problem. In the medical field, three possibilities for providing patient satisfaction exist. In situations in which the patient easily understands the medical problem and the appropriate treatment, the doctor can make a recommendation and the patient can proceed immediately toward a cure. If the patient does not easily understand the medical problem or solution, the doctor may need to discuss thoroughly with the patient the benefits of the recommended treatment. If the medical problem is not within his or her medical specialty area, the doctor may recommend a specialist to provide the treatment. In consultative selling, the salesperson has these same three counselling alternatives.

Recommend Solution—Customer Buys Immediately The selection and recommendation of products to meet the customer's needs may occur at the beginning of the sales call, such as in the product approach; during the presentation, just after the need discovery; or near the end, when minor resistance has been negotiated. At any of these three times, the presentation products that are well matched to the prospect's needs may result in an immediate purchase.

Recommend Solution—Salesperson Makes Need-Satisfaction Presentation This alternative requires a presentation of product benefits, including demonstrations and negotiating objections, before the sale is closed. In this situation, the prospect may not be totally aware of a buying problem and the solution may not be easily understood or apparent. Because of this, the salesperson needs to carefully define the problem and

Selling Today

Action Selling at Carquest

CARQUEST Auto Parts (**www.carquest.ca**) promises to deliver what customers need. To achieve this lofty goal, the company enrolled its 1200 outside sales force members in Action Selling. A major objective of this sales training program is to help salespeople become trusted business consultants. They learned that asking—not telling—is the key to sales success. Emphasis throughout the course is placed on asking more and better questions. Duane Sparks, who developed Action Selling, says "The success rate of sales calls rises significantly when more than two specific customer needs are uncovered by questioning."[b]

communicate a solution to the customer. The need-satisfaction presentation will be discussed in Chapter 12.

Recommend Another Source Earlier, we indicated that professional salespeople may recommend that a prospect buy a product or service from another source, maybe even a competitor. If, after a careful needs assessment, the salesperson concludes that the products represented do not satisfy the customer's needs, the consultative salesperson should recommend another source.

Paul Roos, a sales representative for Hewlett-Packard, once met with a customer who wanted to buy a newly introduced HP product for an application where it would not work. Paul explained why the product would not work and then took time to configure a competing product to meet the customer's needs. He lost that sale to a competitor, but the assistance provided confirmed his integrity and made a lasting impression on the customer. That customer later became a high-value account.[38] In situations like Paul Roos's, where the unique needs of a customer cannot be solved and an alternative recommendation is made to buy from another supplier, long-term partnerships are often created that result in future sales and/or referred business. This creates value for the customer who is looking for a unique solution.

Need Discovery and the Transactional Buyer

Throughout this chapter, you have been given a comprehensive introduction to the consultative sales process. It is important to keep in mind that the fundamentals of consultative selling must be customized to meet the individual needs of the customer. For example, some of the guidelines for developing an effective consultative presentation must be abandoned or greatly altered when you are working with a transactional buyer. In most cases, transactional buyers understand what product they need and when they need it. The Internet has armed many transactional buyers with a great deal of information, so the salesperson who spends time asking survey questions or making a detailed informative presentation may be wasting the customer's time. Most of these buyers want the salesperson to configure a product solution that focuses on pricing and delivery issues.[39]

When working with the transactional buyer, it is important to understand the difference between a transaction and a consultative relationship. Transactions create one-time value; consultative relationships create long-term value and a stable business foundation.[40]

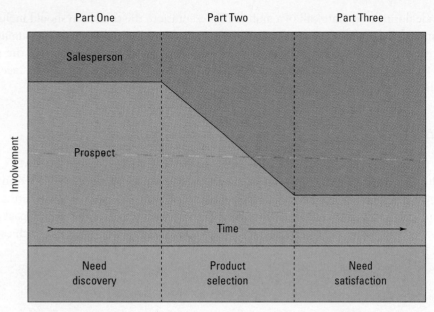

Figure 11.5 Time used by both the salesperson and the prospect during each part of the consultative sales process.

Involving the Prospect in the Need Discovery

In most selling situations, there is a certain amount of time pressure. Rarely does a salesperson have an unlimited amount of time to spend with the customer. As noted earlier, the salesperson is often allotted only 30 minutes for the sales call. Some buyers limit all their appointments to 30 minutes or less.

Figure 11.5 illustrates an ideal breakdown of time allocation between the salesperson and the prospect during three parts of the sales process. In terms of involvement, the prospect assumes a greater role during the need discovery stage. As the salesperson begins the product selection process, the prospect's involvement decreases. During the need-satisfaction stage, the salesperson is doing more of the talking, but note that the prospect is never excluded totally.

Transitioning to the Presentation

As we note in Chapter 10, there is a need to make an effective transition from the approach to the need discovery stage. There is the same need to transition from the need discovery/product selection stage to the need-satisfaction presentation stage. As noted earlier, if your customer buys immediately, you will transition to the close and conduct those activities associated with servicing the sale. Those activities will be discussed in Chapters 14 and 15. If you and your customer decide another supplier might better meet his or her needs, you might transition directly to servicing the sale to achieve a future sale or a referral.

If it is decided that a need-satisfaction presentation is needed to communicate specific features and benefits, make a statement such as "I would like to point out some of the specific benefits of the solution we have agreed upon." If the need-satisfaction presentation is made during a separate call of a multi-call presentation, the transition should include a summary-confirmation question covering the buying conditions discussed. The summary-confirmation question would be used in closing the existing call and opening the next call. Creating and involving the prospect in the need-satisfaction presentation stage will be discussed in detail in Chapter 12.

PLANNING AND EXECUTION—FINAL THOUGHTS

THE IMPORTANCE OF STRATEGIC PLANNING AND EXECUTION OF THE NEED DISCOVERY AND product selection parts of the consultative sales presentation model is explained in this chapter. Figure 11.6 summarizes the key concepts that must be addressed during the planning and execution process. These planning and execution activities will impact your ability to create customer value and build a partnering relationship. This approach can be used in the three major employment settings: service, B2B, and B2C.

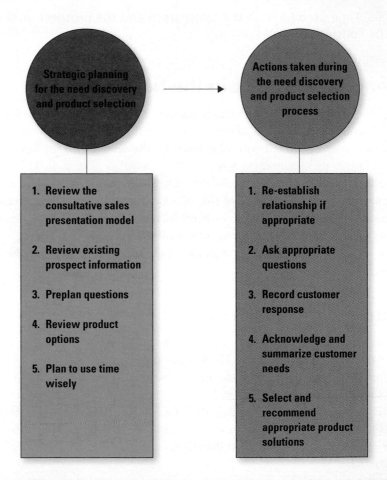

Figure 11.6 Strategic Planning for Need Discovery and Product Selection
Need discovery and product selection activities are the first steps in creating value and building a partnering relationship with your customer.

REVIEWING KEY CONCEPTS

- Outline the benefits of the consultative sales presentation.

  Salespeople use the consultative sales presentation because this customer-focused selling model results in increased customer satisfaction, more closed sales, and more repeat and referred business. Research indicates that high-performance salespeople have learned how to skilfully use the consultative model to diagnose and solve their customers' buying problems better than their competitors.

- Describe the four parts of the need-satisfaction model.

  A well-planned and well-executed consultative sales process is an important key to success in personal selling. To be most effective, the presentation should be viewed as a four-part process: need discovery; selection of the solution; need satisfaction through informing, persuading, or reminding; and servicing the sale.

- Discuss the use of questions to discover needs.

  The most effective sales process is characterized by two-way communication. It should be encouraged with survey, probing, confirmation, summary-confirmation, and need-satisfaction questions.

- Describe the importance of active listening and the use of confirmation questions.

  Beware of assuming information about the prospect, and be sure the language of your presentation is clearly understood. Listen attentively as the prospect responds to your questions or volunteers information. The effective use of confirmation questions to enhance active listening assures a mutual understanding of buying motives.

- Select solutions that match customer needs.

  After making a good first impression during the approach and getting the customer's full attention, the salesperson begins. During the process of, or shortly after determining and/or confirming customer needs, the process of configuring a solution begins. The salesperson's ability is tested during this part of the sale because this is where the prospect's buying motives are matched with benefits, a solution is configured, and appropriate solutions are recommended.

Key Terms

active listening **273**

buying conditions **269**

closed questions **267**

confirmation questions **268**

general survey questions **265**

need discovery **263**

need-satisfaction questions **270**

open questions **267**

probing questions **268**

specific survey questions **266**

summary confirmation questions **269**

survey questions **265**

Review Questions

1. List and describe the four parts of the Consultative Sales Process Guide.

2. Describe the findings of the two major research projects on the strategic use of questions in selling.

3. List and describe the four types of questions commonly used in the selling field.

4. Define the term *buying conditions*. What are some common buying conditions?

5. Describe the process of active listening, and explain how it can improve the listening efficiency rate.

6. Discuss the three dimensions of need discovery.

7. Describe the three dimensions of selecting a product solution.

8. Describe the ideal time allocation for each part of the consultative sales presentation between the salesperson and the prospect.

9. Describe the nature of the need discovery process when working with a transactional buyer.

10. Discuss how time is used by the salesperson and the customer as the consultative sales presentation proceeds.

ROLE-PLAY APPLICATION EXERCISES FOR "QUESTIONING" VIDEO SERIES

Most sales skill development exercises used in the classroom are product-oriented. As noted on page 258, "Product-oriented selling can easily lapse into product evangelism." This three-part video series on questioning focuses on the customer's buying process, consultative selling, and building high-quality partnerships.

The goal of this series is the identification and clarification of the customer's problem and finding a solution. The first video focuses on the appropriate use of survey and confirmation questions to identify the customer's problem. The second video introduces the use of probing and need-satisfaction questions. Probing questions examine and clarify the potential issues surrounding the customer's problem, while need-satisfaction questions focus the sales process on the appropriate solution. The third video demonstrates the use of these questions in a challenging, yet typical, contemporary sales setting.

The role-play exercises presented below challenge the participant to understand, apply, and integrate questioning skills presented in this chapter and in the video series. Product information for these exercises is found in "Partnership Selling: A Role Play/Simulation" online in the Student Resources section at **www.pearsoncanada. ca/manning**. See pages 5 to 26. Customer information will be found in the B. H. Rivera Contact Report presented on page 26 (disregard any other information on this page). You will assume the role of a newly hired salesperson as described in the Position Description on page 8. Refer to the questioning material and examples presented on pages 244–51. Use a need discovery worksheet like the one on page 248 for developing your questions.

After viewing the video *Questions—Discovering and Confirming Customer Problems*, study the online role play/simulation material (pages 5 to 26). Refer to the Contact Report on page 26 (as noted, disregard any other information on this page). Assume you were assigned to this account and you are meeting B. H. Rivera to inquire about additional information regarding when the meeting will be held and what audiovisual equipment might be needed.

Prepare a list of general survey and specific survey questions that reveal when, during the next month, the meeting will be held and what, if any, audiovisual equipment (see pages 21–22) might be needed. Plan to use a summary-confirmation question to verify the existing four items on the Contact Sheet. Using the questions you have created, role-play this part of the need discovery process.

After viewing the video *Questions—Discovering Pain and Pleasure* and reviewing the information you prepared in the role play above, prepare three probing questions. These questions should clarify and reveal a mutual understanding of issues and consequences regarding food service, facility design, and audiovisual equipment. Also, using the information on pages 5 to 24, prepare five need-satisfaction questions that reveal how the features of your convention centre provide a solution to the buying situation. Select appropriate proof devices to demonstrate these specific benefits. Using these questions, meet again with B. H. Rivera and role-play this part of the questioning process. Prepare and use confirmation questions as the need arises.

After viewing the video *Questions—Getting it Right* and using the information in the first two role plays, prepare a need-satisfaction presentation to Cameron Rivera, a new meeting planner just hired at Graphic Forms. Cameron, a cousin of B. H., was previously employed as a training coordinator at West College. Due to extensive growth in the company, B. H. has turned all meeting planning over to Cameron. Cameron will make the final selection of a facility for the meeting described on page 26, plus 11 more identical meetings to be scheduled in the next 12 months. You have also been informed that the Marriott and Sheraton hotels will be making presentations (note the comparative room, parking, and transportation rates). You will travel to Graphic Forms to make your presentation. Prepare appropriate survey, probing, confirmation, and need-satisfaction questions and presentation strategies that will help secure this important account—then role-play this presentation.

CASE PROBLEM

When Deborah Karish wakes up in the morning, she does not have to worry about a long commute to work. Her office is in her home. As an Amgen (www.amgen.com) pharmaceutical sales representative, Deborah spends most of her day visiting hospitals, medical clinics, and doctors' offices. She spends a large part of each day serving as a consultant to doctors, head nurses, pharmacists, and others who need information and advice about the complex medical products available from her company. As might be expected, she also spends a considerable amount of time conducting informative presentations designed to achieve a variety of objectives. In some situations, she is introducing a new product, and in other cases she is providing up-to-date information on an existing product. Some of her presentations are given to individual health care professionals, and others are given to a group. Each of these presentations must be carefully planned.

Deborah uses informative and reminder presentations almost daily in her work. Informative presentations are given to doctors who are in a position to prescribe her products. The verbal presentation often is supplemented with audiovisual aids and printed materials. Reprints of articles from leading medical journals are often used to illustrate the success of her products in treating patients. These articles give added credibility to her presentations. Some of her informative presentations are designed to give customers updates on the prescription drugs she sells. Reminder presentations are frequently given to pharmacists who must maintain an inventory of her products. She has found it necessary to periodically remind pharmacists of product delivery procedures and policies, and of special services available from Amgen. She knows that without an occasional reminder, a customer can forget information that may be important.

In some cases, a careful needs analysis is required to determine if her products can solve a specific medical problem. Each patient is different, so generalizations concerning the use of her products can be dangerous. When doctors talk about their patients, Deborah must listen carefully and take good notes. In some cases, she must get additional information from company support staff. If a customer needs immediate help with a problem, she gives the person a toll-free 1-800 number to call for expert advice. This line is an important part of the Amgen customer service program.

Deborah's career in pharmaceutical sales has required continuous learning. In the beginning she had to learn the meaning of dozens of medical terms and become familiar with a large number of medical problems. If a doctor asks, "What is the bioavailability of Neupogen?" she must know the meaning of the medical term and be knowledgeable about this Amgen product.

Deborah also spends time learning about the people with whom she works. She recently said, "If I get along with the people I work with, it makes my job a lot easier." When meeting someone for the first time, she takes time to assess his or her communication style and then adapts her own style to meet his or her needs. She points out that in some cases the competition offers a similar product at a similar price. In these situations, a good relationship with the customer can influence the purchase decision.

Questions

1. Would need discovery be an important part of Deborah Karish's sales process with a new medical practice? Explain.

2. Would Deborah use the same questioning strategy with medical personnel such as the office manager or receptionist that she would with medical professionals such as nurses or doctors?

3. Describe the nature of the multi-call sales process that Deborah might use.

4. Describe what Deborah might plan to do in the first call, in the second call, and in a third call on the same medical practice.

PARTNERSHIP SELLING: A ROLE PLAY/SIMULATION

Visit the role play/simulation materials provided in the Student Resources section of your companion website at **www.pearsoncanada.ca/manning**. *A contents page lists appropriate page references for the activities.*

UNDERSTANDING YOUR CUSTOMER'S BUYING STRATEGY

Read *Sales Memorandum 2* ("A" or "B" depending on the account category you were assigned in Chapter 10). Your customer has called you back because you made such a good approach in call 1 and wants to visit with you about a convention recently assigned. In this call, you are to use the information gathered in sales call 1 to re-establish a good relationship, discover your customer's convention needs, and set an appointment to return and make a presentation.

Follow the instructions carefully and prepare survey questions prior to your appointment. Keep your survey questions general and attempt to get your customer to share information openly. Use specific survey questions later during the appointment to gain more insight. Be careful about doing too much of the talking. In the need discovery, your customer should do most of the talking, with you taking notes and using them to ask confirmation and summary confirmation questions in order to check the accuracy of your perceptions concerning what the customer wants. After this meeting, you will be asked to prepare a sales proposal using the information you have gathered.

Your instructor may again ask you to assume the role of a customer in the account category that you are not assigned as a salesperson. If so, you will receive detailed customer instructions, which you should follow closely. This will provide you with an opportunity to experience the strategic/consultative/partnering style of selling from a customer's perspective.

Chapter 12
Creating Value with the Sales Demonstration

Learning Objectives

After studying this chapter, you should be able to

1 List and describe three types of need-satisfaction presentation strategies.

2 Present guidelines for creating consultative presentations that add value.

3 Describe the elements of a persuasive presentation strategy.

4 Describe the elements of an effective group presentation.

5 Develop selling tools that add value to your sales demonstration.

 Reality Selling Today Video Series

Chris Wylie (see page 286) is a sales representative for Ecolab. With more than $6 billion in global sales, Ecolab is the global leader in cleaning, sanitizing, food safety, and infection control products and services. The company has more than 26 000 employees worldwide. Ecolab serves customers in more than 160 countries across North America, Europe, Asia, Latin America, the Middle East, and Africa. The company delivers comprehensive programs and services to various industries, including food service, food and beverage processing, hospitality, health care, government and education, retail, and others.

Chris Wylie is a territory manager in Ecolab's Institutional Business unit, which is the core of Ecolab. In his territory, Chris serves approximately 80 customers throughout the month. Most of his customers are restaurants, but he also calls on some hotels and a few hospitals. When visiting a customer, he first meets with his contact, which would typically be the general manager, procurement manager, or executive chef. He asks them a series of questions about their business and operations (e.g., how busy they have recently been, whether they had any problems or repairs, or whether a big event like a banquet is coming up). Through these questions, Chris gains insight into his customer's operations, which will later help him create his solutions and sales presentation.

As a part of his call, Chris also has to take care of servicing Ecolab's products by making sure that the dispensers for the products and the dishwashers are working properly, that the calibrations are set correctly, and so forth. Throughout his presentation, Chris constantly tries to discover different needs such as determining needed repairs, identifying

up-selling or cross-selling opportunities, and expanding the business with that customer by showing him or her new products.

Besides serving his existing customer base, Chris also engages in new business selling. In a typical prospecting type of sales call, Chris would meet with the general manager or the executive chef, introduce himself and Ecolab, and eventually ask them whether he can conduct a needs discovery survey of their kitchen to see what their operation looks like and assess whether he can provide any additional value with some of Ecolab's products and services. Then Chris would typically do a series of tests on the current chemicals and equipment that the prospect is using to see if they are functioning effectively and efficiently. Based on these tests, Chris creates a value proposition in terms of cost savings or results improvements (e.g., improved glassware or dishware results). Since Ecolab products are not sold on price, Chris then presents those improved results to demonstrate to the prospect the Ecolab value of excellent service and quality products.

NEED SATISFACTION—SELECTING A PRESENTATION STRATEGY

CONDUCTING BUSINESS IN THE TWENTY-FIRST CENTURY INFORMATION ECONOMY, WHICH IS based on the assets of knowledge and information, requires that we think about ways to improve the sales presentation. Here is how one author described this challenge:

The Six-Step Presentation Plan

Step One: Approach	☑ Review Strategic/Consultative Selling Model ☑ Initiate customer contact
Step Two: Need Discovery	☑ Ask strategic questions ☑ Determine customer needs ☑ Select Product Solution
Step Three: **Presentation**	☐ Select presentation strategy ☐ Create presentation plan ☐ Initiate presentation
Step Four: Negotiation	☐ Anticipate buyer concerns ☐ Plan negotiating methods ☐ Initiate win-win negotiations
Step Five: Close	☐ Plan appropriate closing methods ☐ Recognize closing clues ☐ Initiate closing methods
Step Six: Servicing the Sale	☐ Follow through ☐ Follow-up calls ☐ Expansion selling

Service, retail, wholesale, and manufacturer selling

Figure 12.1 Creating Value with the Presentation

As we move from the rutted byways of the Industrial Age to the electronic thoroughfares of the Information Age, business presentations become a measure of our ability to adapt to new surroundings. The most successful and forward-thinking companies already have assigned presentations a new, fundamental and strategic importance.[1]

After you have configured a solution that matches the customer's needs, you must select which presentation strategy to emphasize. Need satisfaction can be achieved through selecting an informative, persuasive, or reminder presentation strategy; creating the presentation plan; and initiating the presentation (see Fig. 12.1). The salesperson can, of course, use a combination of the three presentation strategies, in some cases (see Fig. 12.2).

Need-Satisfaction—The Informative Presentation Strategy

To be informative, a message must be clearly understood by the customer. Of course, clarity is important in any presentation, but it needs special attention in a presentation in which the primary purpose is to inform. The **informative presentation** emphasizes factual information typically taken from technical reports, company-prepared sales literature, or written testimonials from persons who have used the product.

informative presentation
Emphasizes factual information, which is often taken from technical reports, company-prepared sales literature, or written testimonials from people who have used the product.

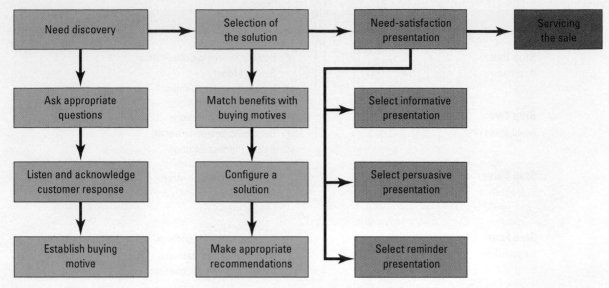

Figure 12.2 The Three Strategies to Use in Developing an Effective Need-Satisfaction Presentation

This type of presentation is commonly used to introduce new products, highly complex products, and services of a technical nature. Salespeople such as Ecolab's Chris Wylie and Hilti's Alim Hirani play a key role in the ultimate success of a firm's new product innovations.[2] Pharmaceutical sales representatives frequently use the informative presentation strategy to describe the details of their products to a physician who may be engaged in an educated search for a prescription drug best suited to meet their patient's medical need.[3] This strategy emphasizes clarity, simplicity, and directness, and in many cases is welcomed by the reflective and directive communication-style customers presented in Chapter 5. Salespeople need to keep in mind the "less is more" concept. Too often the prospect is given far too much information and detail.[4]

It is important to keep in mind the partner/problem-solver role of the salesperson when making an informative presentation. Today information is not just plentiful but available directly to customers in overwhelming amounts. As a result, customers no longer value sales professionals as just information providers. To use the informative presentation strategy effectively, the salesperson must transition from an information conveyer to the role of a trusted business advisor.[5]

Need-Satisfaction—The Persuasive Presentation Strategy

persuasion A communication process by which you motivate someone else to voluntarily do something you'd like them to do.

persuasive presentation A sales strategy that influences the prospect's beliefs, attitudes, or behaviour and encourages buyer action.

Many salespeople believe that when a real need for their product exists, the stage is set for a persuasive presentation. **Persuasion** is a communication process by which you motivate someone else to voluntarily do something you'd like them to. The key word is "voluntarily." Persuasion is not compelling or manipulating others to do what you want. You must present your audience with a legitimate choice of options. True persuasion occurs when someone not only chooses your preferred option but also feels good about it afterward.[6] The major goals of the **persuasive presentation** are to influence the prospect's beliefs, attitudes, or behaviour, and to encourage buyer action. Persuasive sales presentations include a subtle transition stage where the dialogue shifts from an intellectual emphasis to an emotional appeal. This situation may occur when Ecolab's Chris Wylie discovers a safety issue that needs immediate attention. Every buying decision is influenced by both reason and emotion, but the amount of weight given to each of these elements during the decision-making process can vary greatly depending on the prospect.[7]

In the field of personal selling, persuasion is an acceptable strategy once a need has been identified and a suitable product has been selected. When it is clear that the buyer will benefit from ownership of the product or service, an enthusiastic and persuasive sales presentation is usually appropriate. The persuasive presentation strategy requires a high level of training and experience to be effective, because a poorly planned and delivered persuasive presentation may raise the prospect's anxiety level. The persuasive presentation, when handled improperly, can trigger fear or distrust.

Need-Satisfaction—The Reminder Presentation Strategy

Studies show that awareness of a company's products and services declines as promotion is stopped. This problem represents one of the reasons many companies employ *missionary* salespeople to maintain an ongoing awareness of and familiarity with their product lines. Other types of salespeople also use this presentation strategy. Route salespeople rely heavily on a **reminder presentation** (sometimes called *reinforcement presentation*) to maintain their market share. Salespeople such as Tom James Company's Alex Homer, introduced in Chapter 1, know that if they do not make frequent calls and remind customers of their products, customers may turn to the competition.

The reminder presentation is sometimes a dimension of service after the sale (see Chapter 15). Sales personnel, such as the B2B detail salesperson described in Chapter 2, who work with repeat customers are in a good position to remind them of products or services they offer. In a B2C selling situation, retail sales personnel can remind their regular customers of additional products in their own department or another department located in some other area of the business. Some products require special care and maintenance. Busy customers may need to be reminded of the maintenance services offered by your company. In some cases, the service department is a major profit generator, so reminder calls need to be given a high priority.

Reminder presentations are often used by salespeople who may have been unsuccessful in a previous call. Sometimes when the buyer has a strong relationship with a competing supplier, the best you can hope is that the current relationship weakens. You want to be top-of-mind when that happens, and a reminder presentation can often achieve that result. There are also some customers who, after they understand that you are truly committed to getting their business, will eventually give you a trial order.

Some customers get used to the great quality and service you provide and begin to view your product as a commodity. Once this happens, the customer may ask for a price reduction. To keep customers focused on value rather than price, remind them (from time to time) of the value-added services you provide.[8]

reminder presentation
Sometimes called the *reinforcement presentation,* this strategy assumes that the prospect has already been involved in an informative or persuasive presentation and understands at least the basic product features and buyer benefits.

GUIDELINES FOR CREATING A PRESENTATION THAT ADDS VALUE

IT IS IMPORTANT TO DISTINGUISH BETWEEN A PLANNED CONSULTATIVE PRESENTATION AND a **canned presentation**. In most cases, the canned presentation, also referred to as the *memorized* or *scripted presentation*,[9] is built around a standard set of steps, ignores the unique needs of each customer, and is presented in the form of a repetitive speech given to all customers interested in a particular item. Although an effective planned presentation will generally add value from the customer's perspective, a canned presentation today will likely be discounted by the customer and may take away from the value a product has to offer. With the planned consultative presentation, the salesperson is considered a strategic resource and partner for the customer, rather than just a provider of a product or service.[10]

In some group selling situations, a variation of the canned presentation has to be presented because the audience has such a wide variety of needs. In any case, every effort should be made to understand those needs and adapt the group presentation as much as possible to meet the needs of the audience. More will be presented later in this chapter on group presentations.

Strategic planning, of course, sets the stage for an effective consultative presentation that adds value to the sale (Fig. 12.3). Some of the most important ways to create value with the presentation are discussed next.

canned presentation Or *memorized* or *scripted presentation*, is built around a standard set of steps, ignores the unique needs of each customer, and is presented in the form of a repetitive speech given to all customers interested in a particular item.

Adapt the Presentation to Meet the Unique Needs of the Customer

Salespeople who have mastered adaptive selling skills adjust their sales strategies in ways that better fit customer needs and preferences.[11] In consultative selling, each presentation is custom tailored because, as we found in Chapter 11 on need discovery, individual client problems and priorities are unique. In other words, every aspect of the sales presentation should be adapted to the needs or problems mutually identified by the prospect and the salesperson.

It is possible to develop a sales demonstration so structured and so mechanical that the prospect feels like a number. We must try to avoid what some veteran marketing people refer to as the *depersonalization* of the selling–buying process. If the demonstration is overly structured, it cannot be personalized to meet specific customer wants and needs.

Bell Helicopter (**www.bellhelicopter.com**) manufactures helicopters in Canada and the United States. It sells a product with countless custom options, and each option changes its price and performance. One customer may want a helicopter for emergency medical care and another may want one for electronic news gathering. Bell's sales force, all of whom are licensed helicopter pilots, can introduce the Bell product line with a video presentation and then follow up with a demonstration flight if requested. Sales representatives also have access to a sales configuration system that supports the customization process. Price and performance data can be quickly determined for each accessory needed by the customer. The software automatically provides answers to the numerous questions that can surface during the sales presentation.[12]

In most business-to-business selling situations, it would be a mistake to present all of the product benefits. Some benefits may be of no interest to the target customer. Effective precall preparation and well-executed need discovery activities minimize the possibility that you will spend time discussing features that provide no benefit to the customer.

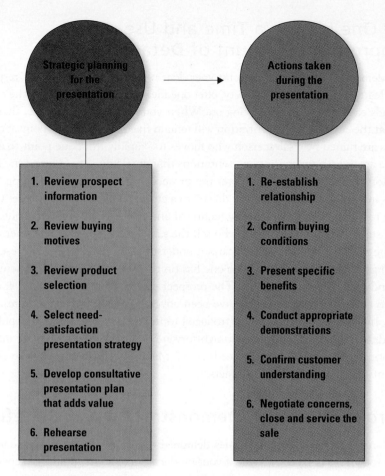

Figure 12.3 Strategic Planning for the Presentation
Salespeople who truly represent value to their customers plan ahead strategically for
the actions taken during the consultative sales presentation.

Global Business Insight

Doing Business in Japan

Many Canadian businesspeople travel to Japan because it
is one of world's largest economies and an important trading partner for Canada. As such, it is important to become
familiar with the Japanese business culture.

- Courtesy is a major key to success in Japan. When you
  address someone, be sure to use titles such as Mr.,
  Ms., or Dr., and wait to be invited before using first
  names.

- The Japanese are very hierarchical, so the business card
  is an important source of information regarding the
  relative status of the other person.

Accept the card with care and then examine it. Do not
put it in your pocket or wallet. Place it in a cardholder.

- In Japan, the culture emphasizes the group over the individual. It would not be appropriate to praise one member
  of a group.

- Decision making in Japan is done very slowly. Be patient
  as the group reaches a consensus. Aggressive sales methods should be avoided.[a]

Cover One Idea at a Time and Use an Appropriate Amount of Detail

Pace the demonstration so that the customer does not become confused. In response to what was learned in the needs discovery, offer one idea at a time, and be sure the customer understands each point before moving on. When you neglect this practice, there is the danger that the customer's concentration will remain fixed on a previous point. Some presentations are ruined by a salesperson who moves too rapidly from one point to another.

There are at least two types of presentations that are doomed to failure. One is a sales presentation that is too basic and leaves the prospect with the feeling of being "patronized." It is important to avoid "talking down" to a customer. The other provides the prospect with too much detail. It is overly technical and leaves the buyer in a confused and frustrated state of mind. Salespeople who sell the same product every day sometimes lose sight of the fact that some customers cannot understand a highly technical presentation.

It is a good idea to assume that no one has time to waste. Make your presentation as concise and to the point as possible. The prospect will be greatly annoyed if you use 10 minutes to make a point that could have been covered in two or three minutes. Several years ago, the "KISS" principle was introduced to the field of selling. This popular acronym stands for "Keep It Simple and Straightforward." Put another way, never make your presentation more complex than it needs to be. Make sure the terms you use and ideas you present are familiar to your customers.

Use Proof Devices to Demonstrate Buyer Benefits

A well-planned and well-executed sales demonstration is one of the most convincing forms of proof. This is especially true if your product has dramatic points of superiority.

When salespeople use effective visual proof devices in their presentations, research indicates that retention increases from 14 to 38 percent and the time needed to present a concept is reduced by up to 40 percent.

In a complex sale, it is imperative to check every part of your demonstration prior to the presentation. During the presentation, you should cover one idea at a time and secure agreement before moving on.

Business-to-business salespeople representing Epson, Canon, Hewlett-Packard, and other manufacturers can offer the customer a wide range of printers. What is the real difference between a $2000 printer and an $8000 printer? The most effective way to provide proof of this buyer benefit is to show the customer material that has been printed on both printers. By letting the prospect compare the samples, the salesperson is converting product features to a buyer benefit. Be prepared to prove every claim you make with tests, findings, and performance records.

Proof Devices We have noted that when trust is present, customers are more open to the sales presentation. One way to build trust is to use a proof device that enhances your credibility. A **proof device** can take the form of a statement, a report, a testimonial, customer data, or a photograph. A salesperson selling conference services for a large hotel/conference centre might use the following proof statement: "We were selected by *Training* magazine as one of Canada's top 10 conference centres." Later, the salesperson shows the customer photographs of the conference facilities and guest rooms. Then the customer is given a copy of a testimonial letter from a satisfied customer. The statement, photos, and letter help build the customer's confidence in the product. Later in this chapter, in the Selling Tools section, we will examine proof devices in more detail.

proof device A device such as a statement, report, testimonial, customer data, or photograph that is used to enhance the salesperson's credibility during a sales presentation.

Appeal to As Many Senses as Appropriate

In conducting a sales demonstration, it is a good idea to appeal to all appropriate senses. Each of the five senses—sight, hearing, smell, touch, and taste—represents an avenue by which the salesperson can attract the prospect's attention and build desire. Although

Bell Helicopter sales representatives have access to a sales configurations system that supports customizing the demonstration. Sales representatives, all of whom are licensed helicopter pilots, conduct customized demonstration flights to meet their customers' unique needs.

sight is considered the most powerful attention-attracting sense, it may not be the most important motivating force in every selling situation. When presenting a food product, the taste and aroma may be critical. Designers and decorators tell us that most furniture buyers still want to touch and feel the product before they buy it.

Christa-Lee McWatters understands the importance of reaching the prospect through as many senses as possible. She sells approximately 30 different wines bottled by Sumac Ridge Estate Winery Ltd. in Summerland, British Columbia, to beer and wine stores, to restaurants, and even to individuals and companies.[13] The sales presentation for a quality wine usually highlights four areas:

- *Consumer demand.* The wine's sales potential is described in realistic terms.
- *Marketing strategies.* Suggested ways to merchandise the wine are discussed.

- *Bouquet.* The distinctive fragrance of the wine is introduced.
- *Taste.* A sample of the wine is given to the prospect in a good-quality wineglass.

Note that a sales presentation featuring these appeals will reach the prospect through four of the five senses. Collectively, these appeals add value. When you involve more than one sense, the sales presentation is more informative and persuasive.

Balance Telling, Showing, and Involvement

A Chinese proverb says, "Tell me, I'll forget; show me, I may remember; but involve me and I'll understand."[14] Some of the most effective sales demonstrations combine telling, showing, and involvement of the prospect. To plan an effective demonstration, consider developing a demonstration. Simply divide a sheet of paper into four columns. Head the first column "Feature to Be Demonstrated." Head the second column "Proof Device to Be Used." Head the third column "What I Will Say," and head the fourth column "What I or the Customer Will Do." List the major features you plan to demonstrate in proper sequence in the first column. In the second column, describe the proof devices you will use. In the third column, describe what you will say about the feature, converting the feature to a customer benefit. In the fourth column, describe what you (or the customer) will do at the time this benefit is discussed. A sample demonstration worksheet appears in Figure 12.4.

When appropriate and possible, try to involve the customer in the sales presentation. The best way to highlight the aesthetics, technology, and ergonomics of Teknion's AL3 executive swivel chair is to have the customer sit in it. Toronto-based Teknion is a leading international designer, manufacturer, and marketer of quality office systems and related furniture. To fully appreciate its products, customers really need to see and try them.

Demonstration Worksheet

Feature to Be Demonstrated	Proof Device to Be Used	What I Will Say (Include Benefit)	What I or the Customer Will Do
Special computer circuit board to accelerate drawing graphics on a colour monitor screen	Monitor and software	"This monitor is large enough to display multiple windows. You can easily compare several graphics."	Have the customer bring up several windows using the computer keyboard.
Meeting room setup at a hotel and conference centre	Floor plan	"This setup will provide a metre of elbow space for each participant. For long meetings, the added space provides more comfort."	Give the customer a tour of the room and invite her to sit in a chair at one of the conference tables.

Figure 12.4 The Demonstration Worksheet
The demonstration worksheet enables the salesperson to strategically plan and then rehearse demonstrations that strengthen the presentation.

From the Field

Selling a Product That Doesn't Exist

Some creative entrepreneurs start selling their product before it even exists. Greg Gianforte wanted to start an Internet-software company in the late 1990s. He noted that no one seemed to be making a good product that would help companies respond to email from customers. Armed with a product feature sheet, Gianforte started trying to sell a nonexistent product. He called customer-support managers at hundreds of companies. After reviewing the product features, he explained that the product would be ready in 90 days. Some of these potential customers mentioned features he had not thought of.

This input helped him develop a better product. After two weeks of cold calls, he knew exactly what customers wanted and began the development of RightNow software. It was ready for customer use in 90 days. He then hired his first three employees—all of them salespeople. Gianforte says, "Sales is really the most noble part of the business because it's the part that brings the solution together with the customer's need." Today, more than 1200 organizations worldwide use RightNow solutions.[b]

If it is not possible for the prospect to participate in demonstrations or handle the products, sales literature, pictures, or brochures placed in the person's hands may help. After the sales call, these items remind the prospect of not only who called but also why.

Develop Creative Presentations

Presenting product features and buyer benefits in an interesting and appealing way requires some amount of creativity. Creativity is needed to adapt a sales presentation that can gain attention, increase desire, and add value. The ability to come up with problem-solving

Secrets of Question Based Selling (www.qbsresearch.com), used in sales organizations around the world, focuses on asking the right questions that pique customer interest, build credibility, uncover greater needs, and solicit more accurate information.

"Following the program, even our most experienced salespeople raved, saying QBS was the best sales training they had ever experienced!"

Secrets of QUESTION BASED SELLING

How the Most Powerful Tool in Business Can Double Your Sales Results

Thomas A. Freese

answers or different ways of looking at situations is greatly valued in today's fast-changing business environment. Creativity is enhanced by expertise in the field of endeavour. For salespeople, this means knowledge of the sales process, product knowledge, and an understanding of human behaviour. Creativity is also enhanced by the capacity for divergent thinking and a willingness to take risks.[15]

Consider the Use of Humour—in Moderation

According to Burt Teplitzky, author of *Sell It with Humor,* humour, if used in moderation and used appropriately, can work wonders to break down barriers, build rapport, and foster long-term and mutually beneficial customer relationships. If used improperly, it can distance you from your customer. Teplitzky suggests that one should never tell jokes off the cuff when speaking to customers. He suggests that your use of humour should be preplanned and communicate that you don't take yourself too seriously.

One part of the sales process in which he likes to use humour is the transition to the presentation. He might open his presentation with a line such as, "Before we get started, I promise not to bore you with a long presentation. . . . I'm sure I can do it with a short one." As he says, this would never go over in a comedy club, but in an environment where people are glad for any release, they appreciate the humour. Humour should never be used to attack anybody, nor should it be used during your transition to the close.[16]

Choose the Right Setting

The location of the sales demonstration can make a difference. Some companies routinely rent space at a hotel, motel, or conference centre so that the demonstration can be conducted in a controlled environment free of noise and other interruptions. However, in these busy times, prospects are often unwilling or unable to participate in a presentation held off premises. In these situations, many organizations do have conference rooms that can be reserved with advance notice.

Document the Value Proposition

In Chapter 7, we defined *value proposition* as a set of key benefits and values the salesperson promises to deliver to satisfy the customer's needs. Salespeople must be prepared to substantiate the points presented during the sales presentation. Recent research indicates that salespeople often make claims of savings and benefits to the customer but fail to back them up. Failure to demonstrate and document claims is a common barrier to closing the sale.[17]

In many cases, the most effective value proposition is one that focuses on favourable points of difference between your product and *the next best alternative.* The salesperson recognizes that the customer can purchase the product from one or more competitors. Once the customer's requirements and preferences are clearly understood, and knowledge of the competitor's product is acquired, the salesperson can focus on key points of difference.

The most effective value proposition describes the few elements that matter most to your customer. This approach recognizes that today's buyers are extremely busy and want to do business with salespeople who fully grasp the critical issues in their

The value proposition includes a mix of key benefits to meet the needs of the customer. This ad illustrates the three parts of Durkee's value proposition: support, flavour, and performance.

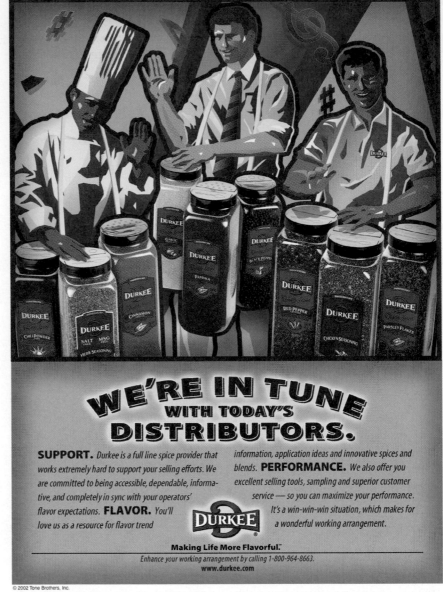

business and are able to deliver a value proposition that is simple yet powerfully captivating. Focus on favourable points of difference between your product and the *next best alternative*.[18]

Quantifying the Solution

In Chapter 6, we explained that the process of determining whether a sales proposal adds value is called *quantifying the solution*. If the cost of the proposal is offset by added value, closing the sale will be much easier. In business-to-business selling, quantifying the solution is very common. Let's assume you represent a manufacturing company that sells robots—programmable machines capable of performing a variety of tasks.

The two primary benefits are (1) payroll cost savings and (2) vastly improved quality. One way to quantify the solution in this case is to use simple **cost–benefit analysis**. This involves listing the costs to the buyer and the savings to be achieved from the purchase of the robots.

Another way to quantify the solution is to calculate the net profits or savings—or **return on investment (ROI)**—expressed as a percentage of the original investment. Using the following formula, you can determine the return on a given investment:

$$ROI = Net\ Profits\ (or\ Savings) \div Investment \times 100$$

If the robotic system costs $16 000 but saves the firm $4000, the ROI is 25 percent ($4000 ÷ $16 000 × 100 = 25%). Some companies set a minimum ROI for new products or cost-saving programs. Salespeople typically acquire this information at the need assessment stage, then include it in the written proposal.

Space does not permit an in-depth review of the many methods of quantifying the solution, such as payback period, opportunity cost, net present value, after-tax cash flow, turnover, and contribution margin.

cost–benefit analysis An analysis of the costs versus the benefits to the customer as a result of making a particular purchase.

return on investment (ROI) The net profits or savings that the customer will see from investing in a particular purchase.

Check Sales Tools

Be sure to check every item to be used in conjunction with the sales demonstration. If you are using audiovisual equipment, be certain that it is in good working condition. Always carry an extension cord and a spare bulb. If you are making a laptop presentation, be sure you can go online in front of the customer. If you plan to demonstrate a website, save it on a hard disk instead of going online. Be prepared for technological snags by having multiple backups. Always carry extra batteries for your laptop.[19]

Summarize Major Points

The allotted time for a presentation usually provides the opportunity to present a significant amount of information. Most people talk at a speed of about 125 words per minute. In a short time span of just 15 minutes, the customer may be bombarded with approximately 1900 words. For this reason, the salesperson should occasionally use a summary-confirmation question to summarize and confirm major points. The customer needs this form of value-added assistance.

GUIDELINES FOR A PERSUASIVE PRESENTATION STRATEGY THAT ADDS VALUE

EARLIER IN THIS CHAPTER, WE INTRODUCED YOU TO THE PERSUASIVE PRESENTATION STRATEGY as one of the three strategies you could choose in creating a need-satisfaction presentation. A study on persuasion in the *Journal for Management in Engineering*, published by the American Society of Civil Engineers, reported that effective communicators recognize that conviction (emotion) is more vital to persuasion than position (logic). People make decisions based primarily on what they feel and then test or rationalize their choice with logic. Table 12.1 illustrates the contrast between traditional technical communication and persuasive communication.[20]

Table 12.1 Technical vs. Persuasive Communication	
Technical Communication	**Persuasive Communication**
Impersonal, objective	Personal, subjective
Intellectual response	Emotional response
Emphasizes features	Emphasizes benefits
Information-driven	Influence-driven

Technical communication, illustrated in the first column of Table 12.1, would be more appropriate for the *informative presentation strategy* introduced in Chapter 11. Persuasive communication, appropriately used, will enhance the success of the *persuasive presentation strategy*.

There are many ways to incorporate persuasion into a presentation strategy and most, if used appropriately, will create value for the customer. In this section, we review a series of guidelines that should be followed during preparation of a persuasive presentation.

Place Special Emphasis on the Relationship

Relationships are enhanced by the salesperson's ability to communicate in compelling and creative ways.[21] Throughout this book, we emphasize the importance of the relationship strategy in selling. Good rapport between the salesperson and the prospect establishes a foundation for an open exchange of information. Robert Cialdini, writing in the *Harvard Business Review*, says the science of persuasion is built on the principle of liking: People like those who like them.

Salespeople, acting as relationship managers, play a key role in the development and management of partnering relationships.[22] Establish a bond with the prospect early by uncovering areas of common interest, using praise when it's appropriate, and being completely trustworthy.[23] Don't forget to adapt your communication style to accommodate the needs of the customer (see Chapter 4). Also remember that good salespeople today use smart social-media strategies to enhance customer relationships. They make it their business to stay connected to their customers through Twitter, Facebook, and LinkedIn.[24] When building important partnering relationships, remember that most people don't care how much you know until they know how much you care.

Target Emotional Links and Use a Persuasive Vocabulary

emotional links The connectors that link a salesperson's message to the customer's emotions and increase the chances of closing a sale—for example, quality improvement, on-time delivery, service, innovation.

Emotional links are the connectors between your messages and the internal emotions of your prospect.[25] Some common emotional links in the business community are quality improvement, on-time delivery, increased market share, innovation, customer service, and reduction of operating expenses. Targeting just a few emotional links can increase your chances of closing the sale. When you target emotional links, use persuasive words. Research conducted on persuasion suggests the following list of words to use in persuasive communication. Consider the appropriate use of these words when planning a persuasive presentation strategy:

*you	*advantage
save	guarantee
money	security
health	discovery
easy	*new
now	*benefits
safety	positive
results	proven

Note: *Many marketing people agree that the words with asterisks are probably the most important in selling and advertising.

Sell Specific Benefits and Obtain Customer Reactions

People do not buy things; they buy what the things will do for them. At Mattress Firm, Edith Botello realizes her customers do not buy a mattress; they buy a relaxing, comfortable, uninterrupted, physically healthy evening of rest. Chief information officers do not buy computers or programming services; they buy timely, easy to access, easy to understand, economically priced information. Every product or service offers the customer certain benefits. The benefit might be ease of operation, greater comfort, security, feelings of confidence, or economy.

If you are selling Allstate insurance, for example, you should become familiar with the service features. One feature is well-trained employees, and another is the convenient location of Allstate offices throughout Canada. The benefit to customers is greater peace of mind in knowing that they will receive good service at a nearby location. Allstate salespeople understand the importance of selling the company, the product, and themselves.

After you state the feature and convert it into a buyer benefit, obtain a reaction from the customer by using confirmation or need-satisfaction questions (refer to Table 11.1). You should always check to see if you are on the right track and if your prospect is following the logic of your presentation. Here are some examples:

Feature	Benefit	Question
Seven-hour battery life*	Fewer work interruptions when travelling	"Battery life is important to you, isn't it?" (*Confirmation question*)
Automatic climate control system for automobile	Temperature in car not varying after initial setting	"Would you like the luxury of setting the temperature and then not worrying about it?" (*Need-satisfaction question*)

*Feature of Fujitsu Lifebook laptop

The feature–benefit–reaction or, as IBM salespeople call it, the FBR approach, is used by many high-performance salespeople. Involving the customer with appropriate questions helps you maintain two-way communication.

Use of Showmanship

showmanship An interesting and attractive way of communicating an idea to others.

Showmanship is defined as an interesting and attractive way of communicating an idea to others. If done tastefully and appropriately, it can do a lot to improve the persuasiveness and effectiveness of a sales presentation. Showmanship in selling need not be equated with sensational or bizarre events. It may be a very subtle act such as the furnishing and accessorizing, or "staging" as it is sometimes called, of a home being shown by PulteGroup's Ashley Pineda, introduced in Chapter 8. Another example of showmanship would be carefully placing a fine diamond on a piece of black velvet before showing the jewel to the customer

Some good examples of showmanship can be seen at trade shows, where new products are displayed. One company demonstrated the fireproof quality of their insulation by holding a piece of it in front of a blowtorch. In simplest terms, showmanship is the act of presenting product features and benefits in a manner that will gain attention and increase desire. It is never a substitute for thorough preparation and knowledge of your customer, company, and product. And effective showmanship is never based on deceit or trickery. It should not be gaudy or insincere. When showmanship detracts from the image, the product, or the salesperson, it is counterproductive.

Minimize the Negative Impact of Change

As we noted earlier, salespeople are constantly threatening the status quo. They sell people the new, the different, and the untried. In nearly all selling situations, the customer is being asked to consider change of some sort and, in some cases, it is only natural for the person to resist change. Whenever possible, salespeople should try to help the prospect view change in a positive and realistic way. Change is more acceptable to people who understand the benefits of it and do not see it as a threat. Always anticipate the one question (spoken or unspoken) that every buyer asks: "How will this product benefit me?" To minimize the impact of change, be sure to personalize the benefit with a specific reference to the customer's need.

Place the Strongest Appeal at the Beginning or End

Research indicates that appeals made at the beginning or end of a presentation are more effective than those given in the middle. A strong appeal at the beginning of a presentation gets the prospect's attention and possibly develops interest. Made near the end of the presentation, the appeal sets the stage for closing the sale.

Use the Power of Association with Metaphors, Stories, and Testimonials

Research reveals that salespeople who use the power of association through sharing information they previously experienced with other clients help their customers better understand their own needs and make smarter buying choices.[26] Metaphors, sometimes

Preparing a sales presentation for a group is more demanding than one-on-one sales calls. Too much reliance on technical devices during a demonstration can affect the relationship, which is important to partnering effectively with prospects.

referred to as *figurative language*, are highly persuasive sales tools. Metaphors are words or phrases that suggest pictorial relationships between objects or ideas. With the aid of metaphors, you can paint vivid pictures for prospects that will command their attention and keep their interest. The success of the metaphor rests on finding common ground (shared or well-known experiences) so that your message gets a boost from a fact already known or believed to be true. A salesperson presenting Cobalt boats, a line of high-quality runabouts selling for $30 000 to $300 000, might refer to his products as "the Steinways of the runabout class."[27] Stories not only help you sell more products but also help you enrich relationships with your customers. Salespeople, such as Liberty Mutual's Marcus Smith introduced in Chapter 2, often use stories about a timely settlement for a large loss to explain the benefits of adequate insurance protection. A good story focuses the customer's attention and can effectively communicate the value of a product or service. The story should be appropriate to the customer's situation, short, and told with enthusiasm.[28]

Many salespeople find it beneficial to quote a specific third party. Third-party testimonials from satisfied customers can help a prospect feel confident about using your product.

GUIDELINES FOR A GROUP SALES PRESENTATION

PREPARING A SALES PRESENTATION FOR A GROUP IS MORE DEMANDING THAN ONE-ON-ONE sales calls. Meeting the diverse needs of the audience can be very challenging. Therefore, *Rule One* is to identify the titles and roles of the people who will attend. Among those attending, who is most likely to influence the buying decision? If you learn that the audience will include the prospect's CEO, your CEO should be there. Anticipate that the audience will include demanding, high-level decision makers who will likely ask some difficult questions. Be prepared![29]

Rule Two is to check out the meeting room in advance. Take note of the room configuration, audiovisual capabilities, seating options, available lighting, and the adequacy of heating or air conditioning. Always arrive at the meeting room about 60 minutes before the meeting begins. Use the first 40 minutes to check and double-check presentation tools, seating arrangements, lighting, etc. Use the other 20 minutes for building rapport with attendees as they arrive.

Rule Three is to be sure your presentation is characterized by clarity and simplicity. Minimize the number of features and benefits you present. Focus on the few benefits that appeal to your prospect. Don't use jargon or technical terms that might confuse persons in attendance. If you are part of a team sales presentation (see Chapter 10), then be sure every team member understands their responsibility and the amount of time they will be given for their presentation. Give the team time for rehearsal before the group presentation.

Rule Four is to anticipate the diversity of questions such as finance, delivery, competition, and service, in addition to traditional product issues you are likely to be asked. You must be prepared with answers that are concise and persuasive. Questions should be welcomed because they help you understand what is truly important to the customer.

Enhancing the Group Presentation with Mental Imagery

mental imagery The ability to visualize an object, concept, or action not actually present.

Mental imagery is the ability to visualize an object, concept, or action not actually present. A sales demonstration can be greatly enhanced with the use of auditory and visual imagery. Today there is no shortage of compact, lightweight portable presentation devices. Sony Electronics, Hitachi Software, and NEC offer sales professionals projectors that weigh only a few pounds and project a clear, bright image. These presentation tools also offer quick and easy setup.[30]

Impatica, a company that specializes in the delivery and viewing of PowerPoint presentations over the Internet and wireless networks, has developed a small, lightweight device that enables salespeople to project presentations wirelessly from a BlackBerry handheld device. Users need only hook the ShowMate to the VGA port projector, LCD, or plasma screen and the BlackBerry will deliver the PowerPoint presentation using Bluetooth technology.[31] Of course, salespeople should never rely solely on presentation tools to sell products. Dianne Durkin, president of the consulting firm Loyalty Factor, offers this advice:

> When a salesperson is tied to the technical device and the presentation, they miss the opportunity to build the personal relationship by asking questions and listening to the customer. A questioning and listening strategy is the secret weapon for the salesperson.[32]

Audiovisual Presentation Fundamentals

Many companies provide their salespeople with such audiovisual aids as videotapes or computer-based presentations. Unfortunately, they sometimes fail to explain how to use these tools in the most effective way. Here are some suggestions on how to use audiovisual presentations to achieve maximum impact.

- As noted above, do not rely too heavily on "bells and whistles" to sell your products. Audiovisual technology provides support for the major points in your presentation, but it does not replace an interactive sales demonstration.

Many firms, like Engineered Machine Products, which produces high-efficiency thermal management systems for cooling engines, have learned that one of the keys to closing a large, complex sale is to conduct a plant tour.

- Be sure the prospect knows the purpose of the presentation. Preview the material and describe a few highlights. Always try to build interest in advance of the audiovisual presentation.

- Be prepared to stop the presentation to clarify a point or to allow the prospect to ask questions. Do not permit the audiovisual presentation to become a barrier to good two-way communication.

- At the conclusion of the audiovisual presentation, review key points and allow the prospect an opportunity to ask questions.

SELLING TOOLS FOR EFFECTIVE DEMONSTRATIONS

NEARLY EVERY SALES ORGANIZATION PROVIDES ITS STAFF WITH PROOF DEVICES OR SALES tools of one kind or another to use in the demonstration part of the consultative presentation. Some companies refer to these as *marketing tools*. Many proof devices and sales tools, when used correctly, add value to the sales effort. If the company does not provide these items, the creative salesperson secures or develops sales tools independently. In addition to technology-based presentations, sales personnel can utilize a wide range of other selling tools. Creative salespeople are continually securing or developing new types of sales tools. The following section summarizes some of the most common proof devices and selling tools used today.

Product and Plant Tours

Without a doubt, the best selling aid is usually the product itself. As noted previously, Bell Helicopter uses an effective video to describe various products—although some customers still will not buy without a demonstration ride. In the growing market for ergonomic office chairs, ranging in price from $700 to $1500, furniture makers know the best way to close the sale is to provide an opportunity for the customer to sit in the chair. With growing awareness of the hazards of poor sitting posture and bad ergonomics, more people are searching for a comfortable work chair.[33]

Doug Adams was the first salesperson hired by a major manufacturer of high-quality optical equipment. Although he was not a technician or an engineer, he quickly realized that the equipment had product superiority that physicians would recognize if they saw it demonstrated. During the first year, he sold 28 machines, far surpassing the expectations of his employer.[34]

As noted in a previous chapter, plant tours provide an excellent source of product information. EMP (Engineered Machine Products) makes high-efficiency thermal management systems for cooling engines. Products are made at its state-of-the-art manufacturing facility, and the company has learned that the key to closing many large, complex sales is a tour of this innovative facility.[35]

Models

Sometimes, it is not practical to demonstrate the product itself because it is too big or immobile. It is easier to demonstrate a small-scale model or cross-section of the original equipment. A working model, like the actual product, can give the prospect a clear picture of how a piece of equipment operates.

With the aid of modern technology, it is possible to create a model in picture form. ClosetMaid (**www.closetmaid.com**), a manufacturer of ventilated wire for commercial closets and other storage products, uses desktop visualization software to create a three-dimensional presentation that allows customers to see exactly what the finished facility will look like. Sales representatives can print out a hard copy so the customer has a picture of the custom-designed model for future reference. With the aid of this visualization technology, ClosetMaid salespeople can modify closet layouts on screen and produce a detailed bill of materials for each project.[36]

Salespeople can add value to their presentations with the aid of photos and illustrations. This salesperson has balanced telling, showing, and involvement by getting the sales literature into the hands of the prospect.

Photos, Illustrations, and Brochures

The old proverb "One picture is worth a thousand words" can be put into practical application by a creative salesperson. A great deal of information can be given to the prospect with the aid of photos and illustrations. Chris Roberts, area manager for Downing Displays (**www.downingretail.com**), a manufacturer of trade-show displays, says that the photo presentation book is the most important item he takes on a first sales call. He says, "Because what we sell is very visual, it's important for the client to *see* the displays."[37]

Many companies develop brochures that visually reinforce specific need or benefit areas. Brochures can be effective during the initial discussion of needs when the salesperson wants to provide a brief overview of possible solutions. Someone planning to remodel a kitchen might be given a number of brochures that feature colour photos of numerous countertop materials and kitchen design examples.[38]

Portfolios

A **portfolio** is a portable case or loose-leaf binder containing a wide variety of sales-supporting materials. The portfolio is used to add visual life to the sales message and to prove claims. Advertising salespeople such as *Texas Monthly*'s Amy Vandaveer, introduced in Chapter 6, customize portfolios to appeal to the unique interests and needs of individual clients. She carefully selects sales tools to include, such as the following items:

portfolio A portable case or loose-leaf binder containing a wide variety of sales-supporting materials. It is used to add visual life to the sales message and to prove claims.

- Sample advertisements used in conjunction with other successful campaigns
- Selected illustrations that can be incorporated into advertisements
- A selection of testimonial letters
- Rate cards
- Market research studies and results on readership and buying habits
- Case histories of specific clients who have used the media with success

The portfolio has been used as a sales aid by people who sell interior design services, insurance, real estate, securities, and convention services. It is a very adaptable proof device that can be revised at any time to meet the needs of each customer.

Reprints

Leading magazines and journals sometimes feature articles that directly or indirectly support the salesperson's product. A reprint of the article can be a forceful selling tool. It is also an inexpensive selling tool. Pharmaceutical and medical sales representatives often use reprints from journals that report on research in the field of medicine. A few years ago, Closure Medical Corporation received approval to sell Dermabond (**www.dermabond.com**), a surgical glue used to close cuts. This innovative product received national attention when the prestigious *Journal of the American Medical Association* concluded that gluing a wound could be just as effective as sewing it shut. Salespeople representing Dermabond used the article to help educate doctors on the product's merits and applications.[39] In many cases, prospects are far more impressed with the good points of your product if a third party presents them than if you do. A reprint from a respected journal can be very persuasive.

Catalogues

A well-designed catalogue shows the range and comprehensiveness of your product line. It may include specifications needed for installation and current price information. If you plan to give customers a copy of your catalogue, review the important features, such as a comprehensive index or important appendix material.[40]

Graphs, Charts, and Test Results

Graphs and charts can be used to illustrate changes in variables such as payroll expense, fuel consumption, or return on investment. For example, a bar graph might be used to illustrate the increase in fuel costs over a 10-year period. While graphs are usually quite descriptive, the layperson may misunderstand them. It is best to interpret the graph for the prospect. Do not move too fast, because the full impact of the message may be lost.

Test results from a reliable agency can be convincing. This is especially true when the test results are published by a respected independent agency, such as J. D. Power and Associates.

Bound Paper Presentations

While many salespeople use some type of presentation technology in conjunction with the sales demonstration, bound paper presentations are still a popular medium for many sales and marketing organizations.[41] With the aid of computer-generated graphics, salespeople find it easy to print attractive graphs, charts, and other proof information. Product guarantees and warranties are sometimes included in a bound paper presentation. Some marketers use guarantees and warranties to differentiate their products from competing products. Customer testimonials represent another common element of bound paper presentations. A testimonial letter from a prominent satisfied customer provides persuasive evidence that the product has support in the industry. Prospects also like bound paper presentations because the document is readily available for future reference.

Laptop Computers and Demonstration Software

A survey conducted by *Selling Power* magazine found that 87 percent of salespeople use laptops during their sales presentations.[42] Many salespeople report that the laptop computer is the single most powerful sales tool they use. Many of the things needed during the demonstration can be stored in the computer. If the customer is interested in a specific product, pull up the appropriate brochure on your laptop screen. If the client wants a copy of printed material or a videotape, you can either print the pages or send them via email. If the customer raises a question regarding product availability, use your laptop to access the information. You can place an order and, in some cases, print an invoice.[43] Thanks to modern computer technology, it's possible to conduct impressive

Social Media and Selling Today

Using YouTube for Presentations/Demonstrations

A sales presentation video posted on YouTube can add value to the sales process. Once reserved for large corporations that could afford professional sales presentation productions, now individual salespeople and small companies have easy access to the Internet and can make their presentations to larger groups of prospective customers.

YouTube and other sites are making it possible for salespeople to easily post a sales presentation on the Internet. YouTube presentations enable salespeople to focus on the key issues involving their customers' needs and their solutions. Different video presentations can be posted that meet the unique needs of individual customers. Various decision makers such as the user and the financial and technical influencers may view a video of a salesperson's presentation at any time during the sales process.

Lack of funds is not a barrier. Small investments are offset by creativity to communicate value. Inexpensive stock pictures, footage, music, and other sounds are available to enhance and add value to your videotaped sales presentation.

To post a sales presentation video on YouTube, follow these steps:

1. Register and sign in to YouTube.com.
2. On the homepage, click "Upload." You will be prompted to browse your computer for the video file of your sales presentation.
3. Select the file and complete the video information and privacy settings form.
4. Copy the Web address for your video.
5. Press "Save Changes."

multiple, simultaneous product demonstrations without leaving your office. Let's assume you are presenting a new employee disability insurance plan to members of the 3M Canada human resources staff. One key decision maker is based in London, Ontario, and the other is in the United States. With the aid of Pixion PictureTalk software or a similar product, you can use the Internet to conduct the demonstration for both persons in real time. Sales managers might use this same approach to train members of their sales team in remote offices.

Personal computers (PCs), with the support of online presentation technologies and presentation software, have played an important role in increasing sales force productivity. Salespeople have instant access to customer data, so they can easily customize the sales presentation. Many salespeople report that PC–based presentations, using graphics software, are very effective. Today's PC can produce striking visuals and attractive printed material that can be given to the customer for future reference.

Enhancing Demonstrations with PowerPoint The PowerPoint software program from Microsoft has been available to salespeople for 20 years. PowerPoint is so common that many prospects will find the standard presentation graphics very familiar, even dull. Salespeople who want their demonstration to look unique and different can create their own corporate template, animate their logo, or put video clips of their company information into the PowerPoint presentation. When developing a PowerPoint presentation, use bold, simple, and large fonts (such as Arial and Verdana) and put graphics on several slides. Limit the number of words to 15 or fewer per slide. Keep in mind two quality alternatives to PowerPoint: Apple's Keynote and Corel's Presentations.[44]

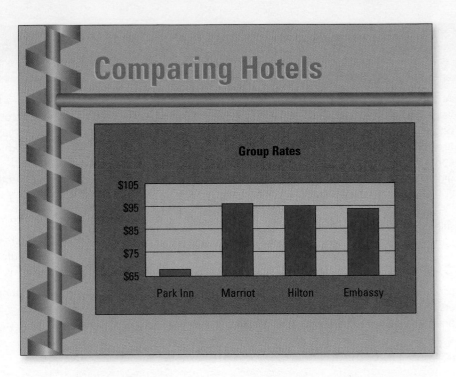

Figure 12.5 Excel Graph
Graphs produced with Excel software can add value and be very persuasive in demonstrating key benefits of a sales presentation. This Excel graph also uses a PowerPoint background design to add more value.

Creating Electronic Spreadsheets For many years, salespeople have been using electronic spreadsheets to prepare sales proposals. The electronic spreadsheet is an excellent tool for organizing the numbers involved in preparing quotes, such as quantities, costs, and prices. CB Richard Ellis's Susana Rosas, introduced in Chapter 3, frequently uses electronic spreadsheets to justify the purchase or rental of commercial properties. The electronic spreadsheet allows the user to answer "What if . . ." questions about the effects of lowering costs or raising prices. Once the preparation work is finished, the electronic spreadsheet itself can be printed and used as the proposal or to accompany the proposal.[45] The spreadsheet data can also be converted to a chart or graph that can enhance the proposal (see Fig. 12.5). When presenting the spreadsheet on a laptop computer, with minor adjustments, client questions regarding alternative proposals can be quickly generated. Many computers sold today include an electronic spreadsheet program. The leading electronic spreadsheet, Excel, is part of Microsoft's Office suite of products. If you have access to Excel or any other electronic spreadsheet software, you can explore the power of this tool for preparing proposals.

Web-Based Demonstrations Salespeople who want to avoid long airport security lines, lengthy terminal wait times, high priced hotels, and expensive rental car rates are turning to Web-conferencing solutions. Popular alternatives to in-person sales presentations include GoToMeeting, WebEx Communications Sales Center, Raindance Meeting

Edition, Adobe's Macromedia Breeze 5, and Microsoft Office Live Meeting. Some salespeople create computerized demonstrations that are stored in a central library and accessed on demand. With a few clicks of a mouse, presenters can call up the information they wish to showcase using a Web browser. The salesperson can show PowerPoint presentations, present product features, and conduct question-and-answer sessions in real time. Prior to scheduling an online meeting, be sure to find out if the customer's firewall restricts the usage of your Web-conferencing software.[46]

Rehearse the Presentation

While you are actually putting on the presentation, you will need to be concentrating on a variety of details. The movements you make and what you say and do should be so familiar to you that each response is nearly automatic. To achieve this level of skill, you need to rehearse the presentation.

Rehearse both what you are going to say and what you are going to do. Say the words aloud exactly as if the prospect were present. It is surprising how often a concept that seems quite clear as you think it over becomes hopelessly mixed up when you try to discuss it with a customer. Rehearsal is the best way to avoid this embarrassing situation. Whenever possible, have your presentation/demonstration videotaped before you give it. Play it back and watch for these things:[47]

- Do you frequently use words that take away from your professional image? Examples include "you know" and "like."
- Check your pace—are you talking too rapidly or too slowly?
- Do you present information with clarity? Are you convincing?

Plan for the Dynamic Nature of Selling

The sales presentation is a dynamic activity. From the moment the salesperson and the customer meet, the sales presentation is being altered and fine-tuned to reflect the new information available. The salesperson must be able to execute strategy instantaneously. In the movie *Top Gun*, Kelly McGillis asks Tom Cruise, "What were you thinking up there?" He replies, "You don't have time to think. You take time to think up there, you're dead." By this he means that one's response must be habit and reflex.[48]

During a typical presentation, the salesperson asks numerous questions, discusses several product features, and demonstrates the appropriate product benefits. The customer is asking questions and, in many cases, voicing concerns. The successful sales presentation is a good model of two-way communication. Because of the dynamic nature of the sales presentation, the salesperson must be prepared to apply several different selling skills to meet the variety of buyer responses. Figure 12.6 illustrates how the various selling skills can be applied during all parts of the sales presentation. In creating effective presentations, the salesperson should be prepared to meet a wide range of buyer responses with effective questions, benefit statements, demonstrations, negotiating methods, and closing methods. Methods for negotiating, closing and confirming, and servicing the sale will be described in the next three chapters.

Consultative Selling Skills	Parts of the Sales Presentation			
	Need Discovery	**Selecting Solution**	**Need-Satisfaction Presentation**	**Servicing the Sale**
Questioning Skills	As a question approach To find needs and buying motives To probe for buying motives To confirm needs and buying motives	To confirm selection	To confirm benefits To confirm mutual understanding To increase desire for a solution	To make suggestions To confirm delivery and installation To resolve complaints To build goodwill To secure credit arrangements
Presenting Benefits	As a benefit approach To discover specific benefits	To match buying motives	To build support for the solution	To make suggestions To use credit as a close
Demonstrating Skills	As a product approach To clarify need	To clarify selection	To strengthen product claims	When making effective suggestions
Negotiating Skills	To overcome initial resistance to sales interviews To overcome buyer's need concerns	To overcome buyer's product concerns	To overcome buyer's source, price, and time concerns	In handling complaints To overcome buyer's financing concerns
Closing Skills	When customer has made a buying decision	When buyer immediately recognizes solutions	Whenever buyer presents closing signals	After suggestion To secure repeats and referrals

Figure 12.6 The Selling Dynamics Matrix
In creating effective presentations, the salesperson should be prepared to meet a wide range of buyer responses with effective questions, benefit statements, demonstrations, negotiating methods, and closing methods.

REVIEWING KEY CONCEPTS

- List and describe three types of need-satisfaction presentation strategies.

Once you have selected a solution that matches the customer's needs, you must decide which presenta-tion strategy to emphasize. Need satisfaction can be achieved through informing, persuading, or remind-ing. The salesperson can, in some cases, use a combi-nation of these presentation strategies.

- Present guidelines for creating consultative presentations that add value.

  The perception of value is enhanced with a well-developed consultative presentation, whether it be the informative, persuasive, or reminder need-satisfaction presentation strategy. A sales presentation that adds value is the result of both planning and practice with the guidelines described in this chapter. An effective, well-organized demonstration helps to make the buying process less complicated.

- Describe elements of an effective persuasive presentation strategy.

  There are many ways to incorporate persuasion into a sales presentation and most will—if used appropriately—create value for the customer. Seven specific methods are presented.

- Describe the elements of a persuasive presentation strategy.

  Group presentations are almost always more challenging than one-on-one sales calls. Be sure you identify the titles and roles of the persons who will attend. Check out the meeting room in advance to assess audiovisual capabilities and seating options. As you prepare your presentation, take into consideration the needs of the audience. In many cases, audiovisual tools can be used to enhance the group presentation.

- Develop selling tools that add value to your sales demonstrations.

  Selling tools, also called *proof devices*, used to demonstrate the benefits of your solution will add value to the sale presentation. Be prepared to use one or more of the 10 tools discussed in this chapter.

Key Terms

canned presentation **290**

cost–benefit analysis **299**

emotional links **300**

informative presentation **287**

mental imagery **304**

persuasion **288**

persuasive presentation **288**

portfolio **307**

proof device **293**

reminder presentation **289**

return on investment (ROI) **299**

showmanship **302**

Review Questions

1. Distinguish among the three types of need-satisfaction presentations: informative, persuasive, and reminder.

2. List the guidelines to follow in planning an effective consultative presentation.

3. Discuss the advantages of using a presentation worksheet.

4. Explain why a salesperson should organize the sales presentation so that it appeals to as many of the five senses as possible.

5. What are the guidelines to be followed when developing a persuasive sales presentation?

6. Develop a list of the sales tools that the salesperson should consider when planning a sales demonstration.

7. Describe the merits of a bound paper presentation. What can be done to strengthen the persuasive power of a bound paper presentation?

8. Explain how magazines and trade journals can be used to assist the salesperson in a persuasive sales presentation.

9. Describe the audiovisual presentation fundamentals.

10. What are some of the common sales functions performed by laptop computers and demonstration software?

Application Exercises

1. In many selling situations, it is difficult, if not impossible, to demonstrate the product itself. List other means that can be used to demonstrate product features and benefits.

2. Develop a list of sales tools you could use in a job interview. What tools could you use to demonstrate your skills and capabilities?

Chapter 13
Negotiating Buyer Concerns

Learning Objectives

After studying this chapter, you should be able to

1 Describe the principles of formal negotiations as part of the win-win strategy.

2 Describe common types of buyer concerns.

3 Discuss specific methods of negotiating buyer concerns.

4 Outline methods for creating value in formal negotiations.

5 Work with buyers who are trained in negotiation.

 Reality Selling Today Video Series

Marriott International Inc. (**www.marriott.com**) is a world-renowned company with approximately 8500 salespeople and 3000 lodging properties around the world—more than 50 of them in Canada. One of its properties is the Marriott Houston Hobby, which is located within a mile of the Hobby Airport in Houston, Texas. Apart from accommodation, the hotel offers comprehensive meeting facilities complemented by expert catering and audiovisual resources. Corporate catering manager Heather Ramsey, in the photo at the top of the next page, is in charge of convention and meeting sales at the Marriott Houston Hobby. She always has a ready response when customers raise concerns about prices and the tranquility of an airport hotel. She emphasizes the value to the customers by describing the state-of-the-art meeting and conference facilities offered by the hotel, its convenience to travellers, as well as other unique features not offered by the competition. Sometimes customers do not communicate openly about their needs and concerns to Heather. She often must work hard to identify their actual needs to offer them the best value and bring benefits to the hotel as well. Her negotiation process with new customers will normally involve identifying their actual needs and then listening to, clarifying, and overcoming their concerns.

NEGOTIATING BUYER CONCERNS AND PROBLEMS

Many sales professionals are very proficient in need discovery and selecting the right solution, but are weak in the area of negotiating an agreement that is favourable both to the customer and to the salesperson's firm. Many buyers with responsibility for

purchasing have formal training in how to negotiate favourable terms. Most customers are studying competitive offers and increasingly attempting to secure the best deal possible. These market conditions require salespeople anticipate buyer concerns and plan collaborative win-win negotiated solutions prior to meeting with their customers (see Fig. 13.1). A recent poll reports that as many as 83 percent of sales executives from 25 industries generally enter negotiations with no formal strategy![1] Another common mistake is making last-minute concessions in order to close the sale.[2] In this chapter, we describe effective strategies for anticipating and negotiating buyer concerns.

We have noted previously that the heaviest time investment in value-added selling is on the front end of the sale. This is especially true for large, complex sales that require a long sales cycle. Identifying the customer's needs and developing the best solution can be very time-consuming. However, when you do these things effectively, you are creating value in the eyes of the customer. When you build value on the front end of the sale, price becomes less of an issue on the back end.[3]

FORMAL INTEGRATIVE NEGOTIATION—PART OF THE WIN-WIN RELATIONSHIP STRATEGY

FRANK ACUFF, NEGOTIATIONS TRAINER AND AUTHOR OF HOW TO NEGOTIATE ANYTHING WITH Anyone, Anywhere Around the Globe, says, "Life is a negotiation."[4] Negotiating skills have application almost daily in our personal and professional lives. Some of the more traditional personal selling books discuss how salespeople should "handle" buyer objections. The message communicated to the reader was that personal selling was a "we versus they"

The Six-Step Presentation Plan	
Step One: Approach	☑ Review Strategic/Consultative Selling Model ☑ Initiate customer contact
Step Two: Need Discovery	☑ Ask strategic questions ☑ Determine customer needs ☑ Select Product Solution
Step Three: Presentation	☑ Select presentation strategy ☑ Create presentation plan ☑ Initiate presentation
Step Four: Negotiation	☐ Anticipate buyer concerns ☐ Plan negotiating methods ☐ Initiate win-win negotiations
Step Five: Close	☐ Plan appropriate closing methods ☐ Recognize closing clues ☐ Initiate closing methods
Step Six: Servicing the Sale	☐ Follow through ☐ Follow-up calls ☐ Expansion selling

Service, retail, wholesale, and manufacturer selling

Figure 13.1 Negotiating customer concerns and problems

process resulting from distributive negotiations: Somebody wins and somebody loses. The win-win solution, where both sides win, was not offered as an option. In this chapter, we focus on integrative negotiations, which are built on joint problem-solving, trust, and rapport to achieve win-win situations.[5]

Ron Willingham, author of two books on integrity selling, says: "When trust and rapport are strong, negotiation becomes a partnership to work through customer concerns. But when trust and rapport are weak, almost any negotiation becomes too combative."[6] Trust and rapport must be established on the front end of the sale and maintained throughout the sales process. High-performance salespeople, like Heather Ramsey, take time to discover the customer's needs and try to recommend the best possible solution. Always keep in mind that any agreement that leaves one party dissatisfied will come back to hurt the other party later, sometimes in ways that cannot be predicted.[7]

negotiation Working to reach an agreement that is mutually satisfactory to buyer and seller.

What is **negotiation**? One definition is "working to reach an agreement that is mutually satisfactory to both buyer and seller." It involves resolving the problems or concerns that prevent people from buying.[8] As we noted in Chapter 1, the salesperson increasingly serves as a consultant or resource and provides solutions to buyers' problems. The consultant seeks to establish and maintain long-term relationships with customers. The ability to negotiate problems or concerns is one of the most effective ways to create value for the customer. Figure 13.2 outlines the steps a salesperson can take to anticipate and negotiate problems.

Adaptive Selling Today Training Video Series

Negotiations—Solving the Tough Problems

One of the biggest challenges to the adaptive selling and partnering strategy is evident as one deals with the tough problems that often come up during the negotiation stage of the sales process. In this new Adaptive Selling Today Negotiations Video, Lana, a medical equipment representative, is faced with the following tough problems: dealing with an angry customer about pricing issues, dealing with skepticism about sourcing and timing issues, dealing with how to be understood about product issues, and dealing with how to walk away yet keep the door open to salvage the order. The customer, Dr. Arroyo, director of a hospital radiology department, has a huge responsibility to make the right selection at the right price, and he therefore has concerns that require an adaptive negotiations strategy. Hopefully, Lana's negotiations skills result in a win-win solution. Refer to the Application Exercises at the end of the chapter on p. 339 for more information.

Dr. Arroyo is a tough negotiator who uses all he knows to get the right solution.

Negotiation Is a Process

By definition, negotiations seek to move polarized parties into the realm of common interests.[9] Negotiations can take place before the sales call or at any time during the sales presentation. Early negotiations may involve the meeting location, who will attend

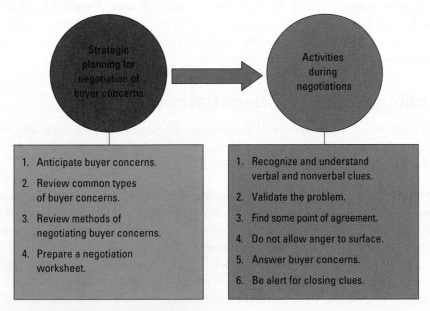

Figure 13.2 Negotiating buyer concerns
Salespeople today must be prepared to anticipate and negotiate buyer concerns and problems.

Negotiation is defined as "working to reach an agreement that is mutually satisfactory to both buyer and seller." It involves building relationships instead of making one-time deals.

the sales presentation, or the amount of time available for the first meeting. Salespeople sometimes make early concessions to improve the relationship. This approach, however, may set a costly precedent for later in the sale.[10] Some concessions can have a negative influence on the sales presentation.

In most cases, you can anticipate that the most important negotiations will take place during stage three of the buying process (see Fig. 8.3). Resolution of problems can sometimes be time-consuming. Establishing a strategic alliance, described in Chapter 1 as the highest form of partnering, requires lengthy negotiations that may extend over weeks, months, or even years. Once the alliance is finalized, negotiations continue when concerns voiced by one party or the other surface.

Planning for Formal Negotiations

Professional buyers are well-trained negotiators. To negotiate with them effectively, salespeople first need to engage in detailed planning. Ironically, one of the most common mistakes negotiators make is not doing their homework in advance.[11]

Gather Information before the Negotiation "Exhaustive preparation is more important than aggressive argument."[12] Robert H. Schuller offers invaluable advice in this crucial step.[13] First, a salesperson should prepare from both counterparts' points of view by identifying the similarities and differences of the goals and objectives of both sides. Then information sources are tapped. The information might be from business associates, buyers' websites, or even previous vendors for the same buyers. The salesperson should bear in mind that negotiation is an information game: the more, the better.[14]

Decide Team versus Individual Negotiations for Both Seller and Buyer The next logical step in this preparatory process is to decide who will be in the negotiations.

For Susanna Rosas, who works in a business-to-business selling context at CB Richard Ellis, it is not unusual to create a cross-functional team consisting of individuals from finance, construction, and zoning to bring to a meeting with the buying centre at the buyer's premises. Other situations might call for her to bring senior managers from her firm. If teams are involved, make sure there is a leader and establish guidelines for information exchange among the team members. Creating a cohesive negotiation team can pay off with higher profits after the conclusion of negotiations.[15]

Understand the Value of What You Are Offering It is important for Salesforce.com's Dave Levitt to know what is of real value to the customer and not consider value only in terms of purchase price. The real value of what you are offering may be a value-added intangible such as expert product knowledge, superior configuration programming, seamless integration with other vendors, short set-up times, effective training, product support, or a reputation for honest dealings. An important aspect of the negotiation process is discovering what is of utmost importance to the buyer (see Table 13.1). The focus of personal selling today should be the mutual search for value. Some salespeople make the mistake of offering a lower price the moment buyer concerns surface. In the customer's mind, price may be of secondary importance compared with the quality of service after the sale. Detailed tactics for creating values in formal negotiations appear at the end of the chapter.

Determine Your Goals and Financial Objectives Two important concepts warrant mentioning. First is **BATNA** (Best Alternative to Negotiated Agreement), defined as "what alternative(s) will be acceptable to you if your negotiation does not succeed."[16] You will likely make concessions in formal negotiations; therefore, you must assess both your own and your customer's BATNA. The second important planning tool is **ZOPA** (Zone of Possible Agreement), defined as the space between the seller's walk-away point and

BATNA Best Alternative to Negotiated Agreement.

ZOPA Zone of Possible Agreement.

Table 13.1 Negotiating Buyer Concerns

Objections are often requests for more information to justify the buying decision. Objections can tell us a lot about the real source of hesitation and what type of information the customer is seeking.

Buyer's Concern	Source of Hesitation	Request For
"Price too high."	Perceived cost vs. benefit	Value articulation
"Think about it."	Afraid to make a bad decision	Create comfort, provide proof
"Talk to boss."	Unable to justify decision	Risk reduction, benefit review
"Need more quotes."	Unsure you're the best option	Targeted solutions, value
"Set with current supplier."	Doesn't see benefit of change	Differentiation
"Bad history."	Past experience is affecting current review	Offer proof of change

Adapted from "Hide-and-Seek," a table from Nancy J. Martini (formerly Stephens), President & CEO, PI Worldwide, Wellesley Hills, MA, "Objections Are a 'Yes' About to Happen," *Selling,* November 1998, p. 3.

the buyer's highest willingness to pay.[17] The walk-away point represents the lowest offer a party would be willing to accept and is also called the *reservation value*. For example, if your walk-away point is $42.65M and the highest price the buyer is willing to pay is $48M, your ZOPA is any offer that falls within this range, or a zone of $5.35M (=$48M − $42.65M).[18]

Ed Brodow (**www.brodow.com**), popular speaker, international consultant, and author of *Negotiating Bootcamp*, contends it is best to aim high when configuring your solution. In his new training video *Six Principles of Negotiation*, he suggests doing your homework and preparing a range of terms that include the maximum you could expect to receive, what you would hope to receive, and your bottom line or the minimum you could accept before having to walk away from the sale. In many buying situations today, buyers expect there to be alternative solutions with alternative pricing.

Prepare an Agenda An agenda outlines what will and will not be discussed and in what sequence. As the seller, you want to achieve "small wins" to create goodwill before dealing with tough issues. Therefore, you want to prioritize these items on your proposed agenda. Sometimes items should be discussed simultaneously rather than sequentially.[19] Experienced buyers, however, also come to the meeting table with a detailed agenda. Negotiations might start with a discussion about the agenda itself.

Review Adaptive Selling Styles The successful negotiation of buyer concerns is based in large part on understanding human behaviour. This knowledge, coupled with a good measure of common sense, helps us overcome most buyer concerns. In one-on-one negotiations, adaptive selling styles are useful (see Chapter 4). The Platinum Rule of negotiating is, "Do unto others as they want to be done unto."[20] When negotiations are conducted in teams, the situation gets more complicated. The role of the negotiation leader is to maintain smooth information exchange and foster strong relationships despite various communication styles.[21]

Prepare a Negotiations Worksheet Your planning must be systematically organized. It helps to predict and classify possible resistance with the aid of a negotiations worksheet. To illustrate how this form works, let us review an example from the food industry. Mary Turner is a salesperson for Durkee Famous Foods. She represents more than 350 products. Mary calls on supermarkets daily and offers assistance in the areas of ordering and merchandising. Recently, her company decided to offer retail food stores an allowance of $1 per case of olives if the store purchased 15 or more cases. Prior to talking with her customers about this offer, Mary sat down and developed a negotiations worksheet, shown in Figure 13.3. We cannot anticipate every possible problem, but it is possible to identify the most common problems that are likely to arise. The negotiations worksheet can be a useful tool.

Conducting the Negotiation Session

During the formal negotiation session, it is beneficial to master the skills presented throughout this book—i.e., good social contact, asking good questions, listening actively, using proof devices, and applying methods of negotiating objections. There are a number of golden rules that a salesperson should internalize to be successful in formal negotiations. These include understanding the problem, creating alternative solutions, periodically recapitulating what has been agreed, and making wise concessions in a timely manner.

Negotiations Worksheet		
Customer's concern	Type of concern	Possible response
"Fifteen cases of olives will take up valuable space in my receiving room. It is already crowded."	Need	**Combination direct denial/superior benefit** "You will not have to face that problem. With the aid of our merchandising plan you can display 10 cases immediately on the sales floor. Only 5 cases will become reserve stock. You should move all 15 cases in about two weeks."
"This is a poor time of the year to buy a large order of olives. People are not buying olives at this time."	Time	**Combination indirect denial/third-party testimony** "I agree that it has been a problem in the past, but consumer attitudes seem to be changing. We have found that olives sell well all year long if displayed properly. More people are using olives in the preparation of omelets, pizza, and other dishes. Of course, most relish trays feature olives. We will supply you with point-of-purchase material that provides kitchen-tested ways to use this high-profit item."
"I have to stay within my budget."	Price	**Superior benefit** "As you know, olives represent a high-profit item. The average margin is 26 percent. With the addition of our $1.00 per case allowance, the margin will rise to about 30 percent. This order will give you a good return on your investment."
"I am very satisfied with my present supplier."	Source	**Combination question/trial order** "What can I do to get you to take just a trial order?"

Figure 13.3 Negotiations worksheet
Before the presentation, it is important to prepare a negotiations worksheet.

Understand the Problem David Stiebel, author of *When Talking Makes Things Worse!*, says we need to understand the difference between a misunderstanding and a true disagreement. A *misunderstanding* is a failure to accurately understand the other person's point. For example, the salesperson believes the customer is primarily interested in price, but the customer's primary need is on-time delivery. A *disagreement*, in contrast, is a failure to agree that would persist despite the most accurate understanding.[22] Be certain that both you and the prospect are clear on the true nature of what each party's needs are

Global Business Insight

Negotiating Across Cultures

Negotiations in the global economy vary from one country to another because of cultural differences. German buyers are more apt to look you in the eye and tell you what they do not like about your product. Japanese buyers, on the other hand, do not want to embarrass you and, therefore, bury their concerns beneath several layers of courtesy. In China, now one of the most important markets for Canadian businesses, negotiations are more straightforward. People who have been doing business in China for many years suggest a very direct approach to negotiations. However, do not become antagonistic or discourteous. Do get involved in Chinese business rituals that are intended to create a friendly atmosphere.

When you enter into negotiations in foreign countries, it is important to understand and accommodate the customer's culture. You may not get every detail exactly right, but you will win respect by trying. Selling in certain cultures often requires more time spent bonding and building rapport. Several meetings may be needed to lay the groundwork for the actual sale.[a]

regarding the issues to be negotiated (see Table 13.1). When the prospect begins talking, listen carefully and then listen some more. With *probing questions*, you can fine-tune your understanding of the problem.

Create Alternative Solutions That Can Add Value When the prospect finishes talking, it is a good practice to validate the problem using a *confirmation question*. This helps to isolate the true problem and reduce the chance of misunderstanding. The confirmation question might sound like this: "I think I understand your concern. You feel the warranty does not provide you with sufficient protection. Is this correct?" By taking time to ask this question, you accomplish two important objectives. First, you are giving personal attention to the problem, which pleases the customer. Second, you gain time to think about the best possible response.

logrolling Offering an alternative solution.

The best possible response is very often an alternative solution. In formal negotiations, this is often referred to as "**logrolling**."[23] Many of today's customers do not want to hear that there is only one way to do things, or a single solution. In the age of information, people have less time to manage their work and their personal lives, so they expect new levels of flexibility. For Marriott's Heather Ramsey, there are many issues such as group pricing, alternative menus, complimentary rooms, etc. that can be introduced into the negotiations for convention services. In many cases, these additional issues take the focus off price and can actually create value for the customer and possibly for the seller. Here are additional issues that can be introduced into negotiations when a buyer is focused on price: delivery dates, financing, contract length, quality, exclusivity clauses, levels of service support, and warranties.

Periodically Review Acknowledged Points of Agreement Negotiating buying problems is a little like the art of diplomacy: It helps to know what points of agreement exist. This saves time and helps establish a closer bond between you and the prospect. At some point during the presentation, you might summarize by using a *summary-confirmation question*: "Let us see if I fully understand your position. You think our product is well constructed and will provide the reliability you are looking for. You also believe our price is fair. Am I correct on these two points?"

Once all the areas of agreement have been identified, there may be surprisingly few points of disagreement. The prospect suddenly sees that the advantages of ownership far outweigh the disadvantages. Now that the air is cleared, both the salesperson and the customer can give their full attention to any remaining points of disagreement.

The business environment is sometimes turbulent. Hence, it might be advisable in negotiations to "pack a reserve parachute." To avoid buyers' frustration when things do not go as agreed upon, lay the groundwork for the unexpected and be open about backup plans with the buyers.[24]

Do Not Make Concessions Too Quickly Give away concessions methodically and reluctantly, and always try to get something in return. Negotiations consultant Ed Brodow suggests that when preparing to make a concession, we should prepare to get something in return by asking, "If we do this for you, will you do this for us?" A concession given too freely can diminish the value of your product.[25] Giving a concession too easily may also send the signal that you are negotiating from a position of weakness. Neil Rackham, author of several books on spin selling, says, "Negotiate late, negotiate little, and never let negotiation become a substitute for good selling."[26]

Timing and the Pareto Law Time plays a critical role in negotiations. In negotiations, experience with the Pareto Law reveals that 80 percent of your results are generally agreed upon in the last 20 percent of your time. Since influence tactics are more likely to exert an effect when their target is under time pressure, negotiators should use time as a strategic weapon by buying more time to fully consider concessions or by giving a deadline to speed up agreement.[27]

Know When to Walk Away

For many reasons, salespeople must sometimes walk away from a potential sale. If the customer's budget doesn't allow the purchase of your product, don't press the issue. If the customer's best offer is not favourable for your company, don't continue to waste your time. If the buyer is only interested in the lowest possible price and you represent a marketer committed to a value-added sales strategy, consider withdrawing from negotiations. If you discover that the prospect is dishonest or fails to keep his word, discontinue negotiations. Be aware of how much flexibility (your BATNA and ZOPA) you have in terms of price, specifications, delivery schedules, and so forth, and know when you have reached your walk-away point.[28]

Finally, when appropriate, document negotiated settlements in writing. These will be helpful when formal contracts are drawn up. Negotiation minutes will also serve as a control tool for follow-up actions.

COMMON TYPES OF BUYER CONCERNS

SALESPEOPLE LEARN THAT PATTERNS OF BUYER RESISTANCE EXIST AND, THEREFORE, THEY CAN anticipate that certain concerns may arise during the sales call. With this information, it is possible to be better prepared for each meeting with a customer. The great majority of buyer concerns fall into five categories: need, product, source, time, and price.

Concerns Related to Need for the Product

If you have carefully completed your precall planning, then the prospect will likely have a need for your product. You can still expect, however, that the initial response may be, "I do not need your product." This might be a conditioned response that arises nearly every time the prospect meets with a sales representative. It may also mask the real reason for not buying, which might be lack of funds, lack of time to examine your proposal carefully, or some other reason. Sincere need resistance is one of the greatest challenges that a salesperson faces during the early part of the sales process. Think about it for a moment. Why would any customer want to purchase a product that does not seem to provide any real benefits? Unless we can create need awareness in the prospect's mind, there is no possible way to close the sale.

If you are calling on business prospects, the best way to overcome need resistance is to prove that your product is a good investment. Every business hopes to make a profit. Therefore you must demonstrate how your product or service can contribute to that goal. Can your product increase sales volume? Can it reduce operating expenses? If the owner of a hardware store says, "I already carry a line of high-quality tools," point out how a second line of less expensive tools will appeal to another large segment of buyers. With the addition of the new line, the store will be in a better position to compete with other stores (discount merchandise stores and supermarkets) that sell inexpensive tools.

Concerns about the Product or Service

You will recall from Chapter 8 that consultative process buyers may lack needs awareness or need help evaluating possible solutions. As such, the product (solution) often becomes the focal point of buyer resistance. When this happens, try to discover specific reasons why the prospect has doubts about your product or service. Often you may find that one of the following factors has influenced the buyer's attitude:

1. *The product or service is not well established.* This is a common form of buyer resistance if you are selling a new or relatively new product. People do not like to take risks. They need plenty of assurance that the product is dependable. Use laboratory test results, third-party testimonials from satisfied users, or an effective demonstration to create value.

2. *The present product or service is satisfactory.* Change does not come easily to many people. Purchasing a new product may mean adopting new procedures or retraining employees. In the prospect's mind, the advantages do not outweigh the disadvantages, so buyer resistance surfaces. To overcome this resistance, you must build a greater amount of desire in the prospect's mind. Concentrate on a value proposition that gives your product or service a major advantage over the existing one, or reconfigure the product and offer customized services to better meet the customer's needs.

Concerns Related to Source

Concerns related to source can be especially challenging when the prospect is a relationship buyer. The buyer may already have well-established partnerships with other companies. If the prospect feels genuine loyalty to his or her present supplier, you will have to work harder to establish a relationship and begin the need discovery process.

When dealing with the loyalty problem, it is usually best to avoid direct criticism of the competing firm. Negative comments are apt to backfire because they damage your professional image. It is best to keep the sales presentation focused on the customer's problems and your solutions.

There are positive ways to cope with the loyalty concern. Here are some suggestions:

1. *Work harder to identify problems your company can solve with its products or services.* With the help of good questions, you may be able to understand the prospect's problems better than your competitors do.

2. *Point out the superior benefits of your product or company.* The logic of your presentation may override the emotional ties that may exist between the prospect and the present supplier.

3. *Work on recruiting internal champions to build more support for your message.* Use referrals whenever possible.[29]

4. *Try to stay visible and connected.* Every contact with the prospect is one more step in building a relationship. David Haslam, president of Toronto-based Presidential Plumbing Ltd., devotes time to a number of community projects. He says, "I believe in community involvement, but I'm also gaining invaluable experience, getting contacts."[30]

Concerns Related to Time

If a prospect says, "I want time to think it over," you may be encountering concerns related to time. Resistance related to time is often referred to as the **stall.** A stall usually means the customer does not yet perceive the benefits of buying now. In most cases, the stall indicates that the prospect has both positive and negative feelings about your product. Consider using *probing questions* to determine the negative feelings: "Is it my company that concerns you?" "Do you have any concerns about our warranty program?"

stall Resistance related to time.

It is all right to be persuasive if the prospect can truly benefit from buying now. If the price may soon rise, or if the item may not be available in the future, then you should provide this information. You must, however, present this information sincerely and accurately. It is never proper to distort the truth in the hope of getting the order.

Renewing a contract also calls for renegotiations. In these cases, be up front and explain the benefits in precise terms as to what additional values the new price will bring to the client. Sometimes it is advisable to offer a break in the payment schedule to overcome the client's adverse feelings about the price hike.[31] To enhance the relationship with long-term business partners, the seller sometimes has to look at the market to re-evaluate what is really fair pricing and voluntarily renegotiate with the buyer to lower the price before the buyer asks for it.[32]

Concerns Related to Price

Price objections are one of the biggest obstacles salespeople have to conquer.[33] There are two important points to keep in mind concerning price resistance. First, it is one of the most common forms of buyer resistance in the field of selling. Therefore, you must learn to negotiate skilfully in this area. Second, it may be nothing more than an excuse. If you are selling a product or service to a transactional buyer, price may be the primary barrier to closing the sale. When people say, "Your price is too high," they probably mean,

"You have not sold me yet." In the eyes of most customers, value is more important than price. Always try to position your product with a convincing value proposition. Customers who perceive added value are less likely to choose a competing product simply on the basis of price. We will present specific tactics to deal with this issue shortly.

SPECIFIC METHODS OF NEGOTIATING BUYER CONCERNS

THERE ARE EIGHT SPECIFIC METHODS OF NEGOTIATING BUYER CONCERNS. IN ANALYZING each buyer concern, we should try to determine which method can be most effective. In most cases, we can use a combination of the following methods to negotiate buyer concerns.

Direct Denial

direct denial Involves refuting the prospect's opinion or belief. The direct denial of a problem is considered a high-risk method of negotiating buyer concerns.

Direct denial involves refuting the opinion or belief of a prospect. The direct denial of a problem is considered a high-risk method of negotiating buyer concerns. Therefore, you should use it with care. People do not like to be told they are wrong. Even when the facts prove the prospect is wrong, resentment can build if we fail to handle the situation properly.

When a prospect offers buyer resistance that is not valid, we sometimes have no option other than to openly disagree. If the person is misinformed, we must provide accurate information. For example, if the customer questions the product's quality, meet the concern head-on with whatever proof seems appropriate. It is almost never proper to ignore misinformation. High-performance salespeople counter inaccurate responses from the prospect promptly and directly.

The manner in which you state the denial is of major importance. Use a win-win approach. Be firm and sincere in stating your beliefs, but do not be offensive. Above all, do not patronize the prospect. A "know-it-all" attitude can be irritating.

Indirect Denial

indirect denial Often used when the prospect's concern is completely valid, or at least accurate to a large degree. The salesperson bends a little and acknowledges that the prospect is at least partly correct.

Sometimes the prospect's concern is completely valid or at least accurate to a large degree. This method is referred to as the **indirect denial.** The best approach is to bend a little and acknowledge that the prospect is at least partially correct. After all, if you offered a product that is objection-proof, you would likely have no competitors. Every product has a shortcoming or limitation.[34] The success of this method is based in part on the need most people have to feel that their views are worthwhile. For this reason, the indirect denial method is widely used. An exchange that features the use of this approach follows. The salesperson is a key account sales representative for Tele-Direct Atlantic.[35]

SALESPERSON: The total cost of placing your one-quarter-column ad in the Yellow Pages of the five different directories you have chosen is $32 000.

PROSPECT: As a builder, I want to reach people who are planning to build a home. I am afraid my ad will be lost among the hundreds of ads featured in your directories.

SALESPERSON: Yes, I agree that the Yellow Pages in our directories do feature hundreds of ads, but the section for general contractors features less than 30 ads. Our design staff can prepare an ad that can be highly visible and can set your company apart from ads placed by other contractors. In addition, we will do the same with your website. Note that the salesperson used the words, "Yes, I agree" to reduce the impact of denial. The prospect is less likely to feel that her point of view has been totally disproved. One note of caution: Avoid the "Yes . . . but" response. When you use the word *but*, it invalidates anything preceding it. A more effective response would be, "I understand your concerns, Ms. Thomas; however, there is another way to view this issue."[36]

Feel–Felt–Found Successful salespeople are sensitive to clues that indicate that the client feels something is wrong. One way to empathize with the client's concerns is to use the "feel–felt–found" strategy. Here is how it works. George Hutchison, chairman and CEO of North Bay, Ontario–based Equisure Financial Network Inc., is an ace negotiator who regularly uses this method. When someone raises a major concern, he will often say to the person, "I know how you *feel*. Others have *felt* the same way. However, we've *found* that . . ." Hutchison says that, besides offering empathy, this method reassures the person that others have successfully overcome the same concerns.[37]

Questions

Throughout this chapter, we have described several situations where probing or confirmation questions can enhance the negotiation process. We must also keep in mind the important role of need-satisfaction questions. In Chapter 11, we noted that *need-satisfaction questions* are designed to move the sales process forward toward commitment and action. These questions focus on the solution.[38] Consider the following exchange that involves a price concern:

BUYER: It would be difficult for our human resources department to absorb the cost of your psychological tests.

SELLER: Would a 10 percent reduction in employee turnover save your company?

In these examples, the questions are designed to get the customer's attention focused on the solution. These questions also give ownership of the solution to the prospect. See Chapter 11 for more examples of the need-satisfaction question.

Superior Benefit

Sometimes the customer raises a problem that cannot be answered with a denial. For example: "Your television commercial proposal does not include payroll costs for actors who will be used during the shoot. This means we must cover this expense." You should acknowledge the valid objection and then discuss one or more superior benefits: "Yes, you are correct. We do conduct the talent search and coach the actors throughout the development of the commercial. In addition, if you are not happy with the performance

In their best-selling book *The New Conceptual Selling,* authors Heiman, Sanchez, and Tuleja recommend using the question "What are your concerns with this proposal?" They also suggest that you ask questions in a positive rather than negative manner, and that you "wait for answers."

THE **NEW** CONCEPTUAL SELLING®

WARNER BOOKS 0-446-67449-4

THE MOST EFFECTIVE AND PROVEN METHOD FOR FACE-TO-FACE SALES PLANNING

REVISED AND UPDATED FOR THE 21ST CENTURY

STEPHEN E. HEIMAN, DIANE SANCHEZ WITH TAD TULEJA
FOREWORD BY JOHN PHILIP COGHLAN, PRESIDENT, SCHWAB INSTITUTIONAL

superior benefit A benefit that will, in most cases, outweigh the customer's specific concern.

of the actors, we will conduct a second search for new actors and remake the commercial at no additional cost to you." A **superior benefit** is a benefit that in most cases outweighs the customer's specific concern.

Demonstration

If you are familiar with your product as well as that of your competition, this method of negotiating buyer resistance is easy to use. You know the competitive advantages of your product and can discuss these features with confidence.

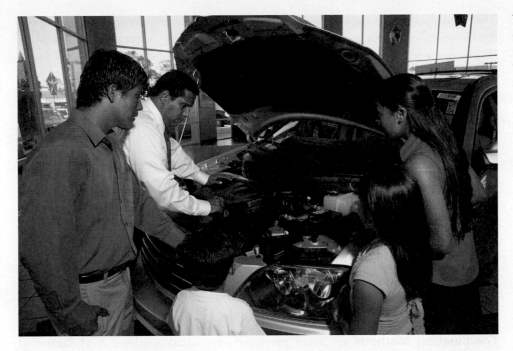

The product demonstration is one of the most convincing ways to overcome buyer skepticism.

At Mattress Firm, Edith Botello realizes product demonstration is one of the most convincing ways to overcome buyer skepticism her customers might have. With the aid of an effective demonstration, you can overcome specific concerns. Sometimes a second demonstration is needed to overcome buyer skepticism. This demonstration can provide additional proof. High-achieving sales personnel know when and how to use proof devices to overcome buyer resistance.

Trial Offer

A **trial offer** involves giving the prospect an opportunity to try the product without making a purchase commitment. The trial offer (especially with new products) is popular with customers because they can get fully acquainted with your product without making a major commitment. Assume that a buyer for a large restaurant chain says, "I am sure you have good cooking oil, but we are happy with our present brand. We have had no complaints from our managers." In response to this comment, you might say, "I can understand your reluctance to try our product. However, I do believe our oil is the finest on the market. With your permission, I would like to ship you 20 litres of our oil at no cost. You can use our product at selected restaurants and evaluate the results. If our oil does not provide you with superior results, you are under no obligation to place an order."

trial offer Involves giving the prospect an opportunity to try the product without making a purchase commitment.

Third-Party Testimony

Studies indicate that the favourable testimony of a neutral third party can be an effective method of responding to buyer resistance. Let us assume that the owner of a small business states that he can get along without the services of a professional landscaper.

The salesperson might respond in this manner: "Some business owners feel the way you do. However, once they contract for our service, they do not regret the decision. Mark Williams, owner of Williams Hardware, says our service completely changed the image his business projects to the public." Third-party testimony provides a positive way to solve certain types of buying problems. The positive experiences of a neutral third party almost never trigger an argument with the prospect.

Postpone Method

postpone method A method salespeople use to delay a response when a customer raises a concern that would be better handled later in a sales presentation.

Today's customers are well informed and may want to engage in negotiations early in the sales process. The customer may raise concerns that you would prefer to respond to later in the presentation. Let's assume you are calling on an office manager who is interested in well-equipped cubicles for eight employees. Soon after you present some product information, the customer says, "How much will eight well-equipped cubicles cost us?" Using the **postpone method,** your response might be, "I would prefer to answer that question in a few minutes. Once I learn what features you prefer, I can calculate a cost estimate." Every customer concern should be taken seriously. Always try to explain why you want to postpone the response.

Combination Methods As noted previously, consultative selling is characterized by flexibility. A combination of methods sometimes proves to be the best way to deal with buyer resistance. For example, an indirect denial might be followed by a question: "The cost of our business security system is a little higher than that of the competition. The price I have quoted reflects the high-quality materials used to develop our system. Wouldn't you feel better entrusting your security needs to a firm with more than 25 years of experience in the business security field?" In this situation, the salesperson also might consider combining the indirect denial with an offer to arrange a demonstration of the security system.

A salesperson might attempt to turn the objection into a *trial close* by concluding the sale without prejudicing the opportunity to continue the selling process with the buyer should they refuse to commit themselves. This might take the form of, "If I can address this final concern of yours, will you buy it?[39] See Figure 13.3 on p. 323 for more examples of combination methods.

CREATING VALUE DURING FORMAL NEGOTIATIONS

THE CHALLENGE A SALESPERSON FACES IN ALMOST EVERY NEGOTIATION IS TO SELL PRODUCTS and services based on fair and unique value propositions, not simply on the basis of price.[40] "If salespeople rely on price only to capture and retain business, they reduce whatever they're selling to a commodity. Once that happens, there is no customer loyalty."[41] In this section, we focus on how a salesperson can tactfully create value for buyers during formal negotiations without compromising profits.

The Pitfalls of Paying Too Little

It's unwise to pay too much. But it's worse to pay too little.

When you pay too much, you lose a little money, that is all.

When you pay too little you sometimes lose everything, because the thing you bought was incapable of doing the thing it was bought to do.

The common law of business balances prohibits paying a little and getting a lot. It can't be done.

If you deal with the lowest bidder, it is well to add something for the risk you run.

—*John Ruskin, British Writer*

How to Deal with Price Concerns

As we have noted, price resistance is common, so we must prepare for it. There are some important "dos and don'ts" to keep in mind when price concern surfaces.

Do Clarify Price Concerns with Questions When you are confronted with a price objection, determine what the customer is really saying. You will recall from Chapter 11 that *specific survey questions* encourage the customer to give you more details. The following questions might be used when price concerns surface:

> When you say our prices are higher, could you be more specific, please?
>
> What did you anticipate the price to be?

When the customer says budget is the primary reason for delaying the purchase, you might ask, "If you had the budget, would you buy?" Questions can help you determine what the customer is really thinking.[42]

Do Add Value with a Cluster of Satisfactions As noted in Chapter 7, a growing number of customers are seeking a cluster of satisfactions that includes a good product, a salesperson who is truly a partner, and a company that stands behind its products (see Fig. 7.1). Many business firms are at a competitive disadvantage when the price alone is considered. When you look beyond price, however, it may become obvious that your company offers more value for the dollar.

Stephen Smith, senior account manager for Bell Atlantic, says that price is like the tip of the iceberg—it is often the only feature the customer sees. Salespeople need to direct the customer's attention to the value-added features that make up the bulk of the iceberg that is below the surface (Fig. 13.4).[43] Do not forget to sell yourself as a high-value element of the sales proposal. Emphasize your commitment to customer service after the sale. Listen carefully to identify and reconfirm what intangibles in addition to the product or service the customers *actually* value.[44]

Do Not Make Price the Focal Point of Your Sales Presentation You may need to discuss price, but do not bring it up too early. The best time to deal with price is after you have reviewed product features and discussed buyer benefits. You increase the chances for a win-win outcome by increasing the number of issues you can resolve. If you negotiate price along with delivery date, support services, or volume purchases, you increase the opportunities for a trade-off so you and the customer both win something of value.[45]

Do Not Apologize for the Price When you do mention price, do so in a confident and straightforward manner. Do not have even a hint of apology in your voice. Convey to the prospect that you believe your price is fair and make every effort to relate price to value. Many people fear paying too much for a product or service. If your company has adopted a value-added strategy, point out this fact to the prospect. Then discuss how you and your company add value.

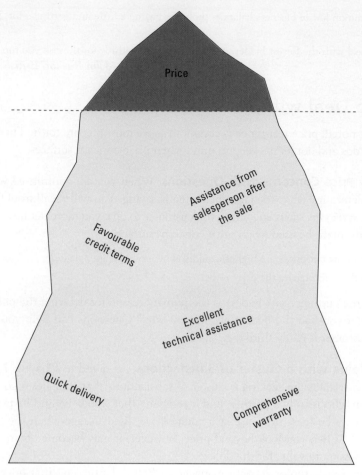

Figure 13.4 The price iceberg
A sales proposal is sometimes like an iceberg. The customer sees the tip of the iceberg—the price—but does not see the value-added features below the surface.

Do Point Out the Relationship between Price and Quality In our highly competitive, free enterprise economy, there are forces at work that tend to promote fair pricing. The highest quality can never be obtained at the lowest price. Quality comes from the Latin word *qualitas,* meaning, "What is the worth?" When you sell quality, price is more likely to be secondary in the prospect's mind. Always point out the value-added features that create the difference in price. Keep in mind that cheap products are built down to a price rather than up to a standard.[46]

Do Explain and Demonstrate the Difference between Price and Cost Price represents the initial amount the buyer pays for the product. Cost represents the amount the buyer pays for a product as it is used over a period of time. The price–cost comparison is particularly relevant with a product or service that lasts a long time or is particularly reliable. Today, airlines are comparing the price and cost of small regional jets manufactured by Bombardier of Canada with large jets sold by Boeing and Airbus. Sales representatives at Bombardier compare their smaller $21 million cost of the 50 passenger CRJ200 with the larger $150 million cost of the 150 passenger A320 offered by Airbus, and point out the fast speed (534 MPH) and low fuel consumption of the CRJ200 (see Fig. 13.5).

	CRJ200	A320
Passengers (seats)	50	150
Cost of aircraft	$21.0 million	$48.2 million
SHORT TRIP (925 km)		
Cost per seat per km	3.34¢	2.85¢
Total cost of trip	$961	$2460
LONG TRIP (1850 km)		
Cost per seat per km	2.79¢	2.16¢
Total cost of trip	$1604	$3722

Figure 13.5 The winner in the short run
Airlines are comparing the price and cost of small regional jets with large jets sold by Boeing and Airbus. The cavernous Airbus leads on seat cost per kilometre, but the much lower price per trip of the CRJ200 makes it a winner in the minds of some buyers.
Adapted from *Fortune*, 9/4/00 © 2000 Time Inc. All rights reserved.

Negotiating Price with a Low-Price Strategy

As noted in Chapter 7, some marketers have positioned their products with a price strategy. The goal is to earn a small profit margin on a large sales volume. Many of these companies have empowered their salespeople to use various low-price strategies such as quantity discounts, trade discounts, seasonal discounts, and promotional discounts. Some salespeople are given permission to match the price of any competitor. Many *transactional buyers* are primarily interested in price and convenience during negotiations, so consider eliminating features that contribute to a higher selling price.

Sales Training Centre
- Over 12,000 trained, of which...
  - 95% increased their sales
  - 98% recommend it
- Zero risk investment with our 100% money back guarantee

Why choose the Canadian Professional Sales Association?
- We have been the leader in serving and training sales professionals since 1874
- We provide a total package training solution for all sales levels and roles
- All training programs are skillfully delivered by experienced facilitators
- We are a not-for-profit association of nearly 30,000 sales and marketing professionals across Canada
- The CPSA Sales Institute is the only certifying body offering the Certified Sales Professional (CSP) designation - a standard for sales excellence
- You are fully protected by our 100% money-back guarantee

www.cpsa.com Sales@cpsa.com 1.888.267.2772 (CPSA)

The Canadian Professional Sales Association helps salespeople master the negotiation process.

WORKING WITH BUYERS WHO ARE TRAINED IN NEGOTIATION

IN RECENT YEARS, WE HAVE SEEN AN INCREASE IN THE NUMBER OF TRAINING PROGRAMS developed for professional buyers. Some salespeople are also returning to the classroom to learn negotiation skills. Learning how to negotiate is one of the linchpins of effective selling.[47] The Canadian Professional Sales Association offers a popular course, "Effective Negotiating Strategies," which is designed to provide salespeople with the keys to successful negotiation.

Professional buyers often learn to use specific tactics in dealing with salespeople. Homer Smith, author of *Selling through Negotiation*, provides these examples:

Budget Limitation Tactic[48]

The buyer may say, "We like your proposal, but our budget for the convention is only $8500." Is the buyer telling the truth, or is the person testing your price? The best approach in this instance is to take the budget limitation seriously and use appropriate negotiation strategies. One strategy is to reduce the price by eliminating features or items, sometimes described as **unbundling.** In the case of a truck fleet sale, the salesperson might say, "We can deliver the trucks with a less powerful engine and thus meet your budget figure. Would you be willing to purchase trucks with less powerful engines?"

unbundling Eliminating features or items that contribute to a higher selling price.

Take-It-or-Leave-It Tactic[49]

How do you respond to a buyer who says, "My final offer is $3300. Take it or leave it"? A price concession is, of course, one option. However, this is likely to reduce profits for the company and lower your commission. An alternative strategy is to confidently review the superior benefits of your product and make another closing attempt. Appealing to the other person's sense of fairness also may move the discussion forward. If the final offer is totally without merit, consider calling a halt to the negotiation to allow the other party to back down from his or her position without losing face.[50]

Selling Today

You Don't Get What You Deserve, You Get What You Negotiate

Chester L. Karrass, creator of the Effective Negotiating seminar, says, "In business, you don't get what you deserve; you get what you negotiate." This is good advice for the job seeker. Most employers will not propose the highest wage possible at the beginning of the offer. If you want a higher starting wage, you must ask for it. Employers often have a predetermined range for each position and the highest salary is reserved for the applicant who brings something extra to the job. To prepare for a productive negotiation, you must know your own needs and you must know some-thing about the worth of the position. Many employers will tell you the salary range prior to the interview. The Internet can be a good source of salary information for certain types of jobs. In terms of your needs, try to determine what you care about the most: Interesting work? Future promotion? A flexible work schedule? If you are willing to negotiate, you can increase your pay by hundreds or even thousands of dollars. Be prepared to sell yourself, negotiate the salary you feel is appropriate, and achieve a win-win solution in the process.[b]

Let-Us-Split-the-Difference Tactic[51]

In some cases, the salesperson may find this price concession acceptable. If the buyer's suggestion is not acceptable, then the salesperson might make a counteroffer.

"If . . . Then" Tactic

This approach involves the buyer saying something like, "Unless you agree immediately to a price reduction of 20 percent, we'll have to look elsewhere for a supplier." In this situation, the consequence could be serious. The correct response depends upon the outcome of the assessment of the balance of power conducted during the preparation. If the buyer does have a number of options, all of which offer the same kind of benefits as yours, then you may have to concede. If your product offers clear advantages over the competition, then you may be able to resist the challenge.

"Sell Low Now, Make Profits Later" Tactic

In this situation, also referred to as the "Reward in Heaven" tactic, the buyer may say something like, "If you can reduce the price another $500 on this job, I will give you all my future work." This may be a genuine statement, and in fact may meet your own objective of gaining a foothold in your buyer's business. You might respond with "Because of the price I have quoted, I am unable to discount this job. However, if you do give me this job and your future jobs, I will discount your future work." This negotiation approach can actually create value for both you and your customer.

These tactics represent only a sample of those used by professional buyers. To prepare for these and other tactics, salespeople need to plan their negotiating strategies in advance and have clear goals. Decide in advance on the terms you can and cannot accept. It is important that you have the authority to set prices. Buyers want to do business with someone who has decision-making authority. Daniel Skarlicki, a specialist in organizational behaviour at the University of British Columbia, says, "Simply put, negotiations are won or lost in the planning and preparation, not at the negotiating table. Don't wing it."[52]

From the Field
Renting Pandas

Ron Barbaro, chairman of The Brick Group Income Fund and former chairman and CEO of the Ontario Lottery and Gaming Corporation, says that when he first started in sales, he was not a good salesperson but he had determination and was a good worker. It was this determination and hard work that enabled him to sell more than $1 million worth of insurance in his first year. He went on to become president of Prudential Insurance Company of America's Canadian and worldwide operations. His determination—

and undoubtedly the negotiating and problem-solving skills he learned while selling—helped him close what he refers to as his toughest, but most rewarding, sale.

When Ron Barbaro was chairman of the board for the Metro Toronto Zoo, he was instrumental in bringing the first giant panda exhibit to Canada from Asia. "They wouldn't give the pandas to us, nor would they sell them to us," says Ron. He eventually succeeded in negotiating a panda exhibit rental.[c]

REVIEWING KEY CONCEPTS

- Describe the principles of formal negotiations as part of the win-win strategy.

  Negotiations play a central role in the selling profession. Generic principles of formal integrative negotiations include preparing for negotiations, knowing the value of what you are offering, understanding the problem, creating alternate solutions, finding some point of agreement, and knowing when to walk away. If a salesperson uses a negotiations worksheet, then it can be much easier to plan systematically.

- Describe common types of buyer concerns.

  Sales resistance is natural and should be welcomed as an opportunity to learn more about how to satisfy the prospect's needs. Buyers' concerns often provide salespeople with precisely the information they need to close a sale. These concerns fall into five broad categories: need, product or service, source, time, and price. Whatever the reasons, the salesperson should *negotiate* sales resistance with the proper attitude, never making too much or too little of the prospect's concerns.

- Discuss specific methods of negotiating buyer concerns.

  We describe seven specific methods of negotiating buyer concerns: the direct denial, indirect denial, need-satisfaction questions, superior benefits, demonstration, trial offer, testimony, and postpone methods. The use of these methods and combinations thereof varies depending on the particular combination of salesperson, product, services, and prospect.

- Outline methods for creating value in formal negotiations.

  We have described several specific methods for creating value in formal negotiations, but you should remember that practice in applying them is essential and that there is room for a great deal of creative imagination in developing variations or additional methods. With careful preparation and practice, negotiating buyer concerns about price should become a stimulating challenge to each salesperson's professional growth.

- Describe how to work with buyers who are trained in negotiation.

  Buyers who are trained in negotiation resort to a number of tactics that a salesperson should be prepared for. In any case, the ultimate goal of formal integrative negotiations is to achieve win-win solutions by offering buyers the value they appreciate without compromising the sellers' benefits.

Key Terms

BATNA **321**

direct denial **328**

indirect denial **328**

logrolling **326**

negotiation **318**

postpone method **332**

stall **327**

superior benefit **330**

trial offer **331**

unbundling **336**

ZOPA **321**

Review Questions

1. Explain why a salesperson should welcome buyer concerns.

2. List the common types of buyer concerns that might surface in a presentation.

3. How does the negotiations worksheet help the salesperson prepare to negotiate buyer concerns?

4. Explain the value of using *probing* and *confirmation* questions when negotiating buyer concerns.

5. List eight specific strategies for negotiating buyer resistance.

6. John Ruskin says that it is unwise to pay too much when making a purchase, but it is worse to pay too

little. Do you agree or disagree with this statement? Explain.

7. What is usually the most common reason prospects give for not buying? How can salespeople deal effectively with this type of concern?

8. Professional buyers may have learned to use specific negotiation tactics in dealing with salespeople. List and describe two tactics that are commonly used today.

9. When a customer says, "I want time to think it over," what type of resistance is the salesperson encountering? Suggest ways to overcome this type of buyer concern.

10. Discuss the merits of using need-satisfaction questions to negotiate buyer concerns.

Application Exercises

1. Research for this Adaptive Selling Today Training Video revealed that anger does surface during the sales presentation and can be very challenging to negotiate. Anger can be something the other party experiences outside of the sale itself, or it can be caused by some aspect of the sale. Lana, the medical equipment salesperson, received an angry call from the doctor she was working with and had to prepare for solving both the anger problem and the reason for it. What three actions did she learn to use in negotiating with an angry customer? Describe how she adapted these actions during the sale to move the doctor's apparent position of "I am going to win, I don't care if you win;" to "I want to win and I want you to win also."

2. As was shared by the doctor, it is not unusual for a customer to experience skepticism and doubt about the pricing, timing, supplier, need, and/or product solution during the sales process. Skepticism creates an "I may not win" customer reaction and can prevent the other party from making a good and correct decision, resulting in a "no sale." What three actions did Lana use to help her customer overcome the skepticism he was experiencing?

3. Research also reveals that the most common problem in negotiations is the price problem. Customers often want to be sure they are getting the best price possible, as well as the best product solution. What three actions did Lana use to attempt to achieve a win-win solution with the doctor's concern about staying within a budget? Describe them in detail.

4. The action of "walking away" from a potential sale is often considered a high-risk negotiations strategy. What three actions did Lana employ before she walked away from the sale?

↻ ROLE-PLAY EXERCISE

You work for the sales department of an apparel manufacturing company. Montreal Fashions, a company you met with during a recent trade show, is going to visit your facilities next week. You understand that this company wants to "buy low" but normally places large orders. However, you want to "sell high." Your company might not be able to deliver very large orders unless you invest in new facilities. Montreal Fashions says it will send over a team of three people: the vice president of marketing, the purchasing manager, and a designer. They are interested in developing a collection for the next season and going over a "price exercise" with you. In addition, they are interested in placing a trial order at the price of a bulk order (i.e., large order). Delivery of the order is to be made in two weeks. Unfortunately, this trial order is well below the minimum quantity you're willing to accept, and your company normally needs one month to fill a new order.

1. How do you convey this information to the other departments within your company to prepare for this meeting? Will you invite your boss to the meeting? Why?

2. Using a negotiations worksheet, plan your response to the following statements made by the purchasing manager: (a) We are concerned that you will not be able to meet our quality requirements, (b) Your price is too high, (c) Either take this trial order or we will look for another vendor. Decide at what point in the negotiations on price and delivery date you will turn down or accept the offer. Role-play your response to each of these statements.

Reality Selling Today Video Case Problem

Each year, public and private organizations send thousands of employees to meetings held at hotels, motels, convention centres, conference centres, and resorts. These meetings represent a multimillion-dollar business in Canada and the United States. Airport hotels such as the Marriott Houston Hobby, introduced at the beginning of this chapter, are a good example of the venues typically selected for these meetings The Marriott Houston Hobby is conveniently located only one mile from the Hobby Airport in Houston, Texas. It has a competitive edge over its competition because it lies outside of the flight path. In addition to convenience and tranquility, the goal of the hotel is to provide guests with outstanding meeting and conference services. The hotel offers 235 deluxe guest rooms, 52 suites, 13 soundproof meeting rooms with state-of-the-art audiovisual technology, and continuous break service that can accommodate any agenda. Lavish customized meal events from a wide variety of international cuisines are a specialty of the Marriott Houston Hobby.

In an ideal situation, Heather Ramsey, corporate catering manager at the hotel, tries to get prospects out for an inspection of the property. Prospects might also sample hors d'oeuvres or lunch during a site tour. This tour, in some ways, fulfills the function of a sales demonstration. Throughout the tour, Heather describes special amenities and services offered by the hotel. She also uses this time to get better acquainted with the needs of the prospect. Once the tour is complete, she escorts the prospect back to her office and completes the needs assessment. Next, she prepares a detailed sales proposal or, in some cases, a contract. The proposal needs to contain accurate and complete facts because when signed, it becomes a legally enforceable sales contract.

For big events, the sales proposal is rarely accepted without modification. Professional meeting planners are experienced negotiators and press hard for concessions. Some have completed training programs developed for professional buyers. The concessions requested may include a lower guest room rate, lower meal costs, complimentary suites, or a complimentary event such as a wine and cheese reception. It might take as long as two months to reach an agreement with sophisticated buyers.

Of course, some buyer resistance is not easily identified. Heather Ramsey says that she follows four steps in dealing with buyer concerns:

1. *Identify the actual needs of the prospects.* To achieve win-win deals, Heather spends time asking specific questions about the customer's needs, such as the audience for the event, the size and timing of the event, and the customer's budget. The prospects normally focus on negotiating details of the food menu, group rates for room rental, and audiovisual facilities.

2. *Locate the resistance.* Some prospects are reluctant to accept the offer, but the reason may be unclear. Heather has discovered that asking open-ended questions goes a long way in understanding the actual resistance. Once the reason for resistance is uncovered, Heather knows how to deal with it.

3. *Clarify the resistance.* If a prospect says, "I like your facilities, but your prices are a little high," then the salesperson must clarify the meaning of this objection. Is the prospect seeking a major price concession or a small price concession?

4. *Overcome the objection.* Heather says, "You must be prepared for negotiations by understanding both your flexibility and the customer's needs." The hotel must earn a profit or publicity, so concessions can be made only after careful consideration of the bottom line and other intangible benefits.

Heather has discovered that the best way to negotiate buyer concerns is to make sure both the prospect and the resort feel like winners once the negotiations are finalized. If either party feels like a loser, a long-term relationship will not be possible. During peak seasons, Heather might also need to negotiate the schedule of events with prospects to minimize opportunity costs for the hotel while keeping the customers happy by offering off-season concessions. Refer to the opening vignette on page 316 and Reality Selling Today Role Play 7 in Appendix 1 on page 447 for more information.

Questions

1. If you were selling convention services for a hotel located in a large city, what types of buyer concerns would you expect from a new prospect?

2. Let us assume that you are representing the Marriott Houston Hobby and you are meeting with a new prospect at the hotel for a site tour. This prospect is planning to host an important event for 200 guests at your hotel. List the questions that you might ask the prospect to identify her actual needs. In doing so, be specific about the alternatives (e.g., high-end, medium, or regular packages) you can offer and the order you present them.

3. If you meet with a professional buyer who is trained in negotiation, what tactics can you expect the person to use? How would you respond to each of these tactics?

4. What subtle questions will you ask to ascertain that the negotiator is the decision maker without hurting her feelings? What actions will you take if you find out she is not the decision maker?

PARTNERSHIP SELLING: A ROLE PLAY/SIMULATION

Visit the role play/simulation materials provided in the Student Resources section of your companion website at **www.pearsoncanada.ca/manning**. A *Contents page lists appropriate page references for the activities*.

Developing a Presentation Strategy—Negotiating

Refer to *Sales Memorandum 3* and strategically plan to anticipate and negotiate any buyer concerns that may arise during your presentation. You should prepare a negotiations worksheet to organize this part of your presentation.

The instructions for item 2e direct you to prepare negotiations for time, price, source, and product concerns. You will note that your price is approximately $200 more than your customer budgeted for this meeting. You will have to be very effective in negotiating a value-added strategy because your convention centre is not a low-price supplier. (See Chapter 6 on value-added product strategies.)

During the presentation, you should use proof devices from the product strategy materials provided in *Employment Memorandum 1* to negotiate concerns you anticipate. You may also want to use a calculator to negotiate any financial arrangements, such as savings on parking or airport transportation, etc. Using spreadsheet software, you may want to prepare graphs to illustrate competitive pricing. Place these materials in the front pocket of your three-ring binder (portfolio) so that you can easily access them during your presentation. You may want to secure another person to be your customer, instructing him or her to voice the concerns you have anticipated, and then respond with your negotiation strategies. This experience will provide you with the opportunity to rehearse your negotiation strategies.

Chapter 14
Adapting the Close and Confirming the Partnership

Learning Objectives

After studying this chapter, you should be able to

1 Describe the proper attitude to display toward closing the sale.

2 List and discuss selected guidelines for closing the sale.

3 Explain how to recognize closing clues.

4 Discuss specific methods of closing the sale.

5 Explain what to do when the buyer says yes and what to do when the buyer says no.

 Adaptive Selling Today Training Video Series

Ask For the Order—or **AFTO**, as it is also called—is the third training video in the Adaptive Selling Today Training Video Series. The video begins with a salesperson who has a fear of closing the sale. Research shows that many sales are lost because salespeople fear asking for the order, and that even when they do, it is not unusual to have to ask three or four times. Along with many successful examples of how to ask for the order, AFTO presents a three-dimensional approach to overcoming any fear one may have of asking.

AFTO presents many closing methods, described in this chapter, that illustrate the importance of adapting your closing questions to the customer's particular buying situation. Specific methods of asking for the order are clearly presented in dramatic sequences, representing a wide variety of selling situations.

AFTO presents a system to use throughout the sales process to gain a better understanding of your customer's needs and ultimately help your customers make sound buying decisions.

ADAPTING THE CLOSE—AN ATTITUDE THAT ADDS VALUE

SUSAN MINNS, VICE PRESIDENT OF CLIENT SERVICES AT EVENT SPECTRUM IN TORONTO, looks at closing from the prospect's point of view. Although the special event plan she has prepared may seem perfect, she realizes that the customer may have a different point of view. A special event for her company may involve a national sales conference, a

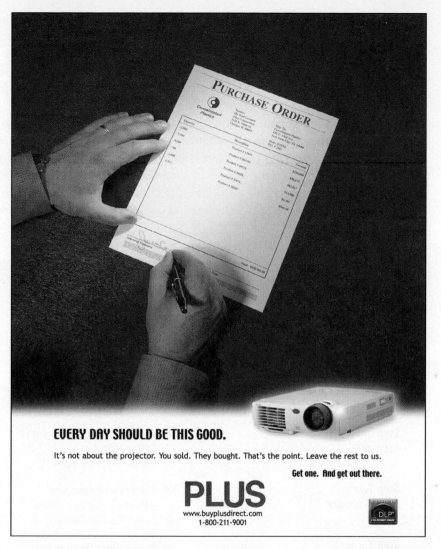

PURCHASE ORDER

EVERY DAY SHOULD BE THIS GOOD.

It's not about the projector. You sold. They bought. That's the point. Leave the rest to us.

Get one. And get out there.

PLUS

www.buyplusdirect.com
1-800-211-9001

DLP

Closing the sale is easier if you review the value proposition effectively from the prospect's point of view.

corporate executive retreat, a new product launch, or even a client appreciation event for large or small companies that want to recognize and thank their important customers. She must try to see the actual event through the eyes of the Event Spectrum customer and, from this insight, use adaptive closing questions to confirm the sale and begin to build a long-term partnership. Susan believes that relationship-building skills must be applied at every step of the sales process. If she is continuously adding value throughout the sales presentation, closing a sale and getting a contract will be much easier. This is especially true in those cases in which price might be a barrier to closing.[1]

Throughout the evolution of personal selling, we have seen major changes in the way closing is perceived. Prior to the introduction of consultative selling and the partnering era, closing was typically presented as the most important aspect of the sales process. The early sales training literature also presented closing methods that encouraged manipulation of the customer. Use of any closing method that is perceived by the customer as pushy or manipulative will damage your chances of building a long-term partnership, even if you do get the sale.[2]

Closing should not be viewed as a strategy to win at the expense of the customer. The proper attitude should be "If this is the best solution for the customer, I should help her make the correct decision."[3] Once the best solution is determined, *asking for the order* is the next logical step.

We take the position that in many selling situations, the salesperson needs to assume responsibility for obtaining commitment from the customer. Some closing methods can move the customer from indecision to commitment. When these methods are used effectively, the prospect will not feel pressured. In some cases, we need to simply replace defence-arousing language—such as "This is the lowest price available anywhere"—with a positive *need-satisfaction question*, such as "Wouldn't this new software help you achieve more efficient inventory control?"

Asking for the order is less difficult if the salesperson is strategically prepared for the close. Preparation for the close involves understanding customer needs, custom-fitting solutions, and planning appropriate closing methods. Throughout the sales presentation, the salesperson should recognize closing clues and be prepared to use effective closing methods (Fig. 14.1).[4]

The Six-Step Presentation Plan	
Step One: Approach	☑ Review Strategic/Consultative Selling Model ☑ Initiate customer contact
Step Two: Need Discovery	☑ Ask strategic questions ☑ Determine customer needs ☑ Select Product Solution
Step Three: Presentation	☑ Select presentation strategy ☑ Create presentation plan ☑ Initiate presentation
Step Four: Negotiation	☑ Anticipate buyer concerns ☑ Plan negotiating methods ☑ Initiate win-win negotiations
Step Five: Close	☐ Plan appropriate closing methods ☐ Recognize closing clues ☐ Initiate closing methods
Step Six: Servicing the Sale	☐ Follow through ☐ Follow-up calls ☐ Expansion selling

Service, retail, wholesale, and manufacturer selling

Figure 14.1 Effective closing methods require careful planning.

Review the Value Proposition from the Prospect's Point of View

Closing the sale is usually easier if you look at the *value proposition* from the prospect's point of view. Have you effectively summarized the mix of key benefits? Will your proposal provide a solution that solves the customer's problem? Is your proposal strong enough to win over a customer who is experiencing buying anxieties?

Gene Bedell, author of *3 Steps to Yes*, reminds us that buying often causes emotional stress, sometimes referred to as "buyer's remorse." The following buying anxieties help explain why some customers are reluctant to make a commitment to your proposal.[5]

Loss of options. If the customer agrees to purchase a $5000 design proposal, then that money will not be available for other purchases or investments. Agreeing to purchase a product or service often means that some other purchase must be postponed. Anxiety and stress build as the customer thinks about allocating limited resources.

Fear of making a mistake. If the customer believes that agreeing with a closing request may be the wrong thing to do, he or she may back away just when the decision seems imminent. Fear of making a mistake can be caused by lack of trust in the salesperson.

Social or peer pressures. Some customers make buying decisions with an eye on the opinions and reactions of others. A business buyer may have to justify a purchase to her boss or to employees who will actually use the product. Be prepared to deal with these anxieties as you get closer to closing the sale. Sometimes a little gentle persuasion will help the anxious customer make a decision.

Closing the Sale—The Beginning of the Partnership

Tom Reilly, in his book *Value-Added Selling*, says, ". . . you don't close sales; you build commitment to a course of action that brings value to the customer and profit to the seller."[6] There is a process that begins with an interesting approach and need discovery. It continues with effective product selection and presentation of benefits, which build desire for the product. After a well-planned demonstration and after negotiating sales resistance, it is time to obtain commitment. Closing should be thought of as the beginning of a long-term partnership.

GUIDELINES FOR CLOSING THE SALE

A NUMBER OF FACTORS INCREASE THE ODDS THAT YOU WILL CLOSE THE SALE (see Fig. 14.2). These guidelines for closing the sale have universal application in the field of selling.

Focus on Dominant Buying Motives

Most salespeople incorporate the outstanding benefits of their product into the sales presentation. This is only natural. However, be alert to the *one* specific benefit that generates the most excitement. The buying motive that is of greatest interest deserves special attention. Vince Peters, director of sales training and development for Wyeth-Ayerst

Noted author Gene Bedell reminds us that buying often causes emotional stress. A loss of options, fear of making a mistake, and/or social pressures can cause high levels of anxiety. Salespeople must be prepared to help the anxious customer make a decision.

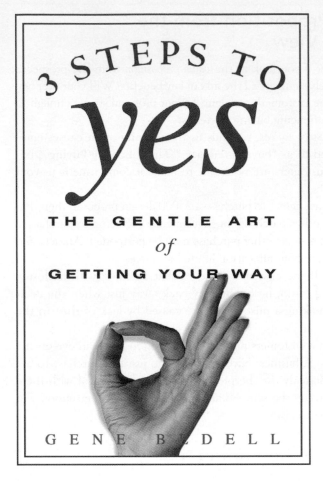

3 STEPS TO

yes

THE GENTLE ART *of* GETTING YOUR WAY

GENE BEDELL

International, tells his 8000 pharmaceutical salespeople that the key to closing "is to find out exactly what a prospect is looking for."[7]

Throughout the need discovery stage, pay close attention to the buyer's interests. Focus your closing efforts on the point of greatest interest and give the prospect a reason for buying.

Longer Selling Cycles and Incremental Commitments

Longer selling cycles have become a fact of life in many industries. One reason for this change is that more decision makers are involved in purchasing some products. A survey of 1300 companies by sales analysis firm CSO Insights indicates that increased competition, more complex buying processes, and higher buyer workloads are also adding time to the sales cycle. The buying cycle for many products can be measured in months and some buying cycles can be measured in years.[8]

incremental commitment
Gradually moving the customer to total commitment (i.e., closing on a purchase) by gaining cumulative commitment with each sales call.

When you are working on a large, complex sale, you should try to achieve **incremental commitment** throughout the sales process. Some form of incremental commitment should be obtained during each step in a multi-call sales presentation. At the conclusion of the first sales call, for example, you may obtain commitment to an agenda for the second call. At the second call, you might obtain commitment for the prospect to

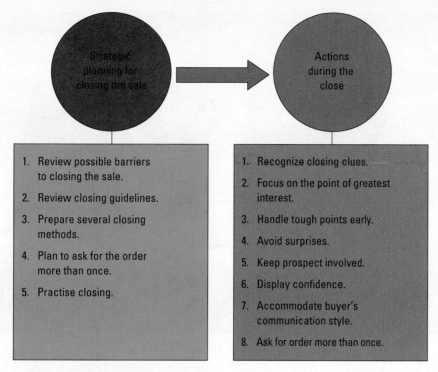

Strategic planning for closing the sale

1. Review possible barriers to closing the sale.
2. Review closing guidelines.
3. Prepare several closing methods.
4. Plan to ask for the order more than once.
5. Practise closing.

Actions during the close

1. Recognize closing clues.
2. Focus on the point of greatest interest.
3. Handle tough points early.
4. Avoid surprises.
5. Keep prospect involved.
6. Display confidence.
7. Accommodate buyer's communication style.
8. Ask for order more than once.

Figure 14.2 The presentation strategy should include reviewing these guidelines for closing and confirming the sale.

tour your company facilities. Each commitment should move the sale forward toward a signed order.

In some cases, the best way to shorten a sales cycle is to create an entirely new way to locate and approach customers. The customer base for Telegraph Hill Robes is upscale hotels and spas. When Maria Spurlock assumed the duties of CEO, the typical sales cycle was six months to two years. Most Telegraph Hill Robes clients were large, established hotels, and decisions regarding the purchase of robes often involved the general manager and the head of housekeeping. Spurlock decided to focus more sales efforts on hotels still under construction. The key decision maker for a hotel under construction is often just one person, the interior designer. By working with designers, she reduced the sales cycle to three months or less.[9]

Negotiate the Tough Points before Attempting the Close

Many products have what might be thought of as an Achilles heel—in other words, the product is vulnerable or appears to be vulnerable in one or more areas. Negotiate a win-win solution to the tough points before you attempt to close the sale. Such factors can lose the sale if you ignore them. The close should be a positive phase of the sales presentation. This is not the time to deal with a controversial issue or problem.

In the case of Rolex watches, BMW automobiles, or Banff Springs Hotel conference facilities, for example, the Achilles heel may be price. Each of these products may seem

Closing should be viewed as part of the selling process—the logical outcome of a well-planned presentation strategy.

expensive in comparison with competing ones. People who sell them find ways to establish the value of their product before attempting the close.

Avoid Surprises at the Close

Some salespeople make the mistake of waiting until the close to reveal information that may come as a surprise to the prospect. For example, the salesperson quotes a price but is not specific concerning what the price includes. Let us assume that the price of a central air-conditioning unit is $4000. The prospect believes that the price is competitive in relation to similar units on the market and is ready to sign the order form. Then the salesperson mentions casually that the installation charge is an extra $975. The prospect had assumed that the $4000 price included installation. Suddenly the extra fee looms as a major obstacle to closing the sale.

The surprise might come in the form of an accessory that costs extra, terms of the warranty, customer service limitations, or some other issue. Do not let a last-minute surprise damage the relationship with the buyer and threaten the completion of a sale.

"Tough-Mindedness"—Display a High Degree of Self-Confidence at the Close

Do you believe in your product? Do you believe in your company? Do you believe in yourself? Have you identified a solution to the customer's problem? If you can answer yes to each of these questions, then there is no need to display timidity. Look the prospect in the eye and ask for the order. Do not be apologetic at this important point in the sales presentation. The salesperson who confidently asks for the sale is displaying the boldness that is so effective in personal selling.

Ask for the Order More Than Once

Too often, salespeople make the mistake of not asking for the order or asking just once. If the prospect says no, they give up. Michael LeBoeuf, author of *How to Win Customers and Keep Them for Life*, reports that almost two-thirds of all sales calls conclude without the salesperson asking for the order. He also says that a majority of customers say no several times before saying yes.[10] Some of the most productive salespeople ask for the order three, four, or even five times. A surprising number of yes responses come on the fourth or fifth attempt. Of course, not all these closing attempts necessarily come during one call. Determination is a virtue if your product solution solves the customer's problem.

RECOGNIZE CLOSING CLUES

As the sales presentation progresses, you need to be alert to closing clues (sometimes called *buying signals*). A **closing clue** is an indication, either verbal or nonverbal, that the prospect is preparing to make a buying decision. It is a form of feedback, which is so important in selling. When you detect a closing clue, it may be time to attempt a close.

Many closing clues are quite subtle and may be missed if you are not alert. This is especially true in the case of nonverbal buying signals. If you pay careful attention—with your eyes and ears—many prospects will signal their degree of commitment.[11] As we noted earlier in this text, one of the most important personality traits salespeople need is empathy—the ability to sense what the other person is feeling. Recognizing situational clues allows you to modify your self-behaviour to use the appropriate strategy for the close.[12] In this section, we will review some of the most common verbal and nonverbal clues.

closing clue An indication, either verbal or nonverbal, that the prospect is preparing to make a buying decision.

Verbal Clues Closing clues come in many forms. Spoken words, or verbal clues, are usually the easiest to perceive. These clues can be divided into three categories: (1) questions, (2) recognitions, and (3) requirements.

Questions. One of the least subtle buying signals is the question. You might attempt a trial close after responding to one of the following questions:

> Do you have a credit plan to cover this purchase?
> What type of warranty do you provide?
> How soon can our company get delivery?

Recognitions. A recognition is any positive statement concerning your product or some factor related to the sale, such as credit terms or delivery date. Some examples follow:

> We like the quality control system you have recommended.
> I have always wanted to own a boat like this.
> Your delivery schedule fits our plans.

Requirements. Sometimes customers outline a condition that must be met before they will buy. If you are able to meet this requirement, it may be a good time to try a trial close. Here are some requirements that the prospect might voice:

> We will need shipment within two weeks.
> Our staff will need to be trained in how to use this equipment.
> All our equipment must be certified by the plant safety officer.

From the Field

Brand Development Starts with Personal Selling

Building a brand name for a line of "unmentionables" (bras, underwear, and camisoles) can be a challenge. Alka and Mona Srivastava, sisters and business partners, readily agree that they didn't know what they were getting themselves into when they started Florentyna Intima, a lingerie company. The two economics majors knew very little about design, manufacturing, and marketing. Once they had a business plan and some money borrowed from their parents, Alka and Mona began the search for a designer and manufacturer. They needed prototypes to show to customers. Once the prototypes were completed by a firm in Bangkok, they tried to hire a sales representative to present the new line. Unfortunately, no one was willing to represent a line sold by an inexperienced manufacturer. That's when they decided to become salespeople. They hit the road, calling on owners of lingerie boutiques coast to coast and visiting trade shows. Soon buyers were calling with orders. Sales have grown about 30 percent each year.[a]

In some cases, verbal buying clues will not jump out at you. Important buying signals may be interwoven into normal conversation. Listen closely whenever the prospect is talking.

Nonverbal Clues Nonverbal buying clues will be even more difficult to detect. Once detected, this type of signal is not easy to interpret. Nevertheless, you should be alert to body movement, facial expression, and tone of voice. Here are some actions that suggest that the prospect may be prepared to purchase the product.[13]

- The prospect's facial expression changes. Suddenly the person's eyes widen and genuine interest is clear in the facial expression.
- The prospect begins showing agreement by nodding.
- The prospect leans forward and appears to be intent on hearing your message.
- The prospect begins to examine the product or study the sales literature intently.

When you observe or sense one of these nonverbal buying clues, do not hesitate to ask for commitment. There may be several opportunities to close throughout the sales presentation. Important buying signals may surface at any time. Do not miss them.

SPECIFIC METHODS FOR CLOSING THE SALE

THE SALES PRESENTATION IS A PROCESS, NOT A SINGLE ACTION. EACH STEP DURING THE process should create another layer of trust and move the customer closer to making the purchase. Throughout the sales process, you are moving closer to the close by positioning yourself as a valued resource.[14]

There is no *best* closing method. Your best bet is to preplan several closing methods and adapt the ones that seem appropriate to each customer (see Fig. 14.3). Given the complex nature of many sales, it is often a good idea to be prepared to use a combination of closing methods that fit the customer.[15] Do keep in mind that your goal is not only to close the sale but also to develop a long-term partnership.

Closing Worksheet		
Closing clue (prospect)	Closing method	Closing statement (salesperson)
"That sounds fine."	Direct appeal close	"Good. May I get your signature on this order?"
"What kind of financing do you offer?"	Multiple options close	"We have two financing methods available: 90-day open credit or two-year long-term financing. Which of these do you prefer?"
"Well, we don't have large amounts of cash available at this time."	Assumptive close	"Based on your cash position, I would recommend you consider our lease–purchase plan. This plan allows you to pay a very small initial amount at this time and keep the cash you now have for your everyday business expenses. I will be happy to write up your order on the lease–purchase plan."
The prospect completes a careful reading of the proposal, then looks satisfied (a nonverbal clue).	Combination summary-of-benefits/direct appeal close	"That solution surpasses your quality requirements, meets your time deadlines, and provides your accounting department with the details it requested. Can you get your chief financial officer's signature on the order?"

Figure 14.3 Closing worksheet
Preparing for the close requires the preplanning of several closing methods. Research indicates that in many selling situations, several closing attempts will be necessary.

Trial Close

A **trial close,** also known as a *minor point close,* is a closing attempt made at an opportune time during the sales presentation to encourage the customer to reveal either readiness or unwillingness to buy. When you are reasonably sure that the prospect is about to make a decision but is being held back by natural caution, the trial close may be appropriate. It is a good way to test the buyer's attitude toward the actual purchase. The trial close can also be effectively adapted to achieving incremental commitment in more complex multi-call sales. A trial close is often presented in the form of a probing or confirmation question. Here are some examples:

We can arrange an August 1 shipment. Would this date be satisfactory?

Would you rather begin this plan on July 1 or July 15?

Is the timing right to do a presentation to the executive committee?

Will a $2000 down payment be possible at this time?

trial close A closing attempt made at an opportune time during the sales presentation to encourage the customer to reveal either readiness or unwillingness to buy.

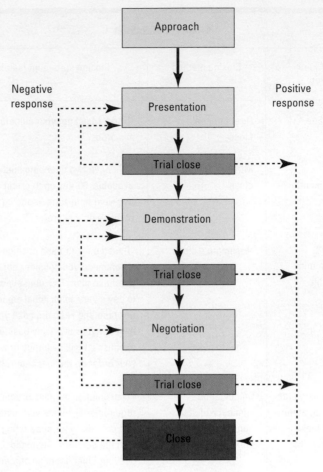

Figure 14.4 The trial close

The trial close should be attempted at an opportune time during the sales presentation. It is appropriate to initiate a trial close after steps two, three, or four of the six-step presentation plan.

Some salespeople use the trial close more than once during the sales presentation. After the salesperson presents a feature, converts that feature to a buyer benefit, and confirms the prospect's agreement that the benefit is important, it is appropriate to use a trial close.

In broader terms, it would be appropriate to attempt a trial close after steps two, three, or four of the six-step presentation plan (see Fig. 14.4).

Direct Appeal Close

direct appeal close Involves simply asking for the order in a straightforward manner.

The **direct appeal close** has the advantages of clarity and simplicity. This close involves simply asking for the order in a straightforward manner. It is the most direct closing approach, and many buyers find it attractive. Realistically, most customers expect salespeople to ask for the sale.

The direct appeal should not, of course, come too early. It should not be used until the prospect has displayed a definite interest in the product or service. The salesperson must also gain the prospect's respect before initiating this appeal. Once you make the direct appeal, stop talking. John Livesay, a magazine ad director, says being patient at the close is his "secret weapon." He remains silent after asking the customer to buy. He avoids asking more questions or making additional statements. This approach gives the customer time to think about the proposal.[16]

A variation of the direct appeal close involves using a question to determine how close the customer is to making a buying decision. The question might be "How close are we to closing the sale?" This direct question calls for a direct answer. The customer is encouraged to reflect on the progress of the sale.[17]

Assumptive Close

The **assumptive close**—sometimes called *take-it-for-granted* close—asks for a minor decision, assuming that the customer has already decided to buy.[18] This closing approach comes near the end of the planned presentation. If you have identified a genuine need, presented your solutions in terms of buyer benefits, presented an effective sales demonstration, and negotiated buyer concerns satisfactorily, it may be natural to assume that the person is ready to buy. Noted sales consultant Jeffrey Gitomer (**www.gitomer.com**) says the assumptive close is appropriate when the salesperson has removed perceived risks and the prospect has confidence in the salesperson.[19] The assumptive close usually takes the form of a question that focuses on a minor point. Here are some examples:

> If you feel that Model 211 gives you the major benefits you are looking for, let's schedule delivery for next Tuesday.
>
> Since our production systems provide you with the order fulfillment flexibility you require, let's go ahead and place your order.

Most customers will view either of these statements as the natural conclusion of the events that preceded it. Assumptive closes often include a benefit with your request for action.[20]

assumptive close The salesperson asks for a minor decision, assuming that the customer has already decided to buy.

The assumptive close asks for a minor decision, assuming that the customer has decided to buy.

This closing method provides a subtle way to ask for a decision when you are quite certain the customer has already decided to buy. You are only bringing the selling/buying process to a close.

Summary-of-Benefits Close

summary-of-benefits close Involves summarizing the most important buyer benefits, re-emphasizing the benefits that will help bring about a favourable decision.

Let us assume that you have discussed and demonstrated the major benefits of your product and you detect considerable buyer interest. However, you have covered a great deal of material. There is a chance that the prospect will not be able to put the entire picture together without your help. At this point, you should provide a concise summary of the most important buyer benefits. Your goal in the **summary-of-benefits close**—also referred to as the *step-by-step close*—is to re-emphasize the value-added benefits that will help bring about a favourable decision. This closing statement gives you the opportunity to restate how the benefits will outweigh the costs.[21]

Let us see how this closing method works in the management education industry. Foster Zanuto, a representative for Brock University's Management Development Centre, recently called on Ray Busch, director of marketing for a large corporation. Near the end of the sales presentation, Foster summarized the major benefits in this manner:

> Mr. Busch, we can provide you with a state-of-the-art seminar room that will seat 30 people comfortably and four smaller rooms for the workshops you have planned. Our staff will serve a noon lunch. The cost will be $295 per person, including the instructor's fees. Finally, we will see that each of your employees receives a pad of paper, a pen, and a copy of the workshop program. Today I can reserve these facilities for November 24, which is your first preference for a meeting date. Can I go ahead and enter your reservation into our computer?

Notice that Foster has reviewed all the important elements of the value proposition and then asked a *need-satisfaction question*. This question is designed to move the sales process toward commitment and action.

Special Concession Close

special concession close Offers the buyer something extra for acting immediately.

The **special concession close** offers the buyer something extra for acting immediately. A special inducement is offered if the prospect will agree to sign the order. The concession may be part of a low-price strategy such as a sale price, a quantity discount, a more liberal credit plan, or an added feature that the prospect did not anticipate.

You should use this closing approach with care, because some customers are skeptical of concessions. This is especially true when the concession comes after the salesperson has made what appears to be the final offer.

Nicholas Graham, founder and chairman of Joe Boxer Corporation, spends considerable time presenting his novelty underwear line to retailers. Graham recalls that one of his most difficult sales involved Saks Fifth Avenue, the prestigious department store company. He wanted the company to carry Joe Boxer underwear and suggested a Daniel Boone–inspired boxer with a detachable raccoon tail. Graham says, "They had never seen anything so absurd in their life." To close the sale, he let the store take 24 pairs on consignment. "They sold out in one hour," Graham says. Saks has been a committed customer ever since.[22]

Multiple Options Close

In many selling situations, it is a good idea to provide the prospect with options regarding product configuration, delivery, and price. This is especially true when you are dealing with the price-conscious *transactional buyer*. As noted in the previous chapter, today's customer expects new levels of flexibility. In the **multiple options close,** allow the person to examine several different options and try to assess the degree of interest in each one. As you near the point where a close seems appropriate, remove some of the options. This will reduce confusion and indecision.

multiple options close When the salesperson gives the prospect several options to consider and tries to assess the prospect's degree of interest in each.

The multiple options technique is often used in office equipment sales. If a small business owner wants to purchase a copy machine, most vendors will offer several models for consideration. Let us assume that the prospect has examined four models and seems to be uncertain about which one would be the best choice. The salesperson might determine which copier is least appealing and eliminate it as an option. Now the prospect can choose among three copiers. If the prospect seems to favour one copier, it would be appropriate to ask for the order.

When using the multiple options close, follow these simple steps:

1. Configure more than one product solution.

2. Cease showing product options when it appears that the prospect has been given ample selection. Too many choices can result in confusion and indecision.

3. Remove products (or features) that the prospect does not seem genuinely interested in and concentrate on the options the prospect does seem to be interested in.

Balance Sheet Close

The **balance sheet close** appeals to customers who are having difficulty making a decision even though they have been given plenty of information. Let's assume that the customer feels he or she has a choice: Buy now or buy later. The salesperson draws a T on a sheet of paper and writes the captions below on each side of the crossbar.

balance sheet close A visual way of showing the customer the reasons for making a decision now versus not making a decision now.

Reasons for buying now	Reasons for not buying now
1.	1.
2.	2.
3.	3.
4.	4.

To get the process rolling, the salesperson might say, "Let's see how many reasons we can list for buying now." On the left side of the T, the salesperson lists some reasons for buying now. These should be benefits in which the customer has already expressed an interest. On the right side, reasons for not buying now are listed. Throughout the listing process, the salesperson should engage the customer in a dialogue. This closing method will not be effective if the salesperson is doing all the talking.

Global Business Insight

Doing Business in South America

Although specific customs vary in the countries of South America, some generalizations can be made. For example, residents of Brazil, Argentina, and other countries have a different idea of what is appropriate personal space. They tend to stand closer to you during conversations. To step back may be viewed as being impolite. You should expect more physical contact such as pats on the back and hugs. Lunch is the main meal of the day and it's not uncommon for a business meal to last several hours. Latin Americans often arrive late for appointments. Be patient with decision makers and do not use the hard-sell approach. Be aware of language preferences. Brazilians speak Portuguese; addressing them in Spanish would be insulting. Business associates in Argentina will likely speak English and Spanish. However, your business card should be translated into Spanish.[b]

Management Close

management close A close that involves bringing the sales manager or senior management to the sales presentation as a way to help close a sale.

In previous chapters, we have discussed the merits of involving the sales manager or senior executives in sales calls. To close a major account, salespeople sometimes call on top management for help. This is the **management close.** Ryan Hegman, who works for Hegman Machine Tool Inc., recalls a sale that involved a $1.5 million automated manufacturing system. During the sales process, he brought in the president of the company, the vice president of sales, and the lead engineer. "Each added value in a separate way," Ryan explains. One important reason to involve management is to make prospects feel that your whole company's resources will be available to support the customer.[23]

Impending Event Close

impending event close Involves making positive use of a negative point.

The **impending event close**—also known as the *positive/negative technique*—involves making positive use of a negative point. This technique of closing requires that you know the needs of the prospects well enough to turn their objections into your selling points. More often than not, you will need to have a good relationship with your prospects to make the method work.

For example, the salesperson might say, "As you have agreed, our product does have several advantages over the competing offerings. I also want to share with you that we cannot make delivery before the middle of next month (the negative point) due to high demand (the positive point). However, I believe you're not looking for delivery until the end of next month (make sure you know this as a fact), so if you place this order today, delivery will not be a problem."

Combination Closes

In some cases, the most effective close is one that combines two or more of the closing methods we have discussed. To illustrate, let us observe Colleen White as she attempts to close a sale in the office of a buyer for a large department store. Colleen represents a firm that manufactures a wide range of leather clothing and accessories. Near the end of her planned presentation, she senses that the prospect is quite interested in her products but seems reluctant to make a decision. This is how Colleen handles the close:

> Ms. Taylor, I have described two benefits that seem especially important to you. First, you agree that this line will be popular with the fashion-conscious shoppers your store caters to. Second, you indicated that the prices I quoted will allow you excellent profit margins and third, if we process your order now, you will have the merchandise in time for the pre-holiday buying period. With this in mind, let's go ahead and process your order today.

Notice that this close starts with a summary of benefits and ends with an assumptive close.

Adapting to the Customer's Communication Style

In Chapter 4, we examined the concept of communication styles and achieving versatility through style flexing. We noted that people with different behaviour styles will make their decisions in very distinct ways. We need to take the prospect's style into consideration when deciding how to approach the close.[24]

Directive Most Directives are goal-oriented individuals who are ready to make quick decisions once they believe your solution meets their needs. They like doing business with salespeople who display confidence that they can give customers the benefits they want. The Directive may reject your trial close just to test your confidence level. The highly assertive Directive will respect persistence and determination.

Emotive The Emotive needs social acceptance, so provide support for their opinions and ideas. Maintain good eye contact and be a good listener. Don't let this buyer's emotional statements throw you off balance. Spontaneous statements, spoken dramatically and impulsively, should be expected.

Supportive You can expect the Supportive customer to be slow in making the buying decision. This buyer is more apt to worry about change or taking risks. It's important to understand his or her perceived risks so that you can provide reassurance before asking for a buying decision. Curb the desire to put pressure on the Supportive customer—it may make this buyer more indecisive. Patience is important.

Reflective Before you ask the Reflective customer for a buying decision, make sure you review important factual information. These buyers are less likely to be influenced by emotion. Ask Reflectives, "Is there any other information I can provide before you make a decision?" Never pressure the Reflective customer to make a quick decision.

Practise Closing

Your success in selling will depend in large part on learning how to make these eight closing methods work for you. Gaining experience using adaptive selling techniques can result in increased recognition of opportunities and greater effectiveness.[25] You will not master these approaches in a few days or a few weeks, but you can speed up the learning process with preparation and practice. Role playing is the best-known way to experience the feelings that accompany closing and to practise the skills needed to close sales. To prepare the role play,

Applying the Platinum Rule: People with different behaviour styles will make their buying decisions in very distinct ways. Therefore, the prospect's communication style must be taken into consideration when deciding how to adapt the close.

anticipate various closing scenarios and then prepare a written script of the drama.[26] Find someone (your sales manager, friend, or spouse) to play the role of the customer and give that person a script to act out. Practise the role play in front of a video recorder and then sit back and observe your performance. The video monitor provides excellent feedback. Use the closing worksheet (see Fig. 14.3) to prepare for practice sessions.

CONFIRMING THE PARTNERSHIP WHEN THE BUYER SAYS YES

CONGRATULATIONS! YOU HAVE CLOSED THE SALE AND HAVE ESTABLI-SHED THE BEGINNING of what you hope will be a long and satisfying partnership with the customer. Before preparing to leave, be sure that all details related to the purchase agreement are completed. Check everything with the buyer, and then ask for a signature if necessary.

confirmation step Reassuring the customer after the sale has been closed, pointing out that he or she has made the correct decision. This may involve describing the satisfaction of owning the product.

buyer's remorse Feelings of regret, fear, or anxiety that a buyer may feel after placing an order.

Once the sale has been closed, it is important to take time to reassure the customer. This is the **confirmation step** in closing the sale. Before you leave, reassure the customer by pointing out that he or she has made the correct decision, and describe the satisfaction that will come with ownership of the product. The reason for doing this is to resell the buyer and to prevent buyer's remorse. **Buyer's remorse** (sometimes called *cognitive dissonance*) is an emotional response that can take various forms such as feelings of regret, fear, or anxiety.[27] It is common to wonder whether we have made the right decision. Compliment the customer for making a wise choice. Once the sale is closed, the customer may be required to justify the purchase to others. Your words of reassurance will be helpful.

Before leaving, thank the customer for the order. This is very important. Everyone likes to think that a purchase is appreciated. No one should believe that a purchase is taken for granted. Even a small order deserves words of appreciation. In many cases, a follow-up thank-you letter is appropriate.

In several previous chapters we said that a satisfied customer is one of the best sources of new prospects. Never hesitate to ask, "Do you know anyone else who might benefit from owning this product?" or a similar question. Some customers may even agree to write an introductory letter on your behalf.

What to Do When the Buyer Says No

High-performance salespeople learn to manage disappointment. A strong display of disappointment or resentment is likely to close the door to future sales. Losing a sale may be painful, but it can also be a valuable learning opportunity. Doing some analysis of what went wrong can help you change the outcome of future sales. Here are some things you should do after a lost sale.[28]

1. *Make sure the deal is really dead.* There is always a chance that the prospect's decision can be changed. You might want to mount a last-ditch effort and reopen the presentation.

2. *Review the chain of events.* When you experience a no-sale call, try to benefit from the experience. If you were part of a sales team, get each member's reaction. Soon after the prospect has said no, schedule a debriefing session. If you worked alone, engage in honest self-analysis. If you carefully look at your performance during every aspect of the sales process, you may be able to identify weaknesses that can be corrected.

3. *Interview the customer.* Obtaining feedback requires a delicate approach. If you probe too aggressively, you may appear argumentative. If your approach is too passive, and the client's comments are general, you will not know how to improve. The key is to couch your questions in neutral terms. Rather than asking, "Why didn't we get the order?" try this approach: "Thank you for considering our company. We hope to do business with you at some time in the future. Would you mind helping me understand any shortcomings in our sales proposal?"

Before leaving, thank the customer for the order. This is very important. Everyone likes to know that a purchase is appreciated.

Always keep the door open for future sales. Tell the prospect you would love to work with him or her at some time in the future. Then put this person back on your prospect list, record any new information you have learned about the prospect, and continue to keep in touch. Marvin Gottlieb, president of The Communication Project, recalls the loss of a very large piece of business from a large IT firm. This company decided to begin doing its own training rather than outsource it to Gottlieb's company. Rather then give up hope, Gottlieb continued to maintain relationships with key people at the IT firm. After four years, he was invited to present information on a needed service. He closed a $50 000 sale in less than a month.[29]

Prepare the Prospect for Contact with the Competition Some prospects refuse to buy because they want to take a close look at competing products. This response is not unusual in the field of selling. You should do everything possible to help the customer make an intelligent comparison. It is always a good practice to review your product's strong points one more time. Give special emphasis to areas in which your product has a strong competitive advantage. Make it easy for the person to buy your product at some future date.

REVIEWING KEY CONCEPTS

- Describe the proper attitude to display toward closing the sale.

  The early sales training literature presented closing methods that sometimes encouraged manipulation of the customer. Use of any closing method that is perceived by the customer as pushy or manipulative will damage your chances of building a long-term partnership. Closing should not be viewed as a strategy to win at the expense of the customer. Once the customer's need has been confirmed, salespeople should determine the most ethical and effective method of moving the buyer from indecision to commitment.

- List and discuss selected guidelines for closing the sale.

  Long sales cycles require multiple commitments. These commitments need to be obtained from the prospect throughout a multi-call sales presentation. The buying motive that is of greatest interest deserves special attention at the close. Always negotiate tough points before attempting the close, display a high degree of confidence, and ask for the order more than once.

- Explain how to recognize closing clues.

  The salesperson must be alert to *closing clues* from the prospect. These clues fall into two categories:

verbal and nonverbal. Verbal clues are the easiest to recognize, but they may be subtle as well. Again, it is important to be an attentive listener. The recognition of nonverbal clues is more difficult, but careful observation helps in detecting them.

- Discuss specific methods of closing the sale.

  Several closing methods may be necessary to get the prospect to make a buying decision; therefore, it is wise for the salesperson to preplan several closes. These closing methods should be chosen from the list provided in this chapter and then customized to fit the product and the type of buyer with whom the salesperson is dealing. In some selling situations, the use of *combination closes* is very effective. Flexing to the customer's communication style is important.

- Explain what to do when the buyer says yes and what to do when the buyer says no.

  The professional salesperson is not discouraged or offended if the sale is not closed. Every effort should be made to be of further assistance to the prospect— the sale might be closed on another call. Continue to keep in touch. Even if the sale is lost, the experience may be valuable if it is analyzed in order to learn from it.

Key Terms

Review Questions

1. List some aspects of the sales presentation that can make closing and confirming the sale difficult to achieve.

2. Describe three buying anxieties that sometimes serve as barriers to closing the sale.

3. What guidelines should a salesperson follow for closing the sale?

4. Why is it important to review the value proposition from the prospect's point of view?

5. Define the term *incremental commitment*. Why is it important to achieve incremental commitments throughout the sale?

6. Explain how the multiple options close might be used in the sale of men's and women's suits.

7. Is there a best method to use in closing the sale? Explain.

8. What is meant by a trial close (the minor point close)? When should a salesperson attempt a trial close?

9. Explain the summary-of-benefits close (step-by-step close).

10. What confirming steps should a salesperson follow when the customer says yes? What should be done when the customer says no?

Application Exercises

1. Which of the following statements, often made by prospects, would you interpret as buying signals?

   a. "How much would the payments be?"

   b. "Tell me about your service department."

   c. "The company already has an older model that seems good enough."

   d. "We do not have enough cash flow right now."

   e. "How much would you allow me for my old model?"

   f. "I do not need one."

   g. "How does that switch work?"

   h. "When would I have to pay for it?"

2. You are an accountant who owns and operates an accounting service. You have been contacted by the president of an advertising agency about the possibility of having you audit her business on a regular basis. The president has indicated that she has investigated other accounting firms and thinks that they price their services too high. With the knowledge you have about the other firms, you know you are in a strong competitive position. You also realize her account would be profitable for your firm. You would really like to capture this account. How will you close the deal? List and describe two closing methods you might use in this situation.

3. Zig Ziglar, Brian Tracy, and Tom Reilly are well-known authors and speakers on the subject of closing the sale. Access each of their websites—**www.zigziglar. com, www.briantracy.com, www.tomreillytraining. com**—and research the books, courses, and videos they have available for companies and individuals to purchase and learn more about closing the sale. Prepare a summary of what you find available. Does the material in this chapter parallel the kind of information these individuals present?

4. If the prospect is ready to buy before you have presented all of your selling points, should you make an effort to complete your sales presentation? Explain your answer.

5. Books have been written explaining hundreds of different closes that salespeople can use. One close that some salespeople commonly use is called the impending doom close. This is one of many closing techniques we would never recommend in our book. Using your search engine, find out how this particular close works. (Search for impending doom technique as well as impending doom close.) Explain why you would never expect to see this close recommended in our book.

⟳ ROLE-PLAY EXERCISE

Examine the superior benefits of the convention centre identified in "Partnership Selling: A Role Play/Simulation" online in the Student Resource section at **www.pearson-canada.ca/manning**. Specifically, research the qualities of the "five-star" executive chef, the award-winning renovation of the facility, the cost of parking and transportation to and from the airport, and the easy highway access to and from the facility. You should assume the role of director of sales and, with this information, prepare a closing worksheet on the combination of summary-of-benefits and direct appeal closes for a prospective customer. Using the information from the audiovisual presentation guide, prepare a special concession close, allowing free use of the laser pointer and wireless microphone (a $107.50 value) for a group presentation to the 23 people who will be staying in single rooms at the hotel. Role-play the close of a sale using these closing methods to a prospect who is seriously considering using one of your competitors.

CASE PROBLEM

The team at Event Spectrum can help make your dreams come true. The team can help you plan a special event—large or small—in almost any venue. If you want to show appreciation to your retiring chief executive officer, the Event Spectrum team will make sure the party is truly special. They can help organize employee reward and recognition programs, strategy planning retreats for executives, or even corporate team-building events. One special event involved approximately 850 employees of Unilever Canada who were brought to Las Vegas over a two-week period to launch a new company vision.

Susan Minns, vice president of client services, enjoys working with customers. Her customers vary greatly in terms of age, education, income, and social class. The key to working effectively with all of these people is relationship building. Once she builds rapport with clients and establishes a foundation built on trust, they are more likely to open up and discuss their needs. Event planners have at their disposal a wide range of planning tools, including facilities and event production expertise, but customer needs guide the use of these resources.

Susan finds that if the sales presentation is well planned and delivered, closing the sale and confirming a contract is easier. She believes that good listening skills and careful probing can help uncover dominant buying motives. For example, the client who wants an event with a special theme may have difficulty expressing her thoughts. Susan must probe and listen closely in order to understand the customer's desires. She must also create value throughout the presentation in order to set the stage for the close. A special event can cost anywhere from a few thousand dollars to—at the other extreme—several million dollars, so price can be a barrier to closing.

Questions

1. What closing clues should Susan look for?

2. What trial closes would be appropriate?

3. What tough points should be negotiated before attempting to close?

4. Can you visualize a situation in which Susan might use a multiple options close? Explain.

5. Assume that a large corporation wants to schedule a recognition event for 40 people. This event will begin with cocktails and appetizers and end with a served meal. Special entertainment will precede the meal. What items might be included in a summary-of-benefits close?

PARTNERSHIP SELLING: A ROLE PLAY/SIMULATION

Visit the role play/simulation materials provided in the Student Resources section of your companion website at **www.pearsoncanada.ca/manning.** *A Contents page lists appropriate page references for the activities.*

Developing a Sales Presentation Strategy—Closing the Sale

Refer to *Sales Memorandum 3* and strategically plan to close the sale with your customer. To consider the sale closed, you will need to secure the signature of your customer on the sales proposal form. This will guarantee your customer the accommodations listed on the form. These accommodations may change depending on the final number of people attending your customer's convention. This is an important point to keep in mind when closing the sale; however, you still must get the signature to guarantee the accommodations.

Follow the instructions carefully and prepare a closing worksheet listing at least four closes using the methods outlined in this chapter. Two of these methods should be the summary-of-benefits and the direct appeal. Remember that it is not the policy of your convention centre to cut prices, so your methods should include value-added strategies.

Use proof devices to make your closes more convincing and place them in the front pocket of your three-ring binder/portfolio for easy access during your presentation. You may want to ask another person to be your customer and practise the closing strategies you have developed.

Chapter 15
Servicing the Sale and Building the Partnership

Learning Objectives

After studying this chapter, you should be able to

1   Explain how to build long-term partnerships with customer service.

2   Describe current developments in customer service.

3   List and describe the major customer service methods that strengthen the partnership.

4   Explain how to add value with expansion selling.

5   Explain how to deal effectively with complaints.

Introduction

customer service All the activities that enhance or facilitate the sale and use of a product.

WFS Ltd.—formerly Windsor Factory Supply—is one of Canada's largest general-line industrial distributors. The company started as a two-man operation in Windsor, Ontario, in 1955. Jerry Slavik and Cliff Cretney, both 22 years old, decided to leave another distributor and begin their own company. They had $500 between them and raised an equal amount from relatives. Joe Sobocan joined the company a few months later, and Cliff soon left for personal reasons. Jerry and Joe began an employee profit-sharing plan as the company grew, with the intention that it would someday become 100 percent employee-owned. This occurred in 1995, shortly after Jerry and Joe retired. WFS now has 10 Canadian branches, one branch in South Carolina, and a warehouse near Detroit, Michigan. Currently, there are more than 220 WFS employees. Sales are approaching $100 million, far beyond the first-year sales of approximately $50 000. WFS currently has more than 3500 suppliers and more than 4000 customers. How has it achieved its tremendous growth? The company has a strong internal culture and a healthy business philosophy. The company's foundation is built on *quality*, *satisfaction*, and *dependability*, and it is known for outstanding **customer service**. President Rick Thurston describes the company philosophy as one based on the belief that being able to service existing customers is more important than gaining new customers, since a large amount of incremental business comes from the current customer base. He says, "Our business is built on relationships. Of course, we are always looking for opportunities, but we know that sometimes it is important to curb growth so that quality service to existing customers is not compromised. A great example is our most recent expansion into the United States. We had been asked on many occasions to open up more facilities to

The Six-Step Presentation Plan	
Step One: APPROACH	☑ Review Strategic/Consultative Selling Model ☑ Initiate customer contact
Step Two: PRESENTATION	✔ Determine prospect needs ✔ Select solution ✔ Initiate sales presentation
Step Three: DEMONSTRATION	✔ Decide what to demonstrate ✔ Select selling tools ✔ Initiate demonstration
Step Four: NEGOTIATION	✔ Anticipate buyer concerns ✔ Plan negotiating methods ✔ Initiate win-win negotiations
Step Five: CLOSE	✔ Plan appropriate closing methods ✔ Recognize closing clues ✔ Initiate closing methods
Step Six: SERVICING THE SALE	● Follow-through ● Follow-up calls ● Expansion selling
Service, retail, wholesale, and manufacturer selling.	

Figure 15.1 Servicing the sale
Servicing the sale involves three steps: follow-through, follow-up calls, and expansion selling.

support customer growth there, but we recognized that our successful Canadian approach would not necessarily be a fit for all U.S. markets. After many years of fine-tuning our relationship with one key customer, we finally decided to open a South Carolina branch."[1]

Servicing the sale encompasses a variety of activities that take place during and after the implementation stage of the buying process (Fig. 8.3). In this chapter, we present servicing the sale as a three-part process: follow-through on assurances and promises; follow-up with ongoing communication after the sale; and expansion selling, which involves the identification of additional needs and providing solutions (Fig. 15.1). Each of these strategies can add value and build the partnership.

BUILDING LONG-TERM PARTNERSHIPS WITH CUSTOMER SERVICE

IN A WORLD OF INCREASED GLOBAL COMPETITION AND NARROWING PROFIT MARGINS, customer retention through value-based initiatives can mean the difference between increasing or eroding market share. Progressive marketers are searching for ways to differentiate their service from that of competitors and build emotional loyalty through value.[2]

A sales organization that can develop a reputation for servicing each sale is sought out by customers who want a long-term partner to help them with their buying needs. Satisfied customers represent an "auxiliary" sales force—a group of people who will recommend customer-driven organizations to others. If customers are pleased with the service they receive after the sale, be assured that they will tell other people. Research shows that when someone has a good customer service experience, he or she tells an average of six people; when someone experiences outstanding customer service, he or she tells twice as many.[3]

Achieving Successive Sales

In Chapter 1, we defined *partnering* as a strategically developed, long-term relationship that solves the customer's problem. A successful partnering effort results in successive sales and referrals.

Many of today's large companies want to partner with suppliers who sell and deliver quality products and services that continually improve their processes and profits. The first sale is only the beginning of the relationship—an opportunity to earn a repeat sale. Repeat sales come after the supplier demonstrates the ability to add value in various ways.[4] This value may take the form of timely delivery, superior installation, accurate invoicing, technical know-how, social contacts, or something else that is important to the customer. In business-to-business sales, the relationship should intensify as the supplier delivers extensive postsale support. Taking the customer's point of view and acting in the customer's interest, often described as *customer advocacy*, is a major factor underlying repeat business.[5]

Responding to Increased Postsale Customer Expectations

According to Ted Levitt, author of *The Marketing Imagination*, people buy expectations, not products. They buy the expectation of benefits you promised. Once the customer buys your product, expectations increase. Levitt points out that after the sale is closed, the buyer's attitude changes. The buyer expects the salesperson to remember the purchase as a favour bestowed on him or her by the buyer. Nitin Nohria, business professor and co-author of *What Really Works: The 4-2 Formula for Sustained Business Success*, says, "Customers are enormously punishing when companies don't meet their expectations."[6]

Increased customer expectations after the sale is closed require a strategic plan for servicing the sale. Certain aspects of the relationship, product, and customer strategies can have a positive influence on the customer's heightened expectations.[7] In most business-to-business sales, the salesperson cannot service the sale alone. To manage the account properly, the salesperson will need assistance from shipping, technical support, engineering, and other departments. Customer service is increasingly a team effort.[8]

How do you respond to a customer who has increased expectations?

- *First, you should be certain your customer strategy is on target.* You must fully understand the needs and wants of the customer. What is the customer trying to accomplish, and how can you help him or her do it better?

This salesperson is preparing a thank-you note that will strengthen the relationship with the customer.

- *Second, you should focus like a laser beam on follow-through and follow-up activities.* Throughout every sales presentation, the salesperson will offer assurances and make some promises. The salesperson's credibility will be tarnished if any of these commitments is ignored.

- *Third, you should re-examine your product strategy.* In some cases, you can enhance customer satisfaction by suggesting related products or services. If the product is expensive, you can follow through and offer assistance in making credit arrangements. If the product is complex, you can make suggestions concerning use and maintenance. Each of these forms of assistance may add value to the sale.

Selling Today

Job Searches Require Widening the Net

You have a good education but you don't have a job. This scenario is playing out in the lives of thousands of people throughout Canada. Before you send out another thousand résumés via the Internet or spend more time searching for employment opportunities, consider the results of a study conducted by Drake Beam Morin (DBM), a workplace-consulting firm. Networking is the top tactic for landing a job, outpacing other strategies such as the Internet and newspaper ads. The report indicates that 66 percent of DBM clients found new jobs via networking, whereas just 6 percent found employment through the Internet. Don't overlook the value of personal contact that gives you the opportunity to sell yourself.[a]

High Cost of Customer Attrition

Financial institutions, public utilities, airlines, retail stores, restaurants, manufacturers, and wholesalers face the problem of gaining and retaining the patronage of clients and customers. These companies realize that keeping a customer happy is a good strategy. To regain a lost customer can be four to five times more expensive than keeping a current customer satisfied.[9]

There is no longer any doubt that poor service is the primary cause of customer attrition. Surprisingly few customers (12 to 15 percent) are lost because of product dissatisfaction. No more than 10 to 15 percent of lost customers leave because of price considerations. Some studies have found that from 50 to 70 percent of customer attrition is because of poor service.[10] A carefully developed strategic plan to reduce customer defection will pay big dividends.

Larry Rosen, chairman and CEO of Harry Rosen Inc., fully embraces the customer-for-life philosophy. He says, "We don't look at a person who walks into our store as an immediate sale. We look at him with a potential lifetime value. If we can provide enlightened service and advice and earn a man's trust, chances are he will be loyal to our organization for life. This relationship-based aspect of our selling is perfectly captured in our brand promise—'Harry Rosen is in the business of assisting men develop a personal, confident image, in all aspects of their life—any day, any time and any occasion.' To help us develop these quality relationships with our clients we spend over a million dollars annually training our selling associates about providing ongoing service and expertise."[11]

CURRENT DEVELOPMENTS IN CUSTOMER SERVICE

IN HIS BOOK *Business @ The Speed of Thought*, BILL GATES PREDICTS THAT IN THIS millennium, customer service will become the primary value-added function.[12] He recognizes that customer service is the primary method of building and extending the partnership. Customer service, in its many forms, nourishes the partnership and keeps it alive. Salespeople are in a unique position to enhance *customer satisfaction* and *trust*, the two major contributors to relationship quality.[13] With adequate orientation and training, members of the sales force can build long-term, profitable customer relationships. Recent research indicates that the building process involves five important service behaviours that are especially important in the context of business-to-business selling.[14]

- **Diligence.** Diligence combines two types of service behaviours: responsiveness and reliability. In today's highly competitive, time-starved business environment, salespeople must provide service in a timely manner. Service behaviours that demonstrate both reliability and responsiveness include following up on commitments, returning phone calls, fulfilling customer requests, and being available when needed.

- **Information communication.** This service behaviour involves regularly relaying product information to the customer in a clear and concise manner. Communicating information must encompass the entire sales process. Early on, this may involve drawing objective comparisons between your product and competitive offerings, and continually reiterating a clear case for your product. After the sale is closed, information communication often involves providing updated information on product usage.

- **Inducements.** This service behaviour is aimed at personalizing the relationship with the customer. In Chapter 3, we noted that the manner in which salespeople establish,

Bill Gates, author of *Business @ the Speed of Thought,* predicts that in the new economy, customer service may become the primary value-added function.

build, and maintain relationships is not an incidental aspect of personal selling. Some service behaviours provide the customer with an incentive, or an inducement, for maintaining the relationship with the salesperson. Becoming genuinely interested in the customer, talking in terms of the customer's interests, or doing special favours can strengthen the relationship with the customer.

- **Empathy.** As the information age unfolded and the global economy heated up, we learned that it takes more than quick and accurate information communicated through advanced technology to retain customers. Empathy is one of those high-touch abilities that mark the fault line between salespeople who are highly productive and those who are average or below average in terms of productivity.[15] Salespeople who display a strong willingness to help customers and make an effort to understand them are demonstrating empathetic behaviour.

- **Sportsmanship.** This service behaviour can be defined as a salesperson's willingness to tolerate setbacks and disappointments without displaying negativism. It means demonstrating good social judgment and professionalism during all customer interactions. If you have a 10:00 a.m. appointment with a customer but are required to wait until 10:30 a.m. for the meeting to begin, how will you handle this disappointment?

Computer-Based Systems

Customer-friendly computer-based systems are frequently used to enhance customer service, loyalty, and sales growth.[16] Computers give both the salesperson and the customer ready access to information and problem-solving alternatives. Nantucket Nectars provides a good example of a company that has enhanced customer service with computer-based systems. The 150 distributors can log on to **www.juiceguys.com** to place and check

Maggie Chung, a sales manager at Harry Rosen in Vancouver, uses a customer relationship management system to help manage relationships with customers.

orders. Nantucket Nectars's 85 field salespeople can log on to NectarNet, a dedicated company website, from their homes to check on the status of customer orders and determine inventory levels.[17]

The sales staff at Harry Rosen Gentlemen's Apparel, the highly successful clothing retailer introduced in Chapter 2 and mentioned earlier in this chapter, use technology to establish a more personal relationship with the customer. In a matter of seconds, salespeople can review a customer's complete buying history, his or her birthday and anniversary, clothing sizes, favourite colours, children's names, or any other information that the customer has willingly provided. With this information, salespeople are better able to bond with their customers. Maggie Chung, a sales manager in the Vancouver store, says, "At Harry Rosen, I've really learned the value of customer relationships. I have some customers who visit me almost monthly."[18]

CUSTOMER SERVICE METHODS THAT STRENGTHEN THE PARTNERSHIP

CUSTOMER SERVICE ENCOMPASSES ALL ACTIVITIES THAT ENHANCE OR FACILITATE THE SALE and use of one's product or service. The skills required to service a sale are different from those required prior to the sale (Fig. 15.2). High-performance sales personnel do not

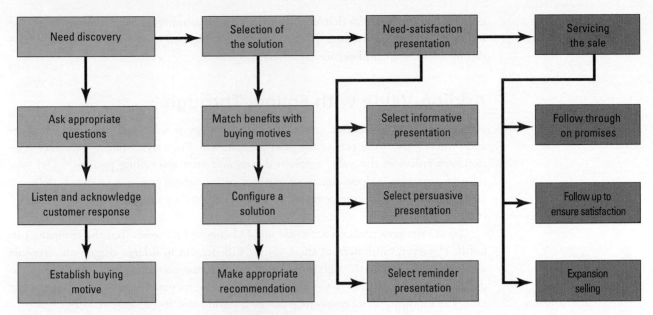

Figure 15.2 Consultative sales presentation guide

The completed consultative sales presentation guide illustrates the ways in which high-performance salespeople use value-added strategies to service the sale and build repeat business and referrals. Customer service provides many opportunities to strengthen the partnership.

A follow-up phone call to thank the customer and find out if he or she is pleased with the product will strengthen the relationship after the sale.

abdicate responsibility for delivery, installation, and warranty interpretation or other customer service responsibilities. They continue to strengthen the partnership with follow-through, follow-up, and expansion selling.

Adding Value with Follow-Through

A major key to an effective customer service strategy is follow-through on assurances and promises that were part of the sales presentation. Properly managing customer relationships enhances the value creation during and after the selling process.[19] Did your sales presentation include claims for superior performance; promises of speedy delivery; assistance with credit arrangements; or guaranteed factory assistance with installation, training, and service?

Most sales presentations are made up of claims and promises that the company can fulfill. However, fulfillment of these claims will depend to a large degree on after-sale action. Postsale follow-through is the key to holding that customer you worked so hard to develop. The first sale can be the beginning of a long-term partnership or it can be the last sale. The following services can help ensure a second sale and successive sales.

Make Credit Arrangements Credit has become a common way to finance purchases. This is true of industrial products, real estate, automobiles, home appliances, and many other products. Closing the sale will often depend on your ability to develop and present attractive credit plans to the customer. Even if you do not get directly involved in the firm's credit and collection activities, you must be familiar with how the company handles these matters. Salespeople need to establish a relationship with the credit department and learn how credit analysts make their decisions.[20]

Making credit decisions gets a lot tougher when you are conducting business in foreign countries. Overseas transactions can be complex, and in some cases there is little recourse if a customer does not pay. Doron Weissman, president of Overseas Brokers, a freight forwarder and export brokerage firm, says, "When I sell my services, I automatically qualify the account to make sure they're financially able to meet my demands. If not, I move on."[21]

Schedule Deliveries Many organizations are adding value with on-time deliveries. A late delivery can be a problem for both the supplier and the customer. To illustrate, let us assume that the supplier is a manufacturer of small appliances and the customer is a department store chain. A late delivery may mean lost sales because of out-of-stock conditions, cancellation of the order by the department store, or loss of future sales.

The causes of late delivery may be beyond your control. It is your responsibility, however, to keep the customer informed of any delays. You can also take steps to prevent a delay. Check to be sure your order was processed correctly. Follow up to see if the order was shipped on time. Always remember: "Every time an order is handled, the customer is handled. Every time an order sits unattended, the customer sits unattended."[22]

Be Present During Delivery When the first delivery is made, be there to be sure the customer is comfortable with the purchase. Check to determine if the order is complete and be available to offer assistance.[23]

Selling Today

The Moment of Magic

Tony Alessandra is a well-known author, sales trainer, and national speaker (**www.alessandra.com**). He says that there are three possible outcomes when a customer does business with an organization:

■ *The moment of truth.* In these selling situations, the customer's expectations were met. Nothing happened to disappoint the customer, nor did the salesperson do anything to surpass the customer's expectations. The customer is apt to have somewhat neutral feelings about his or her relationship with the salesperson. The moment of truth will usually not build customer loyalty.

■ *The moment of misery.* This is the outcome of a selling situation where the customer's expectations were not met. The customer may feel a sense of disappointment or even anger. Many customers who experience the moment of misery will share their feelings with others and often make a decision to "fire" the salesperson.

■ *The moment of magic.* This is the outcome of a sale where the customer received more than he or she expected. The salesperson surpassed the customer's expectations by going the extra mile and providing a level of service that added value to the customer–salesperson relationship. This extra effort is likely to establish a foundation for increased customer loyalty.[b]

Monitor Installation Buyer satisfaction is often related to proper installation of the product. This is true of consumer products such as security systems, central air-conditioning, solar heating systems, and carpeting. It is also true of industrial products such as electronic data processing equipment and air-quality control systems. Some salespeople believe it is to their advantage to supervise product installation; they are then able to spot installation problems. Others make it a practice to follow up on the installation to be sure no problems exist.

Offer Training in the Use or Care of the Product For certain industries, it is essential that users be trained in how to use the new product. This is true of factory equipment, electronic cash registers, farm implements, and a host of other products. Technology has become so complex that many suppliers must provide training as part of the follow-up to ensure customer satisfaction. Most organizations that sell computers and other types of electronic equipment for office use now schedule training classes to ensure that customers can properly use and care for the products. These companies believe that users must be skilled in handling their equipment.

Provide Price Change Information Price changes need not be a serious problem if they are handled correctly. The salesperson is responsible for maintaining an up-to-date price list. As your company issues price changes, record them accurately. Customers expect you to quote the correct price the first time.

Preventing Postsale Problems

There are ways to prevent postsale problems. The key is conscientious follow-up to be sure everything has been handled properly. Get to know the people who operate your shipping department. They are responsible for getting the right products shipped on time, and it is important that they understand your customers' needs.

Doing Business in Russia

The Cold War is over and Russia has become an important trading partner with the West. In recent years, Russia has changed politically, socially, and economically. Prior to doing business in the new Russia, get acquainted with the business etiquette and ethics of this important market for Canadian products and services.

■ Meetings may not start on time, but it's still a good idea to be punctual.

■ The first meeting with your Russian counterparts may be just a formality. They will attempt to assess your credibility and relationship skills, so be warm and approachable.

■ Cultivate relationships with government agencies at all levels. Politicians and government agencies continue to have arbitrary power.

■ Most Russians enjoy having a drink and a good meal. Take this opportunity to establish goodwill. Some restaurants and bars do not accept credit cards, so bring cash.[c]

CREATING THE LIFETIME CUSTOMER

When we build a plant or purchase a computer—when we acquire just about any new asset—by accounting conventions, it begins to depreciate on day one. But there is one asset that can appreciate over the years. That asset is the well-served customer, who becomes the most significant sustainer of the business, the lifetime customer. (www.tompeters.com)

Tom Peters

Tom Peters believes there is one asset that can appreciate over the years. That asset is the wellserved customer, who becomes the most significant sustainer of the business, the lifetime customer.

Source: Toby Talbot/AP Wide World Photos

Become acquainted with people in the credit department. Be sure that they maintain a good, businesslike relationship with your customers. This is a delicate area; even small mistakes—a "pay now" notice sent too early, for example—can cause hurt feelings. If your company uses customer support staff to resolve postsale problems, be sure to get acquainted with the people who provide this service.

Schedule regular account reviews to determine the level of customer satisfaction. The focus of these reviews should be key decision makers. Are there lingering service-type issues that make you vulnerable to the competition? You want to be certain there are no open doors for your competitors. If you discover a problem, act quickly to resolve it. In some cases, these formal account reviews will uncover opportunities to improve customer service. You will also become more of a consultant in the eyes of the customer.[24]

Adding Value with Customer Follow-Up

Customer follow-up methods usually have two major objectives. One is to express appreciation for the purchase and thus to enhance the relationship established during the sales presentation. You no doubt thanked the customer at the time the sale was closed, but appreciation should be expressed again a few days later. The second purpose of the follow-up is to determine whether the customer is satisfied with the purchase. Both of these methods will strengthen the buyer–seller relationship and build a partnership that results in additional sales.[25]

In survey after survey, poor service and lack of follow-up after the sale are given as primary reasons people stop buying from a particular supplier. Most customers are sensitive to indifferent treatment by the sales representative. With this fact in mind, you should approach follow-up in a systematic and businesslike way. There are five follow-up methods.

Personal Visit This is usually the most costly follow-up method, but it may produce the best results. It is the only strategy that allows face-to-face, two-way communication. When you take time to make a personal visit, the customer knows that you really care.

Use the personal follow-up to keep the customer informed of new developments, new products, or new applications. This information may pave the way for additional sales. Use the personal visit to reassess where you stand with the account. The reassessment process should involve something more than a "How's it going?" question. If you want the customer to see you as a partner, ask the tough questions: "Are there any problems that I need to address?" "Can you suggest any ways we can better serve your business?" Tom Reilly, author and sales trainer, says, "Your perceptions of your performance are meaningless. It's the customer's perceptions that count."[26]

Personal visits provide a wonderful opportunity to engage in **value reinforcement**. Value reinforcement means getting credit for the value you create for the customer. You might review all of your follow-through activities so the customer realizes the many ways you have added value. Whenever possible, document your value-added services and point out any benefits that the customer has received. In some cases, positive bragging is an effective value reinforcement technique.[27]

value reinforcement
Reinforcing to the customer the value they are getting from their purchase.

Telephone Call The telephone provides a quick and efficient way to follow up a sale. A salesperson can easily make 10 or 12 phone calls in a single hour, and the cost will be minimal. If you plan to send a thank-you card or letter, follow it up with a thank-you call. The personal appeal of the phone call will increase the effectiveness of the written correspondence. The telephone call has one major advantage over written correspondence:

It allows for a two-way exchange of information. Once an account is well established, you may be able to obtain repeat sales by telephone.

Email Message In many cases, it is a lot quicker to send an email message than to make a phone call. Salespeople report that they waste a lot of time playing "phone tag." Some customers prefer email messages and may become irritated if you do not adhere to their wishes. If you know that a customer is not in the habit of checking their email all that often, use the telephone as a back-up method. When in doubt, use parallel channels of communication.

Letter or Card Written correspondence is an inexpensive and convenient way to thank the customer for the order and to promise continued service. Some companies encourage their salespeople to use a formal letter typed on company stationery. Other companies have designed special thank-you cards, which are signed and sent routinely after a sale is closed. The salesperson may enclose a business card. These thank-you cards do have one major limitation: They are mass produced and therefore lack the personal touch of hand-written cards and envelopes. Personalized notes, birthday cards, and anniversary cards can make a positive impression.

call report A written summary that provides information on a sales call to people in the sales organization so that follow-up action can be taken as necessary.

Call Report The **call report** is a form that serves as a communications link with persons who can assist with customer service. The format varies, but generally it is a simple form with only four or five spaces. The sample call report form that appears in Figure 15.3 is used by a company that installs security systems at banks and other financial institutions.

A form such as this is one solution to the problem of communication between company personnel and the customer. It is a method of follow-through that triggers the desired action. It is simple yet businesslike.

Follow-up programs can be as creative or ingenious as you wish. Every sales organization competes on value, so you must continually think of new ways to add value. Creative use of your interpersonal communication skills can keep your messages fresh and personalized. Keep in mind that people buy both from the head and from the heart. Let customers know how much you care about their business.[28] You can use these five methods independently or in combination. Your main consideration should be some type of appropriate follow-up that (1) tells customers you appreciate their business, and (2) determines whether they are satisfied with the purchase.

Sales Call Report Date: January 26, 2012

To: Walt Higgins, service engineer

From: Diane Ray, sales representative

Action Promised: Visit the bank's Ottawa location within the next week to check on installation of our security system.

Assistance Needed: System B-420 was installed at the bank's main Ottawa branch on January 23. As per our agreement, you should make a follow-up call to check the installation of the system and provide bank personnel with a Form 82 certification checklist. The form should be given to Mr. Sandeep Khosla, the branch manager.

Copies to: Mr. Sandeep Khosla

Figure 15.3 The call report

Adding Value with Expansion Selling

Personal selling is the process of identifying and filling the customer's needs. As the salesperson learns more about the customer and establishes a relationship based on trust and mutual respect, opportunities for expansion selling will arise. Expansion selling can take three forms: full-line selling, cross-selling, and upselling.

Full-Line Selling Sometimes called *suggestion selling*, **full-line selling** is the process of recommending products or services that are related to the main item sold to the customer. The recommendation is made when, in the salesperson's judgment, the product or service can provide additional satisfaction. To illustrate, let's look at the sale of new houses. Many contractors offer customers who want to differentiate their home a variety of options, including marble in the entryway, granite countertops, gourmet kitchen appliances, or Jacuzzi-like tubs for the bathroom. Customization is an important value-added service for many customers.[29]

full-line selling The process of suggesting products or services that are related to the main item being sold to the customer.

Full-line selling is no less important when selling services. For example, a travel agent has many opportunities to suggest related products. Let us assume that a customer purchases a two-week vacation in Ireland. The agent can offer to book hotel reservations or schedule a guided tour. Another related product would be a rental car. Sometimes, a new product is simply not "right" without related merchandise. A new business suit may not look right without a new shirt and tie. An executive training program held at a fine hotel can be enhanced with a refreshment break featuring a variety of soft drinks, fresh coffee, and freshly baked pastries.

Customers will view full-line selling as a form of value-added service when it is presented correctly. There is a right way and a wrong way to make recommendations. Here are some guidelines to follow:

1. *Plan for full-line selling during the preapproach step.* Before meeting with the customer, develop a general plan that includes your objectives for this important dimension of selling. Full-line selling is easier when you are prepared.

2. *Make recommendations after you have satisfied the customer's primary need.* While there are some exceptions to this rule, it's usually best to meet the primary need first. In the case of a new home purchase, for example, the customer should first select the model home and then make decisions regarding the upgrades.

3. *Make your suggestions thoughtful and positive.* "We will deliver your new copy machine on Monday. Would you like us to deliver some quality copy paper?" Avoid questions such as, "Can we ship anything else?" This question invites a negative response.

4. *When appropriate, demonstrate the suggested item or use sales tools to build interest.* If you have suggested a shirt to go with a new suit, allow the customer to see it next to the suit. If you are calling on a business or commercial account, show the customer a sample or at least a picture if the actual product is not available.

Full-line selling is a means of providing value-added service. When you use it correctly, customers will thank you for your thoughtfulness and extra service. It is also a proven sales-building strategy.

Cross-Selling We have seen an increase in the use of cross-selling to grow sales volume. **Cross-selling** involves selling products that are not directly associated with products that you have sold to an established customer. A bank customer who has a home equity loan might be contacted and asked to consider the purchase of a mutual fund. The customer

cross-selling Selling to an established customer products that are not directly related to products the customer has already bought.

Follow-up calls allow for a two-way exchange of information. In many cases, once an account is well established, you may be able to obtain repeat sales by telephone.

who has purchased a townhouse might be a candidate for a security service. One financial services company, Quick & Reilly, has trained its 600 customer service representatives to use cross-selling when customers call regarding their current investments. By completing the cross-selling training program, the representatives learned how to assess the caller's financial goals and develop a tailored proposal of products and services. Quick & Reilly achieved a 35 percent sales increase after developing the cross-selling program.[30]

More and more companies use cross-selling to discover additional sources of business within established accounts. Buyers generally welcome cross-selling efforts because they are searching for ways to consolidate purchases. They like the convenience of buying several items from the same source.[31] Cross-selling is most effective in those situations in which the salesperson and the customer enjoy a true partnership.

Salespeople who have a good understanding of the customer's needs and have earned the customer's respect will face less resistance when recommending a product or service. To achieve success with cross-selling, you need to use *survey questions* and *probing questions* (see Chapter 11). A general survey question such as "Can you tell me more about your expansion plans?" may uncover information needed to position your cross-selling sales strategy. However, you will likely need to use probing questions to uncover and clarify a buying problem that may open the door to a cross-selling opportunity. Keep in mind that cross-selling has to be a well-thought-out part of your strategy and process.[32]

upselling The effort to sell better-quality products.

Upselling The effort to sell better-quality products is known as **upselling**. It is an important selling method that often adds customer value. Mike Weber, sales manager at Young Electric Sign Company, offers us two important tips on upselling. First, you need a well-established relationship with the customer—a relationship built on trust. Second, you need to continually qualify the prospect throughout the buying process. As you hear customers tell you more about their needs, you may see an opportunity to upsell. Weber says his salespeople usually engage in upselling at the design stage. The customer is shown a rough sketch of the desired sign and another rendition of something better. The added value of the more expensive

Rackham and De Vincentis, in their best-selling book *Rethinking the Sales Force,* say that success no longer depends on merely communicating the value of products and services, but rather on the critical ability to create value. They state that value is created by making the purchase painless, convenient, and hassle-free, and that salespeople can create significant value by showing customers how to install and use the product.

option will become obvious to the customer.[33] In many selling situations, such factors as durability, comfort, or operating economy help justify the higher-priced product. A professional salesperson explains to the customer why it is in his or her best interest to spend "just a little more" and get the best value for their dollar. Most customers are more concerned with making the right purchase than they are with making the least expensive purchase.[34]

Preplan Your Service Strategy

Servicing the sale is a very important dimension of personal selling, so a certain amount of preplanning is essential. It helps to preplan your service strategy for each of the three areas we have discussed: follow-through, follow-up, and expansion selling. You cannot anticipate every aspect of the service, but you can preplan important ways to add value once the sale is implemented. Develop a servicing-the-sale worksheet, like the one shown in Figure 15.4, prior to each sales presentation.

Partnership-Building Strategies Should Encompass All Key People

Some salespeople do a great job of communicating with the prospect but ignore other key people involved in the sale. To illustrate how serious this problem can be, let us look at the

Method of Adding Value	What You Will Say or Do
Follow-Through	
Set up a secure website or Extranet so the client can track the production and delivery of custom-engineered seed research equipment.	Set up the secure website in a timely manner and then contact the customer when it is operational. Explain how to access the website and review the benefits of using this source of assistance.
Schedule training for persons who will be using the new technology.	Send the training schedule to the customer and confirm the dates with a follow-up call.
Follow-Up	
Send a thank-you letter to each member of the team who made the purchase decision.	Express sincere appreciation for the purchase and explain the steps you will take to ensure a long-term partnership.
Check to be certain that the training was effective.	Visit the customer's research facility and talk with the employees who completed the training. Answer questions and provide additional assistance as needed.
Expansion Selling	
Suggest the purchase of global positioning (GPS) technology to enhance use of seed research equipment.	"GPS technology will enable you to track all your research and plot the findings on your computer."

Figure 15.4 Servicing-the-sale worksheet
Follow-through on assurances and promises, customer follow-up, and expansion selling must be carefully planned. Use of this worksheet will help you preplan ways to add value.

approach used by Jill Bisignano, a sales representative for a major restaurant supply firm. Jill had called on Bellino's Italian Restaurant for several years. Although she was always very friendly to Nick Bellino, she treated the other employees with nearly total indifference. One day she called on Nick and was surprised to learn that he was retiring and had decided to sell his restaurant to two long-time employees. As you might expect, it did not take the new owners long to find another supplier. Jill lost a large account because she had failed to develop a good personal relationship with other key employees. It pays to be nice to everyone.

Here is a partial list of people in your company and in the prospect's company who can influence both initial and repeat sales:

1. *Receptionist.* Some salespeople simply do not use common sense when dealing with the receptionist. This person has daily contact with your customer and may schedule most or all calls. To repeatedly forget this individual's name or display indifference in other ways may cost you dearly.

2. *Technical personnel.* Some products must be cleaned, lubricated, or adjusted on a regular basis. Take time to get acquainted with the people who perform these duties. Answer their questions, share technical information with them if necessary, and show appreciation for the work they are doing.

3. *Stock clerks or receiving clerks.* People who work in the receiving room are often responsible for pricing incoming merchandise and making sure that these items are stored properly. They may also be responsible for stock rotation and processing damage claims.

4. *Management personnel.* Although you may be working closely with someone at the departmental or division level, do not forget the person who has the final authority and responsibility for this area. Spend time with management personnel occasionally and be alert to any concerns they may have.

This is not a complete list of the people you may need to depend on for support. There may be other key people who influence sales. Always look beyond the customer to see who else might influence the sale as partnerships can be built upon different levels of the organization.[35]

PARTNERING WITH AN UNHAPPY CUSTOMER

WE HAVE LEARNED THAT UNHAPPY CUSTOMERS GENERALLY DO NOT INITIATE A VERBAL OR written complaint. This means that postsale problems may not come to the attention of salespeople or other personnel within the organization. We also know that unhappy customers do share their negative experiences with other people. A dissatisfied customer will typically tell eight to ten people about their problem.[36] A double loss occurs when the customer stops buying your products and takes steps to discourage other people from buying them. When complaints surface, salespeople should view the problem as an opportunity to strengthen the business relationship. Conflict resolution is another aspect of problem solving important to the customer–salesperson relationship.[37] To achieve this goal, follow these suggestions:

1. *Give customers every opportunity to disclose their feelings.* Companies noted for outstanding customer service rely heavily on telephone systems, such as toll-free hotlines, to ensure easy access. At Federal Express, Cadillac Division of General Motors, and IBM—to name a few companies—specially trained advisers answer the calls and offer assistance. When a customer purchases a Ford vehicle, the salesperson introduces the customer to service staff who provide a key role in providing postsale service. The goal is to personalize the relationship with another member of the service team. Ford has discovered that after-sale contact builds a perception of value.[38] When customers do complain, by telephone or in person, encourage them to express all their anger and frustration. Do not interrupt. Do not become defensive. Do not make any judgments until you have heard all the facts as the customers see them. If they stop talking, try to get them to talk some more. How you deal with anger is very important. Encourage the angry customer to vent his or her feelings. By asking questions and listening carefully to the response, you can encourage the person to discuss the cause of the anger openly. After venting feelings and discussing specific details, the angry customer will expect a response. Briefly paraphrase what seems to be the major concern and express a sincere desire to find ways to solve the problem.[39]

2. *Keep in mind that it does not really matter whether a complaint is real or perceived.* If the customer is upset, you should be polite and sympathetic. Do not yield to the temptation to say, "You do not really have a problem." Remember, problems exist when customers perceive they exist.[40]

From the Field

When to Say Goodbye to a Customer

Today's salespeople often find that they must devote considerable time to establishing and building partnering relationships with important customers. Some salespeople are recognizing that they often have too many customers—or even some wrong customers—and are deciding to reduce their customer base selectively. Too many customers drain precious sales resources and endanger a salesperson's ability to serve his or her most important accounts. Wrong customers often demand customized products and services at prices so low they cannot be served profitably. Further, they frequently complain or demand a level of service that is unjustified for their current sales or future sales potential.

Jeff Multz, director of sales and marketing at FirstWave Technologies, found he was serving too many customers. He relates an example that occurred when he owned his own consulting business. He realized that 80 percent of his customers were a drain on his business, so he called 3000 of them to explain that he could no longer serve them. Partly as a result, his sales increased by 50 percent the next year, but his profit increased by 50 percent in just five months.

David Sutcliffe, CEO of Richmond, B.C.–based Sierra Wireless, found he was serving the wrong customers. He discovered the value of not focusing on price-sensitive customers who typically buy small quantities but demand special attention. He says, "I give them a competitor's name, phone number, or email address. I know they're thinking I'm out of my mind. But if your competitors are so busy choking on those small orders, you can focus on and win the more profitable opportunities."

There is a growing trend today for salespeople to focus more on territory profit than simply on sales.[d]

3. *Accept responsibility.* Avoid the temptation to blame the shipping department, the installation crew, or anyone else associated with your company. Never tear down the company you work for. The problem has been placed in your hands, and you must accept responsibility for handling it. "Passing the buck" will only leave the customer with a feeling of helplessness.

4. *Politely share with the customer your point of view concerning the problem's cause.* At least explain what you think happened. The customer deserves an explanation. At this point, a sincere apology is usually appropriate.

5. *Decide what action must be taken to remedy the problem.* Take action quickly and offer a value-added atonement. Don't just do what is expected; delight the customer by exceeding their expectations. Winning customer loyalty today means going beyond making it right.[41]

The value of customer complaints can emerge in two forms. First, complaints can be a source of important information that may be difficult to obtain by other means. Second, customer complaints provide unique opportunities for companies to *prove* their commitment to service. Loyalty builds in the customer's mind if you do a good job of solving his or her problem.[42]

A Word of Caution When you are dealing with major or minor customer service problems and an apology is necessary, do not use email. When a minor problem surfaces, call the customer personally. Do not delegate this task to someone else in your organization. If you need to apologize for a major problem that has occurred, meet with the customer in person. Schedule the meeting as soon as possible.[43]

REVIEWING KEY CONCEPTS

- Explain how to build long-term partnerships with customer service.

  Servicing the sale is a major dimension of the selling process, with the objectives of providing maximum customer satisfaction and establishing a long-term partnership. Servicing the sale encompasses a variety of activities that take place during and after the buying process. In this chapter, we present servicing the sale as a three-part process: follow-through on assurances and promises, follow-up with ongoing communication after the sale, and expansion selling.

- Describe current developments in customer service.

  In the new millennium, customer service has become a primary value-added function. Salespeople are in a unique position to enhance customer satisfaction and trust by displaying five important service behaviours: diligence, information communication, inducements, empathy, and sportsmanship.

- List and describe the major customer service methods that strengthen the partnership.

  A major key to an effective customer service strategy is follow-through on assurances and promises that were part of the sales presentation. Follow-through services may involve making credit arrangements, scheduling deliveries, monitoring installation, training in the use or care of the product, providing product updates, and similar services. Salespeople can also add value with a sincere expression of appreciation. Follow-up methods include personal visits, telephone calls, email messages, letters, or call reports.

  A salesperson depends on the support of many other people in servicing a sale. Maintaining good relationships with support staff members who help service your accounts is well worth the time and energy required.

- Explain how to add value with expansion selling.

  As the salesperson learns more about the customer, opportunities for expansion selling will arise. Expansion selling can take three forms: full-line selling, cross-selling, and upselling.

- Explain how to deal effectively with complaints.

  Dealing effectively with an unhappy customer should be thought of as an opportunity to strengthen the business relationship. Always give the customer every opportunity to disclose feelings. Encourage the angry customer to vent his or her feelings and listen closely to what is said. Briefly summarize what seems to be the major concern and express a sincere desire to find ways to solve the problem.

Key Terms

call report **376**

cross-selling **377**

customer service **364**

full-line selling (or suggestion selling) **376**

upselling **378**

value reinforcement **375**

Review Questions

1. You are currently a sales manager employed by a company that sells long-term care insurance. Tomorrow you will meet with five new sales trainees. Your major goal is to explain why it is important to service the sale. What important points will you cover?

2. Define *customer service*. List the three major activities associated with this phase of personal selling.

3. Explain how full-line selling fits into the definition of customer service. How does *full-line selling* differ from *cross-selling*?

4. List and describe three current developments in customer service.

5. Adding value with follow-through can involve several postsale services. List five possible services.

6. How does credit become part of servicing the sale?

7. This chapter describes the value of the lifetime customer. Is it realistic to believe that people will become lifetime customers in our very competitive marketplace?

8. Define *upselling* and explain how it can add value.

9. What types of customer service problems might be prevented with the use of a call report?

10. What are five things you should do when trying to re-establish a partnering relationship with a dissatisfied customer?

Application Exercises

1. You are a salesperson working in the paint department at a Canadian Tire store. A customer has just purchased 75 litres of house paint. Assume that your store carries everything in the painting line and list as many items as you can think of that could be used for expansion selling. Explain how your suggestions of these items could be a service to the customer.

2. You work as a wholesale salesperson for a plumbing supply company. One of your customers, a contractor, has an open line of credit with your company for $10 000 worth of products. He is currently at his limit; however, he is not overdue. He just received word that he has been awarded a $40 000 plumbing contract at the local airport. The contract requires that he supply $9000 worth of plumbing products. Your customer does not have the cash to pay for the additional products. He informs you that unless you can provide him with some type of financing, he may lose the contract. He says he can pay you when he finishes his next job in 60 days. Explain what you will do.

3. You have just interviewed for a job that you would really like to have. You have heard that it is a good idea to follow up an interview with a thank-you note or letter and an indication of your enthusiasm for the position. Select the strategy you will use for your follow-up and explain why you chose it.

4. Using your search engine, examine the Internet for information on customer satisfaction. Type in "customer satisfaction + selling." Are you surprised by the number of queries on this subject? Examine some of the queries related to what customers have said about specific company customer service programs. Be prepared to discuss some of what you find in class.

5. *Buyer remorse* was explained in Chapter 14. It is a common response customers have after making an important purchase. You are a salesperson who has been very successful selling cars to young families. Knowing that buyer remorse is a common response, how can you use this to help service a sale and build a partnership? Explain.

ROLE-PLAY EXERCISE

Visit the role play/simulation materials provided in the Student Resources section of your companion website at **www.pearsoncanada.ca/manning**. A *Contents page lists appropriate page references for the activities.*

An important aspect of personal selling is the need to add value with follow-through and follow-up. Both of these account management activities can be time-consuming, especially if the salesperson is not skilled at setting up appointments that fit into a busy schedule. In this role play, you are to set up three follow-through meetings with a customer who has just purchased conference services from the convention centre you represent. First, you must contact your client three days from today to confirm the availability of the Revolving Platform Room (see Partnership Selling, p. 47) for the meeting of 300 people. Second, you must contact this same client a week from today to get approval on the number of chicken Wellington banquet-style dinners needed (see Partnership Selling, p. 15, and Guarantees on p. 25). And, third, because your client isn't sure about the need for a microphone (see Partnership Selling, pp. 21–22), you need to call your client the day before the meeting, which is scheduled four weeks from today, to verify whether you or your client will supply a microphone.

Equipped with a calendar, you should establish dates and times when your client will be available to talk or meet with you. Before you meet with your client, plan to recommend at least two times of the day that fit into your schedule for each of your meetings. If your client cannot meet at either of these times, ask your client to recommend a time. Do not start out by asking when your client is available because this could conflict with your busy schedule. Write the agreed-on times and dates in your calendar, suggesting your client do the same, so there will be no misunderstandings. Because these dates are deadlines, suggest that your client call you back if, for some reason, the schedule changes. Inform your client that you will plan to be at the hotel when the client's meeting starts and that you will be available to make sure everything is properly scheduled. Give your client your phone number and email address and ask him or her to contact you if there are any questions between now and the meeting date. Have another student role-play the customer and, after the role play, assess your customer service.

CASE PROBLEM

WFS Ltd., introduced in the opening vignette, is one of Canada's most respected industrial distributors. Many customers remain loyal to WFS because they value outstanding service; a broad range of industrial, automotive, and construction products; and a supplier that will work closely with them to solve their buying problems. The success of WFS can be traced to a number of factors:

- *A desire to build as many relationships and the strongest relationships possible with all customers.* WFS frequently moves employees to new positions within the company: A warehouse person may become an outside salesperson and later be transferred to inside sales; an outside salesperson may be transferred to purchasing or back to inside sales. (Rick Thurston, now president, began as a driver/delivery person at the Leamington branch in 1984.) This creates maximum flexibility within the company but, more importantly, means that inside salespeople know the difficulties that outside salespeople face, and they often have personal contacts within customer firms. It also means that outside salespeople have had the benefit of training and learning while in the warehouse and on the inside sales desk. As a result, customers frequently have strong relationships with and trust in several WFS employees who they know can help them.

- *A strong belief that work should be rewarding for all employees.* "Employee happiness is very important to us. Happy employees help build positive relationships with customers," says Rick Thurston. Employees share many experiences, from going to major sporting events to having company parties and picnics. Twice, for example, all of the employees shared an expense-paid trip to Las Vegas. The company also sponsors many community events and encourages volunteerism among its employees. There is an excellent employee benefits package, which includes education

and recreation allowances. This employee investment has been rewarded many times over. At one point, the company had gone four years without a single absentee day. Employees even provide important input on management. In fact, a management committee, including the president, is elected each year.

- *An investment in customer service and a strong service culture.* The company has invested in computer equipment and programming and is able to tell customers immediately how much inventory it has and where that inventory is located. Purchasing, payables, invoicing, receivables, account profiles, sales and other financial reports, and vehicle maintenance schedules are all computerized. Employees are empowered to make decisions whenever customer service is an issue. On one occasion, two employees took a company van and left Windsor to get some material in Pittsburgh, Pennsylvania, for a customer who urgently needed it, and they returned immediately with the material. If a customer calls to order something that is urgently needed but the delivery truck has left for the day, the customer is never told to wait for the next delivery. Someone else within the company will see that the order gets delivered.

- *A willingness to experiment and grow to meet changing customer needs.* In 2008, WFS acquired Keep Industrial Supply, which provided three new locations, and its customer relationships and business solutions complemented those of WFS. With the addition of the South Carolina operation, the company now has 10 branches and numerous on-site customer integrated-supply agreements. Many WFS customers now check inventory, place orders, or check order status online. The company has also established commodity management programs with its best customers, whereby it manages all of the general supply items for these companies. WFS is always willing to add items to its inventory for customers who will buy them, and an increasing number of customers are taking advantage of this service.[44]

Questions

1. How might a WFS salesperson add value with full-line selling? Cross-selling?

2. What types of follow-through activities and follow-up calls should WFS salespeople be prepared to initiate? How can inside salespeople be used to help maintain value-added customer relationships?

3. How can commodity management programs and other special inventory management programs be used to add value for WFS? How can such programs contribute to the company's long-term success?

4. Assume that you have just received a phone call from an important customer who says, "We just received a shipment that is needed urgently, but there are some problems with it. We need you to take some action fast." What will you do? Be specific. How might you partner with this unhappy customer?

PARTNERSHIP SELLING: A ROLE PLAY/SIMULATION

Visit the role play/simulation materials provided in the Student Resources section of your companion website at **www.pearsoncanada.ca/manning**. *A contents page lists the appropriate page references for the activities.*

Developing a Sales Presentation Strategy—Servicing the Sale

Refer to *Sales Memorandum 3* and strategically plan to service the sale with your customer. After closing the sale—getting the customer's signature—there are several steps to take in order to add value and build customer confidence and satisfaction. These steps are important to providing total quality customer service and should provide for repeat sales and a list of referred customers.

Following the instructions in item 2g of your presentation plan, you need to schedule a future appointment to telephone or personally call and confirm the number of people attending the convention, as well as the final room and menu needs (see the convention centre policies). Also during this conversation you might suggest beverages for breaks, audiovisual needs, and any other items that will make this an outstanding convention for your customer.

You should have your calendar available to suggest and write down dates and times for this future contact. Any special materials, such as a calendar, can be placed in the back pocket of your portfolio. You may want to ask another person to be your customer and practise the customer service strategies you have prepared.

At this point, you should be strategically prepared to make the presentation to your customer as outlined in *Sales Memorandum 3*. Your instructor will provide you with further instructions.

PART V
ROLE-PLAY EXERCISE
Developing a Presentation Strategy
SCENARIO

This role play is a continuation of the Part IV role-play exercise. You recently met with Gabriela Ansari,

founder and chief executive officer of Cantrol Security Inc. The purpose of the first sales call was to begin the relationship-building process and present selected value-added guest services and amenities offered by the Park Inn International Hotel and Convention Centre. You also obtained some information regarding the customer's buying process.

CUSTOMER PROFILE

Prior to starting Cantrol Security, Gabriela Ansari spent 12 years working in sales and sales management at General Electric Corporation (GE), described by *Fortune* magazine as America's most admired company. Working for GE was a great learning experience for Gabriela, who is trying to apply the GE success formula to Cantrol Security. She is the classic extravert, a person who combines high sociability and high dominance.

SALESPERSON PROFILE

You are new to the field of selling, but you are a quick learner. The first visit with Gabriela Ansari went well, and now she is preparing for the second sales call. Gabriela is planning a large banquet to recognize her employees but has not yet selected a location for this event. While working for GE, Gabriela attended more than 25 business conferences and was disappointed by many of them. Too often, they were held at look-alike hotels that served bland food typically served by poorly trained waiters who displayed little enthusiasm. You took notes throughout the meeting and will address these concerns during the second sales call.

PRODUCT

The Park Inn is a full-service hotel and convention centre. After completion of a recent $2.8 million renovation, the Park Inn received the Excellence in Renovation Design Award from the Ontario Architectural Association.

INSTRUCTIONS

The first sales call was basically an informative presentation. Near the end of the visit, Gabriela Ansari did disclose her plans for a large recognition banquet to be held on October 25, the company's second anniversary. No other information was provided, but Gabriela agreed to a second meeting to be held the following week.

Based on the information collected during the first call, you are now planning a persuasive presentation that will involve the first three steps of the six-step presentation plan (see Fig. 15.1). At the office of Gabriela Ansari—to be role-played by another student—you will need to re-establish the relationship and then initiate the agenda approach (see Chapter 10). Begin the presentation with appropriate survey, probing, and confirmation questions. These questions should be preplanned using information found in Chapter 11.

As the need discovery phase of the presentation progresses, the customer's buying criteria or buying conditions should surface. Prior to the second sales call, you should also select and be prepared to demonstrate appropriate selling tools (proof devices). A variety of selling tools suitable for reproduction can be found in "Partnership Selling: A Role Play/Simulation" online in the Student Resource section at **www.pearsoncanada.ca/manning**. Ensure that you preplan feature/benefit selling statements that appeal to Gabriela Ansari's needs. The importance of selling specific benefits and obtaining customer reactions cannot be overemphasized (see Chapter 11).

A major objective of the second sales call is to move the sale forward by convincing Gabriela Ansari that the Park Inn offers an outstanding combination of value-added guest services and amenities and is prepared to meet her needs. The sale will not be closed during the second call, but you will try to obtain a commitment to prepare a formal sales proposal to be presented to Gabriela Ansari within 48 hours. (See Partnership Selling, p. 45, on your companion website for a sample sales proposal form.)

Part VI
Management of Self and Others

The primary cause of success in life is the ability to set and achieve goals. That's why the people who do not have goals are doomed forever to work for those who do. You either work to achieve your own goals or you work to achieve someone else's goals.

—Brian Tracy

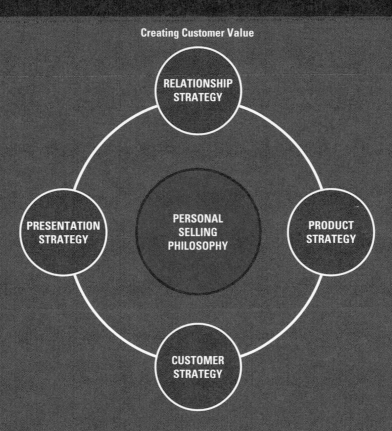

Creating Customer Value

RELATIONSHIP STRATEGY

PRESENTATION STRATEGY

PERSONAL SELLING PHILOSOPHY

PRODUCT STRATEGY

CUSTOMER STRATEGY

Personal selling requires a great deal of self-discipline and self-direction. Chapter 16 examines the four dimensions of opportunity management. The final chapter examines the fundamentals of sales force management.

Chapter 16
Opportunity Management: The Key to Greater Sales Productivity

Learning Objectives

After studying this chapter, you should be able to

1 Discuss the four dimensions of opportunity management.

2 List and describe time management strategies.

3 Explain factors that contribute to improved territory management.

4 Identify and discuss common elements of a records management system.

5 Discuss stress management practices.

Introduction

Many of the best salespeople we know had no intention of pursuing a career in sales, but had experiences early in their lives that helped them develop personality traits and abilities that have certainly contributed to their success. During her school years, Paula Shannon acted in plays, practised public speaking, and participated in a number of competitive sports, most notably gymnastics. She spent a year studying in Belgium, where she learned to adapt to another culture and social setting and learned a third language. Paula now speaks six languages.

Paula credits managing a large paper route at a young age with helping to teach her about responsibility. Later, she worked as a waitress, did some interpretation on a tour bus, sold clothing and other retail items, and spent a summer in customer service for a large commercial waste management firm. In Europe, Paula worked as a management trainee for Berlitz International. This program helped give her a solid grounding in general business: operations, finance, accounting, human resources, and sales. Following her management training, Paula Shannon began to handle sales for several Berlitz language centres. Paula says her belief and confidence in the product she was selling was evident. She credits her boss at the time, Anita Komlos, whom she describes as "one of the most natural and effective salespeople I have ever known," with helping her learn how to probe effectively and how to know when to "shut up."

Paula Shannon has managed to learn something of value from everything she has done. She is clearly focused on managing herself and her career. Today, Paula Shannon is senior vice president and chief sales officer for Boston-based Lionbridge Technologies, Inc. She manages its global sales force of 70 from her home office in Montreal.[1]

Most people who achieve success in selling have a strong work ethic. They are "self-starters" who are committed to achieving their personal and professional goals.

OPPORTUNITY MANAGEMENT—
A FOUR-DIMENSIONAL PROCESS

WHAT MAKES A SALESPERSON SUCCESSFUL? SOME PEOPLE BELIEVE THE MOST IMPORTANT factor is hard work. This is only partly true. Some people work hard but do not accomplish much. They lack purpose and direction. This lack of organization results in wasted time and energy. Hard work must be preceded by careful planning. Every moment spent planning, according to some experts in self-management, saves three or four moments in execution.[2]

Wasting time and energy is the slippery slope to failure in the age of information. Many salespeople are drowning in information and the flood of messages each day leaves little time to think and reflect. Sales and sales support personnel, like most other knowledge workers, are working under tighter deadlines. The response time to customer inquiries has been shortened and customers are less tolerant of delays. Thus, prioritizing different sales force decisions becomes important to managing productivity.[3]

As pressures build, it's easy to overlook opportunities to identify prospects, make sales, and improve service to customers. The ability to perceive opportunities and seize them is an important characteristic of high-achieving salespeople.[4] **Opportunity management** should be viewed as a four-dimensional process consisting of the following components:

opportunity management
A four-dimensional process consisting of time, territory, records, and stress management.

1. *Time management.* There are only about 250 business days per year. Within each day, there is only so much time to devote to selling. Selling hours are extremely valuable. When salespeople are asked to evaluate the major challenges they face in their work, "Not enough time" is often rated number one. Dealing with information overload and achieving balance in life are also major challenges.

sales territory A group of customers and prospective customers assigned to a single salesperson.

2. *Territory management.* A **sales territory** is a group of customers and prospective customers assigned to a single salesperson. Every territory is unique. Some territories consist of one or two cities or counties, while others encompass several provinces. The number of accounts within each territory also vary. Today, territory management is becoming less of an art and more of a science.

3. *Records management.* Every salesperson must maintain a certain number of records. These records help to "systematize" data collection and storage. A wise salesperson never relies on memory. Some of the most common records include planning calendars, prospect forms, call reports, summary reports, and expense reports.

4. *Stress management.* A certain amount of stress comes with any selling position. Some salespeople have learned how to take stressful situations in stride. Others allow stress to trigger anger and frustration. Learning to cope with various stressors that surface in the daily life of a salesperson is an important part of the self-management process.

TIME MANAGEMENT

A SALESPERSON CAN INCREASE SALES VOLUME IN TWO MAJOR WAYS. ONE IS BY IMPROVING selling effectiveness, and the other is by spending more time in face-to-face selling situations. The latter objective can best be achieved through improved time and territory management.

Improving the management of both time and territory is a high priority in the field of selling. These two closely related functions represent major challenges for salespeople.

Let us first look closely at time management. There is definitely a close relationship between sales volume and number of customer contacts made by the salesperson. You have to make calls to get results.

Time-Consuming Activities

Some salespeople who have kept careful records of how they spend their time each day are surprised to learn how little they spend in face-to-face selling situations. A national survey of 1500 salespeople from 13 industries found that on average, salespeople spend 60 percent of their time on administrative duties or travel.[5] Administrative duties can include such things as completion of sales records and time spent on customer follow-through and follow-up. Salespeople need to examine carefully each of these activities and determine whether too much or too little time is spent in any area. One way to assess time use is to keep a time log. This involves recording, at the end of every hour, the activities in which you were engaged during that time.[6] At the end of the week, add up the number of minutes spent on the various activities and ask yourself, "Is this the best use of my time?" Once you have tabulated the results of your time log, it should be easy to identify the "time wasters." Pick one or two of the most wasteful areas, and then make plans to correct the problem. Set realistic goals that can be achieved. Keep in mind that wasting time is usually a habit. To manage your time more effectively, you need to form new habits. Changing habits is hard work, but it can be done.[7]

Managing His Time to Manage His Personal Self-Development

Alex Pettes believes in the power of personal goals and self-development. As a 35-year-old vice president of sales and marketing, he set a personal goal to become company president by age 40. Four months before his fortieth birthday, he achieved his goal. Many who know Alex were not surprised. Alex has his own personal mission statement that he repeats to himself three times each day. He is a strong believer in and continually practises self-development: physically, spiritually, socially, and academically. He believes that education does not end with a degree, and he has two of them.

Early in his career, Alex decided he didn't have a lifetime to get a lifetime of experience, but he found a solution: read books by people who have spent their time and effort to present their experiences and philosophies to others. Alex says, "By reading books, you bypass all the tons of earth that was required to be mined to get at the ounce of gold, the few nuggets of wisdom that it took others years to learn."

Alex's advice: Get out of bed twenty minutes earlier than usual and spend that time reading books related to your job, your industry, or your personal self-development. Early in the morning, your mind is fresh, and you will find that the routine quickly becomes an important part of your life. People who do this will, over a year, read 15 to 20 books. Chances are good that your peers and competitors are not doing this, so you will quickly out-distance them with knowledge and new ideas.

Alex says, "I consider myself Alex Pettes Inc., a personal services corporation dedicated to maximizing the income and potential of Alex Pettes. I am committed to investing in my own business (myself and my personal development) regardless of whether my employer or someone else is doing it." After all, he adds, "Who cares more about you than you?"[a]

Time Management Methods

Sound time-management methods can pave the way to greater sales productivity. The starting point is forming a new attitude toward time conservation. You must view time as a scarce resource not to be wasted.[8] The time-saving strategies presented here are not new, nor are they unique. Time-conscious people in all walks of life are using them.

Develop a Series of Personal Goals According to Alan Lakein, author of *How to Get Control of Your Time and Your Life*, the most important aspect of time management is knowing what your goals are. He is referring to all goals—career goals, family goals, and life goals. People who cannot or do not sit down and write out exactly what they want from life lack direction. Brian Tracy, who developed the "Law of Direction" says, "Your ability to set clear, specific goals will do more to guarantee you higher levels of success and achievement than any other single skill or quality."[9]

The goal-setting process requires that you be clear about what you want to accomplish. If your goal is too general or vague, progress toward achieving that goal is difficult to observe. Goals such as "I want to be a success" or "I desire good health" are much too general. The major principles that encompass goal setting are outlined in Table 16.1.

Goals have a great deal of psychological value to people in selling. Sales goals, for example, can serve as a strong motivational force. To illustrate, let us assume that Mary Paulson, sales representative for a cosmetic manufacturer, decides to increase her sales by 15 percent over the previous year. She now has a clear goal to aim for and can begin identifying specific steps to achieve the new goal.

Mary Paulson has established a long-term goal as part of a yearly plan. Some goals require considerable time and should be part of a one-year plan. Next, Mary should set

Table 16.1 Goal-Setting Principles
The following goal-setting principles give you the power to take control of the present and the future.
1. *Reflect on the things you want to change in your life.* Then prepare written goals that are specific, measurable, and realistic.
2. *Develop a written goal-setting plan that includes the steps necessary to achieve the goal.* Review your plan daily—repetition increases the probability of success.
3. *Modify your environment by changing the stimuli around you.* This may involve finding a mentor or spending less time with persons who are negative.
4. *Monitor your behaviour, and reward your progress.* Reinforcement from yourself and/or others is necessary for change.
Source: Barry L. Reece and Rhonda Brandt, *Effective Human Relations: Personal and Organizational Applications,* Boston: Houghton Mifflin Company, 2005. Reprinted by permission of the publisher.

aside an hour or so at the end of each month to decide what she wants to accomplish during the coming month. Weekly planning is also important. Once a week—Friday is a good time—set goals for the next week and develop a plan for reaching them. Finally, Mary should develop a daily plan.[10]

Figure 16.1 Daily to-do list
A daily list of activities can help a salesperson set priorities and save time.

Prepare a Daily To-Do List Sales professionals who complete the time management course offered by FranklinCovey are encouraged to engage in event control. This involves planning and prioritizing events every day.[11] Start each day by thinking about what you want to accomplish. Then write down the activities (Fig. 16.1). Putting your thoughts on paper (or in your computer) forces you to clarify your thinking. Investment firm regional director Heather Gardner records her daily planned activities in her BlackBerry and Microsoft Outlook calendar. On a typical day, the BlackBerry will show entries for every half hour. Gardner works through her detailed to-do list by adhering to one unshakable rule: Avoid nonpaying activities during working hours.[12]

Now you should prioritize your "to-do" list; do not let outside distractions interfere with your plan. Begin each day with the highest-priority task.

Maintain a Planning Calendar Ideally, a salesperson needs a single place to record daily personal and business appointments, deadlines, and tasks. Unfortunately, many salespeople write daily tasks and appointments on any slip of paper they can find: backs of envelopes, business cards, napkins, or Post-it notes. Hyrum W. Smith, author of *The 10 Natural Laws of Successful Time and Life Management,* calls these pieces of paper "floaters." They just float around until you either follow through on them or lose them. It's a terribly disorganized method for someone who wants to gain greater control of his or her life.[13] The use of floaters often leads to the loss of critical information, missed appointments, and lack of focus. Select a planning calendar design (the FranklinCovey Day Planner is one option) that can bring efficiency to your daily planning efforts. You should be able to determine at a glance what is coming up in the days and weeks ahead (Fig. 16.2).

personal digital assistant A small, personal device that stores information and provides many of the features common to laptop computers.

Many salespeople use a **personal digital assistant** (PDA) to organize information. Small, pocket-size PDAs, such as those available from Apple or BlackBerry, offer many of the features common to laptop computers. The salesperson can send and receive emails or

June 2011

	MAY 2011		JULY 2011
	S M T W T F S		S M T W T F S
	31 ... 1 2		... 1 2 3 4
	3 4 5 6 7 8 9		5 6 7 8 9 10 11
	10 11 12 13 14 15 16		12 13 14 15 16 17 18
	17 18 19 20 21 22 23		19 20 21 22 23 24 25
	24 25 26 27 28 29 30		26 27 28 29 30 31

NOTES

SUNDAY	MONDAY	TUESDAY	WEDNESDAY	THURSDAY	FRIDAY	SATURDAY
	1	**2** 10:30 Wheat First Securities 12:00 Lunch with Roy Williams 3:00 Farrell's Service Centre	**3** 9:00 Demonstration at Ryerson University 11:00 Demo at Mills, Inc. 3:30 Meet with Helen Sisson	**4** 9:00 Austin & Son Storage 10:30 Demo at CMP Sporting Goods 1:00 Attend Computer Trade Show	**5** 9:00 Sales Meeting at Holiday Inn 1:30 Demo at Omega Homes	**6** 10:00 Take Dana to soccer game
7	**8** 8:00 to 12:00 Sales Training 1:30 Meet with M.I.S. staff at Mohawk College	**9** 9:30 Park Realty 11:00 White Tire Service 2:00 Demo at Ritter Seafood	**10** 9:00 Demonstration at Ross accounting services 11:00 Prospecting 2:30 Meet with technical support staff	**11** 8:30 Meet with Helen Hunt 12:00 Lunch with Tim 1:00 Demo at Collins Wholesale 4:00 Parent-Teacher conference	**12** 9:00 Demo at Seneca College 1:00 to 5:00 Update sales records	**13** 9:00 10-K run (starts at YMCA building)
14	**15**	**16**	**17**	**18**	**19**	**20**

Figure 16.2 Monthly planning calendar sample

Shown are 11 days of a monthly planning calendar for a computer service sales representative. Monthly planning calendars such as this one are now a key function of most CRM systems.

text messages and download important customer information. Salespeople can also input their customer notes immediately after a sales call. The PDA also serves as an electronic memo pad, calendar, expense log, address book, and more. These organizers can be used to keep track of appointments and serve as a perpetual calendar.

Organize Your Selling Tools You can save valuable time by finding ways to organize sales literature, business cards, order blanks, samples, and other items needed during a sales call. You may waste time on a callback because some item was not available during your first call. You may even lose a sale because you forgot or misplaced a key selling tool.

If you have a great deal of paperwork, invest in one or more file cabinets. Some salespeople purchase small, lightweight cardboard file boxes to keep their materials organized. These boxes can easily be placed in your car trunk and moved from one sales call to another. The orderly arrangement of selling tools is just one more method of time conservation.

The key to regular use of the four time-saving techniques already described is *commitment*. Unless you are convinced that efficient time management is important, you will probably find it difficult to adopt these new habits. A salesperson who fully accepts the "time is money" philosophy will use these techniques routinely.

Saving Time with Meetings in Cyberspace and Other Methods of Communication

As the cost of travel increases, more and more salespeople are asking the question, "Is this trip necessary?" Instead of travelling to a customer's office, some salespeople schedule a telephone conference call. A modern alternative to this type of conference call is a meeting in cyberspace. The voice of each meeting participant travels over a phone line and attendees view visuals—PowerPoint presentations—on their desktop computers. Nerac Inc., an information-services company, often schedules Web conferences for potential customers. The sales representative can bring online a Nerac researcher who presents an introduction to the company's closely guarded databases. Clients get to watch the researcher at work over the Internet.[14]

Some customers actually prefer telephone contact for certain types of business transactions. Here are some situations in which the phone call is appropriate.

- Call the customer in advance to make an appointment. You will save time and the customer will know when to expect you.

- Use the telephone to keep the customer informed. A phone call provides instant communication with customers at a low cost.

- Build customer goodwill with a follow-up phone call. Make it a practice to call customers to thank them for buying your product and to determine whether the customer is satisfied with the purchase.

Some customers prefer to be contacted by email, and it would be a mistake to ignore their preference. Busy people often discourage telephone calls to minimize interruptions.

Voice-mail telephone systems are now being used by companies of all sizes. These systems not only answer the phone and take messages but also provide information-retrieval systems that are accessible by telephone. This technology is especially useful for salespeople who need to exchange information with others. For many salespeople, the cell

With the aid of fax machines and computer scanning equipment, salespeople can send and receive documents in seconds. Hard-copy documents are often needed to move the sales process to a successful outcome.

phone has become a convenient and time-saving sales tool. A pager also can be used to facilitate communication with customers and the main office.

Fax machines and computer scanning equipment take telecommunication a step further. With this equipment, salespeople can send and receive documents in seconds, using standard cable or telephone lines. Detailed designs, charts, and graphs can be transmitted across the country or around the world.

TERRITORY MANAGEMENT

MANY MARKETING ORGANIZATIONS HAVE FOUND IT HELPFUL TO BREAK DOWN THE TOTAL market into manageable units called sales territories. As noted earlier in this chapter, a *sales territory* is the geographic area where prospects and customers reside. While some firms have developed territories solely on the basis of geographic considerations, a more common approach is to establish a territory on the basis of classes of customers. Territories are often classified according to sales potential. Some marketers assign sales representatives to key industries. The *Ottawa Citizen* newspaper divides its customer base into major business lines, such as real estate and automotive.[15] Regardless of how the sales territory is established, it is essentially a specific number of present and potential accounts that can be called on conveniently and economically. Although uncontrollable by the salesperson, it is acknowledged by managers and researchers as an important factor in enabling salespeople to perform well.[16]

What Does Territory Management Involve?

To appreciate fully the many facets of territory management, it will be helpful to examine a typical selling situation. Put yourself in the shoes of a salesperson who has just accepted a position with a firm that manufactures a line of high-quality tools. You are responsible for a territory that covers Manitoba and Saskatchewan, which includes 88 auto supply firms that carry your line of tools. It also includes 38 stores that do not carry your tools. On the basis of this limited information, how would you carry out your selling duties? To answer this question, it will be necessary to follow these steps:

Step 1: Classify All Customers. Salespeople often divide their territory by area code, by industry, by product, or by projected sales volume. Always divide your territory in a way that makes sense.[17] If you classify customers according to potential sales volume, then you must answer two questions: What is the dollar amount of the firm's current purchases? What amount of additional sales might be developed with greater selling effort? Store A may be purchasing $3000 worth of tools each year, but potential sales for this firm amount to $5000. Store B currently purchases $2000 worth of tools a year, and potential sales amount to $2500. In this example, store A clearly deserves more time than store B.

It is important to realize that a small number of accounts may provide a majority of the sales volume.[18] Many companies get 75 to 80 percent of their sales volume from 20 to 25 percent of their total number of customers. The problem lies in accurately identifying which accounts and prospects fall into the top 20 to 25 percent category. Once this information is available, you can develop customer classification data that can be used to establish the frequency of calls and the level of resources to be allocated to these customers.[19] Jennifer Kline, a pharmaceutical salesperson employed by Schering-Plough's animal care division, gives a high priority to loyal customers. Kline says, "The people who are writing for you will continue to write for you if you serve them well."[20]

The typical sales territory is constantly changing, so the realignment of territories from time to time is necessary. One division of AT&T uses MapInfo ProAlign software to realign its sales territories. Accounts are segmented based on industry, size, dollar volume, and complexity. The sales manager enters a variety of account information and then produces maps that show accounts in different configurations.[21]

Step 2: Develop a Routing and Scheduling Plan. Many salespeople have found that travel is one of their most time-consuming nonselling activities. A great deal of time can also be wasted just waiting to see a customer. The primary objective of a sales routing and scheduling plan is to increase actual selling by reducing time spent travelling between accounts and waiting to see customers.

If a salesperson called on only established accounts and spent the same amount of time with each customer, routing and scheduling would not be difficult. In most cases, however, you need to consider other variables. For example, you may be expected to develop new accounts on a regular basis. In this case, you must adjust your schedule to accommodate calls on prospects. Another variable involves customer service. Some salespeople devote considerable time to adjusting warranty claims, solving customer problems, and paying goodwill visits.

Selling Today

Balancing Career and Family

Women today know that they will probably be working for pay for part or all of their adult lives. Most will also perform multiple roles that can be stressful and tiring. Many women who work full-time in sales also assume the responsibilities of wife and mother. Ellyn Foltz, vice president of sales and marketing for Dataline Incorporated, maintains a fully equipped personal computer (PC) and Internet hookup at her home. She gets up early and usually spends about 90 minutes on her work while family members are eating breakfast. In the evening, she logs on and completes two or three hours of work after her son is in bed. Foltz has structured her life so that she does not have to make "impossible choices" between work and family. She turned down a high-profile job that would have required constant travel.

Jill Doran, director of national accounts for National Car Rental, says that her employer gives her the tools and support she needs to maintain balance in her life. She took maternity leave for each of her children and now has the freedom to work from her home part of each week. When she is at home, Doran checks her voice mail and email frequently to be sure she is responsive to each of her national accounts. She records everything in her daytimer to avoid work–family conflicts.

As women struggle to balance career and family choices, many employers are doing more to help. Women, as well as men, who work in sales, often have the option of spending part of every week working from home.[b]

There are no precise rules to observe in establishing a sales routing and scheduling plan, but the following guiding principles apply to nearly all selling situations:

1. Obtain or create a map of your territory and mark the location of present accounts with pins or a marking pen. Each account might be colour-coded according to sales potential. This will give you a picture of the entire territory. Many companies are using mapping software to create a territory picture that can be viewed on the computer screen. With the aid of TerrAlign (www.terralign.com) mapping software, salespeople can align sales territories by account size or geography, analyze sales information, generate maps and reports, and produce territory recommendations.[22]

2. If your territory is geographically quite large, consider dividing it into smaller areas. Postal codes provide one option. You can then plan work in terms of several trading areas that make up the entire territory.

3. Develop a routing plan for a specific period of time. This might be a one- or two-week period. Once the plan is firm, notify customers of your anticipated arrival time by phone, letter, or email.

4. Develop a schedule that accommodates your customers' needs. Some customers appreciate getting calls on a certain day of the week or at a certain hour of the day. Try to schedule your calls in accordance with their wishes.

5. Think ahead and establish one or more tentative calls in case you have some extra time. If your sales calls take less time than expected or if there is an unexpected cancellation, you need optional calls to fill the void.

6. Decide how frequently to call on the basis of sales potential. Give the greatest attention to the most profitable customers. Many salespeople use the 80/20 rule. They spend 80 percent of their time calling on the most productive customers and 20 percent calling on smaller accounts and prospects.[23]

Sales Call Plans

sales call plan A plan developed with information taken from the routing and scheduling plan. The primary purpose of the plan is to ensure efficient and effective account coverage.

You can use information from the routing and scheduling plan to develop a **sales call plan.** This proposal is a weekly action plan, usually initiated by the sales manager. Its primary purpose is to ensure efficient and effective account coverage.

The form most sales managers use is similar to the one shown in Figure 16.3. One section of the form is used to record planned calls. A parallel section is for completed calls. Additional space is provided for the names of firms called on.

The sales manager usually presents the sales call plan to individual members of the sales staff. The plan's success depends on how realistic the goals are in the eyes of the

Sales Call Plan

Salesperson _____   For week ending _____

Territory _____   Days worked _____

Planned Calls	**Total Completed Calls**
Number of planned calls _____	Number of calls only _____
Number of planned presentations _____	Number of presentations _____
Number of planned telephone calls _____	Number of telephone calls _____
Account Category Planning	Number of orders _____
A. Account calls _____	Total km travelled _____
B. Account calls _____	A. Account calls _____
C. Account calls _____	B. Account calls _____
	C. Account calls _____

Companies called on	Address	Date	Customer rating	Comments about call

Figure 16.3 Sales call plan
The sales call plan is part of most CRM systems and is sent electronically.

sales staff, how persuasive the sales manager is, and what type of training accompanies the plan's introduction. It is not unusual for members of the sales force to respond with comments such as, "My territory is different," "Do not put me in a procedural straitjacket," or "My territory cannot be organized." The sales manager must not only present the plan in a convincing manner but also provide training that helps each salesperson implement the plan successfully.

RECORDS MANAGEMENT

ALTHOUGH SOME SALESPEOPLE COMPLAIN THAT PAPERWORK IS TOO TIME-CONSUMING AND reduces the amount of time available for actual selling, others recognize that accurate, up-to-date records actually save time. Their work is better organized and quick accessibility of information often makes it possible to close more sales and improve customer service.[24]

A good record-keeping system gives salespeople useful information with which to check their own progress. For instance, an examination of the sales call plan at the end of the day provides a review of who was called on and what was accomplished. The company also benefits from complete and accurate records. Reports from the field help management make important decisions. A company with a large sales force operating throughout a wide geographic area relies heavily on information sent to the main office.

Common Records Kept by Salespeople

A good policy is never to require a record that is not absolutely necessary. The only records worth keeping are those that provide positive benefits to the customer, the salesperson, or the personnel who work in sales-supporting areas of the company. Each record should be brief, easy to complete, and free of requests for useless detail. Where possible, the format should provide for the use of check marks as a substitute for written responses. Completing sales record forms should not be a major burden.

What records should you keep? The answer to this question will vary depending on the type of selling position. Some of the records most commonly kept by salespeople are described in this section.

Customer and Prospect Files Most salespeople find it helpful to keep records of customers and prospects. Each of these files has space for name, address, telephone and fax numbers, and email address. Other information recorded might be the buyer's personal characteristics, the names of people who might influence the purchase, or appropriate times to make calls. Most salespeople have replaced their card files with computerized record systems.

Call Reports The call report (also called an *activity report*) is a variation of the sales call plan described earlier in this chapter. It is used to record information about the people on whom you have called and what took place. The call report is one of the most basic records used in the field of selling. It provides a summary of what happened during the call and an indication of what future action is required. The call reports (daily and weekly) featured in Figure 16.4 are typical of those used in the field.

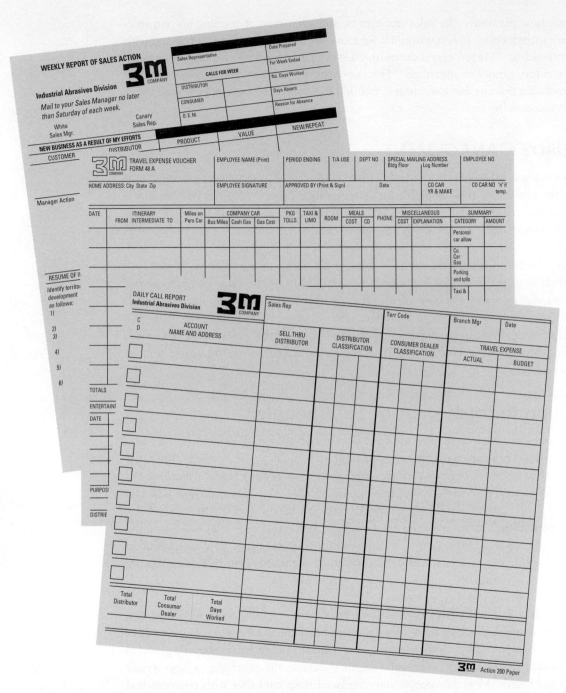

Figure 16.4 Call report, expense voucher, and weekly sales report
These are three of the records most commonly kept by 3M salespeople.

We are seeing less emphasis on call reports that require only numbers (e.g., calls made each day, number of proposals written). With increased interest in customer relationship management and customer databases, companies are putting more emphasis on collecting information that will expand the customer's profile and provide knowledge on current buying behaviour and short- and long-range buying plans.

Expense Records Both your company and the government agencies that monitor business expenses will require a record of selling expenses. These usually include such items as meals, lodging, travel, and, in some cases, entertainment expenses. Several expense-reporting software packages are now available to streamline the expense-reporting process. Automated expense reports save the salesperson a great deal of time and allow expenses to be reimbursed while the salesperson is still on the road.

Sales Records The records used to report sales vary greatly in design. Some companies require daily reports, others weekly ones. As you would expect, one primary use of the sales report is to analyze salespeople's performance.

You can take certain steps to improve a reporting system. Charley Cohon, president of Prime Devices, wanted his salespeople to turn in sales call reports each Monday. However, sales representatives often delayed writing these reports until well after the calls were made. His salespeople were anxious to call on prospects but not eager to write reports. To improve his reporting system, Cohon offered his salespeople a dedicated phone number just to receive and retrieve voice mail. Sales reps could call in their reports, which would be transcribed by a clerk in the office.[25]

Some records should be completed right away, while you can easily recall the information. Accuracy is always important. It can be embarrassing to have an order sent to the wrong address simply because you transposed a figure. Take time to proofread forms and use a spell checker.

You should re-examine your territory management plan continually. Update it often so it reflects the current status of your various accounts. When possible, use a laptop computer or PDA and appropriate software to improve your records management system. Computers can help you achieve increased selling time and enhance customer service.

Salespeople often use CRM systems to record handwritten notes taken during meetings with the customer.

Maintaining Perspective

Personal selling is often characterized by emotional highs and lows. It's easy to lose perspective and drift into an emotional low during what seems like a sales slump. Carefully prepared records can serve as a reality check. For example, you may be upset by low first-quarter sales. A check of your records, however, could indicate that first-quarter sales were low during the previous year.[26]

STRESS MANAGEMENT

PERSONAL SELLING PRODUCES A CERTAIN AMOUNT OF STRESS, IN PART FROM THE NON-routine nature of sales work. Each day brings a variety of new experiences, some of which may cause stress. Prospecting, for example, can be threatening to some salespeople. Long hours on the job, the loss of leisure time, and too little time for family members can also be stressful and cause burnout if not coped with properly.[27] While "variety is the spice of life," there is a limit to how much diversity one can cope with. One of the keys to success in selling is learning how to bring order to the many facets of the job. We also must be physically and mentally prepared to handle work-related stress.

stress Refers to two simultaneous events: an external stimulus called a stressor, and the physical and emotional responses to that stimulus.

Stress refers to two simultaneous events: an external stimulus called a stressor, and the physical and emotional responses to that stimulus (anxiety, fear, muscle tension, surging heart rate, and so on). Negative, threatening, or worrisome situations accumulated over time can cause depression and burnout and make you sick.[28] In personal selling, too much negative stress hurts relationships and productivity. Some stress is beneficial because it helps keep us motivated, but too much stress can be unhealthy if left unchecked.

Stress might be caused by trying to figure out ways to meet a sales quota or schedule travel throughout a sales territory. Missed appointments, presentations before large groups, and lack of feedback concerning your performance also can create stress. Ironically, some of the time-saving tools used by salespeople (e.g., cell phones, pagers, and email) make it difficult for them to escape the pressures of their job. Many salespeople feel they are on call 24 hours a day.

As noted in Chapter 1, information surplus has replaced information scarcity as an important new problem in the age of information. Increasingly, knowledge workers report tension with colleagues, loss of job satisfaction, and strained personal relationships as a result of information overload. Too much information also crowds out quiet moments needed for reflection and to restore balance in our lives.[29] It is not possible to eliminate stress from your life, but you can adopt stress management strategies that can help you cope with it. Four stress management strategies are discussed next.

Develop a Stress-Free Home Office

Many salespeople maintain a home office. With a little effort, it's possible to create a less stressful home office environment. Install a business line for phone, email, and fax that rings only in the office. It's not professional to have other family members answering business calls. If your office is not an appropriate meeting space, meet with clients at their office or at a restaurant. Establish set hours. Try not to let work hours extend into evenings and weekends. Let your neighbours and friends know you keep office hours and cannot be disturbed during "working" hours.[30]

Doing Business in England

Linda Phillips, co-director of Executive Etiquette Company, says, "First and foremost is the British attention to detail." English businesspeople also tend to be more formal in terms of dress and person-to-person communication. It's helpful to study English business customs before visiting that country.

■ Introductions in England tend to be very formal. The British look for whose name is spoken first. If you are calling on a client named Robert Timmons, the introduction of your sales manager would be, "Mr. Timmons, I would like you to meet Raymond Hill, my sales manager." In this case the client's name is first because he is the more important person. Never address someone by his or her first name unless you are invited to do so.

■ Making decisions is often a time-consuming process, so don't expect a quick close.

■ Do not use aggressive sales techniques, such as the hard sell, and avoid criticism of competing products. Focus on objective facts and evidence during the presentation.

■ It would be poor manners to discuss business after the business day in England. This is true even when you have drinks or a meal with a businessperson.[c]

This salesperson is using a personal digital assistant (PDA). It serves as an electronic memo pad, calendar, expense log, address book, and more. It is valuable to salespeople who want to add value with efficient time and territory management.

Maintain an Optimistic Outlook

Optimistic thoughts give rise to positive attitudes and effective relationships with customers. According to Martin Seligman, professor of psychology and author of *Learned Optimism*, optimists are more likely to view problems merely as temporary setbacks. They focus on their potential success rather than on their failures. Pessimists, in contrast, tend to believe bad events will last a long time and tend to give up more easily when faced with a challenge.[31]

Seligman reminds us that optimism is a learned behaviour. For example, you can spend more time visualizing yourself succeeding. If you want to succeed at something, picture yourself doing it successfully. The visualization process needs to be repeated over and over again.[32]

Practise Healthy Emotional Expression

When stress occurs, you may undergo physiological and psychological changes. Your heartbeat quickens, your blood pressure rises, and tension builds. To relieve the pressure, you may choose a *fight* or a *flight* response. With a fight response, you might unleash an avalanche of harsh words or ignore a person with whom you are dealing. These reactions, of course, are not recommended. This behaviour may damage relationships with team members, customers, or customer support personnel.

A flight response is running away from the problem. Rather than facing the issue squarely, you decide to turn your back on it. Flight is usually not satisfactory, as the problem will seldom go away by itself. If you feel stress from an impractical quota, for example, talk to your sales manager and try to get the quota reduced. Don't just give in to the feeling of being overwhelmed. Diminished personal accomplishment can add to further burnout and stress.[33] If you are spending too much time away from family and friends, take a close look at your territory management plan and try to develop a more efficient way to make sales calls. It is not possible to eliminate those elements that cause us stress, but we can find ways to cope with daily stressors. There are stress management activities that can be used during brief pauses in your day (see Table 16.2).

Table 16.2 Five-Minute Stress Busters

- Take five minutes to identify and challenge unreasonable or distorted ideas that precipitated your stress. Replace them with ideas that are more realistic and positive.
- Take a five-minute stress-release walk outdoors. Contact with nature is especially beneficial.
- Enjoy stress relief with a gentle five-minute neck and shoulder massage.
- Spend five minutes visualizing yourself relaxing at your favourite vacation spot.
- Take a five-minute nap after lunch.
- Spend five minutes listening to a recording featuring your favourite comedian.

Source: Barry L. Reece and Rhonda Brandt, *Effective Human Relations: Personal and Organizational Applications* (Boston: Houghton Mifflin Company, 2008). Reprinted by permission of the publisher.

Increasingly, in the age of information, physical exercise is a very important part of a stress management program. Exercise also helps us maintain peak mental performance.

Maintain a Healthy Lifestyle

An effective exercise program—jogging, tennis, golf, racquetball, walking, or some other favourite exercise—can counter the harmful chemicals that build up in your bloodstream after a prolonged period of stress. Salespeople at Owens Corning formed a sales wellness advisory team (SWAT). The team organized a health screening for Owens's 600 salespeople and instituted an incentive program that rewarded those who reached exercise goals.[34]

The food you eat can also play a critical role in helping you manage stress. Health experts agree that the typical Canadian diet—high in saturated fats, refined sugars, additives, caffeine, and even too much protein—is the wrong menu for coping with stress. Employees of Husky Injection Molding Systems Ltd. in Bolton, Ontario, enjoy fresh, healthy food at the company cafeteria. The company's wellness centre sponsors programs for weight management, fitness instruction, physical therapy, and smoking cessation.[35]

Leisure time can provide you with the opportunity to relax and get rid of work-related stress. One of the most effective strategies for managing the negative aspects of stress is getting enough quality sleep. The number of hours of sleep required for good health varies from person to person, but seven or eight hours seems to be about right for most people. The critical factor is whether you feel rested in the morning and prepared to deal with the day's activities. In many respects, salespeople must possess the same self-discipline as professional athletes. Sales work can be physically demanding. Lack of proper rest, poor eating habits, excessive drinking, and failure to exercise properly can reduce one's ability to deal with stress and strain.

REVIEWING KEY CONCEPTS

- Discuss the four dimensions of opportunity management.

  All salespeople can learn more about their products and improve their selling skills. However, there is no way to expand time. Our only option is to find ways to improve in the four dimensions of opportunity management discussed in this chapter: time management, territory management, records management, and stress management.

- List and describe time management strategies.

  Effective time management methods can pave the way to greater sales productivity. To achieve greater time conservation, salespeople should adopt the following timesaving strategies: Develop a series of personal goals; prepare a daily "to-do" list; maintain a planning calendar; organize your selling tools; and save time with meetings in cyberspace and other methods of communication.

- Explain factors that contribute to improved territory management.

  The first step in territory management is the classification of all customers according to sales volume or some other appropriate criteria. You should normally spend the most time with accounts that have the greatest

  sales potential. The second step requires developing a routing and scheduling plan. This plan should reduce time spent travelling between accounts. Salespeople are often guided by a *sales call plan*.

- Identify and discuss common elements of a records management system.

  A good record-keeping system provides many advantages. Accurate, up-to-date records can actually save time because work is better organized. The company also benefits because sales reports provide an important communication link with members of the sales force. Today, computers are used to develop more efficient record-keeping systems. Common records kept by salespeople include customer and prospect files, call reports, expense records, and sales records.

- Discuss stress management practices.

  There is a certain amount of stress associated with sales work. This is due in part to the non-routine nature of personal selling. Salespeople must learn to cope with factors that upset their equilibrium. Stress management strategies include developing a stress-free home office, maintaining an optimistic outlook, practising healthy emotional expression, and maintaining a healthy lifestyle.

Key Terms

opportunity management **391**

personal digital assistant **394**

sales call plan **400**

sales territory **392**

stress **404**

Review Questions

1. The From the Field boxed feature (p. 393) describes how Alex Pettes manages his time for self–improvement. Why is it important for salespeople to have a self-improvement plan?

2. Opportunity management has been described as a four-dimensional process. Describe each dimension.

3. List and briefly describe the four goal-setting principles.

4. How can a salesperson use a time log to improve time management?

5. List four techniques the salesperson should use to make better use of valuable selling time.

6. Effective territory management involves two major steps. What are they?

7. What is a *sales call plan*? Explain how it is used.

8. Describe the records most commonly kept by salespeople.

9. What is *stress*? What are some indicators of stress?

10. Table 16.2 describes six "five-minute stress busters." Which of these do you think are most important for persons employed in the sales field? Explain.

Application Exercises

1. The key to successful time management lies in thinking and planning ahead. You must become conscious of yourself and decide what you want from your time. You can manage your time only when you have a clear picture of what is going on within and around you. To assess the quality of your working time, it is helpful to keep a careful record for a certain amount of time showing exactly how you have used your day. Over this period of time, write down everything you have done and how long it took. Next you can appraise your use of time and decide whether or not it was put to good use. Some pertinent questions you might ask yourself in appraising your use of time are suggested by the following "time analysis" questions:

   a. What items am I spending too much time on?

   b. What items am I spending too little time on?

   c. What items offer the most important opportunities for saving time?

   d. What am I doing that does not need to be done at all?

   e. How can I avoid overusing the time of others?

   f. What are some other suggestions?

2. Deciding on a goal can be the most crucial decision of your life. It is more damaging not to have a goal than it is not to reach a goal. It is generally agreed that the major cause of failure is the lack of a well-defined direction. A successful life results not from chance, but from a succession of successful days. List three goals for yourself in these four categories: career, family, education, interpersonal relations.

3. Interview someone you know who uses a planning calendar. What kind is it: pocket, desk, or some other type? How long has the person been using it? How important is the calendar to daily, weekly, monthly, and yearly planning? Has the person ever considered discontinuing its use? What are the person's suggestions for someone who does not use one? Write down your answers.

4. Time management is an important part of a successful salesperson's job. Using your search engine, examine the Internet for information on time management. Type "time management + selling." Examine the training products and services available on this topic. Be prepared to discuss some of what you find in class.

5. Territory management involves classifying customers and developing a routing and scheduling plan. You have just been hired to demonstrate—not sell—a new inventory management product to stores that sell grocery products. As your first task, the manager has asked you to prepare a list of up to 20 stores in your territory—try looking within a one-mile radius of your college or university or home. Classify these customers. Prepare a scheduling plan and be prepared to defend the plan you have made.

↻ ROLE-PLAY EXERCISE

Using the information in the Chapter 15 role-play exercise, develop a contact plan regarding the future contacts you set up (see p. 384). Your sales manager has scheduled a status report meeting to go over your activities with this account. With this information and with the information written in your calendar, plan to meet with your sales manager to talk about the account management meetings you have scheduled. Plan to cover how this schedule enhances both your time and territory management and adds value to the sale.

CASE PROBLEM

Paula Shannon, introduced at the beginning of this chapter, spends part of most weeks away from her Montreal home-based office, managing a global team of 70 sales professionals for Boston-based Lionbridge Technologies, Inc. Some indicators of her success: 1) Under her direction, Lionbridge placed second for Best Sales Team in the American Business Awards; 2) Paula was recognized with the inaugural International Stevie Award as Best Sales Executive; and 3) Among more than 600 entrants, Paula received a second Stevie Award as Best Canadian Executive. Some qualities recognized by the Stevie awards include leadership, innovation, perseverance, creativity, teamwork, and integrity. There are many things that must come together to create success at this level. Paula Shannon is a person who has managed herself and her career with meticulous detail; her success is not an accident. Paula Shannon notes six principles that she believes have contributed to her success:

1. *Be self-confident, but be humble and respectful.* Customers buy from salespeople who are confident and professional, not from those who are arrogant or self-centred. Paula says, "Some of the best people I have worked with have been able to combine self-confidence with a genuine interest in and respect for our customers' business issues and needs."

2. *Communicate clear, simple customer solutions in a language they understand.* Some salespeople have a tendency toward bafflegab—sprinkling their discussion with technical jargon without explaining it—mistakenly believing that this will impress their customers. Yet most customers want a clear, simple solution to their buying problems. Paula says, "The art of making complex issues simple seems to be one of the most important things a salesperson can do. When done well, this results in a 'call to action' and a sense of mission or purpose to see the job through."

3. *Be a prolific reader.* Paula Shannon reads both fiction and nonfiction for pleasure. She also reads the *Wall Street Journal* daily, *Fortune, CIO Insight, Selling Power, The Economist, Harvard Business Review,* and numerous reports, industry newsletters, and specialized publications. Paula says, "I know that the ability to digest large volumes of information has always been a key to my success. Whether I am getting up to speed on a project, a new deal, or an opportunity, or staying current on business trends or technology shifts, my reading is something that has helped me at every level of my secondary education and my career."

4. *Have fun and love what you do.* Salespeople who work too hard are often subject to burnout. You need time for yourself and to relax. Paula logs more than 240 000 kilometres by air a year. There is no doubt she works hard, but she also plays hard. Paula says, "I rarely schedule work for myself over the weekends and save time for my family, sports, friends, and fun. As a result, I remain energetic, positive, and upbeat. These are all things that are important when interacting with both colleagues and customers."

5. *Develop competence with technology.* At one point in her career, Paula purchased her own laptop. She recognized that she could improve her own efficiency if she could work on correspondence and client proposals while away from her office. Paula says, "Sales requires extraordinary time management, immediacy, customer focus, and access to and the exchange of information. Technology is an essential tool in the equation." Speaking of the impact of technology on herself and her sales team, she adds, "Our ability to respond to customers, solve problems, and deliver information has improved five-fold. Remote access to a shared store of centralized information has helped us, as service providers, to manage global projects, report on status, improve quality, and coordinate worldwide teams."

6. *Develop both depth and breadth of knowledge.* Paula credits some of her success to the fact that she has taken several "career meanderings" during her career—lateral moves and an occasional step downward. Speaking of this, Paula says, "In sales—deep technical or product and service—offering expertise is crucial to your success and credibility with customers. However, those skills alone, without broader business or cultural context, result in someone whose options become increasingly limited as their career progresses."

Questions

1. Which of Paula Shannon's "six principles for success" will make the most important contribution to a career in personal selling? Explain.

2. Reflect on your own approach to accomplishing things. Then select two of Paula's principles that you would find easy to adopt. Also select two principles you would find difficult to adopt. Explain your choices.

3. What things, among the many that Paula does, do you think help her manage stress most effectively? Explain.

4. How important do you think time management is to Paula? Records management? Territory management?

Chapter 17
Management of the Sales Force

Learning Objectives

After studying this chapter, you should be able to

1   Describe how leadership skills can be applied to sales management.

2   List and discuss the qualities of an effective sales manager.

3   Discuss recruitment and selection of salespeople.

4   Describe effective orientation and training practices.

5   Explain effective sales force motivation practices.

6   Develop an understanding of selected compensation plans.

7   List and discuss criteria for evaluating sales performance.

 Reality Selling Today Video Series

If you enter the field of personal selling and experience success, you may be given the opportunity to manage a sales force. Some salespeople are asked to accept the promotion but decline the offer. They do not want to give up a job they thoroughly enjoy. Many of the salespeople who do move into management positions, however, become exemplary leaders and advance to positions that offer even greater challenges.

Jaime Barauh, pictured at the top of the next page, district sales manager for McKesson Pharmaceutical (**www.mckesson.com**), started her career at this largest North American pharmaceutical distributor company as a salesperson calling on retail independent pharmacies. She attributes her success to the training she received from the company and from her previous managers. In a highly competitive and ever-changing pharmaceutical industry, continuing training about new products and services is critical. McKesson adopts a multi-layer training program. This includes a comprehensive online curriculum covering all products and services the company is offering, hands-on training with current managers, and frequent updates. The company also runs regional and national sales conferences where managers can network with peers and receive updated information. All new recruits also spend two weeks in the corporate distribution centre working as actual distribution staff to familiarize themselves with an extensive line of products.

An avid learner, Jaime Barauh was soon promoted to district sales manager of McKesson's distribution hub. Working under her supervision are five account managers who are responsible for approximately $750 million in sales. As a sales manager, she makes sure that her subordinates are empowered to fulfill their responsibilities. At the same time, she sets a good example for her subordinates with her strong work ethic. She subscribes to the principle that a good leader should keep regular and open communication with followers without micro-managing, which is the enemy of creativity and motivation. She is also actively involved in recruiting and training new staff because she believes that such early involvement in the process will help build a strong sales team.

APPLYING LEADERSHIP SKILLS TO SALES MANAGEMENT

THANKS TO THE EFFORTS OF JAMES KOUZES AND BARRY POSNER AND THEIR MANY YEARS OF research on this topic—summarized and reported in their best-selling book, *The Leadership Challenge*—we know a great deal about leadership. Their book is based on countless interviews and observations conducted around the world.

Lindsay Levin, managing director of Whites Limited, was one of many exceptional leaders cited by the authors of *The Leadership Challenge*. Whites Limited, based in London, is an auto dealership built around three departments—sales, service, and parts. Soon after assuming her new management position, Lindsay began searching for answers to one important question: "What do our customers really think of us?" She visualized Whites as a company where every customer would say, "My experience at Whites was amazing." With input from customer focus groups, she was able to identify some areas that needed improvement. She then asked employees to talk about changes they would like to implement and to form small, voluntary teams to work on them.

Lindsay Levin also visualized a company where everyone is treated with respect and feels involved and valued. She took the position that leaders can never have enough communication with their people. She never hesitated to let the employees know what she was thinking and what she believed. She talked about her values often and listened attentively when employees expressed their views. Levin also recognized employee accomplishments with personal thanks and formal awards.

People who rise to the position of sales manager must understand the difference between leadership and management. Managers who lack certain leadership skills can actually deteriorate salesperson performance.[1] Leadership is the process of inspiring, influencing, and guiding employees to participate in a common effort.[2] Stephen Covey, author of *The 8th Habit*, says, "Leadership is communicating people's worth and potential so clearly that they come to see it in themselves."[3] Leaders are made, not born. Leadership is a series of skills that can be acquired through study and practice.

Sales management is the process of planning, implementing, and controlling the personal selling function.[4] The sales manager typically performs such management functions as planning, recruiting, training, budgeting, development of compensation plans, and assessing sales force productivity. Managing the sales force is an external management function focused on bringing in orders and revenue from outside the company. However, it also requires coordination and cooperation with almost every internal department, including marketing, finance, and distribution.[5]

The true essence of sales management has been captured by Lisa Gschwandtner, editor-in-chief of *Selling Power* magazine. She describes the sales manager as a leader, coach, mentor, facilitator, goal setter, motivator, number cruncher, and communicator.[6] Figure 17.1 describes the most popular topics covered in training programs designed for sales managers. Needless to say, it's a job that requires many qualities and skills. Today's sales

sales management The process of planning, implementing, and controlling the personal selling function.

Planning and Organizing Activities (total = 13 topics)

Topic	%
Goal setting for salespeople	76%
Developing sales strategies	58%
Strategic sales planning	56%
Recruiting new salespeople	52%
Organizing salespeople	52%
Sales forecasting	50%

Management and Development Activities (total = 19 topics)

Topic	%
Motivating salespeople	82%
Leading salespeople	66%
Training salespeople	64%
Territory management	62%
Time management	60%

Evaluation and Control Activities (total = 10 topics)

Topic	%
Evaluating salespeople	64%

Figure 17.1 Most popular topics covered in training programs for sales managers

Source: Adapted from Rolph Anderson, Rajiv Mehta, and James Strong, "An Empirical Investigation of Sales Management Training Programs for Sales Managers," *Journal of Personal Selling & Sales Management*, Summer 1997, Table 6, p. 61. Used by permission of M.E. Sharpe, Inc.

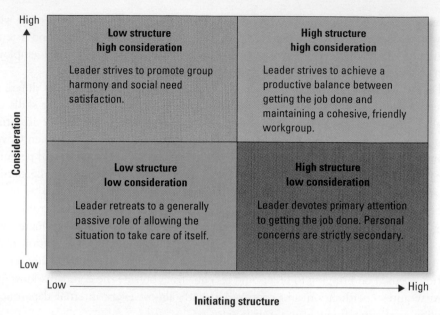

Figure 17.2 Basic leadership styles from the Ohio State study
This matrix is similar to the Leadership Grid (formerly called the Managerial Grid) developed by Robert Blake and Jane Mouton. The Leadership Grid is based on two leadership style dimensions: concern for people and concern for production.
Source: Robert *Kreitner, Management,* 10th Ed. (Boston: Houghton Mifflin Company 2007), p. 449. Reprinted by permission of the publisher.

manager is more likely to function in a virtual office environment. Sales force automation permits salespeople to receive data on their laptops or home computers. The use of other technology—videoconferencing, teleconferencing, email, and voice mail—reduces the need for frequent face-to-face contact with members of the sales team.[7]

Sales managers can have a dramatic influence on the salespeople they supervise. Depending on the leadership qualities adopted, sales managers can have an advantageous, neutral, or even detrimental effect on the performance of sales subordinates.[8] Effective leadership has been discussed in hundreds of books and articles. A careful review of this material indicates that most successful supervisory-management personnel have certain behaviours in common. Two of the most important dimensions of leadership—consideration and structure—have been identified in research studies conducted by Ohio State University researchers.[9] By making a matrix out of these two independent dimensions of leadership, researchers have identified four styles of leadership (see Fig. 17.2).

Structure

structure A leadership characteristic displayed by sales managers who clearly define their own duties and those of the sales staff, and who assume an active role in directing their subordinates.

Sales managers who display **structure** clearly define their own duties and those of the sales staff. They assume an active role in directing their subordinates' work. Policies and procedures are clearly defined and subordinates know what is expected of them. Salespeople also know how well they are doing because the structured supervisor evaluates their productivity and provides feedback. Structure is the set of written and unspoken policies, practices, and expectations that surround the job of the salesperson. It can include job descriptions, territory definitions, call reports, and sales process definition.[10] The following behaviours provide evidence of structure:

1. *Planning takes place on a regular basis.* The effective sales manager thinks ahead and decides what to do in the future. Strategic planning is the process of determining the company's current position in the market, determining where you want to be and when, and making decisions on how to secure the position you want. Strategic planning gives meaning and direction to the sales force.

2. *Expectations are clearly communicated.* The law of expectations, according to Brian Tracy, states, "Whatever you expect, with confidence, becomes your own self-fulfilling prophecy."[11] There is a strong connection between what you expect to accomplish and what you actually achieve. Sales managers must effectively formulate their expectations and then communicate them with conviction to the sales force.

3. *Decisions are made promptly and firmly.* An effective sales manager is willing and able to make decisions in a timely way. An ineffective manager often postpones important decisions, hoping the problem will go away. Of course most decisions cannot be made until all the facts are available. A good sales manager keeps the lines of communication open and involves subordinates in making the truly important decisions.

4. *Performance of salespeople is appraised regularly.* All employees want to know "where they stand" with the manager. An effective sales manager provides regular feedback. When a salesperson is not performing up to established standards, the sales manager takes immediate action.

Although structure is an important aspect of sales management, too much structure can sometimes create problems. In an effort to become better organized and more systematized, some sales organizations have developed detailed policies and procedures that rob salespeople of time, energy, and creativity. Filling out endless reports and forms, for example, can cause unnecessary frustration and may reduce productivity. Overcontrolling sales managers aren't just annoying, they are also inefficient.[12]

Consideration

A sales manager who displays the leadership dimension of **consideration** is more likely to have relationships with salespeople that are characterized by mutual trust, respect for salespeople's ideas, and consideration for their feelings. A climate of good two-way communication usually exists between the manager and the employee. The following behaviours provide evidence of consideration:

1. *Regular and effective communication receives a high priority.* Whenever possible, the effective manager engages in face-to-face communication with salespeople. They do not rely entirely on email, letters, or sales reports for information sharing but arrange for face-to-face meetings. John Morrone, vice president of sales for Pitney Bowes Management Services, frequently travels with his salespeople. He says, "My claim to fame is reaching out and touching people."[13] The effective sales manager is a good listener and creates an atmosphere of cooperation and understanding.

2. *Each salesperson is treated as an individual.* The sales manager takes a personal interest in each member of the sales force. No one is treated "like a number." The interest is

consideration A leadership dimension displayed by sales managers who have relationships with salespeople that are characterized by mutual trust, respect for the salesperson's ideas, and consideration for their feelings.

Besides supervising the sales force, sales managers often are involved in establishing sales quotas, developing long- and short-term forecasts, and seeing that goals are achieved.

genuine, not artificial. The effective sales manager does not endanger effectiveness by showing favouritism to anyone.

3. *Good performance is rewarded often.* Positive reinforcement is one of the strongest morale-building factors in the work environment. Ken Blanchard, co-author of *The One-Minute Manager*, says, "The key to developing people will always be to concentrate on catching them doing something right instead of blaming them for doing something wrong."[14] Recognition for a job well done is always appreciated.

The recognized standard of sales excellence

CSP - When these three letters follow your name, they pack a powerful message

- 86% gained a competitive advantage in the marketplace
- 72% rank in the top 25% of sales within their respective organizations
- More than half earn personal annual incomes over $75,000 per year
- 9 out of 10 CSPs recommend becoming a Certified Sales Professional (CSP) to others

The CPSA Sales Institute has been committed to excellence in the sales profession by maintaining progressive competency standards for sales professionals since 1994. It is the only organization in Canada that offers the Certified Sales Professional (CSP) designation.

Situational Leadership

Mastery of consideration and structure skills is an important first step toward achieving success in sales management. The next step is to match your leadership style to the various situations that surface among members of your sales force. Paul Hershey is credited with the development of **situational leadership.** This leadership approach is based on the theory that the most successful leadership occurs when the leader's style matches the situation.[15]

Let us assume that a member of your sales team has almost totally abandoned customer service and follow-up activities. She is devoting nearly all of her attention to calls on new customers. Many of her regular customers have complained about poor service, and a crisis is developing. At this point, the leadership dimension of *structure* will require the most time and attention. This situation must be corrected immediately.

The Character Test Sales managers who develop consideration and structure skills and the flexibility required to be a situational leader must pass one additional test. If you fail the character test, you fail as a sales manager. Character is composed of your personal standards of behaviour, including your honesty and integrity. If you are seen as an honest broker of advice and assistance, as someone who always tells the truth, trust and respect will build. But building trust is a slow process and it can be irreparably destroyed by a single lie or deception.[16]

situational leadership Matching your leadership style to the particular situation you face with individual members of your sales force.

Coaching for Peak Performance

"When you die there is an express line at the Pearly Gates for coaches," jokes Canadian consultant, international speaker, and award-winning retailer Donald Cooper (**www.donaldcooper.com**). He recognizes that the ability to be a good coach—to improve the attitudes and skills of others—is both rare and important.[17] A sales manager who develops a leadership style that combines structure and consideration behaviours possesses the skills needed to be an effective coach. **Coaching** is an interpersonal process between the sales manager and the salesperson in which the manager helps the salesperson improve performance in a specific area. The coaching process has two primary areas of focus: helping the salesperson recognize the need to improve his or her performance, and developing the salesperson's commitment to improving performance.[18]

Coaching is often used to correct a specific performance problem such as ineffective prospecting, poorly developed sales presentations, or failure to create value for the customer. We will outline a four-step coaching strategy:

coaching An interpersonal process between a sales manager and a salesperson in which the manager helps the salesperson improve performance in a specific area.

> **Step one** in the coaching process involves documentation of performance problems. In some cases the best approach is to observe and assess performance during actual sales calls. Make note of things the salesperson is neglecting to do.

> **Step two** involves getting the salesperson to recognize and agree that there is a need to improve performance in a specific area. Sales managers should never assume the salesperson sees the problem in the same way they do.

> **Step three** involves exploring solutions. At this point it's often best to let the salesperson suggest ways to improve performance.

Valuable Advice for Those Who Would Be Leader

Tom Gunter has spent most of his life in sales: Scott Paper, Frito-Lay Canada, Molson Canada, and now as vice president of sales for ConAgra Foods in Toronto. Tom has eight directors of sales who report to him, and each of them is responsible for four to six account managers. Tom has lots of good advice for aspiring sales leaders. The following are some of Tom's comments:

■ *Managing change*. When you must change a culture, you have to create stability and put the appropriate structures and processes in place to succeed. The biggest challenge is getting some people to understand the importance of change, and then training them so they can make the change. The ones who can't get to where you want them may have to go elsewhere.

■ *Plateaued salespeople*. Every company has a number of people who don't want to move up in the organization, and you need those steady performers as long as they are open to new concepts and ideas. But if they have lost their motivation, you must have an open and honest talk with them about where they fit and let them decide whether they want to stay. Some may become re-motivated and get excited about helping someone else develop into the company's next senior executive.

■ *Sales meetings*. Attendees must be aware of the preparation required and the decisions to be made at the meeting. In addition, the facilitator, timekeeper, and note-taker should be briefed on their roles and responsibilities. If a meeting room is unfamiliar or if there are materials to set up, the manager should arrive early to prepare. This ensures that the meeting starts on time, as starting late shows disrespect to the participants.

■ *Coaching*. You should involve the salesperson when delivering feedback. You must offer praise where due, but rather than spout criticism, you are better off asking questions that create a dialogue about possible ways to improve results.

■ *Alcohol and drug abuse*. If a salesperson has identified the problem and is seeking help to deal with it, you are required to provide employee assistance to help them overcome the problem. If they fail to acknowledge the problem and continue with the abuse, in spite of your efforts to offer assistance, you should move to termination. It is always advisable to seek legal counsel and involve human resource professionals in these situations as they are delicate and can put your organization in jeopardy if handled poorly.

■ *Harassment*. Personalities and outcomes of harassment are very diverse and each situation requires a different course of action. If a salesperson reports harassment, a sales manager must reserve judgment, listen actively, take many notes, and begin an investigative process. The outcome could include third-party counselling, a meeting with the two individuals, a written apology, suspension of duties, or termination.

■ *Termination*. Termination should be the last step after all other options are exhausted, but sometimes it is inevitable. If the employee leaves and feels as though he was treated fairly and respectfully, even if he does not agree with the assessment, it reflects well on the company and manager. It will be recognized internally by other staff and externally by potential hires. Your organization will be known for its good practices.

■ *Final thoughts*. A great employee is focused on his or her own development, whereas a great leader is focused on the development of others. Some final words of wisdom: Be clear and consistent, be honest, maintain a sense of humour, and, most important, never ask someone to do something that you wouldn't do yourself.[a]

Step four involves getting a commitment from the salesperson to take action. This step may involve development of a contract—written or verbal—that clarifies the coaching goals, approaches, and outcomes.

A major goal of coaching meetings is to improve performance while enabling sales managers and salespeople to maintain a relationship based on mutual respect and trust. Most salespeople welcome coaching, even when it involves constructive criticism.[19]

RECRUITMENT AND SELECTION OF SALESPEOPLE

CAREFUL RECRUITMENT AND SELECTION OF SALESPEOPLE IS VERY IMPORTANT. THIS IS ONE OF the most significant tasks sales managers perform because sales organizations have been forced to become more sophisticated. The authors of *How to Hire and Develop Your Next Top Performer: The Five Qualities That Make Salespeople Great* say that about half of the people working in sales should be doing something else. In addition, they say that about 20 to 25 percent of the salespeople currently employed are selling products or services not suited to their personality.[20] If the research reported by these authors is accurate, then it appears that sales managers are frequently hiring the wrong people.

Successful salespeople are often difficult to identify. The selection of sales personnel today is more of a science and less of an art. Sales managers no longer need to rely on "gut feelings." The ability to identify sales aptitude accurately can be acquired. Many progressive sales organizations recognize the need to help sales managers develop the interviewing skills necessary to make profitable hiring decisions. It is impossible to avoid occasionally hiring a poor performer, but sales managers can improve their average by using some established recruitment and selection guidelines.

Determine Actual Job Requirements

To decide what type of applicant is needed, the manager should first outline the duties the person will perform. The sales manager must have a clear picture of the job requirements before beginning the recruitment process.

Some sales managers make every effort to discover the success factors that contribute to the achievements of their high-performance salespeople. Success factors are the skills, knowledge, abilities, and behaviours considered critical for successful performance. This information may be collected through interviews with salespeople or customers, by observing the salesperson during sales calls, or by some other method.

After a careful study of the duties the salesperson will perform and identification of the success factors, the sales manager should prepare, or have human resources prepare, a job description. A *job description* is an explanation of what the salesperson will do and under what conditions the work will be performed. It is a good idea to spell out in as much detail as possible the abilities and qualities that the applicant needs to be successful. This can be accomplished by answering a few basic questions about the position.

1. Will the person be developing a new sales territory or assuming responsibility for an established territory?
2. Is the product or service well established, or is it new to the marketplace?
3. Will the salesperson work under the sales manager's close supervision or independently?
4. What amount of travel is required? What is the likelihood of eventual transfer? Promotion?

Once the job description has been prepared, the foundation has been established to determine the type of person to be hired. There is no substitute for knowing what the job requires.

Search Out Applicants from Several Sources

To identify the best possible person for the job, sales managers usually seek applicants from more than one source. As a rule of thumb, they try to interview three or more applicants for each opening. Some suggested sources of new employees follow.

1. *Candidates within the company and employee referrals.* One of the first places to look is within your own company. Is there someone in accounting, engineering, customer service, or some other area who aspires to a sales position? These people have the advantage of being familiar with the company's products, policies, operations, and what it takes to please the customer. Companies are also increasingly using referral programs because employees often know of people with similar skills in other organizations. General Mills Canada gives bonuses to employees who refer new hires. It recognizes that current employees know what it takes to be successful within the company. Referred employees often have better skills, more loyalty, and achieve superior performance.[21]

2. *College and university students.* Many business firms are turning to college and university campuses to recruit salespeople. As noted in Chapter 2, several colleges and universities have developed personal selling certificate and degree programs. Placement offices are usually cooperative about publicizing openings.

3. *Trade and newspaper advertisements.* A carefully prepared newspaper advertisement will often attract well-qualified job applicants. A well-written ad should accurately describe the job requirements and spell out the opportunities. The ad should "sell" the position, but it should not exaggerate its benefits.

4. *Employment agencies and listings.* Canada Human Resources Centre helps companies across Canada assess job applicants and select the best among them, helping to reduce employee turnover, increase productivity, and improve job satisfaction. There are also many private employment agencies across Canada. These firms specialize in matching applicants to the job and usually do some initial screening for employers. A fee is assessed for the services these agencies provide.

5. *Internet.* Many companies are using the Internet to recruit for sales positions: Monster.ca, Workopolis, CareerOwl, Canjobs, Canada JobSearch, and CPSA.com are popular websites that advertise thousands of sales jobs across Canada. Job boards can reach candidates in distant places and can locate talented salespeople who are not actively searching for jobs. Vancouver human resources executive Shirley Quinn finds job boards convenient and cost-effective when hiring the best sales and management people.[22]

Select the Best-Qualified Applicant

Once you have identified qualified applicants, the next step is to select the best person. This is becoming more difficult as products become more complex, customers become more sophisticated, and competitors become more aggressive. Selecting the best-qualified applicant will never be easy, but there are some qualifications and characteristics that all sales managers should look for. One of the most important qualities is a high level of interest in and enthusiasm for the job and a high degree of self-motivation. Salespeople have to be self-starters.

Another very important quality is integrity. Dana Telford and Adrian Gostick, authors of *Integrity Works,* say that managers spend about 90 percent of their time on capability-related questions and almost no time on character-based questions. They suggest checking backgrounds and interviewing for character by asking ethics-based questions. Here are a few examples.[23]

What are your three core values?

What does integrity mean to you?

Who are your role models and why?

What would your past manager say about you?

Tell me about a time when you were asked to compromise your integrity.

Bruce Diamond, vice president of sales for a large office equipment company, says, "Our salespeople now need to be much more professional, much more educated about the market, customers, products, and business in general."[24] His strategy for finding good salespeople includes discussions of business trends and developments. During the interview, he poses business situations and asks the candidate to come up with solutions. Diamond says he is impressed when a candidate displays an understanding of profitable revenues and finding the right customers to do business with.

Personality and Skills Testing

To increase the quality of new hires, many companies are placing more emphasis on personality and skills testing. The HR Chally Group developed the Chally Talent Audit, an instrument that can be used to predict performance in a variety of sales positions. The audit provides a skills profile that helps determine strengths and weaknesses in several roles. For example, a candidate may possess the skills needed to develop new accounts, but lack the skills needed for strategic account management. Chally assessment instruments are fully compliant with equal opportunity regulations and are non-discriminatory.[25]

Western Psychological Services developed the Sales Achievement Predictor. This instrument assesses self-confidence, personal diplomacy, competitiveness, and other qualities equally importantly in sales.[26] Caliper Corporation, a testing service with more than 40 years of experience, developed Caliper Profile, an instrument for personality assessment. Caliper's basic personality profile can be taken online.[27] Online testing has become more popular in recent years. John Wood, vice president of business development at HR Chally Group, recommends that firms rely 30 percent on predictive assessment instruments, 30 percent on a structured interview, 30 percent on references and background checks, and 10 percent on personal reactions to the applicant.[28] Test results should always be used *in conjunction* with information obtained from the interview with the candidate and the findings of reference checks.

ORIENTATION AND TRAINING

ONCE YOU HAVE SELECTED THE BEST-QUALIFIED SALESPERSON, TWO STEPS SHOULD BE TAKEN to ensure that this person becomes a productive member of your staff. First, give the new employee a thorough orientation to your business operation. Provide the orientation

Selling Today

Are You Ready for Today's Sales Interview?

The personal interview is an important part of the selection process when filling sales positions. When companies use a series of interviews, the first one often is used to eliminate unacceptable candidates—those who lack maturity, lack enthusiasm, or display poor appearance. Subsequent interviews are used to match people to job qualifications. At Hewlett-Packard, candidates may have as many as six interviews with various people. At Smith Kline, a team approach is used so that candidates do not learn the "right" answers from one interview to the next.

Although interviews vary from one company or interviewer to another, there are some popular questions and requests that you should be prepared to handle:

- Tell me about yourself.
- Describe the sales process as you understand it.
- What books have you read recently on selling or for personal development?

- What is your greatest weakness? Strength?
- What was the most boring job you ever had, and how did you handle it?
- How do you feel about your present (or previous) employer?
- What was the biggest contribution you made to your last employer?
- Sell me this pen (ashtray, laptop computer, lamp).
- Why should we hire you?

Some employers also ask you to complete a test to demonstrate your written communication skills or your ability to handle "the numbers." These are both important skills sales professionals require for success.[b]

before the person begins working. This should include a review of your company's history, philosophy of doing business, mission statement, business policies, compensation plan, and other important information.

Second, initiate a training program that will help the person achieve success. Sales training that is carefully planned and executed can make a major contribution to the performance of every salesperson.[29] Nabisco Corporation developed a two-day Professional Selling Program that helps sales reps plan for and deliver professional presentations. The cost of the training is about $1000 per enrolee. A careful evaluation of the program indicates that the training has resulted in additional sales of more than $122 000 per salesperson and yielded almost $21 000 of additional profit per rep.[30] Study results indicate that salespeople have a more positive view of their job, greater commitment, and improved performance when their sales managers clarify their job role, how to execute their tasks, and how their needs will be satisfied with successful job performance.[31] Figure 17.3 provides a framework for developing an effective sales training program.

Even salespeople with great potential are handicapped when the company fails to provide adequate training. Keep in mind that in the absence of formal training, employees will develop their own approaches to performing tasks.

The size of the firm should not dictate the scope of the training program. Even the smallest marketing organization should have a formal sales training program. Online training often reduces training costs. A program should have three dimensions:

- Knowledge of the product line, company marketing strategies, territory information, and business trends

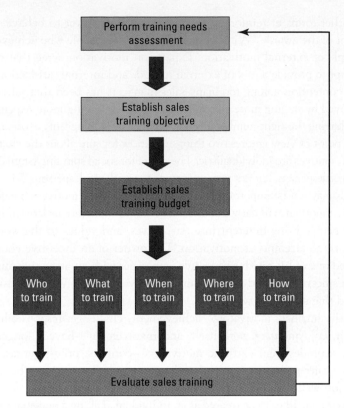

Figure 17.3 A framework for training salespeople

Source: H. F. (Herb) MacKenzie, *Sales Management in Canada* (Toronto, ON: Pearson Prentice Hall, 2008), p. 229.

- Attitude toward the company, the company's products and services, and the customers to be served

- Skill in applying personal selling principles and practices—the "doing" part of the sales training program[32]

An important part of the sales training program is foundation-level instruction. This aspect of sales training focuses on the *basics*. If salespeople are to plan and execute a sales call successfully, they must first master certain fundamental selling skills—the skills that form the foundation for everything salespeople do in their careers. The steps that make up the Six-Step Presentation Plan (i.e., approach, presentation, demonstration, negotiation, close, and servicing the sale) represent fundamental selling skills (see Fig. 15.1).

SALES FORCE MOTIVATION

IT IS HELPFUL TO NOTE THE DIFFERENCE BETWEEN INTERNAL AND EXTERNAL MOTIVATION. AN **internal motivation** is an intrinsic reward that occurs when a duty or task is performed. If a salesperson enjoys calling on customers and solving their problems, this activity is in itself rewarding, and the salesperson is likely to be self-motivated.[33] Internal motivation is likely to be triggered when sales positions provide an opportunity for achievement and individual growth. **External motivation** is an action taken by another person involving

internal motivation An intrinsic reward that occurs when a duty or task is performed.

external motivation Action taken by another person that involves rewards or other forms of reinforcement that cause the worker to behave in ways that ensure receipt of the reward.

rewards or other forms of reinforcement that cause the worker to behave in ways that ensure receipt of the award.[34] A cash bonus given to salespeople who achieve a sales goal is one example of external motivation. Experts on motivation agree that organizations should attempt to provide a mix of external rewards and internal satisfaction.

A basic contention among too many sales managers has been that sales productivity can be improved by staging more elaborate sales contests, giving more expensive recognition awards, having the right number of prize winners, or picking truly exotic meeting locations.[35] This point of view ignores two things we know for sure about the characteristics of motives. First, motives are individualistic. The desire for social standing (status) may be very strong for one salesperson, but not very important to another salesperson. What satisfies one person's needs may not be important to someone else. Second, motives change throughout our lives. What motivates us early in our career may not motivate us later in life.

Because people bring different interests, drives, and values to the workplace, they react differently to attempts at motivation. The owner of an incentive consulting company rewarded one of his highly productive employees with an attractive mink coat. She thanked him sincerely, took the coat home, but never wore it. When he asked her why, she explained that she didn't wear fur.[36]

Frequently, intrinsic motivators—achievement, challenge, responsibility, advancement, growth, enjoyment of work itself, and involvement—have a longer-term effect on employee attitudes than extrinsic motivators—contests, prizes, quotas, and money. In many cases, sales performance is linked directly to the appreciation the sales manager shows for a job well done. The importance of one-on-one communication cannot be overstated. Everyone likes to be treated as an individual. Taking a personal interest means learning the names of spouses and children, finding out what employees do during their leisure time, and acknowledging birthdays.[37]

Sales training that is carefully planned and executed can make a major contribution to the performance of salespeople.

Effective Use of External Rewards

While criticisms of external rewards have a great deal of merit, the fact remains that large numbers of organizations continue to achieve positive results with carefully developed incentive programs. It is possible to design programs that have long-range benefits for both the organization and the individual employee if you follow these guidelines:

1. Design reward programs that focus on several important aspects of the salesperson's job, such as developing new accounts, expanding sales of existing accounts, and improving customer service after the sale. Keep contest time frames short so more salespeople have an opportunity to win. However, don't use short-term motivation contests too often and don't use the same incentive plan over and over again.

2. Evaluate your incentive program often to determine which plan has the most impact.[38] Is it cash bonuses? Travel? Merchandise? Bill Grassie, manager of compensation and business planning for Sprint, likes to use non-cash incentives because he believes Sprint salespeople have a solid compensation package. He feels non-cash incentives provide a lasting memory, whereas a cash bonus is just one more way to earn money.[39] Of course, a salesperson who is not earning a lot of money in salary and commission might favour a cash incentive.

3. Avoid setting goals that are unrealistic. Some companies are under enormous pressure to meet sales and profit targets. In many cases, sales targets increase while resources decline. One salesperson made President's Club for being 220 percent above quota, and her whole team did well and was recognized as tops in the company. Her boss, the vice president for sales, immediately raised their overall quota by 65 percent for the next year. This was an impossible target and team morale plummeted.

Pressure to reach unrealistic sales goals can produce negative results. Employee loyalty and teamwork erode quickly, and in some cases so do business ethics. Salespeople who fear loss of their job if they do not meet established targets are more inclined to engage in unethical behaviour.[40]

Should sales managers encourage their salespeople to *compete* or encourage them to *cooperate*? This is one of the dilemmas facing managers who want highly motivated salespeople but also want members of the sales team to share important information and become resources to each other. One answer is to develop a plan that rewards sales collaboration and the achievement of specific sales goals, whether individual goals, team goals, or both.[41]

COMPENSATION PLANS

A **compensation plan** FOR SALESPEOPLE COMBINES DIRECT MONETARY PAYMENTS (i.e., salary and commissions) and indirect monetary payments (such as paid vacations, pensions, and insurance plans). Compensation practices vary greatly throughout the field of selling. Furthermore, sales managers are constantly searching for the "perfect" sales force compensation plan.[42] Of course, the perfect plan does not exist. Each plan must be chosen to suit the specific type of selling job, the objectives of the firm's marketing program, and the type of customer served.

As noted in Chapter 2, the highest amount of total compensation is earned by salespeople involved in value-added selling. Salespeople who use this approach realize

compensation plan A pay plan for salespeople that combines direct monetary pay with indirect monetary payments such as paid vacations, pensions, and insurance plans.

Global Business Insight

Doing Business in Switzerland

Trudi Gallagher, a real estate sales associate born and raised in Switzerland, offers some advice on doing business there:

- The Swiss are very private people, and it takes quite a while for them to get to know you and invite you to their home. They are more likely to entertain in restaurants and hotels.

- The Swiss are very punctual, very correct, and when they give their word, they mean it.

- Although four languages are spoken in Switzerland, businesspeople will almost always speak English.[c]

that the solution to the customer's buying problem is more important than price. They are frequently involved in team selling and in some cases they are rewarded with a team compensation plan.

Increasingly, companies are abandoning compensation plans that are linked to a single target such as a sales quota. At Siebel Systems, an e-business software provider, 40 percent of each salesperson's incentive compensation is based on the customer's reported satisfaction with service and implementation of the products they have purchased. This plan encourages continual customer follow-up, which generates repeat business.[43]

In the field of selling, there are five basic compensation plans. Here is a description of each:

1. *Straight commission plan.* The only direct monetary compensation comes from sales. No sales, no income. Salespeople under this plan are very conscious of their sales. Lack of job security can be a strong inducement to produce results. However, these people may also concentrate more on immediate sales than on long-term customer development.

2. *Commission plan with a draw provision or guaranteed salary.* This plan has about the same impact on salespeople as the straight commission plan. However, it gives them more financial security.

3. *Commission with a draw or guaranteed salary plus a bonus.* This plan offers more direct financial security than the first two plans. As such, salespeople may adhere more to the company's objectives. The bonus may be based on sales or profits.

4. *Fixed salary plus bonus.* Salespeople functioning under this compensation plan tend to be more company-centred and to have a fairly high degree of financial security if their salary is competitive. The bonus incentive helps motivate people under this plan.

5. *Straight salary.* Salespeople who work under this compensation plan are usually more company-centred and have financial security.

According to a *Sales & Marketing Management* research study, most companies participating in the survey used some form of compensation plan that combined base salary and incentive.[44] The salary plus bonus and salary plus commission plans are both quite popular, while determining the right proportion of salary versus incentive depends on many factors.[45]

Strategic Compensation Planning

Many sales managers admit that their current compensation plan does not drive behaviours needed to achieve specific sales objectives. The purpose of strategic compensation planning is to guide salespeople in the right direction. Compensation plans can be designed to achieve a variety of sales objectives:

- *Specific product movement.* Bonus points can be given for the sale of selected items during a specified "push" period.

- *Percentage sales increase.* Sales levels can be established with points that are given only when those levels are reached.

- *Establish new accounts.* A block of points can be awarded for opening a new account, or for expansion selling to existing accounts.

- *Increase sales activity.* For each salesperson, points can be awarded based on the number of calls.[46]

There is no easy way to develop an effective compensation plan. There are, however, some important guidelines for your efforts to develop a good plan.

1. Be sure that your sales and marketing objectives are defined in detail. The plan should complement these goals. If sales and marketing objectives are in conflict with the compensation plan, problems will surely arise.

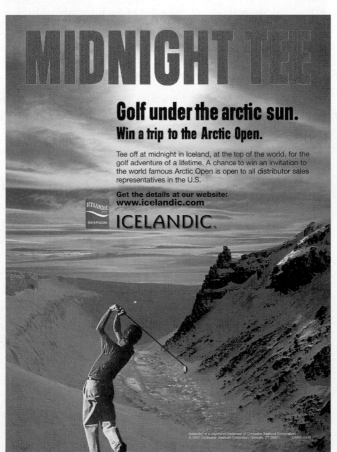

Icelandic® offers a very attractive incentive program to its distribution sales representatives.

2. The compensation plan should be field tested before full implementation. Several questions should be answered: Will the new plan be easy to administer? How does the proposed plan differ in terms of payout compared with the existing plan?

3. Explain the compensation plan carefully to the sales force. Misunderstanding may generate distrust of the plan. Keep in mind that some salespeople may see change as a threat.

4. Change the compensation plan when conditions in the marketplace warrant change. One reason for the poor showing of many plans is that firms fail to revise their plan as the business grows and market conditions change. Review the compensation plan at least annually to ensure that it's aligned with conditions in the marketplace and the company's overall marketing strategy.

ASSESSING SALES FORCE PRODUCTIVITY

As the cost of maintaining a sales force increases, sales managers must give more attention to measuring productivity. The goal is to analyze the profitability of each salesperson's sales volume. This task is complicated because sales territories, customers, and business conditions vary.

The problem of measuring sales force productivity is more complicated than it might appear at first glance. In most cases, sales volume alone will not tell you how much profit or loss you are making on the sales of each member of the sales force. A small manufacturer was losing money until he analyzed the profitability of sales generated by each person. He found that one salesperson created a loss on almost every order. This salesperson was concentrating on a market that had become so competitive that she had to reduce the markup to make sales.

Some sales managers view the frequency of calls as an indicator of success. This information is only helpful when compared with the profit earned on each account. The number of calls made on an account should bear some relationship to the sales and profit potential of that account. In some cases, it is possible to maintain small accounts without frequent personal calls.

To compare a salesperson's current productivity with the past can also be misleading. Changes in products, prices, competition, and assignments make comparisons with the past unfair—sometimes to the salesperson, sometimes to the company. It is better to measure cumulative quarterly, semi-annual, or annual results in relation to established goals.

Some sales managers use performance evaluation criteria that communicate to the sales force which elements of their jobs are most important and how they are doing in each area. Evaluating salespeople involves defining the bases on which they will be evaluated, developing performance standards to determine the acceptable level of performance desired on each base, monitoring actual performance, and giving salespeople feedback on their performance.[47] Some of the most common criteria for assessing the productivity of salespeople are:

Quantitative Criteria

Sales volume in dollars or units

Sales volume compared with previous year's sales

Chally's research suggests that the decision to promote salespeople into sales management should not be taken lightly. Their Chally Sales Talent Audit is designed to provide important insights into the potential success of a salesperson being considered for a sales management position.

Sales volume by product or product line

Number of new accounts opened or accounts lost

Amount of new account sales

Net profit dollars in total, per account, or per product line

Number of customer calls

Qualitative Criteria

Attitude

Product knowledge

Communication skills

Personal appearance

Customer goodwill generated

Selling skills

Initiative

Team collaboration

In most cases, it is best to emphasize assessment criteria that can be expressed in numbers (i.e., quantitative). The preceding quantitative items are especially significant when accompanied by target dates. For example, you might assess the number of new accounts opened during a six-month period. Of course a sales manager should not ignore the other criteria listed here. The other items can affect a salesperson's productivity, and you have to make judgments in these areas.

Some sales managers ask their salespeople to complete a self-evaluation as part of the overall evaluation process. Many salespeople believe that self-evaluation contributes to their personal development.[48]

REVIEWING KEY CONCEPTS

- Describe how leadership skills can be applied to sales management.

  Many capable salespeople have advanced to the position of *sales manager*. This job involves such diverse duties as recruiting, selecting, training, and supervising salespeople. The sales manager is part of the management team and therefore must be a strong leader. Those who rise to the position of sales manager must understand the difference between leadership and management.

- List and discuss the qualities of an effective sales manager.

  Effective sales managers help members of their sales force feel confident, strong, and capable of fulfilling their duties. Although the qualities of effective leaders are subject to debate, most research tells us that such people display two dimensions: *structure* and *consideration*. Sales managers who develop a leadership style that combines structure and consideration possess the skills needed to be an effective *coach*.

- Discuss recruitment and selection of salespeople.

  Most sales managers are involved directly or indirectly in recruiting and selecting salespeople. This is an important responsibility because mistakes can be costly. A company's profit and its image can be influenced positively or negatively by each member of the sales force. To increase the quality of new hires, many companies are placing more emphasis on personality and skills testing.

- Describe effective orientation and training practices.

  Orientation and training for salespeople are almost daily concerns of the sales manager. These duties

should always be viewed as an investment in human resources. They help members of the sales force reach their fullest potential. Figure 17.3 provides a comprehensive framework for training salespeople.

- Explain effective sales force motivation practices.

  We discussed the difference between *internal* and *external motivation*. In many cases, intrinsic motivators (achievement, challenge, responsibility, involvement, and enjoyment of work itself) have a longer-term effect on employee attitudes and behaviour than extrinsic motivators (contests, prizes, and money). Sales managers need to discover the individual differences between salespeople to select the most effective motivation strategies.

- Develop an understanding of selected compensation plans.

  Compensation plans for salespeople combine direct monetary payments (salary and commissions) and indirect monetary payments, such as paid vacations, pensions, and insurance plans. Compensation practices vary greatly throughout the field of selling. Strategic compensation planning can be used to guide salespeople in the right direction.

- List and discuss criteria for evaluating sales performance.

  Assessing sales force productivity is a major responsibility of the sales manager. Sales managers use both quantitative and qualitative criteria. In most cases, it is best to emphasize assessment criteria that can be expressed in numbers (quantitative).

Key Terms

coaching **417**

compensation plan **425**

consideration **415**

external motivation **423**

internal motivation **423**

sales management **413**

situational leadership **417**

structure **414**

Review Questions

1. What is the difference between leadership and management?

2. Are all sales managers' duties the same? Explain.

3. What are the two main leadership qualities displayed by most successful sales managers? Define and explain each of these qualities.

4. List and describe the four basic steps involved in coaching.

5. What is a job description? Explain the importance of job descriptions when selecting salespeople.

6. What are four sources for recruiting new salespeople?

7. What should sales managers look for when selecting new salespeople? Describe at least three important qualities.

8. List and describe three guidelines that should be followed when you design a sales motivation program based on external rewards.

9. List and describe the five basic compensation plans for salespeople.

10. What are the *best* criteria for measuring a salesperson's performance? List additional criteria that should be considered in evaluating individual performance.

Application Exercises

1. Assume that you are a manager of a wholesale electrical supply business. Sales have increased to a level where you need to hire another salesperson. What sources can you use to recruit a good professional salesperson? What criteria can you use in selecting the person you hire?

2. Carefully analyze the following types of selling positions:

   a. A territory selling position for a national manufacturer that requires the salesperson to provide customer service to a large number of accounts plus open up several new accounts each month

   b. A retail sales position in the cosmetics department of a department store

   c. An automobile salesperson who sells and leases new and used cars

   d. A real estate salesperson who sells residential real estate

      Assuming that each of the preceding positions is full-time, identify the type of compensation plan you think is best for each. Supply an explanation for each of your answers.

3. Schedule an appointment with two sales managers. Interview each of them, using the following questions as a guide:

   a. What are your functions as a sales manager?

   b. How do the functions of a sales manager differ from those of a salesperson?

   c. What criteria do you use when selecting salespeople?

   d. What kinds of training programs do you have for new salespeople?

   e. What method of compensation do you use for your salespeople?

   f. How do you evaluate the performance of your salespeople?

   g. What personal qualities are important for becoming a sales manager?

      Write down the answers. Summarize the similarities and differences of the sales managers' responses.

4. SalesForce Training & Consulting has been providing sales training and consulting for nearly 30 years. What types of services does this company provide that would benefit sales managers? Visit its website (**www.salesforcetraining.com**) and hit "Right People," "Right Skills," and "Right Tools." Be prepared to discuss in class what you have discovered.

5. You have just been hired as sales manager for the Calgary branch office of a national industrial distributor. It has been five years since you finished your education, and since that time you have had a very successful

career selling to mines and manufacturing plants in Ontario and Quebec. As you take over your new position, you notice that if you are not the youngest person in the branch, you are very close to it. At least two salespeople are 20 years older than you. Will *structure* or *consideration* be most important in determining your success as a sales manager? (Note: Do not be a fence-sitter. Make a choice and be prepared to defend it.)

ROLE-PLAY EXERCISE

For the purpose of this role play, assume the role of a sales manager who is currently supervising a sales team made up of 22 salespeople. Your employer manufactures and sells radio equipment for private aircraft. You plan to open a new sales territory in western Canada and need a self-motivated salesperson to assume the position. You have identified a person who seems to be a qualified applicant and you have scheduled a meeting to discuss the position. Using information in this chapter, prepare a list of questions you will ask during the role play. Use these questions to interview another class member who will assume the role of the applicant. After the role play, review the interview process.

CASE PROBLEM

One of the more interesting developments in sales force management is the use of customer feedback to improve the performance of salespeople. Most of these programs are relatively new and go by a variety of names, such as *360-degree feedback, customer-conscious compensation,* and *customer satisfaction rewards.* Organizations that have adopted this assessment strategy believe salespeople can benefit from feedback collected from the customers they serve. Information collected can also be used by the company to improve customer service.

The use of customer-driven evaluation programs is on the increase because of the rising regard for the role of sales at many companies. Tom Mott, a consultant with Hewitt Associates, says, "Salespeople who were volume pushers are now becoming the manager of their company's relationship with the customer." Tom points out that customer feedback is likely to reflect on the performance of the salesperson and the performance of the company. If problems surface in either area, customer dissatisfaction may need attention.

Data collection methodology is not uniform at this point. Some companies use telephone surveys while others use mailed questionnaires. IBM has experimented with a series of in-person meetings that bring together corporate customers, their IBM sales representatives, and the salesperson's boss.

Some salespeople have not welcomed the use of customer evaluations. Maryann Cirenza, senior account executive at Teleport Communications Group (TCG) of New York, said that she felt betrayed when she saw the questionnaire the company was sending to her customers. One of the questions asked, "Does your sales rep know your industry?" Maryann said, "I thought the company was checking up on me." Later, her anger subsided when she learned the survey was not simply a monitoring system but a trial run for a new compensation plan. After field testing the surveys, TCG used customer feedback to set bonuses. MaryAnn Cirenza was actually rewarded for good customer service by earning a bonus of about 20 percent of her base pay.

Greg Buseman, an IBM salesperson, believes the shift to compensation through customer feedback has improved personal selling at his company. He now spends more time understanding the customer's business and learning to be a problem solver for his clients.[49]

Questions

1. Should the customer be given a major voice in determining how salespeople are performing? Explain.

2. Should sales force compensation be linked to customer feedback? What are the advantages and disadvantages of this approach?

3. Assume you are a sales manager preparing to develop and implement a customer feedback system. How might you gain support for this system from members of your sales force? What data collection method would you use?

4. Research indicates that customers rank "understanding of our business" as an important criterion used to evaluate salespeople. Why is this criterion ranked so high?

APPENDIX 1

Reality Selling Today Role-Play Scenarios

 The 11 role-play scenarios in this appendix are all extensions of the Reality Selling Today Videos presented throughout the text. Using the information presented in the chapter opening vignettes, case problems, and videos, and the information presented in this section, you will have available the most detailed and realistic setting for selecting, preparing, and presenting a role play.

As you discovered in the videos and related material, these are real salespeople in real selling situations, enjoying successful and rewarding careers in the profession of selling. In these Reality Selling Today role-play scenarios, you assume these same responsibilities by selecting a similar position in the same office as the sales professionals presented in the videos. Just as they do in the evolution of their careers, you will need to learn about your new company, its products, and, specifically, the customer you will be calling on.

Detailed information is presented in each of the scenarios. Websites are presented to provide more information about the company, its products, and the industry. Reference is made to reviewing the chapter opening vignettes and corresponding case problems for learning more about your new company and selling responsibility.

The role plays presented in this appendix are also specifically designed to prepare for professional selling role-play competitions at the annual college and university competitive event conventions (refer to **http://coles.kennesaw.edu/ncsc** and **www.deltaepsilonchi.org/compevents/SRP.html** for more information).

The following companies, sales positions, and customer types are presented:

- The Tom James Company, Alex Homer, **www.tomjames.com**, Custom Clothing—See Chapter 1.
- Liberty Mutual, Marcus Smith, **www.libertymutual.com**, Financial Services—See Chapter 2.
- CB Richard Ellis, Susana Rosas, **www.cbre.com**, Commercial Real Estate Services—See Chapter 3.
- Mattress Firm, Edith Botello, **www.mattressfirm.com**, Mattress Retailing—See Chapter 5.
- *Texas Monthly*, Amy Vandaveer, **www.texasmonthly.com**, Advertising and Sales Promotion—See Chapter 6.
- PulteGroup, Ashley Pineda, **www.pultegroupinc.com**, Home Building—See Chapter 8.
- Salesforce.com, Dave Levitt, **www.salesforce.com**, CRM Software—See Chapter 9.
- Hilti Corporation, Alim Hirani, **www.hilti.com**, Construction Products and Services—See Chapter 10.
- Ecolab, Chris Wylie, **www.ecolab.com**, Cleaning and Sanitizing Products and Services—See Chapter 12.
- Marriott International, Heather Ramsey, **www.marriott.com**, Meeting and Convention Services—See Chapter 13.

■ McKesson Pharmaceutical, Jaime Barouh, **www.mckesson.com**, Pharmaceutical Sales—See Chapter 17.

Using the sales information you have learned throughout the book and the sales worksheets presented, prepare to make your sales call.

Reality Selling Today Role Play 1: Tom James Company

Alex Homer *Tom James*

(This mock sales call role-play scenario was created exclusively for use with the *Selling Today: Partnering to Create Value* textbook.)

Your Role at Tom James

You will be a sales representative (professional clothier) for Tom James Company(**www.tomjames.com**), working out of the same office as Alex Homer, featured in the Chapter 1 opening and Reality Selling Today Video. Tom James specializes in offering complete lines of custom, made-to-measure, and ready-made executive apparel. Clients have the opportunity to create a personality for their wardrobe by selecting from the company's more than 500 suit and 250 shirt fabric options. In addition, the company carries an assortment of accessories such as ties, scarves, belts, and shoes to assist in the completion of the client's wardrobe. In business since 1965, Tom James serves more than 300 000 clients through its 107 offices. Each Tom James client purchases directly from one of the company's professional clothiers, who always come to their clients, as appointments are conducted at the client's location of choice. Refer back to the Chapter 1 opening vignette and case problem, and review the Chapter 1 Reality Selling Today Video for more information.

Your Customer: John Leonard

You are calling on John Leonard, a partner at Leonard & Franklin, a small marketing consulting company. John, who has been in the consulting business for the past 10 years, has built a reputable name for himself and his company after several years of experience with McKinsey & Company. He is a graduate of a prestigious business school, where he graduated with honours. John has a wife and two kids, ages six and eight. John enjoys outdoor activities near Lake Michigan with his family and is a huge fan of the Toronto Blue Jays.

You were referred to John by Mike Kerbanian, who is one of John's former coworkers at McKinsey and one of your repeat customers. Mike had mentioned John's hobbies, his current professional success, and that he runs a very busy consulting firm.

When you called John on the phone, he was extremely busy but mildly receptive. He said that because you came well-referred, he'd be glad to give you 15 minutes as he does not have a lot of time to sacrifice. John expresses that he is very protective of his personal time with his family and, though interested in refreshing his wardrobe, is reluctant to spend time clothes shopping at local boutiques or department stores. You agree to honour his time and he agrees to the appointment.

Quick Facts about John Leonard's Needs

- In the short phone conversation, John said he is not sure what he might need, but that it has been a while since he last freshened up a suit.

- He wears primarily dark grey, black, and navy—both in solids and stripes. His black solid suit is still in workable condition, though his grey and navy suits have become a little threadbare. He was not sure about the condition of his black and navy pinstripe suits.

- He had mentioned in passing that for the time being, his off-work attire is in good shape, although he has some older shirts and sweaters that could need replacing.

- John typically wears a combination of shirts and either jeans or slacks to the office on casual Fridays, when he is not with a client. When he is with a client, he prefers to wear dark-coloured suits.

Your Call Objectives

You hope to turn John Leonard from a prospect into a first-time customer. This is not an easy job, as John will raise two major objections during the sales call:

- He perceives your price as too expensive and asks you for a 20 percent discount for this first-time purchase of the whole bundle that you offered him.

- He mentions that he once had a suit tailored when he was in Bangkok. When he received it in the mail a few weeks later, he was disappointed. The suit just did not fit him properly, and the cloth did not feel as comfortable as the swatches. So he wonders what his options are if he does not get the quality that he expects.

If his questions are sufficiently answered, he will agree to a sale to try things out.

Reality Selling Today Role Play 2: Liberty Mutual

Marcus Smith *Liberty Mutual*

(This mock sales call role-play scenario was created exclusively for use with the *Selling Today: Partnering to Create Value* textbook.)

Your Role at Liberty

You will be an independent insurance broker for Liberty International Underwriters (**www.libertyiu.com**), working out of the same office as Marcus Smith, featured in the Chapter 2 Reality Selling Today Video. Liberty International Underwriters is a division of Liberty Mutual Group, a company that operates in both personal and commercial insurance markets. Liberty Mutual's personal insurance products include auto, home, life, and personal liability. In addition, it also offers a wide range of products and services for business. Property insurance, including ocean cargo insurance, represents one of its important lines of business. Liberty International Underwriters was formed in 1999 as a global specialty business with an emphasis on niche insurance products distributed through the independent broker network. (Refer to the Chapter 2 opening vignette and case problem, and review the Chapter 2 Reality Selling Today Video for more information.)

Your Customer: Farris Footwear Inc.

You will meet with Pat Stanley, the import director at Farris Footwear Inc. Founded in 1980 in Los Angeles, California, this large import–export company serves as a one-stop shop for its customers for a wide variety of footwear, from beach slippers, indoor slippers, sports sandals, sports shoes, and ladies' shoes to cowboy boots. Although its customer base includes retail shoe stores, department stores, and discount stores, the company is shifting its focus to the premium market, where profit margins are higher. Farris Footwear Inc. imports footwear from a number of countries in Asia, Europe, and Latin America. Imports are generally bought under FOB (free on board) shipping point terms of trade, according to which Farris Footwear, rather than the seller, arranges insurance of the goods. Most shipments are made by sea. Monthly imports might reach $1 million during peak seasons. Every two years, Farris Footwear reviews its relationship with its insurance and forwarding agents.

Ocean Cargo Insurance As globalization sweeps across nations, U.S. imports have risen some 40 percent over the past five years. So has the U.S. ocean cargo insurance market.

The basic ocean cargo policy covers perils of the sea (e.g., stranding, sinking, fire, and collision) and perils on the sea (e.g., heavy weather and theft). Other risks such as war and civil commotion might be added to the policy. For shipments that involve multiple modes of transportation, such as a combination of marine transportation and inland transit, additional insurance coverage is required. The client normally signs a contract (called a policy) with an insurance broker, who will then work with insurance company underwriters. Big players in the market are members of the American Institutes of Marine Underwriters (**www.aimu.org**).

The insurance premium (i.e., price) is a function of the sums insured, market conditions, loss experience, and other factors such as risks idiosyncratic to the country of departure. Under an open cargo policy, all goods shipped during the year will be covered, with a maximum amount per shipment.

Quick Facts about Farris Footwear Inc.'s Needs

- Farris Footwear Inc. currently uses two insurance companies: Mandarin Insurance Company for all its imports from Asian countries, and Sasser Insurance Company for its imports from the other countries. Mandarin has been working with Farris for six years, while Sasser signed its contract with Farris two years ago.

- Farris Footwear Inc. receives shipments year round, although peak seasons are from October to February. The main warehouse is located in its headquarters in California due to its proximity to the port of Long Beach, but it also owns two other transit warehouses in Houston, Texas, and New Jersey.

- Footwear is normally packed in carton boxes, with a small sachet of anti-mould chemical, especially for leather shoes.

- Because of the competitive nature of the ocean cargo insurance market, insurance premiums tend to be similar across companies. Farris Footwear Inc. is more interested in value-added services such as shipment tracking, claim resolution, risk management resources, and training.

- Most Farris Footwear Inc. imports are from China, Indonesia, Vietnam, Italy, and Brazil.

Your Call Objectives

In your meeting with Pat Stanley, you hope to identify the decision maker of the insurance agent review process, which will start in a month. You also want to know more about Farris's insurance needs. In addition, you hope to convince Pat that your company can offer outstanding services that go beyond basic ocean cargo insurance.

Reality Selling Today Role Play 3: CB Richard Ellis

Susannah Rosas *CB Richard Ellis*

(This mock sales call role-play scenario was created exclusively for use with the *Selling Today: Partnering to Create Value* textbook.)

Your Role at CB Richard Ellis

You will be a sales representative for CB Richard Ellis (**www.cbre.com**), working out of the same office as Susannah Rosas, featured in the Chapter 3 Reality Selling Today Video. The company offers a variety of premium real estate services, both commercial and industrial. Headquartered in Los Angeles, California, the company has a network of more than 400 branch offices worldwide, with some 30,000 well-trained employees. (Refer to the Chapter 3 opening vignette and case problem and review the Chapter 3 Reality Selling Today Video for more information.)

Your Customer: Norman Flooring Company

You will meet with Kerry Nelson, the owner of Norman Flooring Company. The company was established in 1996 and specializes in flooring solutions for both residential and industrial markets in Texas. Despite the slowdown of the U.S. economy, Norman Flooring has been enjoying a healthy annual growth rate in revenue of 10 percent in the past few years. In its headquarters in Houston, Texas, the company has two warehouses that are rented on a short term of six months to a year. Each warehouse also has an office where administrative staff control inventory, deliver flooring materials to subcontractors, and handle other clerical issues. The company realizes that with the current growth rate, it will soon see itself constrained by its somewhat limited warehousing facilities. As a result, it is actively looking for larger industrial properties at locations that are not only easily accessible from highways and ports but also close to major developing residential areas.

The Industrial Property Market Surprisingly, the U.S. industrial property market has not been strongly influenced by the recent U.S. economic slowdown. The three major industrial property markets include distribution hubs, port facilities, and high-tech centres. Last year, rent growth was greatest in the latter two markets, standing at roughly 3 percent, and the lowest in the former market, at about 0.5 percent. The industrial property market is no exception to the supply and demand rule. Net absorption, defined as the balance between increasing demand and new supply, has been very healthy in markets such as Houston, where availability has been falling. Warehousing represents the largest segment of the industrial property sector. About 25 percent of this warehousing segment was new supply. The industrial market outlook is optimistic, with rent growth expected to remain positive over the next few years.

Quick Facts about Norman Flooring Company's Needs

- The company is looking for industrial warehousing facilities that are in very good condition, with little to no deferred maintenance. The area should be at least 16 000 square feet.
- The location should be easily accessible from the Houston port, in an area that is known to be free from flooding risks.
- The initial lease term will be one year, with the possibility of rent-to-own.
- Preferably, the property site should offer available space for expansion.
- The office building is preferably attached to the warehouse.
- The property should have digital surveillance and perimeter fencing with computer-controlled keypad entry access.

Your Call Objectives

In your meeting with Kerry Nelson, you hope to identify the company's warehousing needs. In addition, you hope to convince Kerry that your company can offer outstanding value-added services, such as nationwide property maintenance consulting.

Reality Selling Today Role Play 4: Mattress Firm

Edith Botello *Mattress Firm*

(This mock sales call role-play scenario was created exclusively for use with the *Selling Today: Partnering to Create Value* textbook.)

Your Role at Mattress Firm

You will be a sales representative for Mattress Firm (**www.mattressfirm.com**), working in the same store as Edith Botello, featured in the Chapter 5 opener and Reality Selling Today Video. Your company offers sleep solutions, including conventional and specialty mattresses, as well as bedding-related products. Mattress Firm carries the top mattress brands such as Sealy, Stearns & Foster, Tempur-Pedic, Simmons, Serta, Sleep to Live, and more. From the very beginning, the company set out to be a different kind of mattress retailer, focused on creating a unique shopping experience.

One aspect that sets Mattress Firm apart from competition is the buying process. Customers are invited to get fitted for a mattress, just as they do with suits, shoes, and gowns. This is accomplished through the company's so-called Sleep Diagnostic System, which asks the customer a series of questions about their sleep quality and then measures their weight distribution and postural alignment. After this is done, it recommends a type of support and eliminates 80 percent of the beds in the showroom, thus making it simpler for customers to find the right mattress without trying out every single bed. Taking the risk out of buying a mattress by letting the customer know what mattresses are best for them is something that only Mattress Firm offers. (Refer back to the Chapter 5 opening vignette, and review the end-of-chapter Reality Selling Today Video Case for more information.)

Your Customer: Mark Boomershine

Mark and Kelly Boomershine have been married for eight years. They have two kids, Lisa and Marcus, ages three and five. The Boomershines are a typical middle-class family, living in a residential area on the outskirts of a large city. They have an Airedale terrier that Kelly loves and that occupies their bed quite frequently. Mark works as a motor mechanic and Kelly is a hospital nurse who works primarily on night duty. Mark is into sports, but he has had some severe problems with his back recently due to a slipped disk. He went to hospital just a week ago and is now recovering from the surgery at home. For the past couple of days, he has been waking up stiff and hurting. Mark and Kelly have had a relatively inexpensive queen size mattress for six years. They were not planning to replace that mattress, but Mark's back problems have forced them to find a supportive mattress for his recovery as soon as possible. Kelly dislikes sleeping on firm mattresses, which is why their current mattress is fairly soft. However, the couple has doubts that another soft mattress would be the ideal solution for Mark, as friends have been telling them that Mark would need a very firm mattress to support his recovery. Today, Mark enters your store to try out some mattresses that would fit his needs. He needs a supportive mattress quite urgently, but wonders whether he and Kelly might actually need two separate mattresses to fit both of their needs.

Your Call Objectives

In your sales call with Mark Boomershine, you hope to build rapport with him, identify his sleeping needs, and sell him a sleeping solution based on these needs. You have to overcome two major objections raised by Mark: (1) What if his back pain persists over a longer time—even on the new mattress that you recommend? Can he simply exchange the mattress at your store for a new one? (2) Since the mattresses you offer him as possible solutions would mean a fairly high expenditure for the couple, he asks you for a substantial rebate of around 20 percent in case of a purchase. However, the particular mattresses that come into consideration are price regulated (i.e., the contract with the manufacturer dictates that price negotiation is not allowed). If you manage to overcome these objections and present a good solution, Mark would be ready to buy. Since he needs a supportive mattress urgently, Mark would bring Kelly into your store tomorrow to get her blessing and make the final choice among the options under consideration.

Reality Selling Today Role Play 5: *Texas Monthly*

Amy Vandaveer *Texas Monthly*

(This mock sales call role-play scenario was created exclusively for use with the *Selling Today: Partnering to Create Value* textbook.)

Your Role at *Texas Monthly*

You are a sales representative for *Texas Monthly* magazine (**www.texasmonthly.com**), working out of the same office as Amy Vandaveer, featured in the Chapter 6 Reality Selling Today Video. Your magazine covers politics, business, and culture, but focuses largely on leisure activities and events in Texas. It has a large real estate advertising section, as well as classified sections in which nearly all advertisers are Texas-based businesses appealing to a prospective buyer who is interested in connecting with Texas history and culture. Through you, your potential customers have access to a large, loyal reader base all over Texas—mostly urban, well educated, and affluent. (Refer to the Chapter 6 opening vignette and case problem and review the Chapter 6 Reality Selling Today Video for more information.)

Your Customer: Roger Linville Properties

You will meet with Kim Pratt, the marketing director at Roger Linville Properties, a property management company. Kim was referred to you by a family friend, who told you that although Roger Linville Properties has reached most of its residents through simple word-of-mouth publicity, it is now considering increasing its magazine advertising. According to your friend, who met Kim through their daughters' Girl Scout troop, Kim's career began at an advertising agency specializing in real estate, then moved to the client side. In all, Kim has 15 years of experience in the marketing of high-end real estate.

Roger Linville Properties started selling units in its first condo building in 1987 and now has 12 upscale high-rise condo buildings in Houston and Galveston. Each property has a sales manager and a marketing manager, and the individual properties do some advertising controlled by those managers, but Kim is ultimately in control of the company's marketing and advertising strategy.

Your supervisor at *Texas Monthly* has some connections to Roger Linville Properties, and he has been able to tell you more about its current advertising situation. According to him, Roger Linville Properties does the majority of its advertising in magazines available for free in the Houston area. You've seen these glossy magazines in the waiting areas of restaurants and hotels; they cater to an affluent readership with society pages, event news, and ads for upscale products and services. The company also uses some billboards, and individual properties use direct mail and well publicized open houses to attract prospective residents.

The majority of the Roger Linville buildings are within the city of Houston. You've learned from their website that there are several buildings in the Galleria area, surrounded by luxury shopping and restaurants, and one near the Rice Village shopping arcade in West University. They also have buildings in the downtown theatre district, which has recently become an increasingly popular location for luxury lofts and condos. In Galveston, they have one building in the historic Strand area and several resort-like condos on the beachfront. Judging by the prices and the amenities they offer, such as concierge service and in-building spas, you can tell that their prime market is affluent people looking for a low-maintenance home that they will rarely have to leave. Most of the properties are advertised as second homes, particularly the Galveston condos, which are promoted as the perfect local vacation home.

While on the website, you noticed that the company is currently in the process of building two new properties: one in the River Oaks area, Houston's most exclusive residential neighbourhood, and one in the Woodlands, an affluent master-planned community north of Houston. They will begin preselling units in these two properties in the next few months. In addition, your supervisor has recently heard rumours that Roger Linville has been negotiating to acquire land in the Dallas area, suggesting that the company may be planning expansion there as well.

Your Call Objectives

In your meeting, you hope to convince Kim Pratt that magazine advertising can be more successful than it has been so far, and that *Texas Monthly* is the magazine to use. Hopefully, you will close a deal by the end of the meeting.

Reality Selling Today Role Play 6: PulteGroup

Ashley Pineda *PulteGroup*

(This mock sales call role-play scenario was created exclusively for use with the *Selling Today: Partnering to Create Value* textbook.)

Your Role at PulteGroup

You will be a sales representative for PulteGroup (**www. pultegroup.com**), working in a similar community as Ashley Pineda, featured in the Chapter 8 Reality Selling Today Video. PulteGroup offers a one-stop shopping experience for prospective customers. Sales reps help clients to finance their homes (with Pulte Mortgage) and to close their homes with PGP Title. Being able to offer everything under one roof and walk the customers through each step of the entire home-buying process makes their home-buying experience very comfortable. PulteGroup offers different product lines: homes for first-time homebuyers, move-up homes, and active adult communities. Just like Ashley Pineda, you will sell the company's

Centex product line (see **www.centex.com**), which is primarily geared toward first-time homebuyers. One central purpose of your sales presentations is to educate your prospects on renting versus owning and the benefits of owning a home. You also give prospects information about the neighbourhood, the area, the schools zoned to the neighbourhood, and the amenities of the community, describing the pools and shopping areas in and around the neighbourhood in order to help your customers envision raising their children in one of Pulte's communities. Refer back to the Chapter 8 opening vignette and case problem, and review the Chapter 8 Reality Selling Today Video for more information.

Your Customer: Mary Bartone

Mary Bartone is 37 years old. She is a single mother and has two little kids, Laura and Fred, ages four and two. Mary had been married to Tom Bartone for almost seven years. The first years of their marriage were happy. The Bartones lived in a nice, large apartment in an uptown neighbourhood. They really enjoyed living in this trendy and vibrant part of their city. Both Mary and Tom liked going out to restaurants, cafés, and bars together with their friends, many of whom also lived in or close to the uptown area. In their leisure time, Mary and Tom frequently enjoyed horse riding and going to all kinds of cultural events. Money was never a big issue, since Tom made good money as a design engineer for Honeywell Building Solutions and Mary earned a decent salary as a senior contact representative for the government benefits office. After some years, however, things started to become worse in their relationship, and about one year ago Tom and Mary decided to split up. They went through a painful divorce. After a tedious court battle, custody of the two children was awarded to Mary, with Tom seeing them every other weekend.

For almost a year, Mary and her two kids have been living in a 790-square foot, two-bedroom apartment close to the uptown area, just about three kilometres away from their old apartment, where Tom still lives. Mary feels that the apartment is too small and that the area is not really suited to raising children. Knowing that the apartment would only be an interim solution, Mary has been dreaming about a new home for quite a while.

Quick Facts about Mary Bartone's Needs

- Mary is looking for a house with at least 1200 square feet and three bedrooms.
- Like most parents with young children, Mary is very concerned about her children growing up in a safe and sheltered environment with decent daycare facilities and schools.
- As a single mother who wants to raise her children in the new home, Mary is very much interested in the warranties that PulteGroup can offer as a builder.
- Mary pays great attention to the warmth and feel of a home and having a large backyard for the children to play.
- Mary has bank savings of approximately $60 000. Her annual income (including some alimony) is currently around $55 000. Therefore, a solid financing solution that is comfortable within her budget is needed.
- Mary is a true family person. Her parents and her younger sister Susan, who live about 400 kilometres away, come to visit her quite frequently. Before signing a contract for a new home, she will make sure she has her father's blessing.

- Mary is of two minds concerning the location of the house. On the one hand, she knows that having more square footage and a large backyard would require her to move farther out of the city. On the other hand, she does not want to move too far away from the uptown area where her office is located and where Tom and many of her friends live.

Your Call Objectives

In your meeting with Mary, you hope to build rapport with her and identify her needs and requirements for owning a home. You also hope to convince Mary that you can offer her an excellent home in which to raise her children.

Reality Selling Today Role Play 7: Salesforce.Com

Dave Levitt *Salesforce.com*

(This mock sales call role-play scenario was created exclusively for use with the *Selling Today: Partnering to Create Value* textbook.)

Your Role at Salesforce.com

You are a sales representative for Salesforce.com (**www. salesforce.com**), just like Dave Levitt in the Chapter 9 Video Case Problem. Your company is the world leader in on-demand customer relationship management (CRM) services. Unlike most CRM applications, companies that use your services store customer and sales data on Salesforce.com. One of the benefits of on-demand CRM services is that customers incur neither up-front capital investment nor on-site administration costs. Your company also offers solutions that are customized to specific customer needs, such as creating different interfaces for different departments and work groups, and providing limited access to data for specific authorized work groups.

Your Customer: Rename Clothing Company

You will meet with Jesse Golden, the marketing director at Rename Clothing Company. A family-owned business in Garden Grove, California, the company is expanding at a fast pace not only in the United States, but also in Latin American markets that the company entered into two years ago. The company currently has a sales force of 20 people and outsources its selling activities for overseas operations to local firms. Each salesperson is responsible for three to four customers. While outsourcing has the advantages of capitalizing on market knowledge of local partners, the company realized it does not have full control over its selling efforts. Domestically, the company has strong relationships with its buyers, but there have been signs of work overload among the sales force. While Rename has three in-house brands that it distributes using its own channel, it does provide sourcing solutions to mid-range and high-end department stores under their private labels. Rename works closely with its suppliers in more than five countries, mainly in Europe and Asia. It also has a small manufacturing facility in California for sample development and small-batch order production.

Quick Facts about Rename Clothing Company's Needs The apparel industry is a sophisticated, fast-moving industry with several designs launched every season, and repeat orders must be met as fast as possible before end-users change their tastes. As a company that operates in mid-range to high-end markets, Rename positions itself as a sourcing company with a fast turnaround for its customers. The nature of the industry requires salespeople to be highly diligent in market information gathering, processing, and dissemination across geographic areas and departments.

At present, the in-house salespeople use spreadsheets for almost all of their selling activities, such as recording sales calls, reporting to sales managers, and tracking delivery of orders, to name just a few. Jesse joined the company two months ago and realized that the current system showed clear signs of overload. Mistakes have started to occur more often, and the company has received quite a few complaints about shipment delays, wrong labelling on products, and wrong packaging. As marketing director, Jesse spent several days making sense of disparate information about Rename's domestic sales and has heard mixed reports about its overseas operation. Jesse's secretary lamented that the spreadsheets provided by the sales force are not in a uniform format, making it difficult to consolidate the database. Meanwhile, salespeople claim that their customers are not all the same and they need to customize their spreadsheets so that they can keep track of things more easily.

With high pressure for growth, Rename is looking for an efficient way to consolidate and manage its customer database. Jesse is also in the process of establishing a branch office in Mexico and will staff three local salespeople to manage Rename's business in this growing market. In overseas markets, the focus is more on customer acquisition and lead management, while in domestic markets, Jesse is more concerned with keeping Rename's existing customers happy.

Your Call Objectives

In your meeting with Jesse Golden, you hope to convince him that Salesforce.com is the right CRM solution for Rename. You can do this by providing him with interesting facts and benefits Salesforce.com can offer (see more information at **www.salesforce.com**). Hopefully, you will close a deal by the end of the meeting.

Reality Selling Today Role Play 8: Hilti Corporation

Alim Hirani *Hilti Corporation*

(This mock sales call role-play scenario was created exclusively for use with the *Selling Today: Partnering to Create Value* textbook.)

You will be a sales representative for Hilti (**www.hilti.com**), working out of the same office as Alim Hirani, featured in the Chapter 10 Reality Selling Today Video. The company provides the global construction industry with innovative products and services. In addition to a wide variety of high-end products such as measuring systems, drilling and demolition, installation systems, foam systems, and screw fastening systems, the company also offers its customers customized training programs and consulting services. Hilti sales representatives work directly with customers rather than through intermediary parties. (Refer to the Chapter 10 opening vignette and case problem, and review the Chapter 10 Reality Selling Today Video for more information.)

Your Customer: Ellis Exhibition Inc.

You will meet with Casey Smith, procurement manager for Ellis Exhibition Inc. The company owns a 100 000-square-foot exhibition centre that hosts several local and regional events in Atlanta, Georgia. Some of these events have become a must-see for the local business community. Depending on the theme and the products being showcased, Ellis Exhibition offers exhibitors outstanding display services that include floor plans, display solutions, display installation, and booth dismantlement. After an event, the installation systems are reused, while installation accessories are generally discarded. Casey Smith believes that by buying the right type of installation accessories, Ellis can save a lot of money and therefore offer its exhibitor customers more competitive prices.

Quick Facts about Ellis Exhibition Inc.'s Needs

- Ellis Exhibition Inc. spends about $500 000 a year on installation accessories. These accessories are galvanized, but they can also be painted to match the colour theme stipulated by exhibitors.

- Ellis uses a wide variety of installation accessories, from hexagon nuts and head screws to distance holders.

- Ellis does not want to stock these accessories. Exhibitors who want to use Ellis display services are required to place their order three months in advance. Then, an Ellis accountant will calculate the necessary accessories needed for each event.

- Ellis is extremely concerned with the quality of all of its installation systems and accessories.

Your Call Objectives

In your meeting with Casey Smith, you hope to identify the specific types and the expected quantity of installation accessories. You also want to know about delivery requirements. In addition, you might be able to cross-sell other Hilti products and services, such as sprinkler systems.

Reality Selling Today Role Play 9: Ecolab

Chris Wylie *Ecolab*

(This mock sales call role-play scenario was created exclusively for use with the *Selling Today: Partnering to Create Value* textbook.)

Your Role at Ecolab

You are a sales representative for Ecolab (**www.ecolab.com**), working in a similar territory as Chris Wylie, featured in the

Chapter 12 Video Case Problem. With sales of $6 billion and more than 26 000 associates, your company is the global leader in cleaning, sanitizing, food safety, and infection prevention products and services. Ecolab delivers comprehensive programs and services to foodservice, food and beverage processing, healthcare, and hospitality markets in more than 160 countries. You work in the Institutional Business Unit, which is the core of Ecolab—and the world leader in providing cleaning and sanitation products, programs, and services to customers in a variety of industries. Specifically, you serve the foodservice market, calling on restaurants, cafeterias, etc. Today, you will try to get access to the kitchen facilities of one of the largest prospects in your territory, Angelo's Restaurant.

Your Customer: Francesco Manchini, Owner of Angelo's Restaurant

The owner of the restaurant is Francesco Manchini (known as Frankie by his restaurant friends and patrons). Angelo's is located south of downtown Vancouver in a trendy neighbourhood. Manchini had a great deal of insight into the potential of this area and now has three restaurants located within a three-block radius. His other two restaurants are Pasta e Basta and LaTorre. Based on some initial inspection and speculation, you can assume that each of these restaurants is probably worth $10 000. Angelo's currently uses Swisher, a North American competitor. Swisher was started back in 1986 with the conviction that business people would welcome the opportunity to have their facilities maintained by a true hygiene specialist. You are familiar with the competition and are aware of Swisher's strategy. Typically, they gain the bathroom hygiene business and then look for opportunities in the back of the house. This is exactly what happened at Angelo's. Francesco Manchini has three primary concerns that reflect his problems with Swisher. First, product performance is not to his standards. The Swisher Program is not getting the dishes clean and spotty dishes are unacceptable for fine dining. Second, the people at Swisher know a lot about bathroom care and maintenance, but they lack a great deal of experience and knowledge about back-of-the-house operations. Third, product service is lacking. Swisher was always front-and-centre when they were trying to get the business, but now never show up and seldom return service calls in a timely manner.

Francesco has an expressive personality style. He is talkative and very low on self-monitoring. He is a very emotional person and quick to get red-faced when someone angers him or slap them on the back when they please him. He never leaves a conversation without getting in the last word and saying whatever he feels. He is quick to tell someone that they are wrong, particularly salespeople, if he thinks they are giving him a load of garbage. Francesco acknowledges that Swisher's bathroom hygiene services are good but the decision to move them into the back of the house may not have been such a great idea. He is quick to tell everyone within earshot why he is unhappy with Swisher. Even though there are some problems, he is not sure what the solution is.

You have a 9:30 a.m. meeting scheduled and realize that you probably have about 20 minutes before the lunch push begins to happen.

Quick Facts about Francesco Manchini's Needs Thanks to the approval by Francesco's executive chef, Nino Trappatoni, you have already completed a survey of the kitchen prior to your initial meeting with Francesco Manchini. You uncovered several areas of concern and issues that can be leveraged as opportunities. These may be latent and the prospect may not realize that there are problems or potential problems.

- Floors are covered in grease by the fryer. Floors are slippery and there are no mats or protective coverings in place.
- Limited drying racks. Dishes stacked on top of each other, including glasses.
- Poor results. Food soil left on dishes was found by doing a Mikroklene test.
- Some dishes on the racks are spotty and covered with soap residue.
- There are no safety devices or equipment, such as eye wash stations, first-aid, etc.
- No product dispensers are in place. It looks as if everything is being poured or sprayed from a bottle.

Your Call Objectives

Since this is your first meeting with Francesco Manchini, you have to introduce yourself and Ecolab to him and try to build rapport. Based on the survey of the kitchen, you then try to convince Francesco to buy from you. To that end, you will have to overcome his objections:

- "We used Ecolab at one of our other properties a few years back. The service was terrible."
- "I am sure that if I sign-up with Ecolab, you will forget about me once I commit to the change. What guarantees do I have that you will be there when I need you?"
- "I heard that Ecolab uses more soap than necessary to inflate their sales and rip off the customer."
- "We cannot afford downtime. I am sure that switching over to Ecolab would put the kitchen out of commission for too long. We can't afford to shut our kitchen down to make the change to Ecolab."

Reality Selling Today Role Play 10: Marriott International, Inc.

Heather Ramsey *Marriott International Inc.*

(This mock sales call role-play scenario was created exclusively for use with the *Selling Today: Partnering to Create Value* textbook.)

Your Role at Marriott

You will be a sales representative for Marriott International Inc. (**www.marriott.com**), working out of the same hotel as Heather Ramsey, featured in the Chapter 13 Reality Selling Today Video. Founded in 1927 by J. Willard and Alice S. Marriott, Marriott has grown from a root beer stand to a multinational company with more than 3000 lodging properties located in some 70 countries around the world. Apart from luxurious hotel accommodation under several well-managed brands, the company also offers outstanding services for meetings and events. From weddings to corporate meetings, Marriott's clients know that they are always in good hands. (Refer to the Chapter 13 opening vignette and case problem, and review the Chapter 13 Reality Selling Today Video for more information.)

Your Customer: Hiroshi Watanabe/Chris Scott

You will meet with Chris Scott, personal secretary to Mr. Hiroshi Watanabe, owner of a chain of high-end tailor stores in California. Mr. Watanabe and his wife were married 25 years ago in a simple wedding ceremony. The couple immigrated to the United States with only five dollars between them. They worked very hard to make ends meet, and their fate took a turn when both were hired full-time for the first time by a small tailor shop—Mr. Watanabe as a deliveryman and his wife as a helper.

With strong entrepreneurial spirit and incessant learning, they soon opened their own business using their meagre savings. Initial clients were mainly friends, but they soon found a niche in the market by combining traditional Japanese garment making with American contemporary fashion. Before they knew it, celebrities started knocking on their door, asking for custom-made evening gowns and suits. A couple of years later, they opened their first concept store under the name Watanabe and positioned it as a high-end custom-made tailor house. They also provided customers with a full range of custom-designed accessories.

Their two sons soon joined the team, managing stores and franchisees in prime locations in Los Angeles and San Francisco, California. As their silver wedding anniversary is approaching, Mr. Watanabe asks Chris to organize something very special for his wife to make up for the years of hard work the couple has been through.

Event Planning

More information on event planning is available at **www.marriott.com**. You should also be able to get more information on anniversary party ideas from the Internet.

Quick Facts about the Clients' Needs

- The anniversary has to be formal as many celebrities will be invited.
- The menu has to be as bountiful and sumptuous as possible.
- Costs are not a major concern. However, Chris should be shopping for the best offer.
- Chris is in charge of information gathering and screens offers from three major hotels. Chris already has an offer from a Marriott competitor.
- The goal is not only to impress the guests but also Mrs. Watanabe.
- The highlight of the anniversary is a recount of the couple's happy marriage.

Your Call Objectives

In your meeting with Chris Scott, you hope to identify Mr. Watanabe's needs. In addition, you hope to convince him that you provide the best event planning services, which your competitor cannot offer. In doing so, you should be prepared to offer Chris a number of creative ideas to make the event both formal and memorable.

Reality Selling Today Role Play 11: Pharma Supply

Jaime Barouh McKesson
Pharmaceutical

(This mock sales call role-play scenario was created exclusively for use with the *Selling Today: Partnering to Create Value* textbook.)

Your Role at Pharma Supply

You will be a pharmaceutical sales representative for Pharma Supply, a respected pharmaceutical wholesaler that sells medical supplies and drugs to medical clinics, hospitals, and other health care institutions, and to retail pharmacies, including many small independent retail pharmacies, large pharmacy chains, and pharmacies that are part of large retail operations such as Walmart, Costco, and various supermarket chains. Your company has recently signed an agreement to represent a generic drug manufacturer. You will be introducing a new generic antidepressant drug, fluoxetine (see websites at **www.drugs.com/fluoxetine** and **www.fluoxetine.com**), for Pharma Supply. Competing branded drugs include Eli Lilly's Prozac (see **www.prozac.com/index.jsp**).

You will start by contacting walk-in clinics and multi-doctor family health practices to get acceptance of your generic drug so that doctors will be comfortable writing prescriptions for a generic alternative. (Refer to the Chapter 17 opening vignette and review the Chapter 17 Reality Selling Today Video for more information on the nature of a respected pharmaceutical wholesaler. McKesson Pharmaceutical (**www.mckesson.com**), the featured company in the Chapter 17 Reality Selling Today Video, is a wholesale pharmaceutical distribution business similar to Pharma Supply.)

Your Customer: Family Health Services Clinic

Family Health Services is a downtown clinic. Many of its regular patients live in the immediate area and would be described as lower- to lower-middle income patients. You will meet with Payton Diaz, the clinic manager. Payton has been recently hired at this clinic, but you have met him a number of times previously at another clinic. You would describe Payton as a Supportive (see Chapter 4). Payton always seems quiet and polite, and although you have a friendly relationship, you believe Payton would have a friendly relationship with all salespeople.

Family Health Services has four doctors and two registered nurses:

- Dr. Tom Brown is 36 years old and has been at the clinic for less than a year. He is one of two doctors and begins work at 8:00 a.m. He works each day until 5:00 p.m., but stays on Monday nights until the clinic closes at 8:00 p.m.
- Dr. Lu Bingyu is a bit younger than Tom. She works the same hours as Tom but works late on Friday rather than Monday evenings.
- Dr. Tony Bander is the senior doctor at the clinic and is likely to retire within the next five years. He visits hospital patients each morning and seldom gets to the clinic before noon. He works until 8:00 p.m. Tuesday through Thursday.

- Dr. Jane Blenko works each day from noon until 8:00 p.m. Jane's husband is a doctor at one of the local hospitals.

- Nurse Connie Small comes to the clinic each morning when it opens and works until 5:00 p.m. Ben Brothers, the second nurse, comes to work at noon and works each night until 8:00 p.m.

Quick Facts about Selling to Health Clinics and Medical Practices

- Doctors usually resist seeing salespeople and, when they do, the average duration of a sales call is limited to just one or two minutes.

- Doctors will sometimes meet with salespeople in a group situation, but only when there are very important reasons to do so. Even then, it is common to arrange somewhat of a social meeting as well—perhaps lunch or a small catered meal.

- A typical sales call by a pharmaceutical wholesaler salesperson to a health clinic would normally involve talking to the clinic manager to check inventory, take orders, and ensure that there are no service issues or other problems. Rarely would a wholesaler salesperson have to see the medical practitioners.

- When drugs are involved, the amount of product knowledge required is usually beyond what a wholesaler salesperson would be expected to have, so a product specialist would also be involved in the sales call. When such calls are made, it is important to get to see as many members of the medical staff as possible during a single sales call. This requires working with the clinic manager to coordinate a meeting when everyone can attend.

- Doctors are sometimes reluctant to prescribe generic drugs unless they are certain the drug will be as effective as its branded competitor, even though the cost for a generic alternative can be half the cost of a known brand. However, for patients who must pay for their own prescriptions, doctors will often consider prescribing generic drugs.

Your Call Objectives

During your initial contact, you have developed three call objectives. The first is to re-establish your relationship with Payton. The second is to establish who would be the important people at the clinic who should attend a meeting. Your third objective is to arrange a meeting with the clinic staff, within approximately two weeks, so that the product expert who will accompany you on the subsequent sales call can make a presentation and answer questions for attendees. Your product expert is a well known medical researcher and is widely published in medical journals on the efficacy of the generic antidepressant you distribute.

You are concerned that Payton has been employed with this clinic for only a short time. Payton may not be comfortable trying to arrange a meeting on your behalf unless you can be convincing that the meeting will be worth everyone's time.

Endnotes

Chapter 1

1. Michael R. Solomon, Greg W. Marshall, and Elnora W. Stuart, *Marketing: Real People, Real Choices*, 5th ed. (Upper Saddle River, NJ: Prentice Hall, 2008), p. 445.

2. Christian Homburg, Jan Wieseke, and Torsten Bornemann, "Implementing the Marketing Concept at the Employee-Customer Interface: The Role of Customer Need Knowledge," *Journal of Marketing*, July 2009, p. 64–81.

3. Lucy McCauley, "Voices: The State of the New Economy," *Fast Company*, September 1999, p. 124.

4. Stan Davis and Christopher Meyer, *Blur: The Speed of Change in the Connected Economy* (New York: Addison-Wesley, 1998), p. 9.

5. David Shenk, *Data Smog: Surviving the Information Glut* (New York: HarperEdge, 1997), pp. 27–29.

6. Michael R. Solomon, Greg W. Marshall, and Elnora W. Stuart, *Marketing: Real People, Real Choices*, 5th ed. (Upper Saddle River, NJ: Prentice Hall, 2008), p. 445.

7. Gary L. Frankwick, Stephen S. Porter, and Lawrence A. Crosby, "Dynamics of Relationship Selling: A Longitudinal Examination of Changes in Salesperson–Customer Relationship Status," *Journal of Personal Selling and Sales Management*, Spring 2001, p. 135.

8. Liz C. Wang, Julie Baker, Judy A. Wagner, and Kirk Wakefield (2007), "Can a Retail Web Site be Social?", *Journal of Marketing*, Vol. 71, p. 143–157.

9. Greg Ip, "Why High-Fliers, Built on Big Ideas, Are Such Fast Fallers," *Wall Street Journal*, April 4, 2002, p. A–1.

10. Würth Canada Website, www.wurthcanada.com and BlueSky Personnel Solution Website, www.blueskypersonnel.com (both accessed May 9, 2011).

11. "Sales Reps, Teachers among Most in Demand," www.msnbc.msn.com/id/17858379 (accessed May 31, 2010).

12. Gabrielle Birkner, "Who Says Titles Don't Matter?" *Sales & Marketing Management*, July 2001, p. 14.

13. "America's Best-Paying Jobs," www.forbes.com/2009/05/04/america-best-paying-leadership-careersjobs-slide.html (accessed May 31, 2010).

14. "Top-Paying Jobs," http://jobs.aol.com/articles/2009/12/10/top-paying-jobs (accessed May 31, 2010).

15. Christine Galea, "The 2004 Compensation Survey," *Sales & Marketing Management*, May 2004, pp. 28–34.

16. Michele Marchetti, "What a Sales Call Costs," *Sales & Marketing Management*, September 2000, pp. 80–81.

17. Theodore B. Kinni, "Fast Track to the Top: How to Start Out in Sales and End Up as CEO," *Selling Power*, July/August, pp. 56–61.

18. "Women in the Labor Force: A Databook (2009 Edition)," www.bls.gov/cps/wlftable10.htm (accessed May 31, 2010).

19. Carol Hymowitz, "Women Put Noses to the Grindstone, and Miss Opportunities," *Wall Street Journal*, February 3, 2004, p. B1.

20. Bonnie Harris 2007, "Wanted: Women in Finance, Why: Client Base Changing," *The Des Moines Register*, Monday, Jan 29, 2007, p. 4D.

21. Brett A. Boyle, "The Importance of the Industrial Inside Sales Force: A Case Study," *Industrial Marketing Management*, September 1996, p. 339.

22. David L. Kurtz, H. F. (Herb) MacKenzie, and Kim Snow, *Contemporary Marketing*, 2nd Canadian edition. (Scarborough, ON: Nelson Education, 2010).

23. Erin Munro and Samantha Cheuk, personal interviews, July 24, 2008.

24. Canadian Bankers Association, "Your Guide to Financial Services," www.cba.ca/eng/Tools/Brochures/tools_financialservices2.htm (downloaded April 18, 2002).

25. Pearl Paul, personal interview and correspondence, July 29, 2008.

26. Grant Robertson, "What Your Broker Doesn't Want You To Know," *Globe and Mail*, December 22, 2010, p. 4.

27. Gerald L. Manning and Barry L. Reece, Intelecom Video Library, *Selling Today*, 9th ed.

28. Ibid.

29. Chris Mckee, personal interview, July 28, 2008; The Hitch house Website, www.thehitchhouse.com (accessed July 27, 2008).

30. Stoney Creek Furniture Website, "Home Furnishings Industry To Salute Stoney Creek Furniture National Home Furnishings Association North American Retailer of the Year 2010, www.stoneycreekfurniture.com/current/retailer_of_the_year.aspx (accessed May 9, 2011).

31. Direct Sellers Association of Canada, personal correspondence from Joan Lee, Director of Operations, July 25, 2008.

32. John R. Sparks and Joseph A. Schenk, "Socialization Communication, Organizational Citizenship Behaviors, and Sales in a Multilevel Marketing Organization, *Journal of Personal Selling and Sales Management*, Spring 2006, p. 161–80.

33. Stanley Marcus, "Sales School," *Fast Company*, November 1998, p. 105.

34. Thomas A. Stewart, "Knowledge, the Appreciating Commodity," *Fortune*, October 12, 1998, p. 18.

35. Martin Gargiulo, Gokhan Ertug, and Charles Galunic (2009), "The Two Faces of Control: Network Closure and Individual Performance Among Knowledge Workers," *Administrative Science Quarterly*, Vol. 54, p. 299–333.

36. Sudheer Gupta (2008), "Channel Structure with Knowledge Spillover," *Marketing Science*, Vol. 27(2), p. 247–61.

37. John Naisbitt, *Megatrends* (New York, Warner Books, 1982), p. 18.

38. Dennis Jenkins, "Entrepreneurial Endeavors for Sales & Marketing Professionals," *American Salesman*, August 2007.

39. Beth Belton, "Technology Is Changing Face of U.S. Sales Force," *USA Today*, February 9, 1999, p. A2.

40. Brian Tracy, *The 100 Absolutely Unbreakable Laws of Business Success* (San Francisco: Berrett-Koehler Publishers, Inc., 2000), p. 192.

41. Linda Corman, "Look Who's Selling Now," *Selling*, July–August 1996, pp. 46–53; "Everyone's a Seller," *Sales & Marketing Management*, March 2003, p. 12.

42. Gerry Khermouch, "Keeping the Froth on Sam Adams," *BusinessWeek*, September 1, 2003, pp. 54–56.

43. Simon J. Bell, Seigyoung Auh, and Karen Smalley (2005), "Customer Relationship Dynamics: Service Quality and Customer Loyalty in the Context of Varying Levels of Customer Expertise and Switching Costs," *Journal of the Academy of Marketing Science*, Vol. 33(2), p. 169–83.

44. Harry Beckwith, *Selling the Invisible* (New York: Warner Books, 1997), p. 38; see Norm Brodsky, "Street Smarts," *Inc.*, June 2004, pp. 53–54.

45. Alfred M. Pelham and Pamela Kravitz (2008), "An Exploratory Study of the Influence of Sales Training Content and Salesperson Evaluation on Salesperson Adaptive Selling, Customer Orientation, Listening, and Consulting Behaviors," *Journal of Strategic Marketing*, Vol. 16(5), p. 413–35.

46. Heather Johnson, "Field of Sales," *Training*, July 2004, p. 34.

47. Gerhard Gschwandtner, "Rendezvous with a Rainmaker," *Selling Power*, May 2001, pp. 98–100.

48. Kristine Ellis, "Deal Maker or Breaker?" *Training*, April 2002, pp. 34–7; Michele Marchetti, "Sales Training Even a Rep Could Love," *Sales & Marketing Management*, June 1998, p. 70.

49. Terry Loe in Henry Canaday, "You Can Do It," *Selling Power*, January/February 2007, pp. 23–6.

50. Henry Canaday, "In the Trenches," *Selling Power*, March 2007, pp. 25–7.

Sources for Boxed Features

a. Michael Hammer, *The Agenda* (New York: Random House, 2001), p. 6.

b. CBC News, "A Criminal Mind: The Life and Times of Eddie Greenspan," aired January 20, 2005, www.cbc.ca/lifeandtimes/greenspan.html (accessed June 13, 2005); "My Greatest Sale," Eddie Greenspan, interviewed by Laura Pratt, *Profit*, May 2005, p. 36.

c. Based on John F. Tanner and George Dudley, "How U.S. Salespeople Differ from Their Peers Overseas," *Value-Added Selling*, February 14, 2005, p. 4.

d. The Jim Pattison Group Web site, www.jimpattison.com (accessed January 4, 2011); Government of British Columbia, Protocol and Events Branch, "Jim Pattison—Vancouver," www.protocol.gov.bc.ca/protocol/prgs/obc/1990/1990_JPattison.htm (accessed February 7, 2010); Diane Francis, "What Makes Jim Pattison Run—and Whistle," *Financial Post*, March 5–7, 1994, p. S3.

Chapter 2

1. For a comprehensive description of the distinct stages in the evolution of personal selling, see Thomas R. Wotruba, "The Evolutionary Process of Personal Selling," *Journal of Personal Selling and Sales Management*, Summer 1991, p. 4.

2. Phillip Kotler and Gary Armstrong, *Principles of Marketing*, 12th Ed., (Upper Saddle River, NJ: Prentice Hall, 2008), p. 10.

3. Louis E. Boone and David L. Kurtz, *Contemporary Marketing*, 11th Ed. (Mason, OH: Southwestern Publishing, 2004), p. 11.

4. Norihiko Shirouzu, Gregory L. White, and Joseph B. White, "Beyond Explorer Woes, Ford Misses Key Turns in Buyers, Technology," *Wall Street Journal*, January 14, 2002, p. A–1.

5. Jeff Bennett, "Ford Expects Auto Industry Sales Pace to Continue," *Wall Street Journal Online*, May 2010, online.wsj.com (accessed June 1, 2010).

6. Malcolm Fleschner, "World Wide Winner—The UPS Story," *Selling Power*, November/December 2001, p. 58; "50 Best Companies to Sell For," *Selling Power*, November/December 2004, pp. 94–5.

7. "America's 25 Best Sales Forces," *Sales & Marketing Management*, July 2000, p. 59; "The 25 Best Service Companies to Sell For," *Selling Power*, November/December 2004, p. 95.

8. Gary Armstrong and Philip Kotler, *Marketing—An Introduction*, 7th Ed. (Upper Saddle River, NJ: Prentice Hall, 2005), p. 57.

9. Andris A. Zoltners and Prabhakant Sinha, "Sales Territory Design: Thirty Years of Modeling and Implementation," *Marketing Science*, vol. 24, no. 3 (Summer, 2005), pp. 313–31.

10. Robert M. Peterson, George H. Lucas, and Patrick L. Schul, "Forming Consultative Trade Alliances: Walking the Walk in the New Selling Environment," *NAMA Journal*, Spring 1998, p. 11; Beth Belton, "Technology Is Changing Face of U.S. Sales Force," *USA Today*, February 9, 1999, p. 2A.

11. Charles Gottenkieny, "Proper Training Can Result in Positive ROI," *Selling*, August 2003, p. 9.

12. Tim Smith, "Between Solution and Transactional Selling," www.wiglafjournal/selling (accessed June 1, 2010).

13. Thomas R. Wotruba, "The Evolutionary Process in Personal Selling," *Journal of Personal Selling & Sales Management*, Summer 1991, p. 4.

14. Christian Homburg, Nicole Koschate, and Wayne D. Hoyer, "Do Satisfied Customers Really Pay More? A Study of he Relationship between Customer Satisdfaction and Willingness to Pay More," *Journal of Marketing*, April 2005, pp. 84–96.

15. Michael R. Solomon, Greg W. Marshall, Elnora W. Stuart, *Marketing—Real People, Real Choices*, 4th Ed. (Upper Saddle River: New Jersey, Prentice Hall, 2006), p. 35.

16. Robert E. Miller and Stephen E. Heiman, *Strategic Selling* (New York: Warren Books, 1985), p. 26.

17. Jack Snader, "Is It Consultative Selling or Detailing?" *Newspost*, Fall 1999, pp. 21–32; Patricia Seybold, *The Customer Revolution* (New York: Random House, 2001), p. 1.

18. Fernando Jaramillo, William B. Locander, Paul E. Spector, and Eric G. Harris, "Getting the Job Done: The Moderating Role of Initiative on the Relationship between Intrinsic Motivation and Adaptive Selling," *Journal of Personal Selling & Sales Management*, Winter 2007, pp. 59–74.

19. Keith M. Eades, *The New Solutions Selling* (New York: McGraw-Hill, 2004), pp. ix–x.

20. Marvin A. Jolson, "Broadening the Scope of Relationship Selling," *Journal of Personal Selling & Sales Management*, Fall 1997, p. 77.

21. Keith M. Eades, *The New Solutions Selling*, ibid., pp. 102–04.

22. Patricia Seybold, *The Customer Revolution* (New York: Random House, 2001), p. 1.

23. Christian Homberg, Jan Wieseke, and Torsten Bornemann, "Implementing the Marketing Concept at the Employee-Customer Interface: The Role of Customer Need-Knowledge," *Journal of Marketing*, July 2009, pp. 64–81.

24. Jagdish Sheth and Reshma H. Shah, "Till Death Do us Part . . . But Not Always: Six Antecedents to a Customer's Relational Preference in Buyer–Seller Exchanges," *Industrial Marketing Management*, June 2003, pp. 627–31.

25. Erin Strout, "Fast Forward," *Sales & Marketing Management*, December 2001, pp. 37–38.

26. Geoffrey Brewer, "The Customer Stops Here," *Sales & Marketing Management*, March 1998, pp. 31–32.

27. Gary Armstrong and Philip Kotler, *Marketing—An Introduction*, 7th Ed., ibid., p. 23.

28. Jenex Corporation, "The Jenex Corporation Grants Worldwide License to Distribute and Sell Thermapik Device," news release, February 28, 2007, www.jenexcorp.com/pressreleases.asp?ID=109 (accessed May 18, 2008).

29. See Cy Charney, "Choose Your Partners," *Value-Added Selling 21*, December 16, 2003, p. 3.

30. For a discussion of strategic selling alliances that involves the sales representatives from two or more organizations, see J. Brock Smith and Donald W. Barclay, "Selling Partner Relationships: The Role of Interdependence and Relative Influences," *Journal of Personal Selling & Sales Management*, Fall 1999, pp. 21–40.

31. Gary Armstrong and Philip Kotler, *Marketing: An Introduction*, 7th Ed., ibid., p. 16.

32. Michael Hammer, *The Agenda* (New York: Random House, 2001), pp. 38–39.

Sources for Boxed Features

a. Philip Kotler, Neil Rackham, and Suj Krishnaswamy, "Ending the War Between Sales & Marketing," *Harvard Business Review*, July/August 2006, pp. 68–78.; Dave Stein, "Sales and Marketing Alignment, Take 2," *Sales & Marketing Management*, January/February 2007, p. 9.

b. Robert Kreitner, *Management*, 8th ed. (Boston: Houghton Mifflin, 2001), pp. 3–4.

Chapter 3

1. Daniel Goleman, *Working with Emotional Intelligence* (New York: Bantam Books, 1998), pp. 24–28, 317; Geoffrey James, "Use Emotional Intelligence to Improve Sales," *Selling Power*, January/February 2005, p. 43–45.

2. Daniel Goleman, *Emotional Intelligence* (New York: Bantam Books, 1995), p. 34; Cary Cherniss and Daniel Goleman (eds.), *The Emotionally Intelligent Workplace*, (San Francisco, CA: Jossey-Bass, 2001), pp. 22–24. For more information on social competence, see Daniel Goleman, *Working With Emotional Intelligence* (New York: Bantam Books, 1998), pp. 24–28.

3. L. B. Gschwandtner and Gerhard Gschwandtner, "Balancing Act," *Selling Power*, June 1996, p. 24.

4. Ron Willingham, *Integrity Selling For The 21st Century* (New York: Currency Doubleday, 2003), p. 11.

5. Daniel H. Pink, *A Whole New Mind*, New York: Riverhead Books, 2005, pp. 48–63.

6. Ilan Mochari, "In a Former Life," *Inc.*, April 2001, p. 100.

7. J. D. Power Consumer Center, www.jdpower.com (accessed May 4, 2002).

8. *Partnering: The Heart of Selling Today*. VHS (Des Moines, IA: American Media Incorporated, 1990).

9. Paul S. Goldner, "How to Set the Playing Field," *Selling*, April 1998, p. 9.

10. Larry Wilson, *Selling in the 90s* (Chicago, IL: Nightingale Conant, 1988), p. 35.

11. William Keenan, Jr. "Customer Satisfaction Builds Business," *Selling*, March 1998, p. 12.

12. Tim Sanders, *Love Is the Killer App* (New York: Crown Business, 2002), p. 23.

13. Malcolm Fleschner, "World Wide Winner—The UPS Story," *Selling Power*, November/December 2001, p. 58.

14. Neil Rackham and John R. DeVincentis, *Rethinking the Sales Force* (New York: McGraw-Hill, 1999), pp. 79–83.

15. Phillip C. McGraw, *Self Matters*, New York: Simon & Schuster, 2001, pp. 69–70.

16. Sharon Begley, "Follow Your Intuition: The Unconscious You May Be the Wiser Half," *Wall Street Journal*, August 30, 2002, P. B1: Sharon Begley, "How Do I Love Thee? Let Me Count the Ways—and Other Bad Ideas," *Wall Street Journal*, September 6, 2002, P. B1.

17. Phillip C. McGraw, "Dr. Phil: Know Your Goal, Make a Plan, and Pull the Trigger," *The Oprah Magazine*, September 2001, pp. 60–61; See Barry L. Reece and Rhonda Brandt, *Effective Human Relations—Personal and Organizational Applications* (Boston: Houghton Mifflin Company, 2005), pp. 95–102

18. McGraw, *Self-Matters*, p. 73.

19. Stephen E. Heiman and Diane Sanchez, *The New Conceptual Selling* (New York: Warner Books, 1999), pp. 48–49. See Stephen R. Covey, "Win-Win Strategies," *Training*, January 2008, p. 56.

20. David Mayer and Herbert M. Greenberg, "What Makes a Good Salesman," *Harvard Business Review*, July-August 2006, p. 166. For information on how empathy training helps sales representatives improve, see Cliff Edwards, "Death of a Pushy Salesman," *Business Week*, July 3, 2006.

21. Ibid.

22. Shoshana Zuboff, "A Starter Kit for Business Ethics," *Fast Company*, January 2005, p. 91.

23. Carol Hymowitz, "Management Missteps in 04 Hurt Companies, Endangered Customers," *Wall Street Journal*, December 21, 2004, p. B1; "Edward Jones Agrees to Settle Host of Charges," *Wall Street Journal*, December 21, 2004, p. C1; John Hechinger, "Putnam May Owe $100 million," *Wall Street Journal*, February 2, 2005, p. C1; Erin McClam, "Witness Tells of Coverup," *News & Observer*, January 29, 2005, p. 3D.

24. Nathaniel Branden, *Self-Esteem at Work*, p. 35.

25. Barbara Killinger, *Integrity: Doing the Right Thing for the Right Reason* (Montreal & Kingston: McGill-Queen's University Press, 2007), p. 13.

26. Eli Jones, Jesse N. Moore, Andrea J. S. Stanaland, and Rosalind A. J. Wyatt, "Salesperson Race and Gender and the Access and Legitimacy Paradigm: Does Difference Make a Difference?" *Journal of Personal Selling and Sales Management*, Fall 1998, p. 74; "Danielle Sacks, The Accidental Guru," *Fast Company*, January 2005, pp. 65–71.

27. Barry L. Reece and Rhonda Brandt, *Effective Human Relations—Personal and Organizational Applications*, 9th ed. (Boston, MA: Houghton Mifflin, 2005), p. 35–37.

28. Roy M. Berko, Andrew D. Wolvin, and Darlyn R. Wolvin, *Communicating*, 8th ed. (Boston: Houghton Mifflin Company, 2001), p. 45.

29. Ibid., p. 50.

30. Susan Bixler, *The Professional Image* (New York: Putnam Publishing Group, 1984), p. 216.

31. Barbara Pachter and Marjorie Brody, *Complete Business Etiquette Handbook* (New York: Prentice Hall, 1995), p. 14.

32. Adapted from Leonard Zunin, *Contact: The First Four Minutes* (New York: Nash Publishing, Ballantine Books, 1972), p. 109; and Jerry La Martina, "Shake It, Don't Crush It," *San Jose Mercury News*, June 25, 2000, p. 4PC.

33. Deborah Blum, "Face It!" *Psychology Today*, September/October 1998, pp. 32–69; See Julia Chang, "Selling in Acting," *Sales & Marketing Management*, May 2004, p. 22.

34. Barbara Pachter and Mary Brody, *Complete Business Etiquette Handbook* (Englewood Cliffs, NJ: Prentice Hall, 1995), p. 27; "The Eyes Have It," *Sales & Marketing Management*, January 2002, p. 20.

35. Appropriate clothing for work is discussed in Christina Binkley, "Case Study: Dressing for the Naked CEO," *Wall Street Journal*, August 23, 2007, p. D8.

36. Melinda Ligos, "Does Image Matter?" *Sales & Marketing Management*, March 2001, p. 52–55.

37. Margaret Webb Pressler, "Camouflage for the Cubicles," *News & Observer*, April 25, 2004, p. 4–E.

38. Susan Bixler and Nancy Nix-Rice, *The New Professional Image* (Adams Media Corporation, 1997), p. 11–15; Barbara Pachter and Marjorie Brody, *Complete Business Etiquette Handbook*, p. 72.

39. Paul Galanti, "Talking Motivates—Communication Makes Things Happen," *Personal Selling Power*, November–December 1995, p. 88.

40. Susan Berkley, "Hone Your Sharpest Sales Weapon," *Sales & Field Force Automation*, July 1997, p. 24.

41. Joann S, Lublin, "To Win Advancement, You Need to Clean up Any Bad Speech Habits," *Wall Street Journal*, October 5, 2004, p. B.1.

42. David E. Weliver, "My Fair CEO," *Inc.*, October 30, 2001, p. 112.

43. "Is Etiquette a Core Value?" *Inc.*, May 2004, p. 22.

44. Tim Sanders, *Love Is the Killer App* (New York: Crown Business, 2002), p. 18.

45. Steven Covey, *The 7 Habits of Highly Effective People* (New York: Simon & Schuster, 1989), pp. 240–41.

46. L. B. Gschwandtner, "Mary Lou Retton," *Personal Selling Power*, Fifteenth Anniversary Issue, 1995, p. 99.

47. Jack Canfield, *The Success Principles* (New York: Harper Collins, 2005), pp. 342–43.

48. Colleen DeBaise, "Offbeat Hobbies May Help Build Relationships with Some Clients," *Wall Street Journal*, February 9, 2005, p. B2.

49. Anne Murphy Paul, "Self-Help: Shattering the Myths," *Psychology Today*, March/April 2001, p. 64; Arnold A. Lazarus and Clifford N. Lazarus, *The 60-Second Shrink* (San Luis Obispo, CA: Impact Publishers, 1997), pp. 3–4.

50. Phillip C. McGraw, *Self Matters* (New York: Simon & Shuster, 2001), pp. 69–76.

51. Rick Saulle, "Honor Diversity," *Selling Power*, May 2004, p.54.

Sources for Boxed Features

a. Dean Keating and Brian Rogers, Janssen Inc., March–June, 2011.

b. Adapted from "Secrets of Power Persuasion for Salespeople," by Roger Dawson. See Roger Dawson, "And Your Name Was Again?" *Value-Added Selling 21*, July 16, 2007, p. 2.

Chapter 4

1. Mike McNamee and Christopher Schmitt, "The Chainsaw Al Massacre," *Business Week*, May 28, 2001, p. 48; Dennis K. Berman and Joann S. Lublin, "Restructuring, Personality Clashes Led to Lucent Executive's Exit," *Wall Street Journal*, May 17, 2001, p. B1; Charles Fishmann, "Jeff Bezos," *Fast Company*, February 2001, pp. 80–82.

2. Douglas A. Bernstein, Louis A. Penner, Alison Clarke-Stewart, and Edward J. Roy, *Personality*, 6th ed. (Boston: Houghton Mifflin, 2003), p. 518.

3. Robert Bolton and Dorothy Grover Bolton, *People Styles at Work* (New York: AMACOM, 1996), p. 10.

4. Fernando Jaramillo, William B. Locander, Paul E. Spector, and Eric G. Harris, "Getting the Job Done: The Moderating Role of Initiative on the Relationship Between Intrinsic Motivation and Adaptive Selling," *Journal of Personal Selling & Sales Management*, Winter 2007, pp. 59–74.

5. David W. Merrill and Roger H. Reid, *Personal Styles and Effective Performance* Radnor, PA: Chilton Books, 1981), p. 1.

6. For a more complete description of *The Versatile Salesperson* training program visit the Wilson Learning Corporation Web page, www.wilsonlearning.com (accessed January 20, 2005).

7. Robert J. Sternberg, *Thinking Styles* (New York: Cambridge University Press, 1997), p. 8.

8. Robert Bolton and Dorothy Grover Bolton, *People Styles at Work* (New York, AMACOM, 1996).

9. Geoff James, "Inside the Psychology of Selling," *Selling Power*, January/February 2004, pp. 25–28.

10. The dominance factor was described in an early book by William M. Marston, *The Emotions of Normal People* (New York: Harcourt, 1928). Research conducted by Rolfe LaForge and Robert F. Suczek resulted in the development of the Interpersonal Checklist (ICL), which features a dominant–submissive scale. A person who receives a high score on the ICL tends to lead, persuade, and control others. The Interpersonal Identity Profile, developed by David W. Merrill and James W. Taylor, features a factor called "assertiveness." Persons classified as being high in assertiveness tend to have strong opinions, make quick decisions, and be directive when dealing with people. Persons classified as being low in assertiveness tend to voice moderate opinions, make thoughtful decisions, and be supportive when dealing with others.

11. David W. Johnson, *Reaching Out—Interpersonal Effectiveness and Self-Actualization*, Eighth Edition (Boston, MA: Allyn and Macon, 2003), p. 83.

12. The research conducted by LaForge and Suczek resulted in identification of the *hostile–loving continuum*, which is similar to the *sociability continuum*. Their Interpersonal Checklist features this scale. L. L. Thurstone and T. G. Thurstone developed the Thurstone Temperament Schedule, which provides an assessment of a "sociable" factor. Persons with high scores in this area enjoy the company of others and make friends easily. The Interpersonal Identity Profile developed by Merrill and Taylor contains an objectivity continuum. A person with low objectivity is seen as attention seeking, involved with the feelings of others, informal, and casual in social relationships. A person who is high in objectivity appears to be somewhat indifferent toward the feelings of others. This person is formal in social relationships.

13. Sam Deep and Lyle Sussman, *Close the Deal* (Reading, MA: Perseus Books, 1999), p. 157.

14. Len D'Innocenzo and Jack Cullen, "Chameleon Management," *Personal Selling Power*, January–February 1995, p. 61.

15. "A Global Profiling Tool," Wilson Learning Corporation, Eden Prairie, MN. 1999.

16. Tom Ritchey, *I'm Stuck, You're Stuck*, San Francisco, CA: Berrett-Koehler, Inc. 2002, p. 5.

17. Ron Willingham, *Integrity Selling for the 21st Century* (New York: Currency Doubleday, 2003), pp. 20–21.
18. Stuart Atkins, *How to Get the Most from Styles-Based Training* (Beverly Hill, CA: Stuart Atkins, 1996), p. 1.
19. Gary A. Williams and Robert B. Miller, "Change the Way You Persuade," *Harvard Business Review*, May 2002, p. 65.
20. Robert Bolton and Dorothy Grover Bolton, *People Styles at Work*, p. 65.
21. David Merrill and Roger Reid, *Personal Styles and Effective Performance* (Radnor, PA: Chilton Books, 1981), p. 2.
22. Roger Wenschlag, *The Versatile Salesperson* (New York, NY: John Wiley & Sons, 1989), pp. 165–71.
23. Nina Munk, "How Levi's Trashed a Great American Brand," *Fortune*, April 12, 1999, p. 85.
24. "The Top 25 Managers of the Year," *Business Week*, January 14, 2002, p. 65.
25. Stuart Atkins, *How to Get the Most from Styles-Based Training*, p. 3.
26. Ron Willingham, *Integrity Selling* (New York: Doubleday, 1987), pp. 21–23.
27. Eric F. Douglas, *Straight Talk* (Palo Alto, CA: 1998), p. 92.
28. Ron Willingham, *Integrity Selling*, p. 37.
29. David W. Merrill and Roger H. Reid, *Personal Styles and Effective Performance*, pp. 134, 135.
30. Stuart Atkins, *The Name of Your Game* (Beverly Hills, CA: Ellis & Stewart, 1981), p. 51.

Sources for Boxed Features

a. Personal interview with Ruth Todd, February 9, 2011.
b. Christopher Caggiano, *Psychopath, Inc.*, July 1998, p. 83.
c. "The Platinum Rule," www.platinumrule.com (accessed May 4, 2008).

Chapter 5

1. O. C. Ferrell, John Fraedrich and Linda Ferrell, *Business Ethics*, 5th ed. (Boston: Houghton Mifflin Company, 2002), p. 6. The importance of character at the leadership level is described in Noel M. Tichy and Warren G. Bennis, "Making the Tough Call," *Inc.*, November 2007, pp. 36–38.
2. Shankar Ganesan, Steven P. Brown, Babu John Mariadoss, and Hillbun (Dixon) Ho (2010), "Buffering and Amplifying Effects of Relationship Commitment in Business-to-Business Relationships," *Journal of Marketing Research*, 47 (2), pp. 361–73.
3. Stephen R. Covey, *The Seven Habits of Highly Effective People* (New York: Simon & Schuster, 1989), pp. 18, 92. See Adam Hanft, "The New Lust for Integrity," *Inc.*, February 2004, p. 104.
4. Jan Yager, *Business Protocol* (Stamford, CT: Hannacroix Creek Books, 2001), pp. 199–200.
5. Sharon Begley, "A World of Their Own," *Newsweek*, May 8, 2000, pp. 53–56; Jaren Sandberg, "Office Sticky Fingers Can Turn the Rest of Us into Joe Fridays," *Wall Street Journal*, November 19, 2005, p. B1.
6. John A. Byrne, "How to Fix Corporate Governance," *Business Week*, May 6, 2002, pp. 69–78.
7. Josh Freed, "Investigators: Drug Salesman Foiled Pharmacist," *The News & Observer*, August 26, 2001, p. 12A.
8. Robert Simons, Henry Mintzburg, and Kunal Basu, "Memo to CEOs," *Fast Company*, June 2002, pp. 117–21.
9. Marjorie Kelly, "Waving Goodbye to the Invisible Hand," *Business Ethics*, March/April 2002, p. 4. For a somewhat different point of view, see George Stalk, "Warm and Fuzzy Doesn't Cut It," *Wall Street Journal*, February 15, 2005, p. B2.
10. Yochi J. Dreazen, "Pressure for Sales Fostered Abuses at WorldCom," *Wall Street Journal*, May 16, 2002, p. B1. See Norm Kamikow, "Ethics & Performance," *Workforce Performance Solutions*, March 2006, p. 4.
11. Beth Schultz, "Ethics under Investigation," *Network World Framingham*, April 26, 2004, pp. 72–74.
12. Robert Simons, *et al.*, "Memo to CEOs," pp. 120–21.
13. Patrick Smith, "You Have a Job, But How About a Life?" *Business Week*, November 16, 1998, p. 30.
14. Mitchell Pacelle, "Citigroup Works on Reputation," *Wall Street Journal*, February 17, 2005, p. C3.
15. Patricia B. Gray, "Business Class," *Fortune*, April 17, 2006, p. 336; Margery Weinstein, "Survey Says: Ethics Training Works," *Training*, November 2005, p. 15; "ERC Survey & Benchmarking," www.ethics.org (accessed October 8, 2007).
16. Patricia Gray, "Business Class," *Fortune*, April 17, 2006, p. 336; Philip Kotler and Gary Armstrong, *Principles of Marketing*, 12th ed. (Upper Saddle River, NJ: Prentice Hall, 2008), p. 568.
17. Alan M. Webber, "Are All Consultants Corrupt?" *Fast Company*, May 2002, pp. 130–34.
18. Brenda Bouw, "In praise of an ethical education," *Globe and Mail*, March 18, 2002, p. C1.
19. Gary Armstrong and Philip Kotler, *Marketing*, 6th ed. (Upper Saddle River, NJ: Prentice Hall, 2003), p. 619.
20. Betsy Cummings, "Ethical Breach," *Sales & Marketing Management*, July 2004, p. 10.
21. Sun Life Financial website, www.sunlife.com, and "Code of Business Conduct" (accessed June 26, 2008).
22. Michele Krebs, "All the Marketing Men," *Autoweek*, February 16, 1998, p. 11.
23. Joseph A. McKinney and Carlos W. Moore (2008), "International Bribery: Does a Written Code of Ethics Make a Difference in Perceptions of Business," *Journal of Business Ethics*, 79 (1-2) pp. 103–111.
24. Ken Brown and Gee L. Lee, "Lucent Fires Top China Executives," *Wall Street Journal*, April 7, 2004, p. A8; Carl F. Fey, "How to Do Business in Russia," *Wall Street Journal*, October 27, 2007 p. R4.
25. Steven Sack, "Watch the Words," *Sales & Marketing Management*, July 1, 1985, p. 56.
26. Patricia S. Eyres, "Steps for Staying Out of Court and Trouble," *Selling*, April 2002, p. 10.
27. Michael Schrage, "Internet: Internal Threat?" *Fortune*, July 9, 2001, p. 184.
28. Mary C. Gentile, "Managing Yourself: Keeping Your Colleagues Honest," *Harvard Business Review*, March 2010, http://hbr.org/2010/03/managing-yourself-keeping-your-colleagues-honest/ar/1 (accessed July 7, 2010).
29. Rob Zeiger, "Sex, Sales & Stereotypes," *Sales & Marketing Management*, pp. 52, 53.
30. Barry L. Reece and Rhonda Brandt, *Effective Human Relations—Personal and Organizational Applications*, Tenth Edition (Boston, MA: Houghton Mifflin, 2008), p. 110.
31. Betsy Cummings, "Do Customers Hate Salespeople?" *Sales & Marketing Management*, June 2001, pp. 50–51.
32. Ron Willingham, *Integrity Selling for the 21st Century* (New York: Currency Doubleday, 2003), p. 1.

33. Ron Willingham, "Four Traits All Highly Successful Salespeople Have in Common," (audiotape presentation), Phoenix, AZ, 1998.

34. Price Pritchett, *The Ethics of Excellence* (Dallas, TX: Pritchett & Associates, Inc., n.d.), p. 14.

35. Research on how cheaters justify their actions is cited in Romy Drucker, "The Devil Made Me Do It," *Business Week*, July 24, 2006, p. 10.

36. Robert Kreitner, Barry Reece, and James P. O'Grady, *Business*, Second Edition (Boston, MA: Houghton Mifflin, 1990), pp. 647–48.

37. Karin Schill Rives, "Workers Find Clause Has Teeth," *News & Observer*, July 29, 2001, p. E1.

38. Dawn Marie Driscoll, "Don't Confuse Legal and Ethical Standards," *Business Week*, July/August 1996, p. 44.

39. Nancy Henderson Wurst, "Who's Afraid of Ethics?" *Hemisphere Magazine*, November 2006, pp. 120–23.

40. Carol Wheeler, "Getting the Edge on Ethics," *Executive Female*, May/June 1996, p. 47.

41. Ron Willingham, *Integrity Selling for the 21st Century*, ibid., p. 11.

42. Sharon Drew Morgan, *Selling with Integrity*, (San Francisco, CA: Berrett-Koehler Publishers, Inc., 1997), pp. 25–27.

43. Ibid., pp. 27–28.

44. Tom Peters, *Thriving on Chaos* (New York: Alfred A. Knopf, 1988), p. 521.

45. Gerhard Gschwandtner, "Lies and Deception in Selling," *Personal Selling Power*, Fifteenth Anniversary Issue, 1995, p. 62.

46. Price Pritchett, *The Ethics of Excellence* (Dallas, TX: Pritchett & Associates, Inc., [n.d.]), p. 18.

47. Price Pritchett, *The Ethics of Excellence* (Dallas, TX: Pritchett & Associates, Inc., n.d.), p. 18.

48. Neil Rackham and John R. DeVincentis, *Rethinking the Sales Force* (New York: McGraw-Hill, 1999), pp. 83–84. A discussion of the trust factor is included in Jacqueline Durett, "A Matter of Trust," *Sales & Marketing Management*, January/February 2007, pp. 36–37.

49. Geoffrey Colvin, "The Verdict on Business: Presumed Guilty," *Fortune*, November 15, 2004, p. 78.

50. "The World Is Flat: A Brief History of the Twenty-First Century," www.thomaslfriedman.com (accessed October 10, 2007).

51. Matthew McKay, Martha Davis, and Patrick Fanning, *Messages: The Communication Skills Book* (Oakland, CA: New Harbinger, 1995), p. 108.

52. O. C. Ferrell, John Fraedrich, and Linda Ferrell, *Business Ethics: Ethical Decision Making and Cases*, 5th ed. (Boston: Houghton Mifflin Company, 2002), p. 208.

53. Barry L. Reece and Rhonda Brandt, ibid., pp. 125–26.

54. William M. Pride, Robert J. Hughes, and Jack R. Kapoor, *Business*, 7th ed. (Boston: Houghton Mifflin Company, 2002), p. 40.

Sources for Boxed Features

a. Michael T. Kenny, "Research, Observe Chinese Protocol to Land Sale," *Selling*, May 2001, p. 10; Jan Yager, Business Protocol, 2nd ed. (Stamford, CT: Hannacroix Creek Books, 2001), p. 113.

b. Beth Schultz, "Ethics under Investigation," *Network World*, April 26, 2004, pp. 72–73; "Living the Values: A Guide to Ethical Business Practices at Nortel Networks. www.nortel-networks.com/corporate/community/ethics/collateral/code_of_conduct_ nolinks.pdf (downloaded December 30, 2004).

c. Sonia Verma, "I Don't Have So Much Faith in Law," *Globe and Mail*, January 15, 2011, p. F3.

Chapter 6

1. Interview with Amy Vandaveer on April 13, 2007. For additional information regarding *Texas Monthly* magazine, visit www.texasmonthly.com.

2. Keith M. Eades, *The New Solution Selling* (New York: McGraw-Hill, 2004), pp 4–5.

3. Geoffrey James, "Solution Selling," *Selling Power*, May 2006, pp. 45–48. This article is based on an interview with Keith Eades, author of *The New Solution Selling*.

4. Michael R. Solomon and Elnora W. Stuart, *Marketing: Real People, Real Choices*, Third Edition (Upper Saddle River, NJ: Prentice Hall, 2008), p. 237.

5. "Strategic Vista International Inc. Introduces a Revolution in? Safety and Security Protection to Consumers," *Canada NewsWire*, Ottawa, July 28, 2004, p. 1.

6. "Loki Management Systems Is Selected as Finalist in Microsoft 2004 Impact Awards," *Canada NewsWire*, Ottawa, October 29, 2004, p. 1.

7. Neil Rackham and John R. DeVincentis, *Rethinking the Sales Force* (New York: McGraw-Hill, 1999), p. 79.

8. Department of Finance Canada. www.fin.gc.ca/toce/2002/cmfi_e.html (accessed May 6, 2002).

9. Karen E. Starr, "Simple Solutions," *Selling Power*, July/August 2001, p. 22.

10. Christopher Whittier, "Quotation Management: The Revolution is Here to Stay," www.resultsonline.com (accessed August 27, 2007).

11. John Fellows, "A Decent Proposal," *Personal Selling Power*, November/December 1995, p. 56.

12. Adapted from John Fellows, "A Decent Proposal," *Personal Selling Power*, November–December 1995, p. 56. See Neil Rackham, "Seven Rules for Creating Winning Sales Proposal's," *Value-Added Selling* 21, December 16, 2003, p. 20.

13. "Feeling under the Gun? Check Your Proposal," *Selling*, October 2001, p. 3.

14. Neil Rackam, "Seven Rules for Creating Winning Sales Proposals," *Value-Added Selling 21*, December 16, 2003, p. 20.

15. "What Kind of Rep Is Most Trustworthy?" *Sales & Marketing Management*, February 2001, p. 90.

16. Robert W. Palmatier, Lisa K. Scheer, and Jan-Benedict E.M. Steenkamp (2007), "Customer Loyalty to Whom? Managing the Benefits and Risks of Salesperson-Owned Loyalty," *Journal of Marketing Research*, 44(2), pp. 185–99.

17. Tom Peters, *Re-Imagine! Business Excellence in a Disruptive Age* (London: Dording Kindersley Limited, 2003), p. 224.

18. Reimer Express news release, "Reimer Express and Its Parent? Roadway Express Receive System Wide ISO 9002 Certification," www.reimerexpress.com/news/reimerpressers/2000-04-04.html (accessed June 29, 2008).

19. Betsy Cummings, "Welcome to the Real Whirled," *Sales & Marketing Management*, February 2001, pp. 87–88.

20. Ian Gelenter, "Build Satisfaction with a Service Contract," *Selling*, May 1998, p. 7.

21. Tom Reilly, "Should You Set Prices?" *Selling*, August 2000, pp. 1, 14.

22. Gerhard Gschwandtner, "ROI Selling," *Selling Power*, November/December 2004, p. 10.

23. William M. Pride, Robert J. Hughes, and Jack R. Kapoor, *Business*, Eighth Edition (Boston, MA: Houghton Mifflin, 2005), pp. 456–57.

24. Michael Aherne, C. B. Bhattacharya, and Thomas Gruen (2005), "Antecedents and Consequences of Customer-Company Identification: Expanding the Role of Relationship Marketing," *Journal of Applied Psychology*, 90(3), pp. 574–85.

25. "*Financial Post*'s 10 Best Companies to Work For 2011," available at http://dl.dropbox.com/u/16692492/fp10_2011.pdf (accessed March 1, 2011).

26. Michael L. Askew, "What I Know Now," *Fast Company*, November 2005, p. 108.

27. Michael R. Williams and Jill S. Attaway, "Exploring Salespersons' Customer Orientation as a Mediator of Organizational Culture's Influence on Buyer-Seller Relationships," *Journal of Personal Selling & Sales Management*, Fall 1996, pp. 33–52.

28. "Dealer Merchandising Portfolio," *Views: The Inner Circle News*, Winter 2000, p. 10.

29. "Grassroots Problem Solving," *Inc.*, March 1996, *p.* 92.

30. See Brian Tracy, "Analyzing the Competition," *Value Added Selling 21*, September 16, 2003, p. 2.

31. Jim Dickie, "Lowest Price Isn't the Answer," *Selling*, August 2000, p. 14.

32. Bob Mundson, "A Personal Blend," *Training*, February 2004, p. 11.

33. "Ontario Global Traders Awards," *Profit*, September 2001, Advertising Supplement.

34. Margery Weinstein, "Selling Points," *Training*, June 2007, p. 51.

35. Raj Agnihotri, Adam Rapp, and Kevin Trainor (2009), "Understanding the Role of Information Communication in the Buyer-Seller Exchange Process: Antecedents and Outcomes," *Journal of Business & Industrial Marketing*, 24(7), pp. 474–86.

36. Jill Rosenfeld, "Unit of One," *Fast Company*, April 2000, p. 98.

37. Neil Rackham, *The SPIN Selling Fieldbook* (New York: McGraw-Hill, 1996), pp. 149–52; *Value-Added Selling 21*, December 26, 2006, p. 4.

38. Gary Hamil, Leading the Revolution (Boston: Harvard Business School Press, 2000), p. 87; Neil Rackham, "Improve This Skill and Boost Sales Up to 27 Percent," *Value-Added Selling 21*, March 2, 2004, p. 1; *Value-Added Selling 21*, December 26, 2006, p. 4.

Sources for Boxed Features

a. Rhea Seymour, "Ideas That Work," *Profit*, June 2002, p. 69.

b. "International Snapshot," *Sales & Marketing Management*, March 2000, p. 72; Jan Yager, *Business Protocol*, 2nd ed. (Stamford, CT: Hannacroix Creek Books, 2001), p. 111.

Chapter 7

1. Peter Egan, "The Best of All Worlds Bunch," *Road & Track*, July 2002, pp. 52–78. "2005 Geneva: Lexus Finesses Next IS Sport Sedan," www.autoweek.com (accessed March 1, 2005). Greg Kable, "Audi A4 Debuts at Frankfurt," *Autoweek*, September 3, 2007, p. 10. Joe Rusz, "Saab 9-3 & XWD" *Road & Track*, October 2007, p. 60.

2. Neal E. Boudette, "The Luxury-Car Market Gets More Crowded," *Wall Street Journal*, March 3, 2005, p. D1; J. P. Vettraino, "2006 BMW 3 Series: Technology Update," www.autoweek.com (accessed July 6, 2010).

3. Wayne S. Desarbo, Rajdeep Grewal, and Crystal J. Scott (2008), "A Clusterwise Bilinear Multidimensional Scaling Methodology for Simultaneous Segmentation and Positioning Analyses," *Journal of Marketing Research*, 45(2), pp. 280–92.

4. Michael R. Solomon, Grey W, Marshall, and Elnora W. Stuart, *Marketing: Real People, Real Choices*, 5th ed. (Upper Saddle River, NJ: Pearson Education, 2008), p. 220.

5. D. Lee Carpenter, "Return on Innovation—the Power of Being Different," *Retailing Issues Letter*, May 1998, p. 3.

6. Brian Tracy, "Keeping the Customers You Make," *Selling*, November 2003, pp. 1, 4.

7. Tom Reilly, "You Must Differentiate to Win," *Selling*, April 2001, pp. 1, 10.

8. Gary Armstrong and Philip Kotler, *Marketing: An Introduction*, 7th ed. (Upper Saddle River, NJ: Prentice Hall, 2005), p. 12.

9. Tom Leverton, "Five Questions," *Sales & Marketing Management*, July 2004, p. 13.

10. Theodore Kinni, "The Value Proposition," *Selling Power*, July/August 2005, p. 75.

11. Michael Arndt, "Built for the Long Haul" *Business Week*, January 30, 2006, p. 66.

12. Carl K. Clayton, "Sell Quality, Service, Your Company, Yourself," *Personal Selling Power*, January/February 1990, p. 47.

13. Elaine Parker, "How I Made the Sale," *Value-Added Selling 21*, June 17, 2003, pp. 1–2.

14. Suein L Hwang, "It Was a WOMBAT for the Meatware, But It Was a Good Sell," *Wall Street Journal*, May 15, 2002, p. B1.

15. J. Thomas Russell and W. Ronald Lane, *Kleppner's Advertising Procedure* (Englewood Cliffs, NJ: Prentice-Hall, 1996), pp. 46–47.

16. Kevin Zheng Zhou and Kent Nakamoto (2007), "How Do Enhanced and Unique Features Affect New Product Preference? The Moderating Role of Product Familiarity," *Journal of the Academy of Marketing Science*, 35, pp. 53–62.

17. Lawrence B. Chonko and Eli Jones (2005), "The Need for Speed: Agility Selling," *Journal of Personal Selling and Sales Management*, 25(4), pp. 371382.

18. Mark Leslie and Charles A. Holloway, "The Sales Learning Curve," *Harvard Business Review*, July/August 2006, p. 121.

19. Jess McCuan, "Reeling In the Big One" *Inc.*, August 2004, pp. 43–44; "What Is IntraLinks?" www.Intralinks.com (accessed March 2, 2005).

20. Sun Life Financial websites, www.sunlife.ca and www.sunlife.com (accessed April 3, 2011).

21. Michael R. Solomon and Elnora W. Stuart, *Marketing: Real People, Real Choices* Fourth Edition (Upper Saddle River, NJ: Prentice Hall, 2006), pp. 347–48.

22. Carlos Tejada, "The Allure of Bundling," *Wall Street Journal*, October 7, 2003, p. B 1.

23. Michael Treacy, "You Need a Value Discipline—But Which One?" *Fortune*, April 17, 1995, p. 195.

24. Robert Shulman and Richard Miniter, "Discounting Is No Bargain," *Wall Street Journal*, December 7, 1998, p. A30.

25. Andy Cohen, "Survey Says: Service Beats Price Online," *Sales & Marketing Management*, July 2002, p. 18.

26. Geoffrey James, "Solution Selling," *Selling Power*, May 2006, p. 46.

27. Adapted from a model described in "Marketing Success through Differentiation—of Anything," *Harvard Business Review*, January/February 1980.

28. Joanna Johnson, "A New Perspective on Marketing," *Construction Dimensions*, April 1990, p. 14.

29. Ted Levitt, *Marketing Imagination* (New York: Free Press, 1983), p. 80.

30. Neil Rackham, "Boost Your Sales 20% by Improving This Skill," *Value-Added Selling 21*, June 17, 2003, pp. 1–2.

31. Beth Davis-Sramek, Cornelia Droge, John T. Mentzer, and Matthew B. Myers (2009), "Creating Commitment and Loyalty Behavior among Retailers: What Are the Roles of Service Quality and Satisfaction?" *Journal of the Academy of Marketing Science*, 37, pp. 440–54.

32. Thomas A. Stewart, "A Satisfied Customer Isn't Enough," *Fortune*, July 21, 1997, pp. 112–13.

33. Martin Reimann, Oliver Schilke, and Jacquelyn S. Thomas (2010), "Customer Relationship Management and Firm Performance: The Mediating Role of Business Strategy," *Journal of the Academy of Marketing Science*, 38, pp. 326–46.

34. "Business Bulletin," *Wall Street Journal*, September 24, 1998, p. A1.

35. Chuck Salter, "On the Road Again," *Fast Company*, January 2002, pp. 50–58.

36. "Study: What Really Matters to Your Customers," *Value-Added Selling 21*, February 14, 2005, p. 4.

37. Ted Levitt, *Marketing Imagination*, p. 84.

38. Rebecca Smith, "Beyond Recycling: Manufacturers Embrace 'C2C' Design," *Wall Street Journal*, March 3, 2005, p. B1.

39. Neil Rackham and John R. DeVincentis, *Rethinking the Sales Force* (New York: McGraw-Hill, 1999), p. 89.

40. Ibid., pp. 89–90.

41. Ibid., p. 90.

42. Francy Blackwood, "The Concept That Sells," *Selling*, March 1995, pp. 34–36; *Systems Furniture Overview*, Steelcase Incorporated, November 1995, pp. 48–50. Rebecca Smith, "Beyond Recycling: Manufacturers Embrace 'C2' Design," *Wall Street Journal*, March 3, 2005, p. B1.

Sources for Boxed Features

a. Adapted from discussion in Leonard L. Berry, A. Parasuraman, and Valerie A. Zeithaml, "The Service-Quality Puzzle," *Business Horizons*, September–October 1988, pp. 35–43; Robert Kreitner, *Management*, 5th ed. (Boston: Houghton Mifflin Company, 1992), pp. 613–14.

b. Personal interview with and correspondence from Laura Ricciuto, April 2011.

Chapter 8

1. "Nighttime Reading for Daytime Success," *Sales & Marketing Management*, May 2007, p. 44.

2. Michael Hammer and James Champy, *Reengineering the Corporation: A Manifesto for Business Revolution* (New York: Harper Business, 1993), p. 18.

3. Keith M. Eades, *The New Solution Selling* (New York: McGraw-Hill, 2004), pp. 32–33.

4. Tom Peters and Nancy Austin, *A Passion for Excellence* (New York: Random House, 1985), p. 71.

5. "How Well Do You Know Your Customers?" *Sales & Field Force Automation*, January 1999, p. 141.

6. Gary Armstrong and Philip Kotler, *Marketing: An Introduction*, Sixth Edition (Upper Saddle River, NJ: Prentice Hall, 2003), pp. 191–92, 215.

7. Michael R. Solomon and Elnora W. Stuart, *Marketing: Real People, Real Choices*, 5th ed. (Upper Saddle River, NJ: Prentice Hall, 2008), p. 184.

8. Gary Armstrong and Philip Kotler, *Marketing: An Introduction*, 7th ed. (Upper Saddle River, NJ: Prentice Hall, 2005), p. 169.

9. Michael R. Solomon and Elnora W. Stuart, *Marketing: Real People, Real Choices*, 2008, p. 182.

10. Ibid., pp. 182–83.

11. Philip Kotler and Gary Armstrong, *Principles of Marketing*, Twelfth Edition (Upper Saddle River, NJ: Prentice Hall, 2008), pp. 163–66.

12. FedEx, www.fedex.com (accessed July 6, 2010).

13. Philip Kotler and Gary Armstrong, *Principles of Marketing*, Twelfth Edition, pp. 146–47.

14. Ibid., p. 147.

15. S. Sajeesh and Jagmohan S. Raju (2010), "Positioning and Pricing in a Variety Seeking Market," *Management Science*, 56(6), pp. 949–61.

16. Philip Kotler and Gary Armstrong, *Principles of Marketing*, Twelfth Edition, pp. 145–146.

17. Keith M. Eades, *The New Solution Selling*, pp. 32–33. Betsy Cummings, "Proving the Sale Process," *Sales & Marketing Management*, June 2006, p. 12.

18. Keith M. Eades, *The New Solution Selling*, p. 31.

19. Stephen E. Heiman and Diane Sanchez, *The New Conceptual Selling* (New York: Warner Books, 1999), pp. 190–91.

20. Research reported in Tom Atkinson and Ron Koprowski, "Sales Reps' Biggest Mistakes," *Harvard Business Review*, July–August 2006. p. 1, indicates that 26 percent of the business-to-business buyers say salespeople "don't follow my company's buying process."

21. Gary Armstrong and Philip Kotler, *Marketing*, Seventh Edition, p. 160.

22. Neil Rackham and John R. DeVincentis, *Rethinking the Sales Force* (New York: McGraw-Hill, 1999), p. 66.

23. Bill Stinnett, "Reverse-Engineer the Buying Process," *Selling*, December 2004, p. 16.

24. Neil Rackham and John DeVincentis, *Rethinking the Sales Force*, p. 68.

25. Monika Kukar-Kinney and Angeline G. Close (2010), "The Determinants of Consumers' Online Shopping Cart Abandonment," *Journal of the Academy of Marketing Science*, 38, pp. 240–50.

26. Hean Tat Keh and Jun Pang (2010), "Customer Reactions to Service Separation," *Journal of Marketing*, 74(2), pp. 55–70.

27. Neil Rackham and John DeVincentis, *Rethinking the Sales Force*, p. 69.

28. Neil Rackham and John DeVincentis provide extensive coverage of these three selling modes in *Rethinking the Sales Force*. See also Neil Rackham and John R. DeVincentis, "Let the Customer Define Value—and Sales Will Rise," *Value-Added Selling 21*, January 13, 2004, pp. 1–2.

29. Neil Rackham and John R. DeVincentis, "Let the Customer Define Value—and Sales Will Rise," pp. 1–2.

30. Ken Brown, "Little-Known Avaya Tackles Cisco in Internet Calling Gear," *Wall Street Journal*, October 26, 2004, p. B1.

31. Neil Rackham and John DeVincentis, *Rethinking the Sales Force*, p. 74.

32. Philip Kotler and Gary Armstrong, *Principles of Marketing,* 10th Ed. (Upper Saddle River, NJ: Prentice Hall, 2004), p. 28.

33. Stan Davis and Christopher Meyer, *Blur: The Speed of Change in the Connected Economy* (New York: Addison-Wesley Publishers, 1998), p. 16.

34. Leilei Gao, S. Christian Wheeler, and Baba Shiv (2009), "The 'Shaken Self': Product Choices as a Means of Restoring Self-View Confidence," *Journal of Consumer Research,* 36(1), pp. 29–38.

35. William M. Pride and O.C. Ferrell, *Marketing,* Tenth Edition (Boston, MA: Houghton Mifflin, 1997), pp. 143–48.

36. Douglas A. Bernstein, Alison Clark-Stewart, Edward J. Roy, and Christopher D. Wickens, *Psychology,* 6th ed. (Boston, MA: Houghton Mifflin, 2003), p. 648.

37. C. Page Moreau and Kelly B. Herd (2010), "To Each His Own? How Comparisons with Others Influence Consumers' Evaluations of Their Self-Designed Products," *Journal of Consumer Research,* 36(5), pp. 806–19.

38. Gary Armstrong and Philip Kotler, *Marketing: An Introduction,* 7th ed., pp. 147–48.

39. Douglas A. Bernstein, et al., *Psychology,* 6th ed., p. 21.

40. Gary Armstrong and Philip Kotler, *Marketing: An Introduction,* 7th ed., p. 145.

41. Louis E. Boone and David L. Kurtz, *Contemporary Marketing,* Eleventh Edition (Mason, OH: Southwestern Publishing, 2004), p. 267.

42. "Phaeton Doesn't Deserve Its Ill Fate," July 29, 2006, available www.wheels.ca/article/2911 (accessed April 3, 2011); Roger Hart, "Luxury, VW's Way," *AutoWeek,* December 27, 2004, pp. 18–19; Tom Reilly, "All Sales Decisions are Emotional for the Buyer," *Selling,* July 2003, p. 13.

43. Roy Chitwood, "Hidden Buyer Motives: Handle Them With Care," *Value-Added Selling 21,* April 2, 2007, p. 4.

44. Phil Kline, "Dominant Buying Motive Is the Result of Strong Emotions," *Marketing News,* May 24, 1993, p. 4.

45. Stan Davis and Christopher Meyer, *Blur,* p. 52.

46. Hakkyun Kim, Kiwan Park, and Norbert Schwarz (2010), "Will This Trip Really Be Exciting? The Role of Incidental Emotions in Product Evaluation," *Journal of Consumer Research,* 36(6), pp. 983–91.

47. Robert McGarvey, "The Buyer's Emotional Side," *Selling Power,* April 2006, p. 35.

48. Ibid., p. 36.

49. Gary Armstrong and Philip Kotler, *Marketing,* 6th ed., p. 216; Sid Chadwick, "New Twists in Price vs. Perceived Value," *Sales and Marketing Advisory Magazine,* July/August 2001, p. 6.

Sources for Boxed Features

a. Judith C. Tingley and Lee E. Robert, *GenderSell: How to Sell to the Opposite Sex* (New York: Simon & Schuster, 1999).

b. Dave Stein, "Selling Across Generation Gaps," *Sales & Marketing Management.* October 2007, p. 9.

Chapter 9

1. Gerhard Gschwandtner, "Thoughts to Sell By," *Personal Selling Power,* Fifteenth Anniversary Issue, 1995, p. 122.

2. Dorothy Leeds, "Where Are the Real Decision Makers?" *Personal Selling Power,* March 1993, p. 62; Gerhard Gschwandtner, "Getting Squeezed," *Selling Power,* May 2002, p. 10.

3. Terry Hill, "How Do You Sustain and Grow Your Customer Relationships," *American Salesman,* October 2007, p. 26.

4. Paul Tindall, "Prospecting: It Separates the Best from the Rest," *Sales Exchange,* November 17–23, 2003.

5. For additional information on Joe Girard see "Joe Girard on? Becoming The World's Greatest Salesperson," *Harvard Business Review,* July–August 2006, p. 25.

6. Gerhard Gschwandtner, "The Funnel Concept," *Personal Selling Power,* May/June 1993, p. 23.

7. Joel R. Pecoraro, "Panning for Gold," *Sales & Marketing Management,* November 2004, p. 56.

8. Jim Domanski, "Referrals: The Easy Way to Prospect," in *Top Dog Sales Secrets,* Michael Dalton Johnson, ed. (Carlsbad, CA: Penny Union, 2007), pp. 13–15.

9. Geoffrey James, "How to Earn Customer Referrals," *Selling Power,* July/August 2004, pp. 25–28.

10. BNI-International website, www.bni.com (accessed February? 14, 2005).

11. Thomas Petzinger, Jr., "Selling a 'Killer App' Is a Far Tougher Job Than Dreaming It Up," *Wall Street Journal,* April 3, 1998, p. B1.

12. Daniel Tynan, "Tricks of the Trade Show," *Sales & Marketing Management,* January 2004, p. 27.

13. Ron Donoho, "Steering New Sales," *Sales & Marketing Management,* November 2001, pp. 31–35.

14. Henry Canaday, "Carefully Composed," *Selling Power,* May 2007, pp. 44–46.

15. Ibid., pp. 45–46.

16. Henry Canaday, "Zeroing In On Prospects," *Selling Power,* March 2006, p. 82.

17. Ibid., pp. 84–85.

18. Andy Cohen, "Man About Town," *Sales & Marketing Management,* June 2000, p. 29.

19. John Boe, "Selling is a Contact Sport: Keys to Effective Phone Calling." *American Salesman,* January 2008, p. 26. For more information on cold calls see Scott Stears, "Cold Calls Have Yet to Breathe Their Last Gasp," *Wall Street Journal,* December 14, 2006, p. D2.

20. Maxwell Maltz, Dan S. Kennedy, William T. Brooks, Matt Oechsli, Jeff Paul, and Pamela Yellen, *Zero-Resistance Selling* (Paramus, NJ: Prentice-Hall, 1998), p. 167.

21. Stacy L. Bradford, "Ten Job-Networking Tips," *The News & Observer,* January 30, 2005, p. E7.

22. Tuba Üstüner and David Godes, "Better Sales Networks," *Harvard Business Review,* July–August 2006, pp. 102–12.

23. Michele Marchetti, "Do You Have the Knack for Networking?" *Sales & Marketing Management,* January 1996, p. 30; Deb Haggerty, "Successful Networking Begins as a State of Mind," *Selling,* December 2006, p. 13.

24. Maxwell Maltz, et al., pp. 179–80.

25. Steve Atlas, "Trouble Connecting?" *Selling Power,* September 2001, p. 27.

26. "Are You Generating and Using Quality Leads?" *Value-Added Selling 21,* September 16, 2003, p. 4.

27. Thomas R. Watruba, "The Evolution of Selling," *Journal of Personal Selling and Sales Management,* Summer 1991, p. 7.

28. This example was adapted from "Skills Workshop" by William F. Kendy, *Selling Power,* January/February 2000, p. 26.

29. Mitchell Pacelle, "Former SEC Chairman Levitt Decries Business Ethics in the U.S.," *Wall Street Journal,* June 17, 2002, p. C7; Shoshana Zuboff, "A Starter Kit for Business Ethics," *Fast Company,* January 2005, p. 91.

30. Rick Page, *Hope Is Not a Strategy* (Atlanta, GA: Nautilus Press, 2002), pp. 69–71.

31. "Senior Execs Share Insider Tips," *Selling*, March 2000, pp. 1, 14; Tom Reilly, "Selling to Mr. Big Is Tough, But . . . ," *Selling*, February 2001, pp. 1, 12.

32. Henry Canada, "Fishing for Big Ones", Personal Selling Power, Source Book 2008, p. 46.

33. Jim Dickie and Barry Trailer, "Proactive Sales Intelligence: The New Requirement for Getting Into the Game," Salesforce.com 2007.

34. Ibid., pp. 46–47.

35. H. F. (Herb) MacKenzie, *Sales Management in Canada* (Toronto, ON: Pearson Education Canada, 2008), p. 140.

36. Tony Parinello, "Keeping Track of Prospects," www.entrepreneur.com/article/0,4621,306013,00.html (January 13, 2003, downloaded February 14, 2008).

37. Don Thomson, *Keeping the Funnel Full* (French Creek, BC, Mardon Publishing, 2004), p. 7.

38. H. F. (Herb) MacKenzie, ibid, p. 141.

Sources for Boxed Features

a. Barbara Pachter and Marjorie Brody, *Complete Business Etiquette Handbook* (Upper Saddle River, NJ: Prentice Hall, 1995), p. 278; "International Snapshot," *Sales & Marketing Management*, August 2001, p. 64; Jan Yager, *Business Protocol*, 2nd ed. (Stamford, CT: Hannacroix Books, Inc., 2001), pp. 116–17.

b. Interview with Gene Chahley, Polaroid Canada Inc., May 19, 1997; Barbara Siskind, *Seminars to Build Your Business* (North Vancouver, BC: Self-Counsel Press, 1998), pp. 9–12; Sheldon Gordon, "Punch Up Your Profits," *Profit*, May 1999, pp. 17–22.

c. Mariya Yurukova, personal interview and correspondence, August 25, 2011.

Chapter 10

1. Malcolm Fleschner, "Too Busy to Buy," *Selling Power*, March 1999, p. 36.

2. Gina Rollins, "Prepped to Sell," *Selling Power*, September 2006, pp. 74–77.

3. Bradford Agry, "Every Client Meeting Provides a Dynamic New Opportunity," *Selling*, April 2002, pp. 1, 4.

4. Malcolm Fleschner, "Anatomy of a Sale," *Selling Power*, April 1998, p. 76; Gina Rollins, "Prepare for the Unknown," *Selling Power*, July/August 2003, pp. 26–30.

5. Tom Reilly, "Prepare Like a Pro," www.TomReillyTraining.com (accessed April 8, 2007).

6. "Set the Agenda," *Personal Selling Power*, May/June 1995, p. 79.

7. Donna Fenn, "Because His Family Business Makes an Art of Customer Service," *Inc.*, April 2005, p. 94; Telephone interview with Pamela Miles, *staff member at Mitchells/Richards*, March 22, 2005.

8. Philip Kotler and Gary Armstrong, *Principles of Marketing*, Tenth Edition (Upper Saddle River, NJ: Prentice Hall, 2004), p. 531.

9. Rick Page, *Hope Is Not a Strategy* (Atlanta, GA: Nautilus Press, 2002), p. 25.

10. Betsy Cummings, "Group Dynamics," *Sales & Marketing Management*, January/February 2007, p. 8.

11. James F. O'Hara, "Successful Selling to Buying Committees," *Selling*, February 1998, p. 8.

12. George R. Franke and Jeong-Eun Park, "Salesperson Adaptive Selling Behavior and Customer orientation: A Meta-Analysis" *Journal of Marketing Research*, November 2006, pp. 693–702; Leroy Robinson, Jr., Greg W. Marshall, William C. Moncrief, and Felicia G. Lassk, "Toward a Shortened Measure of Adaptive Selling," *Journal of Personal Selling & Sales Management*, Spring 2002, pp. 111–19.

13. The role of confidence in adaptive selling is discussed in Leroy Robinson, Jr., Greg W. Marshall, William C. Moncrief, and Felicia G. Lassak, "Toward a Shortened Measure of Adaptive Selling," *Journal of Personal Selling & Sales Management*, Spring 2002, pp. 111–19.

14. Neil Rackham and John R. Vincentis, *Rethinking the Sales Force* (New York: McGraw-Hill, 1999), p. 217.

15. Graham Roberts-Phelps, "How to Add Value to Every Sales Call," *Selling Power*, March—April 2010, p. 19.

16. Ibid.

17. Thomas A. Freese, *Secrets of Question Based Selling* (Naperville, IL: Sourcebooks, 2003), p. 114.

18. John Fellows, "Your Foot in the Door," *Selling Power*, March 1996, pp. 64–65.

19. Adapted from Art Sobczak, "Please, Call Me Back!" *Selling*, March 1999, p. 12.

20. *Ibid*.

21. Deborah Dumaine, "Managing Customers with E-Mail," *Selling Power*, March 2004, p. 94.

22. Rachel Zupek, "Reply all and Other Email Gaffes," *Business.com*, September 2007, p. 26.

23. Susan Bixler and Nancy Nix-Rice, *The New Professional Image* (Holbrook, MA: Adams Media Corporation, 1997), p. 3.

24. Steve Atlas, "How to Cultivate New Turf," *Selling Power*, January/February 2003, p. 26.

25. Maxine Clayton, "60 Seconds on Small Talk," *Fast Company*, November 2004, p. 43.

26. Dean A. Goettsch, "Make Your First Meeting Count," *Selling*, July 2004, pp. 1, 4.

27. Melissa Campanelli, "Sound the Alarm," *Sales & Marketing Management*, December 1994, pp. 20–25.

28. Carolee Boyles, "Prewarm Cold Calls," *Selling Power*, July/August 2001, p. 30.

29. Abner Little, "Selling to Women Revs Up Car Sales," *Personal Selling Power*, July/August 1990, p. 50.

30. "Six Great Upselling Questions," *Personal Selling Power*, April 1993, p. 44.

31. Interview with Larry Short, June 9, 1997.

32. Theodore Kinni, "How to Identify and Remove the Problems Underlying Call Reluctance," *Selling Power*, November/December 2004, pp. 69–71; "Types of Call Reluctance," *Value-Added Selling 21*, February 14, 2005, p. 4.

33. Alan Farnham, "Are You Smart Enough to Keep Your Job?" *Fortune*, January 15, 1996, pp. 34–42.

34. "The Disappointment Trap," *Selling Power*, January/February 1999, p. 14.

35. Roy Chitwood, "Still Trying to Slip Past Gatekeepers? Forget It!" *Value-Added Selling 21*, December 16, 2003, pp. 1–2.

Sources for Boxed Features

a. Foreign Affairs and International Trade Canada website, www.international.gc.ca (accessed May 1, 2011); Richard R. Gesteland, *Cross-Cultural Business Behavior* (Copenhagen:

Handelshøjskolens Forlag, Copenhagen Business School Press, 1999), pp. 19–23.

b. Bryan Ziegler, "Your Business Card Can Be a Powerful Tool," *Des Moines Register,* August 2, 1999, p. 17–B; Kemba J. Dunham, "Here's My Card," *Wall Street Journal,* May 14, 2002, p. B12.

Chapter 11

1. Olaf Ploetner, "The Development of Consulting in Goods-Based Companies," *Industrial Marketing Management,* 37, February 6, 2008, p. 329.

2. V. Kuman, Rajkuma, Rajkuman Venkatesan, and Werner Reinartz, "Performance Implications of Adopting a Customer-Focused Sales Campaign," *Journal of Marketing,* 72, September 2008, p. 50.

3. *Going the Distance: The Consultative Sales Presentation* (Pasadena, CA: Intelecom); "The Amgen Difference," www.amgen.com (accessed June 11, 2010).

4. Louis E. Boone and David L. Kurtz, Contemporary Marketing, 11th Ed. (Mason, Ohio: Southwestern Publishing, 2004), p. 576; Geoffrey James, "Consultative Selling Strategies," *Selling Power,* April 2004, pp. 17–20.

5. Jack R. Snader, "Developing Consultative Sales Skills," *Pace,* October 1985, p. 49.

6. Jeff Thull, *The Prime Solution,* (Chicago, IL: Dearborn Publishing, 2005), p. 35.

7. Othman Boujena, Wesley J. Johnston, and Dwight R. Merunka, "The Benefits of Sales Force Automation: A Customer's Perspective, *Journal of Personal Selling and Sales Management,* 24, Spring 2009, p. 137.

8. Duane Sparks, *Questions-The Answer to Sales,* The Sales Board: Minneapolis, MN 2005, p. vii.

9. Rose A. Spinelli, "Listening: A Priority in Shopping for Others," *Chicago Tribune,* November 30, 2003, p. 55.

10. Gerhard Gschwandtner, "What Makes Sales Relationships Work?" *Selling Power,* May–June 2010, p. 9.

11. Research for the SPIN model was conducted in the late 1970s and early 1980. Neil Rackham, *SPIN Selling* (New York: McGraw-Hill, 1988); www.huthwaite.com.au/research-ip.html (accessed June 8, 2010).

12. Geoffrey James, "Driving the High-Stakes Sales," *Selling Power,* May 2007, p. 51.

13. "What Do Good Salespeople Have in Common?" *Training,* December 1984, p. 21.

14. Research for the Professional Selling Skills model was conducted in the late 1960s and early 1970s. "Professional Selling Skills," www.achieveglobal.co.nz/_literature/Professional_Selling_Skills (accessed June 7, 2010).

15. Michael D. Hargrove, "Using the Socratic Selling Method," www.bluinc.com/news/socraticselling.html (accessed June 6, 2010).

16. Ibid.

17. Robert Jolles, *Customer-Centered Selling: Mastering the Art of Urgency,* 2nd ed. (New York: The Free Press, 2009), pp. 105–106.

18. Ann Demarais and Valerie White, *First Impressions—What You Don't Know About How Others See You* (New York: Bantam Books, 2004), pp. 68–69.

19. Fernando Jaramillo and Douglas B. Grisaffe (Spring 2009), "Does Customer Orientation Impact Objective Sales Performance?" *Journal of Personal Selling and Sales Management,* 24(1), p. 167.

20. Barry L. Reece and Rhonda Brandt, *Effective Human Relations: Personal and Organizational Applications,* 10th edition (Boston, MA: Houghton Mifflin, 2008), p. 40.

21. Ibid.

22. Demarais and White, *First Impressions,* p. 70.

23. Abner Little, "Are You Listening," *Selling Power,* May–June 2010, p. 34.

24. William F. Kendy, "The Silence Play," *Selling Power,* July/August 2007, pp. 29–30.

25. Matthew McKay, Martha Davis, and Patrick Fanning, *Message: The Communication Skills Book* (Oakland, CA: New Harbinger, 1995), p. 15; Susan Scott, *Fierce Conversations* (New York: Viking Penguin, 2002), p. 157.

26. William F. Kendy, "How to Be a Good Listener," *Selling Power,* April 2004, p. 43.

27. Tom Reilly, *Value-Added Selling* (New York, NY: McGraw-Hill, 2003), p. 130.

28. Adam Rapp, Raj Agnihotri, and Lukas P. Forbes (Fall 2008), "The Sales Force Technology–Performance Chain: The Role of Adaptive Selling and Effort," *Journal of Personal Selling and Sales Management,* 28(4), p. 335.

29. Olaf Ploetner, "The Development of Consulting in Goods-Based Companies," p. 329.

30. Geoffrey James, "How to Use the Intuitive Model to Sell," *Selling Power,* May–June 2010, p. 40.

31. Decorating Den Interiors, www.decoratingden.com/meet-our-decorators.html (accessed June 12, 2010).

32. Tom Riley, *Value-Added Selling,* pp. 17, 167.

33. Kerry L. Johnson, "The Things Dales Masters Do," *Value-Added Selling 21,* April 16, 2007, p. 3.

34. Consona Corporation, www.configsc.com (accessed August 12, 2010).

35. Big Machines, www.bigmachines.com/salesforce.php (accessed September 14, 2010).

36. Rapp, Agnihotri, and Forbes, "The Sales Force Technology–Performance Chain: The Role of Adaptive Selling and Effort," p. 335.

37. Willem J. Verbeke, Frank D. Belschak, Arnold B. Bakker, and Bart Dietz (July 2008), "When Intelligence Is (Dys)Functional for Achieving Sales Performance," *Journal of Marketing,* 72, p. 44.

38. Paul F. Roos, "Just Say No," *Selling Power,* October 2003, p. 50.

39. Neil Rackham and John DeVincentis, *Rethinking the Sales Force* (New York: McGraw-Hill, 1999), p. 17.

40. Ibid., p. 9.

Sources for Boxed Features

a. Interview with and correspondence from Sybil Taylor, Communications Director, Steam Whistle Brewing, April–May, 2011.

b. Duane Sparks, Questions—The Answer to Sales, The Sales Board, Minneapolis, MN. 2005, p. vi; "CARQUEST Cares," www.carquest.com (accessed November 7, 2007).

Chapter 12

1. "Presentation-Wise, We've Lost Our Tails," *Sales & Field Force Automation,* July 1999, p. 4.

2. Jan Wieseke, Christian Homburg, and Nick Lee, "Understanding the Adoption of New Brands Through Salespeople: A Multilevel Framework," *Journal of the Academy of Marketing Science,* July 7, 2007, p. 278.

3. Franklin J. Carter and Ravindra Chitturi (Winter 2009), "Segmentation Based on Physician Behavior: Implications for Sales Forecasting and Marketing-Mix Strategy," *Journal of Personal Selling and Sales Management*, 29(1), p. 81.

4. Dean A. Goettsch, "Guidelines for Rethinking Sales Presentations," *Selling*, October 2001, p. 14.

5. Ryan Kibacki, "The Changing Role of the Sales Professional," *Selling Power*, May/June 2010.

6. "Communicating Technical Ideas Persuasively." This article originally appeared in the May-June 1998 issue of the *Journal for Management in Engineering*, published by the American Society of Civil Engineers, accessed May 26, 2010.

7. Gary A. Williams and Robert B. Miller, "Change the Way You Persuade," *Harvard Business Review*, May 2002, p. 6; Renee Houston Zemanski, "Subtlety Can Sell," Selling Power, January/February 2007, pp. 42–44.

8. Mike Coyne, "How I Made the Sale," *Value-Added Selling 21*, August 12, 2003, pp. 1 and 4.

9. John M. Hawes, "Leaders in Selling and Sales Management," *Journal of Personal Selling and Sales Management*, November 5, 1985, p. 60.

10. Randall Murphy, "The Consultative Approach to Selling," *Selling Power*, March–April 2010, p. 32.

11. Fernando Jaramillo and Douglas B. Grisaffe (Spring 2009), "Does Customer Orientation Impact Objective Sales Performance?" *Journal of Personal Selling and Sales Management*, 29(2), p. 167.

12. Lambeth Hochwald, "Simplify," *Sales & Marketing Management*, June 1998, pp. 66–67; "Company Information," www.bellhelicopter.textron.com (accessed April 13, 2005).

13. Personal correspondence from Christa-Lee McWatters, May 22, 1997.

14. Cindy Waxer, "The Lighter Side," *Selling Power*, January/February, 2005, p. 91.

15. Douglas A. Bernstein, Alison Clarke-Stewart, Edward J. Roy, and Louis A. Penner, *Psychology*, 6th ed. (Boston: Houghton Mifflin Company, 2003), pp. 373–74.

16. Malcolm Fleschner, "Funny You Should Say That," *Personal Selling Power*, May–June 2010, pp. 14–16.

17. James C. Anderson, James A. Narus, and Wouter van Rossum, "Customer Value Proposition in Business Markets," *Harvard Business Review*, March 2006, pp. 1–9.

18. Ibid.

19. Corbin Ball Associates, "Avoiding Death by PowerPoint," www.corbinball.com (accessed April 12, 2005).

20. "Communicating Technical Ideas Persuasively." This article originally appeared in the May–June 1998 issue of the *Journal for Management in Engineering*, published by the American Society of Civil Engineers, accessed May 26, 2010.

21. Gerhard Gschwandtner, "What Makes Relationships Work?" *Selling Power*, May–June 2010, p. 9.

22. Kevin D. Bradford and Barton A. Weitz (Winter 2009), "Salespersons' Management of Conflict in Buyer—Seller Relationships," *Journal of Personal Selling and Sales Management*, 29(1), p. 25.

23. Robert B. Cialdini, "Harnessing the Science of Persuasion," *Harvard Business Review*, October 2001, p. 74.

24. Ibid., p. 9.

25. Stephanie G. Sherman and V. Clayton Sherman, *Make Yourself Memorable* (New York: AMACOM, 1996), pp. 58–59.

26. Willem J. Verbeke, Frank D. Belschak, Arnold B. Bakker, and Bart Dietz, "When Intelligence Is (Dys)Functional for Achieving Sales Performance," *Journal of Marketing*, 72, July 2008, p. 44.

27. John Grossmann, "Location, Location, Location," *Inc.*, August 2004, p. 83.

28. Rich Mesch, "Spinning Yarns—Seven Tips for Using Stories to Enhance Simulations and Learning," *SPBT Focus*, Spring 2007, pp. 42–46.

29. Carol Burke, "How to Create and Deliver a Winning Group Presentation," www.salesvantage.com (accessed November 4, 2007). For more information see Joann S. Lublin, "Improve Troup Teaches Managers How to Give Better Presentation," *Wall Street Journal*, February 6, 2007, B1.

30. Cindy Waxer, "Light is Right," *Selling Power*, January/February 2007, pp. 100–102.

31. Cindy Waxer, "Shine On," *Selling Power*, April 2007, p. 98.

32. Cindy Waxer, "Light is Right," p. 102.

33. Joseph B. White, "New Ergonomic Chairs Battle to Save the Backs of Workers, for Big Bucks," *Wall Street Journal*, June 8, 1999, p. B–4B.

34. Rick Page, *Hope Is Not a Strategy* (Atlanta, GA: Nautilus Press, 2002), p. 126.

35. Geoffrey James, "Flight to Profit," *Selling Power*, September 2004, p. 74.

36. Lambeth Hochwald, "Simplify," pp. 65–66.

37. Ginger Trumfio, "Ready! Set! Sell!" *Sales & Marketing Management*, February 1995, pp. 82–84.

38. Landy Chase, "Master the Art of Brochure Selling," *Selling*, March 2005, pp. 8–9.

39. David Ranii, "Dermabond's Debut Disappoints," *News & Observer*, July 31, 1999, p. D1.

40. "Three Guides to Using Your Catalog as a Sales Tool," *Value-Added Selling 21*, June 17, 2003, p. 4.

41. "The Presentation Paper Trail," *Sales & Marketing Management*, March 1995, p. 49.

42. Heather Baldwin, "Star Light Star Bright," *Selling Power Source Book 2002*, p. 55.

43. Heather Baldwin, "Up Your Powers," *Selling Power Source Book*, October 2001, pp. 88–92.

44. Kevin Ferguson, "Reinventing the PowerPoint," *Inc.*, March 2004, p. 42; Corbin Ball Associates, "Avoiding Death by PowerPoint"; Stacy Straczynski, "PowerPoint and Beyond," *Training*, October 2006, p. 46.

45. Gerald L. Manning and Jack W. Linge, *Selling-Today.com* (Upper Saddle River, NJ: Prentice Hall, 2004), pp. 26–30.

46. Cindy Waxer, "Presenting the Power," *Selling Power*, (Source Book) 2005, pp. 70–71; Cindy Waxer, "Wired to Sell," *Selling Power*, June 2007, pp. 88–90.

47. Renee Houston Zemanski, "Play It Back," *Selling Power*, September 2007, p. 43.

48. Rick Page, "Hope Is Not a Strategy."

Sources for Boxed Features

a. "International Snapshot," *Sales and Marketing Management*, November 2001, p. 63; Jan Yager, *Business Protocol*, 2nd ed. (Stamford, CT: Hannacroix Books, 2001), pp. 120–121.

b. Emily Barker, "Start with . . . Nothing," *Inc.*, February 2002, pp. 67–73; "About RightNow Technologies," www.rightnow.com (accessed April 4, 2005).

Chapter 13

1. *Selling Power*, June 2007, p. 32.
2. Geoff James, "The Art of Sales Negotiation," *Selling Power*, March 2004, pp. 25–28.
3. Tom Riley, *Value-Added Selling* (New York: McGraw-Hill, 2003), p. 17.
4. Hal Lancaster, "You Have to Negotiate for Everything in Life, So Get Good at It," *Wall Street Journal*, January 27, 1998, p. B1.
5. Joydeep Srivastava and Dipankar Chakravarti (2009), "Channel Negotiations with Information Asymmetries: Contingent Influences of Communication and Trustworthiness Reputations," *Journal of Marketing Research*, 46(3), pp. 557–72.
6. Ron Willingham, *Integrity Selling for the 21st Century* (New York: Currency Doubleday, 2003), p. 154.
7. Brian Tracy, *The 100 Absolutely Unbreakable Laws of Business Success* (San Francisco, CA: Berrett-Koehler Publishers, 2000), p. 235.
8. Ron Willingham, *Integrity Selling for the 21st Century*, p. 153.
9. Brenda Goodman, "The Art of Negotiation," *Psychology Today*, January/February 2007, pp. 64–65.
10. Gregg Crawford, "Let's Negotiate," *Sales & Marketing Management*, November 1995, pp. 28–29.
11. Michael Soon Lee, *The American Salesman*, August 2007, pp. 25–28.
12. Rob Walker, "Take It or Leave It: The Only Guide to Negotiating You Will Ever Need," *Inc.*, August 2003, p.81.
13. Robert H. Schuller, "Preparing to Negotiate," in *The Only Negotiating Guide You'll Ever Need: 101 Ways to Win Every Time in Any Situation* by Peter B. Stark and Jane S. Flaherty, Chapter 10, pp. 81–85.
14. Deepak Malhotra and Max H. Bazerman, *Negotiation Genius* (New York: Random House, 2007), p. 102.
15. Klaus Backhaus, Jenny van Doorn, and Robert Wilken (2008), "The Impact of Team Characteristics on the Course and Outcome of Intergroup Price Negotiations," *Journal of Business-to-Business Marketing*, 15(4), pp. 365–396.
16. Peter B. Stank and Jane Flaherty, *The Only Negotiating Guide You'll Ever Need* (New York: Broadway Books, 2003), p.84.
17. Deepak Malhotra and Max H. Bazerman, ibid., pp. 20–23.
18. Ibid.
19. P. V. Balakrishnan, Charles Patton, and Phillip A. Lewis (1993), "Toward a Theory of Agenda Setting in Negotiations," *Journal of Consumer Research*, 19(2), pp. 637–54.
20. Peter B. Stank and Jane Flaherty, ibid., p. 79.
21. Nicholas G. Paparoidamis and Paolo Guenzi (2009), "An Empirical Investigation into the Impact of Relationship Selling and LMX on Salespeople's Behaviors and Sales Effectiveness," *European Journal of Marketing*, 43(7/8), pp. 1053–75.
22. David Stiebel, *When Talking Makes Things Worse!* (Dallas, TX: Whitehall & Norlton, 1997), p. 17.
23. For details, see Deepak Malhotra and Max H. Bazerman, ibid., pp. 59–64, p. 82.
24. Don Maruska, *Value Added Selling 21*, April 30, 2007, p. 2.
25. Robert Wilken, Markus Corneliben, Klaus Backhaus, and Christian Schmitz (2010), "Steering Sales Reps Through Cost Information: An Investigation into the Black Bock of Cognitive References and Negotiation Behavior," *International Journal of Research in Marketing*, 27, pp. 69–82.
26. Joseph Conlin, "Negotiating Their Way to the Top," *Sales & Marketing Management*, April 1996, p. 62; Neil Rackham, "Winning the Price War," *Sales & Marketing Management*, November 2001, p. 26.
27. Deepak Malhotra and Max H. Bazerman, ibid., p. 175.
28. Lain Ehman, "Not a Done Deal," *Selling Power*, November/December 2003, pp. 42–44; "Negotiate the Right Price Despite Customer Pressure," *Selling*, July 2004, p. 2.
29. William F. Kendy, "Solving the 'Friendship Buying' Problem," *Selling Power*, November/December 2001, pp. 40–44.
30. Steven J. Schwartz, *How to Make Hot Cold Calls*, revised edition (Toronto, ON: Stoddart Publishing, 2001), p. 42.
31. Marc Freeman, "Say It and Sell It," *Sales & Marketing Management*, November/December 2006, p. 13.
32. William F. Kendy, "The Price Is Too High," *Selling Power*, April 2006, pp. 30–33.
33. Ibid.
34. Jeff Keller, "Objections? No Problem," *Selling Power*, September 1996, pp. 44–45.
35. Adapted from Nanci McCann, "Irate over Rates," *Selling*, July–August 1996, p. 25.
36. Tom Reilly, ibid., p. 189.
37. Rick Kang, "Management by Defiance," *Profit*, June 1999, pp. 63–64.
38. See Neil Rackham, *The New SPIN Selling Fieldbook*, (New York: McGraw-Hill, 1996), pp. 127–45.
39. David Jobber and Jeff Lancaster, *Selling and Sales Management*, 7th ed. (Prentice Hall/Financial Times, 2006), p. 261.
40. Arnaud De Bruyn and Gary E. Bolton (2008), "Estimating the Influence of Fairness on Bargaining Behavior," *Management Science*, 54(10), pp. 1774–91.
41. William F. Kendy, ibid., p. 30.
42. Tom Reilly, ibid, p. 191–92.
43. Joseph Conlin, "Negotiating Their Way to the Top," *Sales & Marketing Management*, April 1996, p. 58.
44. William F. Kendy, ibid, pp. 30–33.
45. Sam Deep and Lyle Sussman, *Close the Deal: Smart Moves for Selling* (Reading, MA: Perseus Books, 1999), p. 225.
46. Roland M. Sandell, "Five Sure-Fire Methods to Overcome Objections to Price," *American Salesman*, October 1976, p. 38.
47. William F. Kendy, "Negotiation Tactics," *Selling Power*, September 2006, p. 31.
48. Homer Smith, "How to Cope with Buyers Who Are Trained in Negotiation," *Personal Selling Power*, September 1988, p. 37.
49. Ibid.
50. Robert Adler, Benson Rosen, and Elliot Silverstein, "Thrust and Parry," *Training & Development*, March 1996, p. 47.
51. Homer Smith, ibid.
52. Laura Pratt, "Everyone's a Winner," *Profit*, November 2001, p. 47.

Sources for Boxed Features

a. "Getting to Yes, Chinese Style," *Sales & Marketing Management*, July 1996, pp. 44–45; Sam Deep and Lyle Sussman, *Close the Deal: Smart Moves for Selling* (Reading, MA: Perseus Books, 1999), pp. 279–81; James K. Sebenius, "Six Habits of Merely Effective Negotiators," *Harvard Business Review*, April 2001, p. 90.
b. Hal Lancaster, "You Have to Negotiate for Everything in Life, So Get Good At It," *The Wall Street Journal*, January 27, 1998, p. B1; Amy Lindgren, "Want a Raise? Don't Daydream; Polish

Your Negotiating Skills," *Des Moines Register*, April 26, 1998, p. 1L.

c. Mary Klonizakis, "A Class Act," *Contact*, September 2000, p. 18.

Chapter 14

1. Susan Minns, vice president of client services, Event Spectrum, Personal interview and correspondence, July 9, 2008.
2. Subhra Chakrabarty, Gene Brown, and Robert E. Widing II (2010), "Closed Influence Tactics: Do Smugglers Win in the Long Run?" *Journal of Personal Selling and Sales Management*, 30(1), pp. 23–32.
3. Ron Willingham, *Integrity Selling for the 21st Century* (New York: Currency Doubleday 2003), p. 179.
4. Sergio Roman and Dawn Iacobucci (2010), "Antecedents and Consequences of Adaptive Selling Confidence and Behavior: A Dyadic Analysis of Salespeople and Their Customers," *Journal of the Academy of Marketing Science*, 38(3), pp. 363–82.
5. Gene Bedell, *3 Steps to Yes* (New York: Crown Business, 2000), pp. 72–80.
6. Tom Reilly, *Value-Added Selling* (New York: McGraw-Hill, 2003), p. 176.
7. Andy Cohen, "Are Your Reps Afraid to Close?" *Sales & Marketing Management*, March 1996, p. 43.
8. Michele Marchetti, "Make Process a Sales Priority," *Sales & Marketing Management*, September 2006, p. 16. See John Graham, "How to Profit From Customer Buying-Cycle Basics," *The American Salesman*, May 2007, pp. 19–23.
9. Susan Creco, "The Need for Speed—How to Rev up Your Sales Cycle," *Inc. Magazine*, April 2007, p. 38.
10. Graham Denton, "The Single Biggest Closing Mistake," Graham Denton Skills Center (Web page) May 4, 1999, p. 1.
11. Ray Dreyfock, "Is the Buyer Ready?" *Selling Power*, January/February 2002, p. 52.
12. Ralph W. Giacobbe, Donald W. Jackson Jr., Lawrence A. Crosby, and Claudia M. Bridges (2006), "A Contingency Approach to Adaptive Selling Behavior and Sales Performance: Selling Situations and Salesperson Characteristics," *Journal of Personal Selling and Sales Management*, 26(2), pp. 115–42.
13. "The Closing Moment," *Personal Selling*, October 1995, p. 48; Lain Ehman, "How to Read Hidden Signals," *Selling Power*, June 2004, pp. 36–38.
14. Ron Karr, "Expert Advice—The Titan Principle," *Selling Power*, October 2001, p. 32.
15. Richard G. McFarland, Goutam N. Challagalla, and Tasadduq A. Shervani (2006), "Influence Tactics for Effective Adaptive Selling," *Journal of Marketing*, 70(3), pp. 103–17.
16. Jenny McCune, "Closing Sales with a Splash," *Selling*, September 2004, p. 15.
17. "Selling Tips," *Selling*, May 1999, p. 13.
18. Ron Willingham, *Integrity Selling* (New York: Doubleday, 1987), p. 133.
19. Jeffrey Gitomer, "Did You Get the Order? If You Didn't, Here's Why," *Business Record*, May 7, 2007, p. 36.
20. Tom Reilly, ibid., p. 179.
21. Ron Willingham, *Integrity Selling for the 21st Century* (New York: Currency Doubleday, 2003), p. 184.
22. Jenny C. McCune, "The Brief Story of Underwear's Stupendous Success," *Selling*, March 2000, p. 15.

23. Joan Leotta, "The Management Close," *Selling Power*, November/December 2001, pp. 26–28. See Megan Sweas, "Heavyweights on Call," *Sales & Marketing Management*, December 2003, p. 14.
24. Ron Willingham, *Integrity Selling for the 21st Century*, ibid., pp. 185–187.
25. George R. Franke and Jeong-Eun Park (2006), "Salesperson Adaptive Selling Behavior and Customer Orientation: A Meta-Analysis," *Journal of Marketing Research*, 43(4), pp. 693–702.
26. Mel Siberman, *Active Training* (Toronto, ON: Maxwell Macmillan Canada, 1990), pp. 96–99.
27. T. J. Becker, "That Queasy Feeling," *Chicago Tribune*, July 21, 2002, p. W1.
28. Betsy Wiesendanger, "When a Sale Goes South," *Selling Power*, November/December 2003, pp. 65–67.
29. Betsy Cummings, "Done Deal—How One Sales Pro Closed a Big Customer," *Sales & Marketing Management*, September 2006, p. 13.

Sources for Boxed Features

a. Barbara Hagenbough, "Economics Majors Build Brand Name with Unmentionables," *USA Today*, May 20, 2002, p. 3–B.
b. "International Snapshot," *Sales & Marketing Management*, October 2001, p. 70; Jan Yager, *Business Protocol*, 2nd ed. (Stamford, CT: Hannacroix Books, 2001), pp. 116–17.

Chapter 15

1. Windsor Factory Supply website, www.wfsltd.com (accessed May 23, 2011); Rick Thurston, personal interview, May 25, 2011.
2. Bob Johnson, "Loyalty Lessons from the Pros," *Customer Support Management*, July/August 1999, p. 115; Ranjay Gulati and James B. Oldroyd, "The Quest for Customer Focus," *Harvard Business Review*, April 2005, pp. 92–97.
3. Ibid.
4. Gary Armstrong and Philip Kotler, *Marketing: An Introduction*, Sixth Edition (Upper Saddle River, NJ: Prentice Hall, 2003), p. 553.
5. Don Peppers and Martha Rogers, "Customer Loyalty: A Matter of Trust," *Sales & Marketing Management*, June 2006, p. 22.
6. Theodore Levitt, *The Marketing Management* (New York: Macmillan, 1983), pp. 117–18; Tahl Raz, "The '4 + 2 Formula' for Success," *Inc.*, August 2003, p. 42.
7. Brett Boyle, F. Robert Dwyer, Robert A. Robicheaux, and James T. Simpson (1992), "Influence Strategies in Marketing Channels: Measures and Use in Different Relationship Structures," *Journal of Marketing Research*, 29(4), pp. 462–73.
8. See Tom Reilly, "Value Added Service is a Team Sport," Tom Reilly Training, www.tomreillytraining.com (accessed April 8, 2007).
9. Geoffrey Brewer, "The Customer Stops Here," *Sales & Marketing Management*, March 1998, pp. 31–32; See Ron Zemke and Chip Bell, *Service Magic* (Chicago: IL: Dearborn Trade Publishing, 2004).
10. "Why Customers Leave," *Sales & Marketing Management*, May 1998, p. 86; Tom Peters, *The Circle of Innovation* (New York: Vintage Books, 1997), pp. 138–39.
11. Larry Rosen, personal correspondence, May 17, 2011.
12. Bill Gates, *Business @ the Speed of Thought* (New York: Warner Books, 1999), p. 67.

13. Ruth Maria Stock and Wayne D. Hoyer (2005), "An Attitude-Behavior Model of Salespeople's Customer Orientation," *Journal of the Academy of Marketing Science*, 33(4), pp. 536–52.

14. Michael Ahearne, Ronald Jelinek, and Eli Jones, "Examining the Effect of Salesperson Service Behavior in a Competitive Context," *Journal of the Academy of Marketing Science*, December 2007, pp. 603+.

15. See Daniel H. Pink, *A Whole New Mind* (New York, NY: Riverhead Books, 2005), pp. 48–53.

16. Frederick Hong-kit Yim, Rolph E. Anderson, and Srinivasan Swaminathan (2004), "Customer Relationship Management: Its Dimensions and Effect on Customer Outcomes," *Journal of Personal Selling and Sales Management*, 24(4), pp. 263–78.

17. Steve Ham, "Oracle—Why It's Cool Again," *Business Week*, May 8, 2000, pp. 115–19.

18. Maggie Chung, personal interview, July 25, 2008.

19. Maxim Sytch and Ranjay Gulati (2008), "Creating Value Together," *MIT Sloan Management Review*, 50(1), pp. 12–13.

20. Chad Kaydo, "An Unlikely Sales Ally," *Sales & Marketing Management*, January 1999, p. 69.

21. Sally J. Silberman, "An Eye for Finance," *Sales & Marketing Management*, April 1996, p. 26.

22. Benson P. Shapiro, V. Kasturi Rangon, and John Sviokla, *Harvard Business Review*, July/August 2004, p. 162.

23. Daryl Allen, "Relationship Selling Is Key to Success," *Selling*, March 2002, p. 12.

24. Dave Kahle, "Protecting Your Good Accounts," *The American Salesman*, June 2007, p. 12.

25. Gary L. Frankwick, Stephen S. Porter, and Lawrence A. Crosby (2001), "Dynamics of Relationship Selling: A Longitudinal Examination of Changes in Salesperson-Customer Relationship Status," *Journal of Personal Selling and Sales Management*, 21(2), pp. 135–46.

26. Tom Reilly, "Create Satisfied Customers: Always Be Sure to Exceed Their Expectations," *Selling*, January 2001, p. 3; Mary Salafia. "Reassessment Planning," *Selling Power*, May 2004, p. 56.

27. Tom Riley, *Value-Added Selling* (New York: McGraw-Hill, 2003), p. 117.

28. Andrea Nierenberg, "Eight Ways to Stay Top of Mind," *Selling*, April 1998, p. 7.

29. Queena Sook Kim, "For Sale: Super-Model Home," *Wall Street Journal*, August 6, 2002, p. D-1.

30. Melinda Ligos, "The Joys of Cross-Selling," *Sales & Marketing Management*, August 1998, p. 75.

31. Tom Riley, *Value-Added Selling*, pp. 124–25.

32. William F. Kendy, "Add-Ons Add Up," *Selling Power*, January/February 2007, p. 30.

33. William F. Kendy, "Skills Workshop," *Selling Power*, June 2000, pp. 33–34.

34. Jo Ann Brezette, "Smart Answers to Clients' Questions," *Window Fashions Design & Education Magazine*, September 2001, p. 120; Lain Ehman, "Upsell, Don't Oversell," *Selling Power*, January–February 2004, pp. 30–32.

35. John Hagedoorn (2006), "Understanding the Cross-Level Embeddedness of Interfirm Partnership Formation," *Academy of Management Review*, 31(3), pp. 670–80.

36. "Inspirations from Michele," *Inspiring Solutions*, February 1999, p. 3.

37. Jahyun Goo, Rajiv Kishore, H. R. Rao, and Kichan Nam (2008), "The Role of Service Level Agreements in Relational Management of Information Technology Outsourcing: An Empirical Study," *MIS Quarterly*, 33(1), pp. 119–45.

38. Bob Johnson, "Loyalty Lessons from the Pros," *Customer Support Management*, July/August 1999, p. 115.

39. Barry L. Reece and Rhonda Brandt, *Effective Human Relations: Personal and Organizational Applications*, Tenth Edition. (Boston, MA: Houghton Mifflin Company, 2008), p. 215.

40. Bradley E. Wesner, "From Complaint to Opportunity," *Selling Power*, May 1996, p. 62.

41. Gerald A Michaelson, "When Things Go Wrong, Make It Right," *Selling*, March 1997, p. 12.

42. Michael Abrams and Matthew Paese, "Winning and Dining the Whiners," *Sales & Marketing Management*, February 1993, p. 73.

43. "How to Diffuse a Customer Problem," *Sales & Marketing Management*, May 2000, p. 14.

44. Rick Thurston, ibid.; Windsor Factory Supply website, ibid.

Sources for Boxed Features

a. Based on Jeff Barbian, "It's Who You Know," *Training*, December 2001, p. 22.

b. "Relationships with Customers Must Be Job Number 1," *Food-Service Distributor*, July 1989, p. 74; Joan O. Fredericks and James M. Salter II, "Beyond Customer Satisfaction," *Management Review*, May 1995, pp. 29–32.

c. Jan Yager, *Business Protocol*, 2nd ed. (Stamford, CT: Hannacroix Books, 2001), p. 123; "Selling in Russia," *Sales & Marketing Management*, March 2002, p. 60; Carl F. Fey and Stanislow Shekshnia, "How to Do Business in Russia," *Wall Street Journal*, October 27, 2007, p. R4.

d. Betsy Cummings, "You're Outta Here," *Sales & Marketing Management*, June 2001, pp. 65–66; Rhea Seymour, "Ideas That Work," *Profit*, June 2002, pp. 66–70; Betsey Cummings, "The Perfect Plan," *Sales & Marketing Management*, February 2002, p. 53.

Chapter 16

1. Paula Shannon, personal correspondence, May 2005 and November 30, 2007.

2. Renee Houston Zemanski, "A Matter of Time," *Selling Power*, October 2001, p. 82.

3. Bernd Skiera and Sonke Albers (2008), "Prioritizing Sales Force Decision Areas for Productivity Improvements Using a Core Sales Response Function," *Journal of Personal Selling and Sales Management*, 28(2), pp. 145–54.

4. Eugene Greissman, "Seven Characteristics of High-Achieving Salespeople," *Value-Added Selling 21*, March 16, 2004, p. 4.

5. Betty Cummings, "Increasing Face Time," *Sales & Marketing Management*, January 2004, p. 12.

6. Barry J. Farber, "Not Enough Hours in the Day," *Sales & Marketing Management*, July 1995, pp. 28–29.

7. If you are interested in how to break bad habits and form good ones, see James Claiborn and Cherry Pedrick, *The Habit Change Workbook* (Oakland, CA: New Harbinger Publications, 2001).

8. See Alison Stein Wellner, "The Time Trap," *Inc.*, June 2004, pp. 42–44.

9. Brian Tracy, *The 100 Absolutely Unbreakable Laws of Business Success* (San Francisco: Berrett-Koehler Publishers, Inc., 2000), pp. 40–47.

10. Charles R. Hall, "Create Excitement, Get Motivated Through Planning," *Selling*, February 2000, p. 13.

11. Ed Brown, "Stephen Covey's New One-Day Seminar," *Fortune*, January 1999, p. 138.

12. Besty Wiesendanger, "Time to Spend," *Selling Power*, November/December 2003, pp. 28–32.

13. Hyrum W. Smith, *The 10 Natural Laws of Successful Time and Life Management* (New York: Warner Books, 1994), p. 108.

14. Thomas E. Weber, "Meetings in Cyberspace May Soon Be as Routine as the Conference Call," *Wall Street Journal*, June 4, 2001, p. B1.

15. Michele Marchetti, "Territories: For Optimal Performance, Segment Your Customer Base by Industry," *Sales & Marketing Management*, December 1998, p. 35.

16. Ken Grant, David W. Cravens, George S. Low, and William C. Moncrief (2001), "The Role of Satisfaction with Territory Design on the Motivation, Attitudes, and Work Outcomes of Salespeople," *Journal of the Academy of Marketing Science*, 29(2), pp. 165–78.

17. Lain Chroust Ehmann, "In the Details," *Selling Power*, September 2007, p. 34.

18. Rajkumar Venkatesan, V. Kumar, and Timothy Bohling (2007), "Optimal Customer Relationship Management Using Bayesian Decision Theory: An Application for Customer Selection," *Journal of Marketing Research*, 44(4), pp. 579–94.

19. V. Kumar, Rajkumar Venkatesan, Tim Bohling, and Denise Beckmann (2008), "The Power of CLV: Managing Customer Lifetime Value at IBM," *Marketing Science*, 27(4), pp. 585–99.

20. Ibid., p. 36.

21. Ken Liebeskind, "Where Is Everyone?" *Selling Power*, March 1998, p. 35; Marie Warner, "Take Careful Steps When Redefining Territories," *Selling*, June 2001, p. 10.

22. Alison Smith, "Plan Your Territory," *Selling Power*, March 2003, pp. 37–38.

23. Daryl Allen, "Maximize Your Territory Coverage, Increased Sales and Higher Profits Will Follow," *Selling*, June 2001, p. 10.

24. Paul Clark, Richard A. Rocco, and Alan J. Bush (2007), "Sales Force Automation Systems and Sales Force Productivity: Critical Issues and Research Agenda," *Journal of Relationship Marketing*, 6(2), pp. 67–87.

25. Henry Canaday, "Automated Reports Boost Sales Productivity," *Selling Power*, June 2007, p. 13.

26. "Maintaining Perspective by Keeping Good Records," *Value-Added Selling 21*, August 20, 2007, p.4.

27. Jeffrey E. Lewin and Jeffrey K. Sager (2008), "Salesperson Burnout: A Test of the Coping-Mediational Model of Social Support," *Journal of Personal Selling and Sales Management*, 28(3), pp. 233–46.

28. Bruce Cryer, Rollin McCraty, and Doc Childre, "Pull the Plug On Stress," *Harvard Business Review*, July 2003, pp. 1–2.

29. David Shenk, "Data Smog," *Perdid*, Spring 1999, pp. 5–7.

30. "More Useful Tips for Running Your Home Office," *Selling*, January 2001, p. 11; "Home Office Etiquette," *Sales & Marketing Management*, January 2000, p. 74.

31. Patricia Sellers, "Now Bounce Back," *Fortune*, May 1, 1995, p. 57.

32. Martin Seligman, *Learned Optimism*, (New York, NY: Knopf, 2001), p. 4; Annie Murphy Paul, "Self-Help: Shattering the Myths," *Psychology Today*, March/April 2001, p. 64; Arnold A. Lazarus and Clifford N. Lazarus, *The 60-Second Shrink* (San Luis, Obispo CA: Impact Publishers, 1997), pp. 3, 4.

33. Caleb T. Hayes and Bart L. Weathington (2007), "Optimism, Stress, Life Satisfaction, and Job Burnout in Restaurant Managers," *Journal of Psychology*, 141(6), pp. 565–79.

34. Sandra Lotzs Fisher, "Stress—Will You Cope or Crack?" *Selling*, May 1996, p. 31.

35. Husky Injection Molding Systems, "Working Together," available www.husky.ca/abouthusky/careers-220-223.html (accessed August 4, 2008).

Sources for Boxed Features

a. Alex Pettes, *From the Flight Deck* (Bloomington, IN: iUniverse, 2010); Correspondence and personal interviews, 2006–2011.

b. Michael Adams, "Family Matters," *Sales & Marketing Management*, March 1998, pp. 61–65.

c. "International Snapshot," *Sales & Marketing Management*, February 2001, p. 92; Jan Yager, *Business Protocol*, 2nd ed. (Stamford, CT: Hannacroix Books, Inc., 2001), pp. 114–15.

Chapter 17

1. Jan Wieseke, Michael Ahearne, Son K. Lam, and Rolf van Dick (2009), "The Role of Leaders in Internal Marketing," *Journal of Marketing*, 73(2), pp. 123–45.

2. Robert Kreitner, *Management*, 9th ed. (Boston, MA: Houghton Mifflin Company, 2004), p. 503.

3. "Stephen Covey Talks About the 8th Habit: Effective Is No Longer Enough," *Training*, February 2005, pp.17–19.

4. Michael R. Solomon, Greg W. Marshall, and Elnora W. Stuart, *Marketing—Real People, Real Choices*, 4th ed. (Upper Saddle River, NJ: Pearson Education, 2006), p. 444.

5. Jack Falvey, "Fly by Night, Sell by Day," *Wall Street Journal*, June 9, 1997, p. A-18.

6. Lisa Gschwandtner, "What Makes an Ideal Sales Manager," *Selling Power*, June 2001, p. 54.

7. William Keenan Jr., "Death of the Sales Manager," *Sales & Marketing Management*, April 1998, pp. 72–79.

8. Alan J. Dubinsky, Francis J. Yammarino, Marvin A. Jolson, and William D. Spangler, "Transformational Leadership: An Initial Investigation in Sales Management," *Journal of Personal Selling & Sales Management*, Spring 1995, pp. 17–29.

9. These dimensions are described in Edwin A. Fleischman, *Manual for Leadership Opinion Questionnaire* (Chicago: Science Research Associates, 1960), p. 3. The dimensions of consideration and structure are also described in Robert Kreitner, *Management*, 9th ed. (Boston: Houghton Mifflin Company, 2004), p. 506.

10. Dale Kahle, "It Takes More than Just Compensation to Unleash a Sales Force!" *The American Salesman*, October 2007, p. 5.

11. Brian Tracy, *The 100 Absolutely Unbreakable Laws of Business Success* (San Francisco: Berrett-Koehler Publishers, 2000), pp. 19–20.

12. Jared Sandberg, "Overcontrolling Bosses Aren't Just Annoying; They're Also Inefficient," *Wall Street Journal*, March 30, 2005, p. B1.

13. Sarah Lorge, "In the Box," *Sales & Marketing Management*, April 1998, p. 15.

14. Ken Blanchard, "3 Secrets of the One-Minute Manager," *Personal Selling Power*, March 1993, p. 48.

15. Robert Kreitner, *Management*, 9th ed., (Boston: Houghton Mifflin, 2004), p. 508, Paul Hersey, *The Situational Leader* (Escondido, CA: Center for Leadership Studies, 1984), pp. 29–30.

16. Ron Zemke, "Trust Inspires Trust," *Training*, January 2002, p. 10; Barry L. Reece and Rhonda Brandt, *Effective Human*

Relations: Personal and Organizational Applications (Boston, MA: Houghton Mifflin Company, 2008), p. 110; Noel M. Tichy and Warren G. Bennis, "Making the Tough Call—Great Leaders Recognize When Their Values Are On the Line," *Inc.*, November 2007, pp. 36–37.

17. Rhea Seymour, "The Mentor's Reward," *Profit*, November 2001, p. 35.

18. Kenneth R. Phillips, "The Achilles' Heel of Coaching," *Training & Development*, March 1998, p. 41.

19. Anne Fisher, "In Praise of Micromanaging," *Fortune*, August 23, 2004, p. 40; Brian Tracy, "Coaching for Success," *Sales & Marketing Management*, July/August 2007, p. 6.

20. Anne Fisher, "Essential Employees Called Up to Serve," *Fortune*, October 2000, p. 210.

21. General Mills website, www.generalmills.com/corporate/careers/lifestyle_canada.aspx (viewed August 4, 2008).

22. Paula Lima, "Talent shortage? That Was Yesterday," *Profit*, February/March 2002, pp. 65–66.

23. Dana Telford and Adrian Gostick, "Hiring Character," *Sales and Marketing Management*, June 2005, pp. 39–42.

24. Andy Cohen, "What Keeps You Up at Night?" *Sales & Marketing Management*, February 2000, pp. 44–52.

25. Henry Canaday, "Search Smarts," *Selling Power*, Source Book 2008, pp. 64, 68.

26. "Sales Achievement Predictor," www.wpspublish.com (accessed June 8, 2005).

27. "Hiring & Selection," www.calipercorp.com (accessed June 8, 2005).

28. Henry Canaday, ibid.

29. Shikhar Sarin, Trina Sego, Ajay K. Kohli, and Goutam Challagalla (2010), "Characteristics that Enhance Training Effectiveness in Implementing Technological Change in Sales Strategy: A Field-Based Exploratory Study," *Journal of Personal Selling and Sales Management, 30*(2), pp. 143–56.

30. Philip Kotler and Gary Armstrong, *Principles of Marketing*, 12th Edition. (Upper Saddle River, NJ: Prentice Hall, 2008), p. 460.

31. Alan J. Dubinsky, Francis J. Yammarino, Marvin A. Jolson, and William D. Spangler, "Transformational Leadership: An Initial Investigation in Sales Management," *Journal of Personal Selling & Sales Management*, Spring 1995, p. 27.

32. Skip Corsini, "The Great (Sales) Training Robbery," *Training*, February 2005, p. 14.

33. Barry L. Reece and Rhonda Brandt, *Effective Human Relations in Organizations*, Tenth Edition (Boston, MA: Houghton Mifflin, 2008), p. 157.

34. Ibid.

35. Noah Lim, Michael J. Ahearne, and Sung H. Ham (2009), "Designing Sales Contests: Does the Prize Structure Matter?" *Journal of Marketing Research, 46*(2), pp. 356–71.

36. Audrey Bottjen, "Incentives Gone Awry," *Sales & Marketing Management*, May 2001, p. 72.

37. Lain Chroust Ehmann, "A Team of Winners," *Selling Power*, November/December 2006, pp. 40–43.

38. William H. Murphy, Peter A. Dacin, and Neil M. Ford (2004), "Sales Contest Effectiveness: An Examination of Sales Contest Design Preferences of Field Sales Forces," *Journal of the Academy of Marketing Science, 20*(10), pp. 1–17.

39. Julie Chang, "Trophy Value," *Sales & Marketing Management*, October 2004, p. 26.

40. Carol Hymorwitz, "When Meeting Targets Becomes the Strategy, CEO Is on Wrong Path," *Wall Street Journal*,

41. Michael Schrage, "A Lesson in Perversity," *Sales and Marketing Management*, January 2004, p. 28.

42. Michael Segalla, Dominique Rouzies, Madeleine Besson, and Barton A. Weitz (2006), "A Cross-National Investigation of Incentive Sales Compensation," *International Journal of Research in Marketing, 23*, pp. 419–33.

43. Eilene Zimmerman, "Quota Busters," *Sales & Marketing Management*, January 2001, pp. 59–63.

44. Christine Galea, "2005 Compensation Survey," *Sales & Marketing Management*, May 2005, pp. 24–29.

45. Dominique Rouzies, Anne T. Coughlan, Erin Anderson, and Dawn Iacobucci (2009), "Determinants of Pay Levels and Structures in Sales Organizations," *Journal of Marketing, 73*(4), pp. 92–104.

46. "Point Incentive Sales Programs," *SBR Update*, Vol. 1, No. 4; Christopher Hosford, "A Carrot That Works," *Sales & Marketing Management*, November/December 2007, p. 10.

47. Donald W. Jackson, Jr., John L. Schlacter, and William G. Wolfe, "Examining the Bases Utilized for Evaluating Salespeople's Performance," *Journal of Personal Selling & Sales Management*, February 1995, p. 57.

48. "Survey of Sales Education Process—What Works, What Doesn't," *Selling Power*, September 1999, p. 115.

49. Lisa Holton, "Look Who's in on Your Performance Review," *Selling*, January/February 1995, pp. 47–55; Barry L. Reece and Rhonda Brandt, *Effective Human Relations: Personal and Organizational Applications*, Ninth Edition. (Boston, MA: Houghton Mifflin, 2005), p. 195; "Customer Ratings Are Misleading," *Selling*, November 1996, p. 1.

Sources for Boxed Features

a. Personal interview with Tom Gunter, vice president of sales, ConAgra Foods, Conducted by Lisa Violo, Brock University MBA student, November 4, 2005; personal interview with H.F. (Herb) MacKenzie, August 9, 2006.

b. Douglas J. Dalrymple and William L. Cron, *Sales Management: Concepts and Cases* (New York, NY: John Wiley &Sons, 1998), pp. 344–47; William Keenan, "Time Is Everything," *Sales & Marketing Management*, August 1993, p. 61.

c. Based on Jan Yager, *Business Protocol*, 2nd ed. (Stamford, CT: Hannacroix Creek Books, 2000), p. 124.

Name Index

infogroup, 206–207, 215
Intel, 180
International Organisation for Standardization (ISO), 131
International Trade Canada, 203
IntraLinks, 155
Investment Dealers Association of Canada, 249
Irish, Jaqueline, 20

J

Jagemann Stamping Company, 136
Jaguar, 148, 186
Janex Corporation, 44
Janssen Inc., 60
J.D. Power and Associates, 33, 56, 121, 192, 244, 308
Jeffries, Mark, 240, 248
Joe Boxer Corporation, 354
Johnson, David W., 80
Johnson & Johnson, 60
Jolles, Robert, 272
Jonsdottir, Birgitta, 115
Journal for Management in Engineering, 299
Journal of the American Medical Association, 307
J.P. Morgan, 155
Jung, Carl, 78

K

Kaizen Marketing & Creative Design House, 163
Kantin, Bob, 129
Karish, Deborah, 19, 282–283
Karrass, Chester L., 336
Keating, Dean, 60
Keep Industrial Supply, 385
Keith Eades, 126
Killinger, Barabara, 61
Kilpatrick, Ann, 112
Kinko's, 151, 175–176
Kinni, Theodore, 12
Klassen, Bruce, 248
Kline, Jennifer, 398
Komlos, Anita, 390
Kouzes, James, 412
KPMG LLP (Canada), 78
Kraft Foods, 8
Kreitner, Robert, 414n

L

Lakein, Alan, 393
Land Rover, 149–150

Langston, Mary, 261
LeBoeuf, Michael, 349
Ledwith, Brad, 207
Lehman Bros., 104
Levi Strauss & Company, 92
Levin, Lindsay, 412–413
Levitt, Dave, 195, 222, 263, 321, 433, 443
Levitt, Lee, 205
Levitt, Ted, 151, 366
Lexus, 163, 163n, 186, 222
Liberty International Underwriters, 435
Liberty Mutual Group, 17, 31, 48, 200, 303, 433, 435
LinkedIn, 206, 272, 300
Lionbridge Technologies, Inc., 390, 409
Livesay, John, 353
Loki Management Systems, 126–127
London Life, 31
Lowe's Canada, 135, 136f, 145
Loyalty Factor, 304
Lucent Technologies, 75, 109
Lyncole Industries, 19

M

MacIntosh, Mac, 205
Mackay, Harvey B., 39, 208
Mackay Envelope Corporation, 39, 44
MacKenzie, Herb, 272, 423n
MacNeil, Rita, 86, 99
Management Development Center (Brock University), 354
Manning, Gerald L., 272
Mansbridge, Peter, 85
Manufacturing Agent National Association (MANA), 158
Manulife Financial, 17, 31
MapInfo ProAlign, 398
Marcus, Stanley, 21
Marjorie Kelly, 104
Marriott, Alice S., 447
Marriott Hotels. *See* Marriott International Inc.
Marriott Houston Hobby, 316, 340–341
Marriott International Inc., 34, 316, 324, 447–448
Marshall, Greg W., 45n
Martini, Nancy J., 321n
Maslow, Abraham H., 182–184, 184f, 184n, 191, 192
Matress Firm, 100–101, 120–121, 301, 331, 433, 438–439
Maytag Corporation, 162
McGill, Arch, 173
McGillis, Kelly, 311
McGraw, Phillip, 59

McGraw-Hill Companies, Inc., 126, 161n, 269n
MCI, 154
McKee, Chris, 20
McKesson Pharmaceutical, 411–412, 434, 449
McKinsey & Company, 106, 434
McWatters, Christa-Lee, 294
Mehta, Rajiv, 413n
Melik, Ludwig, 131
Melik, Rudolf, 131
Mercedes Benz, 186, 192
Mercer, Rick, 82, 99
Mercer (Canada) Limited, 12n
Merck, 61
Merrill, David, 91
Metro Toronto Zoo, 337
Microsoft, 38, 77, 92, 126, 135, 180, 213, 222, 309, 310, 311, 394
Midwest Training Institute, 199
Minnis, Susan, 342–343, 362
Mitchell/Richards, 175, 234
Mitsubishi, 165
Mitsubishi Caterpillar Forklift America, 139
Molson Canada, 418
Monster.ca, 4, 8, 420
Montclair University, 64
Morgan, Sharon Drew, 115
Morrone, John, 415
Motorola, 118
Mott, Tom, 432
Mouton, Jane, 414f
Multz, Jeff, 382
Munro, Erin, 13
Murphy, Rex, 85
Murray, Anne, 86
Myers, Mike, 82

N

Nabisco Corporation, 422
Naisbitt, John, 21
Nalco Chemical Company, 232
Nantucket Nectars, 369–370
National Car Rental, 399
National Home Furnishings Association, 20
National Law Firm Marketing Association, 22
NEC, 304
Neiman Marcus, 21
Nerac Inc., 396
NetSuite, 128, 196, 213
NewLeads, 204
NewsWeek, 103

Srivastava, Alka, 350
Srivastava, Mona, 350
Staples, 151
State Farm, 31
Steam Whistle Brewing, 264
Stearns & Foster, 439
Steelcase Incorporated, 162, 166
Stein, Dave, 185
Stiebel, David, 323
Stoney Creek Furniture, 20
Strategic Vista International, 126–127
Strong, James, 413n
Stuart, Elnora W., 45n, 174n
Sumac Ridge Estate Winery Ltd., 294
Sun Life Financial, 17, 31, 107, 156, 222
Sun Microsystems, 109
Sunbeam Corporation, 75
Sutcliffe, David, 382
Suzuki, David, 85, 87
Swartz, Jeffrey, 106
Sybase Inc., 10n
Sysco Canada, 13

T

Taylor, Janis, 244
TD Canada Trust, 167
TD Waterhouse Discount Brokerage, 135, 159
Teknion, 295
Teleconcepts Consulting, 200
Tele-Direct Atlantic, 328
Telegraph Hill Robes, 347
Teleport Communications Group (TCG), 432
Telford, Dana, 421
Tempu-Pedic, 439
Tenrox Inc., 131
Teplitzky, Burt, 297
TerrAlign, 399
Texas Monthly, 124, 128, 146–147, 307, 433, 440–441
Thomson, Don, 241
3M Canada, 309
Thull, Jeff, 259
Thurston, Rick, 364, 385
Tice, Steve, 18
Tilley Endurables, 159–162
Timberland, 106
Timken Company, 157

Tindall, Paul, 197
Tingley, Judith C., 183
Toddm Ruth, 78
Tom James Company, 4–5, 197, 289, 433, 434
Toyota, 130
Tracy, Brian, 50, 59, 361, 388, 393
Trout, Jack, 226
Trugreen Chemlawn, 244
TSX, 202
TSX Venture, 202
Tudor, 188
Tuleja, Tad, 272, 330
Turner, Mary, 322
Twitter, 6, 8, 103, 206, 300
Tyco, 61

U

Unilever Canada, 362
Unisys, 75
United Way, 245
University of British Columbia, 337
University of Pennsylvania, 251
University of Virginia, 103
University Sales Education Foundation, 16n
UPS Incorporated, 33, 57–58, 135, 211

V

Vandaveer, Amy, 16, 124, 128, 146–147, 307, 433, 440
Vecta.net, 215
Volkswagen, 186

W

Wabi Iron and Steel Corp., 140
Wack, Patrick, 155
Waitley, Denis, 60n
Wall Street Journal, 410
Walmart, 449
Warm Thoughts Communications, 92
Webber, Alan, M., 106
Weber, Mike, 378
Weinstein, Bruce, 114
Weissman, Doron, 372
Wenschlag, Roger, 77, 92
Western Psychological, 421
Westin Grand, 13

WFS Ltd., 364, 385–386
Whirlpool, 132
White, Mike, 66
Whites Limited, 412
Wicker Corporation, 22
Willard, J., 447
Williams, Mark, 332
Williams, Robin, 82, 85
Williams Hardware, 332
Willingham, Ron, 54, 113, 318
Wilson, Larry, 56
Wilson Learning Worldwide, 56, 77, 89
Windsor Factory Supply. *See* WFS Ltd.
Winfrey, Oprah, 82, 85
Women's Wear Daily, 203
Wood, John, 421
Woodlands Town Center, 146–147
Workopolis, 420
World Trade Organization, 107
WorldCom Incorporated, 61, 104, 154
Würth Canada, 9
Würth Group, 9
Wyeth-Ayerst, 345
Wylie, Chris, 285–286, 288–289, 314–315, 445

X

Xerox, 130, 264
Xerox Canada Ltd., 2, 222
Xerox Corporation, 44, 204

Y

Yahoo!, 68
Yale University, 141
Yankee Group, 10
Yellow Pages, 203
York University, 106
Young Electric Sign Company, 378
YouTube, 6, 8, 309
Yurukova, Mariya, 212

Z

Zaleznik, Abraham, 252
Zanuto, Foster, 354
Zemka, Ron, 122
Zhou, Sue, 128
Ziglar, Zig, 361
Zuboff, Shoshana, 61

Subject Index

D

daily to-do list, 394
data dump, 144
Data Smog: Surviving the Information Glut (Shenk), 7
databases, 206–207
defamation, 110–111
deliveries, 372
delivery, 132–135
demonstration software, 308–311
detail, 292
detail sales, 14
detail salespeople, 19
differentiation, 150
differentiation strategy, 161
Dig Your Well Before You're Thirsty (Mackay), 208
diligence, 368
direct appeal close, 352–353
direct contact, 209
direct denial, 328
direct-response advertising, 205
direct salespeople, 20
The Direct Sellers Act, 114
Directive style, 84–85, 84f, 92, 94, 96, 357
directories, 202–203
disagreement, 323
The Discipline of Market Leaders, 157
discounts, 156–157
distribution channels. *See* channels of distribution
distribution sales representative (DSR), 162
dominance, 80
dominance indicator, 81f
dominant buying motive (DBM), 187, 345–346
donors, 212
downline, 21
downsizing, 104
drug abuse, 418
Dun & Bradstreet Reference Book, 212
dynamic nature of selling, 311

E

e-commerce. *See* electronic commerce
economic conflict, 37
educational seminars, 210
"Effective Negotiating Strategies," 336
ego drive, 60–61
The 8th Habit (Covey), 413
electronic commerce, 6, 35
elevator speech, 248

elimination of unnecessary questions, 272–273
email, 205, 242–243
email message, 376
emerging products, 155, 155f
emotional buying motive, 187–188
emotional intelligence, 52–53
Emotional Intelligence (Goleman), 52–53
emotional links, 300
Emotive style, 82–84, 83f, 94, 95–96, 357
empathizer, 55, 60
empathy, 60–61, 158, 369
employment opportunities, 9
employment settings, 13–21
    business goods channel, 18–19
    consumer goods channel, 19–21
    selling through channels, 14
    service channel, 14–18
endless chain referral, 200
England, 405
entertainment, 110
entrance, 62–63
entrepreneurs, 23
erosion of character, 103–104
esteem needs, 184
The Ethical Edge, 115
ethics. *See* business ethics
"The Ethics Guy," 114
The Ethics of Excellence (Pritchett), 113
etiquette, 66–67
evaluation of solutions, 178
Excel, 310, 310f
excess zone, 94
execution, 280, 280f
expansion selling, 377–379
expected product, 160–161
expense records, 403
expense voucher, 402f
explosion of product options, 127
external motivation, 423–424
external rewards, 425
eye contact, 64

F

facial expressions, 61, 64, 64f
family and career, balancing, 399
family members, 201–202
fear of making mistakes, 345
feature, 142
    see also feature-benefit strategy
feature-benefit strategy, 141–144, 143t, 144t
feedback, 359

feel-felt-found strategy, 329
"Ferris wheel" concept, 198f, 199, 219
field salespeople, 18–19
fight or flight response, 406
figurative language, 303
financial services, 16
First Impressions, 273
fixed salary plus bonus, 426
flexibility, 250
follow-through, 372–373
follow-up methods, 375–376
formal integrative negotiation, 317–325
formal negotiations, 332–335
four-part consultative questioning strategy, 265–272
four-part need-satisfaction model, 260–262, 260f
France, 191
friends, 201–202
full-line selling, 377
functional discount, 157
fusion stage, 183

G

gatekeeper, 252
GenderSell: How to Sell to the Opposite Sex (Tingley and Robert), 183
general benefits, 142
general survey questions, 265–266
generation gap, 185
Generation Y, 185
generic product, 159–160
Germany, 203
gift giving, 109–110
global marketplace. *See* international business
goal setting, 69, 393–394, 394t
graphs, 308
group influences, 184–186, 185f
    culture, 186
    defined, 184
    reference group, 186
    role, 185–186
    social class, 186
group sales presentation, 303–305
guaranteed salary, 426

H

habitual buying decision, 176
handshake, 63
harassment, 418
Harvard Business Review, 161
healthy emotional expression, 406
healthy lifestyle, 407

sales training programs, 264–265
salespeople
    see also personal selling
    above-average income, 11
    above-average psychic income, 11–12
    activities performed by, 10–11
    compensation, 11, 12t
    control of one's own time and activities, 10–11
    detail salespeople, 19
    in different channels, 15
    direct salespeople, 20
    ethical dilemmas, 105–106
    ethics and, 105–114
    field salespeople, 18–19
    industrial salespeople, 18
    inside salesperson, 13
    learning to sell, 24–26
    management of. *See* sales management
    missionary salespeople, 19, 289
    opportunity for advancement, 12
    outside salesperson, 13
    personal values, 112–113
    plateaued salespeople, 418
    professional selling position, 10f
    recruitment, 419–421
    retail salespeople, 19–20
    selection, 419–421
    selling skills, 21–24
    titles used in selling today, 11
    women, opportunities for, 12–13
The Salesperson's Legal Guide (Sack), 110–111
satisfactions, 151
saying goodbye to customer, 382
schedule deliveries, 372
scheduling plan, 398
Scott's Directories, 202
scripted presentation, 290
seasonal discount, 157
secondary decision makers, 57
secret payoffs, 101
Secrets of Question Based Selling (Freese), 240, 272, 296f
security needs, 183
selection, 419–421
selective attention, 186–187
self-actualization, 184
self-concept, 58–59
self-confidence, 348
self-development, 393
self-improvement strategies, 69–70
Self Matters (McGraw), 59
self-talk, 69
"sell low now, make profits later" tactic, 337
selling 2.0, 6

selling dynamics matrix, 312t
selling models. *See* personal selling models
Selling Power, 196, 230, 413
Selling Power (Kinni), 12
selling skills, 21–24
selling solutions, 125–127
selling strategy, 37
Selling the Invisible, 24
Selling Today (Manning, Reese, Ahearne and MacKenzie), 272
selling tools, 305–311, 396
Selling with Integrity (Drew), 115
Seminars to Build Your Business (Siskind), 210
sensory appeal, 293–295
service
    concerns, 326
    importance of, 158–159
    quality of, 158
service channel, 14–18
service contracts, 132
servicing the sale, 239, 262
    see also customer service
    building long-term partnerships through customer service, 365–368
    customer follow-up methods, 375–376
    expansion selling, 377–379
    follow-through, 372–373
    key people, 379–381
    preplan your service strategy, 379
    unhappy customer, 381–382
    worksheet, 380f
setting, 297
7 Habits of Highly Effective People (Covey), 41, 102–103
showmanship, 302
simplicity, 65
Situation Questions, 266
situational leadership, 417
Six Principles of Negotiation (Brodow), 322
six-step presentation plan, 237–239, 238f, 259f, 287f, 318f, 344f, 365f
skills testing, 421
slander, 110
sociability, 80–81
sociability indicator, 82f
social class, 186
social contact, 243–245
social media
    buying committees, 234
    Chatter, 234
    customer value, creation of, 8
    ethical use of, 103
    prospecting, 206
    relationship strategy, 67

    rules of participation, 206
    team selling, 234
    YouTube for presentations/ demonstrations, 309
social needs, 184
social network, 209
social pressure, 345
social style. *See* communication styles
Socratic Selling: How to Ask the Questions That Get the Sale (Daley), 265
solution, 125–127
solution evaluation, 178
solution questions, 270–272
solution selection, 261, 275–280
    matching benefits with motives, 276
    product configuration, 276–277
    recommendation strategies, 277–278
solution selling, 125–127, 151
source, 326–327
South America, 356
special concession close, 354
special events, 204
specific benefits, 142
specific survey questions, 266
The SPIN Selling Fieldbook (Rackham), 142, 264, 269f, 272
SPIN Selling model, 264
Spin Selling (Rackham), 22
sports sedan market, 148–149
sportsmanship, 369
spreadsheets, 310
stall, 327
step-by-step close, 354
stock clerks, 381
Stop Acting Like a Seller And Start Thinking Like a Buyer (Acuff), 171–172
stories, 302–303
straight commission plan, 426
straight rebuy, 174–175
straight salary, 426
strategic alliance buyers. *See* strategic alliance selling
strategic alliance selling, 58
    buying-decision process, 180–181
    presentation objectives, 233
    trust, 117
    value creation investments, 162–164
strategic alliances, 175–176
strategic compensation planning, 427–428
Strategic/Consultative Selling Model, 6t, 38–43, 39f
    customer strategy, 41, 172f
    interrelationship of basic strategies, 42–43, 42f
    presentation strategy, 41–42, 231f

Credits

Figure Credits

Fig. 3.3, p. 60: From the book *The Double Win* by Dennis Waitley (Old Tappan, NJ: Fleming H. Revell Co., 1985). **Fig. 7.3, p. 160:** Adapted and reprinted by permission of *Harvard Business Review*. An exhibit from "Marketing Success through Differentiation of Anything" by Theodore Levitt (Jan/Feb 1980). Copyright © 1980 by the President and Fellows of Harvard College, all rights reserved. **Fig. 16.1, p. 394:** iStockphoto/Thinkstock.com. **Fig. 16.4, p. 402:** Used with the permission of 3M Corp.

Advertisement Credits

p. 16: Courtesy of The University Sales Education Foundation. **p. 54:** Jacket Cover copyright © 1998 by Bantam Books, a division of Random House, Inc., from WORKING WITH EMOTIONAL INTELLIGENCE by Daniel Goleman. Used by permission of Bantam Books, a division of Random House, Inc. **p. 161:** Book cover of VALUE ADDED SELLING by Tom Reilly. Copyright © 2003. Reprinted by permission of The McGraw-Hill Companies, Inc. **p. 163:** Courtesy of Lexus. **p. 188:** Courtesy of BMW Group. **p. 189:** Courtesy of Formax Inc. **p. 207:** InfoGroup Canada www.infogroup.ca. **p. 215:** Used with permission of OneSource. **p. 230:** Courtesy of Personal Selling Power. **p. 241:** Book cover from "Keeping the Funnel Full" by Don Thomson, Mardon Publishing Inc, French Creek, British Columbia. **p. 247:** ConAgra Foods Inc. **p. 269:** Book Cover from THE SPIN SELLING FIELDBOOK by Neil Rackham. Copyright © 1996. Reprinted by permission of The McGraw-Hill Companies, Inc. **p. 294:** Courtesy of Bell Helicopter, Textron Inc. **p. 298:** Courtesy of ACH Food Companies, Inc. **p. 335:** Courtesy of CPSA Canada. **p. 416:** Courtesy of CPSA Canada. **p. 427:** Courtesy of Icelandic. **p. 429:** Courtesy of HR Chally.

Photo Credits:

Note: Cartoon credits appear on page.

p. 2: Courtesy of H F (Herb) MacKenzie. **p. 5:** Pearson Education Inc. **p. 17:** Courtesy of H F (Herb) MacKenzie. **p. 20:** Courtesy of H F (Herb) MacKenzie. **p. 26:** Courtesy of CPSA Canada. **p. 32:** Pearson Education Inc. **p. 37:** Yuri Arcurs/Shutterstock.com. **p. 38:** Yuri Arcurs/Shutterstock.com. **p. 40:** Yuri Arcurs/Shutterstock.com. **p. 50:** Comstock/Thinkstock.com. **p. 53:** Pearson Education Inc. **p. 56:** digital vision/Thinkstock.com. **p. 62:** Yuri Arcurs/Shutterstock.com. **p. 65:** Ted Levine/Corbis. **p. 70:** iStockphoto/Thinkstock.com. **p. 76:** Pearson Education Inc. **p. 77:** AFP/Getty Images. **p. 79:** Andresr/Shutterstock.com. **p. 85:** George Burns/Newscom. **p. 85:** 2000/Daily News, L.P. (New York)/Getty

Images. **p. 87:** CP Photo/Larry MacDougal. **p. 88:** Hemera/Thinkstock.com. **p. 90:** Reprinted with permission of the publisher. From I'm Stuck, You're Stuck: Breakthrough to Better Work Relationships and Results by Discovering your DiSC® Behavioral Style, copyright © 2002 by Tom Richey, Berrett-Koehler Publishers, Inc., San francisco, CA. All rights reserved. www.bkconnection.com. **p. 91:** Pearson Education Inc. **p. 94:** Nick White/Thinkstock.com. **p. 101:** Pearson Education Inc. **p. 105:** Yuri Arcurs/Shutterstock.com. **p. 108:** iStockphoto/Thinkstock.com. **p. 112:** Smilla/Dreamstime.com / GetStock.com. **p. 113:** Jacket Cover copyright © 2003 by Doubleday, a division of Random House, Inc., from INTEGRITY SELLING FOR THE 21ST CENTURY by Ron Willingham. Used with permission of Doubleday, a division of Random House, Inc. **p. 116:** Jupiterimages/Thinkstock.com. **p. 122:** iStockphoto/Thinkstock.com. **p. 125:** Pearson Education Inc. **p. 126:** Book Cover from THE NEW SOLUTION SELLING, second edition by Keith Eade. Copyright © 2004. Reprinted by permission of The McGraw-Hill Companies, Inc. **p. 129:** Jupiterimages/Thinkstock.com. **p. 131:** Ablestock/Thinkstock.com. **p. 133:** Reprinted by Permission of Sea Ray. **p. 137:** Comstock/Thinkstock.com. **p. 139:** Yuri_arcurs/Dreamstime.com/GetStock.com. **p. 141:** Fderib/Dreamstime.com/GetStock.com. **p. 149:** Comstock/Thinkstock.com. **p. 168:** wavebreak media ltd./Shutterstock.com. **p. 171:** Pearson Education Inc. **p. 175:** Reprinted by permission of Christina B. Bliss. **p. 179:** Yuri Arcurs/Shutterstock.com. **p. 190:** Deanm1974/Dreamstime/GetStock.com. **p. 196:** Pearson Education Inc. **p. 201:** visi.stock/Shutterstock. **p. 204:** George Doyle/Thinkstock.com. **p. 208:** Yuri Arcurs/Shutterstock.com. **p. 220:** iStockphoto/Thinkstock.com. **p. 226:** wavebreakmedia ltd./Shutterstock.com. **p. 229:** Pearson Education Inc. **p. 235:** Yuri Arcurs/Shutterstock.com. **p. 236:** Pearson Education Inc. **p. 242:** Ed Bock Stock/Shutterstock.com. **p. 243:** Supri Suharjoto/Shutterstock.com. **p. 244:** StockLite/Shutterstock.com. **p. 250:** carlosseller/Shutterstock.com. **p. 258:** Pearson Education Inc. **p. 262:** Custom Medical Stock Photo/Alamy. **p. 271:** Pearson Education Inc. **p. 274:** Lisa F. Young/Shutterstock.com. **p. 286:** Pearson Education Inc. **p. 292:** wavebreakmedia ltd./Shutterstock.com. **p. 293:** Yuri Arcurs/Shutterstock.com. **p. 296:** Copyright © 2003 by Sourcebooks, Inc. **p. 303:** Andresr/Shutterstock.com. **p. 305:** Image Source/Firstlight. **p. 306:** Rido/Shutterstock.com. **p. 317:** Pearson Education Inc. **p. 320:** Hemera/Thinkstock.com. **p. 330:** Reprinted with permission of Warner Books. **p.331:** Barry Austin Photography/Thinkstock.com. **p. 335:** Courtesy of PLUS. **p. 346:** Jacket Cover, copyright 2000 by Gene Bedell, from 3 Steps to Yes by Gene Bedell. Used by permission of Crown Publishers, a division of Random House, Inc.

p. 348: Creatas Images/Thinkstock.com. p. 353: Marcelmooij/Dreamstime/GetStock.com. p. 358: Pearson Education Inc. p. 359: Jupiterimages/Thinkstock.com. p. 367: Creatas Images/Thinkstock.com. p. 369: Stephane De Sakutin/Agence France Presse/Getty Images. p. 370: Courtesy of H F (Herb) MacKenzie. p. 371: Photographer's Choice/Getty Images. p. 374: Pearson Education Inc. p. 378: Abel Mitja Varela/iStockphoto. p. 379: Book Cover from Rethinking the Sales Force: Redefining Selling to Create and Capture Customer Value by Neil Rackham. Copyright © 1999. Reprinted by permission of The McGraw-Hill Companies, Inc. p. 388: wavebreakmedia ltd./Shutterstock.com. p. 391: melhi/iStockphoto. p. 397: Jupiterimages/Thinkstock.com. p. 403: Hemera Technologies/Thinkstock.com. p. 405: Hemera Technologies/Thinkstock.com. p. 407: Jupiterimages/Thinkstock.com. p. 412: Pearson Education Inc. p. 416: Clerkenwell Images/iStockphoto. p. 424: Photo Alto/iStockphoto.